# Practical Public Relations

## Theories & Techniques That Make a Difference

Anthony Fulginiti
*Rowan University*

Donald Bagin
*Rowan University*

**KENDALL/HUNT PUBLISHING COMPANY**
4050 Westmark Drive    Dubuque, Iowa 52002

# Practical Public Relations
## *Theories and Techniques That Make a Difference*

Front Cover Design: *Jennifer Curran*
Figures and Graphics: *Jennifer Curran*
Page Layout and Design: *Claudia Cuddy*
Proofreading: *Nancy Fulginiti*
Publisher Representative: *Steve O'Brien*

# Brief Contents

# *About the authors*

**Don Bagin** is professor of communication at Rowan University (formerly Glassboro State College). He coordinates the graduate program in public relations and has served as chairman of the Department of Public Relations/Advertising.

He has spoken to more than 100,000 people on the topics of public relations and communications.

He's the founding publisher of communication briefings, a newsletter read by more than 500,000 people. He served as president of the National School Public Relations Association and has been a public relations practitioner, serving as public relations director for the New Jersey Commissioner of Education. He's consulted with a large number of corporations and not-for-profit agencies. His graduate public relations textbook is used in more than 150 colleges and universities.

He was named one of the country's top five PR educators by pr reporter.

Bagin holds a doctorate from Temple University and his first two degrees from Villanova University.

# *Dedication*

This book is dedicated to a number of caring individuals who encouraged me to write it. At the top of the list would be many students who appreciated the notes they took in our PR class and suggested we make them available in a text.

Two other major contributors were Dr. Leslie Kindred and Dr. Tom Robinson. Dr. Kindred encouraged me to pursue a doctorate in community relations and invited me to co-author a graduate school public relations text. Dr. Robinson, president of Glassboro State College (now Rowan University), strongly urged me to share my public relations ideas when I served as his PR director.

Especially worthy of this dedication is my wife, Carole Bagin, who invested countless hours in many capacities — inputting data, proofreading, organizing and generally improving the content.

Thanks too to my daughter, Cathy Trimble, for her help on many facets of the book. And to our secretary, Janice Hillman, and my former secretary at *communication briefings*, Eve Alkins, for doing so many things well to make me look good.

Also, thanks to Dr. Suzanne Sparks-FitzGerald, Rowan University PR department chair, who appreciated my need to invest time on this book, sometimes requiring that we volunteer for fewer department responsibilities.

*Don Bagin*

**Anthony Fulginiti** is professor of public relations at Rowan University with graduate degrees from Villanova University and Glassboro State College. He served as chairperson of the Public Relations/Advertising Department.

Tony is a Fellow and accredited member of the Public Relations Society of America. In 1987, he received PRSA's Bronze Anvil as Outstanding Educator.

He served as president of the Philadelphia PRSA Chapter, winning two chapter Pepper Pot Awards. To honor his work, especially in accreditation, the chapter instituted the Anthony J. Fulginiti Award for Outstanding Contribution to Public Relations Education.

Tony founded the Rowan University PRSSA, which has won more than 200 national awards and was six times named best chapter in the nation.

He has trained dozens of groups nationally on PR research, writing, persuasion and planning and written a number of works, including "Power-Packed PR."

Tony still consults with ie communication. He has fashioned facility improvement referenda programs for 50 New Jersey school districts — successfully passing 49.

# *Dedication*

I dedicate this book to my wife Nancy. She inspired me to think these thoughts, understand the joy of relationship, and persevere to write about both. Nancy made this book happen with professional fidelity to researching, categorizing, editing, writing, proofreading, assembling and blessing this work.

I also dedicate this work to my children, Samuel, David, and Jennifer for their hours of proofreading manuscripts and suggesting improvements. Jennie also created much of the graphic support in many of the chapters and the cover. Thank you all so much. This is your book, too.

These pages also contain wisdom, ideas and professional attitudes of all my colleagues at Rowan University and *communication briefings*. I was their student more than they knew. I am grateful to Don Bagin, whom I consider my mentor and pathfinder.

Three decades of insightful association with hundreds of graduate and undergraduate students and Glassboro State College and Rowan University Public Relations Student Society of America members is also between these covers.

I also dedicate this book to my mother, Antoinette, and my father, Samuel, who wanted so much to see my work in print. They didn't have to. The script *is* them.

*Anthony Fulginiti*

# *Acknowledgments*

The authors — and we hope readers of our text — appreciate the contributions of many professionals to this book. We thank the following people:

Ed Moore, associate executive director of the National School Public Relations Association, for contributions to the chapters on writing and publications preparation. Mr. Moore was general manager of Earle Palmer Brown Public Relations at both the Philadelphia, Pa., and Bethesda, Md., offices before serving as chair of the public relations department at Rowan University.

Ken Weir, former director of public relations for the North Penn School District in Lansdale, Pa., and a winner of many national awards for his publications, for his contributions to the publications chapter.

Brian McCallum, former publisher of *communication briefings*, for materials from his thesis on publications preparation.

Dr. Suzanne Sparks FitzGerald, chair of the public relations department at Rowan University and a former public relations practitioner at a number of companies, for the section on advertising.

M. Larry Litwin, associate professor, Rowan University, author of *The PR practitioner's Playbook* and the *ABCs of Strategic Communication* for his contribution to Writing for the Electronic Media.

Don Dunnington, manager of marketing communications, K-Tron America, Inc., for his preparation of the chapter on the use of technology in public relations. Mr. Dunnington is also an adjunct professor in the College of Communication at Rowan University.

Gary Bagin, marketing director for the law firm of Stradley Ronon Stevens & Young, LLP, and former public relations director for LRP Publications, Inc., a major publisher of magazines and newsletters, for his contributions to the media chapter.

Yolette Ross, senior research associate for the New Jersey State Senate for the section on lobbying.

Kathy Schoch-Ziprik, West Virginia public relations building materials consultant, for her contributions to the sections on special events and crisis management. Ms. Ziprik was formerly director of public relations for Six Flags Great Adventure, when the historic fire occurred, Hyatt Regency Hotels, Atlanta, and director of public relations for the Georgia Pacific Company. She is also past national president of PRSSA.

Jerry Klein, lawyer and partner in Anne Klein & Associates, a Mt. Laurel, NJ public relations firm, for his ideas on public relations law, many of which are in this text. Mr. Klein is an authority on PR law and sought lecturer on communication law by PRSA and other communication groups.

Jennifer Curran, design consultant and partner in ie communication, a New Jersey public relations consulting firm, for her book cover design, ideas for graphic expression of complex theory, and 40 graphic figures in the book.

Claudia Cuddy, professor at Rowan University, for her professional attention to every layout detail.

John Moscatelli, APR, senior counselor at Anne Klein & Associates, a Mt. Laurel New Jersey public relations firm, for his insightful contributions to the writing and crisis management chapters.

Jack Gillespie, professor emeritus, Rowan University, and former editor of *communication briefings*, for his many practical suggestions over the years to improve writing; his ideas strongly influenced the chapter on writing.

James Grunig, professor, University of Maryland, for many seminal ideas and research on public relations that are appreciated by the authors and refashioned in the text.

We also appreciate the contributions on specific areas of public relations from Rich Bagin, ASPR, APR, executive director, National School Public Relations Association; David J. Byrd, former associate commissioner, New Jersey Department of Commerce and Economic Development and associate public relations director for the Republican Black Caucus; Joanie L. Flatt, Joanie L. Flatt & Associates, LTD; Albert E. Holliday, former publisher of *Journal of Educational Relations* and publisher of *Pennsylvania Magazine*; Joyce McFadden, vice-president, marketing and public relations, Southern Ocean County Hospital; Dr. John H. Wherry, ASPR, president of The Parent Institute; Wilma Mathews, ABC, public relations seminar leader, writer and consultant; Gregg Feistman, faculty member at Temple University, Philadelphia, PA; Larry Kamer, principal, Kamer-Singer & Associates San Francisco, CA; Pamela Hanlon, vice president communications, American Express Company New York, NY; Mark Gordon, managing director, Asia Associates Ltd., Singapore; Donald S. Knight, senior editor, Intelligent Transportation Society of America, Washington, DC; William J. Banach, president, Banach, Banach & Cassidy Ray, MI; James M. Caudill, vice president, Public Relations & Hospitality, Kendall-Jackson, Santa Rosa, CA.

*Don Bagin and Tony Fulginiti*

# *Preface*

A word about our words …

This is one textbook you may want to keep. Why?

Because you'll probably refer to it throughout your life to promote causes you believe in — whether you want to write an effective letter to the editor, gain support for a candidate for an office, or just build persuasive techniques to gain acceptance for an idea you want others to accept.

Public relations is one area every student will practice, forever. Whether it's moving up the corporate ladder or espousing ideas you want to see succeed, you'll be able to tap into the knowledge that you've accumulated in this course and to revisit this text for ideas when you need them.

Also, one of the most important activities you can engage in during your college years is getting involved in a preprofessional society such as the Public Relations Student Society of America. Your college or university might offer other communication, advertising or marketing societies or clubs. Join one. Attend their meetings, especially those of the professional parent society. You'll network with people and get involved in projects that will lead to internships and jobs.

Thousands of students, like you, joined those societies and worked on worthwhile projects, attended national conferences, and become hugely successful after graduation. Some of those were students of ours who wrote some of the words in this text.

You can make your world, and the world that your children live in, better by learning to champion causes you think will make a serious difference. We hope the ideas in this book will help you do that.

If this book enlightens you, we are satisfied. If it motivates you, we are gratified. And if someday, you recall a few of its words when you most need them, we will be edified that through you, we'll still be teaching.

*Tony Fulginiti and Don Bagin*

# *Detailed Contents*

## Chapter 10 ~
## Communicating in Special Circumstances

### Section 1: Using Special Events in Public Relations

### Section 2: Managing Crises in Public Relations  237

## Chapter 11 ~ Communicating in the Networked Age

# Chapter 1

# Public Relations in Society

---

**PRaxiom**  *Public relations is the right to tell a side of a story.*

---

## What this chapter covers

Public relations is story telling. Persons and organizations have the right to tell their sides of the story. It's a constitutionally protected activity, like journalism and advertising. But public relations differs from journalism because it openly advocates for clients and organizations. And PR differs from advertising because it must earn, not purchase, the reputation so important to organizations.

Public relations practitioners are both counselors and communicators. They both fashion and send information and persuasive messages to important audiences. They're responsible for maintaining the relationships between their organizations and their important publics.

Here are some public relations issues this chapter will cover:
- PR deals with building and maintaining relationships
- PR helps build communities
- PR works to gain and maintain reputation
- PR follows one of several theory/action models depending upon the purpose of the organization
- PR acts in a truthful, socially responsible manner
- PR has a "love/hate" symbiotic relationship with "the media"
- Society's image of public relations is less flattering than the actual practice

## What is public relations?

Public relations explains an individual or organization's activities to key publics to gain a favorable opinion from those publics. Expressed as a simple formula, it would look like this:

### Acts + Interpretation of Acts = Opinion

Most people and organizations do things to make them well thought of, the *acts* and *opinion* parts of the formula. But the middle term is *interpretation* of the activities, story telling, or public relations.

Here's an example to illustrate how PR should be involved in interpreting acts or behavior.

A homeowner has a large tree growing on her property. Its roots are so large and deep they're destroying her sewer line. A plumber tells her that if she wants to avoid a large sewer repair bill, she must cut down the tree. So she cuts down the tree (her *act*). But she never explains to her neighbors why she cut down the tree (no *interpretation*).

As a result, her neighbors say she is "deflowering the neighborhood" and is against beauty and aesthetics (*opinion*).

Had the homeowner simply practiced a little public relations and explained her act, she might have gained positive opinion for herself. The lesson here is that if you don't interpret your activities, or those of your organization, someone else will. And the interpretation might not be true or complimentary to you. Public opinion about you will always result, because someone will usually interpret what you do, but the opinion will be out of your control.

The benefit of practicing public relations is your ability to manage public opinion about you.

## Relationship building

Public relations seeks to establish and cultivate positive relationships and communities with an organization's publics. Even if an organization has no formal public relations function, it will nevertheless have relationships with all sorts of publics — employees, stakeholders, customers and governmental agencies. Relationships either develop on their own or they are cultivated. If relationships develop on their own, without nurturing, they can take on a harmful, nonproductive character.

For example, assume a man and woman marry after spending too little time communicating with each other about their ideas of married life, children, jobs, in-laws and finances. It wouldn't be surprising if the relationship withered as each partner's behavior veered in a direction that did not please the other.

If organizations and publics want to cultivate relationships, then both parties should open communication channels. What flows through the channels are **images of each other,** statements about ambition and descriptions of activities, attitudes and information. The organization can achieve its purposes because it is **relating** to publics important to them in ways the publics accept (hence public relations). Organizations must practice public relations because they must be in relationships to do business. View public relations as taking care of an important part of an organization's activities. Production managers take care of producing things. Financial managers take care of money, investments and taxes. Legal managers take care of regulations. Human resource managers take care of employee development and rights.

But communication can be the most important activity of an organization. Who takes care of that? Relationships with publics will happen. Who takes care of them? Public opinion seriously contributes to an organization's success. Who takes care of that? Public relations does. Public relations takes care of all parts of the process — activity, communication, opinion and relationships.

> *Communication can be an organization's most important activity.*

By why must we manage and organize communication? Why can't organizations and their publics just communicate and let the chips fall where they might?

Ask yourself, what would happen if an organization didn't manage its other functions?

If we don't manage production, we can't control quality.

If we don't accord employees their rights, including appeals about unfair treatment, we inherit chaos and loss of production.

If we don't pay taxes and follow laws, the organization will fold.

What happens if we don't manage communication? Communication is more than telling stories, writing words, or sending pictures to publics.

## Who are publics?

Because an organization deals with many publics, one-size messages and stories won't do the job. Managed communication takes care of avoiding that mistake. Communication managers identify publics, craft messages and select channels appropriate to specific publics. This type of customized communication leads to something so important as vital relationships. And no one else in the organization is responsible for this customized communication and relationship building other than the communication officer or public relations specialist.

Managed communication implies purpose and motive. It results in positive public opinion about an organization. Publics with positive opinion about an organization are already in a relationship with the organization. Mismanaged communication or unmanaged communication can cause negative public opinion and harmful relationships.

So the purpose and work of public relations is to manage communication so an organization achieves its objectives through positive relationships with important publics.

## Public relations models

How do publics help PR practitioners decide what type of customized communication they'll use? In their book, Managing Public Relations, James Grunig and Todd Hunt write about four types of communication depending on the publics involved and the purposes of the organization (Figure 1.1).

### Press agentry

The one-way, press agentry model is a propaganda model. Propaganda is simply gaining attention for an organization by controlling the message — one sided. Relationship with publics in this model is mechanistic; simply gain your publics' attention and your product or service should do the rest. Communication is one-way, from the organization out to its publics.

### Public information

The **one-way, public information** model is a *publicity* model. In this model, information attracts attention and should influence attitudes and eventually opinion. When Ivy Lee first began "public relations" communication, he sent information (today's news releases) to newspapers to gain positive opinion about his client companies. Until Lee came along, companies sent

## PR Models

| One-way communication | | Two-way communication | |
|---|---|---|---|
| Press Agentry (Imaging) | Public Information (Publicity) | Asymmetric (Persuasion) | Symmetric (Negotiation) |
| Propaganda | Attention | Compliance | Consensus |
| Organization paramount/ public unimportant | Organization paramount/ public important | Organization important/ public important | Organization and public paramount |

**Figure 1.1**

Adapted from Grunig and Hunt, *Managing Public Relations*, 1984, p. 22

only paid advertisements to newspapers. Information in this model is sometimes viewed as an obligation to publics to inform them. Many government projects include budgets for informing the public. Communication is one-way.

### Two-way asymmetric

The **two-way, asymmetric** model is also called the *persuasion model*. An organization communicates with its publics to learn the most efficacious messages and channels to use with them in a persuasion campaign. The organization beams back what it discovered to gain positive public opinion and compliance from important publics. Marketers frequently use this type of communication. Communication is two-way.

### Two-way symmetric

The **two-way, symmetric model** seeks satisfaction for both the organization and its publics. The organization has not predetermined a course of action. Instead, it *negotiates* with its publics to discover mutually beneficial policies or actions. Organizations and publics reach consensus about the organization's identity. Communication is two-way.

### Merits of asymmetric and symmetric models

Because asymmetric communication uses feedback research from publics, it's more effective than press agentry or publicity. Those two models are quite unscientific. They work on the old idea that simply giving people information will influence them to behave a certain way. Asymmetry is more scientific and self-serving. To get publics to agree with a decision it has already made, an organization asks publics to identify messages and channels that will persuade its publics to agree with the organization. The organization believes that its decision is in the best interest of the public and there's nothing to negotiate.

*Example*: Organ transplant organizations want people to sign organ donor cards, identify their donor intentions on their drivers' licenses, and discuss their wishes with their family.

They believe organ donation is the right thing to do. So they engage in two-way research communication to discover the best messages and channels to make that happen. In another chapter, you'll see this model used in a public relations campaign to reduce binge drinking on college campuses.

Organizations use the symmetric model when they need their publics' opinion before they decide on a policy or action. This is the model of negotiation.

*Example*: In some states, residents must approve tax increases on their properties to build or renovate their schools. A school board could employ an asymmetric model that simply decides the best kind of building or renovation, get some feedback from the public about workable messages and channels, and mount a persuasion campaign.

Or, it could assemble a residents' task force or advisory group that decides, in concert with the school board, the type of building addition or renovation the public wants and will support. A combination of asymmetric and symmetric communication has yielded a 98% success rate in 50 New Jersey school bond referenda managed by one of the authors.

Both persuasion (asymmetric) and negotiation (symmetric) work. PR practitioners choose the most useful model depending on the organization's purpose, unfolding of issues, and disposition of involved publics.

## Image of public relations

PR people have made significant contributions to organizations, publics and societies they serve. Ask organizations such as the American Red Cross, National

AIDS Coalition and United Way if their PR people helped them fulfill their organization's mission. Ask corporations such as Microsoft, Disney and Nordstrom's if public relations helped market their products through excellent customer relations. In tense times, ask Tylenol, Dow Corning and Exxon if public relations helped repair damaged organizational images.

Despite their effective work, PR practitioners traditionally have a difficult time with their own public relations with the general public. Advertisers too, work to overcome a generally negative image. Why? Both professions can trace much of their negative reputation to images the public receives about them from the media.

> **Public relations has difficulty managing its own PR.**

Movies, television programs, books, magazines and other mass media cast advertisers and public relations practitioners in the same negative light, as professions that manipulate public opinion. But public relations in particular receives most of its negative treatment from the news media.

## The press vs. public relations

Frequently, you'll hear phrases like "PR flack," "PR gimmick," "PR stunt," or "They're not telling the truth; they're just trying to PR you." *PR* has become a negative verb much like postal has become a negative adjective. You'll hear the attack phrases, especially from TV and print journalists, because of the long-standing issues journalists have with the role of public relations in society. And it starts with the United States Constitution.

The "press" is specifically mentioned in the Constitution.

> *"Congress shall make no law respecting an establishment of religion, or prohibiting the free exercise thereof; or abridging the freedom of speech, **or of the press**; or the right of the people peaceably to assemble, and to petition the Government for a redress of grievances.*
>
> (First Amendment to the Constitution of the United States of America)

The press believes its role in society is to tell people truthful information. It also gets to decide what the truth is, and whether to tell some of it, all of it, or none of it for specific stories. Unfortunately, many reporters, editors, columnists and editorial writers believe the role of public relations is to shield the truth from them and from the public.

PR people are also mentioned in the *United States Constitution*. You'll find them included, with all citizens, under the First Amendment guaranteeing free speech.

Free speech means that citizens and organizations have the right to tell their stories. But if the story is not in the form of a paid placement, it's the privilege of journalists to report those stories, or not, as they understand and interpret them. Do all journalists report information from PR practitioners or about their organizations without bias? Absolutely not. Do all public relations practitioners tell their organizations' stories truthfully, without counterbalancing negative facts? Absolutely not. Precisely because there is no government-issued license for either journalists or public relations practitioners, some members of both professions stray with impunity from making valid contributions to society.

It troubles PR practitioners, who perform with a sense of public and social responsibility, when media types continually paint them with the broad brush of opinion manipulation.

The PR profession has struggled to defend itself. Over the years, the Public Relations Society of America has made it a priority to organize, prepare and certify its members as ethically practicing professionals, shy of a government license. Their efforts have explained and clarified how public relations contributes to the welfare of society.

## Public relations and society

How does public relations contribute to the welfare of society? The answer to that question lies in specifying what's good for society, what public relations is and does, and whether there's a connection between communication and society's welfare.

Reasonable people would agree that society needs six contributing behaviors from organizations, businesses, and citizens:

- **Community**. Insiders and outsiders in all organizations should behave as though they're linked in a common purpose based on common values. Such mutually respectful behavior guarantees trustful transactions, even if those transactions involve merely selling and buying a hamburger, or asking for and receiving a blood donation.

- **Reputation**. Trust between publics and organizations depends on whether publics and organizations are what they say they are. Reputation, or repetitive believing, establishes patterns of successful commerce, governance and information flow.

- **Public and social responsibility**. Organizations agree that their policies, practices and products will do no harm. Beyond that, organizations will accept responsibility to effect good in communities in which they function.

- **Respect**. Civility will characterize contracts, employment activities, and other issues where people's interests intersect. Legitimate rules, laws and orders will command respectful compliance.

- **Freedom**. People and organizations will pursue their legitimate objectives unfettered by unfair outside control and self-serving criticism. The "pursuit of happiness" guaranteed by the Constitution does not prohibit free speech criticism. But it does envision responsible criticism.

- **Communication**. The flow of information will be reliable, trustworthy, open and accessible. The agendas, motives and purposes of people and organizations will be clear.

When PR practitioners contribute these six behaviors, and do so with integrity, their work is socially responsible. Some add that when practitioners help immediate publics, like customers and clients, meet their goals, their work is in the public interest. Both publics and society alike should appreciate the contribution of PR to the general welfare. Public relations fulfills the aspiration of the preamble to the Constitution as well.

> *"We the People of the United States, in Order to form a more perfect Union, establish Justice, insure domestic Tranquility, provide for the common defence [sic], promote the general Welfare, and secure the Blessings of Liberty to ourselves and our Posterity, do ordain and establish this Constitution for the United States of America."*
>
> (Preamble to the *Constitution of the United States of America*)

Here are some ways everyday PR fulfills the criteria of public or social responsibility.

## Community building

Organizations use public relations to develop "community relationships" with their important publics. To achieve the common purpose characteristic of communities, PR uses symmetric communication. This type of communication empowers publics to have a say in an organization's behavior, a common purpose with the organization.

Professor Hugh Culbertson calls this a "communitarian" type of PR practice (a version of two-way symmetric communication). Professors Dean Kruckberg and Ken Starck agree that PR practice needs to go beyond narrow persuasion tactics to achieve an organization's goals. They believe that when both parties form a community, both parties win. And so does society.

When a retail merchandise store like Wal-Mart conducts customer focus groups to see how well it's doing with its customer service and modify it according to the research, it forms a community that benefits America's neighborhoods. Afterward, it's important for Wal-Mart to maintain trust with its customers by keeping in touch with them. If continual, two-way communication breaks down, trust breaks down; so does community, and with it, the comfortable neighborhood of buyers and sellers.

> *Decisions made for people, not with people, might not be in the best interests of the people.*

## Reputation

Reputation means organizations repeatedly enjoy positive opinion from their publics. Organizations know they need a good reputation to succeed. So they use public relations to achieve this long-lasting positive regard.

When public relations helps organizations earn long-lasting regard, it helps society as a whole. It's better for the public to know that the organizations they deal with are dependable. They need to know that their insurance companies will pay for what they say they will. They need to know that their car repair will last past the next red light. And they need to know if their next hamburger will have quality beef in it. The trust between citizens and organizations depends on repeated regard. Reputation fosters stability in society.

## Public and social responsibility

Like doctors, lawyers and accountants, PR professionals want to do the right thing for their clients and publics. What type of practice results in the best decisions? Ask clients. Decisions made *for people* instead of *with people* might not be in the best interest *of the people*. Imagine a medical procedure without a consent form, or a lawsuit settlement offer without consultation, or a tax return without a signature. Imagine a society in which government decided what was good and right for groups of citizens without consultation, consent and signature of the groups. Lack of empowerment, it can be argued, is social irresponsibility.

Is public relations exempt from collaborating with its publics to act in their best interests? No. It appears that a blend of both symmetric and asymmetric public relations practice results in socially responsible behavior. PR policies, practices and products should not only do no harm, but should be good for the publics involved. In the practice of public relations, the most important question is, "What is good for my public?"

The most contentious issues in society ask the toughest questions about PR practice. Is manufacturing and marketing (with public relations help) tobacco products in the public interest? Is it "good" for the publics involved? Is it good for society generally? Is the practice socially responsible? What about nuclear-generated electricity, rare hardwoods from South American jungles, sugar-laden candy, fossil fuel cars or high octane cocktails?

*If public relations works for both sides of an issue, can both sides be socially responsible?*

Almost any product or service has merit and demerit according to who regards it. Is tobacco "good" if a tobacco-smoking public wants it? Is it socially responsible to participate in marketing tobacco products, if society must pay for tobacco-related diseases attributable to smoking?

Any of the products or services cited could be in the public interest (be "good") and also be socially irresponsible *at the same time* depending on who makes the call. Society has an endless list: spread democracy in the Middle east, don't spread democracy in the Middle East; pro-life, pro-choice positions; pro-armament, anti-armament policies; pro-buckle up, anti-buckle up legislation; pro-gun control, pro-Second Amendment lobbying; pro-big government, anti-big government; eat beef, don't eat beef; distribute free condoms in high schools, don't distribute free condoms in high schools.

Public relations is involved in all of these issues. If public relations works for both sides of an issue, can both activities be good for the public and be socially responsible? In another chapter, you'll be able to use an ethical decision making model to answer these questions.

Perhaps this guideline will help practitioners and society decide what is the socially responsible activity.

Public relations activity could be in the public interest and be socially responsible if it has significant public support and consensus to support it and significant moral authenticity to validate it.

It's important to note that public opinion alone cannot validate all actions. We have too many tyrannical dictatorships controlling public opinion to assert that public opinion alone validates activity. Before he was deposed by the United States, Iraq's Saddam Hussein received 99% of the vote for "president."

But if PR practitioners use two-way symmetric communication, they can more validly defend their activities because they seek public approval *before* they act.

When publics gather around issues and form valid opinion, they are entitled to express and communicate it. Valid does not mean true, or correct, or right. Those terms imply philosophical, logical and moral standards. Valid means that a significant number of people have concluded their position after considering the pros and cons of an issue and have informed themselves about the premises of their position and the consequences.

Admittedly this guideline will not resolve the issue for those passionately involved in advocating any side of a position. *But public relations activity is democracy's jewel.* Even as PR practitioners eye competitor communication, they must at least conclude that their competitors are also acting in their public's interest and for their good. If the interest has significant support and moral authenticity, it is socially responsible activity. Why? Because in a free society valid publics have the right to be "untrue," "incorrect" and "wrong" as others see it.

*Beware when the media pick sides and tell you whose uniform you should wear.*

Only when PR activity merits near universal condemnation can it be said to be socially irresponsible, despite serving the interest of a narrow public.

This guideline will not satisfy those who believe in absolute right and wrong either. It doesn't have to. Listen to any "Crossfire" type television political talk show. Or belly up to any bar after hours for commentary on the social issues of the day. One would think angels and devils were debating. They're not. They're only people "doing PR" for the position they espouse.

Here's a final note about social responsibility. Beware when the minority public says the majority public is irresponsible, or vice versa. Also beware when the media pick sides, and tell you whose uniform you should wear.

## Respect and free expression

When publics' interests intersect, competitors manage their differences by the etiquette of freedom of expression. All groups in society, but especially public relations practitioners, appreciate the empowering aspect of the *First Amendment*. The *Amendment* powers the activity of journalism, advertising, public relations, and marketing. As these professions practice, they demonstrate to society at large why free expression is important to society's welfare. When these entities conflict, they should remind themselves that how they treat each other predicts the way they might themselves be treated.

Intolerance for opposing viewpoints, unfounded criticism, fabricated charges, and other agenda-driven communication subvert society.

In addition, when public relations practitioners follow all legitimate laws, rules and orders, they invite the rest of society to imitate their behavior. Illegal activity signals the worst aspects of communication practice. No one wants to hear public relations spokespersons defend illegal actions such as lying under oath by organization executives, defending insider trading, or promoting products and services under false pretenses.

But the flip side is equally troubling. The greatest challenge to PR practitioners comes in the form of attack communication, in which the attack is purely agenda driven. In most instances, these factless attacks are politically driven. But it positions PR people and their organizations as "wrongdoers." Defending against these attacks has become the 21st century PR communication daily chore. Such attacks and defenses dominate the news. The attack itself generates media complicity in the attack's authenticity. The PR defense generates media complicity in the organization's "guilt." Anyone who practices public relations in the 21st century will spend significant PR days defending against these attacks.

Neither the attack nor the defense implies social public relations irresponsibility.

## Communication

The flow of information through society must be reliable, trustworthy, open and accessible. Purveyed information carries the implied characteristics of being accurate and truthful and establishing a "fact record" that people should use to form their opinions. The greatest betrayal of society would be for communication experts to use information, the product of communication, to deceive society. The most damaging charge one could make against PR practitioners would be that they poison the public opinion process with untruth.

Public opinion poisoning also takes place when all the information necessary for the public to make an informed decision is not given. Access should be the hallmark of organizational communication. *Access is the constitution of PR practice.* If PR practitioners are supposed to speak for their organizations, they should know their organization's story and be prepared to share it. They should also be prepared to identify their organizations' plans and purposes.

As public relations, advertising, marketing and journalism go, so goes society. Society either gets honest, open, truthful communication resulting in quality decisions and a noble society, or it gets tainted information products and services, resulting in decisions, laws and customs built on deceit.

> *Public relations is organized, systematic, two-way communication between an organization and its publics, resulting in managed relationships that produce understanding and support of the organization s purposes.*

## Overview of public relations history

In its earliest form, public relations dates to cave drawings, spoken languages and written words. The art of communication, the basis for public relations as we know it today, developed through a need to persuade. The persuasive aspect of public relations involves getting others to do what you want. Doors to behavior include communication to inform audiences and incline them to accept proposals.

*Note*: The basic persuasion path is:

**Information → Attitudes → Behavior**

Publics **know** what you want, **like** what you want, **do** what you want.

Either the church or the state sponsored the earliest written works. Virgil's *Aeneid*, although a great Latin poem that advanced Latin literary genre, was propaganda literature for Augustus and the Roman Empire. St. Paul wrote his Epistles to encourage membership in the Church (behavior) and increase morale (attitude).

In 1456, Johann Gutenberg invented the printing press, making the Bible and other books accessible to the masses. From this invention, evolved the age of mass media communication. Newspapers were first published in the early 17th century. As publics gained access to more information and ideas, they gained more power. In response, governments and their leaders became more concerned with public opinion.

The development of public relations into a profession in the U.S. occurred in stages. These stages correspond to periods in United States history. Channels of communication developed from 1600 to 1799 with the colonization of the New World and the American Revolution.

Many colonists did not favor separation from England. But the writing of influential men became the first publicity efforts to persuade a populace. Supporters of the Revolutionary War participated in public relations-like activities as pamphleteers. Thomas Paine's *Common Sense* and writings by Benjamin Franklin, Thomas Jefferson and Samuel Adams gained support for their colonial separatist cause. Throughout that period, they used publications and events to move public opinion.

Revolutionists staged The Boston Tea Party, an early public relations special event, to gain public support at home with the colonists and abroad with England's enemies.

The expansion westward, the Civil War and the Industrial Revolution established the framework for wide dissemination of news and events. The railroad and the telegraph contributed to the evolution of communication and public relations.

> *It doesn t matter what you say about me, just spell my name right.*
> *P. T. Barnum*

The Penny Press in the 1830s gave rise to the practice of advocating with the press. Other practitioner types disseminated publicity about people and events. Without being so named, these communicators were actually practicing an early form of opinion formation, the basis for public relations.

These publicists were so successful, they made mythical heroes of Boone, Crockett, Cody, Hickock and Oakley. Some saw the economic advantage of the power of words to create instant images. Enter P. T. Barnum.

According to P. T. Barnum, there was no such thing as bad publicity. Thus the medium became the message and birthed the adage, "It doesn't matter what you say about me, just spell my name right." Many of Barnum's promotions caused controversy. But he welcomed it for the publicity he received.

Eventually, hired writers became spokespersons for special interests in businesses and government. Position statements and advertisements became common methods for one-way communication with consumers. The hired writers had one purpose: persuade consumers to buy the products and services of their clients. This took place from 1900 to l939, concurrent with the Progressive Era.

At the turn of the century, some investigative journalists attacked the New York police, prompting Theodore Roosevelt to dub them "muckrakers." Attacks on business and industry by muckrakers spawned the rise of journalist/publicists doing publicity for organizations to defend them. Thus publicists became spokespersons for organizations and a public relations/publicity function arose, paving the way for Ivy Lee and Edward Bernays.

These two men played important roles in establishing public relations as a unique field. Both got their start during this period.

Ivy Ledbetter Lee was a newspaper reporter by trade. In 1905, he joined with George Parker to form Parker and Lee, the nation's third public relations agency in New York City. Though the partnership lasted only four years, Ivy Lee continued his work with Lee, Harris & Lee, which opened in 1916. His clients included the anthracite coal operators in 1906 and the Rockefeller family in 1914. For each of his clients, Lee acted from a policy of honesty. If telling the truth could hurt the organization, then the organization must change its behavior, not lie. To Lee, public relations was the art of "counseling on dealing fairly with the press and public and urging business to be on its good behavior." His publicity practice resulted in the first real news release. When he sent copy to newspaper offices, trying to earn space instead of buying it as advertising, he said to the editor, "If you think any of our matter ought properly to go to your business office, do not use it."[1] But the copy he sent was so newsworthy that he began a symbiotic relationship with the press — the era of media relations had begun.

Edward L. Bernays, nephew of Sigmund Freud, was born in Austria and immigrated with his parents to New York as a young child. Like Lee, Bernays got his start in journalism. But unlike Lee, who felt public relations was an art, Bernays saw it as a science. Many of his contemporaries believed that social sciences made mass persuasion possible.

While Bernays made use of social science theories, he knew that the "engineering of consent" is only possible when it is in the public's best interest. In l923, Bernays wrote his first of three books about public relations, *Crystallizing Public Opinion*, in which he moved forward the concept of **public relations counsel** first introduced by Ivy Lee.

Later in American history, during World War II, the American government practiced the most concentrated form of propaganda and

> *During World War II, the government propagandized, using air raids, posters and drives  for lard, rubber and metal.*

persuasion on the American public. Poster, slogan, stamp and bond drives, street collections of lard, rubber and metal and air raids — all mobilized the American public to support the war. Many public relations professionals don't regard this era as true public relations because of the propaganda aspect of the communication between the government and the people. But it was a stage that later led to the blossoming of advertising with controlled images and packaged messages.

During and after World War II, technological advances created new industries and stimulated the economy. Eventually, as government became more involved in people's lives, public affairs departments arose to manage

---

1. Ivy Ledbetter Lee. Declaration of Principles. Wilcox, Cameron, Ault, Agee (2003). *Public Relations Strategies and Tactics*, 7th edition. Boston, MA: Allyn & Bacon, p. 37.

the communication between the people and their government agencies.

Today, public relations works to professionalize itself. PRSA sends representatives to former socialist states to share with their people the art and science of open communication in a formerly closed society. The Internet creates special communication problems because companies face additional message competition. The media exceed their original role in merely reporting news and now create it. It's called "participative journalism." The influence

**The media have exceeded their original role in reporting news and now create it.**

ranges from programs like "60 Minutes," which projects the appearance of objective journalism, to nightly news anchors and reporters telling Americans "that's how it is." But these pseudo-journalists, using ambush interview techniques, and gatekeeper prerogative, actually instigated the public to be wary of accepting TV columnist opinion and politically motivated vetted coverage as fact. In annual polls, the media score among the lowest social groups in credibility. Now alerted, a wary public looked at other vested-interest messages, such as public relations statements and positions, with a jaundiced eye. Public relations practitioners today must earn a hearing with their publics.

Crisis management communication has exploded as a litigious society attacks and accuses itself, its businesses and its organizations. For many, public relations has become litigation communication. Inevitably, charlatans creep under the blanket, forcing professional societies like the Public Relations Society of America to develop a certification process to identify professionals who want respect for their practice.

Public relations, whether it's a social science, a communication skill, a disowned cousin of journalism, or a profession with a scientific and artistic base, has evolved dramatically since Edward Bernays coined the term "public relations counsel" in the 1920s.

## Counseling and communicating

To appreciate the work of public relations practitioners, look at what PR people do on the job every day. You'll find PR people issuing news releases, conducting special events, writing and making speeches, appearing on talk shows, publishing annual reports, taking surveys, making videotapes, etc. All of these activities, however, are communication activities. So most people believe that these are the most important contributions public relations makes to an organization's communication program. But PR does more.

Public relations practitioners are **counselors as well as communicators.** The counseling function of public relations might actually be more important than the communication function. Why? Consider this analogy. Suppose you want to write a letter to a friend with advice on how to shop for the best deal on a car. Now also suppose you're the best writer around. Can you give sound advice simply because you can write well? Hardly. You need to know your stuff about how to strike a bargain before you can write about it.

Writing is a skill. But without substance, it's just a skill. If public relations people simply write what others tell them to, they're simply communicators, not counselors.

In an organization, management expects true public relations practitioners to counsel as well as communicate. They need to know about audiences, messages and channels. By merely being great communicators, they might know how to use channels, but not analyze audiences and fashion messages.

It's true that some organizations don't ask their PR people to advise them. In those cases, the practitioners are publicists, not public relations practitioners. The Public Relations Society of America regards the counseling function of public relations so highly that it will not admit practitioners into the Society unless they counsel management or report to someone who does. In many organizations, the true public relations practitioner reports directly to the top person. Management will always need public relations advice.

**Counseling makes PR people more than mere publicists.**

Here are some examples of the differences between a counselor and a communicator (*Figure 1.2*)

*Note*: When counselors encounter a problem, they must first discover if they're facing an **identity or image** problem. Identity is what an organization is in reality. Image is how the organization's publics perceive the organization.

In an identity problem, the organization "deserves" the image it gets. In an image problem, the organization's image doesn't correspond to its identity.

*Example*: In the deli example (*Figure 1.2*), research shows the deli has a poor reputation (image). People have lost confidence. The deli isn't being talked about in town as the best deli with the best sandwiches.

*Solution*: Conduct research to discover if anything has changed with the identity of the deli to warrant the

## Image ~ Communicator ~ Counselor

| Image | Communicator | Counselor |
|---|---|---|
| The owner of a small neighborhood deli can't figure out why she's losing business. She calls for outside PR help. But will she get a counselor or just a communicator? | A communicator might come in and quickly advise a better publicity campaign – a few news releases, some ads and a better looking menu. Then hopes it works. | A counselor would first establish if the problem is image or identity, conduct research, then advise the owner. If it's an identity problem (with the food), an identity program will help — better beef. If it's an image problem (not known well enough), then a communication program would work. |
| When Sears suffered charges of auto repair fraud, The Sears chairman needed the best advice on how to minimize reputation damage and begin image restoration. He needed a counselor. | Regardless of the message, a communicator might have suggested a personal appearance by the chairman on television and personal statements in print. But what to say? | The PR counselor had four "evasions of responsibility" choices. The counselor selected two: the offensive actions were accidental; the offensive actions were unintentional. Then the counselor turned communicator and beamed the messages. |
| In the 1980s, Goodyear needed to turn its fortunes around. CEO Stanley Gault needed a marketing strategy for its new Aquatred tire that would provide new momentum for the company. | A communicator, using traditional product launch thinking, might have simply carried out a multi-million dollar advertising campaign with some supporting PR. | A counselor, sensing that numerous audiences had to buy into the new "wet traction" tire – dealers, manufacturers, the industry media, financial community and consumers, suggested a strategic campaign to generate word-of-mouth excitement for the new tire. It worked. |

**Figure 1.2**

negative image. Has the food changed (different beef supplier)? Has service changed? Is the deli as clean as it was before? Is the menu the same? Is the cook the same? Are prices the same?

If research reveals that a number of changes have produced a poorer product or inferior service or displeased customers who told others the deli has "lost it," then the counselor faces an identity problem. No amount of pure publicity will create a positive image for a negative product (identity). And a conscientious PR practitioner wouldn't try it.

But if research reveals that nothing has changed and the image is unwarranted, then the practitioner faces a communication problem. The message (the identity) is not reaching the audience, or the message is wrong (doesn't match the identity), or the audience is wrong (doesn't want the identity). All of these problems are solvable by communication techniques. Even here, some counseling is necessary to pick the right message for the right audience through the right channel. But the "heavier" counseling, changing the identity, isn't needed.

It's clear from these examples that top management looks to public relations counselors for advice on how communication can help them get the job done. Lower-level public relations employees, lacking sufficient experience and judgment, might be able to carry out a communication strategy, but not be able to invent one.

## PR practitioners

The Public Relations Society of America has categorized PR practitioners into four groups according to responsibility and activity.

**Senior professional**. Top counselor. Advises management on strategic approaches to problems and issues. Has extensive knowledge of how public opinion works and how communication helps organizations gain their ends. Analyzes the outcomes of specific approaches and evaluates their impact on the organization.

**Professional manager**. Often a director of operations, including planning, creative input to campaigns — themes, audience analysis designs, messages — budgeting, program evaluation and personnel decisions. Supervises other communication employees. Advises senior professionals or top managers on communication strategy.

**Staff professional.** Frequently, a communication specialist. Responsible for carrying out campaign strategies, using knowledge and experience of communication tools — news releases, brochures, video stories, research, etc. Might counsel middle managers and directors on communication strategies.

**Beginning professional.** Usually an entry-level communication generalist who carries out tasks and activities associated with the tactics of a campaign. Performs data collection and research activities.

This list of public relations strategic activities will show the difference between counseling and communicating (*Figure 1.3*).

A few years ago, *pr reporter* summarized the contribution of public relations to an organization in this way:

- **An organization adopts a set of values.** Public relations role: to help management define those values through issue identification and research.

- **The organization shares those values internally.** It shares them among employees and other members of the organizational family. Public relations role: to help management communicate with and motivate employees.

- **The organization expresses those values to outside publics.** Public relations role: to assume responsibility for public relations advertising, publicity, promotion, media relations, special events and participation in marketing.

- **The organization's publics understand and accept those values.** This acceptance leads to a successful organization. Public relations role: to handle crises, customer relations, and community relations.

These activities work best when management respects public relations for its contributions.

## Contest for public opinion

In everyday commerce, the arts, the sciences, indeed, in all social life, organizations need their publics' approval to fulfill their mission. Remember that the definition of public relations includes the idea that important publics understand and accept the ambitions of an organization. It also includes the ambition that publics will behave the way organizations want them to.

Now from the viewpoint of the public, they need reasons to behave a certain way. In our chapter on public opinion, we'll review how opinion forms, what influences it, how we can change it, how long it will last, and how it relates to behavior.

But in the context of public relations practice, public opinion is the golden ring. Opinion is really desired behavior from the viewpoint of public relations. And your PR people aren't the only ones after behavior from certain publics. Other public relations practitioners are after the same public. And inside the minds of target publics are reasons and motives to behave a certain way. Society exerts its pressure on the publics. So do family, religion, government, law, groups, crises, circumstances and dozens of other issues influence those publics every day. It's a war out there for the opinion of your target publics.

## Six Functions of Public Relations

| Six Functions Common to Public Relations Activities | |
| --- | --- |
| Research | What we have done |
| Counseling | What we want/need to do |
| Strategic thinking | What will help us do it – strategies |
| Strategic planning | How we will do it – tactics |
| Communication planning | Doing it – PR plan/campaign/program |
| Evaluation | Did we do it? – evaluation |

**Figure 1.3**

**Public relations is the contest for public opinion.**

Because PR is a contest, it's important to remember the following:

• **Don't take the public's behavior for granted.** Behavior is a complex phenomenon. Many factors influence behavior, and public relations practitioners may not be able to influence, let alone control, all of them.

*Example*: In the impeachment debate in Congress in 1998 about the conduct of President William Clinton, many assumed that Democrats in Congress would automatically vote not to authorize a full inquiry into the impeachment charges against the president. But a majority of Democrats voted for the inquiry. Their motives went beyond party affiliation.

**Symbols burn messages in your public s mind.**

• **Don't take your competitors for granted.** Some people are very savvy about persuading audiences. Know your competitors' agenda, research and techniques. You'll have a better chance to control opinion if you know the nature of the messages your target public receives.

*Example*: In seeking election to office, candidates cannot simply beam their messages to their publics and expect to carry the day. How will candidates know if their opponents are accusing them of opinions or activities that might not be true unless they conduct research?

• **Know if your target public is for you, against you, or neutral.** Their beginning posture will have a lot to do with how much effort you need to apply.

*Example*: When a manager wants to gain approval for one of her proposals at a meeting, she cannot show up for the meeting not knowing how many votes she has or how much resistance she will encounter. Many embarrassing moments at business meetings can be avoided if those seeking to control opinion know who believes what, why they believe it, and how intensely they believe it.

• **Make certain your messages always contain reasons why your target public should do what you're asking.** The audience must identify with the message.

*Example*: In the 1990s American anti-smoking campaign, messages would not have been as effective as they were if they had merely exhorted the public not to smoke. Instead, messages to smokers shared research that disease follows smoking. Messages to nonsmokers sought to bring them on board because they showed that smoking-related illnesses overburdened Medicare, which they paid for with their taxes. Both types of messages sought to have both publics identify with the movement.

• **If you need long-lasting behavior, nurture the target public.** Don't assume that initial behavior will repeat itself without nurturing through message repetition. Also, don't assume that the target public will respond to the same message from day to day. Remember, your target public will hear from other influences daily.

*Example*: A college president wants to change the pattern of classes to include a full schedule of classes on a day that previously had been "unassigned," code for "no classes." He presents his case to assembled faculty on a single occasion. But on following days, others demonstrate how their lives would be disrupted by the change. The faculty switches allegiance from the president to the plan's opponents.

• **Don't underestimate the efficacy of campaign symbols and themes.** When a real contest is underway, "sides" can be symbolically expressed. The target public needs to see your side in consumable symbols they can identify with.

*Example*: In the public opinion campaign on gun control, proponents of control used battle-field-like automatic weapons to symbolize how extreme some pro-gun members of society have interpreted the right to own and bear arms. Control proponents wanted publics to agree with their position by showing pictures of assault weapons.

Opponents of gun control used a symbol of the American flag as a backdrop to their print and electronic ads expressing their position that banning certain types of guns is assaulting a freedom guaranteed by the Constitution. They wanted the public to connect their position with symbols of freedom and dangerous erosion of Second Amendment rights. ■

## Tips

1. The right to tell your side of the story is an exercise of your First Amendment rights under the Constitution.

2. The key to building relationships with important publics is to show a match between what you have to offer and what your publics need or want.

3. The "highest" types of PR allow your publics to change what you offer to meet their needs.

4. Don't try to make a bad or negative thing look better than it is. Public relations is not the act of "perfuming manure."

5. To get along with the media, show them how your information is important to their publics.

6. Before you try a communication strategy to solve a problem, see if the real problem lies with the identity of your client or organization.

7. For each project, write a statement expressing the socially responsible nature of what you're about to do.

8. Make certain that part of your job in public relations involves helping management make decisions that affect the organization's relationships, image and identity.

9. Always tell the truth. Your personal reputation and the reputation of your client or organization depend on how reputable you are.

10. Never apologize for practicing public relations. But do separate yourself from "wrongdoing" amateurs. Your actions will affect the image of the whole profession. But the image of the whole profession should not affect your actions.

**Questions for classroom discussion**

1. What was the main historical reason public relations developed as a distinct practice?

2. Which model of public relations do you think your school should use? Why?

3. What was your image of public relations when you first began this course? Why? Did others feel the same as you? How do you feel about public relations now?

4. If the words "public relations" bother some, what word or phrase would you use to describe the right of anyone to tell a side of a story?

5. Do you think today's organizations need a special function, like public relations, to tell their stories?

**Internet assignment**

Roam through news organizations' Web sites on the Internet. Identify **three stories** with clear public relations implications. Prepare an outline of the three stories specifying:

- **Issues** the organization is dealing with
- The organization's **position** on the issues
- How well you think the organization **tells its story**

Name_____Date _____

# Dyeing the environment

A public relations counselor works for a clothing manufacturer who uses dyes in the production process. Some social groups are worried about the potential pollution effect on the environment. But nothing has been proven about the harmful effects of the dyes. The media have caught on to the story and, not surprisingly, support the position of the environmental groups.

What is the role of the PR practitioner in telling the manufacturer's side of this story? Focus on the organization's position.

_____

_____

_____

How can the PR practitioner successfully build consumer, governmental and other relationships with so much special interest and media opposition?

_____

_____

_____

What can the PR practitioner and her boss do about untrue rumors and misinformation?

_____

_____

_____

How does communication, especially public relations communication, contribute to a better society?

_____

_____

_____

*See other side*

Name _____ Date _____

**Practical case study**

Why do the media and public relations practitioners get along so well at times and at other times call each other names, such as "flacks" for PR people and "hacks" for journalists?

_____

_____

_____

Is either function of public relations, counseling or communicating, more important than the other? Why?

_____

_____

_____

How can public relations practitioners work for an organization or individual that many believe doesn't act in the best interests of the public?

_____

_____

_____

Name _____ Date _____

_____

Form teams of four students in each team. One student in each team will take the role of a PR practitioner, another the PR practitioner's boss or manager, another a consumer, and the fourth, a reporter for a local newspaper.

Role play the following scenario: A consumer is unhappy with the way she was treated when she tried to return a boxed set of music CDs to the store that she claimed was not recorded properly. The clerk said the store had a "No Return" policy on music CDs and it was clearly posted at the checkout counter. The woman claimed that the policy pertained to music CDs that did not satisfy the customer, not to CDs that did not work. When the customer appealed to a manager, she received the same treatment, no satisfaction. Instead, she was curtly told, "There's nothing more we can do for you. Take it up with the manufacturer. It's not our problem."

The customer went to a consumer columnist (the reporter) who wrote an unfavorable story about the store and its management.

Now, the consumer and the reporter are visiting the PR practitioner and manager to continue the argument and expand it to a major story on store policy, customer service and the organization's reputation.

Role-play that meeting. Then, report to the class how it went. Ask each group to specify a different person to make the report. One group will use the PR practitioner, another will use the customer, etc. Look for differences, not only in the way each group solved the PR problem, but also in the perspectives of each person in this PR challenge.

Consumer's position _____

Consumer's major argument _____

Reporter's position _____

Reporter's main argument _____

Company manager's position _____

Company's manager's main argument _____

PR director's position _____

PR director's main argument _____

*See other side*

Name _____ Date _____

Class notes. How did the positions of each character differ from yours?

_____

_____

_____

_____

Did anyone change position or argument following the meeting? _____

Who changed? Why? _____

_____

What arguments would you offer for each of the characters? Try to see both sides of the issue. But focus on the PR director's role and responsibility, both at the meeting and afterward, for the reputation of the company.

Consumer _____

_____

Reporter _____

_____

Store manager _____

_____

_____

PR director _____

_____

# Chapter 2

# How Public Relations Works

**PRaxiom** *On a foggy night, public relations will do more than light your way; it will also light you, so others notice.*

## What this chapter covers

In this chapter, you'll learn how public relations works to gain positive public opinion for its organizations. You'll acquire a working knowledge of a PR model you can use for any communication challenge.

You'll look carefully at the importance of audiences, messages and channels, the **M-A-C Triad**, which figures in every public relations challenge. Also in this chapter you'll learn about a successful PR practice model. You'll also see how most successful practitioners are precise in their use of the model. As a first step in understanding the model, you'll explore the value of research in public relations practice.

## Who are public relations people?

The title, "public relations," occurs in a variety of places. Someone pursuing a career "doing public relations" could work in a large organization, handling relationships with the media or communicating with employees.

A practitioner might move up to a top executive position, counseling the CEO or top managers. A practitioner could work for a PR firm or agency performing communication tasks, rising from junior account executive to account manager or higher.

Another communication person might work in a school district, hospital or not-for-profit organization. The person might speak publicly for a utility company, gain publicity for a sports team, or promote an entertainment group.

All these communication workers are called "public relations practitioners" and contribute to society and to their organizations in ways different from advertising and marketing. And they make their contributions through two chief activities, counseling and communicating.

## Role of research in public relations

The work of public relations professionals resembles the practice of medicine. In medicine, trained personnel react — they respond to emergencies and crises to solve problems. Or, they're proactive; they get in front of problems and prevent them from happening.

In either case, these professionals won't do anything until they accurately picture the problem. In medicine, it's called a diagnosis. Medical people use x-rays, blood tests and patients' own opinions to form their diagnoses.

Likewise, PR practitioners use opinion tests, literature searches and the opinion of their audiences to decide the nature of the problems they face. After treating their patients, doctors repeat many of the same diagnostic techniques to measure their success.

PR people use surveys and other feedback techniques to see if they accomplished what they set out to do.

In both professions, guessing at problems and their solutions is a foolish waste of time and resources, and dangerous. It could also be unethical. Real professionals use research or they risk acting like amateurs. What's at stake is nothing less than their clients' survival.

## Basic public relations model

You can solve most public relations challenges and problems using a basic model that blends communication and public relations processes (*Figure 2.1*).

As you work through each part of the model, think of it as a step-by-step process. Each step is important. A practitioner can't skip any step for lack of experience or resources. Some practitioners have bosses or clients who don't appreciate the value of providing sufficient resources in each step. These practitioners will be marginally successful, if at all.

In each step of the model to reduce campus binge drinking, consider the relevance of research (R).

## Public Relations Model

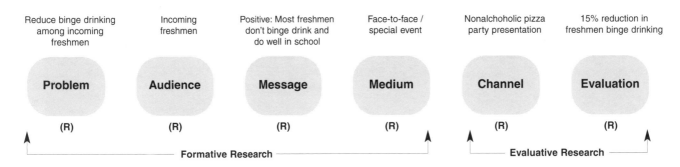

Figure 2.1

Notice how research (R) plays a role in each part of the public relations model.

- Research narrows and defines the **proper challenge or problem** to solve, saving the practitioner from going off into unproductive directions.

- Research identifies the **right audiences** to approach. Research can fracture a large, unmanageable audience into smaller manageable target segments.

- Research helps fashion **appropriate messages** for each audience. In a persuasion campaign, these messages become benefits to influence audiences to know, feel or do something.

- Research picks the **correct channel**, matching it to both audience and message. Note the importance of the **M-A-C Triad** in successful communication planning. (Message-Audience-Channel match)

- Research helps construct the most workable **action plan**.

- Research helps **measure success** of the action plan. Bosses and clients want to know if public relations reached its stated goals. Public relations people also want to know if they correctly identified the issues, audiences, messages and channels on the way to a successful campaign. Research can tell practitioners what worked, what didn't, and how they could improve the process in the next campaign.

## Research challenges

Research identifies the **true issues** in a problem by distinguishing symptoms from causes. For example, if a group of employees is unhappy with management, research can determine the cause for the unhappiness as opposed to the symptom of merely being unhappy.

Solving the problem of unhappiness by providing employees with an additional day off might not solve the problem. Perhaps these employees want more say in

decisions that affect them. Offer them anything less, and the symptoms will remain.

Research also highlights the separate issues within a problem or challenge. One of the most important parts of public relations practice is identifying issues and stating them correctly.

> *Only research can distinguish symptoms from causes within issues.*

## Identify issues

All successful public relations practice begins with successful issue identification. Express issues by writing an "issue statement." Here's a model issue statement:

"**Employees** are **upset** because they feel left out of the **decision-making process** about issues that affect them."

Notice how the statement has three parts: an audience, an issue and an attitude.

- Audience – employees

- Issue – decision making

- Attitude – upset

In issue statements, the audience might be a company, a government agency, or pending legislation. The attitude can be a strength, weakness, opportunity, threat, danger or challenge. And there's always an issue, the right issue, identified by research. Here are examples of issues:

- *Our hospital faces loss of market share because a new HMO regulation requires us to reduce the number of tests we can administer to patients.*

- *The mayoral candidate strongly supports additional nighttime street patrols.*

- *The new international court cannot get the prestige it needs unless the United States supports it.*

In public relations practice, practitioners use issue statements like these to go to work.

## Identify audiences

Four types of audiences comprise public relations practice: **internal**, **external**, **intermediary** and **special**.

- **Internal audiences** are members of the organizational family. They have a vested interest in what happens to the organization. They are also part of the organization's operation. They could be executives, managers, employees, legal counsel, accounting firms, public relations firms, or others. They could even be families of employees for certain issues.

- **External audiences** are individuals or groups outside the organization, but with an interest in the fate of the organization. They could be customers, clients, vendors, suppliers, regulatory agencies, or the media.

- **Intermediary audiences** are "gates" PR practitioners go through to reach the organization's target audiences. For example, in a program to reduce violence in schools, parents might be considered an intermediary audience to students, the real target group. In this case, campaigners beam messages to parents to persuade them to influence the real target audience, students.

- **Special audiences** are usually external and have a special relationship with the organization that's not always positive. In a litigious society, these audiences could include action groups suing an organization. Or, they might be protest groups, boycotters, TV "talking heads" who nightly applaud or deride organizations, depending on media agendas. The media are considered a special audience when they're targets or objects of a public relations effort. If they only convey information and attitudes, they're considered an intermediary audience.

*Example*: If the local newspaper doesn't publish any of the sports stories from the local high school because the editor and principal don't get along, then the media are direct targets for public relations work.

*Example*: If an organization wants to get coverage of its community relations program to improve the parks in a community for residents and its own employees, it might seek to get messages to the community through "gatekeeper" media. It also helps when the PR person persuades the media of the merits of the project.

To properly practice, public relations practitioners must correctly identify the audiences important to their ambition. In doing this, practitioners must avoid stopping their research too early.

If they say for example, **employees** are unhappy, is that sufficient audience analysis to find the real cause and solve the real problem? What does research say about employees? It says they're workers. But janitors and managers are also workers. Are they unhappy about the same issues? A lack of research should cause practitioners to pause before they leap into a communication program. They might make crucial errors if they don't examine audiences and ask three questions:

- **Have I properly identified the right audience for this issue?**

- **Have I narrowly defined this audience?**

- **Do I know what this audience is like and how important it is to my ambition?**

To answer these questions, you should apply these four steps to your audiences:

**I-S-P-R**
    **I**dentify
        **S**egment
            **P**rofile
                **R**ank

Properly identified, audiences form the basis for public relations activity — in other words, audience identification activity **IS PR** if it follows these four steps.

## Step one: Identify the audience

Most issues contain an audience in the issue statement. Ask yourself, "Who should do what for me to succeed?" It's helpful if you use a design to identify some typical audiences. The following *Audience Identification Wheel* could prove helpful (*Figure 2.2*).

### Audience Identification Wheel

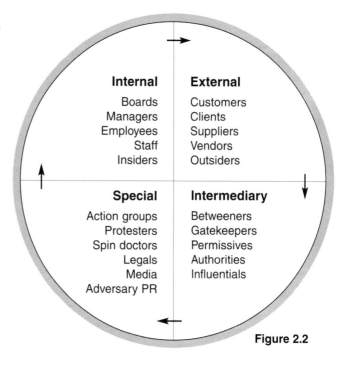

| Internal | External |
|---|---|
| Boards | Customers |
| Managers | Clients |
| Employees | Suppliers |
| Staff | Vendors |
| Insiders | Outsiders |

| Special | Intermediary |
|---|---|
| Action groups | Betweeners |
| Protesters | Gatekeepers |
| Spin doctors | Permissives |
| Legals | Authorities |
| Media | Influentials |
| Adversary PR | |

**Figure 2.2**

Use the wheel to identify important audiences for your issues. Make a wheel for each issue. Make the list all-inclusive. Later, you can refine the list to include only those audiences you'll actually target.

## Step two: Segment the audience

Segment your audiences in several ways: by ...

- Relevance and involvement with issues (publics — media, activists, etc.)

- Importance to PR goals

- Relationship with the organization

- Management imperatives

- **By relevance and involvement with issues**. When we divide issues into important, logical parts, we also divide audiences.

*Example*: You can divide "lack of involvement in decision- making" into decision-making about working conditions, or project selection, or input that controls decisions. Each of these aspects of this issue involves a different audience.

- *Unions* (a segment of "employees") might need public relations attention about working conditions.

- *Managers* (another segment of "employees") might need more communication about which projects the organization will work on.

- *Secretaries* and other staffers (a third segment of "employees") might need to be included on the list of information providers at the beginning of decision-making.

Each segmented audience needs a different message and possibly a different channel.

How well we segment audiences determines if we will be effective practitioners. Approaching audiences at the big, "broad stroke" level signals sloppy, amateur guessing and a lack of commitment to research.

*Note*: Many clients will not want to sufficiently invest in formative research at the beginning of their public relations projects. But they must do the research if they are to succeed. How to solve the problem?

Some practitioners in public relations firms will simply conduct the research and absorb the cost. But they might charge it back to the client in other aspects of the program. It's a trade-off. An unprofessional action for a practitioner is to proceed with a communication program without research. The client deserves, indeed, *needs* the research even if the client doesn't appreciate it. More

frequently, clients favor evaluative research at the end of a project because they're eager to discover whether and why a communication effort did or did not work.

Full-time practitioners working for organizations must convince their superiors that they should spend time on necessary research. A logical argument, bolstered by case studies of organizations that conducted research prior to successful campaigns, should make the point.

*PR is accurate if it Identifies, Segments, Ranks and Profiles audiences I - S - P - R.*

## Step three: Profile the audience

Profiling means getting to know your audience as well as possible. It includes the essential opinion trinity: knowledge, attitudes and behavior. It also includes sources of knowledge and attitudes; how audiences acquire and process information; how key influentials affect an audience segment; appropriate messages for each segment; accommodating channels; and latent audience wishes and ambitions.

A classic research study is a demographic profile of an audience, listing the characteristics that detail "what" audiences are like — their geography, age, sex, marital status, and other important information, such as ergraphic characteristics, their occupational profile.

In addition, psychographic studies can identify "who" audiences are, their likes and dislikes, preferences, inclinations, or positions on issues.

Psychographic studies include a VALS examination of audiences. VALS stands for Values and Lifestyle Study partly invented by SRI International, business researchers and consultants. In a VALS study, researchers categorize audiences according to behavior patterns. (*See the chapter on research for a description of the VALS method.*)

An early classic study of audiences using VALS dealt with marketing yogurt. A yogurt manufacturer wanted to introduce fruit into its yogurt product and wanted to know the best way to produce and market the concept. The company wanted to discover the ideal market niche for the new product.

The company developed a VALS psychographic profile of the typical yogurt eater. It asked focus groups of yogurt eaters how they preferred to eat their yogurt. The study resulted in a profile that revealed an interesting blend of "experiencers" and "actualizers" who not only eat yogurt for lunch but also want to be involved in "creating" their lunch. Apparently, the profiled group wanted a combination of a prepared lunch (yogurt in a container) and the opportunity to participate in making their lunch.

So the company placed the fruit on the *bottom of the yogurt container* so consumers could manually stir the fruit to the top and participate in "making their lunch." Manufacturers still place fruit at the bottom of yogurt containers where a VALS study told them to place it years ago, waiting for experiencers and actualizers to stir it to the top.

You can profile your audiences in other ways.

Focus groups can efficiently discover consumer behaviors, attitudes toward issues, and levels of knowledge. They can also detect your audience's ability to process information. You should not embark on a persuasion campaign until you clearly know the ability of your audiences to process information. You must know if your audience can take your concepts and messages and understand your application of those ideas to their lives. Your audience's ability to process information determines the level and types of persuasive messages you can use. Focus groups can help you identify constraints to getting desired behavior from audiences.

Obviously, research that asks audiences:
- what they know and what they need to know
- what they're like and what they like
- what they've done and what they will do

and provides the best profiles for your campaigns.

## Step four: Rank the audience

Consider two factors in ranking your audiences — the *need* to reach them and the *ability* to reach them.

Not every audience is important enough to justify expenditure of time and other resources. Not every audience will cooperate to make the effort worthwhile.

Consider need first. How can you measure the importance of an audience?

Audience value rises in proportion to the importance of its relationship with the organization. Remember, this is public relations and maintaining, improving and strengthening certain relationships are crucial to an organization. Also, when your organization is under attack, you must know how important and damaging the attack is and whether you should deal with the attacking audience directly or indirectly.

Because you'll plan your public relations activities, your plan's objectives will determine your audiences' importance.

*Example*: A bakery wants to establish a positive relationship with a community. But the bakery's trucks stir a lot of complaints when they travel through the community's streets early in the morning. The public relations department decides to do something about it. Through research, they discover four separate audiences embedded in four issues:

- Issue: Some neighborhood residents are publicly complaining about the noise the trucks make so early in the morning
  *Audience*: **Directly affected residents**
- Issue: Negative editorials appear in local papers
  *Audience*: **Newspaper editor**
- Issue: Bakery employees are criticized in public during social, religious and shopping occasions
  *Audience*: **Employees (unsegmented)**
- Issue: Trucks deliver food in early morning for the community hospital
  *Audiences*: **Hospital audiences, executives, patients, hospital personnel, and patients' families**

How will you rank these audiences? Which relationships most benefit the company? Which audiences will respond to the company's efforts to explain the situation and reduce tension? Why rank them at all? Why not deal with all of them?

That's a fair question. But suppose the PR department has a limited budget, or limited resources, or the attitudes are so firmly held that no reasoning, amount of money, or effort will make a difference? How do you decide which audiences are worth pursuing and which you can let go?

## Informal ranking formula

Rank audiences using two factors based on the PR counselor's motive. Notice that this informal ranking looks only at the organization and its needs. The two factors:

- The **need** to reach an audience
- The **ability** to reach an audience

The *need* depends on the importance of the audience to the purposes of the organization. Looked at this way, the need is connected to how important the issue is to the organization because the audience is part of the issue.

Next, convert the need to two categories: **must influence** the audience; and **should influence** the audience. This is a judgment call. But it's not a guess. Use research to see if there's a match between audience, issue and organizational purpose. Thus:

### Need = Must / should influence

Next, judge how likely you are to influence your audience. Use research to see if you have sufficient resources, time and access to the audience. Also, judge if the audience is available for influence and not severely constrained in any way. Thus:

### Ability = Likely / unlikely to influence

The resulting merger of the two criteria results in a simple 2 x 2 grid (*Figure 2.3*). You decide which audience goes into each cell in the grid. The result is a visual ranking of your audiences. The grid looks like this:

**Audience Ranking Grid**

|  | *Priority targets*<br>**Must influence** | *Secondary targets*<br>**Should influence** |
|---|---|---|
| **Likely to influence** | Do the most | Do the required |
| **Unlikely to influence** | Do the necessary | Do the least |
|  | Maximum PR effort | Significant PR effort |

**Figure 2.3**

Now apply this formula to the case of the baking company delivering its products to the hospital in the morning. Assess each of the four audiences according to the two criteria. Then place each in its appropriate cell in the grid. Here's one assessment: (*Figure 2.4*)

**Affected residents** are irritated. They want the trucks stopped. No manner of public relations will convince them that the baked goods, even for a hospital, is more important than their sleep. Influencing them should be difficult, if not impossible.

**Media** smell a story that can have legs for a more than a couple of days. Besides, it's a baking company, a business versus their readers. They will butter their readers' bread, even if it means they will ask the hospital to "be reasonable" and force the baking company to deliver a little later, or take a different route. They will pretend to be fair, and although the company PR people will make every effort to get them to end the negative editorials, they won't. PR should reach them but won't have much luck. The media are set against them.

**Company employees** are interested in their paychecks and their reputation when they go shopping. They want the unfair editorials ended. And they want the company to get the hospital on their side to help fight the neighbors and the media. They promise to do all they can so everyone will see their side of the story. They are easy to reach and very persuasible.

**The hospital family** can be extremely helpful in protecting the company's image. The company can probably get them on its side but their influence on the neighbors and the media is unknown. After all, the hospital is an important customer, but only a customer. When the company looks at the whole issue, it might conclude that affected neighbors could boycott the baking company and cause serious economic hardship. It's hard to see how the hospital, even patients' families, can shake residents and the media off the company's back.

Using this analysis, here's the audience ranking:

**Ranking Grid Example**

|  | **Must influence** | **Should influence** |
|---|---|---|
| **Likely to influence** | Company Employees | Hospital personnel |
| **Unlikely to influence** | Media | Affected residents |

**Figure 2.4**

This type of informal ranking can work for many challenges. Its chief merit lies in its simplicity and ease of use. If you get all you need from this type of ranking, then use this formula. But if you want a more formal and more quantitative ranking system, look at the next formula.

## Formal ranking formula

Try using the following formula to rank the relationship between audience and organization. The formula is based on six relationship factors:

• Importance of the relationship to the immediate issue at hand or the general mission of the organization (two factors)

• Likelihood the organization can influence the relationship and likelihood the audience wants to be in relationship with the organization (two factors)

- Importance of the relationship to applicable law and to ethical principles (two factors).

Allocate value points from 1–5 (five being *important*, and one being *unimportant*,) to each of six aspects of each audience.

5   Important
4   Somewhat Important
3   Neutral
2   Somewhat Unimportant
1   Unimportant

- **Issue/Mission**. How important is the issue and the audience involved to the mission of the organization? Estimate the importance based on the organization's own management or business plan. Don't estimate it on sentiment, whim or bias. This is the logic portion of the decision.

- **Ability/Capability**. How capable is the organization to influence the knowledge, attitudes or behavior of the affected audience? How capable is the audience to process information, to understand and agree with the organization's mission and purpose, and to be free from constraints so as to offer supporting behavior as the organization wishes?

Consider the organization's ability to influence this audience with available resources (time, money and human capital). Consider the audience's capability to respond because of involvement in the issue and history of responding in the past.

- *Ethics/Law*. What are the public interest, social responsibility and fiduciary relationships with the audience? What **must** the organization do (legal question)? What **should** the organization do (ethical question)? To estimate the importance of the audience in this area, play out different scenarios. Best case? Worst Case?

Remember, none of these factors is more important than any other. Different situations occasionally raise one above another; but none, in itself, is more important.

Here's the formula:

| | |
|---|---|
| Issue/Mission | (5-1) |
| Ability/Capability | (5-1) |
| Ethics/Law | (5-1) |
| **Maximum totals** | **(15-3)** |

*Figures 2.5 and 2.6* show an application of the formula to the case:

## Bakery Trucks Audiences Ranked

| Audience | Issue/ Mission | Ability/ Capability | Ethics/Law | Total |
|---|---|---|---|---|
| Residents | 1 | 2 | 2 | 5 |
| Media | 3 | 2 | 4 | 9 |
| Employees | 4 | 5 | 4 | 13 |
| Hospital | 5 | 4 | 5 | 14 |

**Figure 2.5**

## Audience Ranking Results

| Audience | Points | Rank |
|---|---|---|
| Residents | 5 | 4 |
| Media | 9 | 3 |
| Employees | 13 | 2 |
| Hospital | 14 | 1 |

**Figure 2.6**

## Ranking analysis

*Hospital — Rank: 1 (14 points)*

**Issue/Mission** *(5 points)*. The specific issue of getting the hospital its bakery products on time is crucial to the hospital. But it's also crucial to the bakery to satisfy its customers, to deliver a quality product, on time, to needy people. Nothing, not even upset residents, can change the importance of this relationship. Both the specific issue and the overall mission are about equal in importance because they are intertwined.

**Ability/Capability** *(4 points)*. The company has ready access to its customers and can deliver PR messages to the hospital quickly and directly, without intermediaries. The message can be delivered in a clear and uncluttered fashion, without media bias contaminating the company's position. The hospital wants to hear company PR messages that can solve the double problem, "to get their bread and eat it too," in the form of good relationships with the community. Because the hospital must also hear contravening messages from the media and residents in editorials, letters to the editor, phone calls to its own PR director, and behind the scenes pressure on hospital board members, the company doesn't have free rein to persuade. Hence, the total score is four, not five.

**Ethics/Law** *(5 points)*. The company has a legal contract with the hospital, which it must fulfill. It also holds the ethical high ground that patients need the bread products. The company must tread carefully. It doesn't want the hospital to be the cause of community unrest. So the company must ethically free the hospital from this cloud. PR people must send "freeing" messages to hospital PR people, which they can beam on their own to the media and the community. The two PR directors will work together to solve this problem.

## Employees – Rank: 2 (13 points)

**Issue/Mission** *(4 points)*. Employees are equally crucial to the company's mission. Without a motivated and productive employee group, the company cannot reach its mission. But the hospital must be careful that some employees, perhaps unionized, will assume community arguments that bakery management doesn't need this contract, or the way it's being fulfilled, for the company to survive. Sometimes, PR practitioners need to persuade their own people about the importance of specific issues to the company. Hence, the score is only four, not five, because not everyone at the bakery might see the issue and the mission as the same.

**Ability/Capability** *(5 points)*. The company can reach its employees directly and frequently through its internal communication network. Employees generally agree with company messages, especially when the messages affect their jobs. But the company cannot get 100 percent agreement from its employees. No company can. In this case however, the trucks must get bread to everyone in the larger community early in the morning. Like newspapers, news and bread go stale the longer they take to get to market. The company has time and opportunity to make its point with employees.

> *The best PR analyst looks at all sides of an issue, even those of competitors.*

**Ethics/Law** *(5 points)*. Every company has a fiduciary relationship with its employees to provide the best possible working conditions. Company reputation is the most valuable working condition because everything follows from that — profits, salaries, benefits and jobs. Also, the company has a moral imperative to produce and deliver bread to ill community residents and their caregivers. As employees see it, the benefit to a tired nurse on night shift getting a piece of toast at 6:30 a.m. so she can do a good job in the intensive care unit later in the morning outweighs the community's benefit of a few minutes of uninterrupted sleep.

## Media – Rank: 3 (9 points)

**Issue/Mission** *(3 points)*. The media are sometimes unbiased intermediary audiences. But here, they run articles and editorials against the company. So it's important to get the company's message to them, before there's no company left. But the immediate issue gets in the way of the larger mission. That's why the editor has taken the adversarial stand against the hospital. The conflict between the issue and the mission convinces the company PR director to assess only three points to this aspect of the relationship.

**Ability/Capability** *(2 points)*. The company can easily send messages to the media. But the media just as easily can pay no attention to them, especially if the media have their own agenda on the issue. If the media side with upset residents, the "story value" of a complaining community might exceed the value of the company's explanation. An amateur PR director might assess more points thinking that a sit-down with the editor will change the paper's mind. But this PR director thinks time and money could be better spent on its employees and the hospital community. Besides, the PR director can pay for a message-controlled advertorial (some call these placements op-ed pieces or "opposite editorials," opinion pieces appearing opposite the editorial pages.) But will the editor accept the ad for publication?

**Ethics/Law** *(4 points)*. There's no compelling law for the company or media to follow with respect to information flow. Ethically, the company must issue truthful statements, but it can't promise to garage its trucks during early morning hours without seriously affecting the hospital and its patients. The newspaper knows that a legal contract is at stake. And the editor will not engage the debate on the ethics issue either. It's too risky to favor sleepy residents over hungry patients, the very way the company PR director should fashion the PR message.

## Residents – Rank: 4 (5 points)

**Issue/Mission** *(1 point)*. The company certainly wants to have a good reputation in the community. Reputation affects the company's ability to fulfill its mission. Are residents complaining in the newspaper on the same risk scale as employees demonstrating on the company's sidewalk during a strike? The PR director concludes foodstuffs will almost certainly continue to get through, at the same hour, despite the complaining. The PR challenge is to avoid alienating the small number of residents along the hospital delivery route so much that they decide to boycott the bakery's products. But the whole community will never do that, thinks the PR director, so it's not the best situation, but it's manageable, for now.

**Ability/Capability (2 points).** The company has no direct contact with residents unless it has a key communicator community network. It probably relies on the media to get messages to

> *Today, someone will always find fault in the way an organization does things.*

residents. But that's not a likely scenario, given the media's opposition to the company.

The company could expensively go door to door with its message. But what's waiting for them? If affected residents' highest value is quiet streets, no other value, for any other group, including hospital patients, will prevail. This group is severely constrained from paying attention to the company, let alone end its complaining. No token gesture will work either. If the PR director can't reach this audience, or the audience wouldn't care what the PR director had to say, even a score of two points might be generous. It's not a lower score because the PR director might be able to find a key influencer in the neighborhood to cool heads and tempers, so everyone gets a good night's sleep.

**Ethics/Law (2 points).** A social responsibility issue competes with a public interest issue here. Delivering provisions to the hospital is in the public interest and is socially responsible. Helping some neighbors get some sleep might be in the public interest but is certainly not socially responsible, especially if the hospital community goes hungry. At times, an organization's values directly conflict with community values. That, in itself, doesn't make the organization's or the community's values inferior. In today's litigious society, someone will always fault an organization for doing something someone doesn't like. The PR director assesses two points because the legal contract argument might take the edge off the debate.

On a tight budget, the company PR director will allocate resources according to audience ranking. The director might also approach these audiences in the order of their ranking. The PR tactical plan depends on the public relations strategic plan.

## Messages

Once you have identified, segmented, profiled and ranked audiences, you then would fashion appropriate messages for each. Research plays a major role in this activity.

The most efficacious messages come from an audience itself. That's where research plays a major role.

Some maintain the most important part of the public relations communication process is acquiring, making and expressing messages.

**Acquiring messages.** Audiences reveal messages in focus groups, interviews, surveys, speeches, writings, signs, complaints and congratulations, almost any manner in which the audience reveals its mindset. You need to pay attention to what audiences say and do.

**Making messages.** In fashioning messages for audiences, use research to detect the right nuance coming from audiences.

Messages could be a combination of three types depending on source:

- Messages individuals or organizations want to send
- Messages audiences want to receive
- Messages audiences need to receive

**Expressing messages.** In expressing messages for audiences, research the best channels. Use channels audiences can **access** and **believe**. If either condition isn't present, your message will either not get through

> *Effective channels are both used and believed.*

or will get through but your audience will disbelieve the channel and disregard the message.

Another key factor is the ability of certain channels to carry specific messages without getting in the way.

*Example*: A beach resort sends a nondescript memo to all employees explaining a new payroll deduction system, effects of the system on upcoming paychecks, and advice that employees should go to the business office to change withholding if employees wish it. That's it, no letterhead, no salutation, no examples, and no signature. Without considering the message content, employees are so outraged by the channel that the message never gets a proper reception. Even a channel, like a memo, is public relations and can affect important relationships.

Rely on research to gain feedback from audiences about channels. Research can tell you when the channel might be as important or even more important than the message. In the bakery versus the community example, a respected community organizer (a channel) can get a hearing for a less-than-welcome message the organizer carries.

## Blending messages and channels

*Before you craft messages, ask these questions:*

- What does the audience **already know** about the issue?
- What does the audience **need to know** about the issue?
- What message points will give the audience **greater understanding**?
- What message points should the audience **recall** when it's time for the audience to do what you want?
- How does the audience **feel** about this issue?
- What is the **source** of the audience's feeling about this issue?
- How **free** is the audience to know, feel or do what I want?
- How has the audience **behaved** in the past about this issue?
- What is the audience's likely **future behavior** about this issue?
- Am I researching the **right audience members** about this information?

*Before you send messages, ask these questions:*

- Is the message appropriate to the audience?
- Is the message appropriate to the channel?
- Is the message customized to the audience?
- Would a feature or benefit message work best?
- Would the audience respond to an emotional message?
- Would the audience respond to a logical message?
- Is the message sender's motive identity, image, positioning or marketing?
- Is the message credible to the audience?
- Is the message clearly linked to the issue?

*Before you select channels for messages, ask these questions:*

- Which of the four major channels is most appropriate (face-to-face, electronic, print, or special event)?
- Is the channel appropriate to the message?
- Is the channel appropriate to the audience?
- Is the message clear enough so it's easy to take in and understand?
- Does the audience have access to the channel?
- Does the audience believe the channel?
- Does the audience believe the sender?
- What obstacles in the channel would prevent the message from getting through?
- Does message expression allow audience feedback?
- Is message expression more important than message substance?

These research questions should help you *send the right message, to the right audience, through the right channel*.

Notice how the questions keep your mind open to possibilities. Sometimes law or other circumstances determine the message and you really can't change it.

*Example*: The beach resort memo sender had no choice about the message, only the channel. Even in cases when the substance of the message cannot be changed, research can tell you a lot about how to best picture, write and send messages.

Consider some answers to these questions and how they might affect your messaging decisions.

**Questions about audiences** analyze the *information, attitude* and *behavior* connection. *Note*: PR practitioners refer to this as the important I-A-B connection. You'll learn more about this connection in the chapter on public opinion.

Consider what your audience already knows and what it needs to know. When audiences understand issues, they're more likely to do something about them. So, educate uninformed audiences. And reinforce what informed audiences already know.

Also, it's important you know not only your audience's mindset or position on an issue, but also the *source* of that position. Roots of attitudes, such as education, affiliation with groups, and political or religious beliefs, could make some messages attractive and others unattractive. Failure to identify why an audience feels the way it does could doom a communication transaction.

> **Research helps send the right message to the right audience through the right channel.**

Finally, it's important that you get reliable information about your audience. Make certain your information doesn't come from "representative" members that don't represent the audience.

**Questions about making the message** could provide valuable information, especially for a persuasive communication. Two valuable analyses can almost guarantee success.

Check the connections in the M-A-C triad (Message–Audience–Channel). Your message must complement both your audience and your channel. The **M-A-C Triad** is the most important model for successful public relations communication transactions (*Figure 2.7*).

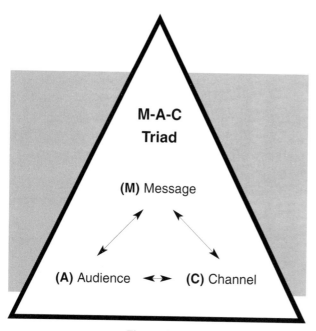

**Figure 2.7**

If any of the links break, effective communication can't happen.

- The right message and the right channel, but the wrong audience, and communication fails.
- The right message and the right audience, but the wrong channel, and communication fails.
- The right audience and the right channel, but the wrong message, and communication fails.

Make certain that all your **M-A-C Triad** connections are valid.

Second, check if your audience is receptive to your message. Your audience will provide you all the information you need. Your research will reveal your audience's best kept secret, the right message to trigger the behavior you want from them.

**Questions about message sending** provide you with important information about the third leg of the **MAC Triad**. Expressing the message gets into areas such as the credibility of the source. Should you send a young or old person to a group of seniors to make a point? Should you send a nonresident to community taxpayers to discuss new taxes for a school construction project?

Source credibility and channel accessibility are two major factors in sending effective messages. Audiences must both believe the source and must use the source. For example, does your audience use e-mail? It will do no good if the audience thinks e-mail is great, but doesn't use it.

A study of the Ewing Township Public Schools in New Jersey revealed that although public relations personnel want to use more electronic channels with residents such as e-mail, school web page, phone mail, and local cable access television station, which the school district controls, every electronic channel showed less use among residents than every print channel tested. PR people in that school district should not give up on electronic messaging. But their work is cut out for them to improve electronic channels, such as the school web page, and better promote their use to residents.

*Note*: Important communication components, such as "noise" in the channel and constraints on your audience, might prevent you from succeeding.

*Example*: A few years ago, the Internal Revenue Service (IRS) public relations personnel for the eastern region wanted some advice about certain messages they wanted to send to their employees about work-related issues. A consultant simply advised the PR people to talk face-to-face with employees to control message content. But union rules said that IRS executives could use only those channels endorsed and approved by the union. In cases like this one, management can communicate with its own employees only through unionized shop stewards. If the union were to take a strong position against management and ask its members to follow suit, then the employee audience would be "severely constrained" from accepting and agreeing to messages from management. That's a tough internal communication system for PR practitioners in those types of organizations.

In researching channels, practitioners frequently separate a *medium* from a *channel*. Four major media disseminate messages — print, face-to-face, electronic and special events.

Channels are variations of each medium. On the next page is an example chart expressing the four media and some of their channels (*Figure 2.8*).

**Face-to-face channels** are the most effective. From the point of view of effectiveness, every other channel could be considered a surrogate for face-to-face communication. If you can physically get in front of your audience, you have the best chance to deliver your message with the least distortion and the best interpretation. In addition, these live contacts allow for instant feedback and redelivery of a more persuasive message.

**Print channels** can be effective even though they suffer from the drawback of lack of feedback and the opportunity to redirect the message. Print products also depend on quality writing and attractive graphics. And the quality of those pieces varies greatly.

## Media Channels

### Print medium

**Channel**

- Advertising
- Advertorial (paid)
- Brochure
- Direct mail
- Flyer
- Letter
- Letter-to-the-editor
- Media kit
- News release
- Newsletter
- Op-ed piece (nonpaid)
- Photography (print)
- Poster
- Report
- Sign
- Stuffer

### Face-to-face medium

**Channel**

- Demonstration
- Dialogue
- Interview
- Lecture
- Meeting
- News conference
- Personal appearance
- Presentation
- Question & answer session
- Sermon
- Speech
- Tour
- Training program

### Electronic medium

**Channel**

- Audio feed
- Broadcast ad
- Broadcast release
- Cell phone
- Customized CD
- E-mail (blast e-mail)
- Files — GIF
  Graphic Image Format
- Files — JPEG
  Joint Photographic Experts Group
- Files — PDF
  *Adobe*, Portable Document Format
- Files: TIFF
  *Adobe*, Tagged Image File Format
- Internet connected chat area
- Internet pop-up ad
- Phone mail
- Photography
- PowerPoint presentation
- Public service announcement
- Radio appearance
- TV talk show appearance
- Videoconference
- Videotape
- Web site and link

### Special events medium

**Channel**

- Anniversary
- Award ceremony
- Banquet
- Book signing
- Boycott
- Celebration
- Commissioning
- Contest
- Demonstration
- Fund raiser
- Ground breaking
- Party
- Protest
- Ribbon cutting
- Sky writing
- Thon

**Figure 2.8**

**Electronic channels** are contemporary. They find a ready audience as more and more people turn to electronic media for news, information and marketing. A drawback to these channels is the need to compete with other electronic channels occupying the audience's attention. When audiences have seen the best in terms of graphics and electronic bells and whistles in their television shows, even news shows, they demand equivalent technical quality from public relations practitioners. But many PR practitioners don't have major media production budgets, so they suffer in comparison. Even a decent PowerPoint presentation can be dull if it doesn't have animation, music, voice-overs and clever graphics, including art work and photography.

**Special events channels** carry messages in important and dramatic ways. Events can change opinion more quickly than mere rhetoric or other opinion-influencing activities. Events can attract audiences who would otherwise pay no attention to PR messages. The mass media will frequently pick up public relations special events messages for the media's own viewership and listenership value. In the process, they transfer the messages to the practitioner's target audiences.

Selection of the best media and channels requires that you profile your audiences. It then demands that you carefully match the best virtues of the channels you select to your audience's communication habits. ∎

# Tips

1. Carefully interview your client or boss before you try to solve related communication problems. Knowing what they know is just a start, but an important one.

2. As soon as you write an issue, write a companion explanation of facts that gives rise to the issue.

3. As part of profiling your audience, also list intermediary audiences that could influence your target.

4. When you use the audience ranking formulas, be as objective as possible. Subjective guesses ruin the very nature of the exercise. Assign some quantitative value to each judgment.

5. When you evaluate an audience's importance to the mission of the organization, don't get sidetracked by emotion or irrelevant issues. Keep a copy of your organization's mission in front of you as you judge.

6. Try not to decide messages for your audiences without getting feedback from them. Of course, you will always have to send certain messages management wants sent.

7. Check your messages with a sampling from your target audience before using them in a fuller, more formal way.

8. Use a S-W-O-T analysis (Strengths, Weaknesses, Opportunities, Threats) to identify appropriate messages (*Figure 2.9*). Remember to combine the SWOT aspects with knowledge, attitude and behavior aspects.

9. Make certain not to underplay the legal/ethical aspects. Sometimes, they can be so demanding they deserve extra value.

10. Pay for formative research yourself if you have to. Later, try to persuade the client to reimburse you because the data were essential to the client's organization.

## S-W-O-T Issues Analysis
Example: Binge drinking
Knowledge ~ Attitude ~ Behavior

| Strengths ~ Students who don't binge drink do better in class | Weaknesses ~ Some freshmen wait until college to act "freely" away from home |
|---|---|
| Opportunities ~ Freshman orientation is a good opportunity to start students on the right path | Threats ~ Some clubs may make nondrinking students feel unwelcome |

**Figure 2.9**

**Questions for classroom discussion**

1. Your boss or client is edgy about spending money to conduct research as part of your public relations work. What argument can you offer to explain why paying for research is the most economical decision a boss or client can make?

2. Evaluate this issue statement for important issue elements:

   *"College students generally care more about their social lives than they do about their academic lives."*

   Does it contain all the necessary elements? Identify them. Can this issue become part of a public relations plan? Why?

3. What are the two chief factors in ranking audiences? If an audience scored high on one factor, but low on the other, would you ignore the audience?

4. In addition to knowing a prevailing attitude in your audience, what else should you know about that attitude to solve a communication challenge?

5. Why are special events such powerful channels in public relations practice?

**Internet assignment**

Use one of the popular PR Web sites such as www.prsa.org. Check the counselor's academy on the PRSA Web site or the Silver Anvil award winners from PRSA. Identify three successful/winning public relations cases on the Internet. Detect how the successful counselors conducted audience research, fashioned messages, selected channels and sent the messages to targeted audiences. Report to your class on the valid connections in the M-A-C Triad in the cases.

Name _____ Date _____

# Where's there's smoke, there's ire

A company with an office in center city has a problem. The company has banned smoking inside the office for some time. So smokers retreated to the foyer and the street area immediately outside the building.

The number of smokers has created a cloud of "offensive" smoke for both nonsmoking employees and guests coming into the building to do business. Meanwhile, a reporter has gotten involved with some of the nonsmoking players to do a major anti-smoking story on: "Where has All the Smoke Gone? To Greet You at the Front Door." And recently, a social rights advocacy group has gotten involved to protect the rights of the smokers.

Management has decided to extend the smoking ban to include the foyer and the sidewalk immediately outside its building leading to the street. (It's legal to do this.) As PR director for the company, you're asked to communicate the new decision to four important audiences and persuade them to go along.

Using the ranking formula in this chapter, identify and rank the important audiences to help management achieve its objective.

## Ranking formula

Use the following formula to rank the relationship between each audience and the company. The formula is based on six relationship factors:

- Importance of the relationship to the immediate issue at hand or the general mission of the organization (two factors)

- Likelihood the organization can influence the relationship and likelihood the audience wants to be in relationship with the organization (two factors)

- Importance of the relationship to applicable law and ethical principles (two factors)

Allocate value points from 1-5 (five being "important," one being "unimportant,") to each of six aspects of each audience.

| (5) Important | (4) Somewhat Important | (3) Neutral | (2) Somewhat Unimportant | (1) Unimportant |
|---|---|---|---|---|

Apply this ranking formula to the case of the company caught in the fog of the smoking debate. The four audiences you are to rank are: smoking employees, nonsmoking employees, the media, and social rights groups. Use the chart on the other side (*Figure 2.9*).

*See other side*

Name _____ Date _____

### Audience Ranking Grid

| Audience | Issue/Mission | | Ability/Capability | | Ethics/Law | | Total |
|---|---|---|---|---|---|---|---|
| Smoking employees | 5 | 5 | 2 | 5 | 5 | 5 | 27 |
| Nonsmoking employees | 5 | 5 | 5 | 5 | 5 | 5 | 30 |
| Media | 2 | 5 | 3 | 5 | 1 | 1 | 17 |
| Social action group | 4 | 4 | 2 | 5 | 1 | 1 | 17 |

**Figure 2.9**

### Audience Ranking Results

| Audience | Points | Rank |
|---|---|---|
| Smoking employees | 27 | 2 |
| Nonsmoking employees | 30 | 1 |
| Media | 17 | 4 |
| Social action group | 17 | 3 |

**Figure 2.10**

Next, explain your ranking for each audience according to the criteria.

## Smoking employees (Total points you assessed 27 )

Issue ___The smokers aren't able to smoke in the building, in the foyer, and on the sidewalk in front of the building.___

Mission ___The smokers would like an area that is designated for them to smoke in.___

Capability to reach _____

Name_____Date _____

_____

## Smoking employees (continued)

Ability to influence _____

_____

Law _____

_____

Ethics _____

_____

## Nonsmoking employees (Total points you assessed _30_ )

Issue _____

_____

Mission_____

_____

Capability to reach _____

_____

Ability to influence _____

_____

Law _____

_____

Ethics _____

_____

*See other side*

Name _____ Date_____

_____

## Media (Total points you assessed 17 )

Issue _____

_____

Mission _____

_____

Capability to reach _____

_____

Ability to influence _____

_____

Law _____

_____

Ethics _____

_____

## Social action group (Total points you assessed 17 )

Issue _____

_____

Mission _____

_____

Capability to reach _____

_____

Ability to influence _____

_____

Name _____ Date _____

_____

Law _____

_____

Ethics _____

_____

Finally, using the informal ranking grid (*Figure 2.11*), place each of the four audiences in the proper boxes. The merger of two criteria, the ability of the organization to influence an audience, and the necessity of the organization to influence an audience, results in a simple 2 x 2 ranking grid. You decide which audience goes into which cell in the grid.

## Informal Audience Ranking Grid

|  | *Priority targets* **Must influence** | *Secondary targets* **Should influence** |
|---|---|---|
| **Likely to influence** | "Do the most" <br><br> (audience) | "Do the required" <br><br> (audience) |
| **Unlikely to influence** | "Do the necessary" <br><br> (audience) | "Do the least" <br><br> (audience) |
| **Figure 2.11** | **Maximum PR effort** | **Significant PR effort** |

# Chapter 3

# Managing Public Opinion

## PRaxiom  *The three R's of public relations are: Responsibility, Relationship and Reputation.*

## What this chapter covers

In this chapter, you'll learn about the importance of detecting and managing public opinion in the practice of public relations. Public opinion drives most of society's culture and mores. But practitioners can influence opinion, both emotionally and rationally.

You'll also learn how public opinion forms, the difference between true and false opinion, and attitude roots for opinion. The chapter will also explore key persuasion concepts as crucial parts of opinion management, including the "Six Moments of Persuasion."

Finally, you'll learn how to profile and rank audiences so you can communicate with and about them using an economy of resources and effort. Also, in this chapter, notice how the phrase *public relations counselor* appears more often than the phrase *public relations practitioner*. Material in this chapter deals with higher level activities in which PR people need to *counsel* their organizations on the best strategic approaches toward difficult issues, not only *communicate* messages.

To begin understanding how PR counselors manage opinion, let's first look at how communication works. In particular, notice how difficult it is for anyone, let alone PR counselors, to communicate a clear meaning to another.

## How communication works: A communication theory primer

To understand opinion, you need first to consider the process of human communication. Public relations practitioners use a communication model to do their work. Most use a combination of Harold Lasswell's model and the Shannon/Weaver mechanistic model. These models form part of the collection of principles called communication theories.

### Lasswell's Model

Harold Lasswell asked five questions to demonstrate how communication works (*Figure 3.1*).

1. Who says...
2. What...
3. To whom...
4. Through what channel...
5. With what effect... ?

### Shannon/Weaver Model

Lasswell's theory sets up the Shannon/Weaver mechanistic model, so called because it resembles the mechanics of a telephone transmission involving a caller, a message, a receiver, a wire, and a return message. Claude Shannon conceived of this model as a result of his work with AT&T (*Figure 3.2*).

### Lasswell's Communication Process

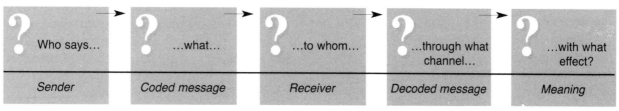

Figure 3.1

## Communication Process
## Modified Shannon / Weaver Mechanistic Model

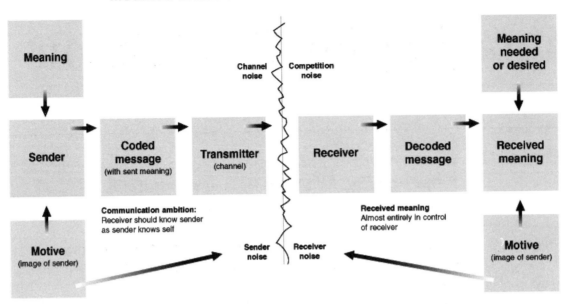

**Figure 3.2**

Notice how each theory resembles the other. Someone sends a message to another through a channel. It gets through or it doesn't depending on the foresight and skill of the sender and the ability of the receiver to "get" the message.

Sender ➤ Meaning ➤ Message ➤ Channel ➤ Receiver ➤ Feedback

To combine the two, let's first look at Lasswell's communication process.

• *"Who says"* means *source credibility*. If the right sender or messenger picks the right audience, there's a good chance the message will get through.

• *"What"* is the right message for the right audience.

• *"To whom"* means the sender considers the audience's frame of mind, attitudes, past behavior and loyalties. If the sender doesn't know these audience predispositions, communication will likely fail.

• *"Through what channel"* means the "carrier" of the message, person, letter, e-mail, advertisement, phone, etc. The right channel, one the receiver uses, can guarantee communication success.

• *"With what effect"* means the result. Did the communication get through?

For example, if a sports organization wants fans to *buy tickets* to an event, it won't matter if the fans like the event, and want to attend, if they don't buy tickets.

When public relations practitioners use these models, they're most often senders of messages. If they're to

succeed, they must pick the right message for the right audience and send it through the right channel. And that requires that they know the difference between information, attitude and opinion. In the example of fans buying sports tickets, *publicity* about the event is *information*; *wanting* to go to the event is an *attitude*; actually *going* is an *opinion*. Here's how it works.

## Information

**Information is the bank of cognitives a person knows about an issue**. Most public relations people send information to their audiences or receivers. What a person **knows** about an issue can determine how a person **feels** about the issue and whether the person will **do** anything about it.

## Attitude

**An attitude is a predisposition to act**. It's a mind set, a readiness to do something. Attitudes don't "do anything." They are simply orientations or the way people are "pointed" before they act or react to things. Frequently, an attitude is a feeling about something.

For example, a jogger might be predisposed or *ready* to defend exercise in the face of a report that exercise might be bad for some people. A college student might be predisposed or *ready* to support aid to education. *Ready* is an in-the-head characteristic of a person.

## Opinion

**An opinion is the outward expression of an attitude**. When someone acts on an attitude, the result is an opinion. An opinion can be a word, action, vote, gesture or even nod of the head. It's an outward and observable act.

For example, when a customer complains about a poor product or service, the complaint is the opinion. The attitude fueling the opinion might be inconvenience, embarrassment or feeling cheated.

Therefore, public relations practitioners can achieve only three effects in their receiver audiences:

- What audiences know     (Information)
- How audiences feel       (Attitude)
- What audiences do        (Behavior)

Opinion is behavior. Information and attitude formation are preambles to behavior. Some early theories of communication maintained that if an audience simply had enough information, it would cause an attitude, which, in turn, would cause an opinion (a behavior). But today, we think we know more about opinion formation and behavior. We believe that to form an opinion (behavior) an attitude must first cause it. For example, to cast a supportive vote, one has to first favor an issue or a candidate. But to look favorably on something, one usually knows what or why to favor it (information). So don't make the mistake of thinking that information alone leads to behavior.

## Influencing attitudes and opinion

This difference between information, attitude and opinion is important because public relations is a *behavioral science* and a *communication art*. Effective public relations communication means influencing attitudes and ultimately opinion.

To influence opinion, PR practitioners first detect, and if necessary, modify attitudes. Here is a model PR action plan:

- Detect behavior
  - Discover underlying attitudes
    - Modify attitudes
      - Influence behavior

The key effect of public relations communication is opinion change. The key activity is attitude detection and change. But it's difficult to change attitudes. Why? Because attitudes are deeply embedded in our mental and emotional makeup. To begin changing an audience's attitudes, the PR practitioner must know the source of the attitudes.

Attitudes come from history, upbringing, education, religion, affiliations, race, gender, and other genetic characteristics such as body size and shape.

For example, research indicates that if a tall person and a short person enter a room at the same time, a group will be more inclined to believe the taller person, thus granting the taller person *unearned credibility*. The shorter person will have to earn credibility and respect. Thus, being short could influence short peoples' attitudes toward the way they behave at business meetings. Shorter people might more aggressively present their ideas to earn credibility and respect.

Because it's so difficult to change attitudes permanently, PR practitioners will try for temporary attitude change. Even a temporary attitude change could lead to an opinion change.

James Grunig demonstrated through his research that an attitude need only be temporary to effect a desired behavior.

*Example*: A shopper needing a new tube of toothpaste might reach for a brand that was just advertised with a discount coupon. The shopper hesitates, because changing brands is a big decision. The shopper recalls the ad, forms a temporary attitude to try the new brand, and reaches for it. It's possible that the quickly formed attitude disappears just as quickly, but not before the shopper

> **It's more difficult to change an attitude than an opinion.**

has tried the toothpaste at home. Indeed, the shopper might feel uneasy about the buying decision almost as soon as it's made. But attitude was formed and behavior (the purchase) followed.

Of course, if the toothpaste manufacturer wants the new customer to continue buying the new brand, a longer-lasting attitude change will be necessary.

So PR people concentrate on installing, reinforcing and modifying attitudes. They can achieve long-lasting behavior only if they work on enduring attitude change. But many times, a temporary change is success for PR practitioners because that's all they can get.

## Public opinion

What is opinion? What is public opinion? How important are these concepts to PR practitioners? How does public relations influence and use public opinion?

Opinion is what people do according to what they think. From the primer on communication theory, you learned that opinion comes from information and attitudes. Public opinion is important in public relations practice because favorable, supportive behavior is the Holy Grail of public relations. The **contest for public approval** of people and organizations drives public relations activity.

When public relations people talk about public opinion, they don't refer to the "opinion" generated by polling firms.

## Message and Meaning

A note about messages and meanings. In the Shannon/Weaver Model, notice that senders always start the process with the *idea* they want to send. The idea is their meaning. To do it, they pick a code, language, symbols or pictures. The code is their message.

On the other end, receivers decode the message to extract the original meaning. If the code is right for receivers, then decoding it to reveal the meaning shouldn't be too difficult. But if the code is too difficult, receivers might not try to "crack it." And the organization's message will never get a hearing.

School administrator and teacher jargon, for example, is a serious code problem for parents who want messages in simple language. The communication process succeeds when the idea (meaning) sent is the same as the one received. Codes (messages) are tools. They are not meanings. Public relations people know that getting the meaning through the communication process unchanged isn't easy or automatic. They know that making effective messages for their audiences is their job. But their job isn't over until they ask for feedback to see **if the meaning sent was the one received**. They also know that sometimes, no matter how accurately they write or picture the message, receivers can get or deliberately take a different meaning.

*Example*: During a committee hearing, tobacco company PR people tell a congressional representative, who is determined to end tobacco use in America, that they will improve their marketing efforts. The meaning sent was clear. The message used was clear. But the meaning received was different. Why? **Because receivers almost always control the meaning of messages.** Because of this phenomenon, public relations practice is always challenging.

That type of opinion can be valuable in public relations research. The end game for PR practitioners is a favorable, supportive action by a targeted audience – not merely a response to a telephone polling firm.

To understand how public relations seeks and uses favorable public opinion, consider first a definition of public opinion and then an analysis of how publics form opinion.

**Public opinion is the accumulation of individual opinion, on an important issue, in public debate,** affecting the lives of a public.

*Example*: Take a complaining customer. Even an amateur customer service representative can detect the opinion — a customer at the counter, or in a letter, complaining about a failed product or service. The customer service representative must satisfy and persuade the customer to give the organization another chance without complaining to other customers and hurting business. First, the company representative must research the attitude causing the complaint. Suppose the representative didn't take time to discover the attitude but simply offered a "stock" reply,

> "O.K. We'll replace the product. Just go down the aisle and get another one."

That response might resolve the attitude of frustration, but not the attitude of inconvenience, embarrassment, or injustice.

For the anger of being inconvenienced, the customer might need a discount on a future product.

For the embarrassment of using the failed product with guests for a special occasion, the customer might want an apology *and* an exchanged product.

For the feeling of injustice that the organization did not provide what it advertised, the customer might want to see the product pulled from the shelves or sound off to a manager to be assured that the message got through to someone who could make a difference.

Unless the customer representative solves the attitude problem, the disturbed customer might act out (another opinion) in a way the company wouldn't like — telling others not to shop at the store.

Notice how a casual response might get *temporary favorable opinion*. The customer goes down the aisle to get a replacement

> **An audience can get the right message, but the wrong meaning.**

product. But real public relations work by the customer representative might "frame the customer's mind" in such a way that the positive attitude about the store replaces a negative one. The result? The disgruntled customer won't tell others about the bad experience. The now-satisfied customer will continue to shop at the store and adopt a long-lasting, satisfying behavior, as far as the store is concerned.

Researching attitudes behind opinions also reveals that communicators can't easily wedge out unfavorable attitudes and replace them with favorable ones. Instead, audiences can maintain negative attitudes about an issue and simultaneously hold positive attitudes toward the efforts of the communicator. James Grunig calls this the "hedging and wedging" phenomenon that disputes old notions that attitude wedging is automatic.

In this case, the customer has a favorable attitude because she gets a replacement product. But she also harbors negative attitudes at the same time. So she likes and dislikes the company at the same time. Result? She'll probably behave (opinion) favorably and unfavorably at the same time. Half a good job by the customer service representative isn't good enough.

## Analysis of the definition

All four elements are necessary for valid public opinion.

### ■ *The accumulation of individual opinion* …

One person's opinion is usually not sufficient for public opinion unless that person is an entire public, such as the president of a country or a company. The accumulation of opinion does not always mean majority opinion. Several public opinions can exist about the same issue without any one of the opinions achieving a mathematical majority.

*Example*: The issue of abortion spawned several public opinions. One group believes in abortion or absolute choice for women at any stage of pregnancy. For them, even so-called late term abortions are constitutional. Another opinion favors choice for women, for any reason, up to 28 weeks. After that, it favors choice only for the life or health of the mother. A third opinion supports choice at any time during the pregnancy but only for rape, incest and the life or health of the mother. A fourth opinion favors the life of the child and allows choice only for rape, incest and the life of the mother, but not "health" because health can be interpreted to mean merely the "mental stress" of being a mother. A fifth opinion favors the life of the child with no exceptions.

> *Don't equate public opinion only with majority opinion.*

Variations of these positions involve issues such as government-paid abortions for military personnel or those on Medicare. Another sub-position involves the amount of freedom in the choice, parental consent, a waiting period, counseling, transporting those under 21 across state lines to obtain abortions, and abortion pills.

It's obvious that the multiplicity of sub-issues creates many opinions on the issue without any of them achieving a majority of the held opinions.

What constitutes a sufficient "accumulation of individual opinion" to warrant the attention of the public

relations communicator? That decision rests with the communicator and with the circumstances. Sometimes, *significant* opinion never becomes *sufficient* public opinion.

*Example*: In the mid-'90s, Native American Indians protested the use of words denoting their culture in America's sports teams. The Washington *Redskins* National Football League team

> *Significant opinion becomes sufficient opinion when it results in some important action.*

particularly offended them. But they also cited the Atlanta *Braves* and Cleveland *Indians* baseball teams. The group protested that the use of "redskins" was a racial offense and said no other group in the nation would stand for a team being called by the skin color of its race.

On this issue, other publics, such as owners and fans of the teams, said "too much history" had occurred to change the teams' names. Besides, they added, the names, chants, mascots and logos all complimented the American Indian and were signs of respect. Who won?

Groups with the critical mass necessary to achieve effective public opinion got their way. Nothing changed. Would the outcome have been the same if a different racial group had an identical complaint? It depends on how much *sufficient* public opinion and political muscle complainers muster.

The debate witnessed public relations practitioners on both sides of the issue trying to generate public opinion for their positions sufficient to effect a behavior change or keep behavior as it was.

*Note*: The St. John's Redmen college basketball team did change its name to the Red Storm.

***Public relations tactic***: Gain support for a message before you beam it to a public. Most publics don't want to be the first to adopt an idea. Show support to gain support.

### ■ *… on an important issue* …

The issue must have serious substance. Why? Because true public opinion can't exist over insignificant issues. Valid opinion represents feelings or attitudes of publics after they *considered* the issue. If a public thinks an issue insignificant, it might only glibly regard it. Less-than-serious regard creates doubt about the validity of the attitude and whether it should be taken seriously.

Was the public response (opinion) reasoned and informed? Did responders take the issue seriously enough to form a serious attitude? Or did the issue generate a mental, "Who cares…"? If that happens, opinion is unreliable.

*Example*: If you tried to detect public opinion about

whether vanilla or chocolate ice cream is the better flavor, you wouldn't get far because the issue isn't substantive enough to generate sufficient consideration for a serious opinion.

An example PR case involved the federal government's antitrust suit against the Microsoft Corporation. The government took Microsoft to court in 1998 to get it to unbundle its web browser from its operating system and relent on other software issues. Microsoft claimed the government was meddling in lawful business decisions.

*Successful PR messages match the audience's values.*

Some organizations polled the general public about its position on the issue.

Most computer users said they were satisfied with their Microsoft operating system and didn't want anything changed. The issues of market dominance and alleged illegal marketing activities by Microsoft didn't seem important enough to consumers to generate valid public opinion. Many didn't understand the issues. They were having enough trouble of their own getting their computers to do what they wanted.

Noncomputer users couldn't generate interest about a technology they didn't use.

*Note*: The lesson for public relations people: If the issue isn't important enough, it will be difficult to generate public opinion sufficient enough to change the behavior of important publics. A serious issue, but not considered serious by a public, might generate unreliable opinion and make the practitioner's work more difficult.

*Public relations tactic*: Control the message so the issue appears important to the public. Always relate the issue message to the public's value structure.

■ .... *in public debate* ...

To generate true public opinion, publics must first know about an issue. Informed decisions yield more reliable opinion than uninformed decisions. Public debate seems to be the best way to air all sides of an issue. Also, the public opinion process requires the public to know alternatives before it can develop valid opinion. Alternatives force thoughtful choice and offer publics competing positions.

*Example*: From time to time in America, the public, the media and the government debate the right of citizens to burn the American flag. But if there were no debate, the public wouldn't learn about the sides of the issue. It would be similar to someone stopping you in a mall and asking,

"Do you favor a citizen's right to burn the American flag in public as a sign of protest against the government?" Without a debate on the issue, you wouldn't know answers to important questions: Is flag burning allowed by the U.S. Constitution? Why do some favor the idea? Why are some opposed to it? Has the Supreme Court ruled on it? Debate reveals positions. And positions yield opinion.

*Public relations tactic*: Expertly use public media to disseminate your messages. Make certain your public believes the channels you use so your information is credible to them. Expert use of television talk shows, the Internet, direct mail and other channels, if believed by the public, can make your messages credible.

■ ... *affecting the lives of people* ...

The issue must be so important to the general public that its opinion on the issue could lead to serious consequences for its members. If the public doesn't perceive important consequences, at least potentially, its "opinion" could be just an unconsidered reaction.

*Example*: Congress occasionally debates the fairness of the federal income tax. The issue implies such important potential consequences that a public, asked for its opinion, knows the opinion could be reported to political leaders who could act on what it says. Resulting congressional action could affect their lives. So the public reports reliable opinion — what it really thinks. Similarly, television ratings sweeps and Neilson ratings have real consequences. So ratings participants take their job seriously, knowing their opinion could affect programming for millions.

On the other hand, a public might be asked if it agreed with a company's new advertising campaign. Depending on whether the campaign theme

*Without a debate about pros and cons, public opinion cannot form.*

were controversial or not (tobacco advertising for example), the resulting opinion might not be valid because expressing the opinion has no consequences on their lives.

*Public relations tactic*: Present issues to your target publics in a way that they believe their responses could affect their lives.

*Example*: A PR practitioner for a local public library was asked by library officials to help prevent the library's takeover by the county library system. The issue would eventually come down to a public vote. Such issues are sometimes "mysterious" to the general public. They don't know what or whom to believe. To appear believable, the practitioner told the public how each system would affect them and their children. She played out how the differences in the number and kind of holdings, borrowing and returning books, censorship and Internet access would affect them. She won the vote.

With an understanding of what public opinion is, let's consider how it forms and the role public relations practitioners play in it.

## Public opinion process

A few years ago, the Public Relations Society of America and Dr. Robert Kendall from the University of Florida published an accreditation prep manual in which they described how public opinion is formed. Notice how the elements of the public opinion definition are fulfilled in this model (*Figure 3.3*). Although it looks like a "cracked egg," it's filled with insight about how public opinion forms and the role of public relations in the process.

The model displays eight stages of opinion formation:

**1. Mass sentiment**. The late, great PR counselor and theorist, Patrick Jackson, calls this quiet inward feeling, *latent attitude*. At any time, publics harbor latent attitudes about issues. For example, diffused throughout society are

> **Important attitudes lie latent until an event triggers a reaction.**

attitudes about gun control. These attitudes reside unexpressed until something occurs to activate them and publics express them. Everyone has many unexpressed or latent attitudes. Some are personal. They share them with families, communities, churches, political organizations, or other societies.

Public relations counselors exploit these latent attitudes when they match their objectives to their publics' attitudes. Counselors conduct research to see where and how deeply these latent attitudes reside in publics.

**2. Incident or issue.** When something happens that agitates these latent attitudes, the attitudes become activated and manifest themselves. For example, in 1999 two students took guns to Columbine High School in Littleton Colorado and killed several students and a teacher. The incident provoked latent attitudes in the general public about school security, gun control, and "youth-of-today" mentality. Incidents powerfully evoke strong attitudes from publics.

*Public relations tactic*: PR counselors can activate latent attitudes for their purposes by introducing incidents such as speeches, demonstrations, letter writing campaigns, ads, research reports, in short, anything that reaches publics with messages clearly expressed and sufficiently

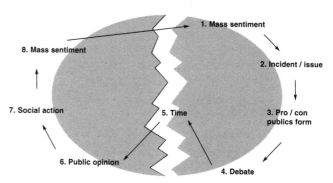

**Public Opinion Formation Model**
"Cracked Egg Model"

1. Mass sentiment
8. Mass sentiment
2. Incident / issue
7. Social action
5. Time
3. Pro / con publics form
6. Public opinion
4. Debate

**Figure 3.3**

powerful to generate response. Counselors who routinely perform public opinion research on their publics already know the attitudes they want to provoke by the incident.

Also, counselors should scan news and everyday events for issues that could trigger latent mass sentiment. PR counselors are most valuable to their organizations when they alert their organizations about impending public opinion.

**3. Pro/con publics form**. As soon as the incident occurs, publics take sides on the issue, both pro and con. Sometimes, more than two sides form as in the abortion example. For example, when the shooting in Columbine High School occurred with easily available guns, pro-gun control and pro-Second Amendment publics quickly formed around the incident. Gun control advocates said there ought to be more gun control. Second Amendment advocates said that deranged students killed the children and teacher, not the guns themselves. They cautioned the public not to overreact by controlling the right to bear arms guaranteed by the Constitution.

*Public relations tactic*: Public relations counselors should monitor events that change rapidly. They must be *social trend detectors* or they'll miss publics as they develop. Also, when incidents like Columbine occur, they should immediately profile emerging publics to detect the strength and sources of attitudes. Trend detection is a crucial public relations activity.

**4. Debate.** When publics form themselves around serious and important issues, a debate must occur about the merit of the positions. Reliable public opinion cannot form without informed positions. It's through debate that publics clarify their own position and adopt theirs, another's, or form a new one.

*Public relations tactic*: Public relations, advertising, lobbying, marketing and journalism have a stake in the outcome of opinion formation. Frequently, all get involved in the debate. PR counselors should establish objectives, strategies and tactics for their involvement. They should also learn what works and what doesn't from similar incidents in the literature and the experience of other counselors. That's one of the chief reasons PR professionals join a public relations professional society, such as the Public Relations Society of America.

> **Initial strong reaction to a 6:00 p.m. news report isn't public opinion.**

Remember, public relations will be on competing sides of the same issue. Ethical questions about who's right are resolved both personally and organizationally. (*See the chapter on ethics on how to make an ethical decision in public relations practice*.)

**5. Time.** For opinion to form, a period of time must elapse so arguments from the debate can "marinate" in the minds of the publics. Without this time, the resulting opinion would be glib.

For example, suppose a television anchor reported to the public on the 6 p.m. news that two deranged students had just killed some students and a teacher in their high school. The anchor ran 15 seconds of tape from spokespersons on either side of the gun control issue, then asked seriously as he peered into the cameras, "What do you think?" Call this number if you agree with controlling guns. Or call that number if you disagree.

Without time for the public to take in the arguments, think about them, add their own positions and test them on others, a phone call at 6:05 p.m. to the television station will capture only spontaneous, emotional reaction, not informed public opinion.

*Note*: The television station might dutifully report results of the "public opinion poll" that night. And unwary viewers will probably believe they're getting true public opinion on the issue when they're really getting only initial, uninformed reactions. But after all, it appeared on television, didn't it?

*Public relations tactic*: Guard against confusing initial reaction for true public opinion. Also, be wary of silently letting others do the same, especially if they're not on your side. When planning public relations campaigns, allow enough time for your messages to penetrate the mindset of target audiences.

**6. Public opinion**. True public opinion is formed after all four characteristics occur:
1. the accumulation of individual opinion
2. on an important issue
3. in public debate
4. affecting the lives of a public

That's when important societal change will happen, one way or the other. In this example, the stage is set for the natural outcome of opinion formation, official action to control guns or not control guns.

*Public relations tactic*: Use public opinion as evidence in your campaign of what society needs to do or not do about an issue. If necessary, cite various stages of the process to validate the opinion.

**7. Social action**. Usually, at the conclusion of the opinion formation process, society, government, groups, families, virtually any public, takes some action based on the opinion to affect society's behavior.

In this case, if the pro-gun-control opinion is stronger than the pro-Second Amendment

> **Law and research move opinion more quickly than any other evidence.**

opinion, laws will pass to control the sale or availability of guns. But if that group's arguments aren't persuasive enough or the political climate isn't right, the pro-Second Amendment forces would win. Remember, no action, no gun control, is as effective as action, gun control, for society to be affected.

*Public relations tactic*: Suggest the action you think should take place as a result of the debate. Remember, there could be multiple opinions on the same issue. So, it's all right to offer something seemingly against what the "majority" wants.

■ **Mass sentiment**. The action society takes can itself influence mass sentiment. In fact, law can influence opinion more firmly and dramatically than almost any other factor or technique.

In the example, new gun control laws would establish an attitude in the public mind that restriction on the availability of guns for youngsters was the "right attitude" to have. Public latent mass sentiment would become, "We legislated a solution to the public angst. We're safer now." Conversely, no new social action would send the signal that people, not guns, commit crimes and that new message could become *latent mass sentiment*, again.

Notice how this same law-drives-attitude phenomenon occurs in issues about stoplights, income tax, driver licensing, copyright and so forth. Wherever there's a law, there's a corresponding mass sentiment, albeit sometimes unwilling, to conform to the law's provisions.

*Public relations tactic*: If you're on the side of the winner, agree publicly with the new mass sentiment. If you're on the side of the loser, disagree publicly with it. Notice how pro-choice counselors agree with the Supreme Court decision *Roe vs. Wade* while pro-life public relations counselors disagree with the split decision.

Other PR counselors disagree with affirmative action, property taxes, and capital gains taxes. In fact, if counselors want to blunt the effect of a new law on mass sentiment, they will publicly make it "uncomfortable" for people to automatically accept the new sentiment. That's the best they can do until the next public opinion contest.

## Two-Step Flow Theory

The benchmark theory in the triad relationship of the media, public relations and publics has been the Two-step Flow Theory of Katz and Lazarsfeld (*Figure 3.4*). The theory contends that the flow of influence begins with media setting the agenda, influentials picking up ideas and messages, endorsing them, and passing them on to target publics. The publics then adopt the ideas. Here's the Two-step flow picture:

## Two-Step Flow Theory

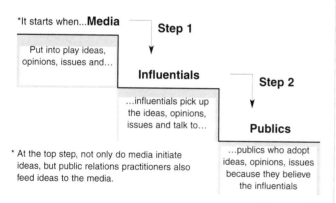

**Figure 3.4**

This process is similar to *diffusion theories*, such as those espoused by Bolen and Beale and others, which try to explain how ideas and opinions are disseminated in society and adopted by publics.

Public relations counselors can use the Two-step Flow Theory to their advantage. Counselors can place their own messages in the media, at the beginning of the process, so they filter down, through influentials, to target publics.

**Media relations is the PR activity in which PR counselors persuade the media to carry their organization's messages.** The media comply with these requests when they see an advantage to their own audiences and to themselves. The connecting interest is news value. If PR counselors can make their messages newsworthy, the media will comply, adopt the messages, and beam them to their publics because it serves their purposes. The other main media activity is advertising. In this activity, PR counselors control messages in the media because they pay to place them.

*PR is the act of influencing the influencers.*

The Two-step Flow Theory recognizes that real opinion formation happens through influentials, people whom the target public respects. In the theory, influentials have greater influence on target audiences than do the media.

## Persuasion

Influence is the effect of the public relations persuasion effort. The dictionary defines **in • flu • ence** as: "A power indirectly or intangibly affecting a person or a course of events."

But the Latin root for influence provides a better picture of what happens. It means to "flow into." The Romans conceived of a idea, force, attitude or ambition flowing from one person or thing into another. That image suggests that the flow be attractive and unimpeded. *Influence works best when one wants to be influenced and wants to gain a value.*

In his book, *101 Ways to Influence People on the Job* (*communication briefings*), Professor Anthony Fulginiti of Rowan University describes influence this way:

Einstein said that gravity curves space. Influence works like gravity. Like gravity, your influence doesn't actually touch others at a meeting or through your advertising copy. You can't force others to think or feel a certain way. Instead, when you present your ideas or write your copy, you "curve the space" of the thoughts and feelings of others. You force them to think, feel and act according to the "curved space" you provide. *People actually persuade themselves.* They follow your "influenced space" because they want to or think they have to. People will always act according to what they think is their own best interest. So to successfully influence others on the job, merely show them what's in their best interest and make it easy to get.[1]

1. Anthony J. Fulginiti. (1998). *101 Ways to Influence People on the Job.* Alexandria, VA. *communication briefings*, p. 1.

The influence formula can be expressed this way:

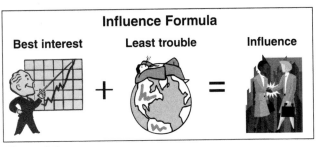

**Figure 3.5**

All influential communication contains three elements — you, your audiences and your messages. The more you know about each, the more effective you'll be. The most effective influencers follow researcher Earl Newsome's four-part advice. The advice follows the acronym F-I-C-A, Familiarity, Identification, Clarity and Action.

## Familiarity

■ Look as much like the audience as possible.

*Example*: A company needed someone to talk to loading dock workers about a change in employee benefits. They selected someone in the public relations office who had roots in the neighborhood where most of the workers came from. The PR person provided similar background and even similar speech patterns.

*Tactic*: In place of physical characteristics, match a spokesperson's expertise to the expertise of the target public. Research suggests that even a neutral message from an expert is better than a positive message from a novice. But a positive message from an expert works best.

What makes someone credible? Here's what research tells us. Credible sources:

   • Have the experience or expertise to solve a problem
   • Place the public's interest above personal interest
   • Belong to groups target publics identify with

When you use experts or appear as an expert solving a problem, cite these three factors.

## Identification

■ Show publics that what you want is the same as what they want. Use messages your public wants to hear.

*Example*: A large stationery store trying to explain to customers why it can't carry certain products shouldn't focus on space and inventory technology. Such a "management-minded" message doesn't work with dissatisfied customers who want to know what you will do for them. The company should train its salespersons to

send "audience-minded messages" so the company's priorities appear to be the same as the customers'.

*Example*: A customer can't find a certain type of file folder in the store. Instead of responding, "We simply can't carry everything everyone wants," a salesperson might instead offer, "but we'll check our other stores, special order it for you, or find another store that carries it."

> **The beginning of persuasion — getting your public to know you as you know yourself.**

*Tactic*: Concentrate on your public's purpose rather than your purpose. Publics must perceive that their interests are part of your organization's mission.

For example, a national department store known for its customer service has as its motto: "In all things, use your own best judgment." No canned customer service jargon or smile campaigns here. Customer service and sales representatives provide the highest customer satisfaction because *they are empowered to provide it*. While the motto doesn't mention customer service, management knows that it will occur. Why? Because empowered to decide, employees will realize customer service is their job, not the owner's or manager's and that they *are* the organizational culture.

## Clarity

To influence others, deliver crisp, clear messages. Weak writing, ineffective speaking and unclear thinking cloud messages. Remember, clarity applies to both the meaning you start with and the messages you craft to send that meaning. Foggy efforts in either activity work against effective persuasion.

*Tactic*: Monitor the clarity of meaning and messages you direct to publics. Make certain more than one mind or one pair of eyes checks both meanings and messages before you send them.

Author Herman Holtz sums it: Persuasion is "sending messages in a clear way that will arrive at the reader's brain with the same meaning they had when they left your brain." [2]

Example of foggy communication:

*From time to time, things have a tendency not to go as planned. Our new electric coffee pot was designed to maintain the optimum temperature for coffee no matter the duration of being attached to the power source. A special computer chip analyzes and reanalyzes the temperature and transmits electronic signals to the interrupt*

---

2. Herman Holz. (1983). *Persuasive Writing*. New York: McGraw-Hill.

*switch at the power entry node. But sometimes, power surges, power drains and even sunspots create uneven power flow and the switch disengages. If that happens to your pot, you should consider trying another plug in your home, taking it back to your dealer, or shipping it back to us for analysis.* (**106 words**)

A clearer communication:

*Our automatic coffee maker is supposed to keep your next cup of coffee at a constant temperature without burning it. If it doesn't, return it to us and we'll replace it.* (**31 words**)

Many organizations work against themselves when they send unclear messages.

## Action

To be influential, ask for what you want. Tie a specific action to your plan or idea. Connecting your purpose to a doable roadmap makes you more influential than the persuader who merely proposes ideas. Some say that you don't have to draw action conclusions for bright people. But why take the chance? Even intelligent people appreciate instant blueprints. Draw action conclusions for all publics.

Newsome's original idea said you shouldn't sing one tune and dance to another. To be persuasive, match your actions to your rhetoric.

*Example*: A bank wouldn't be very credible if it launched a "quit smoking" campaign, while its tellers could be seen smoking in the back room during breaks.

*Tactic*: Use lots of imperative verbs in your persuasive speeches and promotional copy, such as, "Try," "Attend," "Buy," "Vote."

## Your messages

### Know, Feel and Do

The message recipe has three ingredients: knowledge, attitudes and behavior. That's it. You can influence publics to know or believe something. You can motivate them to start feeling, keep feeling or stop feeling a certain way. Or you can prod them to start behaving, keep behaving or stop behaving a certain way.

To be persuasive, decide which combination of the three you want.

*Example*: To persuade the media to attend your special event, you presume the media should know about the event, agree that it will benefit them to attend, and actually cover the event.

If you're in charge of the invitation, you might send these three different message points to the media:

"The special event is a demonstration concerning a major scientific finding, the ability to grow human tissue from frozen embryos to heal major diseases.
(*The knowledge message*)

"Your audiences will consider this research both groundbreaking and controversial."
(*The attitude message*)

"Come to the Bionics Lab at 3:00 p.m. Please bring visual recording equipment for a special demonstration. Scientists and executives will be available for exclusive interviews at 4:00 p.m."
(*The behavior message*)

Persuasiveness is more than merely sending messages you agree with and assuming your audience values what

## Six Moments of Persuasion

| Persuasive question | Persuasive action | Persuasive moment |
|---|---|---|
| Are you there? | Message sent | Right audience receives the right message |
| Are you available? | Message received | Audience is available and attentive for persuasion — channels are clear |
| Do you remember me? | Message retained | Audience recalls message's features and benefits |
| Do you know me? | Information change | Audience knows me as I know myself — meaning is transferred |
| Do you agree with me? | Attitude change | Audience accepts my meaning for itself |
| Will you act for me? | Behavior change | Audience is unconstrained and acts as intended |

**Figure 3.6**

you do. Real influence is creating the right message for the right audience and getting it to them. Here's a checklist of the steps necessary to persuade a public to act for you or your organization.

## Six moments of persuasion

Combining the messages you send with the evolution your audiences must pass through results in six stages or **moments of persuasion** for every persuasive act (*Figure 3.6 – previous page*). Research from the University of Maryland and Yale University shows that these stages, or aspects of them, are necessary to successfully influence publics. Miss a stage, and you probably won't succeed. Figure 3.6 on the previous page shows how they work.

Here's a profile of the various publics during the Six Moments of Persuasion. An easy-to-remember nametag is assigned to each to help counselors identify the type. In actual practice, counselors would conduct research to identify at which moment on the persuasion clock the target public is as the project begins.

The charts below display the failed publics for each "failed" persuasion moment and the successful publics for each successful persuasive moment (Figures 3.7 and 3.8).

### Failed persuasion

| Failed public | Failed persuasive moment |
|---|---|
| Unresearched public | Public or message is incorrect |
| Unavailable public | Public never receives the message |
| Distracted public | Public receives the message but doesn't "get" it |
| Uninformed public | Public gets the message, but not the meaning |
| Indisposed public | Public gets meaning, but doesn't agree with it |
| Constrained public | Public agrees with the meaning, but can't act |

**Figure 3.7**

### Successful persuasion

| Successful public | Successful persuasive moment |
|---|---|
| Researched public | Public and message are correct |
| Available public | Public can receive the message |
| Attentive public | Public recalls the message |
| Informed public | Public gets the message and the meaning |
| Disposed public | Public agrees with the meaning |
| Persuaded public | Public is free to act and acts |

**Figure 3.8**

Figure 3.9 shows how far PR practitioners need to go to persuade audiences.

Read columns vertically in the chart. Notice how persuasion stops when one of the moments doesn't happen. Actually, communicators might still be working, but they have already failed.

For example, in the *unavailable* column (2), if the right message to the right audience has been sent, but the audience doesn't recall it, persuasion stops even though communicators continue to act as though all is going well. They have already failed but they don't yet know it.

Notice that with the *persuaded public*, all the moments must be "yes" for persuasion to occur. With the other publics, where some of the moments are "yes," counselors can claim some success, but the overall behavior objective was not achieved.

### Persuasion Moment Publics

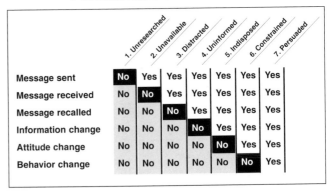

| | 1. Unresearched | 2. Unavailable | 3. Distracted | 4. Uninformed | 5. Indisposed | 6. Constrained | 7. Persuaded |
|---|---|---|---|---|---|---|---|
| Message sent | No | Yes | Yes | Yes | Yes | Yes | Yes |
| Message received | No | No | Yes | Yes | Yes | Yes | Yes |
| Message recalled | No | No | No | Yes | Yes | Yes | Yes |
| Information change | No | No | No | No | Yes | Yes | Yes |
| Attitude change | No | No | No | No | No | Yes | Yes |
| Behavior change | No | No | No | No | No | No | Yes |

**Figure 3.9**

For example, suppose counselors are after a "yes" vote on a referendum to allow the legalization of marijuana in their state. They do a lot of things correctly and almost win, but the referendum issue fails. Did they succeed?

> **Beaming a message to an unavailable public is like talking into a dead phone.**

Not in the larger sense. They lost the election. But they did succeed in alerting many members of the voting public about the need for terminally ill patients to gain pain relief from marijuana. And they successfully got a number of voters to agree with the idea. But when they actually voted, residents couldn't bring themselves to act on their temporary attitude change. They paused, recalled other messages, agreed with those messages, and defeated the issue. Perhaps, the losing counselors reason, next time they put the question on the ballot, they can get more than just a temporary attitude change. Next time, they might convince the public that it's a better idea than any competing idea.

Counselors can make some gains even though they don't gain the overall behavior change. That might comfort the counselors, but their clients will probably see it differently.

Here are some other examples of the types of publics identified in the failed *Six Moments Of Persuasion* model. Students should note how the effect with each public could be reversed with proper PR activity.

**Unresearched public.**The manager of a fast food restaurant misreads customer unhappiness with the restaurant. The manager tells sales representatives to smile and be nicer to customers. But customer unhappiness doesn't improve.

In reality, customers are unhappy with the restaurant because the owner has changed the beef supplier. The food just isn't as good as it was. Right audience. Wrong message. Poor research.

**Unavailable public**. The mayor of a resort community wants to improve the way residents act toward visitors. The mayor decides to send a brochure to all residents outlining a new campaign and asks for their cooperation. But a majority of the community perceives the mailing as a waste of tax dollars and refuse to consider the plan. Many report trashing the brochure as soon as it arrives; result, clogged channel of communication. Message never received.

**Distracted public**. A local civic association wants to clean a local park on a fall Sunday afternoon. Three weeks prior to the event, a leading citizen pleads for 50 people to show up on the given Sunday with rakes and bags. Through the grapevine, the citizen is led to believe a number of residents will show up. Unfortunately for the civic leader, the local football team gets involved in a battle for first place in a must-win game on the same Sunday. Result: Few show up. The public is distracted. They agree with the message, but don't retain agreement long enough to act on it.

*Another example*: Many salespersons can't afford a distracted buying public. They try to close sales before their customers say they need time to "think it over." They know that customer buying attitudes could change when other priorities are allowed to compete. So they frequently ask customers to "decide now."

> **The worst moment for a persuader is when the audience checks the clock.**

**Uninformed public**. NASA seeks public approval for its new space station. It doesn't need the approval for the funding. That's been done by the U.S. Congress and international partners. Instead, it wants the public to understand and accept the reasons for the expensive venture into space. Negative publicity has challenged the agency on the wisdom of the expenditures.

NASA may never be able to convince opposed, vocal publics to relax their criticism. Reason: NASA may never be able to translate the message, "space station exploration is good for America," into the same *meaning* the public will accept. In other words, unless the target public sees NASA the way NASA sees itself, the agency will send the message, the publics will receive it, but they will remain "uninformed" because they won't share the meaning.

**Indisposed public**. A regional clearinghouse for organs for transplantation wants to increase the number of donated organs by getting people to sign organ donor cards. It's had a lot of success. But not enough. It doesn't seem to be able to get young people to agree. That target public gets the message, and fully understands the meaning, including the number of people who die waiting for organs. There's no understanding problem here. Instead, the young target public doesn't agree with the meaning, for itself.

Research tells the agency that young people are afraid that their organs will be taken from them while they're still alive, although in a coma. It isn't true of course. But in this case, the target public is attributing a meaning that is not factual and accepting it. There's little the agency can do unless the target public surrenders the false meaning and makes itself available to agree with the true meaning.

**Constrained public**. A public relations firm is trying to land a big contract with a major client. The account manager responsible for making the pitch wants to bring in someone from another company to endorse the proposal by vouching for the experience and quality work of the PR firm. The person asked to make the endorsement understands the message, agrees with it, and wants to help the firm by making the endorsement. But there's a problem.

The endorser's boss doesn't want his employee to make the endorsement. The firm's client is the boss's competitor. So the potential endorser remains just that, a *potential* ally, because serious constraints prevent her from helping. Her job is on the line if she goes against her boss and there's an ethical question about helping a competitor identify excellent PR counsel who could work against her own company's interests. Green lights for all the persuasion moments until allegiance, duty and ethics prevent the desired behavior.

**Persuaded public**. A number of years ago, the Colonial Penn Insurance Company was told by a senior citizen group that it would lose the group's endorsement. At the same time, the group allowed Colonial Penn to retain as much insurance as it could before the endorsement expired.

In an excellent persuasion strategy, the company secured national radio talk show opportunities for a cadre of trained spokespersons to persuade seniors to retain Colonial Penn as their insurance company. Result: a satisfying retention rate. The right messages were sent to the right audience, using the right channels, convincing seniors to adopt the company's message and meaning. The company was able to overcome the constraint (in the public's mind) of the lost endorsement.

## Case example: College binge drinking

To exemplify how the Six Moments of Persuasion work in every influential act, consider this example using the campus binge drinking campaign. Here's a picture of the situation:

| | |
|---|---|
| Client: | College administration |
| Persuaders: | College public relations professionals |
| Target public: | First-year college students |
| Meaning: | Reduce binge drinking |
| Message: | Most successful students don't binge drink |
| Constraints: | Peer pressure, experimentation |
| Channels: | Print, electronic, face-to-face, special events |
| Resources: | Modest budget, six months, campus cooperation |

## Persuasion moments

• *Are you there?* Send the right message to the right public. Research has shown that national campaigns have been successful with the selected message. Now, you're extrapolating the experience to college first-year students.

• *Are you available?* The messages must come through channels the target public uses and believes. Distracting channel noises must be turned off. "Capture" your public's attention with dramatic copy, dynamic graphics and familiar surrogates. Surrogates are people other than college spokespersons you use as channels the target public believes.

• *Do you remember me?* Research on persuasion stresses message repetition. If your target publics can't, won't or don't recall your messages at the moment they must decide whether or not to binge drink, persuasion stops. Some researchers say you must send your messages up to six times so publics can recall them. Recall is enhanced with memorable messages. Creativity should work with this public.

*If your audience can't recall your message, it won't persuade itself.*

• *Do you know me?* The most efficient information exchange occurs when your public knows your product, service or value as you know it.

You must be a clear, efficient communicator to convince first-year college students that nonbinge-drinking students do better in academic and social life in college than do binge drinkers. Use picture words to convey information and attitudes. Most influence efforts fail when influencers don't get their audiences to see the issue the way they do.

• *Do you agree with me?* Your audience must accept the values you described for themselves. They must see and accept themselves as nonbinge drinkers. They might do this as part of a campus-wide pledge movement or campaign. The benefits from not binge drinking must identify with their core values. Research and values work might precede the actual campaign.

• *Will you act for me?* Getting your audience to do (or not do) what you want is the final moment. Even if all the moment lights were green up to this point, persuasion won't happen unless the audience acts. Your audience must be free to act. If your audience is constrained, you won't get the behavior you seek. A constrained audience negates all the work of the campaign in the first five moments. One "audience-freeing" tactic might be to seek partial or trial behavior, avoiding binge drinking on the next occasion or avoiding it "x" number of times during the year.

## Constrained audiences

Constraint is pressure on an audience to resist providing a desired behavior. To remove constraints, research suggests that counselors discover what publics *know* about issues, and whether the publics are *free* to do anything about them.

To reveal the amount of constraint, counselors can ask two questions about publics. The questions rate publics as easy or difficult to persuade.

- Does the public "see" the problem or issue?
- Can the public do something about it?

Here's a rating chart based on the answers to the questions and adapted from Gruning and Hunt, *Managing Public Relations* (*Figure 3.10*).

### Persuasible Audience Probability

| Audience | Knows about the issue | Free to act | Persuasion probability |
|---|---|---|---|
| Disposed | Yes | Yes | Excellent |
| Available | No | Yes | Good |
| Indisposed | Yes | No | Fair |
| Unavailable | No | No | Poor |

**Figure 3.10**

Notice that an "available" audience ranks higher than an "indisposed audience" because it's easier to inform a audience about an issue than it is to remove its constraints.

Inefficient public relations counselors mistake information for persuasion. The heavy duty work of persuasion is not merely sending messages, but sending the right ones, those that remove constraints. The best PR people are not the practitioners who know how to write, speak and picture things, but counselors who research and craft *what* to write, speak, and picture. You'll always hear the best ask, "Why?" about a certain communication not merely, "How?" Message makers manage persuasion. Message senders serve the managers.

Now apply this chart to four segments of the first-year student population in a college and their availability for persuasion to avoid binge drinking.

*Example*

**Disposed audience**

Incoming first-year students who know how binge drinking affects academic performance and social growth and who have an open mind about drinking while at college

*Know the issue, free to act*

**Available audience**

Incoming first-year students who have an open mind about avoiding excessive alcohol but don't know about the research on binge drinking

*Don't know the issue, free to act*

**Indisposed audience**

Incoming first-year students who know about how binge drinking affects academic performance and social growth, but want to experiment while away from home

*Know the issue, aren't free to act*

**Unavailable audience**

Incoming first-year students who don't know about the research on binge drinking and are pledging into a fraternity that uses excessive drinking as an initiation activity

*Don't know the issue, aren't free to act*

**Disposed students** might not yet have accepted the non-binge-drinking message, but aren't constrained from adopting it. They know the message. It's the meaning of the message that's up for grabs. PR counselors should send attitude-adopting messages to this public. The PR counselor has an *excellent* chance to succeed.

**Available students** have the same open mind, but they haven't heard the message yet. There's an extra step to take with this public. Send both information and attitude-adopting messages to this group. Make certain they recall the message when they face "temptation." The PR counselor has a *good* chance to succeed.

**Indisposed students** are much harder to deal with. They've been exposed to the message and they're resisting adopting the meaning for themselves. Information alone won't work as well with this public as it might with the disposed and available groups. Persuaders must research exactly why this group won't adopt the meaning and try to neutralize those factors. The PR counselor has only a *fair* chance to succeed.

**Unavailable students** are just that. When faced with this kind of public, counselors frequently waste no time or money trying to persuade them. If they wanted to try, counselors must first work on making the public available for the message and the meaning, then send attention getting messages. Afterward, they will have to work on the attitudes again, this time with the message out there. The PR counselor has little to *no chance* to succeed.

## Binge-drinking Case Audience Analysis

| Audiences | Knowledgeable about binge-drinking messages | Free to accept the meaning and avoid binge drinking |
|---|---|---|
| Disposed | Received the message. Seeks information about such issues. | Generally predisposed to adopt behavior leading to personal advantage. |
| Available | Hasn't received the message yet. Not aware of what it means for them. | Generally predisposed to adopt behavior leading to personal welfare. |
| Indisposed | Received the message. Understands what it means. But won't seek more information. | Generally indisposed to commitments restricting personal freedom. |
| Unavailable | Hasn't received the message. Probably will selectively avoid the message (and the meaning) when exposed to it. | Hostile to any message that conflicts with predetermined values. |

**Figure 3.11**

Figure 3.11 (above) shows what the chart looks like for those student publics.

## Characteristics of influence

All persuasive messages share common characteristics:

- Must reach audiences
- Identify with audiences' basic and higher needs
- Bond with audiences' values, and be tailor-made to the moment.

Effective counselors avoid the trap less successful colleagues fall into, that of crafting messages for oneself, for a presumed audience, or from habit or unconcern to get the job done. Influential communication is not busy work, or mere message sending. It's a sharp skill requiring an outside-of-self type of communicating. Influencing is not merely communicating information. That activity is left to communicators who have no behavior or attitude formation purpose.

## Persuasive tactics

All PR counselors use tactics to achieve their ends. The most persuasive counselors use researched strategies to gain the advantage and avoid making persuasion a guessing game. Here are some tactics from research that should help in many persuasion situations.

First, two tactics to help audiences remove constraints

preventing them from providing the desired behavior.

• **Fraction of Selection Formula**. You can remove constraints by following researcher Wilbur Schramm's easy-to-use "Fraction of Selection Formula." To determine how constrained an audience is, divide the benefit an audience will enjoy by the amount of effort it must expend to get the benefit.

$$\frac{\text{Benefit}}{\text{Effort}} = \text{Amount of constraint}$$

If your audience finds it too troublesome to get a benefit, it probably won't go after it. To motivate behavior, emphasize the benefit and diminish the effort for your audience. This will free your audience from its constraints, at least in its mind (*Figure 3.12*).

### Reward/Effort Relationship

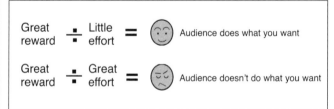

**Figure 3.12**

*Example*: If you ask an audience to try a new product, you'll probably find that brand switching is a big problem to a lot of people. The effort and risk are greater than the promised reward. To counter constraints, identify and refute them:

Effort: *"I'm satisfied with my present brand."*

Benefit: *"But your brand wasn't always your brand. You wouldn't be using it now unless you experimented. By experimenting, you found a more satisfying product."*

Effort: *"It's too much trouble to change."*

Benefit: *"For a single investment of a little time, you can enjoy many pleasurable hours with the new product."*

Effort: *"It costs more than my current product."*

Benefit: *"Better products usually do. But new users love the new features. They're willing to pay a few extra cents for a better product."*

## How to make a winning argument

When most people argue points, they generally use a style they heard before. Unfortunately, they probably failed a lot, too. Here's an example of the style from an employer/employee interaction:

**Behavior**: *"Employees need to use the new customer service policy."*

In the opening statement, the influencer announces the topic and the desired behavior.

**Information**: *"Customer complaints increased 5 percent this past year."*

In the second statement, the influencer offers proof or reason for the behavior.

**Attitude**: *Nothing*

That's the problem. There's no all-important attitude statement to generate the behavior.

What should the "attitude statement" be?

Like glue, the attitude statement bonds the influencer and the audience. In the example, if the manager simply argued that employees should follow the new customer service policy and cite an increase in customer complaints, employees could say,

"So what? What's wrong with five percent?" or,

"So what? We can't please everybody." or,

"So what? What do fewer customer complaints mean to us?"

Unless the manager bonds with employees, the behavior request and information statement by themselves may not produce the desired behavior.

## Listening with Feedback

A note about good listening. Listening is a key feedback skill. Public relations counselors must be effective listeners if they want to capture messages and detect the meanings behind them. Active listening, developed by Joseph DeVito, in his *Interpersonal Communication* book (Harper Collins) can help.

Active listening uses focusing and caring skills. It requires a partnership between the sender and receiver. The technique is called active because of the energy required to focus on the sender's message and the commitment to care that the sender succeeds. The technique has three steps:

• **Paraphrase the sender's meaning**. By feeding back to the sender what you heard (or read through interactive e-mail), you signal the sender that you're interested in the communication, both the message and the meaning.

Ask a question such as, "By your message, do you mean that you don't like the product generally or that the one you selected wasn't right for you?"

Without this first feedback step, there's no way you can know if you have the correct meaning.

• **Accept the sender's attitude about the message**. This takes commitment to make certain both you and the sender succeed in the partnership. By discovering the attitude prompting the message, you engage the sender.

*Example*: "You must have been unhappy when you tried to use our product for your party and it didn't work for you. How disappointing, and embarrassing."

Not many people, even those responsible for customer service, ever try to get to the attitude behind an opinion. Attitude leads to motivation, which leads to meaning.

• **Ask a question about the message's meaning**. This is the ultimate partnership act. Few people engage another in conversation for fear they will be "trapped" in another's circumstance.

*Example*: "Have you ever tried the same product from another company?"

The essence of good listening is willing entrapment for mutual benefit.

How do influencers bond with their audience? They could use Attitude Statements to signal the value of doing what they're asking for. Values bond people. If the manager values satisfied customers and employees value satisfied customers, they bond, and the manager has a great chance to get employees to follow the policy.

> *Good listening is willing entrapment for mutual benefit.*

Here are some Attitude Statements that could bond the manager and employees:

> *"I'm sure you agree that improved service is something we owe our customers."*
> (Value: Provide what we advertised.)

> *"Don't you agree that improved service will help keep our regular customers?"*
> (Value: We don't lose business.)

> *"Don't you agree that improved service will keep enough customers coming to us so we stay in business?"*
> (Value: You don't lose your job.)

Notice how these statements appeal to the values of the audience. If employees value keeping promises, or keeping business, or keeping their jobs, they might use the new service policy.

When you argue, if you don't use a bonding attitude statement, you leave the audience to come up with the attitude on its own. It might not. Why take the chance?

Here's a list of powerful attitude statements to bond with an audience.

■ **Values**. Values are ranked attitudes. If you and your audience share the same value about something, your chances to exert influence improves. Here's an example:

**Behavior statement**:  *"We're taking up a collection in the office for our Sunshine Club — for employees who are sick, get married, have children and other occasions."*

**Information statement**:  *"We need a collection because we're down to our last $20."*

**Attitude statement**:  *"The Sunshine Club helps you take care of your obligation to your colleagues."*

Here, the value is duty, an obligation to show concern for one's colleagues. Probably everyone at work believes the sunshine club serves a worthwhile purpose. Notice that without the attitude statement, the information statement doesn't really motivate. It just informs.

■ Beliefs. These are powerful statements, more powerful even than values, because they cannot be proved or disproved. If you can cite a common belief you and your audience share, and apply it to your topic, you have an excellent chance to win your argument. Here's an example:

**Behavior statement**:  *"As members of the employee group, we're asking for additional refreshment vending machines for the office."*

**Information statement**:  *"Right now, we have only one machine for 100 employees. It's difficult to get proper service."*

**Attitude statement**:  *"You'll agree a company is only as strong as the morale of its employees."*

Notice that the Attitude Statement is a belief. No one can prove or disprove the extent to which a company's strength depends on a certain level of employee morale. But if the audience (management) believes it is and accepts the idea that vending machines and morale are linked, you can probably expect management to plug new machines into that office shortly.

■ **Research/Rules**. These are powerful binders. If you appeal to research, rules or law, audiences generally will respect facts or things they cannot change, and act. Here's an example:

**Behavior statement:** *"Management will monitor the e-mail of all employees to protect the rights of the company and its employees."*

> *Picture words powerfully persuade — they "see" what you "mean."*

**Information statement**: *"Recently, we had several incidents of employee-on-employee harassment and use of e-mail for unauthorized communications."*

**Attitude statement**: *"The law clearly gives management the right to do this. In addition, 92 percent of employees surveyed agree they need management's help to stop the harassment."*

The strength of research or rules as bond elements is self evident.

*Tip*: When you propose an argument, have some research on your side. If it doesn't exist, get it.

## Picture words

Picture words add influence to your speech because they're easy to take in, entertain while they inform, and add personal experiences associated with the images.

For example, you can say,
*"Stay on your diet and you'll achieve your goals."*
Or you can say,
*"Stay on your diet, you'll be able to wear your shirt*

*inside again instead of loosely hanging it outside to hide embarrassing bulges."* Which is more forceful?

## Cases and scenarios

Case studies or scenarios are powerful persuaders, especially with adults. Research shows that adults learn better through real life "walk-through" than through classes or lectures about abstract ideas.

Cases and scenarios help you picture your idea, steps necessary to make it happen, and benefits the audience will enjoy. Help audiences "live out" benefits, like buying a car, sitting behind the wheel and kicking the tires. Make case study presentations story-like, complete with heroes, challenges, problems, crises and solutions.

Cases and scenarios store images in target publics that they can easily recall for decision making.

## Group persuasion

Persuading target publics one member at a time wastes time and could be unrewarding. When counselors need to persuade a large group of people, but don't have the time or resources to do it piecemeal, they try to target the group's leaders. *Members of a group will often do something for the group they won't do for themselves*. Persuading leaders of defined groups to go with the proposal generally inspires group members to follow.

What's working for counselors is the known dynamic that continued membership in a group depends on members conforming to the group's norms and leadership wishes. Members identify with their groups and acquire power and recognition from group association. *Examples*: unions, political parties, cults, families, fraternities and college student bodies. Members sublimate personal preference to group preference. Counselors know that when members decide to follow the group leader, they're ultimately serving their own self interest.

Group leadership depends on the leader taking the middle position on issues at group meetings. Members don't usually select leaders who take extreme positions. Juries, ad-hoc committees and teams all seek compromisers to lead them.

It's interesting that the middle of the road is called the *crown*.

## Motivating employees

Research at Rowan University suggests that nothing except cash will work to motivate nonmanagerial employees to do their jobs the way the boss would. But many organizations can't or won't offer cash to motivate their employees — banks, fast food restaurants, schools, hospitals, government agencies, retail sales associates and even college professors.

Without cash rewards, organizations traditionally look to recognition programs, such as "Employee of the Month," "Outstanding Achiever," "Best Idea," and the like.

But rewards and recognitions have limited value. They seem to work only with "service mentality" employees who respond to recognition because the employees are responsive. They don't seem to work with employees with a "hireling" mentality.

Counselors know that motivating these employees may be an impossible task unless they demonstrate a service mentality. Counselors could help organizations by suggesting that for these programs to work, organizations should hire right. They should select employees with skills **and** a service mentality.

Many service workers, such as teachers and hospital personnel, perform heroically merely for supervisor congratulation and peer recognition. To motivate them for continued superior contributions, congratulate them publicly.

### The Media and Influence

Public relations must deal with the media as an important channel to help tell an organization's story. Chapter One discussed the relationship between the press and public relations as a mutually beneficial and sometimes contentious partnership in the public opinion drama.

But with respect to opinion formation, the question with the media always is: Are media helpful in the contest for public opinion? Are they independently effective? How influential are they with the publics that public relations deals with?

A number of studies over the years have demonstrated that the media are indeed very influential. Most of the earlier studies demonstrated that the media have only an agenda-setting function in society. They don't tell people what to think, but what to think about. More recently, practitioners have questioned whether the media are more influential than that. They have suspected that massive advertising, direct mail, sophisticated political campaign strategies and other techniques might directly influence the attitudes of publics. They also suspect that as more people use media figures, network anchors, talk show hosts and other media types for their sole source of information, the media's influence has increased.

Indeed, the experience of societal observers demonstrates that people who have limited access to influential people might be more influenced by the media than formerly believed.

When so honored, such employees feel obliged to live up to their new reputation. The monthly "star performer" programs in many organizations work on this principle.

When you can't offer a raise, offer praise. ■

## Public opinion challenge:
## Marketing a personality toy

A marketing director for a toy manufacturer wants to create a big holiday demand, even a frenzy, for a new toy power figure. The figure has "multiple personalities." It can become any one of nine lives, an astronaut, an athlete, a teacher, and others.

The marketing director asks you, the PR director, to get favorable public opinion for the action figure. You have to influence four major publics, children, parents, toy outlets and the media. What activities do you suggest for each? Why?

## Persuasion challenge:
## Facing a hostile audience

You are the public relations director of a clothing department store. Once a year, your boss collects letters from disgruntled customers and invites them to the store's auditorium for a meeting with management. Management wants to soften their criticism and explain the store's side of the story. This year, your boss selects you to meet with them.

How will you prepare to meet with this "hostile" audience? What tone will you adopt at the meeting? What game plan will you adopt? Will you bring anyone or anything with you?

# Tips

1. When you're trying to influence a public, do your best to look and sound like them. And always make them feel you're giving them what they need or want.

2. To discover who's on different sides of an issue, start a debate about the issue. To do that, stage an "incident" about it.

3. Don't try to influence opinion without first understanding the attitudes behind it.

4. If you can't convince a public about your point of view, at least try getting it to act on your position.

5. Never assume the meaning of your message got through to your receiver. Always check through feedback.

6. To interest a public in your position, show how it will affect their lives, positively or negatively.

7. To use the Two-Step Flow Process to your advantage, feed the media stories your influential publics would be interested in.

8. Never end your argument until you've included an "attitude statement" that tightly bonds you, the audience and what you want. Use values, beliefs, research or law statements.

9. Never assume the attitudes of your important publics. Always test for them.

10. Always put yourself in the shoes of your target audiences before you create messages for them. Say to yourself, "If I were my audience, what would persuade me to do this?"

**Questions for classroom discussion**

1. Of the five parts of the communication process, sender, receiver, message, channel and feedback, which one most influences the meaning of a communicated message?

2. Which of the *Six Moments of Persuasion* directly affects the meaning a receiver gets from a communicated message?

3. In the formation of public opinion, why is it important that publics be informed before they offer their "opinion"?

4. In your opinion, how important are the media in influencing public opinion? Why?

5. Why is an "indisposed" public a difficult audience to work with? What should you remember about handling this kind of problem?

**Assignments**

1. Look around your college or university. How many efforts at gaining a positive public opinion can you detect? Who's trying? Who are the target audiences?

2. Look in the newspaper tonight for a case involving two competing individuals or organizations. Assume you are public relations counsel for either one. Write a brief analysis of the case and the advice you would give your client on how to gain positive public opinion for your client's position.

3. Look up a recent launch of a new product, perhaps a new drug or computer program. Analyze the market position the company apparently wanted the product to have. Then, analyze how the company managed the public opinion process to gain the desired position.

4. Search the Internet for five corporate Web sites. Analyze their Web page designs to detect the positioning and public opinion for each corporation. Suggest what you might do differently if you think you know what their companies are up to.

5. Search the Internet for public relations Web sites. Try PRSA, IABC, WIC and NSPRA. Look for case studies of public relations challenges. Analyze the public opinion formation process in each one. Log onto the Web sites of large public relations firms like Burson-Marstellar and Ketchum for posted case studies of PR programs. Also, search universities with advanced degree programs in public relations, such as Maryland, Florida and Rowan.

**Internet assignment**

Connect with the Web site, *Influence: Agency for the New Economy*, or a similar Web site, and research the function of influence as it interfaces with marketing to help the public relations function.

Team with two other students online and prepare a position for class discussion on this statement:

> Influence builds market and like-minded leaders in the New Economy by integrating marketing, communication and technology. Influence turns your stakeholders into evangelists. Influence will help you succeed in the new economy.

Name _____ Date _____

## AAA in a CAT Fight

The American Automobile Association of New Jersey, a consumer association serving car owners, published a report stating that pollution for automobile emissions was not the primary cause of air pollution. Specifically, the study cited certain harmful emissions, volatile organic compounds (VOCs) and nitrous oxide, and claimed that stationary sources such as power plants and refineries and mobile sources, such as trucks, caused most of the harmful pollution.

The report stated that cars contribute only 24 percent of the VOCs going into the air. And the percentage is dropping every year as newer model cars replace older, more polluting ones. The group was going to bat for its association members, attempting to get federal and state governments and environmental groups off their backs.

The report was not good news for the Clean Air Team (CAT) that wants the federal government to issue more stringent regulations on auto emissions. In fact, CAT is pushing the state of New Jersey to issue the toughest rules yet on auto emission testing. The group quickly condemned the report. "Baloney," said the clean air people to AAA, "your members' auto emissions are still dangerous and your study must be flawed."

The groups have begun waging a public opinion war for the minds, hearts and votes of the general public and the governments involved.

## PR issues

Both AAA and CAT will have public relations counsel on their sides, trying to persuade the publics involved to see the issue their way and support their positions.

### AAA issues

- Research can affect public opinion more quickly than rhetoric.
- Members want AAA to slug it out in public on their behalf.
- By issuing the study, AAA is trying to release the grip of CAT on controlling public opinion. Whoever wins the public opinion war will win the legislative war.
- AAA knows that the media will probably side with CAT. It also knows that government officials will too. Why? Because the media generally side with groups that appear to be on the "good side" of issues and against organizations that appear to "harm" society on behalf of a select group of people.

Legislators too, will be inclined to side with CAT because the volume of public communication seems to weigh on the side of clean air, not on the side of the lesser publicized public, automobile drivers.

### CAT issues

- It must publicly denounce the report, and it did.
- Public opinion is up for grabs when science disputes long-standing mass sentiment about an issue such as the part auto emissions plays in air pollution.
- Similar attacks on long-held attitudes are occurring, such as global warming, which

Name_____Date_____

new scientific reports say is due more to a 26,000-year earth/climate cycle rather than human-caused attacks on the ozone layer. CAT cannot let the public focus on studies like those.

- CAT must position AAA as a special interest group with a narrow, self-serving public — auto owners and drivers. It must position itself as a general interest group, serving the larger public, including children, the aged, and the ill that need clean air.

## PR activities

### AAA activities

- Follow the report up with another one. Force CAP to keep trying to debunk scientific reports. It's better if it's occupied defending rather than attacking. Public opinion will gradually go to the side that appears reasonable and objective.
- Send a lot of information to legislators. Make certain they understand the issue scientifically as well as emotionally or politically. The political climate will change when their constituents tell them they believe AAA's reports.
- Send the media the same information. Legislators won't be able to hide if the publics they represent are getting the same data they are. Start a controversy in the media about who's right, using letters-to-the-editor, talk show appearances, and editorial board meetings.
- Mobilize AAA members and constituents. Send them form letters they can send to congressional representatives. Make certain the letters contain the new scientific data.
- Redirect the argument to personal freedom guarantees to own and drive cars. Frame any interference, such as CAT's position and government regulation, as an infringement on personal freedom.

### CAT activities

- Find a report that favors CAT and send it to legislators and the media. Both should be willing recipients of the information.
- Get scientists to go public with information favoring CAT's position. Public opinion cannot be controlled until the playing field is leveled.
- Begin a campaign crediting organizations like CAT that say they have the public interest as their top priority. Discredit organization's like AAA. Position it as held captive by special interests. Force public concentration on the message, "All pollution is bad. The percentage doesn't matter. Stopping any auto emission has to be better than letting even a little continue."
- Don't allow AAA to redirect the argument to government intervention in personal freedoms, like owning and driving a car.

*See other side*

Name _____ Date _____

# Public Opinion Formation Model
## "Cracked Egg Model" worksheet

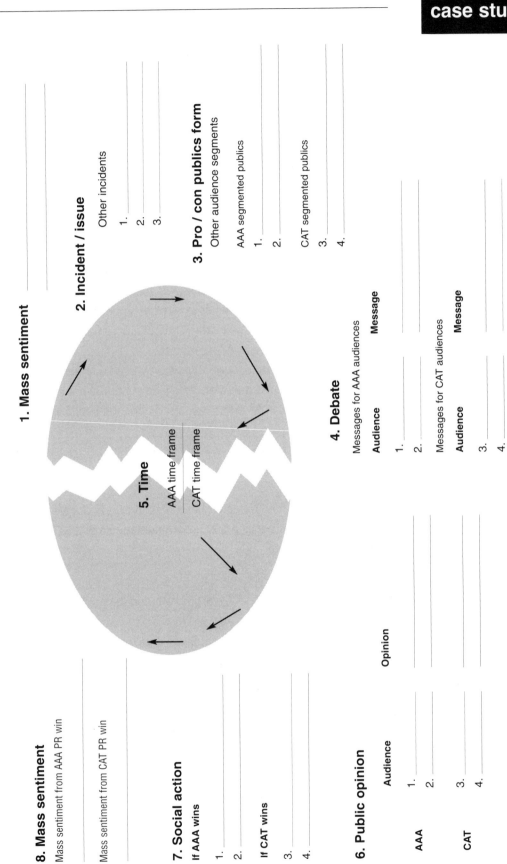

**1. Mass sentiment**

**2. Incident / issue**

Other incidents
1. _____
2. _____
3. _____

**3. Pro / con publics form**

Other audience segments

AAA segmented publics
1. _____
2. _____

CAT segmented publics
3. _____
4. _____

**4. Debate**

Messages for AAA audiences

| Audience | Message |
| --- | --- |
| 1. _____ | |
| 2. _____ | |

Messages for CAT audiences

| Audience | Message |
| --- | --- |
| 3. _____ | |
| 4. _____ | |

**5. Time**

AAA time frame

CAT time frame

**8. Mass sentiment**

Mass sentiment from AAA PR win

Mass sentiment from CAT PR win

**7. Social action**

If AAA wins
1. _____
2. _____

If CAT wins
3. _____
4. _____

**6. Public opinion**

| Audience | Opinion |
| --- | --- |
| AAA | 1. _____ |
| | 2. _____ |
| CAT | 3. _____ |
| | 4. _____ |

Name _____ Date _____

## PR questions

- In addition to issuing a report, think of other **incidents or special events** (2) that could trigger mass sentiment and start the public opinion formation process. Write these in the spaces provided.

- Under each of the four publics mentioned in the case analysis list segments of these **pro/con audiences** (3) you think could be important to either side.

  In the **debate** phase (4) of the chart, list attractive messages for each audience segment.

- In the **time phase** (5), list the length of campaign time you think each side in the controversy should take for maximum effect.

- In the **public opinion** phase (6), list possible large-scale opinions that could emerge from the debate. List at least one for each segmented public. If you think any of the opinions will reach critical mass (majority or significant opinion), place an asterisk next to it.

- In the **social action** phase (7), list the desired social actions you think each side would want to come from this case. Remember, even nonaction can influence mass sentiment.

- In the **mass sentiment** phase (8), predict possible public attitudes that will result from the actions society takes in phase 7.

Write the **best position** you think each side should take **in response to the position stated** in the list of case facts

AAA major position ...

_____

CAT response position ...

_____

CAT major position ...

_____

AAA response position ...

_____

*See other side*

*Name* _____ *Date* _____

What would be your ethical limit on positioning your opponent as the "bad guy" for each competitor?

AAA ethical limit …

_____

Why

_____

CAT ethical limit …

_____

Why?

_____


What **messages**, other than science and freedom, do you think AAA could use? With whom?
Through which channels?

**AAA alternatives**

Audience _____ Message _____ Channel _____

Audience _____ Message _____ Channel _____

Audience _____ Message _____ Channel _____


What **messages**, other than health and special interests, do you think CAT could use? With whom?
Through which channels?

**CAT alternatives**

Audience _____ Message _____ Channel _____

Audience _____ Message _____ Channel _____

Audience _____ Message _____ Channel _____


Finally, picking just one side of this controversy, draw your ideal public opinion formation model — the way you think it should evolve, including the final social action you would want.

Team with another student who selected the opposite contender and debate your ideal PR programs in class.

# Chapter 4

# Using Research in Public Relations

---

**PRaxiom**  *Public relations without research is like shooting an arrow, then frantically moving a target around to catch it.*

---

**What this chapter covers**

In this chapter, you'll learn the research tools necessary to complete most public relations projects. Although they might seem mysterious at first, they're useful, easy-to-use techniques. And the math isn't that difficult either.

You'll learn about surveys, polling, detecting opinion, and using research results to make you an influential persuader. In applying research to public relations activity, practitioners can use a number of techniques. Training, common sense and an analysis of the task will help you select the right tools for the job.

The following chart (*Figure 4.1*) displays the major public relations research techniques. Like the media/channel relationship, each general type has specific versions.

## Types of Research

|  | **Formal** | **Informal** |
|---|---|---|
| **Quantitative** | Probability survey<br>• *Sampling*<br>Content analysis<br>Audit<br>Interview<br>• *Intercept*<br>Controlled experiment | Nonprobability survey<br>Document search<br>Interview<br>• *Casual*<br>• *In-depth*<br>Readability study<br>Data analysis<br>• *Clips* |
| **Qualitative** | Probability survey<br>Audit<br>Interview<br>• *Intercept* | Nonprobability survey<br>Focus group<br>Interview<br>• *Casual*<br>• *In-depth*<br>Case history / study<br>Observation<br>Advisory panel<br>Diaries<br>Data analysis<br>• *Clips*<br>Self-analysis |

**Figure 4.1**

# RESEARCH TYPES

## Formal research

Formal research is organized, methodical, scientific research. It tells you objective truth about an audience or data under study.

In some versions, you can apply results to the larger population from which the data came — from a sample audience to the larger universe audience or from sample data to the larger universe database.

Universe means the entire population under study. Sample means a portion of that universe. In formal research, the sample is randomly and scientifically selected.

Formal research is generally more difficult. It takes longer and costs more.

*Example*: Scientific telephone survey of Americans on their attitudes toward a national health care plan.

## Informal research

Informal research is less organized, less methodical and less scientific. The informal researcher is not concerned with getting a picture of the way things absolutely are — just enough of a picture to satisfy the research purpose.

Informal researchers can't transfer what's learned from a smaller population or database to a larger one. Informal research is less difficult than formal research, takes less time and generally costs less.

*Note*: Just because informal research isn't as transferable as formal research, it doesn't mean it has no value. In fact, in many public relations situations, informal research is the only kind you can do.

Sometimes, data aren't available for a formal study; or your client or boss won't pay for a formal study; or a formal study would be a waste of money, time and other resources.

*Example*: A sole reporter (on deadline for an evening story) asks five people passing by the newspaper building their opinions about a national health care plan.

## Quantitative research

Quantitative research *measures things*. It measures data, audiences' opinions, newspaper clips, and other items. It quantifies things mathematically. The difference between quantitative and qualitative research is the difference between **measuring and describing**.

Quantitative research, especially experiments, is time consuming and tedious. Despite the labor involved, it's a valuable tool for public relations researchers. For example, it's important to know not only that employees are upset with their health care benefits, but also how many are

upset, what aspects they're upset about, and what caused the negative attitude.

## Qualitative research

Qualitative research *describes a situation* without necessarily measuring it.

*Example*: Group of employees called together to give their opinion about their health care benefits.

They describe their feelings about the benefits, management's behavior toward them, and their desires for the ideal package. Management simply wants a *picture* of their opinion, not a scientific measurement of it.

*Note*: If management wants a picture *and* a measurement, it could conduct both quantitative and qualitative research through appropriate questions.

It's possible to conduct both formal and informal quantitative research. For example, PR practitioners could *look at* a few newspaper clips to judge their organization's media relations program (informal). Or, they could look at a scientific sample of the clips, or all of them (formal). In both cases, they're *measuring* the clips. But the more formal measure produces an objective picture that better represents reality.

> **For a casual picture, describe things. For a serious picture, count things. But picture or count only what you need.**

Similarly, it's possible to have both formal and informal qualitative research. For example, PR researchers could ask a few employees to describe their feelings toward their health care benefits (informal). Or the researchers could ask a scientific sample of the employees, or all of them (formal) to do the same.

Here's a definition of each general type and possible versions. Following the definitions, a discussion will accompany examples of their use in public relations practice.

# RESEARCH TECHNIQUES

## Survey

*Questioning an audience through a questionnaire in writing, over the phone, or in person*

If the survey studies a random sample of the population, the study is called *probable* and results are *projectable* to the larger universe from which the sample was derived. If the survey covers the entire audience universe, it's a census and results are not merely probable, but *certain*.

*Example*: Surveying a random sample of 300

customers from a company's 10,000-member customer list about attitudes toward the company's service.

## Content analysis

*Discovery of information about a series of items and factual statements about them*

Content analysis relies on proper coding of each item and effective identification of categories. The technique does not answer *why* items are the way they are. It establishes only that they are that way.

*Example*: Identifying characteristics of an organization's media clips, such as those resulting from a PR news release.

## Audit

*Comprehensive analysis of an organization's communication style*

A communication audit focuses on communication content and style. A public relations audit determines if an organization achieved its PR objectives.

Audits use specific research techniques such as interviews, surveys, network analysis, content analysis, and focus groups to discover how communication occurs and how effective it is. It also lays groundwork to remedy ineffective communication.

*Communication audit example*: Analyzing both content and style of all communication activities of secretaries in an organization.

*PR audit example*: Analyzing a public library's external communication efforts, including an analysis of its marketing efforts, availability of services to customers, and customer opinion.

## Interview

*Focused conversation with a target audience to discover information level, prevailing attitudes, and behavior (actual or potential) about certain issues*

The interview can be in-depth or casual. It can follow a strict protocol of questions or it can be open-ended and focused. It involves listening and recording skills. Interviews can form part of a formal communication audit, or conducted as "day-after-the-event" interviews.

*Example*: A series of in-depth interviews with associates in a law firm to discover willingness to advertise firm services.

## Controlled experiment

*Test of relationship between variables*

The test can be conducted in-house or in the field. Careful control of variables yields a reliable conclusion.

*Example*: "Split-flight" run of baby food advertising messages to discover the most attractive of the pair for parents.

## Focus group

*Controlled discussion with six to eight carefully selected target audience participants to discover attitudes and opinions*

The merit of the focus group is live interaction with a facilitator and the capability to "show" the group test items, such as proposed logos or advertising copy, to elicit reaction. Careful preparation of the questioning protocol and accurate recording of responses results in rich qualitative data.

*Example*: A gas utility conduct of five focus groups (corresponding to customer geographic organization) to discover customer reaction to its annual energy report and ideas for improvement.

## Document search

*Organized analysis of literature on focused issues*

The literature can be an organization's own documents or outside literature. The search can be organized around a type of document, like customer letters to the company. Or, it can be a research question, like identification of industry trends in employee field reports.

Types of documents include standard research data resources and banks, letters to the company, letters to the editor, editorials, newspaper clips, field reports, trade literature, competitor advertising and legislation.

*Example*: Analysis of messages in competitors' ads as part of a high tech company's pre-launch research for a new intranet server. The search analyzes PR story types in industry publications attractive to media and style of marketing brochures and how-to manuals.

## Readability study

*Analysis of the readability of copy in an organization's publications*

Practitioners can use one of the standard formulas in the industry, such as the Gunning-Meuller Fog Index. (*See Chapters 5 and 6 for an explanation of this formula.*)

The study identifies compatibility between copy and an audience's ability to take in and process information. The study can form part of a communication audit of an organization's publications. (Other parts of that audit could be an analysis of story content, placement and frequency, and graphics.)

*Example*: Compatibility match between patient information brochure copy prepared by doctors and a hospital's patients. A dispute between in-house public relations personnel and medical staff to either simplify copy for consumers or retain the original version justifies the study.

## Data analysis

*Critical examination of information according to a purpose*

Information comes in a variety of forms, such as rumors within an organization, results of observations (of customer or business associate behavior), publicity about an organization, interview notes, field reports, economic trends, sales records, adversary activity and legal rulings.

*Example*: A cruise line analysis of guest satisfaction with its ships' special events program.

## Case study/Case history

*Analysis of a situation in marketing, public relations or advertising to detect success or failure with a communication campaign or program*

These studies reveal chief players, objectives, activities, variables and effects. They sometimes are placed in trade literature or entered into national competitions to enhance an organization's image.

*Example*: Complete story (objectives, strategies, tactics, outcomes) about a successful church fund-raising campaign for a new building. The media and sister churches asked how they did it. The case study details the anatomy of the successful campaign.

## Observation

*Systematic visual recording of activities to collect data for analysis*

This frequently overlooked technique is one of the most reliable ways to collect data. If done by a person (not merely a video camera), the observer can add additional information. If done by electronic means only, some of the subjective interpretation could be lost. Organizations that want both subjective and objective aspects should employ both simultaneously.

*Example*: Trained researcher observation of bank teller activity for a fixed period. Customers had been complaining about the bank's service.

*Caution*: Researchers can report only about employee observed behavior in a specific research time period. They can't extrapolate to other employees working in different time periods. Researchers are not scientifically "sampling" the entire employee population through this method. However, researchers could observe the entire employee population in all work periods. Such a census would provide certainty about total employee behavior.

> ## *Observation is one of the most believable ways to collect evidence data.*

## Advisory panel

*Stratified group of representatives from a target public appointed to advise an organization about its policies or activities*

Stratification places specific demographic characteristics, such as age, gender and ethnicity, or ergraphic characteristics, such as occupation and work habits in the selected panel.

These panels can go beyond merely analyzing issues to offering opinion. They can advise on strategic approaches to solve problems. Some panels stay on after the initial job so management can later test changes recommended by the group. Using the same group eliminates a troublesome variable.

*Example*: School-board-appointed resident advisory group study of the feasibility of a board plan to expand school facilities. The board wants public opinion on its side before it asks for voter approval to fund new construction.

The merit of this approach lies in the "sponsorship" of the plan by the representative advisory panel.

A special variation of the advisory panel is a popular and efficient interactive technique known as the "Key Communicator" program. This program is described in detail in Chapter 5.

Briefly, the two-way *Key Communicator Program* envisions a group of influential community members appointed to advise an organization — company, school district, public utility or government agency — about issues, opinions and rumors in the community. In return, the organization sends information about issues to these key people hoping they will pass on the information to key constituents.

## Diary

*Personal record of activities, usually about use of time, selection of activities, or impressions of campaign items*

The value of these highly subjective research documents is predicated on the honor system. The data are as valuable as they are accurate. Interestingly, a comparison of diaries about the same issues or events can reveal bias in research.

*Example*: Organization's secretaries diaries of their communication transactions for a week. As part of a communication audit, a company wants to know how efficiently its secretaries communicate daily with all internal and external publics. The diaries form part of network analysis research within the communication audit.

## Self-analysis

*Record of participants' roles in a communication program and their impressions of the efficacy of the tactics in the program*

If organizations do not use these records to punish employees but to learn where campaigns succeed and fail, they can provide both objective and subjective data. Frequently, these self analyses form part of the organization's exit strategy for voluntarily departing employees.

*Example*: Two key employees from a PR firm leave to join another firm. Before they depart, the organization asks them to recount their impressions of their contributions. They also ask about their relationship with management and other employees, and their satisfaction with the roles they were asked to play during their tenure with the company. These unvarnished reports can contain valuable data about the organization's internal communication style.

## PROBABILITY TECHNIQUES

### Sampling

Sampling is a selection technique to identify target audiences for research. Depending on its purpose, researchers employ two basic types:

- Scientific sampling tries to make the sampled audience reflect the actual universe audience. Some researchers say it's like trying to make the smaller picture of an audience (microcosm) resemble the larger picture (macrocosm).
- Nonscientific sampling makes no attempt to reflect the larger research audience.

The difference between the two lies in the kind of information each yields. Scientific sampling yields probability. Nonscientific sampling does not.

An example of a nonscientific sample is a self-select sample. A college wants to find out how its students feel about the new cafeteria menu. It places a survey in the college paper asking students their opinions. In this study, **the sample selects itself**. Hence, there's nothing scientific about it. It has some merit to define the issues. But it can't be used to project the results onto the entire student body.

### Probability

Probability is a conclusion researchers draw that the information they derive from a scientific sample reliably reflects the larger universe. Only random sampling yields probability.

Probability is not certitude. Only a census (a study of every member of the universe) yields certitude. Instead, a probability study is subject to a certain amount of error — the results are probably right, but in a very small number of cases, they might be wrong. Public relations people accept a certain amount of minimal error because the probability of being right is so high.

*Only random sampling yields probability.*

### Sampling error

Sampling error is the chance that results from a scientific study will differ from reality. Error in a probability study follows mathematical laws. Error is reported in percentage points above or below a finding (e.g., + (plus) or – (minus) 5 means that a closer picture of reality is **five points above or five points below** an actual score).

*Example*: In a scientific study, a PR director finds that 55% of company employees like their company newsletter. The finding is 55%. But when sampling error is applied to the *finding*, a picture closer to reality lies five points above 55% (55% + 5% = 60%) or five points below 55% (55% – 5% = 50%). The *picture closer to reality* lies somewhere between 50% and 60%. Remember, even the gap between 50% and 60% is only probable, not certain.

The **error gap** is the gap between the highest and lowest scores after the error is applied. Here, the error gap

### Sample Size and Error

| Sample size | Error at 95% confidence level |
|---|---|
| 100 | ± 9.8% |
| 200 | ± 6.9% |
| 300 | ± 5.6% |
| 384 | ± 5.0% |
| 400 | ± 4.9% |
| 500 | ± 4.3% |
| 600 | ± 4.0% |
| 700 | ± 3.7% |
| 800 | ± 3.4% |
| 900 | ± 3.2% |
| 1,000 | ± 3.0% |
| 1,250 | ± 2.7% |

**Figure 4.2**

is between 50% and 60%. The table on page 69 shows sample size and related error (*Figure 4.2*).

*Note*: A sample of 384 representatives yields an error of plus (+) or minus (–) 5%, **regardless of the size of the universe.** A major polling organization, such as the George Gallup Organization, will use 1,250 representatives in the sample for an error of plus (+) or minus (–) 2.7%, *for the entire United States.*

Error is related only to the size of the sample in itself, not the size of the sample in relation to the larger universe. Stated another way: there is no relationship between the size of the sample and the size of the universe with respect to sampling error.

*Example*: In the table (*Figure 4.3*), a random sample of 384 employees yields +5 points of error. That's true if there are 3,000, 30,000 or 300,000 employees. The size of the universe doesn't matter — only the size of the sample. It may not seem logical, but the logic of mathematics, not appearances, is working in sampling.

Consider this example. How much soup would a person have to sample to know if it were salty or not? A cup? A bowl? A can? A case of cans? If the soup were made the same way, it wouldn't matter if it were a tanker car full of soup or just a cup to detect saltiness. Sampling works.

### Sampling Size and Sampling Error

| Sample size | Universe size | Sampling error |
|:-----------:|:-------------:|:--------------:|
| 384 | 3,000 | ± 5% |
| 384 | 30,000 | ± 5% |
| 384 | 300,000 | ± 5% |

**Figure 4.3**

*Caution*: Researchers can be confident of results with relatively small sample sizes like 384. But they should confine their confidence to mostly simple dichotomous (two-choice) questions such as,

"Do you **like or dislike** the company newsletter"?

"Do you want to receive the company newsletter **at work or at home**"?

## Confidence level

The chart above shows sample size and error at the 95% confidence level. That means that if a study were done 100 times using the same random selection process to select the sample, the picture closer to reality would fall within the error gap 95 times out of 100. With odds like

that, PR researchers can be confident in their findings.

A greater confidence level, one approaching 99% would involve increasing the size of the sample without increasing sampling error. Thus, a sample of 384 yields + or – 5 points of error at the 95% confidence level; but a sample of 685 also gives + or – 5 points of error, but at the 99% confidence level. Most PR researchers don't usually need or use 99% confidence level sample sizes.

## Random sample

Random sampling is the selection of a sample based on the provision that each member of the larger universe or audience has an equal chance to be selected in the sample. Biased sampling, on the other hand, is the prejudiced selection of the sample and denies each member an equal chance for selection. Biased sampling has its uses in public relations but not for probability studies.

The merit of random sampling lies in its ability to indiscriminately select representatives from the population universe so that the sample reflects the larger reality.

Types of public relations random sampling:

### Simple random sample

Researchers select the sample in lottery fashion. The entire universe must be equally available for selection.

*Example*: A PR director wants to know employee attitudes toward the company newsletter from 30,000 employees in international locations. She uses the company's employee list and selects a sample of 384. Because the employees are randomly selected, the information the director receives from the sample can be projected or "extrapolated" to all 30,000 employees.

Also, you can draw a simple random sampling using a table of random numbers generated by a computer. For example, each of the 30,000 employees is given a number from 1 to 30,000. The computer then generates a list of 384 for the sample. (The list of numbers could look something like this: 13, 2022, 354, 1,196, 12, 28, 2444, 838, etc.) The computer, by lottery technique, randomly selects the employees.

### Systematic interval random sample

In this type of sampling, researchers line up all the items in the universe population, whether they're people, news clippings, ads, or other items. Researchers decide the sample size they want. Then, they divide the universe by the sample size to get the interval. The interval, commonly known as taking every "nth" item on a list, becomes the ruler used to select the sample (*Figure 4.4*).

## Interval Formula

| Universe | ÷ | Sample size | = | Interval |
|----------|---|-------------|---|----------|

*example:*

| Universe | ÷ | Sample size | = | Interval |
|----------|---|-------------|---|----------|
| 3,000 | | 300 | | 10 |

**Figure 4.4**

Thus, the researcher will take every 10th employee or item on the list. To select a starting point for the count, the researcher will select a number from one to ten at random. The number pulled becomes the starting point for taking every "nth" number.

*Example*: Suppose the researcher pulled the number "7" from the lottery pile. The researcher would start the count with the seventh employee on the list and select every tenth employee thereafter.

This valid process will yield probability when the survey is completed because each member or item on the list has an equal chance to be selected. Notice how bias is eliminated from the selection process by the use of a mathematical formula.

When researchers conduct a telephone survey, they can use one of two methods to select their phone number samples.

### Random digit dialing random sample (RDD)

Random digit dialing involves selecting a sample by randomly selecting phone numbers from a computer generated list. Here's what an RDD list looks like:

| 3646 | 3980 | 2203 | 2386 | 0943 | 7009 | 5792 |
| 0020 | 1199 | 1919 | 6439 | 1459 | 0039 | 9161 |
| 7560 | 0401 | 7910 | 3209 | 9911 | 1492 | 0077 |

Because the list has been mathematically and randomly generated, the resulting sample will yield probability. Also, this type of sampling will guarantee that unlisted numbers will be included in the sample. In fact, when calls are made, many respondents with unlisted numbers are surprised that someone "had" their unlisted number. If they recall that any telephone exchange contains 10,000 possible numbers (0000 to 9999), they shouldn't be surprised that their phone number, not their identity, is known.

### Cross-referenced telephone directory sample

Certain telephone directories list all streets, homes and listed telephone numbers in a community. The entries are primarily by street, then by homes or businesses on the street, with accompanying numbers.

The directory differs from a typical phone book, which lists names alphabetically with corresponding phone numbers only.

### Cluster sample

Researchers can take a geographic community or area and arrange clusters from which to pick a sample. The merit of selecting a sample this way guarantees the representation of various geographic areas in the sample. It could be random or nonrandom.

> *A cross-referenced telephone directory lists all the listed phone numbers for residences, by street   perfect for a community study.*

*Example*: A company wants to survey its statewide customer base on its knowledge of the company's activity to protect the environment in its manufacturing process. The PR director draws five circles on a community map reflecting the five geographic areas of its base. Within each circle, the director sets up three additional circles. These are the targeted clusters from which the sample will be drawn. (*See Figure 4.5 on the next page.*)

Two other types of samples help researchers make the smaller sample "look like" the larger universe.

### Stratified sample

A stratified sample is a refined attempt to configure the sample to look as much like the universe as possible. Researchers use characteristics — demographic, psychographic or ergraphic — to make the sample a true microcosm of the universe. Researchers select the characteristics according to their research purposes. It could be random or nonrandom.

*Example*: An organ donor transplant organization wants to know if any religious denomination objects to its members donating their organs after brain death. The organization plans a new organ donation campaign and wants to include research about major religions and objections they might have.

Researchers conclude that their sample should include only representatives of religions that can authoritatively speak to the issue. The stratum they select is "representatives of religions." They could select "high school students" if they wanted to know student attitudes toward the issue.

*Example*: A college wants to know how students feel about a new class schedule. But the strata they're interested in include only junior and senior students, not underclass students. They also want to include males and females, commuters and noncommuters, full- and part-time

# Sampling by Geographic Clusters

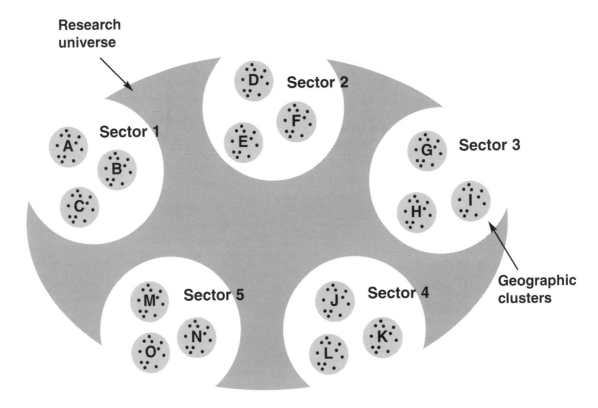

Divide the research universe into large geographic **sectors (1–5).**

Then, divide the sectors into smaller **clusters (A–O).**

You can sometimes consider the sectors "neighborhoods," the clusters "streets," and within the clusters, individual residences.

Selecting a sample using geographic clusters guarantees a representative sample, possibly scientific, if randomly selected.

**Figure 4.5**

students. They stratify their sample according to these characteristics.

## *Proportional sample*

To create a better sample and to guarantee that the sample truly represents the universe, population characteristics occur in the sample in the same proportion as they occur in the larger population. It could be random or nonrandom.

*Example*: In a college survey, commuters make up 60 percent of the population; therefore, the sample should contain 60 percent commuters.

*Caution*: When researchers select the sample, and want to proportionalize the characteristics, they must set quotas for each characteristic in the sample.

The college sample above might contain these quotas: 60 percent commuters, 40 percent residents; 52 percent female, 48 percent male; 45 percent seniors, 55 percent juniors.

Sometimes researchers must establish a quota within a quota. Once the female population of the college (e.g., 52%) is established in a list, then the list can supply other quota characteristics within that population, such as subject majors or sororities.

## OPINION ASSESSMENT

### Surveys

A survey is one of the most effective research techniques available to practitioners. Survey versatility and reliability give PR practitioners the ability to investigate

*Practical Public Relations: Theories and Techniques That Make a Difference*

three important aspects of audiences — knowledge, attitudes and behavior. Practitioners can administer surveys in three ways.

### In-person survey

Audiences respond in-person from a prepared question protocol. Because interviewers conduct these surveys in person, they could erroneously interpret questions, coach respondents, or argue both merit and substance of questions. Interviewers must avoid this temptation or chance contaminating the study. Why? As soon as interviewers involve themselves in assisting respondents, they risk losing "pure" response.

These interviews can be short or long, but if the researcher doesn't have a "captive" audience, it's better to keep the survey brief. Also, researchers can't ask questions with complicated response designs. Respondents have difficulty keeping complicated question and response patterns in mind until they're allowed to answer.

### Intercept interview

Intercept surveys interview respondents in motion, for example, outside a mall ("mall studies"), exiting stores ("exit studies"), on the sidewalk ("person-in-the-street studies"), sitting in service establishments such as restaurants ("roaming studies"), and on transportation vehicles ("transit studies"). These studies are formal if respondents are scientifically selected; informal, if they're not.

### Telephone survey

Telephone surveys are cost-effective and nonintrusive public relations tools. They require little respondent effort and extend researcher reach.

Done properly, telephone surveys provide important information; however, the target audience must be sufficiently motivated, or have vested interest in responding, otherwise the survey will not gain sought information.

Train telephone researchers to stick to the question wording, avoid coaching respondents, and get as much information as possible.

Research questionnaires are marked at the top with the numbers ①, ② and ③ to indicate that the researcher must try three times to get a respondent from that particular phone number. They abandon the number only if it's not possible to get a response. This technique is more important in a probability study than it is in a nonprobability study.

### Two-tiered study

Frequently, public relations practitioners use the telephone survey as a *first tier* of research to get overall data; afterward, they conduct focus group studies to enrich the data in a *second tier*. This pattern is called a *two-tiered study* and works well to unlayer opinion the phone survey only grossly revealed.

### Print survey

Print surveys require respondents personally, and mostly alone, to fill out a questionnaire. Hence, reading and understanding questions and instructions are important. Respondents must also return the survey. If it's a mail return, it could pose a fatal obstacle for respondents. If it's a drop-off survey, perhaps inside an organization, it's less problematic.

*Example*: Mail surveys can include studies of organization members, and product or service satisfaction surveys. Drop-off surveys can include employee payroll stuffers and restaurant surveys.

## Questionnaire

This is one of the most-used research tools by PR professionals. Questionnaires have four parts — administration, invitation, question protocol, and response set.

## Guidelines for questionnaires

■ Before you begin, outline the data you want. Consider these elements in your outline:

- What does your audience already know about these issues? Ask questions that confirm their knowledge or openness to acquire new knowledge.

- What must you learn about how your audiences feel about issues, relationships, conditions and situations, both actual and emerging?

- What variables are in play? Asking a question without considering variables could leave you wondering about the real cause of the reply.

*Example*:

Question without considering variables
*How productive are you with your time in the office?*

Follow-up question considering variables
*List three changes that can make you and your colleagues more productive with time in the office.*

By asking questions in this manner, you'll learn about negative conditions (variables) that might make office workers unproductive. The first question might completely miss those variables.

- How will you analyze the data? Some researchers mistakenly ask "brilliant" questions only to find they can't tabulate or analyze the data or that the analysis takes more trouble than it's worth.

Robert E. Simmons (Longman, 1990) says there are six types of variables to consider in a study:

1. Demographic variables (*age, gender, work, income*)
2. Media or channel variables (*face-to-face, print, electronic*)
3. Knowledge variables (*level of knowledge, ability to process information*)
4. Attitude variables (*roots, nature, intensity and direction of attitudes*)
5. Motivation variables (*persuasive "hot buttons," Maslow's hierarchical needs*)
6. Practice variables (*behavior patterns, tendencies*)

   - What will you do with the data? Who will use it? How? Who will see it? In what form? Does it really fulfill the need that motivated the study?

■ Make questionnaires easy to answer. There's no substitute for clear ideas clearly expressed. Keep words and sentences simple, declarative and short. Avoid jargon. Seek an average of 10–15 words per question.

■ Design a pleasing, functional layout for printed questionnaires. Avoid clutter and distracting elements. The appearance should say, "This looks like fun," not, "This looks difficult and threatening."

■ Keep phone questionnaires brief and to the point. Avoid long introductions, instructions and sentences. Practice saying questions aloud to see if they work as well spoken as they do printed.

■ Embed flow and even structure to in-person questionnaires. Always test your survey on a practice audience before adopting it.

■ Pretest questionnaires. It's better to find out if they will work before you print and administer them.

■ Conduct a focus group of representative audience members before writing your questionnaire. Frequently, a group can help you with appropriate content and wording.

■ Impart logical flow to questions. Skipping back and forth among topics confuses respondents.

### Guidelines for writing survey questions and statements

■ Make certain questions actually ask about choices or encourage respondents to offer personal knowledge and attitudes.

   *Example*: *How do you feel about the new employee handbook?*

■ Statements should be declarations by researchers designed to elicit specific reaction.

*Example*: *I'm going to read a list of statements. Please tell me which one best represents your feeling on how much involvement you want in helping your organization make decisions.*

   a -- I want to be personally involved in all major decisions affecting the company
   b -- I want to be personally involved in all decisions affecting my job in the company
   c -- I want my elected representative to be involved in all decisions affecting the company
   d -- I want my elected representative to be involved in all decisions affecting my job

■ Avoid biased questions. Don't "lead the witness" by suggesting a desired response.

   *Example*:   *Most Americans are upset with the cost of health care. How upset are you?*

   *Better*:   *Do you agree or disagree that health care in America today is too costly?*

   *Even better*:  *In your opinion, do you think health care in America today is generally affordable or generally too costly?*

■ Avoid biased responses. Don't force respondents to select from a list of choices skewed to one side of the issue.

   *Example: Which of the following statements best describes your feeling toward local government?*
   a -- all local politicians should resign
   b -- all local politicians should be investigated for unprofessional conduct
   c -- residents should refuse to pay taxes until local politicians resign or are investigated

■ Avoid unbalanced responses. Don't offer more negative than positive responses and vice versa.

   *Example: Which of the following responses best describes your feeling about your local public library's holdings?*

   1 -- it needs more books
   2 -- it needs more computers
   3 -- it needs more videos
   4 -- it has enough newspapers
   5 -- no opinion

   *Example* : *How would you rate your employee benefit program?*
   a -- excellent
   b -- good
   c -- fair
   d -- poor
   e -- no opinion

*Caution*: Some researchers argue that the use of "fair" in the set above creates a 3 to 1 imbalance toward a positive response. (Is "fair" weather positive or negative?)

■ Avoid questions without necessary background. Some questions assume too much in their presentation. They need some explanation to get a valid response.

*Example*: *Do you agree that your government should increase the local budget this year?*

Without sufficient background knowledge, respondents might offer meaningless information or refuse to answer altogether. For this question, provide explanatory text before asking the question.

*Example*: *This past winter, unusual snowfall caused the government to spend funds reserved to pick up fallen leaves. To restore the reserve, the local budget would have to increase. Should the local budget increase to restore the reserve?*

■ Avoid questions that ask too much. If a respondent is asked for an opinion on more than one item in the same question, researchers won't know which of the choices respondents had in mind when they answered.

*Example*: *Do you think media coverage of our crisis has been fair and comprehensive?*

No matter what the respondent answers, researchers don't know if the response refers to the fair or the comprehensive aspect. Use two questions instead.

■ Avoid threatening questions. Threatening questions can freeze respondents, causing them to abort the study, lie, skip the question, or disguise responses.

*Example*: *How much money do you make each year?*
Even if the questionnaire is anonymous, people believe that somehow researchers can study the demographic responses and personally identify them. And even if respondents answer the question, they could disguise their answers by checking off conflicting responses.

Offer respondents a way out. Try this question:
*Check the response that best represents the range for your annual salary.*
  ☐ $20,000 to $29,999
  ☐ $40,000 to $49,999
  ☐ $50,000 to $59,999

By offering ranges and asking respondents to check a single choice, researchers relax respondents and should get useful information.

*Note*: Responses in this example are mutually exclusive. Write similar exclusive responses for age ranges, decades of employment — any type of response that offers a range.

■ Avoid hypothetical questions. If asked about future behavior that does not affect them in any real way, respondents might glibly answer anything. Responses would unreliably predict future behavior. Hypothetical conditions are unreal scenarios.

*Example*: *If your company is taken over by another corporation, as rumor says, would you favor more overtime for current employees, or would you favor hiring more employees with no overtime for present employees?*

The hypothetical isn't really happening, so respondents don't have to say anything that reflects their true attitude were the company actually taken over. It's better to ask if, in the past, employees preferred overtime to new hires, it might serve as an indication (only) of their future preference.

■ Ask respondents to speak for themselves. Ask about their information, attitudes and behavior. It's more reliable than asking about their friends or neighbors.

*Note*: Sometimes researchers must use data they get from respondents about people they associate with. Focus groups sometimes ask participants what neighbors and friends think about issues. Reported hearsay is reliable, but less reliable than reported personal opinion.

■ Avoid coaching respondents. Offering a set of restricted choices limits what respondents can say and what researchers can learn. To really discover what audiences think, offer "other" as a choice following the structured list of responses. But be prepared to spend extra time tabulating these responses.

■ Use the uncoached/coached pattern for better information. First, ask respondents in an uncoached question before coaching them in follow-up questions.

*Example*: To measure the effectiveness of community relation's outreach, a PR director might ask a community,
  *Uncoached*: *Have you read or heard about any recreational improvements in the community in the last three months?*
  *Coached*: *Have you noticed the new playground at Main and Elm Streets?*
  *Coached*: *Do you know who sponsored the new playground at Main and Elm Streets?*

## Writing questions

Writing questions is the most difficult part of constructing questionnaires. It controls data so completely that if done properly, rich, useful data result. Imprecise, vague and unanswerable questions result in useless data and waste of resources.

Questions comprise three types: closed, unstructured open and structured open. These are often referred to as closed-ended and open-ended because they either confine audiences to a set of limited responses, or allow audiences to supply their own responses.

### Closed questions

Questions are closed when they control or limit audience responses. The researcher doesn't want respondents to wander away from the point of the question. These questions offer response sets or patterns that make it easy for respondents to answer.

*Example*: *Which one of the following statements best reflects your opinion about the number of articles in the company newsletter?* (Circle one)

   a -- too many articles
   b -- too few articles
     c -- right number of articles
       d -- no opinion

In this question, the researcher offers statements that cover all possible choices. Respondents have only to circle or check off one of the mutually exclusive answers. The question tightly controls the subject matter. It deals with articles, not graphics or editorials. It deals with number, not content, length or placement. It deals with the company newsletter, not company memos. And it deals with the employee newsletter, not the consumer newsletter, which employees also receive.

### Open questions

Open questions empower audiences to respond in any manner they wish. Researchers use open questions when they can't or don't want to predict (and force) possible answers. They also want audiences to expand on their answers, and provide richer data.

*Example*: *How do you feel about communication with employees in the company?*
(Answer here)_____

In this question, researchers allow the audience to select any type of communication, not just the newsletter. They also encourage employees to select anything about the array of possible techniques — frequency, effectiveness, type and preference.

Notice that this question also leaves open the possibility that audiences might offer (1) an information response — what they know about communication; (2) attitude response — how they feel about communication; and (3) behavior response — how they use communication.

In open questions, researchers have little control over responses. But it's a tradeoff. What's sacrificed in control, is gained in openness and depth.

The important downside to open questions lies in what researchers cannot do with the information. Because a forced choice set of responses wasn't offered, researchers might have trouble quantifying the qualitative results. Most researchers can't simply count all the (a), (b) or (c) responses and run them through a computer. Some researchers are using new software that actually codes and counts responses to open-ended questions.

### Coding open responses

Denied easy quantification, researchers must code open question responses and quantify them.

*Example*: Suppose the array of employee responses included these phrases: *"very effective," "read the newsletter all the time," "can't meet other managers face-to-face often enough," "voice mail on the phone system frustrates customers," "nobody answers my e-mail."*

*Analysis*: These responses are all over the place. One talks about effectiveness; another deals with behavior (newsletter); another complains about a specific system (voice mail); another deals with attitude.

The way you list responses begins your coding and quantification activities. Picture responses according to the table below. (*See Figure 4.6, attitude column*.)

• Numbers in **parentheses** (**e.g., 25**) represent the number of times the type of comment was offered in the study.

• The **upper** percentage (**e.g., 62%**) represents the percentage of comments related to others in the same row.

• The **middle** percentage (**e.g., 38%**) represents the percentage of comments related to others in the same column.

• The **lower** percentage (**e.g., 16%**) represents the percentage of comments related to all other cells in the table.

*Example*:(*"Attitude" column, "voice mail" row*)
   **(25)  Number of comments of this type**
   62%  Row percentage
   38%  Column percentage
   16%  Overall percentage

The coding pattern might also include under information — knowledge of types or characteristics of types; under attitudes — effective/ineffective; under behavior — frequency of use (preference and manner of use could also be included).

Once they create categories, researchers place each response into one of the category "cells." Then, they count the frequencies (number of times something is mentioned) and calculate percentages of each cell against any combination of other cells.

## Communication Audit Frequencies and Crosstabulations Findings Table

| | Information | Attitude | Behavior |
|---|---|---|---|
| **Voice mail** | "Voice mail on the phone system frustrates customers"<br><br>(10)<br>25%<br>44%<br>6% | "Nobody answers my e-mail"<br><br><br>(25)<br>62%<br>38%<br>16% | "I pester people who don't respond to me immediately"<br><br>(5)<br>13%<br>7%<br>3% |
| **Newsletter** | "I never get the newsletter"<br><br>**(3)**<br>14%<br>13%<br>2% | "Birthdays and bowling scores turn me off"<br><br>**(6)**<br>28%<br>9%<br>4% | "Read the newsletter all the time"<br><br>**(12)**<br>57%<br>18%<br>8% |
| **Meetings** | "Meetings often don't have the right people present"<br><br>**(4)**<br>7%<br>17%<br>3% | "Meetings without agendas waste time"<br><br><br>**(20)**<br>37%<br>30%<br>13% | "I don't meet other managers face-to-face often enough"<br><br>**(30)**<br>56%<br>45%<br>19% |
| **E-mail** | "Unwanted e-mail delays responding to our customers"<br><br>**(6)**<br>15%<br>26%<br>4% | "I'm frustrated when I get e-mail from colleagues who want rapid responses"<br><br>**(15)**<br>36%<br>23%<br>9% | "I answer my e-mail first thing every morning"<br><br>**(20)**<br>49%<br>30%<br>13% |

**Figure 4.6**

For example, they will calculate 10 "voice mail" information responses as opposed to 3 "newsletter" information responses. And they will know that "voice mail" responses comprised 44% of all information responses and "newsletter" comprised 13% of all information responses (*Figure 4.6*). They also will know the number of "newsletter" responses that were information as opposed to "newsletter" responses that were attitudes or behavior.

### Structured open questions

To allow respondents the freedom to respond, but simultaneously confine their responses to a specific area or a specific type, researchers ask structured open questions.

*Example*: Using the response grid above as a guide to the kind of information that could be useful, researchers could ask:

"*How do you feel about the effectiveness of voice mail in communicating with your fellow employees?*"

The question is still open but respondents are confined in their response.

*Note*: Professional researchers ask only for information they need to know. To write effective questions, they ask themselves, "What do I need to know?" Then they write questions to get that specific information.

## Writing response sets

Generally, researchers use a few classic response sets — response patterns designed to acquire information in a form easy to tabulate and analyze.

### Simple dichotomous choices

Dichotomous choices are two mutually exclusive choices such as agree/disagree, effective/ineffective, present/absent, will vote/won't vote.

*Example*: *Check the line for the response that best represents your attitude toward the following*:

|  | Effective | Ineffective |
|---|---|---|
| The new meeting schedule | ――― | ――― |
| The company newsletter | ――― | ――― |
| The voice mail system | ――― | ――― |

### Multiple-choice questions

Respondents select from a series of choices. The choices can be words, phrases or statements. They are usually mutually exclusive.

*Example*: *Circle the response that best represents your attitude toward the following statement*:
*When I try to use the e-mail system I ...*

1 -- always succeed
2 -- frequently succeed
3 -- seldom succeed
4 -- never succeed
5 -- no opinion

*Note*: Design your questionnaire responses in staggered form (see example above). That format makes it easier for researchers or respondents to select choices. You may use numbers or letters, but numbers might be easier to tabulate, report and discuss.

Sometimes, researchers allow respondents to select as many choices as are appropriate.

*Example*: *Circle* **all responses** *that best represent your attitude toward the following statement*:
*"Whenever management issues a policy I disagree with, I ..."*

a -- suffer silently
b -- tell my family about it
c -- complain to colleagues
d -- tell management about it
e -- refuse to follow it
f -- make suggestions to improve it
g -- have no opinion about this

### Likert Scale responses

Developed by Rensis Likert, the Likert Scale generally uses five options in the response set. Options are usually verbs such as "agree/disagree." The scale measures both quality and strength of responses by assigning weight to each response. *Example*:

| Strongly agree | = 5 |
|---|---|
| Agree | = 4 |
| No opinion | = 3 |
| Disagree | = 2 |
| Strongly disagree | = 1 |

Then, average the response scores.

*Example*: *Whenever there's an attack on our product by the media or a special interest group, management always responds quickly.*

a -- strongly agree
b -- agree
c -- no opinion
d -- disagree
e -- strongly disagree

Most researchers include "no opinion" or "don't know" among the five choices. This guarantees widest possible opinion spread. Some researchers decline the "no response" answer. They push respondents to either side of the *agree, disagree* response set. They force respondents to lean for a response with quality. But it's not as valid as including the fifth response.

### Semantic differential responses

Conceived by Osgood, Suci and Tanenbaum in 1957,[1] the semantic differential gives respondents latitude to declare their intensity of response. What would a respondent do if "effective" or "ineffective" were the only choices, but felt a shades of these two would be more valid?

The differential allows respondents to choose from seven interpretations of a response for one that best reflect their opinions. Such variety provides rich qualitative and quantitative data.

At the core of the semantic differential are bipolar adjectives such as good/bad, effective/ineffective, informative/uninformative, etc. Because adverbs modify adjectives, the differential uses six adverbs, three on each side of the scale corresponding to each polar adjective. There's always a neutral choice between the six, dividing the adjectival interpretations.

Researchers use the semantic differential in two ways. First, they can use one set of bi-polar adjectives to investigate multiple questions. Or, they can use multiple sets of bipolar adjectives to investigate a single question.

---

1 Roger Wimmer & Joseph Dominick. (2003). *Mass Media Research* (7th ed.). Belmont, CA: Wadsworth/Thomson Learning.

*Example*: One set of bipolar adjectives with several issues (*Figure 4.7*):

PR practitioners use the semantic differential when they need to refine opinion to the point of gaining shades of gray. Why? Practitioners can make incorrect decisions if their research data are based on simple black-and-white responses. Certain issues require varying semantic shades of responses because that's where actual attitude, and ultimately behavior, might lie.

## Semantic Differential Response Set: One Adjectival Pair, Several Questions

E = Extremely    M = Moderately    S = Somewhat    N = Neutral

| | Effective | | | | Ineffective | | |
|---|---|---|---|---|---|---|---|
| | E | M | S | N | S | M | E |
| Media relations | — | — | — | — | — | — | — |
| Internal communication | — | — | — | — | — | — | — |
| External communication | — | — | — | — | — | — | — |
| Community relations | — | — | — | — | — | — | — |
| Special events | — | — | — | — | — | — | — |
| Crisis management | — | — | — | — | — | — | — |
| Ethical behavior | — | — | — | — | — | — | — |
| Legal behavior | — | — | — | — | — | — | — |

**Figure 4.7**

*Example*: Multiple sets of bipolar adjectives with one question (*Figure 4.8*):

## Semantic Differential Response Set: Several Adjectival Pairs, One Question

*"How would you evaluate our crisis management activities over the past year"?*

E = Extremely    M = Moderately    S = Somewhat    N = Neutral

| | E | M | S | N | S | M | E | |
|---|---|---|---|---|---|---|---|---|
| Effective | — | — | — | — | — | — | — | Ineffective |
| Timely | — | — | — | — | — | — | — | Untimely |
| Ethical | — | — | — | — | — | — | — | Unethical |
| Proactive | — | — | — | — | — | — | — | Reactive |
| Rehearsed | — | — | — | — | — | — | — | Unrehearsed |

**Figure 4.8**

## Delphi study

Olaf Helmer and Norman Dalkey originally developed the Delphi method at the RAND CORPORATION. Delphi is a group process and its goal is to help a group reach consensus. It's a systematic method to seek and collect judgments on a particular topic through a set of carefully designed sequential questionnaires interspersed with summarized information and feedback of opinions derived from earlier responses (*Figure 4.9 on next page*).

Resembling the capital letter Delta from the Greek alphabet, the technique follows these steps:

### Round one

Selected members of an organization, usually a group of 15–20, complete a survey, generally open unstructured questions, usually by mail.

### Round two

After researchers tabulate the group's responses from the original open-ended questions, they develop a series of structured items for a second questionnaire. They send this second questionnaire to Delphi group members to

# Delphi Technique

**500 individual responses** — *Round 1*

**100 refined responses** — *Round 2*

**By question:** Reduce many individual responses to a final shorter list.

**50 useable responses** — *Round 3*

**By audience:** Use small 15-30 participant group to provide research issues. Eventually, entire organization is surveyed.

**15-30 group** — *Round 1*

**Department** — *Round 2*

**Whole organization** — *Round 3*

rank-order the items (for priorities) using a Likert-type rating scale. Group members are invited to comment on their rationale for the rating and add additional items. Members get a copy of their original responses for comparison with responses from other group members.

## Round three

During the third, and any additional rounds, Delphi group members re-rate each item. To help them, they receive:

- statistical feedback related to their own rating on each item
- rating of the same item by other members of the group
- summation of comments by each group member

This feedback process makes the Delphi group member aware of the range of opinions and the reasons underlying those opinions.

Usually, three rounds are sufficient for group members to reconsider and change previous replies in light of the replies of other members of the group. The final group's position is the average of all positions.

Barbara Ludwig,[2] Associate Professor and District Director, Ohio State University Extension Wooster, Ohio, says the Delphi study could run over a period of several weeks.[3] Researchers determine the number of Delphi group members by deciding how many they think will validly represent the general judgment of the entire group they're studying, such as all employees, consumers or vendors.

Public relations researchers could effectively use this technique today in conflict resolution or consensus building. In some Delphi studies, the ranked list becomes content for a further, larger study. For example, the ranked composite list, derived from only selected members of an organization, might go to all employees.

2. Internet address: ludwig@agvax2.ag.ohio-edu.

3. Barbara Ludwig. (1997, October). Predicting the Future: Have you considered using the Delphi Methodology? *Journal of Extension*, 35(5).

PR people can use Delphi data to help a larger group reach consensus on a position because it has evidence of what the similar smaller, representative group thinks.

In consensus building, it's more important to take time to agree than it is to simply sample the population and announce results, thereby creating winners and losers. (See details about another consensus-building technique — the *1-3-6 Method* in the chapter on employee communication.)

## Conducting the telephone survey

Audiences are skeptical about researchers, especially on the phone. Unethical marketers have disguised blatant marketing promotions as legitimate research, even marketing research. Their activity has made it difficult for legitimate researchers to gain the confidence of respondents over the phone. For that reason, the introductory statement and the sequencing of questions is important.

## Administrative section

The survey should contain sufficient instructions so researchers can efficiently conduct the survey. Every instruction must be absolutely clear. Code responses for later tracking.

## Introductory statement

The introductory statement should announce the survey's sponsor (including the name of the researcher making the call), purpose, (without biasing the answers), importance (better product, service, etc.) and sometimes length (in minutes or number of questions).

The researcher should begin the survey at once, without asking for respondent permission. Asking for permission invites the respondent to decline. Researchers have a better chance of getting a completed survey if they ask the first question quickly so respondents can sense the legitimacy of the study.

## Sequencing questions

Avoid asking personal questions too early in the survey. This practice could threaten respondents who might abort the survey.

Save demographic questions for the end of the survey if possible, especially questions about salary. Behavior questions could be more threatening than either information or attitude questions. Save them for the latter part of the survey.

Here are some classic ways to sequence questions:

• By rapport. You'll get a higher response rate if you can build rapport with your audience. Sometimes, researchers will use a "throw away" question just to

> **If you can collect and line things up, you can analyze content scientifically.**

establish rapport. It may not figure in the analysis at all.

*Example*: "*This survey is for residents who believe a school system is an important part of a community's reputation. Do you believe your community's school system influences your community's reputation?*"

• Ask a filter question to qualify the respondent.

*Example*: *Are you a registered voter?*

The filter question will save you time. If you ask it at the end of the survey, and the respondent doesn't qualify, you would have wasted your time.

• By type. Information, attitude and behavior comprise a logical sequence. This sequence offers the best chance for respondent cooperation because it starts with relatively nonthreatening knowledge questions and ends with more personal behavior questions.

*Example*:

First question (information)
*Have you heard about the proposed landfill for your community?*

Second question (attitude)
*How do you feel about a new landfill in your community?*

Third question (behavior)
*Have you ever protested, in any way, a landfill in your community?*

• By issue. A cluster of questions can focus on a specific issue. Complete each issue with a complete set of questions. Complete one set before starting another. Frequently, respondents will get "into" the survey if the first topic is highly relevant to them.

## Closing section

End the survey with demographic questions. Then interviewers debrief themselves, in writing, to recall important aspects of the study.

## Content analysis

Content analysis is a systematic, objective method to quantitatively measure the content of a series of items according to categories. This study eliminates subjective bias.

You can use the analysis to show how a series of media clips or evening news reports covered a company's position. You can measure the content of speeches, campaigns, advertising messages, letters to the editor, political cartooning in newspapers — anything you can physically collect.

You can also use it to test a hypothesis. For example, a national association of drug manufacturers believes that national editors are treating the association unfairly during a crisis. The crisis deals with recent adverse reaction to an approved drug. To test that belief (hypothesis) the association collects all editorials for a fixed period of time on the subject and conducts an objective content analysis.

Here are the steps in the content analysis:

**1. Assemble the items**. Make certain they are all of the same type (e.g., all are editorials and not news articles).

**2. Decide categories for analysis.** Use only categories that fulfill the research purpose.

*Example*:

• Were the editorials (**a**) fair or (**b**) unfair in their argument, even if they disagreed with the company?

   • Do the editorials (**c**) express the association's position or (**d**) ignore it?

   • Do the editorials (**e**) arise from a meeting with the editors or (**f**) develop without a meeting?

   • Do the editorials (**g**) reveal media bias or (**h**) reveal balanced treatment?

These categories can help public relations professionals fashion an effective response to the negative editorials.

**3. Code each of the items**. Coders must be trained very carefully to "see things the same way." Usually, coders don't proceed unless they agree 95% of the time on a series of test items.

*Example*: Each editorial will bear codes for categories they express. For example, an editorial from the Gazette newspaper editorial board, which condemned the association prior to its campaign (**b**), ignored the association's position arguments (**d**), refused to meet with association representatives (**f**), and accused the association of caring more about profit than safety (**g**) might bear these codes

Gazette Editorial = b – d – f – g

**4. Tabulate and analyze data**.

Place the codes across the top of the grid and the newspapers down the side. You can count and crosstabulate the "cells" created by the intersections. And you can generate percentages for cells by row, by column and by all categories.

Figure 4.10 shows an example grid for editorial coverage of the Gazette.

## Focus groups

Focus groups are research interviews. They can be either a first or second tier research technique.

As a first tier technique, they yield new information about topics and questions from a live assembled panel.

As a second tier, they complement a mail or print survey by elaborating on gross results from the first study. In both cases, they acquire comment from stakeholders on information, attitudes and behavior about defined issues.

Sometimes, they simply raise issues and ask participants for comment. Or, they show items to panels and ask for reaction. These groups are also known as focus panels, idea juries or reaction panels.

### *Nonscientific panels*

Focus groups are generally nonscientific panels. They do not attempt to get probability — extrapolation to the larger universe. Instead, they try to get "representative" sentiment.

Panels might "represent" the population by stratifying the sample. In this process, the researcher attempts to replicate the universe by loading the sample with representative types, based upon important characteristics in the general population. These characteristics may include age, sex, race, ethnicity, job description, managerial responsibility, shift, union, nonunion, etc.

## Newspaper Editorial Coverage

| Paper | a | b | c | d | e | f | g | h |
|---|---|---|---|---|---|---|---|---|
| News | | | | | | | | |
| Press | | | | | | | | |
| Report | | | | | | | | |
| Daily | | | | | | | | |
| Post | | | | | | | | |
| Times | | | | | | | | |
| **Gazette** | | (2) | | (3) | | (4) | (5) | |
| Chronicle | | | | | | | | |
| Herald | | | | | | | | |
| Tribune | | | | | | | | |

Numbers (2), (3), (4), (5), indicate the **number of editorials** with characteristics b, d, f, and g.

**Figure 4.10**

## Select participants

- You should select important characteristics and sample the universe based on those characteristics. In most cases, one participant can satisfy two or more characteristics.

- Conduct an information program before selecting the representative panel. If participants know they will be research subjects, they will accept or reject the invitation based upon their willingness to contribute during the study.

- Make certain participants represent the universe.

- Provide sufficient motivation to get panelists to attend the session.

## Communicate with participants

- Send a letter or other communication asking for the panelist's participation. State the importance of attendance. Include the notion that decisions will be made with or without the invited panelist, but should be made with the participant's involvement.

- Send several notices to participants. Emphasize the need for their participation. After the study, inform them about the results.

## Select the site

- Select a room, quiet and apart from other organization personnel. Avoid physical columns or barriers that might prevent participants from seeing each other and the facilitator.

- In some cases, it will be necessary to meet away from the organization to guarantee privacy for the participants.

## Set the agenda

- Select the topic based on research. In some cases, you will already have a general topic, but want participants to pick specific areas to talk about.

- The agenda should always be discussed in terms of benefit to participants. Even management agendas can relate to participants' welfare. You'll gain greater participation if you guarantee the connection.

## Pretest questions, processes, materials and procedures

- Focus panels can validate communication tools before you employ them in a project. Used this way, they are a classic research technique.

- In addition, before you conduct the panel, you should validate processes and procedures you will use in the study. Do this by informally checking with persons who represent the sample. For example, you can ask

secretaries or colleagues about their reactions to materials you intend to use.

## Prepare for the focus group

- Facilitator. Secure an unbiased facilitator, preferably unaffiliated with the organization under study.

- Prepare materials. You'll need questionnaire handouts, tape or video recorders, a projector, screen, easel and other recording assists.

- Select and reserve the site.

- Order or prepare refreshments. Shy away from sugary refreshments such as doughnuts early in the day. They can make audiences lethargic.

- Train recorders. Rehearse stages of the study.

- Communicate with participants.

- Arrange room seating. Make certain it promotes personal interchange and sharing.

## Conduct the focus group

- Make certain no organization person is in the study room, or at least cannot be seen by participants. If necessary, have them observe behind a two-way mirror.

- Greet participants. Call them by their first names. Allow them to call you by your first name.

- Actively listen during the interview.

- If you have a general topic, but can accommodate specification by the audience, go around the room and conduct a brainstorming session and list topics people want to talk about. Use a flip chart to organize comments. Avoid griping about personal issues.

- Don't speak exclusively to one person. Caution: Outspoken participants can dominate the conversation. People who agree with you or the group can also dominate if you let them.

- Incorporate all participants in the conversation. But try not to lock onto a silent person and put that person on the spot. Include them in a general invitation.

   *Example: Mary, Jack, Tony, what do you think about this?*
   Talk to them directly. Don't refer to them in the third person, unless you're quoting their opinion.

- Keep conversation to one topic at a time. Control the agenda. For example, during a discussion of employee expectations, archive a comment about customer expectations by asking your recorders to note it. Leave time to return to that topic.

- Set a time limit for each part of the discussion. Make •

participants feel they're part of an efficient group and their participation is valuable.

- Belong to the group as a facilitator rather than appear as an employee of the organization.

- Stand. Don't sit unless you're not part of a process that's going on or unless the group is very small. Move close to establish personal contact, then step back to make the speaker comfortable. Don't stand over participants and force them to crane their necks upward to see you.

- Don't get involved in a transaction between a company apologist and a participant. You're not a management representative.

- In general, don't allow participants to talk about their personal concerns or peeves if they're representing the general target population on general issues. By doing this, you guarantee the group "represents" the universe.

*PR research can measure three important things: what people know, how they feel, and what they are willing to do.*

If someone continues to dominate, gently move away from focusing on the personal concern by asking whether the concern is general. As a last resort, record the concern and tell the participant that someone from the company will deal with that privately.

- Avoid these potentially harmful communication faults:

**Jargon**. Make certain everyone understands terminology. People might be embarrassed to ask what unfamiliar words mean.

**Interruptions**. Don't dominate the conversation. Don't finish others' sentences.

**Sexist and other comments**. You have to be careful not to offend, even in a joking way, in this area. You can lose all your credibility in a momentary lapse.

**Indifference**. Don't make notes, page through your notes, or talk to others during the discussion.

**Patronizing tone**. This can be very dangerous. Even though your guests are employees or consumers and may not know the issues as well as you, don't talk down to them. Avoid offending sing-song cadences.

- If you must give information, use cases. Adults learn and remember better through cases.

- Involve seemingly shy guests by mingling with them before the session. At a discreet point in the session, invite them by name and jump start them by asking about their issue.

- Set the room in a circle or "horseshoe." Stand in the middle to control the process.

- Allow refreshments during the process. Also, make participants feel they can freely move about.

- Prepare questions to probe certain topics. Comments will fall into one of three categories: What people know. What people feel. What people do.

- Announce the topic you're about to discuss. Have your questionnaires and media helps ready. Control discussion with visuals, PowerPoint presentation, or other support.

## Communication audit

### Audit process

The communication audit procedure comprises seven steps:

- **Focus groups**. Focus groups identify issues for further study. They reveal important qualitative data about target audiences.
- **Surveys**. Surveys discover and quantify data about population groups. You can conduct formal or informal studies.
- **Network analysis**. Network analysis attempts to study communication content and process of each member in an organization. Place the target member in the middle of a circle and draw the network of people who communicate with that person. Then, analyze each strand of the network for content and channel effectiveness.
- **Interviews**. Interviews with key members of an organization discover strengths and weaknesses in communication processes.
- **Content analysis**. A content analysis evaluates all communication products in an organization such as letters, newsletters, brochures and media relations products.
- **Technology assessment**. Technology assessment looks at the effectiveness of all media and technology an organization uses in its daily communication.

## MEASURING AND EVALUATING PR ACTIVITY

One of the most important activities in public relations is measuring results of PR activity. This evaluative function complements formative research at the beginning of activity.

Public relations practitioners and authors have written and spoken extensively about the need to measure and evaluate PR results. PR professionals have chronically complained that too little measurement research accompanies public relations activity.

Here's what they're complaining about. Practitioners who undertake public relations activities must be able to prove to themselves and their clients that they achieved their objectives. And if they didn't succeed, they need to demonstrate why.

Even though many practitioners theoretically agree with the idea of measuring results, they sometimes can't get bosses and clients to spend necessary time and money to conduct research. Consequently, many practitioners don't learn anything from their successes or failures.

Other practitioners are wary of research because they don't know what to measure or how. A number of these problems come from poorly designed campaigns. Without objectives, strategies and tactics controlling their plans, practitioners have no roadmap to follow or benchmark from which to measure success. Without research training, some professionals are wary of doing it.

## Benefits of evaluating PR activity

• Continue or discontinue programs
• Change strategy
• Expand or limit audiences
• Change messages
• Improve practices or procedures
• Allocate resources, including staff
• Change organizational direction
• Improve products, services and marketing
• Identify new strategic relationships

## Content of evaluation

You can conduct a public relations audit. This type of audit differs from a communication audit in that it measures the effects of public relations activities and not just communication activities. Here are the effects a public relations audit measures.

• **Communication**. The intended message is sent to the right audience.
• **Information**. The right audience receives the message and retains it for future use.
• **Attitude acceptance**. The audience agrees that both message and meaning are appropriate for them.
• **Attitude change**. The audience adopts the message's meaning for itself.
• **Behavior**. The audience overcomes any constraints and takes action based on the message and the meaning.

Each of these areas is fruitful for evaluation. Why? Because the communication process can break down at any one of these points. So a phenomenon occurs when PR practitioners are moderately successful in some areas of their work but don't achieve their overall goal. Did they fail? Did they partially succeed? What will they learn from

> ## One of the most important activities in public relations is measuring results of PR activity demonstrating achievement.

evaluating all aspects of the campaign and not just the final outcome?

*Example*: A PR firm designs and carries out a new product introduction. The campaign does not achieve all its objectives, particularly in first year sales. Has the firm "failed"? Consider the campaign objectives.

• Introduce the company to the public
*(Right message sent to the right audience)*

• Get consumers to agree that the product is worthwhile and the company is reputable.
*(Audience agrees that the product has merit.)*

• Coax consumers to say (through surveys) that they intend to try the product or actually try free samples.
*(Audience agrees that the product is good for themselves and their families.)*

• Persuade consumers to buy the product in quantities specified in the campaign.
*(Audience behaves as the company wants and buys the product.)*

It's possible that the organization and its PR counsel achieve the first three of the four objectives. True, they didn't get the sales they wanted. But evaluation research showed they gained company recognition, product familiarity and respect, consumer agreement to try or use the product, and some sales. These are significant public relations successes. Will the client be satisfied?

Not with the sales level. But PR practitioners should point out that they succeeded in the heavy lifting of the campaign. Perhaps sales might improve when the economy improves, or product price comes down, or competitors don't advertise a sale on their well-known name brand as the new company continues its second-year launch.

Only through evaluation can PR people show significant achievement, despite apparent failure to reach the overall goal of the campaign (*Figure 4.11 – next page*).

## Table outlining measurable general PR activity

| Planning | Acting | Achieving |
|---|---|---|
| Issue analysis | Tactics | Goal |
| Audience analysis | Time allocation | Objectives |
| Message analysis | Cost allocation | Strategies |
| Channel analysis | Personnel allocation | Tactics |

## Table outlining measurable PR ambition for audiences

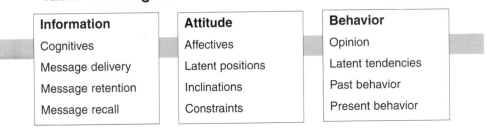

| Information | Attitude | Behavior |
|---|---|---|
| Cognitives | Affectives | Opinion |
| Message delivery | Latent positions | Latent tendencies |
| Message retention | Inclinations | Past behavior |
| Message recall | Constraints | Present behavior |

## Table outlining measurable PR activity for organizational goals

| Reputation | Relationships | Responsiveness |
|---|---|---|
| Social responsibility | Customer | Consensus building |
| Products / services | Community | Issues management |
| Employment practices | Government | Political action |
| Law / ethics | Employee | Accountability |
| Public interest | Investor | Public policy |
| Fairness / mutual benefit | Media | Assessment |

**Figure 4.11**

*Note*: When you select an outside research firm, remember:

- Outside counsel is objective and trained. But it knows less about your program.
- Inside counsel is less objective, but offers continuous evaluation and has connections inside the organization.
- Make certain outside counsel knows your objectives and customizes techniques to what you need or want.
- Ask outside counsel to provide sample reports of research studies. Also ask for references.

*(See Figure 4.12 on the next page for the Public Relations Research Model.)*

## Public Relations Research Model

| Situation | PR Need | Technique | Result |
|---|---|---|---|
| Need valid data about audience information, attitudes or behavior | Data may be formal or informal, but must be valid and easy to analyze and interpret | Survey | Statistical information including frequencies, percentages and cross-tabulations |
| Need analysis of a database, product, activity or test | Data must be in categories expressed in percentages of the whole | Content analysis | Information that relates one piece of information to another and to the whole |
| Need subjective opinion from a representative group | Data must express audiences' latent attitudes and expressed opinions about diverse issues | Focus group | Qualitative information unveiling effective messages to direct a communication program |
| Need valid data about systemic or comprehensive communication activity | Data must be verified by a variety of research techniques | Audit | Picture of a program array: communication activities and their effectiveness |
| Need subjective data from involved audience | Data must be verified by a variety of research techniques | Interview | In-depth consideration of audience opinion |
| Need organized information about trends, patterns or relationships | Data must provide valuable information for planning | Data analysis | Enriched situation analysis for planning |

**Figure 4.12**

# Tips

1. When you're pulling a random sample, make certain that every member of the universe has an equal chance to be selected.

2. You can always use a cross-referenced telephone directory to pull a random sample of a neighborhood. But you won't get unlisted phone numbers.

3. To get unlisted phone numbers, use Random Digit Dialing — 10,000 numbers (0000 to 9999) for any exchange.

4. When you conduct a survey, never help the respondent answer the questions. You might "contaminate" the study.

5. Make your phone calls for your survey during weekday evening hours between 6:00 p.m. and 9:00 p.m. and on Saturdays after 11:00 a.m. and before 5:00 p.m. (Some communities prefer different hours. Check first.)

6. Avoid too many open-ended questions. They are difficult to tabulate. If you must use them, at least make them "structured" open-ended questions.

7. When you practice public relations and also do research, become two persons, a researcher and a counselor, and keep them separate. Researchers just report results. Counselors advise on what to do with results.

8. Don't spend more money for research than necessary. But don't begin a project without it. Experience will show that you'll be much more successful if you have research results to share with your client or boss.

9. Don't let other "researchers" claim that nonprobable data are probable. Example: Don't agree that a self-select survey done through a newspaper or magazine is probable or proves anything.

10. Always remain objective about your research, from fashioning questions to reporting negative, even embarrassing results. Research doesn't lobby. It just says what is.

**Questions for classroom discussion**

1. A deli owner wants you to tell her why she's losing customers. How will you go about designing a study to get what she needs? What must you decide about first?

2. What is probability? How do you get it in sampling?

3. If you want to advise your organization to authorize some focus group studies, what will you tell your managers about their effectiveness? If they ask you to conduct them, what will you tell them you'll need?

4. When would you recommend a communication audit for an organization?

5. Cite three organizational needs that would call for a content analysis.

Name_____ Date _____

## Case study: CEO wants the truth

Assume you're a PR director for a manufacturing company. Your CEO has heard rumors about the way she manages the business. Some are complimentary, others not so complimentary. She wants to know the truth about her management style, and that of her management teams throughout the company.

Your company is large, five plants in the state, with about 10,000 employees. First, answer these questions. They will give you background for the research design you need to construct.

1. What do you think the CEO wants to measure?

_____

_____

_____

2. What do you think she should measure?

_____

_____

_____

3. How will you get the information you both think is necessary?

_____

_____

_____

4. How rich must your data be so she can do something with it?

_____

_____

_____

5. Should your study be formal or informal?

_____

_____

*See other side*

Name_____Date _____

6. Should it be anonymous?

_____

_____

_____

7. What will your role be in the process?

_____

_____

_____

8. Design the research study

**Study objectives**

_____

_____

_____

_____

Name _____ Date _____

## Complete the following chart.

(A portion of the chart, together with some research audiences, is completed to give you a start and demonstrate the information you need to supply.)

| Audience | Data needed | Technique | Process |
|---|---|---|---|
| CEO | • Self-identity<br>• Intended image<br>• Communication awareness<br><br>• _____ | • In-depth interview<br>• _____<br>• _____<br>• _____ | • Outside firm for objectivity and candidness<br>• _____<br>• _____ |
| Top managers | • _____<br>• _____<br>• _____ | • _____<br>• _____<br>• _____ | • _____<br>• _____<br>• _____ |
| Middle managers | • _____<br>• _____<br>• _____ | • _____<br>• _____<br>• _____ | • _____<br>• _____<br>• _____ |
| Line employees | • _____<br>• _____<br>• _____ | • _____<br>• _____<br>• _____ | • _____<br>• _____<br>• _____ |

## Guidance to fill out the chart

**Audiences:** Think about audiences that might have something important to say about the CEO's communication style.

**Data needed:** Identify data that will help you establish the "real state," picture the "ideal state," and improve communication in the company.

**Technique:** Be specific. Name the formal or informal research types. Identify the quantitative or qualitative type. The same technique might be appropriate for different audiences.

**Process:** Consider who will actually conduct the studies. When will you do them? How much will they cost? How will you collect the data?

# Chapter 5

# Managing Relationships with Employees

## PRaxiom

*Two things people want more than sex or money are recognition and praise. – Mary Kay Ash*

## What this chapter covers

This chapter offers information and techniques to help you communicate with employees. It should allow you to improve morale, generate ideas that will make the company more profitable, and help managers communicate more effectively with their employees. The chapter emphasizes the role each employee plays in the public relations effort.

Well informed and well disposed employees are the best front line PR offense for an organization. Employee relations is liking yourself before you ask others to like you.

## Everyone does public relations

Many companies, organizations and people mistakenly equate the public relations effort only with the work of the "public relations office." This mistake prompts an image problem for public relations.

In reality, everyone has a public relations role.

For example, a female secretary in a company goes to a beauty parlor and shares some negative information about the way employees are treated. This has a severe impact on the image of the organization within the community. It discourages other people from applying for jobs and causes the people who heard this comment to think less of the company.

The custodian who is active in the local fire company can cause much damage by bad-mouthing the company because he feels he's underpaid. People in the community tend to believe the secretaries and custodians much more than they tend to believe news releases. That's why it's vital that the public relations leader for the organization conduct workshops for all employees to show them their

role in the way the company is perceived. That perception can have a dramatic impact on the stock price of the company and this, in turn, could affect the holdings of the employees.

Remember this one important principle when dealing with employees: Despite what managers and many top executives think, employees want to be recognized and praised.

Studies over the past nine years have clearly indicated that employees want to be recognized and to be praised. Yet, managers in the same studies said that recognition and praise were ninth on the list of things that employees might want.

A 1997 study, however, shows that the main concern that most managers have is losing a job because of a merger. Robert Half International, an international employment company, found that 51% of the executives surveyed listed this as their number one concern.

For some reason, many top management people and even public relations practitioners fail to invest the time and effort with internal audiences that they do with external ones. Roger D'Aprix says that the organization feels that it can always count on employee loyalty and commitment. Therefore, there is a tendency to short-change the employee audience in organizations.[1]

D'Aprix notes that the greatest communication needs that employees have are the answers to questions such as: How's the organization doing and where is it going? Am I performing appropriately? What do I need to know to do my job better? Does anyone in the organization care about me? How can I help the organization become better?

---

1. Roger D'Aprix, "Employee Communications" in *Experts in Action: Inside Public Relations* by Bill Cantor, New York: Longman.

## Public relations starts from the inside

Many public relations experts strongly urge that the good public relations program must work from the "inside-out." They feel that you can produce excellent news releases and develop wonderful videotapes extolling the virtues of your organization for external audiences. But if you don't have the confidence of employees, and employees don't feel good about where they work, then you won't be able to reach the levels of excellence in your public relations efforts that you seek.

Because of mergers and downsizing (or rightsizing, as some management authorities prefer to call it), the loyalties that employees used to have for companies for many years seldom exist. Many counselors trying to help people get ahead in their careers remind them that they are "working for themselves." These counselors note that it's your reputation that you're building; you should be concerned about that reputation rather than the success of your employer. Naturally, employers don't like this attitude prompted by the lack of security that employees feel.

A general lack of trust has permeated the workforce. Pat Jackson, former editor of the international professional newsletter, *pr reporter*, notes that public relations professionals must solve one particular problem: the loss of trust in our society.

The American Association of School Administrators, a number of years ago, identified the number-one problem facing public schools as the lack of public trust and confidence in educational leaders. Building trust, therefore, becomes one of the greatest challenges facing management in general, and public relations practitioners in particular. Jackson suggested a few years ago that "overcoming mistrust in our society and rebuilding self-esteem within internal and external audiences will be the major challenge with public relations practitioners in the next five years."

---

The Gallup Poll recently asked 55,000 workers to associate workers' attitudes and company productivity.

The survey discovered four attitudes that produced higher profits:

- Workers feel they have the opportunity to do their best every day.

- They feel their opinions count.

- They sense their co-workers are committed to quality.

- They have a direct connection between their work and the company's mission.

---

## What would you believe?

The public relations director for a large school district was coming out of church one Sunday when he ran into his former next-door neighbor. The neighbor admonished the PR director for all of the publicity that was appearing on cable TV, in local newspapers and on radio, as well as in the school district newsletter about the new reading program *The school district had been the recipient of a grant to develop this reading program and the administration knew it was working well.*

The former neighbor said to the public relations director: "I know it's not working and you're just trying to make it look good."

The PR director: "Why do you say it's not working?"

The neighbor: "Because my next-door neighbor works in the school and he told me."

The PR director: "Would you mind telling me who that is?"

The neighbor: "He won't get in trouble, will he?"

The PR director: "No, he won't."

The neighbor: "Well, it's John Glick, custodian. He told me the kids aren't learning anything."

The next day the public relations director just happened to be in the school where John Glick is the custodian. He bumped into him and asked him how the new reading program was going. The custodian said, "The kids aren't learning anything in there. Come on, I'll show you."

The custodian led the PR director to a classroom, where the door was ajar, and the kids were involved in holding up flash cards in groups of three or four. Students were calling out answers. "Hear how noisy it is in there; can't be no learning going on with all that noise," noted the custodian.

When the custodian, age 62, went to school, noise meant no learning was going on. No one had explained to him that this was active noise or that the children were learning by being involved in this process. He then went out and shared his impression with lots of people who then disbelieved what the public relations person was disseminating.

It's imperative that public relations professionals realize that everyone plays a major role in the public relations effort of an organization, and conduct workshops to show employees the importance of their roles.

## Who should be in charge of communicating with employees: human resources or public relations?

Whether public relations practitioners or human resources people should have the primary responsibility for communicating with employees remains a contested point. Human resources proponents explain that they are responsible for overall communication with employees because they are generally responsible for much of the hiring process and orientation procedures. They're also usually responsible for explaining employee benefits and therefore strategically positioned to communicate with employees when they are just hired.

Backers of public relations practitioners take the position that public relations experts are better trained in communication skills and are better prepared to use a variety of communication strategies and techniques to communicate with employees. Compromise might work, allowing both departments to contribute to the overall efforts in orientation, employee benefits, internal newsletters and other internal communication techniques. But little support has been engendered for this approach. Each department considers its turf clearly defined and is seldom receptive to the other department's getting involved.

It would seem to make sense to use the strengths of the people from both departments and realize that the importance of communicating with employees and employee morale dictates that the best talent available in the organization begins to foster a spirit of solid internal communication. Someone at the top of the organization has to make this happen.

## Ways to communicate effectively with employees

A variety of techniques can be used to communicate with employees. As employee communication expert D'Aprix repeatedly points out, it's more important that the communication be on a trusting, regular basis than in an occasional four-color, award-winning publication. Employees want to know now what's happening and what the implications are for them, D'Aprix points out.

As noted earlier in the chapter, face-to-face communication is important. Without it, all of the other efforts combined won't assure an effective employee communication program.

A study of 148 senior-level communication executives in 1994 at the Arthur W. Page Society's spring seminar showed that 88% of the CEOs, according to the communication experts, thought employee communication is important. Their thinking agreed with D'Aprix's pronounce-

ments that internal newsletters are not the most effective ways to communicate with employees.

Among the suggestions made by these communication executives:

- Top management must communicate a vision and organizational values in employee communication. Every employee should know what the company stands for and how this translates into everyday decisions.

- Public relations managers must work more closely with supervisors in the organization and help them improve their ability to communicate with employees.

Complementing that ongoing two-way communication between managers and employees might include some of the following suggestions:

## Print communication

**Employee newsletters**. If your organization already has a newsletter, determine if anybody's reading it. Conduct focus panels to see what readers like and what they want more and less of. Don't forget — content is the most important part of any publication. While it's imperative that it be tastefully prepared (see the chapter on publications), **the most attractive publication won't be read if it doesn't contain the kind of information that employees want.**

*Is anyone reading your newsletter?*

Be sure to address the concerns that readers identify. This might require selling those needs to the CEO. Articles that show how the company is doing always attract readers. So too do articles that focus on successful employee efforts and how new products and services are performing.

When you gather information about employee likes and dislikes, put them to use. *Example*: After conducting such a survey for one organization, we found that employees wanted a chance to buy, sell and swap cars, furniture and other items. Although many managers thought this was a waste of space in the publication, we tested it and found that the publication's readership soared. List only home phone numbers for this kind of information or much of the working day might be spent reacting to the "for sale" items.

When determining the frequency of your newsletter, remember that people would rather have new news in a less fancy format than old news presented in a more attractive way.

After introducing changes to the publication as a result of the focus groups, continue to conduct the groups to see how those changes are being received. The focus groups allow you to make decisions based on research rather than on the whim of an editor or boss.

**Rapid wrap-ups of important meetings**. When the organization has a board meeting or a top-level management meeting that will stir the interest of all employees, provide the outcome of the meeting as soon as possible.

*Distribute meeting summaries as soon as possible.*

By publishing a summary of the results no later than the morning after the meeting, you communicate that you care about employees and want them to be up-to-date about what's happening in the organization.

Be sure the information presented is objective and accurate. Distribute the information as soon as possible during the day of or after the meeting before rumors become rampant. (Work from a tape of the meeting. If you quote various board or audience members in your wrap-up of the meeting, you will undoubtedly be accused of misquoting them. It's a comforting feeling to play the tape and have them at least understand that you were indeed correct.)

**Bulletin board memos**. In this era of high technology, it's surprising to find that some organizations — some of them very large — depend on daily bulletin board memos to communicate with employees.

**Check stuffers**. Take advantage of the regular opportunity to communicate information in the envelope with paychecks. When people use "direct deposit," most companies provide them with a copy of the information sent to the bank. You might use this opportunity to support a charitable fund drive or an undertaking of the organization. The messages should be succinct and focus primarily on ideas of interest to employees. Each insertion might focus on an idea presented by an employee that contributed to the overall success of the organization.

**A series of helpful communication tips**. Many employees never took a course on how to communicate effectively with co-workers and customers. A series of 8" x 11", folded, one-page tips and techniques would be useful. It might include items like "How to Write Better E-mail Messages," "How to Deal with an Irate Customer," and "How to Communicate That You Care" to co-workers and customers. You can prepare these yourself or buy them from a number of companies that prepare videos and publications to help employees communicate better.

Be sure to distribute a copy of any publications being distributed externally to employees before the publications are sent elsewhere.

## Other morale-building techniques

The way to customer satisfaction may very well be through employee satisfaction. Hal Rosenbluth, author of *The Customer Comes Second*, suggests that by caring for and motivating employees, customer satisfaction will follow.

When people feel good about coming to work, they share a certain confidence and attitude that just might become contagious. To help develop this kind of spirit, you might consider using some of these suggestions:

- **Distribute CIA cards.** Give them to all employees and encourage them to give a card to a co-worker "caught in the act" (CIA) of doing something special. It might be going out of the way to help someone meet a deadline. It might be someone who does something special to solve a customer problem. When you see something like this happening, give the person a CIA card. The card might be good for a free lunch in the cafeteria.

- **Distribute 10 "congratulations" cards** to each employee for the year. Similar to CIA cards in intent, the cards are given to people who do something special. The organization decides what the cards are worth. At the end of the year, each employee can turn in the cards. One company gives a free car wash for one card, a free dinner for two at an area restaurant for five cards, and an overnight stay at a casino in the area for 10 cards. Is there a risk that some employees might abuse this technique? Of course. But misuse is usually minimal and the amount of good that comes from the system more than overcomes the occasional abuse.

- Let employees know about **job openings in the organization** before you announce them externally, even if not required by union agreements. As it becomes more and more difficult to attract quality employees, reward employees who recommend others for jobs with your company. If a person stays more than three months in a job, the employee who recommended the person might get a $100 bonus.

*I can live a month on a good compliment.*
*Mark Twain*

- Remember, many employees don't care how much you know until they know **how much you care.** Conduct training workshops for all managers on how to communicate better and how to build better morale. From something as simple as saying "hello" to each employee every day and asking how things are going to following up on suggestions they make, bosses can engender a better spirit.

- **Suggest that all managers hold one-on-one meetings** with employees who report to them. Have managers give each employee a sheet of paper while taking one for themselves. Then, ask the employee to write down three things that you or the organization can do to help the employee do a better job. Explain that you're doing the same thing — writing down three things that the employee can do to help you do a better job. In a candid discussion that follows the listing, the two employees share ideas that should help bring about a better understanding of their needs.

## Setting up an advisory committee

Setting up advisory committees can help build believability in the organization. The public relations director can be instrumental in preparing managers to set up effective advisory committees. The chief executive officer might want to have one advisory committee representing the full spectrum of employees. Other level managers may wish to develop advisory committees to assure the feeling of "we're working together and we want to listen to your questions, suggestions and ideas."

When selecting members for an advisory committee, you may have to work with union officials if such a requirement is stipulated in the contract. Be sure to have broad representation on advisory committees so that all employees feel they do have a voice. It's imperative that it be communicated at the first meeting that the committee is just what it's called — an advisory committee. It is not to establish policy, but to advise management on the thinking of employees.

*Advisory committees influence policy, not establish it.*

Appoint someone to take notes at the meetings and, before the meetings end, summarize the key points made and who needs to follow up on what. A list of topics brought before the advisory committee and the next step regarding the concerns expressed and suggestions made should be published on bulletin boards or in a summary letter from the manager responsible for establishing the advisory committee. One of the most frequent complaints employees have is "nobody listens to what we think." An advisory committee certainly provides the opportunity to share ideas and get responses.

When establishing meeting times, consider the schedules and deadlines of committee members. Meet only when you need to, rather than every second Thursday. Everyone resents going to a meeting when one isn't needed.

When starting the committee, do it at a calm time.

The Opinion Research Corporation has been determining employee opinions of communication in more than 200 organizations for more than 40 years. It found that employees feel that they get most of their useful information from the grapevine, but would prefer to acquire it from immediate supervisors or from meetings with top management.

Don't initiate it in the middle of a crisis because this could be interpreted as a panicky move on the part of management to sway employees' thinking. Don't forget to follow up suggestions with a formal response that lets the people who offered those suggestions know that something has been done with them. If this doesn't happen on a regular basis, people will think that the advisory committee is just window dressing.

## Working with key communicators: An idea that works and works and works

In every organization certain people tend to communicate more effectively and with more people than others do. These people may not have titles that place them on the top of the organizational ladder, but they do have one thing in common: They talk to and are trusted by lots of people. To establish an ongoing, dynamic communication network, you should tap these key communicators.

Some of these people may be secretaries, custodians and others who can be easily identified as people who will be among the first to hear rumors and who will be the people to whom others go to get the latest scoop on what's going on in their place of employment.

The CEO and other managers can establish key communicators at various levels. Set up the key communicators group by meeting with them once and explaining that the goals of the group are to address rumors as quickly as possible and to communicate the latest information all employees need. Usually people are pleased to be chosen to be part of the group.

The group may meet only that one time or may meet occasionally when management must communicate some news quickly. In most situations, communication can take place via telephone or memo to group members. It is expected that they will share the information with colleagues as quickly as possible and will report rumors to the person who set up the key communicators group.

Working with key communicators effectively addresses rumors perpetrated by the grapevine.

## Establishing a rumor control center

Rumors grow quickly and whether or not they're true, people are quick to accept them and tell others about them. One of the keys to dispelling false rumors is to learn about them quickly and issue forthright statements setting the record straight.

In an era of mergers, downsizing and other negative news that prompts employees to be leery of the company, a communication system that addresses rumors can be a giant plus.

One technique is to establish and communicate the existence of a **rumor central number**. People calling this number should be guaranteed anonymity and should get answers as quickly as possible. Questions posed by employees should be rapidly answered and communicated to the entire staff. This might mean using the intranet and key communicators.

When management works hard to help employees understand the rationale behind some tough decisions, the news may be accepted in a way that will help some of the most desirable employees consider staying, while others think about leaving.

Whichever method you use to communicate internally, remember that employees most like to receive news from their bosses.

## Using the 1-3-6 technique

Consider using the one-three-six method with employees to generate ideas that will improve the organization.

How it works: Bring people together from a department or a building. The approach works best when the number of people involved is between 18 and 90. Put them in groups of six — preferably at tables.

Start the session with a positive approach by asking each employee to write down the best communication or public relations technique used in the organization. Then ask two groups of three at each table to agree on which of the three written is indeed the most effective. Then ask for a consensus from each table. List each technique on an overhead projector, chalkboard, or easel tablet and ask for a show of hands to see which ones the group likes best. Each employee has only one vote.

Then get to the fun part. Ask each employee to list the biggest communication or public relations challenge facing the organization. Follow the same procedure after that. After listing each group's major concern, ask each person to vote once to identify the problem deemed most important. Then, asking the people to be part of the solution, allow each table to choose one of the three top concerns and develop a plan to address it. The plan should include a

A 1998 study conducted by Pitney-Bowes, Inc. found that office workers send and receive an average of 190 messages a day. Those same workers are interrupted by messages at least three times an hour. The study surveyed 1,000 workers in large companies and found 12 different forms of communication — including telephone calls, letters, e-mail and courier packages.

*Trends*: Telephone calls reaching the desired party directly fell, but the number of e-mail and voice-mail messages grew.

What are the implications for the public relations person? You've got to come up with ways to be sure your message cuts through the clutter of so many other communication efforts. Use a special color paper that communicates urgency. Have a key word that connotes importance on messages that require instant response. Depend more on word-of-mouth communication, such as through the key communicator group explained earlier in this chapter.

timeline, the amount of money needed to address the challenge, who might be responsible for doing it, and how it would be evaluated. After the session is over, all of the plans would be collected and the public relations director or the CEO would respond to each plan, explaining whether it would be implemented and when it would be implemented.

Employees who see results of their recommendations will feel more a part of the team and realize they can indeed make a difference with their ideas.

## Encouraging employees to generate ideas

What makes one corporation better than another? Frequently, it's something as simple as having employees generate new ideas.

More and more top executives are recognizing that the way to outdo the competition is to create a climate that encourages employees to come up with ways to make the operation more efficient and to offer innovations that keep the company one step ahead of those competing with it.

Yet, not enough companies develop mechanisms within the organization to motivate workers to be idea-conscious. If you want to quickly determine the attitude employees have about coming up with new ideas, ask this one question:

**If you had an idea to improve this organization and it would cost nothing to implement that idea, would you suggest it?**

The authors have conducted research in more than a hundred organizations and found the answers vary dramatically from company to company. In some organizations, more than 80% of the employees said that they certainly would contribute the idea. In some organizations, however, less than 15% said that they would. Why the giant difference?

The answer is relatively simple: In the organizations that prompted employees to be quick to offer ideas, management had established a climate that encouraged and rewarded employees for doing so.

Some things that you can do to effect this kind of spirit:

- If necessary, sell the CEO on the importance of communicating to all managers that **listening to new ideas** is a prime responsibility. Encourage the CEO to let all employees know that this is a priority. "If we're not getting better via new ideas, the competition will pass us," the CEO might say.

- Conduct an **employee survey** to determine how comfortable they are suggesting new ideas and whether they feel ideas they suggest will be implemented. Many studies the authors have conducted show that some employees won't bother suggesting ideas because "nothing ever happens different around here."

- When evaluating each employee, include a question that relates to the number and quality of **new ideas shared** since the last evaluation.

- Make it easy for employees to share ideas. Consider distributing **"I have an idea" cards** to all employees. Prepare them in triplicate so the employee can give the idea to her boss and a copy to the designated idea-mover. If the boss hasn't responded to the idea-contributor within a certain number of days, the idea-mover would get involved by encouraging the boss to respond. This helps identify and overcome idea-blockers, who turn employees off when they don't respond to their suggestions.

- The public relations person might conduct a workshop or **series of workshops** for managers on how to encourage people to be comfortable coming up with ideas that might be rejected. Remember, many managers have become managers with very little training or educational preparation to serve in that capacity. Many will appreciate the opportunity to learn concepts and techniques that will help them do a better job. One of the biggest criticisms of managers is that they don't communicate effectively. Research also consistently shows that employees prefer to get information from their immediate bosses.

Research conducted by University of South Alabama professor Donald K. Rice from 1993 to 1996, showed only about half the employees surveyed consider their immediate supervisors to be effective communicators. [3]

- Use a **suggestion box** or a more modern adaptation of it. The suggestion box should be locked so that only the person in charge of the suggestion box program would have access to it. When those suggesting ideas identify themselves, they should always receive a response to the suggestion—even if it's an explanation as to why the suggestion can't be implemented now.

Teamwork has been a buzzword in management circles for quite a few years.

Whether you establish quality circles or some other form of teamwork in action, the approach can be effective if proper leadership is exerted. Use the "effecktancy" approach. This is a full-blown effort at generating ideas. Companies that have tried it have experienced excellent success in collecting employee ideas and saving thousands — sometimes millions — of dollars with the ideas. They also have come up with new products and services that have brought greater profits to the organization. (Any time you can suggest and implement an idea that improves profits, you solidify your position within the company.)

## How "effecktancy" works

- The CEO or a designate meets with all managers to announce the program. That same person then meets with all employees to share the specifics regarding the program.

- An explanation is given in a letter from the CEO to all employees explaining that each month a prize will be given to a randomly selected person who submitted an idea. The merit of the idea does not enter into the selection. At the end of the six-month period (or what-ever time frame is used), a significant grand prize is offered. (One company offered a trip for two to Hawaii with a one-week vacation.) This prize also was to be chosen randomly.

- The CEO or a designate responded to each suggestion submitted within 10 days. Management thanked the person and explained that any ideas implemented would bring a reward to the submitter.

---

3. Carol Howard, addressing the 1996 Strategic Public Relations Conference in Chicago. She is the retired vice-president of public relations and communication at the Reader's Digest Association, Inc.

Communicating an organization's goals to employees should improve morale. When employees share a sense of spirit, enthusiasm and pride, they're more willing to help their companies achieve their goals. When possible, share plans for growth with employees. Many companies are focusing on restructuring, reorganizing, and re-engineering, according to Robert Tomasco, a managing consultant. Then problems that employees perceive become the focus. Give employees something to believe in as you explain any plans for growth. This approach helps employees look forward to new opportunities.

*Example*: One company gave 10% of the money saved by the idea to the idea-originator and 10% of the profits realized after the first year of the start of a new product or service to the person who came up with the idea.

• Some companies distributed buttons with the words "I'm Effecktant" on them. Also, some of the best ideas submitted each month were printed on placemats in the company cafeteria.

• Ideas submitted were featured in the company publications and, in some instances, on the company video news report.

Overall, a spirit of "we're getting involved to make our company better" permeated workplaces where the idea was undertaken.

What this approach and other ideas to generate ideas will do is to ask employees to use some of their discretionary time to bring forth ideas that will help the company's future as well as theirs. This means that people working together or discussing ideas at lunch or while driving to and from work might be thinking about improving their workplace rather than on other things.

A study, which has been replicated many times around the country with more than 20,000 employees, shows that there is a tremendous difference between what managers think employees want and what employees list as being most important.

One of those studies presented in *The School and Community Relations*[4] showed the following ranking of employee concerns and how managers and employees felt about them (*Figure 5.1*).

The most significant difference for someone practicing public relations is to realize how important it is for employees to feel appreciated for work done and to feel "in" on things.

As rightsizing and mergers increase, it's certainly possible that job security will move up on the employees' list. With younger members of the workforce, interesting work is also gaining more support as one of the top three concerns. The biggest lesson here is that public relations people need to communicate with managers about the need

## Comparison of Manager and Employee Workplace Values

| What workers say they want | What managers think employees want |
| --- | --- |
| 1.  Interesting work | 1.  Good pay |
| 2.  Appreciation of work done | 2.  Job security |
| 3.  Feeling of being in on things | 3.  Promotion and growth |
| 4.  Job security | 4.  Good working conditions |
| 5.  Good pay | 5.  Interesting work |
| 6.  Promotion and growth | 6.  Tactful discipline |
| 7.  Good working conditions | 7.  Loyalty to employees |
| 8.  Loyalty to employees | 8.  Appreciation of work done |
| 9.  Help with personal problems | 9.  Help with personal problems |
| 10. Tactful discipline | 10. Feeling of being in on things |

**Figure 5.1**

4. Donald R. Gallagher & Don Bagin. (2002). *The School and Community Relations*. Boston: Allyn and Bacon.

to show appreciation for work done. It's also vital that employees feel that they are informed about what's going on where they work.

## Communicating about benefits

A master's degree study done by Frank Basso showed that most materials prepared to explain benefits to employees go over their heads. The major problem is that the language used is written at a level that's just not comfortable for people to read. For most employees, it's best to use about a ninth-grade reading level. *(See Chapter 9 for information on how to determine the reading level of what you've written.)*

In addition to booklets or manuals, video or PowerPoint presentations can help. If the human resources department is responsible for communicating benefits, you might be able to work closely with that department to prepare materials.

Some sophisticated companies, including some major automobile manufacturers, have offered instant access to computers located in cafeterias and other areas, so employees can get benefits information or information on borrowing money from the company. This kind of access,

The American Management Association[5] reported on a survey of 10,000 employees nationwide, by Performance Enhancement Group, that shows employees favor daily recognition over bonuses or higher pay. The study also revealed that employees recognized for their work will demonstrate their best effort in their work. The recognition doesn't have to be expensive; however, it does have to be consistent, sincere and personal.

protected by code numbers, can be a major plus for employees.

Some companies, such as Sunoco, have charged a manager with the responsibility of communicating with "alumni." The company keeps in touch with retirees and sometimes will tap them for part-time employment or consulting. The employees feel comfortable about keeping in touch with the company to gain information that might help with financial planning and other areas of interest. ∎

## Use this story to build cooperation and teamwork

### *You Can't Do It Alone*

I am writing in response to your request concerning Block #11 on the insurance form, which asks for "the cause of injuries" wherein I put "trying to do the job alone." You said you need more information so I trust the following will be sufficient:

I am a bricklayer by trade and, on the date of injuries, I was working alone laying brick around the top of a four-story building when I realized that I had about 500 pounds of brick left over. Rather than carry the bricks down by hand, I decided to put them into a barrel and lower them by a pulley, which was fastened to the top of the building. I secured the end of the rope at ground level and went up to the top of the building and loaded the bricks into the barrel and flung the barrel out with the bricks in it. I then went down and untied the rope, holding it securely to ensure the slow descent of the barrel.

As you will note on Block #6 of the insurance form, I weigh 145 pounds. Due to my shock at being jerked off the ground so swiftly, I lost my presence of mind and forgot to let go of the rope. Between the second and third floors, I met the barrel coming down. This accounts for the bruises and lacerations on my upper body. Regaining

my presence of mind, again I held tightly to the rope and proceeded rapidly up the side of the building, not stopping until my right hand was jammed in the pulley. This accounts for my broken thumb.

Despite the pain, I retained my presence of mind and held tightly to the rope. At approximately the same time, however, the barrel of bricks hit the ground and the bottom fell out of the barrel. Devoid of the weight of the bricks, the barrel now weighed about 50 pounds. I again refer you to Block #6 and my weight.

As you would guess, I began a rapid descent. In the vicinity of the second floor, I met the barrel coming up. This explains the injuries to my legs and lower body. Slowed only slightly, I continued my descent, landing on the pile of bricks.

Fortunately, my back was only sprained and the internal injuries were only minimal. I am sorry to report, however, that at this point I again lost my presence of mind and let go of the rope. As you can imagine, the empty barrel crashed down on me. I trust this answers your concern. Please know that I am finished "trying to do the job alone."

5. American Management Association. (1997, January). *HRFocus*, New York, NY 10019

# Tips

1. Communicate to all managers that employees want to be recognized and praised. One of the greatest challenges facing management is building trust with employees.

2. Communicate to all employees that each of them has a role to play in the overall public relations effort.

3. Remember that employees would rather have new news in a less fancy format than old news presented in an elaborate, award-winning way.

4. Use key communicators to help dispel rumors and communicate important ideas quickly.

5. Establish advisory committees to help build believability in the organization.

6. Use the 1-3-6 approach and the "effecktancy" effort to generate ideas to make more money for the organization.

7. Only about half of employees surveyed consider their immediate supervisors to be effective communicators.

8. Consider using up-to-date bulletin boards to communicate with employees. Even though high-tech techniques may be more glamorous, some companies find that the simple bulletin board still works well.

9. Distribute CIA cards to employees and encourage them to give a card to a co-worker "caught in the act" of doing something special.

10. An effective way to improve customer satisfaction is through employee satisfaction. Every employee should know what the company stands for and how this translates into everyday decisions.

Name_____Date_____

## Answer these questions

1. You're a finalist for a position of public relations director for a company that employs 200 people in one location. You would be the first public relations person hired by the company. The CEO asks you this question: "What are the first three things you would do to communicate more effectively with our staff? Right now, we have a quarterly newsletter and that's about it."

_____

_____

_____

_____

2. After you've been on the job for a while as a public relations director, you find that most of the managers are inadequate in communicating with their employees. What would you suggest to the CEO that you might do to help?

_____

_____

_____

_____

3. The CEO challenges you with this statement: "At the end of one year here, I'll want you to point to employee ideas your techniques generated that will more than pay your salary in money earned or saved." Which ideas would you implement?

_____

_____

_____

_____

4. Debate the merits of placing employee relations under either human resources or public relations.

_____

_____

_____

_____

*See other side*

# Chapter 6

# Working with the Media

**PRaxiom** *All you have to do is: know reporters' deadlines; recognize how they like to be pitched; tell the truth; and always be available. Pretty simple, right?*

## What this chapter covers

Working with the media will be one of the responsibilities listed in the job description of just about every entry-level public relations position. This chapter should enable you to feel comfortable in getting to know the media, realizing how they want material presented and how you can enhance your chances of getting your material used.

Section 1 focuses on the print media, while Section 2 deals with the electronic media.

## SECTION 1

### Working with the print media

When working with the media, remember that they have a job to do and it's not always consistent with what you're trying to accomplish. Remember too, that many public relations people started out as journalists and many people in public relations and journalism took some of the same courses while preparing for careers. Know too, that journalists sometimes applied for positions that public relations people are holding. Also, consider that some journalism professors and some journalists consider public relations people as having sold out their journalistic integrity to make more dollars. Other journalists, however, recognize that solid public relations people provide more than 50% of the information for news articles that journalists prepare.

The relationship you can build will help determine your success at least in one phase of the public relations operation. That's why it's imperative that you work hard early in your new position to establish a solid rapport with reporters, editors and others in the journalistic process.

Some public relations professionals would cringe if you asked, "Did you sell any stories today?" In essence, that's what you're doing. You're trying to persuade, or sell, your company's story, message or opinion to your prospect, the media.

Put yourself in the media's shoes. How annoying is it when you sit down to eat dinner and a salesperson calls to offer you 25 percent off your long-distance phone bill While you might like to save money on your phone calls, how many times have you told the salesperson to call back at a more convenient time?

To help you build a relationship that benefits you and the media:

- **Establish a first-name relationship with all reporters** covering your company or organization as quickly as possible. Find out who they are, call them and ask to meet on their turf. They will appreciate your coming to them.

  A cartoon, "Animal Crackers," drove home the importance of building this kind of relationship with a four-panel message. In the first panel, a horse was being harassed by a horsefly. In the second panel, the horse's tail was shown swishing, trying to swat the fly. In the third panel, the fly flew up around the horse's ear and said, "Hi horse, my name's Homer." In the final panel, the horse's tail quieted and the horse said, "It's hard to hurt somebody you know on a first-name basis."

  Building this kind of relationship does not mean that reporters will not write negative things about your organization. It usually does mean that the reporter will be sure to check with you to get your side of the story.

- **Make sure you're contacting the "right" person.** You won't get much coverage for your hospital's new-wing groundbreaking by inviting your local paper's education reporter. Call your healthcare/medical beat reporter, or your city/region reporter. (On smaller papers, one person might cover a variety of categories.)

- **Crunch numbers**. Keep your media list clean and current by regularly updating journalists' phone and fax numbers. Faxing to a first-floor newsroom reporter who was promoted to a second-floor editor's position can make you look inept. At the least, double-check your target media's phone and fax numbers every month, and update them as necessary.

- **Be accurate**. Nothing embarrasses a reporter or a newspaper or a radio or TV station more than making a factual error. If you're responsible for misspelling a name or giving the wrong date for an event, your relationship will be severely hurt. Always go the extra step to check the facts. Related to this, keep any materials presented to you by others in the organization. File them with the release that you prepare. If an error is made, it's a good feeling to be able to go to the file and realize that you were provided with the incorrect information. No one will volunteer that when it hits the fan.

- **Note deadlines**. Calling an hour before the reporter's newspaper "goes to bed" will only annoy the writer. Know each media's deadline. If you're releasing information, be careful to time it so it works for as many sources as possible. *Example*: If the local weekly is published on Thursday, chances are good that its deadline will be Tuesday morning. Getting the editor something Tuesday afternoon could mean that it won't be used for nine days. This dates the story and does not endear you to the editor of the local weekly.

- **Keep a chart showing when you released stories that had no time value.** You may want to balance these, giving equal opportunities to dailies and weeklies. Remember, though: You can't hold stories that have time value. They have to be released when they happen.

- **Determine the best release time**. If you are dealing with a national paper, such as *The Wall Street Journal*, and you want to get something in it knowing that the editor would be interested in the topic, you can determine the best time to release it for that paper. You can also determine when to release the information to other papers. This is an arguable situation; some experts feel that you should provide all the information to all the papers at the same time.

- When dealing with magazines and trade journals, **know their editorial schedules**. Many of these are prepared

> *Regularly update journalists phone, fax and e-mail numbers.*

six months in advance and it's good to know what the general topics being covered in certain months will be. You might be able to prepare a special article to meet the editor's needs.

- **Be available**. If something breaks and reporters need a comment or a bit of information, the last thing they need to hear is, "He's not available now." Let your secretary or whoever might be answering the phone know where you'll be at all times. Instruct all to find you if a reporter says it's a deadline matter. You'll be appreciated for being there — even when negative news hits. Reporters chiefly complain that public relations people aren't available when negative news hits. If you are not going to be available, designate someone to be available for reporters' requests.

- **Establish a climate of trust**. *Never lie to a reporter.* Once you do, you've lost your credibility forever. Remember that time you told your parents you were staying over Pat's house for the evening? Two days later they realized that Pat was not the same sex that you were and they felt you kind of lied. Don't stretch the truth with reporters. Make sure you communicate this to your boss also. It's no way to establish a relationship. When you establish a reputation for dealing off the top of the deck at all times, you'll command respect. If you're caught in one lie, that reputation will follow you wherever you go.

- **Don't say, "No comment."** Teach those who also speak for your organization to avoid this expression. It's like waving a red flag in front of a bull when you say "no comment" to a reporter. You can say something like, "We're checking into this and will get back to you as soon as we have pertinent information." Then do so.

- **Tell the people you work with how a newspaper works**. It's important they realize that reporters don't write the headlines — unless it's for a very small newspaper. Often your colleagues will become incensed over a headline and refuse to talk to the reporter whose byline appears on the story. They just don't know how newspapers work and it's your responsibility to educate them. One veteran on the local police force was irate when the local newspaper ran a photo of him receiving a watch at retirement after serving 25 years as a "defective" on the police force. Also, people need to know that editors will frequently change stories written by reporters. Sometimes the changes are prompted by the need to fit a certain space. Therefore, some of the positive things that the reporter wrote might not remain in the story when it's printed.

- **Know what news is and communicate that knowledge to your colleagues**. Then try to identify as many newsworthy items as possible to share with reporters. When people submit an idea for a story to you, you might explain why it's not newsworthy or how you can come up with an angle that will make it newsworthy. Remember, most colleagues on the management team aren't proud of their writing and are reluctant to write something that might embarrass them. Come up with ways — recordings or interviews — that will allow them to provide the information without having to write it. Consider conducting a workshop for people who are in positions to generate news ideas for you. Bring in a couple of reporters to work with you to present the workshop. Coming up with small group discussions to generate news items would allow reporters to leave the session with some possible stories.

- Teach all of your colleagues who may be responding to reporters' questions that **it's OK to say, "I don't know."** Making something up that you can't later defend will cause all kinds of problems. No one expects people to know the answers to all questions immediately. But an honest effort to get the desired information will be appreciated and help build a solid relationship.

- **Avoid jargon** and encourage your colleagues to do the same. Often managers will become accustomed to using certain terminology with colleagues — terminology that won't be understood by reporters and the public. It's important then that such jargon be converted to everyday language that all can understand.

- **Don't ask a reporter to show you a story** before it's presented to the editor. This is considered unprofessional and will spark negative reactions from reporters.

- When a reporter makes a mistake, **give that reporter a chance to correct it** before you go over the reporter's head. Many newspapers now have a page where they list corrections and they are quick to explain an error. Remember, though, that you wouldn't like to have to admit a mistake to thousands or hundreds of thousands of people. So don't push for a correction if the mistake wasn't a major one. Sometimes you can come up with a new story that will set the record straight without embarrassing a reporter.

- **Determine the best times to place stories** that aren't time sensitive. A little known consideration: The day after the fifth "anything" of the month is usually an excellent time to place a feature story in the local daily newspaper. Why? Because none of the town's governing bodies will be meeting on that fifth "anything."

All meetings are scheduled for the first, second, third or fourth "something" of the month. Therefore, the local editor has more room in the paper for your feature stories that are sent for use on that day after the fifth "something." You also might get some extra mileage from placing stories on the day after a major holiday, such as Thanksgiving or Christmas. Little hard news occurs on those days and the papers still have to fill space.

- **Prepare a list of experts** in your organization and their phone numbers so that when national, regional or local stories break that could benefit from your local expert, the reporters will have some place to go. Alert your colleagues that this might take place. Ask them if it's acceptable to share their home phone numbers with reporters.

## Build rapport

So, you think you have this "PR thing" figured out. All you have to do is: know reporters' deadlines; recognize how they like to be pitched; tell the truth; and always be available. Pretty simple, right?

Unfortunately, it's not that easy.

The competition among PR practitioners for "prime" media coverage can be cutthroat — especially when a major event or crisis happens, such as Princess Diana's death. *The Wall Street Journal* article exemplifies how PR "professionals" can overwhelmingly bombard reporters with any remotely related information, just to score a "hit" (*Figure 6.1 – next page*)

## What's to be learned from these stories?

- Think twice before trying to publicize nonnews. If you're debating whether something's newsworthy, maybe it's not. You'll earn reporters' respect by not calling, faxing or e-mailing every time your CEO or board members think your company or organization has a "hot" media topic or product. Of course, you need to communicate your reasoning with superiors, not just ignore them — to stay employed.

- Realize you're not alone. When a major event happens, assume you're not the only one pitching the media. To stand out from the hundreds of pitch letters and releases, distinguish yourself — without wasting their time. However, don't let potential coverage slip away if you have something newsworthy.

# *Death of a Princess, Birth of a Thousand Press Releases*

*In the public relations business, the name of the game is finding a hook that links your press release to the news. And no news event is off limits. Just look at this sampling of press releases that moved over wire services to news organizations following Princess Diana's death on Aug. 31, 1997.*

*— Joshua Harris Prager*

■ August 31
**AMERICAN PHYSICIANS MOURN DEATH OF PRINCESS DIANA**
*Chicago, PR Newswire*

The physicians of the American Medical Association are saddened at the tragic death of Diana, Princess of Wales…

Although we never worked with Princess Diana directly, the AMA is nevertheless proud of our mutual commitment to the campaign for a worldwide ban on antipersonnel land mines…As the world mourns this stunning loss, the AMA urges physicians everywhere to remember Princess Diana as a woman of courage, compassion and grace…

**HOLLYWOOD PUBLICIST TO LEAD LAW CHANGE FOR PAPARAZZI STALKINGS**
*Los Angeles, PR Newswire*

In response to the death of Princess Diana and Dodi Al Fayed, Hollywood publicist Michael Levine has pledged to lead an effort to change laws to appropriately punish the criminal behavior of stalking tabloid journalists.

Levine, who represented Hollywood producer Fayed for a year in the early '90s, expressed outrage at the totally unnecessary loss of innocent life.

"I have witnessed the behavior of the tabloids go from obnoxious to criminal in the last few years," said Levine. "I'm frankly surprised that something like this didn't happen sooner…"

**PSYCHOLOGIST CALLS [FOR] SELF EXAMINATION OF TABLOID VOYEURISM**
*Los Angeles, Entertainment Wire*

A psychologist in Hollywood reacting to the tragedy in Paris today in which Princess Diana was involved in a serious automobile accident allegedly exacerbated by pursuing paparazzi said: "We are all to blame if this accident is a result of Princess Diana fleeing from tabloid photographers. The photographers are paid huge sums for these photos because we are addicted to them…"

Psychologist Robert R. Butterworth, Ph.D., has assisted radio, TV and print media since 1984 to find answers and provide insight to enhance understanding of psychological issues…

**DIANA'S DEATH – THE TRAUMA THAT HER CHILDREN WILL EXPERIENCE**
*Los Angeles, Entertainment Wire*

A psychologist reacting to the tragedy in Paris in which Princess Diana was killed in an automobile accident says that another tragedy is just beginning. "The trauma faced by her two children and the psychological reactions that they will face today and live with the rest of their lives…"

"There is no way that we can begin to describe what these children are feeling but it's most likely a combination of shock, anger, denial and depression. We might have lost a princess but they lost a mother and they need the help of experienced professionals to sort it all out…"

CONTACT: Robert R. Butterworth Ph.D.

■ September 1
**STATEMENT BY THE REV. BILLY GRAHAM ON THE DEATH OF DIANA, PRINCESS OF WALES**
*Minneapolis, PR Newswire*

Like almost everyone else in the world, the unexpected death of Diana, Princess of Wales, came as a profound shock to my wife Ruth and me. I know that Her Majesty The Queen and the other members of the Royal Family especially [are] carrying a heavy burden during this time, and we are praying for them and for all those who were touched by this tragedy…

This tragedy should remind us again of how fragile life is, and how we should each be ready to enter eternity and meet God at any moment…

■ September 3
**FTD ADDS OPERATORS TO HANDLE CALLS FOR FLOWER ORDERS IN MEMORY OF PRINCESS DIANA**
*Chicago, PR Newswire*

[In] response to numerous calls regarding sending flowers for Princess Diana's London funeral this Saturday, FTD has added additional customer service representatives to process these international flower orders.

"Even given the extraordinary tragedy of the Princess's recent death, we are taken aback by the sheer volume of calls and inquiries we are receiving," said Rob Norton, President and CEO of FTD. "We are seeing to it that all orders received are processed with the utmost expediency and care…"

*The Wall Street Journal*, "Death of a Princess, Birth of a Thousand Press Releases" by Joshua Harris Prager, Sept. 10, 1997.

Reprinted with permission from *The Wall Street Journal*.

Illustrations by Robert Pizzo

**Figure 6.1**

## Deliver your message

Knowing who covers relevant beats is only half the battle. Getting your news release, media invitation or pitch letter in the media's hands is another challenge. Here are a few avenues to reporters' desks. But remember, you need to know how each reporter prefers to receive your materials.

• **Fax**. Probably the most popular way public relations professionals contact media is by facsimile. When fax machines were introduced, public relations professionals could fax a computer-generated or typewritten release to media. Today, practitioners can fax directly from their computers to a newsroom. *Two things to note:* **Be sure you have the correct fax number for all journalists you're trying to reach.** And, avoid tying up an editor's fax machine with a lengthy release that wasn't expected. If the editor's waiting for something more important — or is on deadline — your fax will most likely find the recycling bin. And, that editor won't be too receptive to your next fax or phone call.

• **Phone.** If you remember only one thing when calling reporters, it's this: NEVER call media to ask if they received your fax! Nothing alienates reporters more. Most reporters receive hundreds of faxes a day. Don't waste their time asking if they got your one fax. If you have something to add to the fax and have established a solid relationship with the reporter, a follow-up call might work. If you have an appealing story and the reporter encourages phone pitches, here are a few tips: Be brief. Don't ramble on for five minutes before telling why you called. Get right to the point. Be concise. These "openings" or "greetings" can work well: "Hi (reporter's name). This is (your name) from (your company). Our company just released a product that will save commuters hours a day. Do you have a couple of minutes now to hear about it?"

• **E-mail**. Many journalists are working online. And e-mail can be an effective way to contact media — if used properly. But, make sure the reporter welcomes e-mail. As with phone calls, send brief, to-the-point messages. Reporters don't have time to scroll for the "meat" of your message. Be descriptive in the "RE:" or subject area, so reporters know the gist of your e-mail. *Example*: *New Product Saves Users Money and Makes Travel Easier.* Make sure your message is readable. Use a standard font and size like Courier 10-point, and limit your words per line. Be sure to include the contact person's e-mail as well as her daytime and evening phone numbers. E-mail is a great way to send a quick note to a reporter saying, "I saw your article on X. Our company is working on a way to combine X with Y. If you'd like more details, please contact me at … " However, never send your release as an attachment unless you know the reporter will be able to open the file. Some reporters won't have the same programs as you, and won't be able to access your attachment. When in doubt, copy the text of your release in the message — and keep it short. Track your "bad-address" returned messages. Keep your media e-mail addresses up to date and remember to note reporters who like, and who dislike, e-mail. Also, try sending a PDF file. All reporters will be able to open it and at least read the contents.

• **Wire Services.** Another effective way to release information is through a "wire" service. For a fee, PR Newswire and Business Wire will electronically send your story to the media you designate. Their coverage ranges from regional to national. Many major dailies such as *The Wall Street Journal* and *The New York Times* are included on their lists. These services also post your release to their Web pages for a specified time and link your release directly to your company's home page, if applicable. Interested reporters can simply click on your release to find out more information.

## How to talk with journalists

Whether talking with journalists, colleagues or clients, your ability to speak effectively is crucial. As when writing, speaking clearly and concisely will help get your point across. And, you'll avoid being labeled "a talker" — someone reporters and co-workers detest.

Some things to remember when speaking:

• Ask yourself: "What's my point?" Before phoning a reporter or calling a colleague, ask yourself "why" you're calling. And, after your greeting, tell the purpose of your call. Sounds simple, doesn't it? But how many times have you answered the phone and then cringed because it was your 50th-not-favorite cousin who's thrilled to tell you what every day last month brought. Don't act like your cousin, no matter whom you're calling.

Remember these tips:

• **Enunciate properly.** Take time to pronounce words. Garbled sentences make it hard for the listener to comprehend what you're saying. Speak clearly.

• **Avoid jargon.** Don't confuse or distract your listener by rattling off acronyms or buzzwords that won't be understood or will need time to interpret. Use the complete name for acronyms on your first reference. If speaking in your industry's language, ask the person if she understands what a word means — before using it off-the-cuff and making your listener feel inferior.

• **Open your ears.** Effective communication occurs when two or more people understand each other's message. Take time to hear, understand and digest another's point. Don't interrupt just because you disagree. Pause and acknowledge that you comprehend the position, instead of cutting your correspondent off in mid-sentence.

• **Sound educated.** Most of the media and your colleagues will have college degrees and expect your skills to be on par with theirs. Don't use "ya know" and watch the "ums." Pause to gather your thoughts, and think before you speak. Of course, pay attention to your grammar and usage when talking. Avoid lazy language, such as: "Me and Sue are going to the meeting." Or, "Between you and I," he was wrong.

## Going "off the record" with reporters

Going "off the record" means that you tell the reporter information that can't be used. Whether or not to do this on rare occasions presents one of the toughest challenges for public relations people.

If you were to lock six public relations practitioners and six journalists in a room and tell them they couldn't come out until they had unanimously agreed on whether off-the-record information should be shared, they would probably never come out. Some people have been harmed professionally and even lost their jobs because they offered information off the record that was then used by the journalist. On the other side of the coin, many public relations professionals have confided in journalists in an off-the-record manner to avoid serious problems.

Some suggestions if you are considering going off the record:

• Be sure you have a solid trusting relationship with the journalist. Don't go off the record with someone you don't know very well.

• Realize that providing this information will help the journalist know the situation better and understand the reason for some of your organization's actions. Realize that if the reporter gets the information from someone else on the record, it's fair game to use that information. Such use would, of course, not be violating the off-the-record relationship that you had established.

- Be clear when you are on the record and off the record. Don't jump back and forth from one to the other. This could legitimately confuse the reporter and result in some things being reported that you didn't want mentioned.

Here's an example of a real situation that prompted the public relations person to go off the record with five reporters covering a college board meeting.

The president of the college was asked by a board member to invite a black person to be the commencement speaker. The president said, "We can't do that."

**Exclusives can help you build rapport with select media.**

Given only that information, reporters might have written a story that prompted a headline that could have read, "College President Denies Black Right to Speak at Commencement." The additional fact was that the President of the United States had promised to be the commencement speaker. For security reasons, however, that information could not be divulged.

The public relations person, wanting to avoid the racial overtones of the possible headline, called the reporters over and asked if they would all accept "off-the-record" information. All agreed to do so. He then shared the fact that the President of the United States would be giving the commencement address, but that they couldn't use this information. All honored the "off-the-record" request, but the public relations person didn't sleep well that night until he was sure that none of the wire services had moved the story.

This is one of many situations in the practice of public relations that does not lend itself to a true/false question and answer.

## Exclusives can get you in the door

An effective way to generate coverage and build rapport with media — especially if you have a story of national interest — is through exclusives.

Major daily newspapers compete for subscribers and circulation numbers, and television and radio stations battle for ratings. Giving one newspaper or station the chance to best its competitors by running your national interest story exclusively can get you in that paper's door. However, know that you run the risk of offending other media by not offering the story to them either first, or at the same time as the other paper. But, exclusivity can mean better coverage for you. Remember though that public agencies must provide information to all media reps.

Consider a publishing company's public relations person who faxed a two-page news release at the same time and day to hundreds of national media. The release spurred calls from major media such as *The Wall Street Journal*, *The New York Times*, *Fox News*, and more. After the *Journal* reporter had written her story from the release, she asked the PR contact if he had sent the release to any other media. The practitioner acknowledged that he had, and asked why. The reporter told him that if he had offered the *Journal* an exclusive, the story would have landed on the paper's front page. Instead, the story ended up in the middle of the paper.

While any positive major media coverage should be lauded, front-page placement is the crème de la crème of news clippings.

The next time the public relations person had a national interest story, he called *The Wall Street Journal* first, and offered an exclusive. While the *Journal* reporter was reviewing the PR person's exclusive news release, a *Money Magazine* reporter called inquiring about the information that the PR practitioner had just given to the *Journal*. Knowing to avoid the cardinal sin of lying to the media, the PR person explained that he had offered the *Journal* an exclusive. But, he would provide *Money Magazine* the information as soon as the *Journal*'s story ran.

The result: The *Journal* ran a front-page story in its second section, "Marketplace"; and *Money Magazine* wrote a feature article a week later. Both stories generated calls by other major media.

So remember: Exclusives can help you build rapport with media. But be aware of offending others.

## Useful tools
### Pitch letters

Public relations writers use pitch letters to propose or "pitch" a story to an editor. As a rule, pitch letters are rarely longer than one page. They are short and sweet — no nonsense appeals that describe a good story and encourage the recipient to cover it.

Just as a strong lead is crucial to the success of a news release, pitch letters demand a strong lead, or first paragraph, for success as well.

The opening paragraph of your pitch letter may be your only chance to grab your reader's attention and interest.

Good pitch letters often are no longer than four paragraphs:

- The first paragraph offers a crisp description of the story and makes it clear why editors — and their readers — would be interested in this story.
- The second and third paragraphs offer key

supporting details, including additional information or persons you can offer to help to develop the story.

- The final paragraph concludes the pitch, with a final offer of assistance, such as:

"If you'd like more information on this story, please call. "I'll give you a call Tuesday to see if you'd like to pursue this story, "Our president, Pat Jones, will be in town next week and available to talk with you. I'll call before then to see if you'd like to schedule an interview."

How you close the pitch letter is based on your relationship with the person you're writing to. If you're confident that the person wouldn't mind a follow-up call from you, suggest that you'll make one. If the person doesn't like such calls, then offer the option of calling you.

### News and photo memos

These memos offer a listing of possible newsworthy events and photo possibilities. The date, time and contact people (with phone numbers) are listed.

### Invitation to cover

Informing reporters and editors about upcoming newsworthy events allows them time to plan coverage. Explaining possible news and giving specifics about the event allow the media representatives to determine if coverage is warranted and to schedule it. Share brief important facts facts to encourage coverage.

### Fact sheets

Used to convey additional background data — key names, dates, places, events and so on — that help people understand your story but generally are too detailed to include in the news release.

### Contact lists

Used to offer the names and contact information for other persons and organizations who can be helpful in commenting on your story. Contact lists might offer other company executives as sources. They also might include other outside experts (such as researchers, educators, former employees and so on) who can offer outside endorsements to your story.

### Q & A sheets

(Question-and-Answer Sheets) Used to offer clear answers to commonly asked questions about the issues covered in your news release.

### Backgrounders

Used to offer in-depth information supporting your story. Backgrounders generally are well-sourced and provide supporting details on the issues and research key to your story. They offer readers both more detail and perspective on your story.

### Media Kits

To assist the media in covering your organization, prepare a media kit. The kit might include:

- News release
- Fact sheets
- Question-and-Answer sheets
- Photographs with captions
- Color slides and transparencies — if applicable
- Charts, graphs and logos
- Copies of speeches — if applicable
- Biographical data on people mentioned in the release
- History of the company
- Company publications, including an annual report
- Sources (with phone numbers to contact for more information)

### Preparing a news release

Here are some tips to make sure your news release meets editors' needs:

■ Format: Use company or client letterhead with "News Release" shown prominently.

- Margins: One-half-inch at least for top and bottom margins; three-quarters of an inch at least for left and right margins. *Remember*: Editors need room to edit your release. Don't make them work to find room to write.

- Indent all paragraphs, except your dateline (first) graph.

- Double-space between paragraphs, and provide enough room between lines in graphs for editors to write. Many prefer the entire release be double-spaced.

- Font: Use serif for copy, sans serif for headlines. Courier used to be the accepted "copy font" for releases, but the computer age has created many other suitable readable fonts.

■ Don't try to write a headline. It won't fit and some research indicates editors don't want them. If your editors prefer them, use them. A fairly new approach is to include a one- or two-line summary of the release before the release starts.

■ "For Release" date: Always include the date that you want your news to be "made public" — or reported on by the press. And don't hide the date. Make sure it's easily seen.

- "Embargo" releases are sent with future release dates. If you want to alert the media to something, but don't want them to report on the news yet, send out an embargoed release. But be prepared for questions as soon as journalists receive the release. And be vigilant about reporters who don't respect the embargo. Talk to them and, if necessary, get them the information at the last minute.

■ Contact name and numbers. Make sure journalists can see the contact person's name and phone number. Include the contact's after-hours phone number, so reporters can get in touch with the spokesperson on their time.

- Provide the contact's e-mail address, if applicable. Some reporters prefer e-mail to phone.
- Include another contact person if your number-one person is hard to reach.

Media don't like searching for someone to talk to or waiting for a spokesperson to get back to them. Make sure someone's available.

■ Dateline: The first words after your headline or sub-headline should be the city your release is from. Type it in all caps and include the state, unless the city is well known (see AP Stylebook for guidelines). Example: GLASSBORO, NJ — ; or PHILADELPHIA.

■ Lead: Start your lead graph immediately after the dateline. Keep it succinct.

■ If your release is more than one page, type "---MORE--- " at the bottom of each page except the last — and center them. This will let reporters know there is "more" than just the page they're reading.

■ At the top of subsequent pages, type a headline summary, called a "slug" — something representative of the release — and then "/ADD ONE" or "TWO" or "THREE." If a page gets misplaced, reporters will know what to look for. Also, use the first two or three words of your headline or summary statement on page one.

■ Signify the end of the release with "-30-" or "# # #." Reporters will know there's no more to your release.

■ If you want to notify editors/reporters of something you don't want made public, include your "Editor's Note" after your "end" symbol. Example: "Editor's Note: For a free review copy, please contact Gary Bagin at 1-800-555-7874, ext. 370."

*(Figure 6.2, a sample news release, spans the next two pages.)*

## Reaching the media

When you need to reach media at various locations, the following sources can help: lists, magazines, newsletters, newspapers, radio and TV stations, as well as news bureaus.

- *Bulldog Reporter* newsletter: *Bulldog Reporter* is the most current source for knowing who's who. Every two weeks, the eight-page publication reports media promotions, transfers and beat changes. From the editor of your daily paper to the producer at a network news program, *Bulldog* covers a wide range of media. It includes contact information — phone, fax, address and e-mail — for most reporters, editors and producers mentioned and tells how each likes to be pitched. InfoComGroup also publishes The *National PR Pitch Book* (pricing varies) — a cumulative publication of the year's media moves. Available from: InfoCom Group, 1250 45th St., Suite 200, Emeryville, CA 94608.

- *Bacon's Media Directories*: These annual directories — with midyear updates — list media covering virtually every subject or industry. The encyclopedia-sized books are divided into the following media: television and radio; newspapers; and magazines. They offer contact information for most editors and beat writers and include helpful background such as the circulation number, various bureaus and types of press materials accepted. Bacon's also publishes a *Media Calendar Directory* providing the editorial calendars for more than 2,000 magazines and trade publications. All of Bacon's Directories are on CD-ROM. Available from: Bacon's Publishing Co., 332 S. Michigan Ave., Chicago, IL 60604.

- *Burrelle's Media Directories*: Regional media directories. Available from: Burrelle's, 73 East Northfield Ave., Livingston, NJ 07039.

- *Gale Directory of Publications and Broadcast Media*: Lists more than 37,000 newspapers, magazines, journals and broadcasting stations in the U.S. and Canada, with names, phone and fax numbers for key personnel. Available from: Gale Research, 835 Penobscot Bldg., Detroit, MI 48226.

- *Guide to Free Product Publicity*: Lists magazines, newsletters and trade publications that accept news releases about new products and services. Available from: Todd Publications, P.O. Box 301, West Nyack, NY 10994.

 **... THE LEADER IN SCHOOL COMMUNICATIONS**

***For Immediate Release***
September 1, 2004

For more info: Larry Lhulier (301) 519-0496

## *But is New Better? ...*

### Forget that dreaded note from the teacher;
### These days it's more likely to be an e-mail

Has little Johnny been bad at school? Don't expect a note from the teacher or principal. These days, Mom and Dad are more likely to get a tattle-e-mail — or find a discipline note when they log onto Johnny's Web-based grade book.

Schools have turned to digital communications in a major way in recent years, rewriting a lot of the old rules on how they deal with parents.

More than one-third of the school districts responding to a national survey four years ago reported that they did not have Web sites. But today, developing Web content and maintaining Web sites topped the list of new demands for school-communication professionals, according to a new survey by the National School Public Relations Association (NSPRA). NSPRA, based in Rockville, Md., is a nonprofit association that publishes *Principal Communicator* — a monthly communication newsletter for school principals.

Some 91 percent of the school-communication executives polled said that some or all individual schools in their districts now maintain Web sites for communicating school information. Of those, however, only 13 percent of them said that their schools "do a good job in keeping them up to date." Half of those responding said, "Some (Web sites) are up to date and others aren't."

E-mail now also plays a major role in school communication, the study found. Some 93 percent of those surveyed reported that they use e-mail to "routinely and effectively" communicate with other administrators, and 81 percent use it to reach teachers. In addition, 49 percent said they now use it to stay in touch with community leaders and groups while 36 percent use it to contact parents.

"The rollout of new communication technology in just a few years has been impressive," said Rich Bagin, publisher of *Principal Communicator*. "But while new technology is boosting the quantity of school information, parents and school officials need to remember that good communication is a two-way street.

(more)

National School Public Relations Association • 15948 Derwood Road • Rockville MD 20855 • (301) 519-0496 • FAX (301) 519-0494 • www.nspra.org

**Figure 6.2** (continues on next page)

---

## *NSPRA NEWS ... 2*

"Schools have to hear what people are saying about them and understand what people think about the jobs they're doing," Bagin cautioned. "There is always a danger of losing touch with each other when we depend too much on one-way communication."

The arrival of communication technology means many parents also have had to learn a whole new set of rules and etiquette for staying on top of what's happening in the classroom, according to Bagin.

"But whether it is new-tech or old-style, parents and educators should still insist on clear, open and ongoing communication between schools and homes," he said.

NSPRA has developed a free tip sheet for parents with ideas and suggestions for communicating with schools. For a copy of "The ABCs of Keeping in Touch with Your Child's Schools" by e-mail, send your request to ABC@nspra.org or log on to www.nspra.org/abctipsheet.pdf.

# # #

**Figure 6.2  (continued from previous page)**

---

- *International Media Guide*: A comprehensive multi-volume listing of business and professional publications for Europe, Asia, Middle East, Africa and Latin America. Available from: R.R. Bowker, 245 W.17th St., New York, NY 10011.

- *PR Newswire's ProfNet*: Another solid source for finding out reporters' needs for stories is PR Newswire's *ProfNet*. This service links media with subscribers — public relations professionals. Reporters e-mail questions on topics of upcoming stories to *ProfNet*. When subscribers have experts or information that could aid a reporter, they can e-mail the journalist directly. Available from: PR Newswire, 806 Plaza Three, Harborside Financial Center, Jersey City, NJ 07311.

- *The Internet*: Although time-consuming, another way to track reporters' beats is to surf the net. Many major daily newspapers and news organizations have Web sites or home pages — and most can be accessed free. Almost all media post their daily broadcast or print stories — with bylines — to their Web site. Learn who's covering what by scanning your targeted media's Web sites every day. Some sites offer direct links to reporters'

biographies that include titles, beats covered, educational background, work history and more. "Bookmark" the media's home pages and research reporters' beats before making a pitch.

## Using news conferences

One of the most overdone of all media events, news conferences often disappoint and anger journalists who don't appreciate covering a "hyped" event that doesn't provide news. Use the conference only when you offer a major news event when you want all media to have the same information at the same time.

If conducting a news conference, choose a time that's fair to as many media as possible. Don't schedule it at a time that causes reporters to miss deadlines.

Prepare a media kit and prepare key personnel to answer anticipated questions.

Offer directions to the location from the main entrance and be available after the conference for questions.

Always consider whether you can adequately give the information to the media via some other mechanism, be it news release, telephone conversation, e-mail, briefing or op-ed piece before holding a news conference.

Howard and Mathews give tips for holding a news conference once you have deemed that the information you wish to release to your publics is worthy of the time and effort needed to hold such a media event.[2]

**Location**. A news conference does not have to be held in the grand ballroom of the best hotel in town. Journalists will go where the conference is if the event is worthy of the effort.

**Online news conferences**. Still in its infancy but rapidly growing is the e-conference — press conference on the web. Instead of renting a room, offering or serving refreshments, renting lights and equipment, you create a Web site; instead of giving directions to get to the land site, you designate a URL; instead of copying B-roll onto video, you run it as a video component of the news conference; instead of copying reams of releases, bios, fact sheets and other collateral, material, you load it onto the e-conference site. An online conference can be easily archived and allows the host organization to determine who logged onto the conference.

**Time**. Knowing your local media well means you will have no trouble determining when to hold a conference. You should attempt to have the event at the best "down" time for all media. More than likely, this will be during the late morning, after the television crews have been given assignments (one of which you hope is to cover your conference) and when there still is time for late-breaking news to go into the final edition of the newspaper.

**Notification**. Alert the media a few days in advance, if at all possible. If you alert the media much before that, you take the chance of a leak. If you wait later than that, you may be too late in that reporters and camera crews will already have their assignments. You may contact the media to remind them of the conference but, if your first notification showed the importance of the conference, a reminder contact can be misinterpreted as pushy.

**Protocol**. Each member of the media should be greeted upon arrival at the conference, even an online conference. They should be shown the layout of the conference site, including where the camera crews should go, where print reporters can sit, and the protocol of the online, live-feed or in-person questioning. Start the news conference on time. Just as your speakers have other engagements, so do the media have other events to cover. Stay within the specified time for the announcement itself and try not to let the question-and-answer period linger

---

2. Howard & Mathews. *On Deadline: Managing Media Relations*. Long Grove, IL: Waveland Press, Inc.

## Letter to the Editor

Letters to the Editor are among the best read sections in the newspaper. Frequently, movers and shakers in the community use this vehicle to express themselves and gain the attention of the community.

Remember that many people won't read that particular letter that might bother you. By responding to the letter, you now bring the issue to more people. Remember, too, that if you're considered an "overdog," that people will tend to go with the common citizen who wrote the original letter.

You want to respond to a misstatement of facts, but you don't necessarily want to respond to opinion. In some cases, it's better if someone on your advisory committee or some supporter of your company or organization writes a letter, if, indeed, you feel the letter has to be written.

It is especially difficult to tell the chief executive officer who may have been maligned in a letter that it might be better to just let the issue die than to stir it.

beyond the point where questions become sparse. Finally, thank the media for attending the conference. Do not assume they know you are grateful for their appearance.

**Available material**. The press material you give to the media at the end of the news conference is critically important. The bulk of your preparations probably will center on these items; certainly, the bulk of your time will go into creating and assembling this material into a media kit.

**Emergency conferences**. Clearly, you need to hold a conference if there is a crisis that demands it, such as an industrial accident or natural disaster. Equally clear is that you will not have the time to locate just the right place and prepare all the right material and observe the minute details of decorum. In these cases, you operate under the rules of crisis management — you have a plan to cover any eventuality that may occur. Your decisions will already have been made about details such as site, spokesperson and protocol. The internet has become a critical factor in the way organizations provide information and respond to the media during a crisis.

## Using digital communication

Although learning the new technologies associated with the Internet and related digital media may seem overwhelming, these new tools in the public relations arsenal actually are making it easier to successfully practice good public relations

Public relations practitioners are rapidly finding new ways to use digital communications to reach and influence audiences.

Just a few of the new but already commonly practiced activities include:

- Issuing news releases to media worldwide, in real time, on the Web
- Storing back copies of previous releases and backgrounders on the Web
- Making standard executive bio and corporate background info available around-the-clock on the Web
- Offering digital photography, video or audio, by disk or Web download
- Staging real-time news conferences on the Web, offering either video or audio
- Offering hyperlinks to material of independent organizations to support a corporate position on an issue
- Providing e-mail addresses of corporate spokespersons to media with questions — making spokespersons even more accessible
- Using Web-based searches to review activities and announcements by individuals and organizations involved in issues of interest to the organization
- Making backgrounders and speeches on key issues available on the Web
- Monitoring message boards and news groups to track grassroots opinion about the organization or its issues
- Developing intranets, internal computer networks, offering company information to appropriate employees.
- Using CD-ROM technology to offer interactive informative or training material on vital issues
- Using e-mail to rapidly disseminate information to employees. And, using e-mail to collect questions and feedback from employees.
- Communicating with shareholders by posting current earnings information, annual reports, government filings and other financial information on the corporate web site.
- Posting special event or other community-interest information on Web spaces devoted to communicating with neighbors and special communities.
- Sharing technical resources and expertise with community groups, such as nonprofits and schools, to strengthen relations with the community ■

## Tips

1. As soon as possible, get to know all the reporters covering your company or organization.

2. Pride yourself on accuracy. If you make a mistake that appears under a reporter's byline, chances are you'll never be forgiven.

3. Don't say, "No comment." It's like waving a red flag in front of a bull.

4. Know deadlines of your various media. Calling at the right time makes a difference.

5. Determine how your reporter or editor wants to receive your news releases. Should you send e-mail, a fax, or regular mail?

Name_____Date_____

## Answer these questions

1. Some authorities advise that a public relations person should never go "off the record" with a reporter. Others think it's a good idea. Would you ever go off the record? Why?

_____

_____

_____

_____

_____

_____

_____

2. A reporter who normally covers your organization accurately makes a major error in a front-page story that embarrasses your boss and the organization. What should you do?

_____

_____

_____

_____

_____

_____

_____

*See other side*

Name _____ Date _____

3. This is not the first time the reporter has made such an error. Suppose that reporter had made the same kind of error four times in the last two months. When checking with public relations colleagues in the area, you find that he has done the same thing with them. What would you do then?

_____

_____

_____

_____

_____

_____

4. Your boss — the CEO — suggests that you respond with "no comment" to reporters regarding a controversial topic that has arisen. What's your reaction?

_____

_____

_____

_____

_____

_____

## SECTION 2

### Working with broadcast media

In a broad sense, *news* is defined as "anything of interest to a great number of people." In its broadest sense, news is "whatever the *news* director says it is."

It is the responsibility of the public relations practitioner to convince a news director or news editor of a radio or television station that a story being pitched is news.

Persuading the media to cover an event can be frustrating. Contacting local (or national) media with poorly researched story ideas could even turn off reporters and editors who might react by not considering future coverage.

How can you get your message on the air? Whether it be on radio, commercial television or cable, you can take a number of proven steps to help assure acceptance of your story by a station decision-maker. And, if pitched convincingly, you will also get that all-important on-site coverage of the event.

The persuasion process begins with *relationship marketing* — developing sound relationships and loyalty by making media outlets and their reporters feel good about working with you. It is not unusual to spend six months or even a year or more developing that (mutually trusting) relationship. *Relationship marketing*, many times subliminal, can be a major ingredient in convincing a media outlet to cover your event or to consider your firm or organization a credible news source.

For example, make yourself available when a reporter or editor is working on an enterprising story. And, try not to waste a reporter's time with invitations-to-cover stories or events that might be less than newsworthy.

No matter which outlets are being "pitched," the initial contact or message from the organization or firm to the media representative (news director, assignment editor, etc.) should contain this information.

- Who you are
- What you think about yourself (value to others)
- What you are trying to do
- Why you deserve their support

### Evolution

First, some background on transitions in the medium itself. No one is really certain what Guglielmo Marconi had in mind when he invented radio in the 1890s, opening the way for the first one-way communication to the masses. In 1937, the first live transcontinental broadcast originated from the Lakehurst Naval Air Station in New Jersey.

While that broadcast was expected to be historic, no one could have imagined the impact it would have on the world. With announcer Herbert Morrison at the microphone, the dirigible Hindenburg burst into flames and was quickly consumed. The description, the first true radio on-scene report, is proof that a radio program can be effective in painting pictures with words. Over the years, families spent their evenings either reading the newspaper or a good book or listening to music, comedy, drama or soap operas on the radio. Edward R. Murrow's live broadcasts during World War II are legendary. Murrow, originally a print journalist, possessed the knack that PR practitioners must acquire if they are going to use the electronic media — **painting pictures with words**.

With the postwar years, broadcast executives discovered they could target audiences more precisely. Radio stations found that while their audiences grew to be more homogeneous, they were more loyal. As television's popularity took off with such entertainment programs as Milton Berle, Sid Caesar and Ed Sullivan, radio stations began carrying fewer comedy and dramatic programs, leaving them to the visual medium. Most went with music formats sprinkled with five-minute newscasts — usually once an hour.

*Too many public relations practitioners overlook radio.*

During the 60s, radio began making the transition from music formats to specialized programming. *Talk radio emerged first.* Then came the all-news format. A bonanza for the PR practitioner, right? Not necessarily. The Federal Communication Commission relaxed its rules on the amount of time a station had to devote to public service programming. And, the National Association of Broadcasters (NAB) amended its code to allow far more commercial minutes per hour. Thus, fewer "free" minutes were available on commercial radio and TV.

That's where cable comes in. On the plus side, audiences are even more defined than those in radio and all cable systems must provide local access channels — a terrific opportunity to reach a target audience. However, on the negative side, the audiences are very limited.

Even with rapid changes in electronic media, too many public relations practitioners still overlook radio. Of all the electronic media, radio still has the lowest production costs. It has the greatest flexibility. But it is television that offers the greatest emotional impact.

Whether it be radio, commercial TV or cable, there is

one basic rule to follow to get a story on the air. ***Get to know the local stations.*** Know what types of programming they are carrying.

How do you find out? Conduct your own informal surveys. Watch and listen to news sources in the markets where you are trying to acquire coverage.

If radio is your goal, listen to stations either at work or while driving to and from your job. If it is television, once on the job or at home, pay particular attention to the types of programming (including cable) on TV. Know how to use area stations to your advantage.

## Why radio?

- **It's immediate** — if there is an emergency, radio, like the Internet, can inform the masses, instantly. More people have access to a radio at any given time than they do to either a television set or a computer. Where do you turn during a snowstorm to find out whether you have to report to work that day or your children have school? Probably, your local radio station.

- **It's comfortable** – people who are listening to the radio are usually involved in other activities simultaneously.

- **It's focused** – because audiences are narrowly defined, your message will reach a particular (target) audience.

- **It's captive** – many listeners are confined to a limited space, such as a car or office. That makes it easier to reach them via radio.

## Radio programming

What kinds of programming are available via radio?

- **Spot announcements** – 10-, 15-, 30- and 60-second announcements much like commercials, except they are provided free for nonprofit organizations.

- **Newscasts** – Stories to be used in newscasts must have solid news value. Remember, except for all-news stations and some talk stations, most radio outlets provide little, if any, airtime for local news. They depend on network programming (local affiliates throughout the country that receive their programming simultaneously via satellite or hard wire from such networks as NBC, ABC, CBS, CNN, FOX, MSNBC, CNBC, etc.)

- **Discussion programs** – Short programs offered in non-prime time that could give your organization or firm exposure in a particular area of expertise. These types of programs are usually heard early on a Sunday morning. But don't discount them. There is an audience listening out there, although it is limited.

***Use radio to inform large audiences instantly.***

- **Talk or interview shows** – With the advent of talk radio, more opportunities are available to communicate your message. Remember, your spokesperson must not only be an expert on the topic, but must also be a good communicator.

## Why television?

Of all the media, TV has the greatest emotional impact. If a picture in a newspaper is worth a thousand words, video on an evening newscast or a guest-shot on a TV talk show is worth millions of words. Just ask anyone who watched on that fateful Sunday in November, 1963, two days after President John F. Kennedy was assassinated in Dallas.

NBC carried what might be the most famous of all the early live TV news reports. It was shortly after noon on Nov. 24th with millions of Americans watching live coverage of the events following the assassination. NBC switched to Dallas as accused assassin Lee Harvey Oswald was to be transferred from the city jail to the county jail. Cameras followed Oswald as he walked between two Dallas detectives along a garage ramp leading from the jail to the street where a police vehicle awaited him. Suddenly, there was Jack Ruby entering the corner of the TV screen, then leaping from among a crowd of reporters, gun in hand, pulling the trigger and murdering the accused assassin. Emotional? Yes. High impact? Couldn't be higher.

Why then shouldn't public relations practitioners use television? If properly produced, it will be of infinite value and even though the story you have to tell won't be as dramatic as Dallas, it can be emotional and have the potential to leave a lasting impression.

Some key points about TV:

- **Nearly as immediate as radio** – With the use of electronic news gathering (ENG) equipment, satellites and fiber optics, the only thing that keeps TV from being as immediate as radio is the time needed to transport the equipment to the site and set it up. Radio is absolutely immediate because the only piece of equipment needed is a telephone. With cellular or wireless phones, radio transmission is 100 percent portable.

- **Audience** – No other medium can reach the numbers of people that TV can. More than 98 million homes in the U.S. have at least one TV set. Most have multiple sets. Those sets are turned on an average of 50 hours per week in the American home.

- **Comfort** – Like radio, viewers are usually watching TV because they want to — in the comfort of their homes or at work. It is the PR practitioner's responsibility to provide programming that will interest them.

- **Captive** – While it is true that a viewer can get up from the sofa or chair and walk away from the set, TV is still considered a captive medium. It can and does deliver the message. That's why billions of dollars are spent each year in TV advertising (In 1996, nearly $37 billion was spent on network, local and cable TV. That's nearly 23 percent of all advertising dollars.). Remember, as a PR practitioner, you have two goals — get the attention of the viewer and deliver your message.

## Why cable?

By 2000, the number of U.S. households wired for cable exceeded 70 million. Demographically, cable can reach just about every audience segment. In addition to carrying commercial stations, the same ones that can be received with an outdoor or indoor antenna, cable provides hundreds of specialized programs on dozens of channels with very specific target audiences. The local access channels mandated by the Cable Communications Policy Act of 1984 offer excellent opportunities for local origination programming — ideal for nonprofit organizations, school districts, hospitals, etc.

Depending on financial resources and expertise, programs may be professionally produced at a substantial cost while others are obviously "low-budget." However, low budget does not necessarily mean poor quality. Cable staff or community volunteers may be willing to assist with a production.

## TV programming

What kinds of programming opportunities are available to the public relations practitioner on television?

- News programs
- As guests for entertainment shows like *Today*, *Good Morning America*, *Leno*, *Letterman* or *Oprah*
- Appearances on local talk shows (many markets have locally originated programs)
- Protest demonstrations
- News releases (printed and video) and story pitches to local and network news directors
- General-interest films
- Creative programming such as medical updates, gardening, geriatric reports, education, etc.
- Silent publicity (like product placement) — use of your products or facilities for a TV program
- Public service announcements

## Getting on the air

*(Figure 6.3, a sample news release for broadcast, spans the next two pages.)*

The National Association of Broadcasters (NAB) suggests that if your appeal is to be effective, you should know answers to some key questions before contacting local stations:

- What is your message? Are you clear about the basic idea you want to communicate?
- Who should receive your message? Is it of general interest to a large segment of the audience? Can it be tailored to reach a specific audience?
- How can you best put your message across? Does it have enough general interest for a special program? Would a PSA serve just as well?

Your answers to these questions should help you determine in advance if your pitch will work.

Whether you use radio or television, follow these steps:

1. **Appoint one person** to be responsible for the news of your organization. Preferably, that person should be familiar with the capabilities and limitations of the news media.

2. Have your representative **contact the program director** or general manager of each local radio station. The station representative will suggest the types of programming most likely to be broadcast, the appropriate time limits for spot announcements and programs and who (your organization or the station) will physically produce the programming.

3. During the first meeting between your representative and the station representative, **establish guidelines** for proper microphone and recording techniques. If your organization does not have access to professional broadcasting equipment, it should ask the station for help. If assured good programming, many stations will offer staff assistance and studio time. It should be understood from the start that the program must be professional in quality. Once your group or organization has made a commitment, it must follow through. And remember the importance of deadlines; most stations schedule their programming days in advance.

4. **Messages should be timely and relevant**. They must be in the local interest. In other words, listeners should identify with the programming.

5. **Broadcast presentations should be succinct** — not padded with unnecessary or unimportant content. Your firm or organization should try for variety in program content and presentation.

NEWS RELEASE – Broadcast Media

## Cherry Hill Public Library
1800 Kings Highway North
Cherry Hill, NJ 08034

| Contact | Barbara Shapiro | Phone: | (856) 667-0300 |
| | Library Director | Fax: | (856) 667-4837 |
| | | Email: | bshapiro@cherryhill.lib.nj.us |
| | Dr. Stephen Barbell | Phone: | (856) 489-8990 |
| | Board of Trustees – | | |
| | President | | |

**FOR IMMEDIATE RELEASE:**                    **Dec. 1, 2004**

## CHERRY HILL LIBRARY BOARD NAMES CHILDREN'S LIBRARY FOR FORMER MAYOR LEVIN

(CHILDREN'S LIBRARY)

CHERRY HILL, N.J. – As the new Cherry Hill Public Library nears completion, its board of trustees has announced its children's library will carry the name of former mayor and board member Susan Bass Levin.

Library board President Stephen Barbell says almost any area of the new building could be dedicated in Mayor Levin's honor. However, it is most fitting that it be the children's library because she has always felt the future of the Township and the nation rests with today's young people.

Levin served as Cherry Hill's mayor for nearly 14 years before resigning to become commissioner of the New Jersey Department of Community Affairs in the McGreevey administration.

(MORE)

**Figure 6.3 – first page**

(CHILDREN'S LIBRARY/ Add 11111)

The new multi-level facility is located next to the current library at 110 Kings Highway North.

"Our library will be a new educational, technological, research and cultural centerpiece for our community," Dr. Barbell said. "With so much to offer, the library will help to strengthen our community connections."

The <u>Susan Bass Levin Children's Room</u> features a colorful and creative open story area, program room, "child-friendly" technology, and book, tape, story and craft areas.

In addition, the new 72,000 square foot library contains a young adult area, quiet study rooms, art gallery, a local history room to display and preserve Township artifacts, a multicultural room, conference and community rooms, reading area and expanded parking area.

According to Dr. Barbell, the new library will continue to offer community programming and events, an outstanding collection of 180,000 volumes of print and electronic materials and classes. Plans include a senior citizen area with a large print book collection, videoconferencing capabilities, a spacious multipurpose room for meetings and community events, and an outdoor patio and café — operated by a private vendor.

# # #

**Figure 6.3 – second page**

6. Your group does not have to avoid controversial topics. Problems as well as innovations and current involvement should be presented and explained. **Solutions to problems** should be offered. At all times, be honest and tell the whole story.

7. All types of programming, from 90-minute spectaculars to brief spot announcements, require **planning and cooperation** with local radio stations. Teamwork is the key to success in any project.

8. **Accept suggestions and constructive criticism**. Your representative may be working with experts in a field that may be foreign.

9. Your firm should **know its limitations**. A half-hour interview program might seem ideal, but spot announcements, if well produced, can be more effective than a long program that is inadequately prepared.

10. People who work for radio (or television) stations are usually **pressed for time**. Do not drop in on them unannounced. Telephone first to make an appointment.

11. When writing for radio, **use simple, descriptive words** that form pictures, give dimension and add color. Radio reaches only the ear. The listener must be able to mentally sketch the picture you're trying to create.

12. Make sure all spot announcements (public service announcements) are **accurately timed**. Ten-second spots usually contain 25 words; 30-second-spots contain about 75 words; 60-second spots usually contain 150 words.

13. **Submit all program copy and ideas** to the program director or station manager as far in advance as possible. Ten days is not too soon.

14. **Be on time** for a live program or taping. The clock waits for no one.

15. When preparing for a live broadcast or taping session, **accept instructions** for proper microphone technique-distance from microphone, voice projection and ways to avoid extraneous noises (paper rustling, chair squeaking, etc.) during the production.

16. After the production has been broadcast, **send a letter** to the station expressing appreciation for its help. This practice will strengthen the relationship between your organization and the station and will increase your chances of getting airtime.

17. Your organization should let the station know of any **reactions to the production**. The station tries to serve its community although, legally, it no longer must administer ascertainment surveys for license renewal purposes.

*See Figure 6.4 (Public Service Announcement) on the next page.*

18. News releases for the electronic media should be about one page long, double-spaced. They should be typed (word processed) on one side of a piece of paper, 8½ x 11. (Note: Newspeople don't usually look on the back of a sheet of paper.) The copy should be readable and legible. Releases should be mailed, delivered, faxed or electronically transmitted one week prior to the event. This gives the editor ample time to plan. **Check with each station to determine how it prefers releases be sent.** (The same holds true for a media advisory or an invitation to cover.)

19. And, remember, you are trying to *relate* your image, not *sell* it. This, after all, is public relations.

## Ten top tips when public relations practitioners use television

Though production costs are higher in television, it still offers great potential as a vehicle of communication for many organizations and corporations. Many of the suggestions for the use of radio can be applied when working in the visual media. In addition, consider these 10 tips for the use of TV by an organization, firm or business:

1. Be simple. Messages can be highlighted and the best camera work done when backgrounds are plain, participants are few and movement is minimal. Quick or sudden movements can be distracting and may draw the viewers' attention away from the focal point.

2. Check with the program or public affairs director on the use of PowerPoint slides, films, videotapes and photographs that can help communicate a message. (Many stations would prefer shooting their own video, using a format compatible with their equipment.)

3. Make sure that text (copy) written to accompany visual aids fits. In other words, if a video or film runs 30 seconds, the text should contain about 60 words. A one-minute video should have a text of about 125 words.

4. Keep in mind that digital photo files are preferred over photographs in most cases. They can be made professionally at a minimal cost. When photographs are used, matte or dull-surfaced prints are preferable because glossy prints reflect studio lights.

5. Provide one graphic for each 10-second spot; two for a 20-second spot and so on.

6. When discussing such statistical topics as budgets or surveys, use charts. Be sure they are large enough to

# Public Service Announcement

## COPY

```
1   The Camden County Chapter of the
2   American Red Cross is holding a student
3   blood drive at Cherry Hill High School East
4   on Saturday, October 30th. The drive takes
5   place from 10 a.m. until 4 p.m. in the main
6   gymnasium gym. Members of the general
7   public are encouraged to join with the
8   students in donating blood. Students under
9   the age of 18 need parents' permission.
10  Cherry Hill High School East is on Kresson
11  Road between Springdale and Cropwell
12  Roads. For information, call, (888) 555-1212.
13
14
15                        end
16
17
18
19
20
21
22
23
24
25
26
27
28
29
30
```

Runs = 30
Words = 74
CAMCO RED CROSS
PLEASE RUN THRU
10/30/04

FOR INFO:
Seth Adams
(888) 555-1212
Today's Date:
10/1/04

Communication Specialists  •  P.O. Box 892  •  Cherry Hill, NJ 08003  •  (609) 428-8049

**Figure 6.4 – first page**

be read easily and don't forget to use vivid colors on those bar graphs and pie charts.

7. Ask that visuals be returned immediately after use. Otherwise, they may be discarded.

8. When your representatives go on the air, they will want to look and sound their best. TV personnel will give participants helpful suggestions and appreciate cooperation in return. Cooperate with the director and floor managers during the appearance. They may find it necessary to give hand signals during the show to control the speed of the presentation. Your representatives should ask the director any questions about the show before the show goes on the air.

9. Participants should not worry about the role they are playing. They are appearing on the program not as an actor or actress but rather as an interesting person, representing your firm or organization.

10. Be on time. In producing a TV program, many things must be accomplished in a short time and every minute is important. Once you've completed the productions, and you've sent letters of appreciation to TV and radio stations, your organization should go a step further. A good starting point for a continuing relationship (relationship marketing) with local radio and TV stations is to ask them to consider your personnel as experts in your particular geographic area. The radio and especially TV exposure could be worth thousands of dollars if the time had to be paid for. You might suggest to the media that they check your web page for a current list of experts or mail them updated personnel sketches several times a year.

## Writing for the electronic media

When writing for radio or television, the text or scripts must be tailored to listeners or viewers who might not be paying full attention (passive listeners or viewers). Bearing that in mind, the following suggestions should be implemented:

- Write simple spoken English. In other words, prefer the plain word to the fancy; the familiar word to the unfamiliar.
- Never use a long word when a short one will do as well.
- Try to keep one thought to a sentence. Master the simple declarative sentence.
- Vary sentence length.
- Use short paragraphs.
- Put the words you want to emphasize at the beginning or end of your sentence.

- Use the active voice ... nouns and verbs rather than adjectives and adverbs.
- Use picture nouns and action verbs.
- Use plain, conversational language. Write the way you talk.
- Write clearly.
- Cut needless words, sentences and paragraphs.
- Avoid gobbledygook and jargon.
- Write to be understood — not to impress.
- Write in your natural style.
- Try to use the present (walk) or the present perfect (have or has walked) tense.
- Avoid synonyms. Synonyms can confuse the listener or viewer. (Use school, college or university rather than "educational institution.")
- Do NOT use pronouns. Repeat proper names.
- Avoid direct quotes — paraphrase. (It is safer.)
- Keep adjectives to a minimum. Adjectives tend to clutter speech and obscure the main line of the story.
- Use verbs. Do not drop verbs. Listeners need verbs.
- Appositions. DO NOT use appositions. Most appositions are not natural to speech. Appositions often confuse listeners because they can't see the necessary punctuation.
- Use mostly simple sentences.
- Attribution (in broadcast writing) ... almost always comes at the beginning of a sentence ... NOT at the end. (*Use*: Store manager S. William Kramer pointed out that this year's event will be the biggest ever. *Don't use*: "This year's event will be the biggest ever," said store manager S. William Kramer.)
- Revise and rewrite. Improvement is always possible.

See the sample TV script (*Figure 6.5*) on the next page.

## The video news release

A video news release can be an expensive but effective vehicle to assist in getting your message on TV. To the novice, it can be compared to a "package" or "wrap" on a TV news program. If well produced, a VNR might be carried in total or part by local stations; some networks have been known to carry portions of VNRs on their evening newscasts. The smaller the station, the better the chance the VNR will be carried unedited.

What exactly is a VNR? The best way to see exactly what is contained on a VNR is to watch any evening news program. An effective VNR should mirror just what we are watching — the news anchor introducing a recorded news

# Sample TV Script

**CLIENT: Red Cross**
**TITLE: It's Only Blood**
**LENGTH: 30 Seconds**

| **Video:** | **Audio:** |
|---|---|
| Open on Dr. Roberts standing on square in front of clock tower. Tight...then pull away: | **DOC:** It's called THE GIFT OF LIFE and THE GIFT THAT KEEPS ON GIVING. It's blood. |
| Dr. Roberts talking with donor inside gym: | **DOC:** Here in Fairfield, we are experiencing a major blood shortage. That's why all of us need your help. |
| Student Donor lying on table. Wide shot to close-up for narration: | **DONOR:** It is our obligation as students to get involved as responsible members of the Fairfield community. |
| **ANNCR.:** Standing in front of College Hall with fade back to Fairfield Square: | **ANNCR.:** Parsons College and Fairfield...working together to save lives. For information on how **YOU** can join with **US**, call...555-2121. |
| **TITLE CARD:** Parsons/Fairfield Blood Drive Monday, Sept. 28 Trustee Gym... 9 a.m. – 6 p.m. Call...555-2121 | |

Figure 6.5

report or going "live" to the scene. The piece usually opens with either the reporter doing a "stand-up" or with scenes of the event. That "stand-up" plus the use of the face and voice of a newsmaker, background scenes and the reporter signing off is called a "package" or "wrap."

A good VNR usually contains a *wrap* or *package*, extra tape of the newsmaker (soundbites), extra video or scenes of the area (known as "B-roll"), titles of the reporter and newsmakers that can be superimposed on the screen and in some instances, an anchor type person introducing the *package*. On a separate track on the video, the narrator (in this case, your reporter) might record an entire "voice-over" narration.

It is also a good idea to open your VNR with printed instructions that can be seen on the screen. The instructions should also be included as hard copy (printed on paper) along with a copy of the script so both may be reviewed prior to the news director popping the tape in the VCR (video cassette recorder/player). A number of tape formats are available. Stations should be surveyed to determine which video format they prefer. VNRs can cost anywhere from a few thousand dollars to more than $50,000 to produce. And there are additional fees for distribution. It is not unusual for a firm to charge $5,000 to uplink a VNR on a satellite and to notify television stations that the VNR is available to them so the station can "lift it off" or downlink it. Some stations will use CD files.

Because of the expense, it is important to determine whether the video release will be used. If stations don't buy into your pitch, VNRs are not a very sound investment.

In the case of video news releases relating to new products, TV stations must weigh the value of the news against giving the time for free. Television stations must wrestle with just how biased the presentation might be and whether to identify the "package" when it runs as "provided by XYZ Company."

According to A.C. Nielson, health and medical releases are the most frequently used VNRs. Business stories rank second, followed by political news, fashion and lifestyle, and sports.

TV news directors and news producers now face the same dilemma that print editors have faced since Ivy Lee hand-delivered his first typewritten release in the early 1900s— whether to use and how to attribute material gleaned from VNRs.

Examples of effective VNRs would be when a major children's brand of aspirin implemented the "baby-proof cap" and when a new drug, such as Viagra (male potency drug), was released. How far should the station go in identifying the manufacturer and showing its logo on the screen? That decision rests with individual stations.

Often, newspapers use quotes from printed releases without mentioning the source. In other cases, newspapers attribute the quotes to a company statement. Many major newspapers make the determination on a case-by-case basis. TV stations now must do the same.

**Before taking that first step — deciding to produce a VNR**

- Determine your goal. What do you want to communicate to the audience?
- Once you determine the goal, write down exactly what you want to say to reach the goal.
- Gather your thoughts leading to your goal. You might want to use focus groups to be sure you are developing background information and facts.
- Focus panel members might serve to provide the types of questions needed to help you reach your goal.
- As you write down the supporting points that will let you reach your goal, continually refine the facts into short sentences.

## Eight elements of an effective VNR

1. Timely
2. Newsworthy
3. Excellent quality
4. Good wrap or package that runs 40 seconds to 1:10
5. Use of B-roll
6. Extra cuts (sound bites … voice cuts … actualities with identification)
7. Super-imposition of names and titles
8. Includes script … with intros.

**One or more of the following elements could help you reach your goal as a script is prepared**

- controversy
- conflict
- competition
- consequence
- familiar persons
- humor
- heartstrings/emotion
- problems
- progress
- success
- unknown
- unusual
- wants/needs

## Tips for talking to the media

Chances are that you or a representative of your firm will never be interviewed by a major news analysis show or Oprah Winfrey. But whether it is an interview by a network correspondent, local radio talk show host, or a cable local access reporter, a number of suggestions will help:

1. Be prepared.
2. Anticipate sensitive questions.
3. Be open and honest.
4. Never say "NO COMMENT."
5. Try to avoid OFF-THE-RECORD statements. (See Section I of this chapter for more on "off the record.")
6. Think before you speak.
7. Never lose your temper.
8. Don't let a reporter put words in your mouth.
9. Don't use jargon.
10. Emphasize the benefits of your project to the community.
11. When dealing with television:
    - Talk in "sound bites" (20- to 30-second responses).
    - Think visually.
    - Dress conservatively.
      - Wear suits or dresses of soft, medium colors. Avoid sharply contrasting patterns and colors. Men should consider wearing blue dress shirts. Solid or striped ties are preferred.
      - Jewelry should be simple and uncluttered. Pearls and dull-finished metals reflect less light than sparkling and highly polished jewelry.
      - Don't worry about glasses. The studio crew will arrange lighting to avoid glare.
      - The program's director or floor manager will discuss makeup. Pancake makeup is advisable for men with heavy beards. Women should avoid heavy makeup or overuse of lipstick.
    - Be natural.
    - Forget about the camera.

## Television interview techniques

### 1. Know the facts — don't guess.

There is no such thing as a pleasant surprise on television. Get the latest information available on the subject before the interview.

### 2. Rehearse your message.

Know what you are going to say, and equally important, know how you are going to say it. But don't overrehearse and lose spontaneity.

### 3. Say it in 20 seconds.

Remember, your time within a TV news story is very valuable and very limited. Economize to maximize.

### 4. Help set the ground rules.

Journalists need help getting the story. Assist them with background, locations for good visuals and the exact content of the story.

### 5. Answer questions — stay alert — listen.

Listen to your interviewer. Don't start formulating the answer to a question that is not being asked.

### 6. Prepare for the worst — do your homework.

Don't hope that the journalist won't ask "that question." Assume it will come up and prepare for the worst case.

### 7. Admit mistakes.

No one will fault you for being honest and forthright. But follow the admission with how you have corrected the situation. Place the mistake in its proper perspective.

### 8. Relate to the viewer, not the interviewer.

Think about how the viewer will receive your information — not how the interviewer posed the question. Talk directly to the journalist, not the viewer at home. The camera will provide subjective angles.

### 9. Strive for informality.

Remove the stiffness from your presentation and let the warmth of your personality come through.

### 10. Humanize yourself.

The audience will relate to a real human being, no matter the subject matter.

### 11. Think as reporters think.

What kind of story are they after? How will they most likely tell it? How can you present it in the best possible context?

### 12. Know journalists' language.

Use their language. Don't say "film" when all that is being used today is videotape. You may be asked for a "sound bite," which is a series of short comments. "Cutaways" are visuals that support your story.

### 13. Be politely persistent, but don't get angry.

Try to always finish your statement without being constantly interrupted. Smile, be patient and allow your overall grasp of the situation to come through. Remember, you will always know more about the story than the reporter.

### 14. Localize your story.

If there is a national story that the media is airing locally, give them the local significance of that story. Many times, your efforts will be either better than the national average, or at least, have a positive impact on local citizens.

**15. Lean forward slightly – positive body language.**

Don't lean back, don't swivel and don't fidget. Look interested and professionally aggressive in your body language.

**16. Tell it like it is.**

Candid responses, when thought out, and presented in a professional, warm manner directly to the reporter, are most effective. The interviewer is your audience. The person in command of the interview is you.

**17. Stick to the subject — don't gamble.**

Don't open other situations unnecessarily. Answer questions with enough information to tell your side of the story.

**18. Dress for the occasion.**

Conservative dress and a professional image go a long way on television. Dress in solid color jackets — no plaids or distracting patterns.

**19. Keep it on a one-on-one basis.**

The interview is with one person in the audience, through the interviewer. Keep it personal and direct.

**20. Never say "no comment."**

No matter what anyone says about your right to silence, it is not golden in the media, and no comment is generally perceived as a "guilty" plea. At the very least, tell the reporter that you *can't* comment.

**21. Maintain solid eye contact.**

Don't look to heaven for guidance before answering. Remember, your facial language tells more about you than what you are saying.

**22. Avoid arguments and hostility.**

It is impossible to win an argument with a person who has the editing equipment. The old adage, "Never argue with a person who buys ink by the barrel" is very appropriate.

**23. Provide advance biographical and background data.**

If time permits, provide the correspondent with information about you as well as the story.

**24. Be direct and friendly.**

The directness of your words in those 20 seconds must be balanced by the friendliness of your delivery.

**25. Don't fold your arms.**

Avoid defensive body language. Don't look down. Most interviewers prefer you look at them when responding. The camera will follow you.

**26. Don't clench your fists.**

Remember, the camera can isolate on the various ways that you release tension. Poise yourself before the interview. Then relax and enjoy.

**27. Don't squint at the lights.**

Give yourself enough time in the studio before the interview to adjust to the set and the lighting.

**28. Suggest talking points before the interview.**

Again, help set the agenda. You know the story; reporters only know what they have been told — often, not very much. Help them to help you tell the story.

**29. Always have at least two themes going into each interview.**

Know what the interview is about and have two positive themes that relate to the subject — and get those themes out front.

**30. Anticipate questions.**

If you have done your homework on the subject, you should be able to anticipate areas of tough questions within the story and answer them in the best possible light. Work with a media pro and tape your responses to questions in a mock session.

**31. Know the reporter.**

Watch a different channel or news program every night. Get to know reporters' styles. Know their beats — politics, education, business, etc.

**32. Develop a single sentence/catchy phrase to make a point.**

Audiences have a difficult time remembering comments by interviewees, and you can help make the interview memorable by coming up with a catchy sentence.

**33. Never guess and never, never lie.**

Having to retract or alter your comments is awkward and damaging. Your comments on tape are the essence of your reputation.

**34. Advance work — do it.**

It may seem like extra work to have your staff assist you in preparing for the worst, but it is worth the effort.

**35. Arrive early for questions and pre-talk interview (warm-up) with the reporter.**

Talk about the other stories that the reporter has done (if known) and establish rapport. Establish yourself as a professional in your field early, before the interview begins.

**36. Edit yourself as you speak.**

Be concise, correct and conversational. Don't ramble.

**37. Practice talking about 150 words per minute.**

Any faster and the audience will lose you … any slower and you will sound dull or overly cautious to the audience.

**38. Use the reporter's name in an interview.**

Use sparingly, but use it in front of the statement that

you want to get on the air. It is a "point of sale" technique that we all use at the time we want that person to take notice of what we are going to say.

**39. Practice the art of bridging.**

Bridging is being able to move from a topic you do not want to deal with to one that you do.

**40. The inconsistency trap.**

Avoid spending a great deal of time on questions that ask you old data. ("That was 10 years ago … we have to look at today.")

**41. Prepare yourself mentally before the interview.**

Much like an athlete, you must be physically and mentally prepared for the television interview. This may require relaxation exercises and the mental exercise of answering questions in your mind.

**42. Above all — be yourself.**

Audiences are inundated with TV news magazines. Audiences are more sophisticated than ever. They can usually detect when someone is making an appearance to promote a personal or business interest. Audiences prefer watching someone who is being natural, not someone whose sole purpose is to impress.

### *During the interview*

#### DO

- Use first names.
- Speak to the interviewer and not to the camera.
- Stand up for your rights.
- Deliver your message early.
- Be prepared from the time you leave your office or home.
- Couch your position as necessary.
- Speak only the truth; be ready with facts.
- Be aware of and sensitive to time.
- Know what the interviewer wants.
- Be big enough to learn from your mistakes.
- Thank the interviewer and crew for their time.

#### DON'T

- Let the topic/subject drift.
- Assume anything.
- Be afraid to take a compliment (but keep your guard up).
- Consider the interviewer a friend … or an enemy.
- Gossip, criticize or speculate.
- Use YES and NO answers.
- Put the interviewer on the defensive without good cause.
- Forget the importance of body language.
- Speak too fast or too slow.
- Go into any situation without preparation.
- Be too hard on yourself.
- Ever say "NO COMMENT."
- Ask for a copy of the final interview. ■

## Tips

1. One way to gain coverage is to make your organization's experts available for interviews on entertainment and talk shows.

2. Use simple, mentally descriptive words that form pictures, give dimension and add color when writing for radio.

3. When dealing with television, talk in "sound bites" (20 to 30-second responses).

4. If you're preparing someone for a radio or television interview, anticipate the question, tape the person's responses and suggest improvements.

5. If considering a video news release, weigh the chances of its being used before investing a large chunk of money.

Name_____Date_____

_____

## Answer these questions

1. What are some ways that a news release for radio differs from one for print media?

_____

_____

_____

_____

_____

2. It's vital that you accurately time spot announcements. How many words should you include in a 30-second spot?

_____

3. Asked to offer a 30-minute "top tips" presentation on how to use television effectively, what are five key recommendations you would offer?

_____

_____

_____

_____

4. If preparing someone to go on TV, what would you suggest regarding dress, jewelry and eyeglasses?

_____

_____

_____

_____

# Chapter 7

# Using Advertising, Marketing and Lobbying in Public Relations

---

## PRaxiom
*The credibility of public relations generally outweighs that of advertising.*

---

### What this chapter covers

This chapter should help you understand how advertising, marketing and lobbying contribute to an overall public relations program. These techniques add strategic power to the aim of public relations.

Section I shows how advertising merges purposes with public relations. It also shows how unearned publicity complements the earned recognition of public relations

Section II provides marketing and lobbying information the PR practitioner can use. It explores the new integrated communication concept and delves in global marketing. For the student interested in not-for-profit organizations, the powerful lobbying function is added to the public relations toolkit.

## SECTION 1

### Advertising

Public relations practitioners must sometimes choose how, when and if to use advertising. According to Public Communications/West, a marketing communications firm, no communication plan is complete until it embraces elements of both public relations and advertising. The firm asserts that in the broadest sense, public relations conditions the market for the advertising message and reinforces the message later while contributing to image and name recognition. The advertising tends to focus on a single "buy" message.

And according to Wells, Burnett and Moriarty, this concept of integrated marketing communication (IMC) stresses the importance of reaching a company's publics by integrating its strategies and programs with public relations, marketing and advertising. So, the use of

advertising to serve public relations objectives and issues seems not only relevant, but also wise.

Many people don't know the difference between public relations and advertising. Public relations is usually thought of as unpaid, "earned" publicity. Public relations gives up control of the M-A-C triad or the message, audience and channel to garner third-party credibility from a writer or producer. Advertising allows you to control all three aspects of the M-A-C triad. But, because advertising is considered paid-for space or air, advertising lacks third-party credibility. Public relations uses the goal of changing the attitudes of the public rather than selling a brand or product line. Publicity or cost-free promotion, an important component of public relations, bears no direct media costs but is not free in the sense that someone pays the salary of the PR person, production and the media relations work it takes to gain the cooperation of gatekeepers. Types of publicity include *print*: news releases and publications; *electronic*: public service announcements (PSAs), video news releases (VNRs), films, and talk shows; and *face-to-face*: news conferences, media tours, conventions/trade shows.

During a crisis or when you encounter a particularly controversial issue, you may need to use advertising rather than public relations to get your message out in its original form. If you send a news release, an editor or producer can change the copy, altering the important message you designed. Or that editor or producer could use the release in a way that would not reach its desired audience. But using advertising allows the public relations practitioner the most control.

### Public relations versus advertising

Robert Dilenschneider and Dan Forrestal in the *Public Relations Handbook* define public relations as the use of information to influence public opinion. Advertising, on the other hand, is information from an identified sponsor

## A Word from the Experts

When asked, "What is the difference between public relations and advertising?" these experts said …

Simply stated, advertising is purchased space or time with the message controlled by the advertiser. Public relations delivers messages through various techniques and the media control what the intended target audience actually hears and sees.

*Rene Henry, Director, Office of External Affairs, Environmental Protection Agency*

Advertising is what you pay for; PR is what you pray for.

*John Elsasser, Editor, PR Tactics*

The difference between public relations and advertising is both philosophical and practical.

Public relations can be very specifically directed, while advertising, by its nature and associated costs, is intended for a broader audience. (*Exception*: An ad in the *Washington Post* on a particular issue might be, while pricey, intended primarily to reach the one senator whose vote will carry the day, and thus be more cost effective than a major national public relations campaign.)

Public relations ranges from mass media (publicity) to one-on-one relationships. Advertising is essentially publicity through mass media.

In any case, every communication is a unique experience. Audiences interpret messages individually regardless of the channel of communication. Even mass media address an audience of one.

Some blithely posit that public relations is free and advertising is paid. Public relations is free. Not quite true. Public relations does have a price tag, usually not as large as an advertising campaign, but certainly not "free."

Often the public relations message is mediated by some third party — editor, reporter, influential — while advertising is controlled — the advertiser controls content, placement, timing, size, position (but does not control the audience's reaction, which may be different from the intended reaction of either PR or gatekeeper).

Public relations seeks to understand another's point of view. Understanding implies a willingness to change and adapt to take into account the public's point of view and needs. Advertising seeks to communicate our point of view to others. If we do market research about our advertising, the feedback is intended to help us refine our message and packaging so the intended audience can accept it more readily.

For good or bad, "public relations" exists. Every organization, just because it exists and deals with people, has relationships with its publics, whether it promotes them or not, whether it knows it or not, whether it wants them or not, whether it cares about them or not. Advertising, on the other hand, is consciously created and targeted to specific publics, even if the advertising itself has unintended effects on the organization's relationships with its publics.

*John Moscatelli, Sr. Vice President Anne Klein & Associates*

using mass media to persuade or influence audiences. The two fields are closely related and good practitioners use techniques from both to produce comprehensive communication programs. Public relations and advertising differ in several important ways including:

- the level of control over the M-A-C triad
- the way they use the media
- the credibility factors mentioned previously

**Control**. If PR practitioners need to control the message, audience, channel or all three, advertising would work best. If the level of control is less important than achieving credibility through a third-party endorsement, a public relations tool or technique is the choice.

When selecting types of media, as this chapter will discuss later, keep in mind examples of *uncontrolled* versus *controlled* media. Uncontrolled media include: special events, feature articles and speeches. Controlled media include advertising, sales promotion, point-of-purchase displays, and direct mail.

**Media use**. Public relations practitioners avoid purchasing time or space and rather use media gatekeepers to carry their messages. Public relations practitioners must trust these "gatekeepers" (editors or producers who control the flow of information by deciding how much of a story, if any, to use) to maintain the intended meaning of a story. Advertisers pay for the time or space and thus maintain control over their message, audience and channel while guaranteeing access to the media.

**Credibility**. Although public relations cannot control the way gatekeepers will use the message, audience and channel, it can offer something advertising lacks — another person or organization recommending or conveying information rather than the paying, identified sponsor advertising it. Thus, the credibility of public relations generally outweighs that of advertising.

So, as a practitioner, you must decide whether control over the M-A-C triad or third-party credibility is more important and how you can best deal with media gatekeepers. Then, construct your campaign based on the most important factor.

## Types of advertising

Let's assume you, the PR practitioner, select advertising. What type of advertisement/commercial should you choose? Is the practitioner selecting advertising instead of public relations or working in concert with it? Remember, when choosing any channel or type of advertising, to consider the purpose of the communication, knowledge of the intended audience, the type of message to be delivered and the available resources. The following list describes some of the most common types of advertising.

**Brand**. The name or symbol used to identify a product or service and distinguish it from the competition is a brand. Brand advertising uses that name or symbol to sell a product or service. For example, a company like Nike has only to use the Nike swoop and consumers readily identify the company.

According to *pr reporter*, a brand is a relationship between an organization and its customer defined by word-of-mouth interaction. But, *pr reporter* also indicates that many brands fail to make a promise and deliver it. The value of a brand, according to Jeff Bezos, founder of the Internet bookstore, is as a time saver. Brands save consumers the time and effort of evaluating every entry in a category. (See the section on marketing later in this chapter.)

## Brand slogans and phrases

Many brands use distinctive slogans or memorable phrases to help potential target markets remember their product or service. Can you identify the following companies from their slogans? (*Figure 7.1*)

### Brand and Slogan Quiz

| | | | |
|---|---|---|---|
| 1. | Like a good neighbor | a. | Busch |
| 2. | Head for the mountains | b. | Wheaties |
| 3. | Good to the last drop | c. | State Farm |
| 4. | Melts in your mouth, not in your hands | d. | New York Times |
| 5. | Breakfast of champions | e. | United Airlines |
| 6. | We bring good things to life | f. | Maxwell House |
| 7. | All the news that's fit to print | g. | AT&T |
| 8. | We'll leave the lights on for you | h. | General Electric |
| 9. | Fly the friendly skies | i. | M&Ms |
| 10. | Reach out and touch someone | j. | Motel 6 |

**Figure 7.1**

Answers: 1-c, 2-a, 3-f, 4-i, 5-b, 6-h, 7-d, 8-j, 9-e, 10-g

**Retail**. This type of advertising or sales promotion primarily gets customers into a store. Retailers commonly use local newspapers to entice consumers to come in to their stores because of featured price cuts. These "loss leaders," or products so significantly on sale that the retailer loses profit, draw consumers in to purchase other goods in the store.

**Directory**. Yellow pages or directory advertising can create widespread awareness and use. Research shows that nearly all adults (90 percent) refer to the Yellow Pages in the course of a year.

**Political**. Politicians use political advertising to persuade people to vote for them. Because this form of speech is protected by the First Amendment, it is exempt from the many restrictions other advertising must follow.

**Institutional**. Also called corporate or *image advertising*, these ads try to establish a corporate identity or image. Instead of having a specific product or service orientation, institutional advertising like General Electric's "We bring good things to life," or Kodak's "Times of your life" campaigns emphasize an institution's strengths and desired image.

**Business-to-business**. This type of advertising usually appears in what advertisers call trade journals or the trade press. It features messages from one business to another, like a software company selling its services to accountants, physicians, insurance companies, etc. in their respective journals. Sometimes business-to-business advertising is directed at retailers, wholesalers and distributors.

One of your most basic decisions for trade press advertising may be whether to concentrate on *horizontal* or *vertical* publications. Horizontals reach a broad cross section of your market. Verticals are more narrowly focused: you get a more targeted readership, but it can be more costly if you need to advertise in a number of vertical publications.

Another decision you might face in print media: *Is lead production important to your sales force?* Leads generated from reader response cards are highly valued in some markets. In high cost capital equipment markets, for example, buyers may enter the market just once in five years. Ad leads can help alert the sales force to active buyers. Choosing publications that generate more leads would work in such a case.

Lead management turns reader, listener or viewer responses into leads for your sales force to follow up. It usually includes fulfillment of prospects' requests for sales literature. The system should also include a mechanism for sales people to provide feedback on lead quality and results. You will need to generate reports and analysis of advertising and PR campaign results.

Your analysis should include some measure of the effectiveness of various media, such as *cost per lead*. You should develop a prospect and customer database and, where possible, follow your campaign results through to product or service quotations (bids) and sales.

Service bureaus and software packages can assist with lead management. Effective lead management is an essential part of marketing communications that is too often overlooked. It requires resources (people and money), effort and continuing attention. In some markets, leads can provide fast, tangible evidence of the effectiveness of your communication efforts, as well as contribute directly to your company's sales.

**Direct marketing**. This type of advertising tries to stimulate a direct sale. It makes use of many media, including direct mail and catalogs to solicit immediate customer response by mail or telephone. The product is then delivered directly to the consumer.

## Public relations advertising

The aforementioned types of advertising come to mind when most people think of "traditional" advertising. However, because public relations practitioners often deal with issues like advocacy, image, persuasion and public information, they tend to use certain types of advertising

more frequently. Remember that when public relations uses paid-for media, the purpose is not to sell a product or service, but usually to feature an image or to evoke behavior other than buying.

Practitioners list many reasons for using advertising in public relations programs and campaigns. Some include:

• Develop awareness of an organization and its activities
• Tie a diverse product line together
• Improve consumer relations
• Improve the organization's image
• Take a stand on a public issue

The following section discusses types of public relations advertising commonly used by PR practitioners.

**Advocacy/Issue.** This type of advertising relates closely to public relations because it seeks to change public opinion concerning an issue or organization. Advocacy advertising portrays an image of the company or organization in an indirect manner by adopting a position on a particular issue rather than by promoting the organization or company itself.

Advocacy advertising also communicates views on issues that affect a company's business, promotes the organization's philosophy or makes a political or social statement. Organizations use advocacy advertising for different reasons. Sometimes they use it to counteract public hostility to corporate activities that result from misinformation or to counter misleading information spread by critics of the organization. An advocacy ad might feature the benefits of nuclear energy or for a group of animal activists seeking a change in laws about animal experimentation.

**House ad**. An organization prepares an ad for use in its own publication or a publication over which it exerts some control. No money changes hands. For example, a television station runs a house ad announcing its new fall programming. Because the public relations function usually controls publications, this type of advertising falls under public relations advertising.

**Cooperative ad**. This type of advertising allows a manufacturer to share costs with a retailer, thus saving money because local advertising rates are less expensive than national rates. Cooperative advertising also allows two organizations to "tie in" with one another. For example, Midas Muffler co-sponsored with the Better Hearing Institute to advertise a special event promoting good hearing. Midas benefited from positive public opinion and the Better Hearing Institute enjoyed lower advertising costs.

**Cause-related marketing or sponsorship**. This

technique offers an alternative to advertising in traditional media by allowing an organization to sponsor an event or programming. Sponsorship can reach a wide audience and create brand or corporate name awareness. For example, Virginia Slims once sponsored women's tennis — now Advanta (an insurance company) is seen as a better fit for a sport. Federal Express sponsors a college bowl.

Television sponsorship can have a powerful impact on viewers because of the control the advertiser exerts on not only the placement of commercials, but also on the content of the program. Often several advertisers sponsor a program together, for example, a sporting event.

Cause-related marketing comprises sponsorship, product placement and percentage of profits as techniques. Sponsorship is the most common, although **product placement** on television programming has become a phenomenon in the last few years. A famous "Friends" episode was based on a Pottery Barn catalog.

Paul Newman offers consumers the opportunity to preserve the rain forests by donating a **percentage of profits** from sales of his products to conservationists.

Many companies/organizations who make controversial products like cigarettes or products with possible unsafe byproducts like chemical companies use cause-related marketing to create a more positive image for their organization.

**Institutional**. As discussed previously, corporate or institutional advertising concerns the image of an organization and thus focuses on public opinion formation or change. Commercials like the U.S. Army's "Be all that you can be" feature the benefits someone can derive from a career in the Army. According to *Public Relations Journal*, institutional ads should improve consumer relations, improve community and employee relations as well as enhance organizational image and reputation.

An Association of National Advertisers survey showed that institutional advertising is used to build recognition, especially for organizations that need "umbrella identification" for broadened and diversified lines.

*Figure 7.2 is an institutional ad designed to promote a humane animal zoo.*

**Public service announcement**. Recalling Grunig's public information model, you'll value how public service announcements can disseminate public information. These announcements require no fee to air or print, and many times agencies will produce PSAs on a *pro bono* (for the public good) basis, eliminating all charges for a nonprofit organization.

Unfortunately, because media space and time are donated, much of this advertising is aired at 3 a.m. One of

---

Imagine being born in a traveling circus. You couldn't be happier — shows, clowns, kids and peanuts!

Then, you're suddenly on the side of a road. The circus truck is gone. It's hot. You're lost, without peanuts.

You are a bear cub. The police found you and brought you to a new home with friends, visitors and peanuts!

Come visit me at ...

# PEANUTS PARK ZOO

Rescuing abused and orphaned animals

Aurora, Pennsylvania

Three miles past the dormant volcano on Orsinus Highway

We have a bear cub and peanuts!

www.peanuts.org
215-555-1234

**Figure 7.2**

This ad promotes a humane animal zoo. The ad copywriter places the reader in the zoo — as one of the "residents"! It appeals to the sympathy of potential visitors by first asking the reader to seek visitors for the lonely, then switches to ask readers to become the visitors.

the most successful campaigns of all time, Smokey Bear and prevention of forest fires, is said to have saved lives and property by educating people on fire prevention. Likewise, seat belt dummies increased seat belt usage and thus saved lives.

If a practitioner doesn't find a specific agency to produce the advertisement, the Advertising Council, a private nonprofit organization, conducts public service advertising campaigns in the public interest. The Council receives approximately 400 requests from private organizations and government agencies annually requesting campaign support.

**Infomercial/Advertorial.** In theory, infomercials are *informational videos* sponsored by branded products and services. Infomercials have proven successful and 30- to 60-minute segments provide ample opportunity to demonstrate even complex topics.

However, infomercials lack the guidelines and regulations that limit more traditional advertising. Some even call infomercials misleading or deceptive. If viewers leave the room and miss the disclaimer, they might think the commercial is a regular program.

In many cases, managers of vacation destinations and marketers of exercise equipment, among others, mail infomercials directly to prospective customers. These infomercials have been extremely successful. Consumers who receive infomercials by mail tend to pay more attention to them than they do to television infomercials. They sometimes pass the tapes on to their friends, thus furthering the reach of the infomercial.

**Advertorials are considered cost-effective promotions** using a print format that works much like infomercials. Advertorials allow advertisers to place a sales message in an editorial-like context. But they must use the word "advertisement" on the page, even though the *text is made to look like the other editorial content of the magazine.*

Once you evaluate how to use advertising for public relations purposes, you must develop an advertising campaign.

## DEVELOPING AN ADVERTISING CAMPAIGN

Prior to developing a campaign, most advertisers design a plan comprising a situation analysis, a creative plan, a media plan, a sales promotion plan (optional), evaluation tools and a budget.

### The situation analysis

Similar to the situation analysis used by public relations practitioners, this evaluation of the circumstances surrounding the campaign helps advertisers focus messages in a targeted way. Practitioners and advertisers should consider the following factors in a situation analysis: the advertising problem; a profile of the "consumer" of the advertisement or campaign; industry trends; an analysis of the product or issue; a look at the competitive environment and a **Strengths-Weaknesses-Opportunities-Threats (SWOT) analysis.**

If the campaign were to convince the community surrounding a nuclear power plant that nuclear energy is safe and clean, the *advertising problem* could be lack of information or widespread community fear.

• A *profile of the target audience* would specify demographics, psychographics and lifestyle factors of community members.

• The *industry trends* section might discuss other energy sources and depletion of natural resources.

• The *analysis of the product* or *issue* would look at community relations in similar cases, and scientific findings on the safety of nuclear energy and its byproducts.

• The *competitive environment* section would look at other energy providers, their safety and efficiency records.

• And the *SWOT analysis* would list all the strengths and weaknesses of nuclear energy of that particular power plant; opportunities for persuasion of the target audience and general acceptance of nuclear energy; and reveal threats to both the industry and this particular power plant.

A situation analysis should also include *advertising objectives*, a concise description of the *target audience*, a *Unique Selling Proposition* (USP) and any information on *product positioning*.

For example, the American Red Cross needs blood donation, particularly in summer months. A public relations practitioner decides to use advertising to inform audiences of the benefits the organization offers other than blood and to persuade them to give back to the organization. The *advertising objective* might read, *"Establish a new image for The American Red Cross as an organization that provides worldwide relief and rescue."* Another objective might read, *"Persuade target audiences to give blood to The American Red Cross as a thank you for its worldwide relief efforts."* Research would pinpoint demographics and motivators of the *target audience*.

The USP in advertising relates to the **Unique Persuasive Proposition of UPP in public relations.** Either could be used here. The USP for The American Red Cross might be identifying the organization as the one group of people on-site at disasters to provide immediate relief, regardless of political philosophy. Usually the USP differentiates the product or organization from similar ones. One of the most famous product USPs of all time, created by Rosser Reeves for Doublemint Gum, is "Double your pleasure, Double your fun, Doublemint, Doublemint, Doublemint Gum."

And finally, an activity, in this case organ donation, could be *positioned* as life giving through images associated with birth. Organ donor day is life day—is a birthday (*Figure 7.3*).

## You're invited to a birthday party.

## Sign an organ donor card.

## You'll be there when someone lives again.

**Figure 7.3**

This ad uses positioning to increase the number of organ donor signature cards. It asks potential donors to equate signing a card with a happy celebration.

When positioning a product, advertisers consider the **product's life cycle.**

• For example, in the *introductory stage* of a product, where little competition exists, advertisers might position the product as *the leader in a category*.

• If the product is in the *competitive stage*, advertisers might position the product in relation to a more established competitor as Avis positioned itself as #2, right after Hertz.

• If the product faces the *mature stage* of the life cycle, often marketers create "line extensions" to keep sales up. When Cheerios matured in terms of the life cycle, marketers created line extensions — Multi-Grain Cheerios, Honey Nut Cheerios and Team Cheerios to extend the product line and product life.

• In the *decline stage* of the product life cycle, products become obsolete and advertising becomes ineffective from a cost and practical standpoint. A product in decline would be the phone-only cell phone. Why advertise a product with little or no consumer demand?

After they complete the situation analysis, advertisers formulate a **creative plan**. Creative people, whether in an organization or an agency, develop a list of features and benefits to stimulate creative thinking. Such a list focuses on the target audience, its preferences and motivators.

## Features or benefits?

In public relations, practitioners ask themselves if they're addressing a passive or active audience and adjust the use of features or benefits. Remember that active audiences need features, not benefits, but passive audiences need a reason to pay attention (benefits).

Using Figure 7.4, try creating a feature or a benefit for the following products using the examples:

## The creative plan

After completing the situation analysis, the creative team should prepare **copy platforms** for the client. Copy platforms provide a theme or approach to an ad. These platforms also allow the practitioner and client to agree

### Two Views of Products

| Product | Feature | Benefit |
|---------|---------|---------|
| bar soap | moisturizer | keeps skin soft |
| | 1. deodorant | ? |
| | 2. ? | attracts the opposite sex |
| pen | 3. washable ink | ? |
| | 4. ? | makes you look prosperous |
| television | 5. remote control | ? |
| | 6. ? | life-size viewing |

**Figure 7.4**

Possible answers:
1. evokes a pleasant smell
2. perfume
3. won't stain
4. high price
5. won't have to leave your seat
6. large screen

that the copy approach will accomplish the advertising objective. According to William Arens in *Contemporary Advertising*, good copywriters follow the copywriter's pyramid to develop a "big idea" that gives the advertisement life:

| | |
|---|---|
| **Attention** | Arouse target audience attention |
| **Interest** | Excite the audience |
| **Credibility** | Give proof of claims |
| **Desire** | Satisfy the audience's needs |
| **Action** | Motivate the audience to act |

The creative plan looks at the following ad components for design and development of a completed advertisement.

### Basic ad components

When you design an ad, consider the following: Keep your message simple, speak directly to your publics or audiences, and know the target market for your message.

The following elements of a print advertisement will help you develop your creative approach. The **headline** should grab readers' attention early and entice the reader into the body copy of the ad. According to advertisers, the headline, which usually appears in large type, has four seconds to catch the reader's attention.

Common types of headlines include:

• Benefit
• News/informative
• Provocative
• Question
• Command

Sometimes advertisers use an **overline** or an **underline** to accomplish this task. An overline appears over the headline and an underline appears under the headline. In a Taster's Choice ad (*Figure 7.5*), the overline reads, "The dilemma … ," while the headline reads, "Andrew or Michael?" The underline reads, "It's your choice!" This print advertisement refers to an ongoing soap-opera-like campaign, where a woman who drinks Taster's Choice must choose between her estranged husband and her next door neighbor (both drink Taster's Choice, of course).

The overline is used to draw the reader into the headline and the underline is used to draw the reader into the body copy. Advertisers use both direct and indirect headlines. The previous example was indirect — a more direct headline for the same product might read, "Drink Taster's Choice To Improve Your Romantic Life." A direct headline is straightforward and informative but may not lure the target audience into the body copy. An indirect headline should compel the audience to read on, but provides less information.

**Figure 7.5**
*Taster's Choice* cleverly asks readers to think of coffee as a deliberate choice — as important as sex!

Write the **copy** or main textblock at a level your target market will understand. It should build on the headline, promise, reward or benefit. The copy should heighten your reader's interest and desire; it should also offer proof in the form of facts and testimony. Perhaps most importantly, the copy should encourage your reader to take some type of action.

The **illustration** or artwork should relate closely to the headline and the copy, attract the reader's attention and appeal to their emotions. Many times, creative directors use photography rather than an illustration. Creative directors recommend the use of two-thirds artwork to one-third copy for maximum effectiveness.

The logo should convey the image of the sponsoring organization and should always include an address and phone number. Often a slogan or tagline accompanies the logo. Use devices for memorability. A **slogan** is repeated from ad to ad. A **tagline** wraps up the idea at the end of a particular ad.

According to Sandra E. Moriarty in her text *Creative Advertising*, these checklist items help practitioners write effective copy:

• Use pictures and words together to create impact.

- Write to someone you know who represents the target audience.
- Make it conversational.
- Use short, succinct statements.
- Use short paragraphs.
- Personalize the copy by using the word "you."
- Avoid the word "we."
- Try not to sound preachy.

Visual relief or the use of **white space** directs the eye of the reader, provides separation from adjoining messages and relieves a cluttered feeling that could make the ad difficult to read.

Properly designed, the **layout** of an ad can both attract attention and hold interest. The layout also organizes the elements of the ad and unifies them.

### Commercial components

When preparing an electronic ad or **commercial**, most advertisers use **storyboards** or **thumbnail sketches** to design the advertisement. In both television and radio, you must consider the **time allocation** of 10 seconds, 20 seconds, 30 seconds or less commonly, 60 seconds. Consider the time needed to capture the audience's attention, develop the theme, support the theme, and call for a specific responsive action.

In television commercials, advertisers consider the use of action and motion. The three-dimensional aspect of television advertising often makes it more compelling than print. The elements of television advertising include video, audio, talent, props, setting, lighting, graphics and pacing.

**Video** dominates the message in television and copywriters make use of visuals to convey messages. The **audio** dimensions of both television and radio advertising are similar, using music, voices and sound effects. **Talent** refers to the people in the commercials. They might be announcers, spokespersons, fictional characters or celebrities. **Props** usually refer to the product and a **setting** is where the action happens. **Lighting** can have an impact on the setting by creating moods — romantic, surreal, etc. And **graphics** are generated on the screen by a computer (usually words or still photos). **Pacing** refers to the speed of the action in the commercial.

In summary, the creative plan often makes or breaks the success of the advertising campaign. The strength of the creative effort affects the results of the persuasion. When a campaign causes behavioral change, most practitioners would consider it a success.

### The media plan

Once you have constructed the situation analysis and the creative plan, evaluate which other marketing, advertising and media planning factors to consider.

• Important marketing factors include *pricing*, *regulations* and *segmentation*.

• Important advertising factors to study include *budgeting*, *media usage*, *message design* and *target audience analysis*.

• Then the media planning occurs, considering factors such as *competitive spending, geographic distribution* (local, regional, national), *media mix* (channels or options), *seasonality*, and *timing*.

Usually practitioners, having examined these many factors, develop specific advertising objectives if not already identified in the situation

> *When a campaign causes behavioral change, most practitioners consider it successful.*

analysis. Is the purpose of the advertisement to address a crisis, to build awareness of date rape or seat belt safety? Or to attract blood donors for the summer months of scarcity? To convince audiences that eating meat is still safe? To establish a better corporate image? To gain votes for an upcoming election?

Once you formulate an objective and analyze the competition and budget, look at factors such as geography, seasonality and purchase cycle. Some issues might apply more in certain areas than others; for example, skin cancer is less prevalent in Alaska than Florida.

Advertisers must also consider seasonal timing, holiday timing, day-of-the-week timing and hour-of-the-day timing. Snow shovels don't sell well in July in the southeast. Likewise, holidays sometimes provide good opportunities for advertisers, but often the airwaves and print media are crowded with other competitors. Knowing the purchase cycle of a product helps advertisers schedule their advertising. Retail advertisers tend to run sale advertisements to bring customers in on slow days in the store. If weekends are busy, they schedule a mid-week sale. Burger King took advantage of the hour-of-the-day timing concept when it aired its, "Aren't you hungry?" campaign from 10 -11:30 p.m. to late night eaters.

### Media channels

Knowing an audience helps to identify which media channel to select. Advertisers often consider the concept of *aperture* — when, where and in what conditions the target audience will be most receptive to the message. If practitioners can determine the aperture, selecting the right media channel becomes easier. The advertiser must also consider how many people to reach in the target audience, how often to reach them and how much it will cost. Three key terms explain this process.

First, the concept of **reach**. Reach is the percentage of unduplicated audience members exposed to a media vehicle at least once during a period of time. In simpler terms, reach is how many target audience members a medium reaches. *Frequency* is the number of times an audience has an opportunity to be exposed to a media vehicle in a specified time span. Advertisers debate the frequency necessary for audiences to remember the message versus overexposing them, causing *wearout*. *Cost Per Thousand* (CPM) means the cost of exposing each 1,000 members of the target audience to the message. For example, direct mail is costly but may have a low CPM because of its highly segmented, smaller audience. Many advertisers measure the value of the advertisement in terms of CPM.

> *Frequency is the number of times an audience can be exposed to a media vehicle in a time span.*

Now, let's look at media options, starting with the medium many proclaim as the most credible, persuasive and intrusive — television.

**Television.** The major advantages to using television are its reach and the fact that it involves several senses producing a high impact on viewers. If the advertiser needs to reach a large number of people in the target market to create brand awareness or to get a message out, television advertising works. The use of sight and sound with the benefit of color and a moving image increases the impact of the commercial.

Disadvantages might involve *cost*, both production and air time, *zapping* (changing channels during commercials) and *zipping* (fast forwarding through commercials). Not only is it expensive to produce commercials, but a standard 30-second commercial can cost millions of dollars when aired during the Superbowl.

Another problem with television advertising, in particular, is low recall caused by "vampire creativity" — when the commercial is extremely creative, but no one remembers the specific product or service. Many viewers might mention the commercial to their friends, but won't remember the most important aspect to the advertiser — the product or service name.

You can choose from the following types of television ads:

- *sponsorship* – the advertiser buys the program content as well as the advertisements
- *co-sponsorship* – the organization works with another company to co-sponsor a program
- *participation* – several advertisers buy air time during a program (could be national or local)
- *spot announcements* – local affiliates sell to advertisers who want to show their ads locally during breaks between programs.

Formats for television and radio advertising are similar and include:

- *straight announcement* – one person delivers a message, also known as the lecture format
- *testimonial* – presented by a satisfied user (advertising regulations insist that the person providing the testimonial, celebrity or layperson must have used the product/service. *Example*: Arnold Palmer, the golfer, testifies to the benefits of Pennzoil, must have tried the product himself.
- *demonstration* – relevant to the message
- *slice of life* – a real-life situation similar to a photograph that preserves that moment in time
- *drama* – a series of related commercials like Taster's Choice coffee, which feature a soap-opera-like plot
- *animation* – uses cartoons, puppets, etc.
- *musical* – features jingles or music as a major component

To summarize, consider television if you want to reach a large audience, but remember, you can't present detailed information in 30 seconds. If national television is too expensive, local or cable television can provide more cost-effective alternatives.

**Radio.** While television commercials are costly, radio commercials are *relatively inexpensive*. Radio also provides a *segmented audience* for advertisers. Most radio stations feature specific demographics allowing advertisers to select just the right target audience. The disadvantages of radio include the lack of visuals, zapping and competition with other distractions, like driving. Some all-news radio stations have costly drive-time rates compared to less popular, more segmented stations. Radio makes use of the formats mentioned earlier for television.

Research shows that approximately 96% of the U.S. population listens to the radio each week. Because listeners are often busy doing other things, radio commercials must grab their attention quickly within five to eight seconds. Copywriters note that a 10-second ad uses about 25 words while a 30-second ad uses 75 words.

**Newspapers.** At least two thirds of all Americans read the newspaper. So many advertisers, especially local retailers, select newspaper advertising. Newspapers, like television, reach a mass audience but offer geographic selectivity. Newspapers provide a timely and credible format for advertisers. Advertisements in newspapers tend to be inexpensive, except for national newspapers like

*The Wall Street Journal* and *USA Today*. Most national papers offer regional editions, thus cutting the price for advertisers.

Disadvantages of newspaper advertising include difficulty in targeting specific audiences, short life span and lack of sound.

**Magazine**s. Magazines offer *highly segmented audiences* for advertisers. They provide detailed information about a product or service. Many business-to-business advertisers choose magazines as the medium of choice so they can explain the features or benefits of their product. In a 30-second electronic ad, the advertiser can't present detailed information of any kind. Magazines have a long shelf life as readers often refer back to articles and advertisements for information.

Magazines have two major disadvantages: cost and timeliness. Many trade journals and national magazines charge high prices for an insertion, particularly in color or for a prime position.

When buying magazine space, publishers base prices on circulation. To receive a preferred position like the back cover or inside front cover, advertisers must pay extra and frequently must advertise in each issue to retain their spot. Magazines, like newspapers, often have regional editions like *Time* or *Business Week*, so smaller advertisers can afford to purchase ads.

Often, media buyers consider the advantages of *vertical* versus *horizontal* publications. A vertical magazine reaches all levels of employees within an industry. *Steel Magazine* goes to all employees in that industry, from management to welder. Horizontal publications focus on a particular employee position within an industry like a human resources manager or systems analyst.

**Outdoor**. Outdoor advertising often *reinforces a primary medium* like television or magazines. Cigarette manufacturers usually select magazines as their primary medium and billboards or outdoor advertising as the reinforcing medium.

Billboards, strategically placed on busy highways, reach a *captive commuter audience* who drive across the same bridge or on the same road each day. Outdoor advertising thus offers good reach but is limited in terms of length of message. Most advertising experts recommend you use seven words or fewer on a billboard so commuters can easily read the message as they drive by. Moving billboards, like those in Times Square or on some casinos, are called *spectaculars*.

So, outdoor advertising offers reach, but a limited message opportunity.

> **Use seven words or fewer on a billboard so drivers can capture the message.**

**Transit**. Transit advertising provides another opportunity to reach a captive audience. These ads usually appear on car cards on buses and taxis and in trains and subways. A large audience can view transit advertising inexpensively. Like outdoor advertising, long messages won't work and a simple visual sometimes drives home the point.

The only disadvantages are wearout (if the ad is seen so often it offends) and the graffiti that sometimes accompanies the car cards, cheapening the appearance of the ad.

**Direct mail**. This type of advertising is perhaps the most segmented and thus advertisers can target highly specific prospects. Advertisers can easily track respondents to direct mail, and because of segmentation, may reap a high response rate.

The major disadvantage to direct mail is high production cost. Often, consumers view direct mail as *junk mail* and then a high-cost print piece becomes unread trash.

Carefully consider lists you purchase. Lists of people who have bought by mail are almost always more effective than compiled lists. (See the marketing section of this chapter for more information.)

**Specialty**. The best place to find specialty advertising is a trade show or convention, where merchandise carrying names or logos of advertisers abound. Each year, advertisers struggle to come up with something innovative on which to place their clients' names. Post-it notes and coffee mugs were the rage for a while. Now many companies offer mouse pads and computer-related paraphernalia.

The advantage to specialty advertising is related to how often target audience members *use* it. For example, you use a logo mug every day; you see the advertiser's logo and message several times a day. The disadvantage is cost. Some specialty items can be prohibitive to purchase, even in large quantities.

**POP displays**. As mentioned earlier, *point-of-purchase displays* provide an opportunity for advertisers to display a message at the point of purchase. For example, a computer store. Advertisers design placards to draw a consumer to a piece of hardware or software much as the products on the end of an aisle attract grocery shoppers who never intended to purchase the product that day.

Such sales promotion advertising advantageously appears on-site at the location where the target audience buys. The disadvantage is that retailers don't always display point-of-purchase materials as they were designed, if at all.

## Going Global

Remember to consider that international audiences can complicate advertising messages. According to Michael D. Kinsman, professor at Pepperdine University, here's what happens when practitioners forget the impact of other cultures.

The Dairy Association's huge success with the campaign "Got Milk?" prompted them to expand advertising to Mexico. Unfortunately, the Spanish translation read, "Are you lactating?"

Coors also put its slogan, "Turn it loose," into Spanish, where it was read as "Suffer from diarrhea."

Clairol introduced the "Mist Stick," a curling iron, into Germany only to find out that "mist" is slang for manure. Not too many Germans wanted the "manure stick."

Colgate introduced a toothpaste in France called Cue, the name of a porno magazine.

An American T-shirt maker in Miami printed shirts for the Spanish market promoting the pope's visit. Instead of "I saw the pope" (el Papa), the shirts read, "I saw the potato" (la papa).

Pepsi's "Come alive with the Pepsi Generation" translated into "Pepsi brings your ancestors back from the grave," in Chinese.

Frank Perdue's chicken slogan, "It takes a strong man to make a tender chicken," was translated into Spanish as, "It takes an aroused man to make a chicken affectionate."

And lastly, when American Airlines wanted to advertise its new leather first class seats in the Mexican market, it translated its "Fly in leather" campaign literally, which meant "Fly naked" (*vuela en cuero*).

**Global media**. Satellites have enhanced the ability of global advertisers to use television to reach people across borders. Now newspapers and magazines are quickly moving to capitalize on new international audiences. The *International Herald-Tribune*, a joint venture of *The New York Times* and *The Washington Post* companies, is designed specifically for the international market. *Reader's Digest* produces 48 editions in 19 languages. And the Internet offers an unregulated medium for online transactions. *The Underground Music Archive* has successfully tapped the international advertising value of the Web with at least 30 percent of music sales coming from outside the United States.

An advantage of advertising globally includes solid opportunity to reach new target audiences. The disadvantage is the need to recognize and adjust to *cultural differences and government restrictions*.

## Gaining attention
### Cows along the highway

In recent years, with the proliferation of advertising messages bombarding the public, advertisers have turned to innovative and unique solutions to the problem of clutter. Cows along the highway now wear "coats" that advertise products. Many golfers reaching to pull their ball out of the hole on the green notice an ad at the bottom of the cup. Some grocery carts have screens that "talk" to shoppers about products and sales as they walk through the store. As consumers become less aroused by advertising, advertisers take more drastic measures to gain their attention.

### Innovative advertising

Maxwell House uses the same slogan today that it developed in the 1960s — "good to the last drop." Some advertising however, has changed substantially. *The Wall Street Journal* tracks advertising trends and indicates new types of advertising.

According to *The Wall Street Journal*, NYC is now offering a 20-year contract to outdoor advertisers to include new bus-stop shelters, public toilets, newsstands, trashcans and information kiosks. Referred to as "**street-furniture advertising**," the city may gain as much as $300 million over the 20 years. The winning bidder will install, operate and maintain at least 3,300 bus shelters, 20 public toilets, 330 newsstands, as well as trash cans and information kiosks.

### Content or ad?

According to a Starcom Entertainment senior vice president, we're going to see more advertisers getting closer to entertainment content with their advertising. *situ-mercials* or situational commercials are designed to play off the shows consumers watch. Geico, an insurance company, has successfully run a situ-mercial of what looks like a scene from a crime drama on court shows and dramas like *Law and Order*.

Proctor and Gamble now buys all the advertising time for Lifetime's Friday night movies and creates two-minute spots featuring women with makeovers using Proctor and Gamble products.

Similarly, like an informercial, the BingoTV channel lets players win prizes during a live two-hour broadcast. Rather than airing 30-second spots, the hosts deliver ad pitches about prizes viewers compete for.

### New tie-ins

Advertisers hitch a ride on a mission to Mars — as advertisers link their products to space exploration. Spirit Airlines ran a newspaper ad that read, "Spirit to Mars? Sure, but our fares are $1.2 million less." When the rovers went to Mars in January 2004, Volkswagen's Audi ran an ad stating, "Mars rover still stuck. Quattro all-wheel drive. You never know when you'll need it."

### Video game advertising

Madison Avenue wants a piece of the video game industry. According to Young and Rubicam, families rarely gather together in front of the electronic hearth. *The Wall Street Journal* notes that you can't market to the 18-24 year-old age group today without using gaming in the media mix. Advertising agencies are opening gaming divisions to preserve their status as middlemen.

### Guerrilla and viral marketing

A clever nontraditional type of advertising uses street theater or *brand evangelists* to spread the word about a product. In fact, Miami-based Crispin Porter and Bogusky LLC works with the Miami Ad School to develop new courses with areas of focus in guerrilla marketing (consisting of both street theater and improvisation) as well as viral marketing (promotion spread via word-of-mouth or forwarded e-mail).

The founder of the Miami Ad School, Ron Selchrist, notes that advertising is not just about TV spots — only a handful of schools are looking at marketplace changes and doing something about them. According to Selchrist, today's marketing-savvy consumers are put off by traditional preachy ads that merely recite claims. And marketers are pressuring ad agencies to look beyond 30-second ads as consumers spend less and less time around the electronic hearth.

According to *The Wall Street Journal*, more than 9 million have visited the Subservient Chicken Web site, a viral marketing campaign for Burger King. Visitors to the site type in commands that a man in a chicken suit follows. Links at the bottom of the page promote Burger King's chicken meals.

### Webisodes

Internet advertising features a webisode starring Jerry Seinfeld and Superman. American Express has unveiled this four-minute webisode to find new customers and engage them longer. According to Interpublic Group's Universal McCann, 10-18% of consumer media time is spent on the Web. American Express has taken the best from traditional advertising (celebrities, cartoon icons and humor) and adapted it for the Web.

### Internet versus traditional advertising

The category of new electronic media has expanded rapidly in the last few years. According to Bergh and Katz, all 100 top advertisers have at least several Web sites. Unlike traditional electronic media, online consumers control the ad messages they view. Because of this interactivity, ads must inform and attract attention — much like print advertising. The growth of the World Wide Web is occurring faster than our ability to measure exactly who views its advertising messages. Most futurists predict that interactive and innovative media will increasingly cut into traditional media usage time.

Trends seem to indicate that traditional advertising is still valid, but not sufficient in itself to reach the sophisticated ad-inundated consumer.

## Scheduling the media

Advertising budgets play an important role in media planning and buying decisions. Media planners must determine the best use of reach and frequency and then select a scheduling pattern. Most advertisers use one of three basic patterns: continuity, pulse and flighting. *Continuity* spreads the advertising out continuously throughout the campaign. *Pulsing* is continuous but uneven — first a lower level of advertising is scheduled, followed by a pulse or burst of activity. *Flighting* alternates intense advertising with a hiatus or no advertising. Advertisers hope that a carry-over effect of past advertising will work during the hiatus. This carry-over effect is known as the *sleeper effect.*

Most practitioners will choose a primary and a secondary medium. Often the secondary medium serves as *reminder advertising.* Media planning establishes how the media can best disseminate the advertiser's message. Media planners devise a schedule of different channels to determine how many of the target audience will be exposed to the messages in a given time period and how frequently. After receiving approval for the media plan, media buyers then execute it. Advertisers note the demand for good media negotiators for both agencies and companies.

## Evaluation tools

When evaluating the success of any campaign, consider ongoing monitoring and postmortems.

Monitoring makes it possible to change direction, reallocate resources or redefine priorities to reach the advertising objectives initially devised. For example, perhaps the advocacy ads in one medium work well, but are failing miserably in another. Practitioners should redirect resources or dollars to the preferred medium.

Most postmortems require formal research to uncover

evidence that advertising objectives were or were not achieved. Practitioners generally evaluate the impact of the campaign on public opinion, the effect on the organization's mission or image, and the effect on the attitudes of key publics toward the organization.

Advertising uses **recall tests** (members of the target audience are asked what they remember about specific ads) and **recognition tests** (members of the target audience are shown an ad and then asked if they remember it) to gauge advertising effectiveness. Advertisers also use **persuasion**

> *The best measure of effectiveness for public relations advertising is behavioral change.*

**tests** because they evaluate the effectiveness of the advertising by measuring consumers' intentions or attitude change. The best measure of effectiveness for public relations advertising is **behavioral change**. Since some common objectives of practitioners include informing publics, trying to change the attitudes of certain publics or stimulating an audience to act, measuring persuasion provides a reliable measure of success.

## Budgeting

The budget has an impact on both creative and media plans. A $50,000 sum will stretch only so far and can prohibit network television advertising. Budget levels determine the reach and frequency of a campaign. Some practitioners employ the task-objective method of budgeting. This method looks at the set objectives and determines the cost of accomplishing each of them. According to Wells, Burnett and Moriarty, practitioners calculate the cost to make 50 percent of the people in the target audience aware of the product, issue or message to determine the right budget.

Once you complete the entire advertising plan, comprising a situation analysis, creative plan, media plan, evaluation and budget, look at regulatory issues to ensure compliance with both federal and industry standards.

## Regulation

Because advertising is considered commercial speech, it suffers more restraints than other forms of speech the First Amendment protects. Advertising also tends to be more regulated than public relations speech, which is "freer." The key regulating authorities include: the Federal Trade Commission (FTC), Federal Communications Commission (FCC), Food and Drug Administration (FDA), Bureau of Alcohol, Tobacco and Firearms (BATF), Patent and Trademark Office and the Library of Congress.

**FTC.** The Wheeler-Lea Act of 1938 empowered the

FTC to monitor unfair or deceptive practices in commerce. This act allows the FTC to order advertisers to stop misleading practices and to fine companies who do not heed its orders.

When someone complains against an advertiser, the FTC can take five actions.

1. Issue a *consent order* that a company must sign agreeing to correct or discontinue questionable practices

2. Issue a *cease and desist order* that is enforced by an FTC judge, if the company doesn't sign the consent order

3. Assure *affirmative disclosure* allowing a company to say what it wants to about a product or service, but with a qualifying warning, like cigarette advertising, or face further FTC intervention

4. Assure *advertising substantiation* by insisting that a company include proof or substantiation for claims it makes or face FTC intervention

5. Enforce *corrective advertising* that insists an advertiser rectify previous deceptive or misleading statements by admitting wrongdoing; simply stopping the ad is not sufficient (e.g., Listerine mouthwash's parent company, Warner-Lambert ran $10 million of corrective advertising to correct the false assertion that Listerine prevents colds and sore throats)

Comparative and testimonial advertising also fall under the domain of the FTC. From a consumer standpoint, comparative ads can provide helpful information. Most companies, however, dislike unfavorable comparisons. According to Bergh and Katz, FedEx threatened to sue the United States Postal Service (USPS) for an ad claiming priority mail costs less than FedEx. *USPS* did not pull the ads and reported record increases in use of priority mail.

Testimonials, as mentioned earlier, cannot make false claims. The endorser must actually use the product. The FTC has held an endorser responsible for damages when the testimonial is false.

**FCC.** This agency has jurisdiction over the radio, television and telephone industries. Problems with obscenity and indecency fall under its authority. Keep in mind that cable television is less heavily regulated than network television.

**FDA.** This agency exerts considerable influence on advertising because of its jurisdiction over labeling of both foods and prescription drugs. The FDA also regulates tobacco advertising since tobacco was ruled an addictive substance.

**BATF**. This agency regulates alcoholic beverage advertising. BATF controls warning messages that must be displayed in bars or liquor stores, but aren't required on the actual beverage.

**Patent & Trademark Office**. This agency controls trademarks and servicemarks. Companies protect their trademarks and will sue to maintain them. For example, a healthcare company produced a magazine for disability management clients known as *Forum*. Penthouse lawyers contacted the company to threaten a lawsuit if the company refused to change the magazine's name. *Penthouse Magazine* produced a separate magazine also known as the *Forum*. Even though the clientele was radically different, the healthcare company changed the name of its publication.

**Library of Congress**. Copyrights are registered at the Library of Congress. Advertisers use copyrights to maintain ownership of their original work. Advertisers also protect their right to sue if materials are used without permission.

**Self-regulation**. In addition, the advertising industry regulates itself. Three groups provide leadership in self-regulation: the Better Business Bureau, advertising trade organizations, and the media.

The Better Business Bureau investigates local consumer business complaints. The National Advertising Review Council, an advertising trade organization, monitors national advertising and advises advertisers. The National Advertising Review Council has two divisions — National Advertising Division (NAD) and the National Advertising Review Board (NARB). Most complaints come from competitors. If the advertiser and NAD cannot resolve a complaint, the case goes to the NARB (50 members from agencies, advertisers and the general public). The conclusions of the NARB are binding and if advertisers won't comply, the case is referred to the FTC.

Many trade and professional associations develop sets of standards for their members. One such set of standards of the American Advertising Federation appears here.

## Media self-regulation

A network or magazine must agree to run an ad giving the medium another gatekeeping role as well as the power to self regulate. Some magazines won't accept advertising for alcohol or tobacco products fearing conflict with their image or subscribers. However, according to Scott Donation in *Advertising Age*, as many as 165 magazines would fold without tobacco advertising.

Other media sources refuse to air or print controversial advertising; condoms would be an example. Even though broadcasters can advertise contraceptive products (National

---

### Advertising Principles of American Business of the American Advertising Federation

1. **Truth**. Advertising shall reveal the truth, and shall reveal significant facts, the omission of which would mislead the public.

2. **Substantiation**. Advertising claims shall be substantiated by evidence in possession of the advertiser and the advertising agency prior to making such claims.

3. **Comparisons**. Advertising shall refrain from making, false, misleading, or unsubstantiated statements or claims about a competitor or his products or services.

4. **Bait Advertising**. Advertising shall not offer products or services for sale unless such offer constitutes a bona fide effort to sell the advertised products or services and is not a device to switch consumers to other goods or services, usually higher priced.

5. **Guarantees and Warranties**. Advertising of guarantees and warranties shall be explicit, with sufficient information to apprise consumers of their principal terms and limitations or, when space or time restrictions preclude such disclosures, the advertisement shall clearly reveal where the full text of the guarantee or warranty can be examined before purchase.

6. **Price Claims**. Advertising shall avoid price claims which are false or misleading, or savings claims which do not offer provable savings.

7. **Testimonials**. Advertising containing testimonials shall be limited to those of competent witnesses who are reflecting a real and honest opinion or experience.

8. **Taste and Decency**. Advertising shall be free of statements, illustrations, or implications which are offensive to good taste or public decency.

---

Association of Broadcasters 1982 repealed the ban on advertising contraceptive products), the major networks believe these ads too sensitive to air.

According to *The Philadelphia Inquirer* writer Jane M. Von Bergen, *Good Housekeeping* magazine won't accept ads for condoms either because they aren't 100 percent effective as birth control and the magazine promises a refund if products it advertises don't work.

So, usually each media outlet controls what it will or won't air, based on the demographics and psychographics of its target audience.

Finally, the agency, practitioner and company must observe certain standards of truth and reliability. When Volvo aired an ad where a monster truck drove over a Volvo and didn't crush it, the company failed to mention that it had added steel reinforced panels to the car. The ad was deemed false and misleading and not just Volvo, but the advertising agency, was cited by the FTC for deceptive advertising.

Knowing about advertising regulation protects practitioners from endangering themselves or their clients and avoids difficulty with false or misleading claims. ■

# Tips

1. Use advertising in public relations programs to develop awareness of an organization, to improve consumer relations, to take a stand on a public issue or to improve an organization's image.

2. Public relations efforts bring more credibility than advertising because a third party (reporter or producer) advances the ideas put forth by the public relations practitioner.

3. A good advertising copywriter arouses the target audience's attention and motivates the audience to act.

4. When writing advertising copy, write to someone you know who represents the target audience and personalize the copy by using the word, "you."

5. Check translations thoroughly when "moving" a slogan from one country to another.

Name _____ Date _____

## Answer these questions

1. Show how a company might combine public relations and advertising in a campaign to promote a new product or service.

_____

_____

_____

_____

_____

_____

2. Do you think it's wise to spend part of a public relations budget on advertorials. Why? Give examples of how they might work.

_____

_____

_____

_____

_____

_____

*See other side*

Name _____ Date _____

3. React to this statement: "Public relations mentions are free; ads are not."

_____

_____

_____

_____

_____

_____

_____

4. How can cows be used to advertise?

_____

_____

_____

_____

_____

_____

_____

## SECTION 2

## Marketing and lobbying

In addition to audiences referred to throughout this text, you'll need to communicate with parents, community organizations and government officials. These parties play major roles in many public relations efforts. This section offers suggestions on conducting marketing and lobbying efforts.

### Community organizations

Many community leaders play major roles in community organizations such as the Lions, Rotary and Jaycees. Through their interactions with other members, they influence the thinking of many movers and shakers. These organizations enjoy a reputation of being objective about issues affecting the community and can sometimes be recruited to assist with community-minded projects.

**Most such organizations seek "do-good" projects to compete for state and national recognition. Involving them in your PR project can be a win-win situation for all.**

*Example*: One community seeking voter approval for a bond issue to build a high school wanted to poll residents to determine their opinions on certain issues. School officials invited the Jaycees to distribute and collect the surveys. The Jaycees' involvement brought a spirit to the survey that communicated the project was not just the effort of school board members who wanted to see their names on a building.

Provide speakers for these groups. Often the program chairperson is hurting to find program speakers and will appreciate the offer. The speakers can talk about a topic of interest to the group and can explain some of the efforts being undertaken by their organizations.

### Town officials

Knowing and dealing effectively with town officials can frequently smooth the way to getting things done. Whether it's approval for a fund-raising effort, town recognition for a community improvement effort or needing a titled official to speak, building a friendly relationship with officials will pay dividends.

Offer to provide public relations expertise for candidates running for office and contribute *pro bono* services for a community newsletter or community improvement campaign.

## Marketing

Marketing has taken on new meaning to a variety of audiences. Many groups that never thought of marketing as a practical approach to help meet their needs a number of years ago have embraced it and are looking for ways to market effectively. The American Marketing Association in 1960 said, "Marketing consists of the performance of business activities that direct the flow of goods and services from producer to consumer or user."

Twenty-five years later in 1985, the AMA said, "Marketing is the process of planning and executing the conception, pricing, promotion and distribution of ideas, goods and services to create exchanges that satisfy individual and organization objectives."

> *Nonprofit organizations market ideas and services as businesses market products.*

As noted in the 1985 definition, marketing is no longer limited to businesses. Nonprofit organizations market their ideas and services as well as businesses market products.

*Example*: Ten years ago you couldn't find the word "marketing" in any of the materials of school districts. Now, the National School Public Relations Association offers a special report on how to market schools.

Colleges, a number of years ago, would seldom have anybody in the organization responsible for marketing. Now, marketing is a serious component of the administration as admission offices and department heads work together to attract students to their campuses.

Attorneys, physicians and others who had never allowed marketing now use it in combination with public relations and advertising efforts.

Authorities in the field of public relations and marketing have been wrestling with how the two disciplines might work together effectively. Colleges and universities are looking for the best approach to prepare people to handle the communication activities that a variety of firms will offer.

Many communicators are using the terms "marketing" and "public relations" almost interchangeably. Frequently, when public relations, marketing and advertising people get together, some of their ideas do overlap.

At a colloquium designed to find the distinctions between public relations and marketing, some of the leading names in the fields of public relations and marketing tried to develop distinctions that would help public relations and marketing people better understand each other and work with each other.

After debating for a day, the panelists agreed to this definition of **public relations**: "Public relations is a management process whose goal is to attain and maintain accord and positive behaviors among social groupings on which an organization depends to achieve its mission. Its fundamental responsibility is to build and maintain a hospitable environment for an organization."

They defined **marketing** this way: "Marketing is the management process whose goal is to attract and satisfy customers (or clients) on a long-term basis to achieve an organization's economic objectives. Its fundamental responsibility is to build and maintain a market for an organization's product or products or services."

The panel agreed that *every organization needs a marketing function and a public relations function.*

The notion of **integrated communication** was discussed. This approach permits clients to do one-stop shopping. A constant concern: The long-term goals maintaining positive relationships with consumers, stockholders and regulatory agencies. The Tylenol example showed the importance of a solid public relations program that would have an impact on marketing and on sales. It's impossible, the panel noted, to separate public relations problems from marketing.

Companies realize that special interest groups and government agencies respond when customers express concerns about auto insurance rates, utility rates and profit margins. Whether it's the price of gasoline or oil company profits or chlordane contamination in their homes, people express their opinions. And these opinions trigger more regulation, loss of autonomy and other problems that create both marketing and public relations challenges.

The panelists agreed that we need to do a better job of explaining the two functions because:

- We're dealing with another generation of managers who do not understand how public relations contributes to organizational success.

- We're dealing with another generation of public relations practitioners who can't fulfill the management function.

- One of the greatest challenges is that the two functions are not understood by managers or practitioners.

- CEOs do not know how to use the strengths of public relations and marketing to achieve their missions.[1]

The challenge of practicing in an integrated environmental forces marketing, public relations, advertising, sales promotions and direct response efforts to find common ground to reach customers. To do so, integrated marketing movement has emerged. Large companies, such as 3M and IBM, have been applying the integrated marketing approach and have been training their managers to conduct such efforts. Agencies have also been using internal training programs to prepare their employees to use a more integrated marketing approach to serving clients.

Those who support the integration of public relations, marketing and advertising claim that such a background will enable proponents to be more readily accepted at the higher managerial levels. Those who oppose the integrated approach feel that public relations students need a broad background in communication and the social sciences.

> *The Tylenol challenge showed the importance of a solid public relations program that would impact marketing and sales.*

A 1995 study of 250 managerial-level members of the Public Relations Society of America showed the following:

- 83% reported working in an organization that applies the principles of integrated marketing in planning public relations programs.

- 51% of the respondents familiar with integrated marketing reported preferring to hire public relations practitioners who have been educated to be specialists in the field of public relations.

- 52% encourage training sessions to encourage their public relations practitioners to understand and apply the concepts of integrated marketing.

- Respondents felt that integrated marketing communication will play a larger role in the public relations function in the future.

School districts wishing to gain voter support for budgets and new buildings combine traditional community relations and public relations efforts with marketing strategies.

Cause-related marketing also combines the areas of marketing and public relations. Example: American Express donated a portion of money charged to its card to restoration of the Statue of Liberty.

## Saving buyers time: A marketing must

Just about all marketers conducting research have found that a main concern of buyers is *time*. Whether it's how long an ordered product takes to arrive or how much time it takes to shop and order something, time is becoming more and more important as a buying factor. Ask your parents how long it took for something ordered by mail or phone to arrive up to about three years ago. Now you can receive overnight delivery. People who would think nothing of spending an hour to go to a store and

---

1. Based on an article, "An Essential Double Helix," by Dr. Glen M. Broom and Kerry Tucker, in *Public Relations Journal.*

select a book now purchase that book through the Internet in a couple of minutes. Companies and organizations that don't communicate they value the customer's time will go

> *Companies and organizations that don t communicate they value customers time will go the way of the dinosaurs.*

the way of dinosaurs. It's imperative that you make every effort to market products and services in a way that clearly lets your potential buyer know that your company does indeed do everything possible to make it easy to buy and to receive the needed materials quickly. Some important considerations:

- Prepare marketing materials that *communicate succinctly* what your products are all about. (Of course, when technical information is needed, supply it fully for those people who need to check specifications.)

- *Promise quick delivery.* Be specific and establish ways to maintain quality control on those promises.

- If selling by telephone, check those phone lines to see how many times people get busy signals or are put on hold for a longer time than you would want to wait. Many enlightened companies are including in the recording, when there is a wait, how long that wait will be. Remember that *people will wait longer for an 800 number* than they will when they're paying for the call. Remember, too, that you should be analyzing those waits and eliminating them whenever possible by hiring more people.

- Teach all customer service reps to *take orders as quickly as possible* and respond to questions not only politely but also efficiently.

- Always *ask permission* before placing callers on hold and wait for them to answer. Never leave callers on hold for more than 30 seconds without explaining the delay.

- Before transferring callers, always provide *the name and extension* of the person the caller is being transferred to.

- If accepting orders by fax, evaluate the *effectiveness of your phone system.* If you need more lines, install them. In this time-conscious society, people will frequently switch from one supplier to another because the order is easier to place.

## Developing new products

One of the fastest ways to increase business is to teach sales people—whether in person or on the phone—to identify the need for new products or services. Conduct workshops for employees to teach them how to do this effectively and how to report on the needs. Selling products

that customers need certainly represents one of the quickest, easiest ways to grow. Marketers can indeed help the new product division come up with products and services that will sell.

When looking for new products, heed the advice of the new product development newsletter:

- Think big. Focus on blockbuster ideas.

- Don't invent a better mousetrap. Look for a way to get rid of mice.

- Appoint someone to head up new product development. Don't assign it to a committee.

- As soon as the product is approved, find out early if it can be effectively manufactured, marketed, packaged and financed. Involve marketing people at the earliest stages.

- In the embryonic stages of the development of a new product idea, ask someone in marketing to write the first two paragraphs of the offer that will present the product to potential customers. If solid copy can't be written to explain the benefits succinctly, perhaps you should not develop the product.

## Importance of the second bottom-line in marketing

As noted elsewhere in this book, two bottom lines exist. The traditional bottom line is where companies or organizations measure success in financial or social terms. To enjoy success with new products or services, organizations must depend on their first bottom line — how well they please customers.

When customers are satisfied, and even more than satisfied with the offerings and the services provided by a company, those customers are more receptive to new products and offers. You must insist that your organization make every effort to build that first bottom line to help the marketing of new offerings.

> ### Be obsessed with customers
>
> Successful organizations have one common central focus: customers. It doesn't matter if it's a business, professional practice, hospital or government agency. Success comes to those — and only those — who are obsessed with looking after customers
>
> *Harvey Mackay*

## Managing marketing communications

Marketing is concerned with an array of activities, including new product development, development and management of distribution channels, pricing strategies and brand management. Marketing communications is more narrowly focused on the types of activities that are familiar to advertising and public relations professionals. Public relations, when part of an integrated marketing communication program, is aimed at promoting or positioning a product or service. It is more closely linked to sales results than other PR activities and is frequently closely allied with advertising. Today, public relations is playing an important role in new product introductions, especially among high tech companies.

Al Ries, who, with Jack Trout, wrote numerous books on the concept of positioning, teamed up with his daughter, Laura, to write a book, *The 22 Immutable Laws of Branding.*

In their book, public relations takes center stage in "Law 3: The Law of Publicity," which says that **public relations now surpasses advertising in its ability to build new brands:**

> … for years public relations has been treated as a secondary function to advertising. PR people even used to measure their success in terms of advertising space. Publicity stories were converted into equivalent advertising expenditures …

**But what works in branding today is publicity, not advertising**. This is especially true in the high tech field. All of the big global marketing powerhouses — Microsoft, Intel, Dell, Compaq, Gateway, Oracle, Cisco, SAP and Sun Microsystems — were first created in the pages of *The Wall Street Journal, Business Week, Forbes,* and *Fortune* by publicity, not advertising.

Product publicity involves preparing news releases and photos, staging news conferences at trade shows or other venues, and developing relationships with the trade media and other targeted media. When working for a technology company or a medical products or services company, you must be able to absorb a great deal of raw technical information and make it understandable to nontechnical audiences. Even if you're communicating to a highly technical audience, you'll need to learn how to simplify and to focus on the most important or persuasive information.

You may have to interview engineers or scientists who are unaccustomed to working with marketing. It's important that you persist in making them explain technical aspects that you'll have to promote so that you really understand them. *Chances are your communication will fall short, even with a technical audience, if you try to repeat a message you don't understand.*

When you deal with the trade press, avoid technical complexity. First, you can't assume all journalists have an adequate level of technical understanding about your product to be able to get it right. Moreover, you need to remember that even in a high tech market, it takes simple, understandable, and memorable messages to position your product in the minds of your target audience.

Depending on the size and nature of your market, you may need to place company spokespersons on radio and TV talk shows, work with engineers to write and place technical articles in journals, or help them prepare papers for professional gatherings. You may seek to place cover photos of your product in trade journals. You'll likely visit customers to develop case studies to publish in a journal or in your own sales literature. Those visits can include supervising photography or video taping of your products in a working environment.

Marketing communications professionals manage a variety of video productions, including:

- New product introductions: short videos (about 5-10 minutes) shown by sales people or mailed to prospects

- Sales training videos showing reps or distributors how to sell a new product or service

- Meeting openers for sales or customer seminars

- Customer seminar audio visuals (may be a combination of video and slides)

- Corporate or brand image videos

- Video news releases and infomercials

Increasingly you will also be working with interactive media such as CD ROM/DVD and the World Wide Web. These media offer opportunities for nonlinear and two-way communication and place a premium on your ability to give users easy access to large quantities of useful information.

The Internet and World Wide Web offer a complex and rapidly growing medium for communicating with your

> *In the idea stage of a new product, ask marketing to write the first two paragraphs of the offer aimed at potential customers. If it can t write copy succinctly explaining the benefits, perhaps it should not develop the product.*

target markets. In addition to publishing your own information on a corporate web site, you will need to become familiar with the many Internet venues where your company and its products may be the subject of good and bad publicity.

## Using direct mail

Direct mail and telemarketing are two of the most rapidly growing communication vehicles. For profitable direct mail, consider these suggestions from the Direct Marketing Association:

- Build and maintain mailing lists (use existing customer lists or purchase outside mailing lists).

- Target mailings to customers who bought most recently, frequently or spent the most money.

- Sell benefits, not features. Remember passive or nonseeking audiences need benefits to motivate them.

- Write believable copy that will elicit a response. Use proof or testimony to back up claims.

- The me-to-you approach works best. Use this personal medium to relate to your audience.

- Write to a person, not an occupant. Most people resent unsolicited mail. Use a name if at all possible. If not, resort to *Dear student or homeowner*, not *To whom it may concern.*

- Design mail to be opened and read. Use metered mail and colored stationery for business mailings. Avoid "see-thru" windows that look like junk mail. Most research indicates that teasers on outer envelopes don't work.

- Be clear, concise and straightforward. Use toll-free numbers, addresses, and a business reply card for reader ease.

- Test your mailing. Try out various approaches and frequency of offers and lists. Try your mailing on a small number of recipients first.

### Free still works

Whenever you can, inject *Free* in direct mail letters or ad headlines. Bob Stone, cited in *Kaleidoscope*, suggests considering these three possibilities to sell a product for $10.

Three possibilities:
- Buy one for $9.99; get the other for one cent.
- Buy two; get 50% off.
- Buy one; get one free.

The word *free* exacts the best response.

### Create a "We're Solid" reputation

If you want to build a growing business via direct mail or telephone, look to leaders. What separates one company from another is generally the reputation built by standing behind products and making it easy for customers to be comfortable doing business with your business. Some examples of companies frequently cited for their service: Nordstrom's, L.L. Bean and Land's End.

These suggestions, from *Guerrilla Marketing Excellence*, will help you with ideas that others in your organization haven't considered:

- Constantly present the uniqueness of your company and the prime benefit that you will bring to customers.

- Consider direct response marketing rather than institutional ads.

- Remove all risk from your customers by offering a 100% money-back guarantee.

- Tell people why they should do business with your firm. Know how the customer will benefit from doing so.

- Become a testing fiend. Test your offers, letters, postcards, ads, headlines, typefaces and copy. Examples: Test the same ad in two newspapers to test the pulling power of the papers. Test different ads in the same paper to determine the power of the ads themselves.

> *For most profitable direct mail, choose lists wisely and sell benefits to people who bought by mail recently and frequently.*

- Recognize the power of headlines and realize that very few companies invest much time in coming up with attention-getting headlines for their ads. Response rates can be improved dramatically by doing so.

- Test prices — including higher prices. It's not unusual for a higher price to bring in not only more money but also more orders.

## Marketing online

When you're launching a campaign to market by the Internet, remember that everything you're doing is experimental. See what other people are doing that seems to be working and then develop your plan. If you're successful, you'll know quickly. If you're not, have a little patience and make some changes.

> **Include your Internet address on your materials for print media, TV and radio. Put it on your letterhead, mailers, fliers, print advertising and business cards.**

Here are some tips from Michael Mathiesen in his book *Marketing on the Internet*:

1. To find your objectives, answer the following questions:
   - Do we want to generate direct response orders?
   - Do we want to build a list of prospects for future promotions?
   - Do we want to increase brand awareness or corporate image?
   - Do we want to gather information about customer preferences to help guide future product development?
   - Do we want to test consumer response to special offers?
   - Do we want to improve customer service?
   - Do we want to recruit employees, subscribers, etc.?

2. Identify the products or services you will offer initially. Select a product with a successful sales history through direct marketing. **Concentrate on one product or service in the beginning** and gradually expand those offerings.

3. Get on the online services and see what happens. Ultimately you will probably subscribe to a number of these services, but start with a couple.

4. Create info-tools about your products. An info-tool is a computer file that contains information about your product, services, business, etc. In each of these, you tell the world something about what you do. If you can **make one of your products or services sound new** by giving applications that would be especially recent, do so. Make the product seem newsworthy. Then try to distribute it in many different areas by online services.

5. If you've had some interest in your products or services via marketing in the online services environment, it's time to move to the Internet. For specifics on doing this, get a copy of *Marketing on the Internet*, by Michael Mathiesen, Maximum Press, 605 Silverthorn Road, Gulf Breeze, FL 32561

6. Create **your own news group** and mailing lists on the Internet. By doing so, you can generate a list of thousands of people with interests that make them good prospects for your services. Paying to rent those lists could be expensive.

7. Augment your efforts with traditional promotions. To get the most from your online marketing, include your Internet address on everything else you're doing — materials for print media, TV, radio, etc. Put that Internet address on your letterhead, mailers, fliers, print advertising, business cards, etc.

## Developing a comprehensive marketing program

To develop a marketing program, you might want to follow these guidelines from *Mastering Marketing*, from Briefings Publishing Group. Working in small groups, ask these questions:

What strengths do we have in the marketplace? If you asked your clients to list the organization's strengths, what would they write?

- Of these strengths, which three are the strongest in the marketplace?

- What weaknesses do we have in the marketplace?

- Which three weaknesses do our clients most frequently discuss?

- What are some strengths of the organization that our clients don't know about?

- What weaknesses don't our clients know about? (Identifying them, admitting they exist, and developing action plans to deal with them will strengthen the organization. *Example*: poor staff morale. Outsiders may not know about this.)

- What do we have that people want?

- What do we have that people need?

- What business are we in, anyway? This will lead to a mission statement — something every organization needs but many don't have. A solid mission statement helps establish a direction and focus.

- What are our three major organizational goals? These should be consistent with our strengths. Under each of the three goals, what are three objectives that seem appropriate?

- Where we will target our marketing efforts? List both internal and external audiences.

- Are target audiences learning about our organization, its programs and its services? By identifying how people find out about us and how they feel about us, we'll determine which channels of communication are working best and where we need to improve.

- How can we let people know what we are doing? Start with the staff by asking reactions and suggestions to the mission statement, goals and objectives. Creating your objectives in easy-to-understand plain English helps everyone have a better feel for what the company position is and where the company is headed.

- What do people think about when they think about our organization?

- What do we want people to think about when they think about us?

- What resources do we need to reach each of the goals? This would include personnel responsible to make it happen and money to implement the ideas (human and financial capital).

- How will we know if the marketing effort succeeded? How will we evaluate it?

## Telemarketing tips

1. Choose the right list when trying to telemarket. Determine which audience is most likely to respond to the phone calls.

2. Get to the right person. Find out who has the real buying authority and keep trying to reach that person.

3. Don't try to sell something by telephone that requires a complicated proposal. If you're going to need visual aids or materials to show the customer, the telephone is not the way to go.

4. Use common courtesy to find out if the prospect is available to talk when you call. If the person is in the middle of doing something with a deadline, you are much safer calling back.

5. Work on a proper tone of voice. Have others react to it. Tone means much to people who don't know you.

6. Work on the best rate of speaking. If you speak too rapidly, the person may not understand. If you speak too slowly, a busy person will become impatient.

7. Remember that the person you're talking to has a built-in resistance. You must offer a reason for listening: a *benefit*.

8. Listen. Probing for the customer's needs is a giant step toward making the sale.

9. When the prospect has a question, rephrase it in your own words. This assures the prospect that the message got through.

## How NOT to succeed

According to Ed Burnett in "How not to succeed in direct mail" *Direct Marketing* (March, 1997), try the following if you want to **FAIL** in direct mail/marketing:

- Mail the same piece over and over without trying to find a way to add improvements or changes.

- Make the mistake of thinking direct mail is easy; anyone can use it well.

- Think that a single order equals a customer without follow-up or development of that lead. (Do remember to include follow-up orders, renewals and long-term sales when calculating income and potential income from mailings.)

- Misuse testimonials
  - concoct highly general testimonials
  - use testimonials that promise too much
  - use testimonials not germane to the offered service

- Misuse illustrations
  - place illustrations far from relevant copy
  - use distracting illustrations that direct the eye away from the message

- Use more than one signature on a letter. (Remember direct mail is a one-on-one discussion with the reader.)

- Believe that all factors influencing response are equal.

Of these five factors, copy, package, timing, offer, and lists — *lists are most important*. Many prefer to send a poor mailing to a good list than a good mailing to a poor list.

## Presenting your sales message

When trying to sell by telemarketing, benefit from these suggestions:

- Start by verifying your prospect's name.

- Identify yourself and your company.

- Tell the prospect why you are calling.

- Offer a benefit that the prospect can expect as a result of hearing your proposal.

- Ask fact-finding or "test" questions to determine if your prospect has an interest in your offer. If there is no interest, go to the next person on your list.

- Make your sales presentation.

- Use descriptive words and phrases to describe the features and advantages of your product or service, but don't overdo it. Then — and this is key — explain the benefits the product or service will provide. Don't go on and on; limit the list of advantages and benefits to just a couple. If you're not sure which are most appealing, experiment with a *split run*. Make several hundred calls using the same format, except vary the advantages and benefits. See which work best.

> **How will we know if the marketing effort succeeded? How will we evaluate it ?**

- Ask for the order by giving the prospect a choice. Example: Would you prefer red or blue? Would you like to place the order using MasterCard or Visa?

- When you receive an order, verify the customer's name and address and credit information. Read the information back to make sure the customer understands what's been ordered.

## Lobbying: What you need to know

Although lobbying is considered an ancient art as old as government itself — it is still frequently misunderstood as a profession that is viewed with suspicion. In fact, mention the word *lobbyist* in some circles and it conjures up the image of back room "wheeling and dealing," complete with monetary payoffs. Lobbyists are often viewed as too powerful and untrustworthy. In many instances, they are portrayed as an evil influence on the legislative process, when in fact they are exercising their constitutionally protected right to petition the government.

Over the years, lobbying has evolved into a sophisticated and refined art. Today's lobbyists are thought to be a critical resource within the political process, bringing it into the ranks of acceptability.

> **Telemarketing tip:**
> **When the prospect asks a question, repeat it in your own words.**
> **This assures the prospect that the message got through.**

Through coalition building, grass roots mobilizing, public relations and communications, lobbyists have changed the appearance of lobbying over the years. The principal elements of today's lobbying activities include researching and analyzing legislation and regulatory proposals; monitoring and reporting on legislative developments; and attending state and regulatory hearings. Lobbyists also work with coalitions interested in the same issues and then educate, not only legislators, but also public employees and corporate officials as to the implications of various changes.

Do lobbyists present the facts in a way that will show their organization's needs in a favorable light? Of course. Do the lobbyists, however, try to be accurate in presenting data related to the topic being considered? The good ones do. Why? They realize that if the legislators can depend on the information provided and not be embarrassed later because some of the information was indeed slanted to the point that facts were distorted, they will come back to those same lobbyists for information again.

Just as good public relations people are depended on by journalists to provide information in an accurate way, lobbyists too become sought by legislators who need pertinent facts before making key decisions.

**Good lobbyists get along with legislators' staffs and build rapport with people in key offices so they have access when needed.** They also communicate where they can be reached at all times so that legislators seeking information can quickly find it.

Lobbyists can be full-time employees of organizations and associations, representing strictly the viewpoint of those entities. They can also be lobbying consultants for a variety of companies who seek people with knowledge of a particular state and how its legislators work. Others specialize in specific areas of legislation and serve as high-paid consultants at a national level in specific industries or areas.

Savvy lobbyists realize that just because they establish a solid relationship with legislators it doesn't mean that the votes will go the way they want. They can't sulk and jeopardize their relationship with these legislators because other votes will follow and they want to seek their support again. It's important to realize that legislators have a variety of constituencies to serve and they must weigh the implications of their votes with all those constituencies — not just the ones the lobbyists represent.

Many industries and companies wishing to influence legislators will involve employees and communities in grass-roots attempts to reach the legislators. Lobbyists will frequently provide the information and identify hot buttons that may prompt favorable reactions from the legislators.

Much of what goes on between legislators and lobbyists comes down to basic human relationships. The lobbyist's goal is to make connections and develop close relationships. Legislators and lobbyists naturally gravitate toward one another. They each share a stake in the legislative system and can commiserate and celebrate with each other.

Legislators are more apt to do things for individuals they like and trust. If through a cultivated relationship, the lobbyist proves to be a credible, reliable, loyal, empathic and likeable individual, then the path to effective lobbying is much easier.

One author studying lobbyists' effectiveness said, "One contact by a good lobbyist may be worth a hundred contacts by an amateur."

A study of legislators and lobbyists focused on traits they believed characterized effective lobbyists. The four characteristics most frequently mentioned were: good personality, intelligence and knowledgeability, aggressiveness and honesty.

Today's lobbying activities can be either direct or indirect. Direct lobbying refers to meeting with elected representatives and providing them with information pertinent to a bill that is being voted on or an issue of concern. Indirect lobbying, also known as *grass roots lobbying*, requires long hours on the telephone and writing letters trying to rouse the community to get involved with an issue or cause. Research has shown that the most popular method is direct. When employing the direct lobbying method, lobbyists are reminded of several DOs and DON'Ts that may prove an asset to developing a working relationship with a legislator. They are:

- DO – Become familiar with the personal interests and concerns of a legislator prior to establishing formal contact.

- DO – Develop rapport with your legislators.

- DON'T – Make an appointment with a legislator and another constituent; then, without notifying the staff, show up with five other people. (The only thing worse is to show up with a reporter without having notified the staff.)

*Legislators are more apt to do things for people they like and trust.*
*If the lobbyist is credible, reliable, loyal, and empathic,*
*effective lobbying is much easier.*

- DO – Plan face-to-face visits with legislators in their home districts. They tend to be very effective.

- DON'T – Arrive late to your meeting, be unprepared, have a considerable amount of information and materials with you — and lack an executive summary.

- DON'T – Call a legislator's office only when a crisis hits or you need something.

- DO – Convince legislators that it's important for them to

listen. Convince legislators they have something at stake.

- DON'T – Flood an office with postcards and photocopies of letters during a heated legislative battle.

- DO – Use the "soft sell" approach. Many lobbyists make the mistake of pushing their case too hard. They ask for the whole pie and accept nothing less than everything they asked for. **Know when to compromise**.

- DON'T – Knowingly give a legislator or his staff the wrong, or "not quite completely true," information.

*Use the soft sell approach. Many lobbyists err by pushing their case too hard. They ask for the whole pie and accept nothing less. Know when to compromise.*

- DON'T – Call on an office without an appointment and insist on seeing the legislator.

- DO – Be pleasant and nonoffensive. Because legislators meet with many people every day, it eases their burden considerably if lobbyists and their associates are pleasant.

- DON'T – Expect to have a substantive meeting with a legislator during a legislative session — unless you have an appointment.

- DON'T – Discount the value of meeting with a legislator's staff — particularly if you've had difficulty meeting with the legislator. Remember staff are the "gatekeepers" of information.

- DON'T – Refuse to help a legislator who has been helpful to you.

- DO – Keep the door open for future contact if a particular legislator appears to be opposed to your views. Remember: A legislator can change positions after learning more facts.

- DO – Follow up. Letters of appreciation and a summary of the meeting help keep a record.

Lobbyists are reminded to also:

- Study the power structure of the legislature.

- Recognize the composition, role and powers of the majority and minority parties in each house and understand that politics is an integral part of governing.

- Never lie to a legislator. And learn how to play "hallways politics." *Translation*: Maintain the ability to bounce from one legislator to another in a single bound while making your point with each.

- Build good will — Remember, lobbying is a communication skill. Tact, patience, persuasiveness and good listening skills must be major components of a lobbyist's personality.
- Acknowledge the pros and cons of a controversial issue — unless legislators know all the risks involved, they may resent you, the lobbyist or your client.

**Remember**: A lobbyist's charge is to link the political process of making laws with the people and the environment those laws affect. An effective lobbyist can help a legislator decide how much a vote is worth — or will cost — politically. While it is true that lobbyists are paid to represent their client's interests, they also contribute a great deal to the legislative process.

# Tips

1. As you consider a communications campaign, don't start by separating marketing, advertising and public relations efforts. Begin with your audiences and then determine which combination of marketing, advertising and public relations you should use to reach them.

2. To develop brand recognition and loyalty, use publicity and public relations efforts more than advertising.

3. When preparing direct-mail promotions, write believable copy aimed at a person — not at a large audience.

4. Traits needed for effective lobbyists: a good personality, intelligence, aggressiveness and honesty. If legislators disagree with your position on an issue, keep doors open. They may change their views, plus you'll want to maintain solid rapport for discussion of the next issue.

Name _____ Date _____

## Answer these questions

1. Give examples of how public relations and marketing efforts can help each other.

_____

_____

_____

_____

_____

_____

_____

2. Do you agree the most important component of a direct mail effort is the promotional letter? If you don't, what is?

_____

_____

_____

_____

_____

_____

_____

*See other side*

Name _____ Date _____

3. To determine the success of a direct mail effort, see if the money collected exceeded the cost of the mailing. True or False? Why?

_____

_____

_____

_____

_____

_____

_____

4. List three top suggestions for successful lobbying.

_____

_____

_____

_____

_____

_____

_____

_____

# Chapter 8

# Preparing Public Relations Publications

---

**PRaxiom**  *When you deal with a printer and want quality, price and speed, remember, you can usually have any two.*

---

## What this chapter covers

Whether you're attempting to win awards for your publications or communicate on a low budget to employees, you need to know what works most effectively. Critics will abound in the workplace — from graphic artists who want publications to attract attention, even if they can't be read, to budget-minded accounting types who will be concerned about the use of a second color. Research plays a large role in enabling you to defend your decisions. This chapter shares much of the practical research done to determine what works best in publications — from paper selection to typography to color. It also offers specific tips on preparing materials for printers, proofreading, and ways to determine if anybody is reading your publications.

## Publications

Nearly all organizations face the challenge of publishing some sort of promotional literature. You may need to put together a pamphlet to announce a grand opening, mail a brochure advertising your organization's newest service or produce a catalog describing all of your wares.

Whatever the goal, it's important to first keep in mind that every promotion, flier, brochure or catalog you send out represents your organization. **Printed pieces function as ambassadors.** A poorly conceived piece communicates that you aren't professional. If you produce a poor brochure, your products and services might also be perceived likewise as poor.

Here's the bad news: To get the results you want, you must become a writer, designer, typographer, editor and production manager. You need to tell your organization's entire story concisely and convincingly — usually in just a few paragraphs. You'll be faced with infinite combinations of design techniques that will help your piece look professional and appealing to your audience. You must choose from thousands of typefaces (fonts) with strange names like Gill Sans, New Century Schoolbook and *Zapf Chancery*. And the worst part: you'll have to do this all in what is often an impossibly tight time frame and budget.

Here's the good news: By following the guidelines presented here, you'll find yourself ahead of much of your competition. The following guidelines will help to make your printed pieces effective and attractive. Too many want-to-be designers fail to follow even the simplest graphic communication rules. As a result, they waste effort, time and money. You can see evidence of this in mountains of inadequate promotional pieces that fill mailboxes, flap in the breeze under car windshield wipers, and overstuff brochure racks across the country.

## Step 1: Establish your purpose

So where do you start? Perhaps the best place is to ask yourself one simple question: Why?

Why are you bothering to produce the promotion?

If you don't have a clear understanding of what you're trying to accomplish with the piece, neither will the reader.

Are you trying to get shoppers to take advantage of an upcoming sale? Do you want residents to call for more information or are you using the piece to inform your public about your organization and build credibility in the community?

Few promotional pieces can be all things to all people. If your effort lacks focus, your audience will not put the effort into figuring out what you want from them.

Experts generally agree that your first step in producing any promotional literature is to establish a clear, measurable objective. You should be able to write in one or two sentences exactly what you want the piece to accomplish. Here are examples of mission statements:

- *By January 15, this brochure should result in at least 25 phone calls about my new lawn service. From this I need to get 3 new clients — or $1,000 in business — to pay for the production of the brochure.*

- *By January 15, I want 75 percent of the southeast neighborhood to be aware of my new lawn service. I'll survey residents after the fifteenth to measure awareness.*

Regardless of your objective, write your publication clearly and concisely. Beware if you're creating a brochure just because someone in the organization says, "We just need one."

Not good enough. Ask why. Even if your boss is the one who said it, ask for more direction. Explain that you'll do a much better job if you know whom you're writing to, what you want them to do with the information and how you'll measure the success of your efforts. If your boss resists thinking about it — and you're in a position to do so — offer to write up several mission statements for approval. Your boss will likely appreciate your thoughtfulness and appreciate your effort to make — or save — the organization money.

> **Know what you want your publication to accomplish.**

## Step 2: Plan and craft your message

Know your audience: A primary consideration in planning and crafting your message is knowing your audience. If you're unsure about the people you're trying to communicate with, your chances of succeeding are slim.

Experts agree that you should first consider what your audience might already know about your organization or its message. If you have a well established name and reputation in the community, your message will be much different if you were just starting up and need to gain public acceptance.

Established organizations don't need to write a lot about who they are and what they stand for. This would waste limited space in the promotional piece — and worse — waste readers' time.

Unknown organizations, on the other hand, may need to establish credibility before the audience will listen to them. If you fall into this category, offer some organizational history or background of the key players in the business.

Next, you must consider what you want your audience to know. What information will they need? What are the main points you're trying to communicate?

### Budgeting and Planning

All agencies and offices have some budget limitations. Therefore, all projects and publications have budget constraints. Even though a publication might appear to have an unlimited budget, there clearly is one. It is critical that you know what your budget will permit as you begin your initial planning. Considerations usually fall into a logical list, regardless of the publication. A typical list of cost estimate will include:

- In-house staff time and resources — is there a reasonable limit?
- Consultant help for writing, graphic design, photography and editorial assistance.
- Typography, printing, delivery or shipping charges.
- Mailing costs, including envelopes, mail-house services, and postage.

Is your shop having a sale? When is it? What are the specifics of the offer?

Knowing how much your audience knows about you, your topic or your message, you'll be better able to craft a message they will understand. You'll know what jargon or industry buzz words you can use — if any.

Besides knowing what information to give your audience, you must be very clear about what you want them to do about it. In a very broad sense, consider whether you want to communicate information, present your side of an issue, create or strengthen an image, or persuade readers to buy something.

Again, this relates directly to your mission statement. After all, getting your audience to do what you need them to determines the success of your promotional efforts.

A common strategy in producing promotions and marketing is profiling your audience. By gathering as much information as you can about your readers, you'll be able to anticipate their needs and objections.

Profiling can be a very scientific process of in-depth demographic, psychographic studies and focus group research. But even if you don't have the time and resources to conduct a formal study of your audience, you should write down and organize all that you know about them and try to identify commonalties. A good place to start is to look at your existing customers. Investigate their habits and tendencies. This information can be key in planning and crafting a message that will reach your prospects.

In his book, *Persuasive Advertising for Entrepreneurs and Small Business Owners*, Jay P. Granat, Ph.D., makes

> **Set a specific objective for your PR effort. Example: By January 15, I want 75% of the southeast neighborhood to be aware of my new lawn service. I'll survey residents after that to measure awareness.**

an excellent point about audience evaluation. He cautions that the audience you are trying to reach is not always the user of the product, service or information you're presenting. For instance, while men are the main users of cologne, a lot of the buying is actually done by females who are buying presents.

Many communication professionals suggest that you consider whether your audience is active or passive.

An **active audience** is actively looking to buy, use or listen. They are already in the market for what you're promoting. They just need to be convinced that you're the best to buy from.

To sell to an active audience your promotional copy should highlight **features** of your product or service. If, for example, you sell lawn mowers, some benefits would be 3.5 horsepower, automatic mulching blade, self-propelling drive system, etc. Because active buyers are already sold on the idea of buying a mower, they just need to know the details about which is best for them.

A **passive audience** is not currently looking to buy. They need to be convinced that they will benefit from what you're selling.

To sell to a passive audience, highlight **benefits** in your copy. For example: The powerful engine on this new mower makes cutting even high grass effortless, a convenient no-fuss mulching-blade to save you time and work, and a work-saving drive system that helps the mower cut the grass, almost by itself.

## Organize your message

In most cases, readers spend very little time reading promotional literature. In fact, research shows that readers generally spend just five to seven seconds per page on promotional material like catalogs.

This means you must quickly convey how prospects will benefit from what you have to say or sell. In just seconds, you must let them know what's in it for them and that getting the facts they need will be easy and effortless.

In many cases, the audience will not bother to look hard to find information in promotional literature. It is your job to make it easy for them to find what they need and direct them through the piece.

## How to organize

A good place to start is by outlining all the information you feel is important to your message. Even if it's just a one-page pamphlet or flier, it's vital to write down your main points. You'll sometimes be surprised at how much you come up with.

*Remember*: People often use brochures and promotional material as the final step in their buying decision. Therefore, they want as much information as possible — without having to do much work to get it.

Problem is, you have a limited amount of space. The difficulty, therefore, is including only ideas and information key to getting your message across. You can do this by prioritizing the information chunks you've written down.

Outline what you want to say and determine how much you need to say about each topic. Then, organize your thoughts perhaps chronologically, cause-effect, or problem-solution.

Identify the items essential to conveying your point — be they helpful or extraneous.

Your facts should then be broken up into "chunks of easily digestible information" and arranged into a logical order. For example, you would likely tell your audience about the grand opening of your new restaurant before you start giving them directions to get there. Much of this is common sense, but

> **Your message should tell your audience what to do. Clearly state they should visit your restaurant, call, mail in a coupon, etc.**

the act of writing it all down and seeing the information in units helps you put the pieces together in a logical order.

## Think like your reader

Many writers and communication experts agree that you should make a list of the reasons your audience should buy your product, service or message. This can be a valuable exercise to help you see things from your readers' points of view. You should know how your audience will benefit from what you're communicating in your brochure or announcement.

Bob Bly, noted author and communication consultant, suggests using the "Motivational Sequence" when you organize your messages. He suggests these five steps as a guide to setting up your outline.

1. Make a statement that will get your audience's attention.

2. Point out a problem or need your audience has.

3. Present your product as the solution to their need or problem.

4. Present proof that your service, product or message will

solve the problem or meet the need by using guarantees, testimonials, experimental evidence, comparisons, etc.

5. Tell the audience what you want them to do. Clearly state they should *visit* your restaurant, *call*, *mail* in your coupon, etc.

## Develop the right tone

Another important factor: What language or tone will most persuade your audience? You could argue that this is more of a consideration during the writing phase of the production process, and so it is. But it's just as important to think about the general feel and language of the publication before you actually begin to write.

Do you want to present a soft, caring message that a hospital or retirement community might use?

Are you trying to appear high-tech and cutting edge, the way a computer repair shop might?

Is it important that you set yourself up as an authority on an issue or problem as a business consultant or lawyer might do?

Knowing this before you start writing will help you identify the pieces you must include in your message.

Using the wrong tone with an audience can not only cause your promotional piece to fail, but it can also give your organization an image you don't want. A heart surgeon, for example, doesn't want to promote fast operations, speedy service and a 30-day, money-back guarantee. An auto repair shop would.

## Step 3: Write persuasive copy

To keep your readers interested in what you're saying and to persuade them to think, feel or behave as you wish, consider these guidelines.

## Write just enough

Some experts believe that promotional copy should be short and to the point. They feel that most readers won't spend the time digging through enormous amounts of copy. Therefore, why waste your time writing a lot and their time reading a lot?

Noted author and communications expert Steve Morgenstern states, "Assume your reader hates to read. Let's face it; this isn't a new Stephen King novel you're delivering — it's information about a product or service. The fewer words it takes to convey your message, the more likely you are to get those words read."

Other experts, however, feel that the more copy, the better. As long as you have something important to say, put it in your message. This school of thought supports the idea that people want as much information as possible.

Promotional literature is often the final step in your audience's decision process. The more facts they have, the better.

Advertising legend David Ogilvy, for example, finds that people will read long promotional copy as often as they will short copy. Therefore, if you have a lot to write, and it adds to your message, write it.

So what's the right answer? It depends. There is no right or wrong answer to this question. But a few considerations can help you arrive at the best length.

*One*: What is the *interest level* of your audience? If you've identified that your message is very important to your readers, and they have much to gain by reading it, longer copy is often more appropriate.

*Two*: Always keep in mind how the audience will *use* your message and how much information they need to think, feel or act as you wish. If you're not asking much of your readers, you won't need to tell them much. If you're asking them to do a lot, you may need to write more to convince them to accept your message.

*Three*: The *size* of your promotional piece and the format you choose will also determine how much you can write. Some people choose a size and format first and then write to length. Others prefer to write their message and then pick a size and format that accommodates the length. Remember, however, not all sizes and formats cost the same to produce. The larger and more complicated the piece, the more expensive it will be.

*The bottom line*: Say only what you *need to say* — in as few words as possible. Make it as easy as possible for your audience to read and comprehend your message.

## Writing to persuade

Here are some additional ideas to help you write persuasive copy:

• Use the second person "you." Just as in headlines, the audience wants to know what's in it for them. By using "you," you write your message from their perspective. "Buy this book so I can make some money" is not persuasive copy. A better way: "You'll discover hundreds of ideas to make your promotions effective and profitable by reading this book."

• Offer the audience an "ultimate benefit" of using your product or service. Jim Sinkinson, noted speaker and marketing consultant, used this example. One benefit of driving a Volvo is saving money because it gets good gas mileage. The "ultimate benefit" is surviving if you get into an auto accident.

• Give readers information that they can use to convince themselves your product, service or message is

> *Use you in headlines promoting a product or service. Write from your reader's perspective. You'll discover hundreds of ideas to make your promotions effective and profitable by reading this book.*

best. Do this effectively by offering facts and evidence it the form of guarantees, research findings and testimonials. Readers expect you to tell them that your product is great. Facts and statements from objective sources give them proof they can use to validate their decision to believe you.

• If you use testimonials, consider this suggestion from the booklet, *101 Secrets to Direct Success* by Lakewood Publications. You can offer four basic types of testimonials: customer testimonials, expert testimonials, celebrity testimonials and testimonials from groups of experts. The fourth is the most convincing.

• Tell your readers precisely what you want them to do. To persuade people to change their feeling, attitudes or behavior, you must ask. Never assume that they'll know what to do with your message. If you want them to mail in a coupon, clearly say so — several times if you must. If you want them to call, make sure your phone number is in large easy-to-read type.

• Conclude your message with a thought readers must agree with. Don't give them the opportunity to say "no" to your concluding remarks. If, for example, you're spearheading an anti-smoking campaign, avoid open questions such as, "Don't you want to quit smoking today?" Many smokers will obviously say, "no." Make a statement they can't deny. "It's a proven fact that each year hundreds of thousands die from smoking. We can help you avoid becoming a statistic."

## Use headlines and subheads for organization

Almost without exception, experts agree that including powerful headlines and subheads is vital to the success of promotional literature.

Headlines and subheads serve a number of functions.

*One*: They grab the readers' attention and pull them into your message. Many readers have only a passing interest in what you have to say. But even a reader with little interest will take some time to skim your piece and read the headlines and subheads.

Consider these suggestions:

• Include a benefit statement. Tell readers what they can gain by reading your message. Think of a problem your audience has that your product or service can solve.

If you own a small accounting firm, you might consider something like: "How To Save On Your Tax Return."

• Use the word "you" in the headline. For example, "Ten Things **You** Should Know About Heart Disease."

• Ask a question: "Can You Answer These Questions About Your Children?"

• Include an intriguing statement: "Every Six Seconds in America a Home is Broken Into."

• Make a promise to the reader: "This Amazing New Fertilizer is Guaranteed to Give You the Greenest Lawn on the Block."

*Remember*: The headline must be a clear and concise thought. If readers must work to figure out the point, you're likely to lose them.

*Two*: Headlines and subheads organize your copy into easily digestible chunks of information. Long, unbroken blocks of type are intimidating. Many readers are apprehensive about committing to reading large sections of type. They are likely, however, to read the same information broken up into three very short sections.

*Three*: Headlines and subheads also provide valuable information for readers at every interest level. Keep in mind the 30-3-30 rule. This formula suggests that readers fall into one of three categories: those who merely scan the message, spending just 30 seconds on the piece; those who give the copy a very quick reading of about 3 minutes; and those who read every word, spending 30 minutes or more.

It is very unlikely that your entire audience will fall into just one of these groups. Your objective then is to write your message and organize your thoughts so that you communicate your ideas to each of the three reader types. Headlines and subheads should provide enough of a message skeleton to communicate even to 30-second readers.

> *If you grab your readers with your first 50 words, they'll probably read the next 450 words. Research shows readership drops little after 50 words, giving you 450 more words to convey your message.*

*Four*: Once your headline pulls your readers into your copy, subheads serve as good resting points for the eye. They give your readers places to stop and digest the information they just read and good starting places to move on to the next idea.

Start strong: Just as headlines and subheads play a key role in communicating your message, so do your opening sentences. Your first sentence must establish the tone of your piece and entice the reader to read on. The lead should also express the main idea of the paragraph to follow.

In *How to Get Results with Business Writing*, the editors of *communication briefings* state:

"Experts agree that, if you can keep readers attention for the first 50 words, chances are good they'll read the next 450. Reason: Research shows that readership wanes after the first 50 words but drops very little between 50 and 500. That means your first 50 words must grab readers. And if you agree with the research, you'll have 450 words left to tell them what you want them to know."

Use these techniques to use when writing your lead:

• Open with an *attention-getting statement*. If you used an attention statement in your headline, repeat it or clarify it in your lead.

• Point out some *common ground* you — or others — share with your readers. If, for example, you are promoting your lawn care service, you may suggest that few people have enough time to do their own yard work. The common ground is lack of time.

• Offer ideas that *motivate your reader* to read more of your message. In this case, your opening sentence promises what readers will learn if they continue. For example, a brochure for a weight-loss center can lead with, "By spending just five minutes reading this brochure you'll learn 15 things you can do today to start losing weight."

## Step 4: Choose a size and format that fits your needs

In their book *Desktop Publishing*, Dan Lattimore and Art Terry offer definitions for a few of the most popular formats used for promotional literature. Knowing the distinctions between these various sizes and formats will help you decide which is best for you — and help you communicate clearly with those you'll work with during production and printing.

**Fliers** and circulars are typically single-sheet publications. In most cases, they have one purpose — to announce an event or some similar idea. The primary goal of a flier is to get the audience's attention and communicate a single and simple message. This format is often distributed by hand (technically called a handbill), posted on bulletin boards and telephone poles (called a poster) or placed under car windshield wipers. Check on the legality of such placement.

*Lead and headlines for a promotional flier or brochure must communicate a major reason for readers to invest their time. Example: Spend just five minutes with this brochure, and you'll learn 15 things you can do today to start losing weight.*

**Brochures** are technically six pages or more. They are traditionally produced and distributed to special publics for a specific purpose. While the term *brochure* is commonly used today to describe most forms of promotional literature, you should keep this distinction in mind to avoid miscommunication.

**Booklets** are usually 24 pages and longer. They tend to have more structure, photos and illustrations than brochures.

**Pamphlets** and folders, on the other hand, are smaller than brochures and have fewer photos, illustrations and color. Their general format is a single 8½" x 11" sheet folded twice — creating a total of six panels. This is the most popular format for basic promotional literature. A slightly larger pamphlet format is a single 8½" x 14" sheet folded three times — creating a total of eight panels.

These are the most basic styles. The options you have for style, fold and format are virtually limitless. But in your first efforts, you are better off relying on these tried and true standards. When you become more comfortable with production techniques, let your imagination take over — provided you have a budget to do so.

You must consider your budget when you select your format. While you may want to produce a fancy multi-page, four-color booklet describing your products and services, it may not be worth the money. In general, the larger your format and the more production steps involved, the more expensive and time consuming the piece will be.

That's why the **single-sheet pamphlet format is so popular.** The 8½" x 11" and 8½" x 14" folders are standard size sheets that permit an organized presentation of information. Plus, it is a format many people are accustomed to seeing. If you're on a limited budget and want to go one step further than a single flat sheet, this is your best option.

To get a better idea of cost, meet with your printer. (See Step 9).

The order in which you plan to present your message can also influence format selection. If you have, for example, six key components to your message, a six-panel pamphlet may be just the ticket. A single thought would likely be best delivered by a circular. A historical look at your organization would work well in a booklet or brochure. The page-by-page organization of these formats lends itself nicely to chronological presentations.

Authors Thomas Bivins and William Ryan offer this statement about organizing and presenting your message through format. Good promotional pieces "do not unfold like road maps, but present a logical pathway through their panels." Each panel or section provides a chunk of information that leads logically to the conclusion you want your reader to reach.

While deciding which format is best for you, always consider how your piece will be distributed and how the audience will use the piece. If you plan to post your promotion on a bulletin board, a booklet would be ill-advised. Obviously, the single sheet circular would be more appropriate.

Are you planning to send your piece by mail? If so, the U.S. Post Office has more than a few guidelines you must follow. To avoid a lot of grief, your best bet is to use common sizes. Design your piece to fit into standard-sized business envelopes.

If you're planning to send a promotion by mail, meet with a representative from your local post office to learn what you can and can't do. If you plan to mail a lot, be sure to ask about discounts and what you must do to get them.

If your piece will be displayed in a brochure rack, be certain you choose a size that fits. You may opt for an unusual size to make your literature stand out in the crowd. But if your uncommon size won't fit into a standard brochure rack — your primary distribution vehicle — you've just wasted a lot of time, effort and money.

Also think about how your audience will use your piece. Is it something they will look at once and discard, or hold onto for future reference? If it's a quick-read-and-pitch piece, you may think twice about spending a lot of money producing it. If, however, you plan for the reader to keep the piece for an extended period of time, you should consider a more substantial piece. You'll need to find a format that will fit nicely into a file cabinet or bookshelf and be sturdy enough to hold up over time and use.

## Step 5: Design your piece with form and function

Starting the design of any project can seem an overwhelming task. You have at your disposal an infinite combination of design tools and techniques. The question is: Where to begin?

Start by understanding the purpose of design and the basics that make effective design possible.

Many beginners — as well as professionals — fail to realize that the primary goal of design is to *help the reader understand the message*.

But facilitating understanding is not easy. Countless factors come into play that encourage or discourage your audience from reading your message.

Your role as a designer is vital because design must

not only keep your audience reading through the piece; it must also first get their attention.

*Think about your message in terms of design*: Even during the planning stages of any project you should begin to think about how you will design your message. As you organize your ideas, picture how they will fit onto a page. This does not mean you must have the exact design or format established mentally, but at least have a rough idea of how your message will break down visually.

Examine your messages and think about how they will look, and how your audience might react to that look. If you see in you mind's eye that your design is overwhelmed by one part of your message, break the message up into two sections.

Go back to the process of dividing your text in chunks of information. Think about how you used headlines and subheads to organize your written message.

Robin Williams, a typographical expert and author, writes, "a document's headlines and subheads do more than simply give you a clue as to the content of the stories. They provide an organization to the page, a repetitive element that unifies the publication and visual contrast that attracts the eye."

Establishing visual organization to your message also

> *To produce attractive and effective promotional materials, know basic design components.*

gives the reader good visual entry and exit points. Your reader should be able to see the logic of your message, not have to read every word to understand your point.

### Principles of design

Knowing the basic components of design results in attractive and effective promotional materials.

Most graphics experts recognize proportion, balance, contrast, rhythm and unity as the basic components of design.

Here are some basic definitions and ideas you can use to put these principles to work for you.

**Proportion** refers to the relationship of sizes and lengths of various parts of a printed page. You must consider proportions of the dimensions of the page and the individual elements on the page.

Research shows that a pleasing page shape is one in which the dimensions are in a ratio of about two to three. This is also an appropriate proportion of individual elements on the page (i.e., blocks of text, photographs, boxes).

This proportion fits the design concept known as the *Golden Mean* (or Golden Section). The formula, established by the Greek philosopher Pythagoras, states that the

> *How the eye is drawn to a page: The eye starts a bit to the left and above the geometric center of the page. It then circles up to the left and moves around the page in clockwise fashion.*

relationship of the smaller segment of a line to its larger segment should be equal to the ratio of the large segment to the entire line.

Another important law of proportion is called *Ground Thirds*.

Basically, this concept suggests that you divide your page into thirds and design in ⅓-page and ⅔-page units. You can see this in use in many magazine and print advertisements.

**Balance** defines how the visual (or optical) weight distributes throughout a page. In general, the larger or darker an element, the more its weight.

Most graphic design experts recognize two types of balance: symmetric (or formal) and asymmetric (or informal).

**Symmetric balance** is established when visual weight of the elements on the page is distributed evenly. This often lends a feeling of strong orderliness and dignity to the look of the page.

**Asymmetric balance** is achieved through uneven distribution of visual weight on the page. In other words, most of the elements (text blocks, photographs, boxes, etc.) are placed on one side or to the top or bottom of the page. Informal balance suggests a more modern, less structured feel.

When thinking about balance, remember that you must not only balance elements on each page or panel, but think of the document as a whole. In a six-panel pamphlet, for example, an inside panel might look fine standing alone, but when you open up the piece, the balance of the spread may be off.

Try to maintain a consistent balance throughout. If you start with informal balance on your cover, stick with it throughout the piece. This rule is not carved in stone, but it will help you keep a consistent look throughout.

**Contrast** is a comparison of elements in terms of size, shape, tone, texture, direction and color value (i.e., the deepness and darkness of a color). In basic terms, if an element becomes lighter or darker compared to its background, it becomes more noticeable. In the same sense, an item becomes more noticeable as it becomes larger than the objects surrounding it.

In a Technique article called, "Use Contrast," Nancy Bargine, a specialist in graphic design, suggests these ideas to add contrast to your layout:

- Use bold against light in your type.

- Use thick against thin in your type, rules and artwork.
- Use shallow against deep shapes.
- Use black against white.
- Use big against small.

As a general rule, you should avoid too much similarity in shapes, sizes and emphasis. When all elements on your page are the same relative size, your design can become monotonous. In establishing your proportions, keep in mind the relative importance of each element to your message.

**Rhythm** is the repetition of similar shapes, sizes, textures and like-elements in a design. By seeing pattern or rhythm in the design, the readers can more easily follow the order you want them to follow. Rhythm helps your message unfold logically.

**Unity** (sometimes called harmony) describes how well — or poorly — all of the elements on the page work together. When you establish unity, all of your design items look as though they belong together. Nothing seems out of place.

Unity is vital because it helps carry the eye smoothly through the document. A consistency of look and feel helps confirm that what readers saw on page one relates to what they read on the last page.

You must also consider what that message is in relation to the look of the piece. A perfectly harmonious design with bright, flashy colors and light cheerful graphics would be inappropriate for a funeral home brochure. Unity ties together both visual and written communication.

## Moving the reader's eye

The idea of moving the reader's eye through the layout is key to successful design. If you fail to do so, your audience might get only part of your message.

Individually — and together — the principles of design just reviewed play an important part in pulling your reader through the page. But it is also helpful to understand a little bit about how people typically look at a printed page. These definitions may help:

- *Geometric center*: A point in the exact center of the page. If you draw an X that touches all corners of the page, it is where the lines intersect.

- *Optical center*: The point where the eye naturally falls onto a page. Research shows that this point is approximately five units from the bottom of the page and three units from the top.

- *Focal point*: The main point of visual interest. Where the eye is first drawn because of a headline, visual, color, etc.

You should keep "points" in mind when figuring out where to place your dominant visual elements.

*The focal point of a page is the main point of visual interest where the eye is first drawn because of a headline, visual, color, etc.*

Where you start your readers plays a major role in determining how much of your message they actually read.

A number of studies have been conducted to determine how a reader's eye typically moves through a page. Two studies are particularly useful to planning design.

Studies by H.F. Brandt show that the eye begins on a page at a position a little to the left and above geometric center of the page. It then circles up to the left and moves in around the page in a clockwise direction.

Brandt also investigated how book readers tend to spend time looking at each section of a page. His studies showed that people look at the upper left section of a page 41 percent of the time, upper right 20 percent, lower left 25 percent and lower right 14 percent.

Experts agree, however, that by using graphic design elements effectively, it is possible to change the natural flow of eye movement. However, you should do so with thought and careful planning.

## Tools of design

Principles of design and research findings are important in understanding how to plan your layout. But equally important is knowing the tools and devices that go into design. These are the actual physical building blocks — the components — of your page.

Here's a listing of the major tools of design you have at your disposal:

**Text block**. A text block is a chunk of information. It is the visual unit that contains your written message. Organizing your text blocks with headlines, subheads, and paragraphs is perhaps the most important factor in using design to communicate. Text blocks are usually set in columns — like those you see in newspapers.

**Rule**. Rules are physical lines added to your page. They vary in thickness from a hairline to 24 points or more. Rules play a key role in adding visual separation to elements in your layout. A good example is the thin rule that often runs vertically between columns of type. However, rules also hold elements together by running horizontally above or below two or more individual pieces.

*Caution*: Too many rules can be very distracting. Because they serve as guides and separation points for the eye, poorly placed rules can send your readers to the wrong paragraph or cause them to stop reading where they shouldn't. Each rule you place in your layout should have a purpose.

**Box**. A box surrounds or outlines another element, either to define the element's shape or draw attention. Boxes often highlight display type, guarantees, photographs and charts or graphs. They also effectively "sidebar" information that is related, but not vital, to your message.

Studies have shown, however, that boxes do not boost readership of articles or long blocks of text. This suggests that you use boxes only to highlight short, but important pieces of information.

**Photograph and illustration**. These are standard components of most promotional literature. The following section in this guidebook will cover in detail how to use both effectively.

Select photographs for the power of their message and their ability to attract attention. To be sure that photographs are not selected and sized to fit the available space, block out large areas at the beginning of the planning process.

Excellent writing is soon lost on a "type heavy" page. Any page that blurs into a sea of gray type is bound to discourage readers. The best message can be lost in too much type. While the overall design should allow for

*Every rule in your layout should have a purpose.*

white space and a variety of design elements, large bold photographs enhance nearly every type of publication.

Strong black and white photos attract attention whenever they are carefully cropped and relate to the message. No rule says a photo will be more effective if produced in full color. Many photos have more power and more influence if they are in stark contrast — black and white.

The most eye-catching and prize-winning publications **use images of people** doing whatever they do. People laughing or crying — at work or engaged in active play — attract our attention. Who can resist the face of a child — full of expression, hope and promise?

It's hard to imagine any publication not benefiting from carefully selected images of people living their lives. Fast food chain executives and beverage producers know the power of images of active people. That's why they budget millions of dollars for television commercials of people living life — and in a final scene they have a drink or stop for a cheeseburger. You can learn a lot about selling messages by **critiquing television commercials**.

Photographs of the human face rarely, if ever, look good when printed in green ink — or blue ink — or any color other than black ink. On special occasions, a sepia photo — or a special charcoal brown ink may work — but the best rule is to avoid any single second color for photographs, especially images of the human face.

Large photographs are best. Avoid small photographs in nearly every type of publication. When we want to obtain the full power of the photo — we need to remember that bigger is better. Faces the size of a postage stamp rarely work, no matter how small the publication, or how many photos are needed for the page requirements.

*Research: A story written with short words, sentences and paragraphs is preferred. It's easier to read, and additional paragraphs create more white space.*

Cropping photographs is an art that can be self-taught. Many who work in publications have simple tricks they learned through experimentation. One quick way to see the effect of cropping is to lay sheets of plain paper around the four sides of the photo and move them back and forth to define the area of the image that is most powerful. Another way is to enlarge the photo on the copy machine and trim edges to get the best effect. Copy machines that reduce and enlarge can make the task of sizing photos a quick and easy process.

Photos should be selected with sensitivity to all people. Gender, age and ethnicity are critical issues when you select images of people. Photos of people with physical limitations are still missing from too many publications.

**Lines and shapes**. In this case, lines are different than rules. Lines are not necessarily printed on the page. They are created by the alignment of other elements along the same horizontal, vertical or diagonal visual axis.

In the same sense, shapes are not necessarily printed on the page. They can be defined by the borders of a text block, areas of white space or any combination of graphic elements. Shapes often create rhythm, proportion, direction and unity in a layout.

Like other tools of design, carefully plan and use lines and shapes to help your audience understand your message.

**Elemental forms**. Over the years, graphic designers have found that specific shapes lend themselves to attractive and functional layouts — sometimes called *elemental forms*. The most common of these forms are: L-shape, T-shape, O-shape, Diagonal-shape, S-shape and C-shape. In basic terms, the pieces of your layout are organized around one of the elemental shapes. In other

words, the lines and shapes within the design pattern form an L, T, O, etc.

It may take a while to use these in your early designs. But start by looking for them in magazine and newspaper ads. When you see their function, apply the ideas to your own work.

**Grid**. Grids are formed by nonprinted lines that serve as guides for the horizontal and vertical placement of your layout components. Establish a grid when you plan your design. It will show you in very clear terms where to locate your margins, columns and borders.

**Screen**. Screens are basically tints of a color. For example, a 10 percent screen of black ink will produce a very light gray. A 10 percent screen of red will produce what appears to be a very light pink. Screens are often used to cover an entire page — to give the illusion of colored paper — or to highlight important blocks of text.

**Bleed**. A bleed is ink printed to the very edge of the page. A full-bleed is ink printed to all edges of the page. Designers often use this technique for photographs.

While bleeds can add interest to your layout, they do traditionally cost more to print. Consider whether the added expense is worth the look you're trying to achieve with your design.

**• Margin and column space**. Margins are areas of white space that separate your design elements (or "live area") — established by your grid — from the edges of your page. A good rule of thumb — leave at least ¾" margins on all sides of your document. These margins allow readers to hold your piece without blocking anything in the layout.

*Column spaces* are white areas between columns of text or artwork. In general, you should allow at least 1 pica (⅙ of an inch) between columns. Columns set too closely together may be confusing because readers may jump the space and start reading the next column. Also be careful not to set columns too far apart. Extremely large column spaces give the appearance that the blocks of type do not belong together.

**Typography**. The type of lettering you choose for your document has a major impact on its look and feel. The next section of this chapter covers typographical rules and techniques in some detail.

**Discretion**. Judgment is a powerful design tool. Too many inexperienced designers try to do too much with their documents. As a result, the message gets lost in a puzzle of fancy type, meaningless graphic elements and insufficient white space. Always use discretion when you add elements to your layout. If what you put on the page doesn't help get your message across, leave it out. *Remember*: A plain and simple layout that communicates a message is far more valuable than a slick piece that does not.

## Use white space effectively

White space, as a design element, too often becomes an afterthought, something left on the page when the rest of the design is completed.

White space is simply empty of print. But these unprinted areas are as important to communicating your message as the type itself. Without white space, nothing separates individual design elements. Your entire layout then becomes a mass of unrecognizable text and visual elements. Consider these research findings and observations on use of white space.

• An article titled, "Research in Brief: The Graphics of Prose," reports research by Smith and McCombs indicating that a story written with short words, short sentences and short paragraphs is preferable, not only because it is easier to read, but because additional paragraphs within the story create more white space.

• An article from the *American Journal of Psychology* reports studies that show that you should allow 25 percent of your layout for white space. This effective percentage attracts attention to your piece. The study also shows that attention decreases when white space exceeds 25 percent.

• Experts recommend that you carefully use white space between elements. Too much white space weakens the visual connection between elements and makes them "float" in the layout.

• In their book, *How to Make Type Readable*, authors Tinker and Paterson suggest that you indent the first line of every paragraph. The extra white space within the text block helps reading speed. Material without indentions, they report, is read 7.3 percent more slowly.

• Professional designers and graphic communication experts often advise pushing white space to the outside; avoid trapping it within your layout. In other words, don't have a large area of white space in the center of your page completely surrounded by text or graphic elements. Trapped white space is a design hole that stops readers. White space should guide readers through, not trap them. It should focus attention and make individual elements stand out — as well as work together.

## Importance of cover design

Like it or not, people do judge a book by its cover. They also judge your promotional pieces by their covers. That's why you should take extra care in designing the front page of your piece. It might be the only part of your message your reader will ever see.

In her book *Better Brochures, Catalogs and Mailing Pieces*, Jane Maas, noted advertising and graphic communication specialist, states that four of five readers never get beyond the cover of most promotional pieces. That's certainly not good news when you've just spent a lot of time, effort and money putting your publication together.

> **Indent the first line of each paragraph to help reading speed. Readers digest nonindented paragraphs 7.3 percent more slowly.**

You can take some steps to help overcome these odds. The cover of your piece should tell at a glance what is offered inside. Many experts feel that those interested enough in picking up your brochure or promotion want to know right away what's in it for them.

Your front page or panel should get readers' attention, tell them what the brochure is about, get them interested in what's inside and set up a theme or look that will run throughout the piece. Many experts suggest you do this by using only one dominant element. It might be a photographic, eye-catching graphic or strong headline.

While your cover panel many not offer any real information or persuasive copy about your product or service, it should "hook" the reader to go inside.

## Most publications need an envelope or custom covering

Envelopes come in a variety of stock standard sizes. Designed properly, most publications fit into standard envelopes. Unfortunately many publications are designed with little thought to the envelope. The envelope and the publication must fit together in size and appearance. A handsome publication loses its impact whenever it's folded for mailing. Don't drop a small publication into an oversize envelope. Address this problem before you decide the shape and size of the publication.

Custom envelopes are expensive and rarely required. Printing on standard envelopes is affordable and helps to attract attention to the publication inside. Those who design the publication should also design the mailing envelope so the total effect adds to the impact. Frequently the quality of the envelope design determines whether the audience will open the mail or discard it without opening it. Understanding that the message on the envelope is key to the success of the mailing should help publication designers to create the best possible package.

## Using paper in your design

The paper you choose can dramatically affect the look — and effectiveness — of your promotion. When used properly, paper can add color, texture, look and style to any promotional literature. When used poorly, it can ruin an otherwise effective design.

Discuss paper options with your printer, who will give you information on what's available and what will work best for you. Here are a few points on the role paper plays in design and ideas you should consider:

• Be careful about using a dark paper for your project. If your text and visual elements are too dark to see, your reader won't put in the effort to figure it out. Research shows that black ink on yellow or white paper offers the best legibility. If you decide to go with an off-color paper, remember that **contrast between ink and paper color is the major factor in legibility**.

• In her master's thesis "Research Studies on the Printed Mass Media Into the '90s," Joellen Collins reported on a study about the use of colored papers. The results show that colorful papers are not perceived as less accurate. Nor are they seen as different from white paper in terms of professionalism, responsibility, informativeness, importance or value. They are seen as more pleasant, interesting, active and modern.

• Be careful about using a colored paper if your document contains a lot of photographs. The color can distort the appearance of photographs, especially when people are pictured. You may not want to make the president of your organization look blue, green, purple, etc.

• Also, if your promotion contains a large number of photographs, consider using a coated paper. The ink won't soak in and spread as much as it will on an uncoated sheet. If there is a lot of type in your piece as well, use a matte finish instead of a gloss to reduce glare — and ease readability.

• A highly textured paper can add a nice touch of class to your promotions. However, it can also interfere with legibility if your type is small or very thin. This doesn't mean you should avoid it. Just be aware that its uneven surfaces can distort type and make details appear fuzzy.

Paper quality is always an important consideration. Many basic publications print effectively on "house" paper or paper purchased in large lots and always in stock. Your printer can make this paper available at the lowest possible price. House paper might be compared to house wine — excellent value for the cost.

*Select paper and cover stock that's right for the job.*

Avoid selecting a paper that looks and feels too expensive for the message. A bulky paper that has texture is rarely necessary and should be used with great care. Inappropriate selection of paper quickly detracts from good writing and excellent photographs and design.

Many publications are suitable for a treatment referred to as "self-cover" — that is, the cover paper is the same quality as other pages. Such publications do not require a strong cover stock for protection or for appearance. A publication that will be used a few times and discarded might not need protective cover stock even though it might need a cover that implies its importance. A publication designed for months of use may need a protective cover. The combination of self-cover and house paper is ideal for student publications, certain mandatory financial reporting to shareholders, and internal documents.

The best paper has a texture that permits an easier fold in one direction. It is the printer's responsibility to cut the paper to accommodate a crisp fold.

## Basic steps in graphic production

When beginning a design, most designers follow a series of steps that take a project from a rough idea to a finished product. Following are the main production steps you should take to bring your design to life.

**1. Thumbnail sketches**. These small drawings give a rough idea of the layout of your pages. They seldom include much in the way of detail, but reflect an overall look of the layout. You should do several thumbnail sketches to decide which version you like best. While the thumbnail is a rough version of your layout, try to keep the proportions of your page close. If your final page size will be 6" x 9", consider making your thumbnails 2" x 3".

**2. Rough layout**. Once you've completed your thumbnails and decided on the version you like best, begin work on a rough layout. It is usually the same size as the final project. You will include more detail and accuracy in it than in your thumbnails, but you're still in the experimental stages. Work with different ideas, but make this version

### Choosing the right paper for your printing...

**Colored paper**
• Seen as similar to white regarding professionalism, responsibility, and value
• Seen as more pleasant, interesting and modern
• Not recommended with many photos

**Coated paper**
• Good with many photos

**Textured paper**
• Adds class but reduces legibility

**House paper**
• Helps cut costs

tighter and plan appropriate space and proportions to each element in the design.

**3. Comprehensive layout**. This stage is commonly called a "comp." This drawing, or mock-up, offers a detailed look of the final printed piece. Be sure you're happy with the comp before you proceed. This is the final step before you start the actual final artwork.

**4. Mechanical**. A mechanical (also called a *paste-up*) is your final artwork. Your printer will use this camera-ready design to reproduce your job. Traditionally, mechanicals are boards with type, photos and instruction pasted, waxed or taped on. With desktop publishing, the mechanical stage is skipped and the assembled parts are photographed.

**5. The dummy**. The dummy is a copy of your mechanical put together, folded or collated just as your final product will appear. Dummies show the printer exactly how the final piece should appear.

## Consider the "look" and the message it sends

Publications must have the right look or they will surely send conflicting messages. Some publications should look and feel expensive. It's expected if they're designed to sell high end cars or homes in exclusive neighborhoods. Direct mail advertising for expensive jewelry must have a certain look. Tabloids and newsprint rarely market expensive consumer goods.

Certain messages are best delivered with a publication that appears to be inexpensive and easy to produce. Community newsletters from municipal governments should look appropriately modest. They should be smart, attractive, and eye-catching while looking inexpensive.

Most nonprofit organizations would benefit from considering the impact of a publication that looks expensive. When people are asking other people to give money to a worthy cause, care must be taken that the appearance of the publication does not interfere with the message. Exceptions to this include solicitation of major gifts from eligible potential donors. With these publications, the look is key to the process.

## Step 6: Choose typefaces that work

Choosing a typeface (font) for your project can be a monumental task. Today, designers can choose from thousands of typefaces, each with its own personality and feel.

You should select a typeface that not only fits the tone and feel of your message and design, but one that is also easy to read.

> *Use serif type, such as this, for text.*
> *Pick 10-11 point type for body copy.*
> **Select sans serif type, like this,**
> **for headlines.**

## The purpose of type

Typography is an art form in its own right. Each typeface carries its own mood, look and feel. Set in different type, the same letter set side by side can communicate different feelings.

While it's important to recognize the artistic form and subtlety of type, you must keep in mind the purpose you want it to serve. In most cases, the purpose is to clearly communicate your message. Experts generally agree that type's primary function is to be read. Just like design, an attractive page of type that is hard to read often isn't — and is therefore useless.

Noted English typographer Stanley Morison put it this way. "Of course, typography can — and should — be used as a decorative element in your layout. But the role of decoration should never outweigh the role of communication tool."

## Anatomy of a letter

To begin to understand typography, it is important to understand what makes up a letter. The following definitions are the basic components of type.

- **Baseline**: An imaginary line on which uppercase letters and the bodies of lowercase letters rest.

- **X-height**: The height (or depth) of the bodies of lowercase letters. For example, the lowercase letters "x," "a," "c," etc. This height varies from typeface to typeface.

- **Stroke**: The lines that make up a letter. Some strokes are thick and some thin. The strokes in some faces are of equal thickness throughout the letter, while other faces contain thin to thick strokes within the same letter.

- **Ascender**: The part of a lowercase letter that extends above the x-height.

- **Descender**: The part of a lowercase letter that extends below the baseline.

- **Type size**: A measurement in points from the bottom of the descender to the top of the ascender, or the height of a capital letter.

In general, typefaces are classed into a few major categories: serifs, sans serifs, scripts and novelty types.

**Set reverse type in sans serif font. Use sparingly: Research shows it slows reading by 11 percent and cuts comprehension by 30 percent.**

The serif group further divides into old style, transitional and modern.

*Serif type* is distinguished by the "feet" or decorative strokes at the ends of letters. *Sans serif* type (which means without serifs) has no feet or decorative strokes.

*Script type* generally resembles handwriting. *Novelty* types are a miscellaneous collection — most often used for logos, display boards, posters, etc. You see this type in circus poster headlines.

## Choosing a typeface

As you look at typefaces, you'll notice variety in shape in character. Your job is to find a type that projects the feel you want.

You should seek readability and legibility. *Readability* describes how easily, quickly and accurately the type is read. *Legibility*, however, relates to visibility and how easy the letters are to see. Look for both when you select type.

An article called "Choosing Legible Typefaces," from *communication briefings* (July 1986) offers these ideas.

For best legibility, choose typefaces that:

- Have open counters — ample space within certain letters, such as "o," "c," and "e"
- Have large x-heights
- Do not have excessive contrast in stroke thickness
- Do not have serifs with exaggerated shapes

*Remember*: You want to communicate your message. If your typefaces are both readable and legible, you stand a better chance to meet your goal.

Communication experts and typographers generally agree that your type should not call attention to itself. If your readers focus on a type's fanciness, they aren't paying attention to the message.

## Serif vs. sans serif

Communicators and typographers have long debated the use of these styles.

The traditional school says that serif typefaces should always be used for body copy and sans serif typefaces used for headline and display copy. The theory goes that the serifs, or feet, in serif type help guide the reader's eye in long blocks of smaller text — and therefore have better readability. The serifs also help readers see your message in words and phrases, not just individual letters put together on the page.

Sans serif types, on the other hand, offer better legibility — are easier to see and recognize — and, therefore, make for stronger headlines. For this reason, sans serif types are used on highway signs.

Others argue that sans serif is just as effective for body copy and serif works fine for headlines.

Research supports both sides of the argument. But the vast majority of research supports the traditional view. Studies predominantly show that serif fonts in body copy are read more easily, more quickly and with better comprehension.

Author and typographical researcher Colin Wheildon states, "Many editors and art directors argue that sans serif body type is clean, uncluttered and attractive …. They also argue that people will grow to live with it, and it will soon become comprehensible to all. This is nonsense …. The conclusion must be that body type be set in serif type if the designer intends to be read and understood."

If you feel that sans serif body copy better fits the mood of your piece, take some precautions. Research indicates that you can improve readability of sans serif fonts by adding at least two points of leading, keeping your line lengths short, and allowing for ragged right alignment (unjustified type).

**Most readers (96%) tested reported too much italic type more difficult and time consuming to read than regular lower case letters, like most of this text.**

## Choosing type styles

Here are some ideas about the attention-getting techniques that you can add to your typeface:

**ALL CAPS**. Avoid setting type in all capital letters. Research shows that setting even a few words together in all caps serious affects readability. Studies show that we recognize words by their shapes. Setting type in all caps removes those shapes and creates a page of nothing but rectangles. The reader must read letter by letter instead of in saccadic jumps (looking at a small group of words for a quarter of a second, then moving on to the next group). This slows reading time by 15 percent.

**Bold**. Experts generally recommend that bold type be used only for emphasis — such as headlines, subheads and key words. Some research suggests that bold type fatigues readers more quickly and comprehension drops off. Other studies show that while bold type does not significantly decrease readability, readers do prefer a medium weight type for body copy.

**Research suggests that for text of 9 to 12 points, you should use a line width between 18 and 24 picas. This allows approximately 10 to 12 words per line. In most cases this means that you should set your type in more than one wide column. The number of columns you can fit depends on the width of your page.** ·

This text is 9 points and line length is 18 picas........................

## This text is 12 points and line length is 20 picas.....

**The explanatory text above is 12 points on 2 points of leading, expressed as 12/14.**

**Underline**. Like boldfacing, underlining type effectively calls attention to important pieces of information. But if you overuse it, reading becomes more difficult and nothing in your message gets attention.

**Italic**. Designers generally agree that italic type should be used sparingly. Research shows that 96% of readers tested believe that italic type is more difficult and time consuming to read than regular lower case letters. Another study shows that subjects read italic type up to 20 words per minute slower than regular type. However, another study found that comprehension levels did not decrease from type set in italic style.

**Reverse.** Reverse type effectively makes a line of type stand out. However, like other typographic effects, designers must use it with discretion. Research reports that reversing type not only slows reading by 11 percent, but also cuts comprehension by 30 percent. Another study finds that black text on a white background is up to 40 percent easier to read than white text on a black background. If you do set type in reverse, avoid using small type sizes — and use it sparingly even for display type. Plus, use heavier weight types and sans serif fonts. Increased weight and lack of thin serif strokes help prevent the type from being filled in or overwhelmed by the background. Studies also show that reversed sans serif type offers higher comprehension levels than reversed serif types.

**Picking the best type size**. A common question of many novice designers is, "How large should my type be?"

In his book *Typography: How to Make it Most Legible*, Rolf Rehe states, "A definition of the most legible type size has been hampered by the fact that x-heights for individual typefaces differ greatly." However, the following research findings and rules of thumb may help you choose the most effective size for your publication:

For body copy, experts suggest using a type size of 9, 10, 11 or 12 points. Typefaces with small x-height should be set in 11 or 12. Typefaces with large x-height can be set in 9 or 10 point.

In *Typography and Typesetting,* Ronald Labuz suggests that display type (headlines and subheads) should be from one-and-a-half to three times larger than your body copy. If type becomes too large, it has the tendency to overpower the page.

Research also shows that larger headlines attract more attention, but only up to 36 points.

You should also create a clear distinction between the size of your headlines and the size of your subheads. Your reader must be very clear about the order of importance in your message. Headlines and subheads too close in size don't communicate clearly main and secondary ideas of the message.

**Picking the best leading.** Leading — also called *line spacing* — is white space between lines of type. The amount of leading you use can determine if your message is easy to read. Use too much leading and the text can look disjointed and not appear as a single unit. Use too little leading and your type will look crowded and your message becomes an uninviting block of gray.

These research findings offer some valuable guidance:

• In his book *Typography: How to Make it Most Legible*, Rolf Rehe states, "For optimal type sizes of 9, 10, 11 and 12 points, the most beneficial amount of leading for maximum legibility consists of either 1, 2, 3, or 4 points. Judgment depends on the typeface used. Heavier typefaces need more leading than light ones, but all typefaces are more legible with moderate leading than without any at all."

*Justified type gives a more formal look to design. Unjustified (ragged right) type looks less formal. Don t justify narrow columns. Poor readers don t handle justified type well.*

• A good general rule of thumb is that leading should be 20 percent of the size of your body copy. If, for example, your body copy is 10 point, you would set it on two points of leading — written as 10/12 by designers.

• Typefaces with a small body (or x-height) often require only one point of leading. Because the body is small, the ascenders and descenders are often proportionally longer. Therefore, the space between the baseline of one line and the top of the x-height of the next is larger, giving a more open, lighter look.

• As line-length increases, so does the need for additional leading. Four-point leading, however, gains little unless line measure is extraordinary wide.

• In a *Technique* article called "Headlines and Subheads," designer Robin Williams advises that in headlines, the larger the type size, the less leading you need. If you have few or no descenders, it is particularly important to remove excess space. Your intent is to keep lines together as one visual unit.

• You should always allow more space above a subhead than below it. Keep the subhead visually connected to the text it controls.

**Setting line width**. This will often be determined by the width of your columns. In this case, then, the question becomes, how wide do I make my columns?

Research suggests that for text of 9 to 12 points, you should use a line width of between 18 and 24 picas. This allows approximately 10 to 12 words per line. In most cases this means that you should set your type in more than one wide column. The number of columns you can fit depends on the width of your page.

When we read, we look at small group of words for a quarter of a second, then move on to the next group. Type set too wide makes it difficult for the eye to move from the end of one line to the beginning of the next. On the other hand, type set in very narrow columns causes the eye to spend too much time jumping from one line to the next.

A good general rule to remember — your line width in picas should be about twice your type size in points. For example, type set in 10 point type should have a line length of about 20 picas. Type set in 12 point type should have a line length of about 24 picas.

*To justify or not*

Like the serif versus sans serif debate, the effect of justification is unclear. However, there seems to be no significant difference in legibility between justified or unjustified type.

An important point to remember, however, is that studies find that while good readers are unaffected by justification, poor readers have more difficulty with it.

Justified type does tend to give a more formal, orderly look to design. Unjustified (also called left aligned or ragged right) tends to look somewhat less formal. Think about justification while trying to keep your design consistent with

*Learn if your readers read and enjoy your publications. Conduct focus groups with readers to see if they re reading all or just some of your publication. Ask if they want more articles on some topics and fewer on others.*

the tone of your message. This text is unjustified because left aligned type is easier on the eye path.

Finally, many designers advise that you don't justify very narrow columns of type. If a narrow column is justified, the spaces between words can become too large because there is less type to work with. This creates what are called *rivers of white space* — vertical channels that run through the text block, making reading very difficult.

## Some final suggestions

On every paragraph, an indention of about four spaces should be used. Studies show that not indenting paragraphs can cut reading speed by 7 percent. The eye looks for the indention as a starting point of the next piece of information.

Designers advise you to carefully use script type. Use script type in small doses and only for display type. Also, don't set script types in all caps.

The width of individual letters contributes to legibility. Condensed typefaces — those with squeezed counters — tend to be more difficult to read than moderately extended typefaces.

Designers suggest that you be wary about "tombstoning" headlines. To tombstone a headline means to place the headlines of different stories next to each other on the page. This can confuse readers because they tend to read across both headlines — seeing both as one unit. If you must place headlines next to each other, separate them with a graphic or visual element of some kind.

## Proofreading — do it right or get help!

If you're not a good proofreader, improve your ability. If you still don't get good enough that you're comfortable with your proofreading, identify a co-worker who can help. Don't limit your search to people working in the public relations area. You might want to ask those people who are quick to find typos on the materials that you've already printed and distributed. Ask colleagues in the organization to identify people who are good at proofreading. Then ask their bosses if you can "borrow" them for an hour or two a week.

Use these suggestions to help you proofread more effectively:

• Proofread once to check spelling of names of people and organizations.

• Proofread again to make sure all subjects and verbs agree.

• Consider reading the material backwards so you don't speed read.

## When proofreading:

- Proof once to check spelling of names and organizations.
- Proof again to be sure subjects and verbs agree.
- Read sentences backwards to avoid speed reading.

Check proofed and corrected sentences to be certain that new errors weren't made when corrections are introduced.

- Of course, use the spell-check function; but the spell-check won't help you with "affect" and "effect" usage.
- Be sure you check sentences you corrected after proofreading. You might find that you took care of the correction, but that something else in that sentence was fouled up when you made the change.
- When you think you're spending too much time proofreading, remember, one mistake could embarrass you 200,000 times, if that's how many copies you're printing.

## Step 7: Use color for maximum effect

Color can be a powerful tool to help you communicate your promotional message. Used properly, color can attract attention to your piece, help your audience develop desired associations, aid in reader retention of your message and create a feel or atmosphere in your piece.

**Color attracts attention.** People notice it, especially when surrounded by black and white elements. It stands out. That's why it's used so often to gain attention: road signs, traffic signals, safety clothing, school buses, etc.

According to a study by the Newspaper Advertising Bureau of New York City, *color can attract about three times as much attention* to your story. This is especially true with younger audiences. Of readers studied, 90 percent of those 18 to 24 prefer color; but only 53 percent over 65 prefer color.

The bureau also found that adding just one color to your ad increases response 45 to 53 percent; and using full-color increases notice 75 to 91 percent.

A study reported in *Advertising Theory and Practice* showed that a mail order catalog sold fifteen times more merchandise when printed in color than it did in black and white. While these studies examined a variety of communication channels, the general conclusion holds true for any form of printed material. Color gets attention.

## How to use color

The following tips and techniques will help you use color effectively in your promotions:

- Design experts agree that you should use color primarily on the design elements of greatest importance. If splashed around indiscriminately, color loses impact. If used sparingly and placed on key pieces of information, your major ideas will jump off the page. And because color attracts the most attention, even skimmers will get your message.
- Remember, use color as a tool to not only get attention, but also add excitement to a layout and break up dense sections of type. Carefully placed color subheads, for example, can effectively add visual relief to a dark page — and also add rhythm to the design.
- Color carries a high memory value. Just picture the colors that come to mind when you think of Coca-Cola, Kodak, Budweiser or Arm & Hammer. It's no accident that we know the corporate colors of big-name products. You can use this concept in your promotions. Although you're not likely to have the same budgets as these business giants, you can use color in your promotions to help your audience remember your identity. With some consistency and repetition, you can use color to make your piece stand out in the crowd and be recognized.
- Studies by researchers Dooley and Harkins determined that color has no significant effect on learning. It does, however, increase attention span. *They found that color's principal effect is motivational.* So, while using color may not help your reader learn your message any faster or better, it will keep their attention longer so they will be exposed to your communication for a greater period of time.

> *The power of color: Experts agree that different colors cause a variety of reactions in people.*

- While bright colors have a greater capacity to attract attention, they can also decrease comprehension levels for readers. Studies suggest that, **in headlines, the darker the color, the greater the comprehension**. The idea to consider here then is balance. Select a color that is bright enough to draw attention, but not so overwhelming that it distracts from the message.
- Experienced designers caution against using *spot color* to decorate your layout. Instead, use color as a functional device, not necessarily an artistic one. Of course, you must also see color from a design point of view.

• Studies demonstrate that when bright colors surround a body of type, readers' eyes tend to stray from the message. You should attempt to keep bright colors inside your text to focus attention on your message.

• Research also shows that you can use color for specific purposes. The findings suggest that red is effective to aid recall. Blue is not as strong an attention-getter, so use it to downplay an item. And, because yellow objects are often perceived first, use yellow on must-see elements.

• The ink you choose to print with is not your only color consideration. Remember, the paper you use can also add what some designers call a "free" or "extra" color. In fact, surveys show that *colored paper can boost readership by up to 40 percent and retention by 18 percent.*

By printing black and red ink on a light blue paper, for example, you can give a two-color piece the look of a three-color piece. A word of caution: Never print dark ink on a dark sheet or very light ink on a very light sheet. Remember, contrast is a key ingredient in readability.

## Step 8: Use photography and illustrations

As the saying goes, "A picture is worth a thousand words."

There's probably no research to actually support this word count, but the idea is essential in promotional literature. The photographs and illustrations you include can quickly and powerfully communicate your message. That's why it's essential you carefully consider the visuals you use and consider exactly what they communicate.

Just as the right picture can dramatically boost the impact of your message, the wrong photograph can distract and confuse your reader.

Here are some ideas that can help you select the right visuals and get the best results from them.

**Understanding the basics**. Artwork prepared for reproduction falls into one of two categories: halftone or line art.

*Halftones* are generally photographs, charcoals or other illustrations that contain graduated tones of black and white — or shades of gray. Before a photograph can be printed, its various tones of black and gray must be changed into a pattern of black and white dots — a halftone. The more dots of black you have in a given area, the darker the tone appears to the eye.

A part of the photograph that is black will be solid on the halftone because the dots are so dense they overlap. An area of the photograph that appears to be a middle tone gray — somewhere between black and white — will translate onto a **halftone as an area covered 50 percent by black dots and 50 percent by white space**. The lighter the area in the photograph, the fewer the visible dots on the halftone.

If you look closely at any printed picture, you can see these dots. The process of creating the halftone — or dots — is called *screening*. Using a special camera, the printer shoots a copy of the photograph through a screen of predetermined dot density. The denser the screen, the more dots per square inch — and the sharper the photograph. The reproduction method determines the proper screen.

The more basic category of artwork is called *line art*. Any illustration that consists only of black and white lines and no midtones falls into this category. Pen-and-ink drawings that appear to have gray area are still considered line art because the gray areas are actually made up of a dense area of small black lines.

Your printer will be able to tell you the best way to reproduce your artwork.

**The power of photographs and illustrations**. Expert opinion and research findings support the conclusion that photographs and illustrations help tremendously to communicate a message.

As a general rule, visuals serve four major functions: to attract attention, make a message more memorable, increase understanding, and add enjoyment.

Studies suggest that about twice as many people will read a story if it's supported with photographs or artwork. And surprisingly, audiences with higher education levels like them even more. And a nine-year study by Eastman Research found that in business publications, pictures ranked highest in readership.

Because visuals attract attention and quickly build interest, people are pulled into the message. Readers see a photograph or illustration and want more information — so they read the text that relates to the picture.

Visuals add interesting focal points for readers as their eyes move across the page. Each time they stop to look at a picture, they look at the written information around the picture to better understand the content.

Research also finds that 80 percent of readers enter a page through a photograph, not a headline. That's why it's vital that the text near visuals — such as captions, headlines, blurbs, etc — communicate key ideas. You want to use photographs and the text around them to quickly make your point to readers who simply skim though your piece.

## Selecting photographs and illustrations

Never make the mistake of including a visual in your promotional piece just because you think it should contain a pretty picture.

You should consider a number of criteria before selecting visuals. A number of authorities suggest that you use this checklist before you select:

Is it relevant? Does it add something to the message that will help the reader understand the message or argument?

Does it communicate a key thought quickly and simply? Will your reader know right away what the photograph is saying about the subjects pictured?

Will the picture grab the reader? Does the picture have sufficient impact to make the reader curious?

Here are more tips to keep in mind when you think about what, if any, pictures you should include:

If your photograph or artwork is of poor quality, don't use it. Remember, it may be the first and only thing your reader sees. If it looks bad, that may be the only impression left on the reader about your organization. Again, your printer can guide you on whether your visual is good enough to reproduce successfully.

Be careful about over enlarging a very small original. As a small image gets larger, it also becomes blurrier. A very clear small photo can become very dirty looking or "grainy" when it gets much past twice its original size. If the photograph you wish to use is too small to get to the size you need, select another one. The number of pixels will determine the quality of larger-sized photos.

*Research has shown that people prefer photographs to illustrations.* However, an illustration may work better for the piece you're planning. If you use drawings, the study suggests, you make them as realistic as possible. Readers prefer realistic illustrations to stylized ones because they spend less time interpreting what the picture is and more time examining the meaning of the message.

Computerized and traditional "clip art" is very easy to use — and compared to photography and custom artwork — very inexpensive. Because of this, clip art is both very useful and very dangerous. You must resist the temptation to indiscriminately drop in clip art. Everything you place in

> *Communicate key ideas with text near visuals such as captions, headlines and blurbs (pull-quotes). Use photos and text near them to make your point to readers who skim through your piece.*

your promotion should enhance your message and add to the meaning.

## How to use photographs and illustrations

Now that you've found a quality photograph or illustration that communicates your message, you need to think about how to use it.

The following tips and techniques can help.

As a general rule, *people prefer pictures of other people*, as opposed to buildings, landscapes, etc. Whenever possible, try to make people the main subjects of your visuals, especially in promotional materials. Some think that people do business with people, not organizations and companies. By using people-pictures in your promotional literature, you not only offer the most preferred type of picture, but also you show people offering your product, service or message.

**When picturing people, however, avoid the standard "mug shot"** used in too many annual reports and company history publications. Show people doing something that adds meaning to your message and puts them in their natural environment. Research supports the idea that readers prefer to see pictures of people in action.

Studies also demonstrate readers prefer unposed pictures to posed pictures; however, this trend reversed with readers over 51 years old or those with fewer than 12 years of education.

Many experts advise that in product brochures and literature, you show people using your product. This not only includes the human element but also communicates how easy it is for customers to use what you are selling.

**Use visuals to show things or express thoughts that are difficult to explain**. For example, it would be difficult to explain just how compact your new product is. But showing a photo of its relative size can quickly get this point across.

Advertising guru David Ogilvy found that when a photograph is placed below the text in advertising, readership of the text drops by 10 percent. He suggests that after people look at the picture, they turn the page instead of going back up to find the text. A number of research findings support this conclusion.

Another rule of thumb — use one large photograph instead of several smaller ones. The single large visual serves as a focal point for the message. You can, of course, use several small photos to show off various features or benefits of your product or service, but they should be clearly dominated by the main visual.

Printing a photograph or illustration to the edges of the page is a common technique in promotional literature. This technique, called a "bleed," can be very dramatic and add great visual impact to your piece. However, bleeding a picture off the page can cost about 15 percent extra and, according to research, result in only 2 percent additional reader attention. Always weigh the cost of this process against the value you think it adds to your piece.

Always use a *caption* with your photographs and illustrations. Text placed directly below a visual increases comprehension and helps readers remember your point.

When taking photographs for use in your promotion, take both horizontal and vertical shots of each scene. You may not know at that time how you will use the shots. Taking the pictures both ways saves you from failing to turn a vertical photo into a horizontal format.

Use direction in photographs to create direction in your overall design. *Readers tend to follow the movement of the picture.* Keep people in pictures facing *into* the page so reader attention moves that way. If someone in the picture is pointing, make sure the pointing is into your piece.

For her master's thesis, *A Digest of Research on the Printed Mass Media*, Mary Anne Frenzel conducted extensive research on the use of photographs and illustrations. Here are a few conclusions she drew from her research:

- Readers prefer rectangular pictures to those cut in fancy shapes and silhouettes.
- Pictures should sit squarely on the page, not be placed at angles.
- Readers prefer pictures with smiling, friendly subjects to those with unhappy, unfriendly people.
- Close-up pictures are particularly effective because people like to look at faces.

## Step 9: Get it to press: Selecting and working with a printer

Although printing is one of the last production steps, you should find a knowledgeable and reliable printer in the early stages.

**Selecting a printer**: If you don't already have a working relationship with a print shop, start looking now.

Before you start, narrow your search by knowing what type of shop you need.

In general, you'll find three major types of print shops: quick-print, sheet-fed, and web-fed.

Quick-print shops are the ones you're probably most familiar with: Sir Speedy, Kinko's, Kwik Kopy, PIP, etc. These shops specialize primarily in small runs (one to a few thousand copies). In many cases, quick-print shops simply use high-speed, high-quality photocopy machines and duplicate in black ink (actually toner) only.

Sheet-fed print shops are ideal for medium-sized runs of several hundred to 50,000 plus. Most sheet-fed shops offer high quality reproduction and a full range of pre-press, printing services and bindery options. The advantages of sheet-fed shops are good turnaround time, excellent quality on all types of print work, all colors of ink available, and a wide variety of papers to choose from. The initial setup of the job is somewhat expensive, but increased quantities can offset the cost.

Web-fed print shops specialize in medium to large runs, generally from 30,000 to multimillions. Web-fed shops are best for large runs because their printing presses use large rolls of paper instead of pre-cut individual sheets. Therefore, the presses can move much faster and press time and expense are reduced. The advantage of web-fed shops is the relatively quick turnaround you can get on a large job. Also, depending on the shop you use, quality can be very good. The primary disadvantages are that setup costs are high and you need a lot of pieces to make web runs worthwhile. Plus, in the hands of the wrong press operator, a web press — because in moves so quickly — can produce some very sloppy looking work.

First identify your promotional piece's category. Then, ask the various shops what type of service they provide. Many shops will offer more than one type of printing. If this is the case, ask them what type of work they do most often before you tell them about your job. You're more likely to get an honest answer instead of a sales pitch like, "Sure we handle jobs like that all the time."

You might also remember this old printing industry adage: *Quality, price and speed — you can have any two.*

Decide which are most important to you, but still insist on an acceptable level of all three.

Try to find at least three printers you're comfortable with and ask them for prices on your job. Getting several quotes gives you some assurance that you're not being overcharged. But remember, price should not necessarily be the deciding factor. The best price will not always give you the best quality or service.

Once you've decided, meet the printer about the specifics of your job as soon as possible. You must consider the printing process even in the earliest stages of production. You'll want to know up front if you can afford to print what you're planning. An innovative, creative idea that can't be done within budget — if at all — won't help you meet the goal you've set for your promotional piece.

Work with your printers and exchange ideas with them. They can often offer ideas that can save you a great deal of time, effort and money.

## Basics of the printing process

While you may not need to know the intricate details of printing, it helps to have at least some understanding of how the process works.

**Mechanical**. As discussed in the section on design, the mechanical is your final, camera-ready artwork. (When using desktop publishing this step is sometimes skipped.) Today, printers accept electronic PDF files or QuarkXPress or InDesign files if they have these programs.

• **Negatives**. Step two is placing the mechanical on a special camera and shooting a negative. Multicolor jobs, and jobs with artwork such as halftones, require several negatives.

• **Stripping**. When all the negatives have been shot, they are then "stripped" together so that all items of the same color are placed together on the same piece of film. In general, each color to be printed will ultimately have one negative (or film).

• **Proof**. A common form of proof is called a *blueline*. This proof is a sample of your piece that shows all the pieces put together and all the color breaks; it is the last chance you have to make changes before the job is prepared for the actual press run.

• **Plates**: After you approve the proofs, the printer uses the negatives to make printing plates. These are usually metal photosensitive sheets that carry the ink on the press. The image from each negative is "burned" onto each plate. Each color to be printed has a different printing plate.

• **Printing**. The plates are then put onto the printing press and duplication begins.

• **Folding and bindery**. Once the job is taken off the printing presses — if needed — it is cut, folded and bound.

This is an extremely simplified version of the process, but it should help you see the big picture. For more detailed information, ask your printer to walk you throughout the process. A good printer will be happy to educate you on the printing process. The more you know about it, the better your piece will be prepared and the easier her job becomes.

## Working with your printer

When you take your piece to the printer you need to provide as much information about the job as possible. In the industry this is called "specing" or giving "specs," meaning specifications. To help your job run as smoothly as possible, discuss the following key issues with your printer:

**Quantity**. Let the printer know how many pieces of your promotional piece you plan to print. Naturally, the more you have printed, the more the job will cost. However, the cost per piece usually decreases with larger runs. With many forms of printing, a significant portion of what you pay is for set up and pre-press production. This cost is spread out over more pieces with larger runs. Once the press is up and running, it's very easy and inexpensive to print more. The additional cost of paper, ink and press time can often be nominal. This can depend on a number of factors, so be certain to ask your printer about your options.

> *Exchange ideas with your printers. They can offer ideas that might save you time, effort and money.*

**Page size and count**. Another significant cost of printing is the paper used. You must, therefore, tell your printer how large your pages will be and how many pages the document will have. You want to to use the paper you buy and the printer's capabilities for maximum efficiency. Early in your planning stages, talk with your printer about page sizes that will minimize waste.

If your document consists of multiple pages, find out which page counts will work best with the page size you choose. Booklet formats are printed in "signatures" — groups of pages printed together. An efficient page count is often an eight-page unit (8, 16, 32, etc.). Four-page units can sometimes work, but six-page formats can be wasteful and difficult in printing and binding. Again, ask your printer about what page counts will work best for you.

**Stock**. The paper you choose is vital to both the design and the cost of your promotion. Papers range from very affordable commodity grade stocks, to very expensive and exotic stocks. Think carefully about how you want the paper in your piece to enhance the look and feel. Then measure that against how expensive it will be.

You can choose from thousands of paper types, textures, colors and weights. Ask your printer for samples of papers that are within your budget. When examining the samples, think about *opacity* — how much ink will show through the other side — and weight — how thick and heavy the paper is. In general, the thicker the stock the higher the opacity — and the higher the cost.

You may also ask the printers for alternatives to the paper you select. They can sometimes offer you a very good price on a paper they have in stock or paper left over from someone else's job. Or, if you use the same paper as another job the printer is running, you may be able to get the paper cheaper. Paper gets cheaper by the sheet (or roll) when bought in bulk.

**Ink colors**. The number of colors you use in your publication makes a big difference in cost. The more you use, the more you pay for pre-press set up and printing. Remember: Black is considered a color in the world of printing. So a job that is black and red is a two-color job, not one.

> *Early in the process, communicate to your printer specifications for your printing job.*

Here are a few of the most basic color options you have.

• *One color printing* is the most basic and least expensive. Your entire job will be printed with one ink color. Because the contrast of the ink to the paper is essential to readability, black — or a very dark blue — is your best bet. A blue/black mixture is also an effective one-color choice.

• *Two-color printing* is perhaps the most common for promotional literature. It is more expensive than one color, but the additional color allows you to highlight important parts of your message and add some excitement to the layout. When the second color is used is this way, the process is called "spot color" printing.

• *Three-color printing* (also a spot color process) is an option, but not always the most cost effective way to go. Many small print shops use only a one- or two-color press. This means that on a two-color press, a three-color job must be put through the press two times. This takes extra time and more work — therefore, more money. If you're considering a three-color job, ask your printer how much the same job would cost at two colors and how much with four colors. You may find that a two-color job is much cheaper and the extra color isn't worth it. You may also find that the additional fourth color costs just a little more and would add enough to the design to justify the extra money.

• *Four-color printing* can be both a spot color process, as described above, or run as what is called "four-color process." Process jobs use four colors (black, magenta, cyan and yellow) in various combinations to make up every other color. This process requires any color photographs you're using to be electronically broken down — or "separated" — into the four colors above. This process can be very expensive and used only if your piece requires a very slick look and the extra money will help the piece achieve its goal.

• **Halftones/Separations**. Whenever you add black and white photographs or artwork with tones of gray, your printer will need to shoot *halftones*. The more pictures you include, the more they'll need to shoot and the more the job will cost. Know in advance how many pictures you plan to include so the printer can give you an accurate estimate up front.

If you're printing a four-color process job, tell the printer how many color photographs you will have. Like halftones, each separation costs more money. You'll want to know as early as possible just how much more you'll need to budget.

**Design elements**. Inform your printer about any design elements you're planning. These can be things such as bleeds, colors butting up together or overlapping, printing across the gutter of two pages, etc. Anything that makes the print job more difficult or exacting is more time consuming and more expensive. Reveal your plans; the printer may suggest another option that will serve the same purpose but cost you less.

**Materials supplied**. Your printer will need to know what type of artwork you will supply. The more work you do up front — the closer you get the job to press ready — the cheaper the job will be. Let the printer know if you're providing rough layouts that require typesetting, mechanicals or film.

**Folding**. How you want your piece to be folded is another important item to spec. Standard folds cost less than custom folds. Here's a brief list of the most common formats:

*Single parallel fold*. This is simply folding the piece in half. For example an 8½" x 11" sheet becomes four panels of 5½" x 8½". This is commonly used for items such as menus and church bulletins.

*French fold*. With this process, the paper folds in half one way and then folds in half the other. This works well for large posters and invitations.

*Accordion fold*. This fold — also called a z-fold — opens like an accordion. While this fold can be difficult to stuff in an envelope because it has no closed edges, it works well if you want to direct readers' attention to one side of the brochure at a time.

*Gatefold*. The ends of the piece fold to meet in the middle, forming a "gate." This can be a great device for building excitement about your message on the outside and then delivering the payoff when the reader opens the gate.

*Barrel fold*. This starts at one end and folds in on itself panel by panel. This is a standard and effective fold for pamphlets. The format allows you to deliver your message in a very organized and orderly fashion, one panel at a time. A barrel fold that only has two folds (or six panels) is sometimes called a *letter fold*. Just as its name implies, the piece folds in thirds just like a letter — a common format for pamphlets.

**Binding**: This process does not apply to every job. Binding is the process of putting together multi-page documents. You can choose from a number of options (perfect, saddle stitch, spiral bound, etc.). Ask your printers which services they offer and which would be best for your job.

**Schedule.** Know exactly when you need your job delivered and tell the printer right away. A tight deadline can substantially impact the cost of your job. The faster you want it, the more you are likely to pay. Giving your printer some flexibility and time not only reduces the cost of your job, but can improve the quality because the job doesn't have to be rushed through. It can be a tremendous advantage to work with your printers, instead of thinking that they are working for you. True, you're the customer and the printer's the vendor, but consideration and cooperation go a lot further in the printing business than demands and unrealistic deadlines.

**Delivery.** Tell your printer how you'd like the job packaged and delivered. If it's a multipage document, specify who should collate the job. If the job is small enough, or you have access to a truck, pick up the job yourself. You'll save delivery charges. If the job is to be distributed at a convention or similar event, have it sent directly to that location rather than ship it twice. You should, however, see samples before you send the job. You'll want to guarantee acceptable quality before you give the piece to prospects, clients or customers.

**Final thought**. Many print shops can provide you with preprinted spec sheets. Fill them out as completely as possible. If you have questions, ask. Don't assume you know something if you're not sure. It's much easier to get your job produced on time and within budget when there are no surprises.

If you're in charge of placing printing orders, be sure you protect your reputation. Write clear specifications so a number of printers compete for the job — if you need multiple quotes. Familiarize yourself with laws that guide bids or quotes. Some states demand that orders more than a certain amount (perhaps $2,500) be put out for bid. Do not place yourself in a questionable situation by splitting jobs

so you have two jobs for $1,250 to avoid the $2,500 rule. Practitioners have lost jobs doing this.

## Step 10: Evaluate your publication's effectiveness

Evaluation is one of the most important parts of any business communication. Unfortunately, it is also one of the most overlooked.

A common technique to measure success of your promotion is the coupon. Somewhere on your piece — preferably on an edge of the page so cutting out is easy — place a coded coupon.

*Familiarize yourself with laws on getting bids and quotes from printers.*

Tell readers exactly what you want them to do with it. Do they mail it back to you? Should they bring it to your store when they come in? Is the offer valid without the coupon? Can the coupon or order form be faxed back?

Be very specific. You'll get a much more accurate idea of the success of the promotion if people understand how to respond.

Coding your coupon or promotion is particularly important if you are sending out several versions of the same piece — or sending the same piece to several different groups. By counting the returned coupons and analyzing the codes, you get a feel for the overall success of the campaign, plus a feel for the group or audience more receptive to your message or offer.

If you're testing two different versions of a promotion — for example, version A offers $10 off, version B offers $15 off — you'll want to know which offer is more effective. You may find that the two versions brought in an equal number of orders. You can then "roll out" with the $10 version — offering the extra $5 off isn't a plus so you may not want to offer it. *Note*: Of course, you would not distribute the same offer to the same people. You'd want to split a single audience.

Without evaluating the effectiveness of your promotion, you'd have no idea how your audience reacts. You risk spending even more money on another promotion that may also be the wrong message or offer.

To evaluate effectiveness, check whether the promotional piece meets the goals you set in your planning stages. As you remember, you wrote your mission statement in clearly measurable terms. If the promotion accomplished those goals, it's a success. If it didn't, evaluate the piece and the feedback and look for causes.

## Is anybody reading this stuff?

An often overlooked part of preparing effective publications is determining whether people are reading and enjoying what you're preparing. If you have the opportunity, ask a dozen people who prepare publications when they last asked their audiences if they read the publications. Chances are good that very few will answer that they've done so within the last year.

Winning awards for publications is one way to gain attention for them. Perhaps even better is a track record that indicates that intended readers are indeed looking forward to receiving the publication and getting something out of it.

You can do this in a number of ways. Conduct occasional focus panels with readers to see if they are reading all of the publication, certain parts or none of it. Ask if they want certain topics covered more and others covered less.

Mail-back coupons included in the newsletter or magazine are seldom effective because the response rate is usually notoriously low. Overreacting to comments from three or four percent of the people will not serve any measurement purpose. That's why the focus panel approach is more effective.

When conducting a focus panel, do it yourself, or add objectivity by having an outsider who knows something about publications conduct the effort. *Caution*: Some employees may reluctantly criticize you because they work with you.

# Tips

1. Before you start to produce a publication, ask yourself why you're producing the publication.

2. When preparing a headline, try to include a benefit statement. Tell readers what they can gain by reading your message.

3. Remember that you're usually writing for three kinds of readers. Remember the 30-3-30 rule. Many people spend only 30 seconds on your publication; some will give your copy a quick reading of three minutes; and a few will read every word of the publication.

4. Grab your readers' attention quickly. If you can keep readers' attention for the first 50 words, chances are good they'll read the next 450.

5. If you're going to mail a publication, meet with a knowledgeable representative from the local post office to learn what you can and can't do.

6. Photos work best when they show people living their lives. Whether they're laughing, crying or engaged in active play, images of people doing what they do naturally attract readers.

7. Build a "swipe file." If you're a beginner, and even if you're a seasoned professional, build a collection of brochures, ads, layouts, designs, etc., so you can prime the pump when you're ready to create a layout for a new publication.

8. Indent paragraphs. Research shows that the extra white space helps reading speed.

9. Most research studies show that serif fonts in body copy are read more easily, more quickly and with better comprehension.

10. Proofread to check the spelling of names of people and organizations. Proofread again to make sure all the subjects and verbs agree.

## Examples

The last section of this chapter presents various publications, some good examples, some bad.

---

*Figure 8.1* (on the next page) shows a newsletter that violates many basics of solid layout. It's called *Blunderville Newsletter* because it contains the following "blunders":

- Newsletter uses eight different fonts — too many
- School name in caps; public school is not
- School name in italics and caps
- Flag is only 10% of the layout; should be 20%
- Lead headline has no verb
- Headline ("residents") is too small for space allocated
- Teaser headline is reverse, serif and not bold
- Teaser headline is a "wooden" head, carries no news
- Main Story text is one-column wide, lacks indentions; font overuses bold type
- Main story in sans serif font; should be serif
- Main story typeface (font) is too condensed

### Layout

- Layout switches from one column to three on same page
- Layout violates modular design; modular design is series of complementary nesting rectangles. "Voting and Citizenship" dives into the main copy. "Quick Pix" box not in line with Voting and Citizenship box.
- Graphic "dot" divider is gruesome

### Voting and Citizenship box

- Frame is too thick — called an "obituary frame"
- Type is in italic — too much for one story
- Copy sentence length is 47 words for each; best length should average 17 words
- Copy is pedestrian, sophomoric
- Clip art is elementary and too literal to be artistic; intrudes into the text
- Typos in lines one and two

### Quick Pix Box

- Type is hard to read and "circusy"
- Overuse of bold type and underline
- "Inside" box not set apart from its parent box in a different typeface

# BLUNDERVILLE *Public Schools*

## Special School Bond Referendum Newsletter

VOTE September 30

*Vote September 30, 11 a.m.-9 p.m.*

### RESIDENTS: NEW RATHER THAN OLD SCHOOL

## Important decision for Blunderville residents

On September 30th the Blunderville Township Board of Education will present residents with a school bond referendum to replace our 80 year old buildings with a new pre-kindergarten to 8th grade school.

If voters approve the referendum, the state will give us $10 million in free aid. With state aid we can build a new school for less than we can repair our old buildings. *State aid reduces our local share by 65% and is good for this vote only.*

Scientific survey results show a majority of our community understand the need for a new school and agree with building a new one.

The school board, state, and community agree we need a new school. On September 30th the Blunderville Township Board of Education will present residents with a school bond referendum to replace our 80 year old buildings with a new pre-kindergarten to 8th grade school. If voters approve the referendum, the state will give us $10 million in free aid. With state aid we can build a new school for less than we can repair our old buildings. *State aid reduces our local share by 65% and is good for this vote only.* Scientific survey results show a majority of our community understand the need for a new school and agree with building a new one. The school board, state, and community agree we need a new school.

## Voting and citizenship

*Blunderville resident are invited to exercize the highest form of citizenship possible this fall when they can vote on improving the schools which are in very bad shape because of many years of use and misuse caused by budget failures and state cuts that couldn't be helped.*

*In the past Blunderville residents have always shown that they value what their children are learning in school and want them to continue to learn more and better things that will help*  *them to get into college and get better scores on tests required by the state. Vote this fall.*

## Quick Pix Of What You Should Know

- Portions of the middle school are over 100 years old

- 1998 study found neither school can provide a modern education

- With state aid it would cost us less to build a new school than to repair our old ones

- Even renovations would not meet state codes for safety, handicapped access and modern classes

- State provides more aid to build than to renovate old buildings

- State will pay 65% of new school building through free aid

| | |
|---|---|
| New school | $12,504,247 |
| State aid | 9,023,347 |
| Capital Reserve | 500,000 |
| Local share | 3,982,898 |

- Average property owner would pay $11.68 monthly in tax

- Vote Tuesday, Sept. 30, 11 a.m.—9 p.m. at middle school and municipal building

- Attend public meeting Sept. 25, 7 p.m., middle school library

**Inside...**
- Pixes of problems
- New Pre K-8 school floor plan
- Voting information

**Figure 8.1**

**Figure 8.2**

**4 Blood Types, 4 Diets**

# Eat right

# 4

# Your Type

Diet solutions to staying healthy,
living longer, and
achieving your ideal weight

Offer an incentive to open the publication by
indicating the idea inside will help the reader

**Figure 8.3**

If you're preparing a promotional piece to gain
support for a school budget, be specific with
references to taxpayers' costs and make the
appearance one that doesn't shout "Expensive!"

**Figure 8.4**

These inviting flier pages invite readers to gather information with short chunks of copy that please the eye.

Used with permission from LifeLineScreening Radiology, LLC

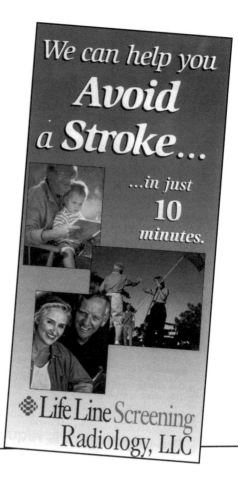

*We can help you*
**Avoid**
*a* **Stroke...**
*...in just*
**10**
*minutes.*

Life Line Screening
Radiology, LLC

## We can help you reduce your risk for stroke...

Thanks to Life Line Screening Radiology, you don't have to wait for a medical problem to be screened for your risk of vascular disease or osteoporosis. Our screenings are fast, painless, accurate and available at an affordable rate.

We have helped thousands of people quickly and inexpensively manage and monitor their wellness.

Call today to schedule a stroke or osteoporosis screening ... **a personal wellness plan is priceless.**

## Top 5 Reasons to Get Screened

**1** Stroke is the third leading killer in the United States. Life Line Screening Radiology offers a carotid vascular test with ultrasound technology that visualizes the buildup of fatty plaque in the carotid arteries that may block the flow of blood to the brain and lead to stroke.

**2** Many people who have aneurysms do not experience symptoms. Therefore, a preventive Life Line Screening Radiology ultrasound aorta screening may identify life threatening health problems early enough for your physician to take corrective action.

**3** Approximately 12 million Americans suffer from Peripheral Arterial Disease (PAD), often referred to as hardening of the arteries or atherosclerosis. This narrowing of the blood vessels in the legs is caused by the buildup of fatty plaque and is a strong predictor of heart disease. PAD may show up in leg arteries before there are any signs or symptoms.

**4** Osteoporosis is responsible for about 1.5 million fractures a year, usually in the spine, hip or wrist. This screening estimates the bone density. Abnormal findings may suggest a risk of osteoporosis.

**5** Life Line Screening Radiology offers painless, inexpensive, and non-invasive (no needles!) preventive health screenings in your neighborhood.

## Pre-registration is required. Call 1-800-778-6097

**1**
*Stroke/Carotid Artery Screening*
Ultrasound scan of the carotid arteries that screens for buildup of fatty plaque — the leading cause of strokes.

**2**
*Abdominal Aortic Aneurysm Screening*
Ultrasound scan that screens for the existence of an aneurysm (enlargement) in the abdominal aorta that could lead to a ruptured aortic artery.

**3**
*Peripheral Arterial Disease Screening*
Screens for peripheral arterial disease in the lower extremities. An abnormal result may indicate a risk for peripheral arterial disease and an increased risk of coronary artery disease.

**4**
*Osteoporosis Screening*
Ultrasound screen for abnormal bone mass density in men and women. Osteoporosis is painless and silent in its early stages.

**Vascular Package**
**(Screenings 1-3) only $99. Save $36!**

**Complete Wellness Package**
**(all 4 screenings)**
**only $125. Save $45!**

Summer 2004

*A Publication for Family and Friends*

Rowan Family

## Message from the President

In this issue of "Family," you'll notice that more of our faculty and students are working and studying abroad than ever before.

This spring, Rowan approved the creation of an international MBA program in Greece. We have started exchange programs with universities in Ecuador and Korea. Our students are helping the Chilean salmon industry, and one of our best and brightest, Fulbright winner Gino Banco, is headed to Germany to study automotive engineering.

Some might expect these types of experiences only to be available at the most elite private institutions or at the largest research universities. Rowan students and faculty know different: their school offers many such opportunities.

We hope that after reading some of these stories you will encourage your student to broaden his or her horizons by either studying overseas for a semester or helping a professor who is undertaking projects based abroad. The experience may change his or her life forever.

# Engineering Team Works to Get Salmon in the Pink

Rowan University College of Engineering students have been working to get Chile – specifically one of its major exports – in the pink.

Under Dr. Zenaida Otero Gephardt, a chemical engineering professor, the students have been experimenting with natural food additives that will turn white, farm-raised salmon the pink hue desired by consumers worldwide.

> "There is a push in the country to strengthen the salmon industry. This is a collaboration where we can make a difference."
>
> - Dr. Zenaida Otero Gephardt

Gephardt, who spent six weeks in Chile last summer teaching and conducting research at the Universidad De La Serena in La Serena, worked with Rowan students Danielle Baldwin, Toms River; Elizabeth DiPaolo, Wenonah; and William Henderson, Bricktown, on supercritical fluid extraction: extracting pigment from algae that can be transformed into a substance to be fed to salmon in salmon farms to make them pink. Their ultimate goal is to grow algae from which pigment can be harvested, extracting the pigment and developing natural food products – such as a powder that can be mixed with fish food – that will turn the salmon pink.

Salmon are not naturally pink; they gain their trademark color because of the pink food – such as algae and shrimp –

that they feed upon in their natural state in the ocean. But salmon farms – large cages that may hold a hundred thousand salmon – don't offer and can't provide the amount of pink-tinged natural wildlife

**Engineering students** have been working to develop a natural additive to turn white salmon pink.

that so many salmon need to consume.

The Rowan work may make a difference in some economies. Gephardt noted the salmon farmers are competing in a world market ripe with pink salmon. "When people think of salmon, they think pink," she said.

Chile, a coastal South American country which in 2002 exported 375,013 tons of farmed salmon, would like to further its standing in the salmon industry.

"There is a push in the country to strengthen the salmon industry," Gephardt said. "This is a collaboration where we can make a difference."

**Figure 8.5** Research shows that employees like to be in on things related to their jobs. The lead story in this publication informs a large university employee group about happenings across the campus — preparing them to speak knowledgeably and well about the university.

communication briefings

*As We See It*

# A Quiz on Using Plain Words

By Jack Gillespie, editor, and Joe McGavin, managing editor

In his classic "Politics and the English Language," George Orwell listed 10 rules for clear writing. One of our favorites: "Never use a long word when a short word will do."

That rule came to mind when we saw some of the words contestants were asked to spell in the National Spelling Bee. Of course, we applaud the purpose of the Spelling Bee—to stretch young minds to excel.

---

## Would you use words such as *hebetude, crambo* or *lapideous*?

---

But we doubt if the contestants—or most people, for that matter—have or ever *will* have much use for many of the contest words. And after looking at some of them, we would add this rule to Orwell's: "Never use an obscure word when a plain word will do." To see if you agree with us, pick one answer for each of these questions. We've italicized the Spelling Bee words and our simpler substitutes:

• **Would you** be likely to say (a) "The employee cafeteria is serving *crambo* again" or (b) "The employee cafeteria is serving *leftover cabbage* again"?

• **After attending** a workshop, would you most likely say (a) "His presentation bordered on *hebetude*" or (b) "His presentation bordered on *dull*"?

• **If your** co-workers lie down on the job, would you describe them as (a) *thesmothetes* or (b) *slackers*?

• **When lunching** with a client, would you say (a) "Please pass a *grissino*" or (b) "Please pass a *bread stick*"?

• **If your** co-workers asked you how the boss reacted to your great idea, would you say (a) "She greeted it with a *lapideous* silence" or (b) "She greeted it with a *stony* silence"?

• **Would you** say to your opposites in a negotiation (a) "I hope we can *ratiocinate* together" or (b) "I hope we can *reason* together"?

• **If you** didn't like the way your brochure photos turned out, would you tell the printer (a) "The photos look *lacteal*" or (b) "The photos look *milky*"?

• **Faced with** some tough questions from the media, would you describe your position as (a) "a *mucilaginous* situation" or (b) "a *sticky* situation"?

*Scoring:* If you picked all "a" answers—or *any* "a" answers—you fail. If you picked all "b" answers, you pass. *Reason:* Picking all "b" answers shows you want to communicate with, not impress, your audiences.

*Face-to-Face Communication*

# Replies You Should Avoid

A co-worker snidely comments to you about a colleague's frequent tardiness. *Caution:* Avoid these disdainful replies that show you object to the:

• **Attitude.** "I don't see it as a big deal if George is late all the time. Who cares as long as he does his share of the work?"

• **Perception.** "In my opinion, when George gets here is nobody's business but his."

• **Language.** "I don't approve of the way you're talking about George."

• **Behavior.** "I don't like gossip. It's wrong to talk about people behind their backs when they can't defend themselves."

• **Person.** "I disapprove of *you* because you're gossiping about George by talking behind his back."

*What you should do:* Agree in the abstract—lateness is a problem—but refuse to respond to the specific issue of George's lateness.

*Example:* "Len, you're right. Lateness is a problem. I've read a lot about it, and no one seems to have a good solution. I'd be interested in hearing your ideas on what you think can be done."

*Source: How to Disagree Without Being Disagreeable*, by Suzette Haden Elgin, John Wiley & Sons Inc., 605 3rd Ave., New York, NY 10158.

# An R&R Day Gets Referrals

This idea can bring you a double benefit—happier customers and new business. Here's how it works at Chorus Communications in King of Prussia, Pa.:

• **Every Tuesday** is R&R—Referral and Retention—Day. For two hours, all 70 salespeople and eight telemarketers call customers to make sure they're happy and to ask for referrals.

• **The calls** yield about four prospects for every 10 customers contacted. And those referrals have accounted for 40% of the company's new business.

*Source:* Stephanie Gruner, writing in *Inc.*, 38 Commercial Wharf, Boston, MA 02110.

---

# A Short Lesson On Productivity

Consider this workplace equation: Force × Distance = Work. And imagine that what you do is like pushing against a rock.

You may shuffle papers, make calls, write reports, open your mail, etc. and say you're working hard. But if your pushing—the force—doesn't move the rock any distance by adding profit—the work—for your organization, you're just busy, not productive.

*Moral:* Ask "Will this move the rock?" about everything you do. If you answer "no," you shouldn't be doing it.

*Source:* O. Keith Backhaus, writing in *Managers Handbook,* 300 Day Hill Road, Windsor, CT 06095.

---

# Trade Show Tip

It takes only 4.8 seconds for someone to pass by a 10-foot trade show booth, so your display must communicate a benefit and invite people to visit.

To do that, your display must use eye-catching and informative graphics that answer the two questions attendees ask most often: "What does your company do?" "What are you showing here?"

*Source:* Brilliant Image, Seven Penn Plaza, New York, NY 10001.

— ideas that work —

3

**Figure 8.6** This management newsletter attracted 500,000 readers by offering succinct sentences loaded with useful information. Also, use of bulleted lists and 1/3, 2/3 layout attract readers.

Name _____ Date _____

1. You've been serving as publications coordinator for a company. The new public relations director, your boss, asks you how effective your publications are. How would you determine this if you haven't already?

_____

_____

_____

_____

_____

_____

_____

2. You've been blessed with a graphic designer in your department. But she wants everything in the most modern typefaces without serifs. How can you convince her to use a serif typeface for body copy in most instances?

_____

_____

_____

_____

_____

_____

_____

*See other side*

Name _____ Date _____

3. You've been asked to make a brief presentation to people who put out newsletters in different parts of your company. In evaluating the ones that have been done, you found that most of them are deadly, with very little white space and type spread across the page, and requiring many eye fixations. What three major tips would you share with the audience to help it prepare a more attractive publication?

_____

_____

_____

_____

_____

_____

_____

_____

4. To protect yourself from critics who think you're paying too much for your printing, be sure you write thorough specifications for printers when you solicit bids. If you were asked to write specifications for a printing job, what major components would you include?

_____

_____

_____

_____

_____

_____

_____

# Chapter 9

# Writing Effective Public Relations Messages

**PRaxiom**     *Writing persuasively is enchanting the willing.*

## What this chapter covers

Successful public relations practitioners share one skill — the ability to write. Many professionals, in books and articles, cite the ability to write as the top skill needed to succeed in public relations. This chapter explores the writing process, types of public relations writing, including the news release, letter and memo, readability scores for writing, tightening writing and editing tips, copywriting strategies, persuasive copywriting, audience writing, and offers many examples of both poor and improved writing.

The special section on persuasive writing will reveal successful strategies to manage opinion — get your audience to know, feel or do what you want — through your writing.

Most public relations professionals consider writing the most important public relations skill. If it's not the most important, it's right up there with strategic thinking, research and ethical decision making.

Read what some leading practitioners think about the importance of writing talent in public relations.

## Care for the audience
*Larry Kamer, Principal*
*Kamer-Singer & Associates*
*San Francisco, CA*

- High on the list of disappointments of public relations employers is the discovery that an otherwise presentable candidate can't write.

- This "ability to write" is table stakes in the public relations business—it's what gets you in. But one does not get very far without the ability to write authoritatively

and cleverly. Public relations is still about convincing people. The writing must feel as if the writer actually believes what it says and could sincerely defend it.

- People who couldn't care less about the words they put on a page, or who can barely mask their skepticism about something they expect others to believe, should probably seek another line of work.

## Avoid thoughtless writing
*John J. Moscatelli, Senior Counselor*
*Anne Klein & Associates*
*Mount Laurel, NJ*

- The fax, the Internet, e-mail, the personal computer, and satellites have all speeded up the communication process. And with that increased speed, good writing becomes more important than ever.

- For the moment, let's not worry about the news release or feature story or fact sheet or formal speech text. Instead, let's focus on simple, straightforward business correspondence. Business writing needs to be clear, crisp, to the point, easily understood, engaging and accurate. Yet, e-mail makes it all too easy to dash off a missive, with little, if any, thought given to what we're saying or how a reader might interpret it. More harm is being done to American business today by "thoughtless" e-mails and dashed off faxes than by all the overseas competitive forces you can imagine.

- So before you start worrying about writing for your Pulitzer, consider those who will be reading your everyday work. Take a moment to re-read what you've written. Make sure it is clear and accurate. Be concise, but not to the point of vacuity. Be thoughtful … in content, in tone, in phrasing and in how your words will impact on the psyche and ego of the person on the receiving end.

- Technology is only a means to an end. Technology does not communicate; only people do. Use technology and write for people.

## Write to gain attention

*Pamela Hanlon, Vice President-Communications*
*American Express Company*
*New York, NY*

- The elements of good public relations writing are the same as those essential to good news writing. As in news writing, the public relations practitioner should create copy based on clear and concise thoughts, simple language, and easy-to-read sentence constructions.

- Experienced public relations professionals always keep in mind that the primary objective of their writing is to get the attention of news reporters. Therefore, common sense dictates that public relations professionals should write in a style that reporters will identify with and appreciate.

## Think before you write

*Mark Gordon, Managing Director*
*Asia Associates Ltd.*
*Singapore*

- Good PR writing is not about the rules of grammar, the richness of adjectives or the density of verbs. Good PR writing is about clear thinking. It is the natural outcome of a disciplined mental process that has, at its heart, logic and reasoned argument.

- Writing is "good" when the flow of ideas is orderly and logical — when the action the writer wishes to elicit from the reader is an inevitable consequence of the act of reading.

## Write easy-to-read copy

*Donald S. Knight, Senior Editor*
*Intelligent Transportation Society of America*
*Washington, DC*

- Keep it short. Not many sentences can be confined to three words but that might be a worthy target for budding wordsmiths. We look for precision, clarity and, yes, brevity in testing candidates for jobs in media relations and other public relations writing slots.

- The longest lead paragraph in a recent edition of the Sunday New York Times contained 46 words, the shortest 11. Somewhere in between might be the ideal paragraph length in crafting a news release, or even a technical paper or essay.

- Material burdened with adjectives also fails our writing

test. Too often, corporate publicity is presented under the guise of news, but in fact reads like advertising copy.

## Think clearly to write well

*William J. Banach, President*
*Banach, Banach & Cassidy*
*Ray, MI*

- The most important skill in writing is thinking. Quite simply, high quality writing can't emerge from low caliber thinking. Given this, I evaluate writing skills by asking these questions, in this order:

  - Did the writer understand the context? It's difficult to communicate if one doesn't know enough about the topic to visualize the big picture.

  - Does the writer have "purpose" to the writing; that is, does the writer know why to write and what to write?

  - Did the writer address the message to the target? Most opera fans aren't interested in brilliant writing about mud wrestling.

  - Was the writing crisp and generally consistent with the rules of respected style? I like short sentences. Small words. Punch!

  - Would someone keep reading after the first sentence?

  - Did the writing do something to me; that is, motivate me, discourage me, move me, relax me, or enlighten me?

  - Is the writer reasonably quick about it? People don't like waiting for anything these days. Not even quality writing.

- His/her, he/she, him/her, s/he and other such attempts at being neutral can destroy good writing. They certainly ruin reading. (See tips in "Handling 'He said, she said' problems," in this chapter.)

## Captivate your audience

*James M. Caudill, Vice President*
*Public Relations & Hospitality*
*Kendall-Jackson*
*Santa Rosa, CA*

- My personal preference is for writing that "sings." I look for a cadence, a certain kind of rhythm, that jumps from the page.

- We can never afford to be unclear, to be sure, but we must also arrest and entertain. Whether memo, fax or news release, you have an audience that you must capture. That audience is increasingly critical, increasingly harried and rushed.

- In the end, readers want information, and they'll only spend time with your writing if there is a perceived reward. So be clear. Be concise. And never forget what a partner of mine once said: "Never underestimate the value of a snappy quote."

• Take risks. Be a bit unconventional. But remember to deliver the goods quickly.

The "ability to write" in public relations means more than possessing good grammar, spelling and proofreading skills. Many great writers couldn't make it as public relations practitioners. So what sets the public relations writer apart from the journalistic writer, the fiction writer, or the technical writer? One characteristic stands out: competence to integrate all of the skills needed by a public relations practitioner, including "the ability to write."

## Writing: PR's output skill

Becoming a successful public relations writer begins by understanding that "writing" is not a stand-alone skill for public relations practitioners. Along with writing, accomplished practitioners cite persuasive speaking, interpretive listening, critical thought, media savvy, decisive decision-making, intellectual inquisitiveness and more.

The successful public relations practitioner synthesizes a range of skills, knowledge and qualities to build awareness, understanding and support.

This synthesis of knowledge and abilities demonstrates why outstanding writing skills are necessary. Most of the critical skills involved in public relations are "input skills" crucial to research, planning and action underlying a good public relations program.

Writing, however, is the principal "output skill." Writing places your research, planning, thoughts, goals and programs before your audiences, internal and external, to gain their understanding and support.

The channels you'll use, face-to-face, print, electronic, special event, digital, make no difference without good copy.

Without words in action, public relations media fall mute. Placing your words into action, by writing them, begins successful public relations practice.

## Separate process from results

The variety of written materials generally falls into four categories: journalistic writing, internal audience writing, external audience writing and marketing writing. Within these four areas, public relations professionals produce a variety of products. Among them:

### *Journalistic writing*
  News releases
  Public services announcements
  Pitch letters
  Backgrounders and fact sheets

### *Internal writing*
  Newsletters
  Letters
  Memos

### *External writing*
  E-mail
  Scripts
  Position papers
  Speeches

### *Marketing writing*
  Brochures
  Advertising
  Proposals
  Plans

Some of the frequently used products will be explained in how-to fashion later in this chapter and throughout this book. In addition to these products, public relations practitioners must produce all types of business-related copy, from research reports to internal briefing materials, critical to the function's significant management role.

But these products are just tools resulting from the planning and writing process. They help to produce the true "product" of public relations: understanding, support and action.

It's important to understand this distinction. As a writer of public relations products, you will not be judged on your technical ability to string words in grammatically correct sentences. Ultimately, you will succeed based on your ability to prompt understanding, support and action for your organization's objectives.

In other words: you'll succeed depending on what your copy does, not on how it reads or sounds.

The importance of this relationship comes through a dialogue between a novice public relations practitioner and her boss:

With three months on the job, she was asked by her boss, "What have you accomplished?"

The novice responded with pride, "I've written more than 50 news releases."

"That doesn't answer my question," the boss continued. "I asked, 'What have you accomplished?'"

Pondering that repeated question, the novice practitioner slowly began to understand the important role "results" play in public relations writing.

Writing 50, or 500, or 5 million technically good news releases means absolutely nothing, if nothing results. Your copy counts if it enlightens, inspires and activates your publics. It counts a whole lot less if it's technically perfect, strung with words in grammatically correct sentences, but doesn't do the job. Creating such impact has nothing to do

## How Much Do Words Really Matter?

### Talking About People:
### A Guide to Fair and Accurate Language
*by Rosalie Maggio*

The brochure promoting Rosalie Maggio's work contained a section headed, "Do Words Really Matter?" It highlighted the following examples, preceded by the comment that "Words matter terribly":

- The difference between "fetal tissue" and "unborn baby" (referring to the same entity) is arguably the most debated issue in the country.
- The United States changed "The War Department" to "The Department of Defense" because words matter.
- When President Bush used the word "hostages" for the first time in August 1990, it made headlines; up to that time he had been using "detainees." The change of terms signaled a change in our posture toward Iraq.

Sometimes, the word is not the thing we mean, and the further the word we use strays from our meaning, the less likely it is we get our meaning across.

We must understand word meaning to make our words meaningful.

with the quantity of copy you produce. It has everything to do with the quality of the copy you generate and the strategy you base it on.

## Set writing objectives

To get results, the public relations writing process must begin with specific copy objectives.

Managers and clients, of course, should never give writing assignments without also giving specific objectives the copy should accomplish. But they do it all the time. That's why the public relations writer, as a first step, must always agree with bosses and clients on the copy's job.

Without agreement on what your copy should do, you have no meaningful benchmark on which to judge it.

Consider, for example:

- Do you simply want your copy to *inform* your audience about a set of facts? or,
- Do you want your audience to also *accept*, or *agree* with, the facts? or,
- Do you want your audience to agree with and *act on* the facts?

Deciding what you want your copy to accomplish plays an important role in deciding:

- The amount of information you should include. (Do you need some background information, a lot, or none?)
- The extent to which your copy must cement your credibility. (Whom should you cite or quote from within your organization? Should you include data or quotes from outside sources?)
- Your copy's tone, to properly reflect your organization and to properly accommodate your audience's existing point of view. (Will a formal tone be too stuffy? Will a conversational tone be too casual? What tone cares for your audience and your purpose at the same time?)
- How will your copy work in the media you'll use? (Will you use a brochure? Will you need copy in supporting publicity? Will you need fact sheets for a face-to-face meeting?)

## Understand your copy strategy

Consider the case of a company whose officials decided to ban smoking at outdoor bus stops used by its employees. The task seemed simple enough when a public relations staff member received the assignment:

"We're banning smoking at company bus stops next week," the public relations director announced. "Write up an announcement and get it to me as soon as possible."

Later in the day, the writer returned with the copy. The boss's reaction to unsatisfactory public relations writing was typical:

"No, no, no," the director huffed while reading it. "This isn't what I wanted at all."

The director's complaint had absolutely nothing to do with the technical quality of the writing. The director wasn't complaining about misplaced modifiers or noun-verb agreement.

The director's complaint was typically nonspecific and fuzzy. "You-haven't-got-it-right" objections frequently frustrate unfocused public relations writers, their managers and clients.

The copy didn't work because the director and the writer didn't agree on what the copy should accomplish. Thus, the copywriter was criticized for producing "poor" copy.

The boss might begin to think she has a weak writer on staff, even though concerns about the copy had nothing to do with the writer's technical skills. Sentences were complete. Grammar was flawless. Spelling was impeccable. Yet the copy, as far as the director was concerned, was useless.

Consider how different the writing would have been as

well as the director's opinion of her staffer had director and writer agreed to the writing's purpose before they began work on this seemingly simple assignment.

In the following list of possible objectives, consider how each objective would have influenced the copy:

- Simply *inform* employees of the smoking ban. Make sure they *know* about the ban. In other words, copy should **educate** them.
- *Inform* employees of the ban and get them to *agree* that it's a good idea. In other words, copy should both **educate** them and **influence** their attitude.
- *Inform* employees of the ban, get them to *agree* that it's a good idea, and make them feel compelled to *obey* the ban. The copy then, should **educate** them, **influence** their attitude, and **prompt** compliant action.

Assume you are the writer for this assignment.

Your writing objectives will influence the type of media you choose to carry your copy. And your media choice will itself influence your copy.

If your writer's task is to simply inform employees of the new smoking ban, a simple, one-page announcement will probably do.

But if your purpose is to generate support for the ban by getting people to comply with it, a one-page announcement might fall short. Using research, you might conclude that your audience's ability to process information and their prevailing practice requires copy for a series of communication efforts — an announcement of the new ban, a brochure explaining reasons for the ban, a presentation to discuss benefits of the ban, and posters at the bus stops reinforcing the compliant behavior you want.

Clearly, the ability to integrate your skill as public relations writer, with your skills as public relations researcher, planner and strategist, ultimately determines how well you succeed as a public relations "writer."

## Target your audience

Defining the target audience for your copy is an important part of this objective-setting stage. The more precisely you target your audience, the more predictably you enhance your chances for success.

By its name, public relations would seem interested in connecting with "the public." But you'll rarely find yourself targeting or writing for that large, poorly defined mass often referred to as "the public."

Your audience usually will comprise specific groups whose understanding and actions are important to you and your objectives. The better you define and understand these groups, the better you'll write copy they'll read or listen to, understand, and accept.

After you've established overall copy objectives, do the same for your target audiences. Precisely determine your target audience and make sure everyone you're working with agrees with your definition.

Begin with the broadest description of your audience. Then narrow it as you consider subsets that are most important to your writing objectives.

*Example*: Assume you're assigned to communicate pending changes in your company's health insurance benefits that would affect coverage of dependents. Begin by broadly targeting your audience:

## Employees

- Through research, you decide you don't need to reach all employees.
- So, you limit your target audience to employees eligible for health benefits.
- Among this group, you might limit your audience to employees who carry dependent health-care coverage.

Now that you've established a specific group of people as your target audience, you can research exactly what members in the group know about this issue, media most likely to reach the greatest number of them, and likeliness of response to your message.

With your copy objectives set, and your audience precisely identified, you have begun the "process" of public relations writing. Only now are you ready to begin putting words into "copy."

## Keep an audience focus

Committing to a strong "audience focus" is key to producing copy that will get results.

Audience focus means simply that you write your copy with your audience in mind. Audience-focused copy:

- Gives information your audience wants and needs
- Uses words and structures your audience is comfortable with
- Respects your audience's time

Unfortunately, many organizations tend to produce only company-focused copy. Audiences generally ignore company-focused copy because it isn't written from their point of view, is difficult to comprehend, and requires a lot of time and effort to decipher.

How you can tell the difference in focus:

- Company-focused copy provides information executives want the audience to know, not necessarily what the audience wants or needs.
- Company-focused copy uses words and structures company executives are comfortable with, not words

and structures audiences are comfortable with.

- Company-focused copy believes that people have nothing else to do but accept executives' copy. It ignores the fact that audiences generally accept copy focused only on their interests.

## Effort vs. benefit ratio

Consider this formula commonly used to describe the transaction between writers and readers. The effort readers must expend (or perceive they must expend) to read copy is proportional to the benefit they perceive. (See the chapter on public opinion for an explanation of Wilbur Shramm's Fraction of Selection Formula, with examples.)

The public relations writer determines how best to manage this ratio. To enhance readership, you can boost the benefit your copy offers your readers. Or, you can decrease the amount of effort it takes to read the copy. Or, ideally, you can do both.

Reducing reader effort your copy requires depends on your ability to produce copy that places your readers in their reading comfort zones. The reading comfort zone is the place where the pain and work associated with difficult reading dissolves.

All of us have been lulled into reading copy that we might otherwise have ignored because the copy gently pulled us into a comfortable reading zone. Consider this typical scenario:

Imagine someone, perhaps you, sitting at a breakfast table. It's early Saturday morning. The person has poured a bowl of cereal and glass of juice and is staring blankly at the back of the cereal box, thinking of nothing, doing nothing, just waking up.

Someone enters the kitchen and takes the cereal box. "Bring that back," the first person demands. "I was reading it."

Half asleep. Totally unfocused. Somehow the person had been lulled into reading copy on the back of a cereal box. Most likely, no great personal benefit screamed from the copy. In other words, the breakfaster had no apparent motive to read the back of the box. Instead, the copy required very little effort on the part of the reader. It was easy to do, even with the person only half-awake. Small familiar words, in short crisp sentences, enhanced with reader-friendly graphics, enticed effortless reading.

## Formulas for success

Writing copy for your readers' comfort zone relies on picking the right words and putting those words to work in the right combination of short- and medium-length sentences.

Several formulas (The Gunning-Mueller Fog Index, The Flesch Formula, The Dale-Chall Formula) can make your copy more comfortable to read. The formulas consider the average length of the sentences you write, along with the number of multi-syllable words you use, to calculate a "grade-level" or "reading level" for your copy.

Some word-processing programs (e.g., Microsoft Word) offer an option for checking the difficulty-level of your copy. Free "shareware" programs for evaluating reading ease also are available.

You need to understand how these formulas work, and how you can use them to make your copy more reader friendly.

One popular and easy-to-use formula is the Gunning-Mueller Fog Index. Although you don't have to use the Gunning-Mueller Fog Index on every paragraph you write, you should use such a formula to periodically check your copy.

The Gunning-Mueller Fog Index can be used to calculate the "grade-level" of copy you've written. The formula used to determine the index considers the average length of sentences in your text, as well as the percentage of larger words in your text. The resulting number is considered the "fog index" for your copy. (*See boxed item on next page.*)

*Remember*: The Gunning-Mueller Fog Index is a reading formula, not a writing formula. It predicts reading ease. It's an excellent tool to keep tabs on your ability to write short sentences and your ability to use short, descriptive words that readers will be comfortable with.

## Improve your score

No matter which formula you use to check what you write, one fact remains clear: If your sentences are too long, and your words are too big, you will lose readers.

Generally, sentences of 17 or fewer words are considered to have a standard-to-fairly-easy level of difficulty. That means about 75 percent of a typical audience will have little trouble reading your copy. But readership falls off dramatically as the length of your sentences increases. At the high end, sentences of 29 words or more generally reach fewer than 5 percent of your readers.

Readability formulas, such as the *Gunning-Mueller Fog Index*, score copy on a difficulty level that compares to a "grade level." For example, your copy might be rated at the "10th-grade level." But keep in mind that your readers' comfort zone for reading will be lower. People usually are "comfortable" reading at least two grade levels below their reading grade-level ability.

This is why you'll find many newspaper front pages

# Defog your writing

Sometimes writing is vague, obscure and hard to grasp. Professional writers call it "foggy" writing because the cluttered message makes it difficult for the audience to get the meaning.

To defog writing, try the Gunning-Mueller Fog Index. It tells writers the "reading ease score" of their copy. Remember, easy-to-read copy influences. Here's a brief explanation of how it works.

- **Step one**: Take a 100-word sample from the copy in question. Estimate the average sentence length (ASL) of the sample by dividing the 100 words by the number of sentences.

*Example*: Suppose you have four sentences in the 100-word sample. Divide 100 words by four sentences and you get an average sentence length of 25. (That's high. A workable average sentence length is 17.)

- **Step two**: Calculate the number of three-syllable words (TSW) or more in the sample. Don't count proper nouns, verbs that become three syllables when you add -*ed* or -*es* (e.g., parad*ed*, compose*s*) or compound words that arise from joining two common words (e.g., count "Internet" but not "butterfly" "briefcases" or "lawbreaker"). Assume you have 22 of these in the 100-word sample.

- **Step three**: Add the average sentence length (in this case 25), to the number of three-syllable words (in this case, 22). The sum is 47. Then multiply that number 47 by .4 (the .4 never changes). Thus: 25

(ASL) + 22 (TSW) = 47 x .4 = 18.8 — the grade level of the copy, or the **reading ease score**.

Most general audience copy should reflect about an 8.5 Fog Index grade level. If you want to reduce the fog in your writing, reduce the ASL, the TSW, or both.

If you exceeded 100 words to complete a sentence, then simply find the average of three-syllable words in the sample.

*Example*: Assume your sample is 110 words and the number of three-syllable words is 22. Divide 22 by 110 and you get 20 percent. Then use 20 percent as your TSW score.

So the new reading ease score would be:

25 (ASL) + 20 (TSW) = 45 x .4 = 18.0 (Grade level or reading ease score.)

Remember, if you want to write influential copy, don't write **up** to a person's ability to process information. Write a couple of levels **below** it. Understanding copy and finding copy easy to understand aren't the same. Even college professors like copy written at levels lower than their abilities — for reading ease.

Also, recall the *Fraction of Selection Formula*. Your readers might read difficult copy because the promise of reward is so great. They must. But if the reward isn't that great, they might quit reading your copy because the reading ease score is too high for them to deal with.

written at the grade 9 reading level or lower. It's not because newspapers' readers have been educated only to the grade 9 level. Rather, it's clear that newspaper editors understand their readers' comfort zones.

In fact, many newspaper readers are college graduates. But while writing produced for them at the 16th grade level might sound important, with big words and long sentences, it would not be read by the majority of subscribers.

*Remember*: Impressive sounding copy, left unread, is useless. Also useless: a writer with no readers.

To understand how reading comfort zones work, consider what you *choose* to read, not what you *must* read. Because you made it through high school, you're probably able to read at the 12th grade reading level or higher. But how much reading do you think you'd really do if everything presented to you were written at this level?

Probably not nearly as much as you now do.

All of us have more to read than we can ever get to. And we decide what to read by looking for the most comfortable copy to read. We also look for copy that promises the biggest personal benefit for reading it. When these two combine, ease-of-reading and personal benefit, readership skyrockets.

## Deflate bloated copy

The best defense against rambling sentences and puffed-up word choices focuses on becoming a ruthless self-editor. Frequently, writers produce bloated copy in their first drafts, so you must practice editing your copy to direct it toward your readers' comfort zones.

Fortunately, by focusing on a few key areas when you edit, you can make dramatic improvements in your copy.

## Effective copywriting principles

### *Use strong verbs*

Ridding your copy of passive constructions and weak verbs adds impact to your writing. Your verbs are your power tools that create attractive flow for your readers. Verbs are, in short, your copy's "sirens."

To improve your writing, analyze your verb use.

Take any sample of your writing and circle all the verbs. See if you wrote strong, active dynamic verbs. Your copy will be forceful if you used strong verbs. Look at these two examples:

*Weak verb example*: The problem with your computer system **is** that you don't **have** a way of getting the results you **want**, when you **want** them. Our company **has** the right answers for you. They**'re** in the enclosed brochure. And there**'s** a phone number in there for you to **call**.

The weak verbs in this example: *is, have, want, has, are, is.*

*Strong verb rewrite*: If your computer system **fails** you when you must **succeed**, our company **fixes** broken systems like yours. **Intrigue** yourself with stories in our brochure of successful clients who **won** by using our services. Want to **win**? **Call** us.

Strong verbs in this sample: *fails, succeed, fixes, intrigue, won, win, call.*

Never underestimate the power of verbs to move people to action or bore them to inaction.

*Tip*: The so-called verbs *be, is, was* and *were* aren't real verbs. Verbs carry action. The "be" words declare state of being without action, and so weaken your writing.

*Example*: The computer **is** on the desk.

The computer isn't doing anything. The statement merely describes the state of the computer, lying passively on the desk.

Here are two examples, one with weak existence verbs, the other with the weak verbs replaced by strong verbs.

*With existence verbs*: "The book **is** blue. **It's** a report about UFOs. **It's** the property of the United States Air Force. **It's** controversial. And **it's** secret."

*Without existence verbs*: "The United States Air Force's secret and controversial Blue Book **reports** on the existence of UFOs."

*Caution*: Sometimes "be" verbs can add brevity and simplicity to copy. Used properly, they could influence. But try to use as few of them as possible, no more than five to ten percent of the verb total.

**Take care of your verbs and your verbs will take care of you.**

Here's a list of short, punchy verbs that communicate clear, specific action.

*Aid, ask, bid, block, dip, drop, gain, mix, pick, push, quit, rip, seek, sway, tell, vie, vow, warn*

Sometimes, sentence construction or syntax can blur the sentence's true action and rob the verb of its power.

## Buried verbs

When this happens, the **buried verb** can't do its job and loses the power of its action. The reader must work harder to decipher just what is going on in the sentence.

Consider these examples:

*Weak*: When we feel it is mandated, we will be offering comprehensive new options and alternatives.

*Better*: When required, we'll offer new options.

*Weak*: The board will take the issue under consideration.

*Better*: The board will consider the issue.

When you unknowingly convert verbs to nouns, you rob them of their power. Consider the difference in the action when you write:

He *made a suggestion* that we adjourn.

Instead of,

He *suggested* we adjourn.

Mary *made an implication* that the product would fail.

Instead of,

Mary *implied* the product would fail.

The committee's report *gave an explanation* for the productivity decline.

Instead of,

The committee's report *explained* the productivity decline.

A few key words can serve as clues to help you spot many nouns that might better work as verbs. These include:

| | | |
|---|---|---|
| *made* – | *made an agreement* | **agreed** |
| | *made an acquisition* | **acquired** |
| | *made a determination* | **determined** |
| *gave* – | *gave her resignation* | **resigned** |
| | *gave authorization* | **authorized** |
| | *gave information* | **informed** |
| *had* – | *had an expectation* | **expected** |
| | *had a reaction* | **reacted** |
| | *had a relapse* | **relapsed** |

Another symptom of verbs disguised as nouns lies in noun endings. Look for four types of noun endings to reveal buried (and more powerful) verbs:

Uncover verbs lurking in nouns ending in:

**...ment   ...ing   ...ance   ...ion**

*Examples*:

**...ment**
*Weak*: We must strive for the recruit*ment* of more minorities.
*Improved*: We must recruit more minorities.

**...ing**
*Weak*: This would have the effect of reduc*ing* the impact of financing charges on corporate earnings.
*Improved*: This would reduce the impact of financing charges on corporate earnings.

**...ion**
*Weak*: These studies will take into considera*tion* the need for the identification of a secure water supply and an environmentally safe ash disposal system.
*Improved*: These studies will consider the need to identify a secure water supply and an environmentally safe ash disposal system.

**...ance**
*Weak*: The therapy involves the applica*tion* of music for the restora*tion*, mainten*ance* and improve*ment* of health.
*Improved*: The therapy applies music to restore, maintain and improve health.

*Tip*: **Convert nouns to verbs** to add verb power in your writing. Let verbs do their work. Take care of verbs and verbs will take care of your writing.

## Be clear

Many beginning public relations writers find it difficult to inject clarity into their writing. Why? Because principles of clear writing can conflict with some poor writing habits.

Sometimes, to be polite, and sometimes to cover ourselves by being purposely vague, many of us use fuzzy language.

This practice shows up in our workplace when we write:
*Please make it a priority to read this new product report.*

It shows up in our personal life when we write:
*Let's get together for dinner soon.*

Statements such as these create confusion rather than transfer information. Avoid confusion by communicating precisely. Use concrete statements. Consider the difference in what we communicate when we rewrite the above examples to read:

*Please make sure you read the new product report before our Thursday meeting.*

*Let's get together for dinner soon. Does Saturday night work for you?* (Unless, of course, the invitation was only a social nicety.)

Public relations writers put pressure on themselves to be specific because much of what they write they want the media to use. Reporters and editors demand clarity and accuracy.

You'll rarely see a news story that reports:
*He has a long and impressive track record in the software industry.*

News writers want specific facts, such as:
*He has worked in the software industry for more than 20 years, producing several programs still being used by most Fortune 500 companies.*

Both sentences communicate the same general idea. The second example, however, paints a much clearer **picture** for the reader.

*Note*: Public relations writers should be even more specific than journalists because, unlike journalists, they promote clients. The information in the example above (number of years, Fortune 500 use, etc.) would never make it into the newspaper if the PR writer didn't tell the journalist about it in the news release. Although journalists like to be specific and accurate, they also lazily decline to dig out facts complimentary to the practitioner's client to avoid seeming to be merely a printing press for PR people.

*Bottom line*: Use words your readers know and understand. Use words that create specific **images** for your readers.

**swimming pool**    *not*    aquatic facility
**library**    *not*    reading resources room
**award-winning**    *not*    accomplished

*Final point on clarity*: Too many adjectives cause clarity problems. Writing more is not necessarily writing better when you want to write clearly.

More copy adds little effect, other than to increase your word count.

*Example*:
Instead of: *Agreement on the plan is ~~absolutely~~ essential to success.*
Write: *Agreement on the plan is essential to success.*
(Even better: *To succeed, we must agree on the plan.*)

Instead of: *Hitting the sales goal is a ~~top~~ priority.*
Write: *Hitting the sales goal is a priority.*
(Even better: *We must hit the sales goal.*)

## Cut extra words

When you're self-editing your copy to cut needless words, consider a few other areas. Cast a wary eye on sentences beginning with *there is* or *there are*. This usually signals a poorly constructed sentence smothering meaning under too many words and usually a weakened verb.

*Example*: ~~There are~~ 40 employees who are demanding a meeting.
*Revised*: Forty employees demand a meeting.
*Example*: ~~There's~~ no excuse that can be used for writing flabby sentences.
*Revised*: Nothing excuses flabby sentence writing.

• Look at prepositional phrases as structures to possibly cut. You can use prepositions to add variety to your copy. But too many of them produce wordy copy. Consider:

*Example*: He is the leader ~~of the band~~.
*Revised*: He leads the band. or, He's a band leader.
*Example*: She has won awards ~~for her work~~ as a writer.
*Revised*: She's an award-winning writer.

• Don't fight for the same ground twice by being redundant. Many redundancies sneak into copy almost unnoticed. Revise two-word combinations that can stand as one to reduce your average sentence length.

*Examples*:

**cancel** *not* cancel out
**disappear** *not* disappear altogether
**innovation** *not* new innovation
**history** *not* past history
**3 p.m. today** *not* 3 p.m. this afternoon

Avoid infectious business writing habits by avoiding word-wasting phrases that add little to a sentence's meaning, such as:

*Enclosed herewith…*
*Kindly be advised…*
*It has come to my attention…*
*Thanking you in advance…*

*Note*: The greatest danger to a PR writer is to "fall asleep at the keyboard" and become a habitual writer. The letter-ending phrases above reveal a writer that doesn't care to write an original idea, and so, doesn't care about the reader. **Borrowed language is not the hallmark of a PR writer who seeks to impress and persuade.**

## Use positive statements

Try to write as many positive statements as you can and need to. Some negative statements can create a pessimistic tone. Negative statements can also come across as less helpful than positive statements.

### Special Tip: Get it Right

Good public relations copy must be accurate. This means your facts, grammar and structure must be correct. Errors will hurt your credibility.

Look out for errors any writer could make, especially when you produce copy quickly. Some common errors:

~~Could~~ care less *should be* **Couldn't** care less
Between you and ~~I~~ *should be* Between you and **me**
~~Here's~~ several ideas *should be* **Here are** several ideas
Her comments ~~inferred~~ I did it *should be* Her comments **implied** I did it
I ~~myself~~ wrote the proposal *should be* **I wrote** the proposal
Mary must ~~of~~ approved this *should be* Mary must **have** approved this

A good stylebook, usage guide and dictionary should be well-worn tools in your public relations writing efforts. Among those you should consider:

*The Associated Press Stylebook and Briefing on Media Law*, New York: Associated Press, 2002.
*Publication Manual of the American Psychological Association*, Fifth Edition, American Psychological Association (APA), 5th Edition, June 1, 2001.
*Webster's New World College Dictionary*, Fourth Edition, Michael Agnes, John Wiley & Sons, June 11, 2004.(For more writing resource texts, see the bibliography for this chapter in the Appendix)

*Negative*: We **can't send** the materials to you until you complete a release form.
*Positive*: We'll **send** you the materials as soon as we receive your completed release form.

*Negative*: We **close** at five o'clock.
*Positive*: We're **open** until five o'clock.

*Negative*: I am not a **crook**.
*Positive*: I'm an **honest** person.

*Note*: Sometimes negative statements are perfect when you want to signal incapability, victimization, and denial.

*Example*: We **can't allow** you more time than the government allows us."

## Use transitions

To help readers move through your copy, use smooth transitions.

Without transitions, your copy will sound very

staccato — isolated statements that seem disconnected. This would force readers to work harder to decipher what you're trying to communicate.

Consider this paragraph:

> The spirit of volunteerism is sweeping corporate America. Becoming a volunteer is a time-consuming task. It's not a task you should take lightly. You can enjoy tremendous rewards by volunteering. You'll get more than you give. To be a successful volunteer you must be ready to make a major, long-term commitment.

Now look at what happens to the paragraph when transitions help readers move through the copy:

> The spirit of volunteerism is sweeping through corporate America. **Although** becoming a volunteer is a time-consuming task, you can enjoy tremendous rewards by volunteering. **But** it's not a task you should take lightly. **To succeed**, you must make a major, long-term commitment. **In short**, you'll get more out of it than you put in.

Transitions fall into these primary categories:

| | |
|---|---|
| Moving copy forward | *and, also, for example* |
| Offering a conclusion | *thus, therefore, so* |
| Offering a new thought | *but, yet, despite, however* |
| Linking events or ideas | *as a result, consequently, this caused* |
| Adding a qualifier | *if, even if, when, provided* |
| Specifying time | *subsequently, meanwhile, frequently* |

## Special PR writing products

### News release writing

Public relations writers use news releases as the primary tool to communicate with the media. And news releases generate a majority of stories that appear in the media. Many journalists receive an overwhelming number of news releases daily. But this shouldn't discourage you. If you have a well-written news release and a solid news story, your news release will attract attention over your competition.

Remember the two simple keys for success: your release must be both **newsworthy** and **well-written**.

The lead (or first paragraph or two) of your news release is critical. You must write it like a typical lead in any news story. And it must offer a compact statement describing precisely the news you're offering.

The balance of your news release, no matter how great, generally will go unread if you fail to entice the editor or reporter into your story with your lead.

The lead contains your story's most important

## Handling "he said," "she said' problems

Singular nouns and pronouns require singular referents. This can create problems if you want to avoid sexist writing.

*Example:*

Everyone is to report to *his* class on Thursday.

Some writers avoid this problem by adding words to accommodate both sexes.

*Example*:

Everyone is to report to *his or her* class on Thursday.

Other writers solve the dilemma by breaking the rules, and creating sentences, such as:

Everyone is to report to *their* classes on Thursday.

Increasingly, such constructions are being accepted in both spoken and written presentations. But why break the rules when often you can simply write around the problem? Some examples:

• **Use plurals**

*Everyone is to report to his class now.* (becomes)
***All students** are to report to **their** classes now.*

*Every student completed his test.* (becomes)
***All students** completed **their** tests.*

• **Avoid the pronoun**

*Everyone should be in **his or her** seat.* (becomes)
*Everyone should be seated.*

*Each teacher should hand in **his** grades.* (becomes)
*All teachers should hand in grades.*

Most writers ignore the suggestions that writers consider using a type of "sexless" pronoun (such as *he/she, him/her,* or "*s/he*"). And for good reason: Although making nouns and pronouns agree with their verbs and referents can present nettlesome problems for writers, careful and creative rewriting or editing can correct them.

information. As your news release progresses, the information becomes less and less essential to the story.

Journalism texts teach that a lead should contain the 5 W's of a story — *Who, What, When, Where* and *Why.*

Your leads don't always have to contain all five of these items. But they should include those vital to your story's most important element. (You'll usually include all five of W's somewhere in your news release.)

Consider how your lead addresses the question an editor asks when evaluating your news release: Why should I, or my readers, be interested in this story?

Be editorially honest. Ask yourself:

*Is my lead truly interesting to an outside reader?*

*Does my lead make the reader want to know more?*

If you can't answer a resounding "yes" to both questions, rewrite your lead.

Consider this lead:

At its regular monthly board of directors meeting yesterday, the Cat'n Dog Pet Food Corporation voted to fund a statewide pet adoption program with a $100,000 contribution to the Allstate Humane Association, Cat'n Dog Pet Food President Rex Rover announced.

It sounds as if a good story lurks in that lead. But that's the problem. The story "lurks" in the lead. It doesn't jump out at the reader.

Ask yourself: *What's the essence of this story?*

The essence of this story is that many homeless pets will soon find a place to live, thanks to a $100,000 donation by a pet-food company.

But the lead, as written, buries this story under too much company information and background. Don't fall into the trap of trying to promote your company, products or people too early in a news release to the detriment of the real news. Stick to the top news in your lead. Later in the story, you can work in promotional details about your company, products or people. As your story progresses, offer less and less vital information.

To emphasize the news in this story, and to offer the reader the essence of the story, a better lead might be:

Thousands of homeless pets in New Jersey got a new lease on life yesterday, when a major pet food company decided to give $100,000 to the Allstate Humane Association.

---

## News Release Excerpts Defining News to Outsiders

All news release writers struggle to define the "news" in their stories. The key: Appreciate what will be important to those outside of your organization. Don't think the information your organization thinks is important will be important, or newsworthy, to outsiders.

Here are news release excerpts showing how some companies have done this:

**United Moves To Improve In-flight Air Quality For**
**Passengers And Flight Crews To Highest Standard Possible**
*Upgraded Cabin Air Filtration Systems To Meet "True HEPA" Standard*
CHICAGO — United Airlines announced today that it expects to be the first commercial airline in the world to upgrade its fleets with air conditioning recirculation filters that provide the best possible air quality for its passengers and flight crews.

United said it will install new filters in all its cabin air filtration systems that meet the "True HEPA" standard, widely considered to represent the highest possible air quality standard.

HEPA is short for High Efficiency Particulate Air. Air filtration systems that meet the True HEPA standard remove at least 99.97 percent of all air particles 0.3 microns in size. (By comparison, a human hair measures about 70 microns, dust-mite debris about 10 microns and bacteria are in the 0.3 micron range.)

"Reaching the True HEPA plateau is an important milestone in our ongoing commitment to provide our passengers and crew members with the best possible air quality while they're in the air," said Andrew P. Studdert, senior vice president of fleet operations. "Air quality always ranks among the top consumer concerns in United's marketing research.

Note that the news release first describes the essence of the story. And because the company itself is vital, the story includes the company's name.

Next it deals with some difficult scientific detail. A human hair comparison aids the nonscientific reader. Then the story quotes a company vice president as sourced opinion—"important milestone."

*See next page for second example*

---

## News Release Excerpts Defining News to Outsiders, continued

**William R. Lewis Named CFO Of Campbell Spinoff: Vlasic Foods International**

Camden, N.J. — Campbell Soup Company today named William R. Lewis Chief Financial Officer of Vlasic Foods International, the specialty foods company Campbell plans to spin off to shareowners at the end of March.

Lewis has 30 years of experience in finance and management at several leading companies, including Nutri/Systems, Simplicity Holdings, Columbia Pictures, Culbro Corp., PepsiCo and Citibank. He will report to Robert F. Bernstock, who will be president and chief executive officer of Vlasic Foods International.

The new company, with sales of approximately $1.4 billion in operations in five countries, will be anchored by "Swanson" frozen foods and "Vlasic" pickles in North America, and "Swift" meats and pates in South America.

"Bill Lewis is an outstanding addition to the senior leadership team of Vlasic Foods International. His wealth of experience in finance, treasury, acquisitions and divestitures at both large and small companies will bring perspective to our management team and build on our entrepreneurial spirit," said Bernstock.

The news release begins by offering the essence of the news in the story, without too much detail. It continues with background on the person in this story, again without much detail, but with enough information to offer the reader a sense of the person's significant background.

Next, it addresses the basic questions readers would have about this new company. The sentence is long, more than 40 words. To enhance readability, it would work better as two sentences. The first sentence could focus on sales and brands. The second sentence could identify the "anchor" brands.

Finally, the news release uses a quote to offer some opinion and commentary.

---

Here are some additional guidelines for writing news release copy:

- **Remember that you are writing news copy, not marketing copy or advertising copy.** Because you're trying to make news, you should avoid unnecessary adjectives, or unsourced opinion or commentary. Descriptions such as "Smith has an outstanding background in telecommunications," present opinion. Who says the background is outstanding? Just report the facts on his background; they will imply its outstanding nature.

- **Keep your sentences and paragraphs as short as possible.** Many paragraphs will contain only one or two sentences, and rarely more than three sentences. One-sentence paragraphs are acceptable in news releases. *Tip*: Most paragraphs should be no longer than five lines of type.

- **Keep your news release brief.** News releases should be as short as possible. Offer lengthy details in additional materials, such as fact sheets, backgrounders, biographies or question-and-answer sheets. As a general rule, keep news releases to no more than two pages.

- **Use quotes to add life to your news release and to work in some opinion or commentary.** Because quotes usually require sources, they can contain opinion or commentary. Just make certain the quote truly adds to the story's news value and isn't simply a self-serving statement. (And clear all quotes with those for whom you wrote them.)

  *Example*: "We're making a donation to Wee-Tots Day Care because it provides an outstanding early learning program for our community," said Jane Davis, president of XYZ Inc.

- **Always be accurate.** Check and re-check the spelling of names and accuracy of all numbers you use (including phone numbers, addresses, ZIP codes and web addresses). One error can destroy an editor or reporter's confidence in you. Remember, any wrong information in print makes the reporter look bad. And if the error resulted from your poor fact checking, don't expect reporters who relied on your copy to be very forgiving.

- **Use news style throughout your release.** Many public relations writers prefer to follow Associated Press style. Consult a news stylebook frequently for guidance.

## Speech Writing

When you write a speech, you should shout to yourself the key point: The audience won't *read* it; it will *hear* it. This will demand a number of changes from your written-to-be-read copy.

Some of those differences:

- Use shorter words. "Use" works better than "utilization."

- Use short sentences.  Even fragments work well. People can grasp three-and four-word chunks more easily than 28-word sentences.

- Select words that form pictures in listeners' minds. Be as descriptive as possible.

- Most speakers insist on telling people what they're going to tell them, tell them, and remind them what they told them. While this sounds unnecessary, remember that listeners can't reread paragraphs.

- When you can, insert a quote or two from a recognizable name that will add credibility to what the speaker's saying.  Choose a name the audience will receive favorably.

- Choose only words the speaker will find comfortable. Don't include tongue-twisters or words listeners won't understand.

- Give three adjectives or three examples to drive home a point.  Audiences respond well to groupings of three.

- Start with a startling statement or a key point designed to grab attention.

- Unless the person delivering the speech is an excellent storyteller, don't start with a joke. If you do use stories, be sure they relate to the topic and make a point, even if humor isn't the mechanism.

- Prepare the speech in a variety of lengths and clearly show what to skip or add as the time constraints change. A speech originally slated for 30-minutes could be changed to 20 or 40 depending on circumstances.

- Remember the writing suggestions earlier in this text. Do your homework on the audience before writing; use active verbs.

- After you write the speech, ask the person who will deliver it to read it for a comfort level. Change statements that don't work for the presenter. Also, after the speech is ready, look for other public relations uses. Use excerpts in a company publication, news release or annual report.

Common areas worthy of caution:

- Numbers (*Example*: Generally spell out zero through nine, but use figures for larger numbers).

- Abbreviations (*Example*: Abbreviate "Avenue" as "Ave.," but never abbreviate "Road." Also: State abbreviations do not follow the two-letter U.S. Postal Service format. Example: "Arizona" is abbreviated "Ariz.," not "AZ").

- Weights and measures (*Example*: The baby weighs 6 pounds, 10 ounces. Also: The 6-pound, 10-ounce baby).

- Titles (Example: Generally don't use courtesy titles such as Mr. or Ms. But use more formal ones, and allowably abbreviate them, such as Dr., Sen., Gov.).

## Persuasive writing

### Guidelines for the persuasive writer

Start by deciding your writing purpose — knowledge, attitudes or behavior. The key to writing successful persuasive copy focuses on knowing what motivates your audience and how to tap into it. It also involves freeing your audience to do what you want. Your job is to send messages that audiences can and will receive. Here are some guidelines for these purposes:

- **Attract audience attention.** Audiences can't receive messages if they're not paying attention. For example, television producers raise the volume at the beginning of commercials and sometimes use a musical intro to capture an audience's attention. Attending to the message or "listening up" is the earliest stage of opinion formation. You need "listen up" copy at the beginning of your piece.

- **Make information valuable.** Once you focus your audience, present your argument so your audience can see it will make a difference in their lives.

- **Make information easy to take in and process.** Use readability formulas. Always write to your audience's lowest ability to process information.

*Tip*: You could write two levels of copy, one your audience can deal with, and one they're comfortable with. Use the one they're most comfortable with. Mass audiences generally find copy easy to understand at approximately grades 8–9. Audiences will not resent the "lower level" copy.

- **Make information memorable.** Audiences need to recall messages before they'll act on them. End your copy with a phrase that sums up your message points.

- **Check your copy.** Edit for readability, legibility, design and content. All factors influence message retention.

For messages intended to change or confirm an audience attitude:

- **Identify the roots of the existing attitude**. You won't have much success changing an attitude if you deal only with its expression and not its cause. Target your copy to offer alternatives to the existing attitude. Or, cancel the effect of the existing attitude by offering another attitude more valuable to your audience. Remember, benefit to an audience has to do with the audience's ranked values. To supplant an existing attitude based on benefit, identify a benefit associated with a value higher in the audience's mind (or heart).

Your audience might feel it must hold the attitude (e.g., ethnic traditions, customs, peer pressure, habit, genetic tendencies, etc. To dislodge these entrenched positions from your audience, make it comfortable for your audience to hold another viewpoint without feeling guilty about abandoning the old one. Never directly attack these attitudes without offering an alternative value safety net.

The *theory of cognitive dissonance* can work for you. Audiences become uncomfortable when they hold an attitude that pulls in one direction but their behavior pushes in another. It makes them uncomfortable. Most audiences don't like the discomfort.

For example, if you want your audience to switch brands and buy your product, make them feel comfortable about owning the new product or uncomfortable about not owning it. Behavior campaigns, such as using car seat belts, or finishing all the pills in a prescription bottle, seek to make audiences uncomfortable about doing the opposite.

- If you want to **change behavior,** you're in for the toughest aspect of persuasion. Why? Because an audience may understand what you're proposing, agree with your proposal, want it for themselves, but can't or won't take the final persuasion step and behave for you.

## Persuasive copywriting tactics

### Catering to active and passive audiences

Writers best serve the needs and interests of their audiences when they properly handle features and benefits. Features are generally known as the "virtues" of a product or service. Benefits are the actual enjoyment of those features by an audience.

Until recently, advertising copywriters suggested routine conversion of features to benefits in ads.

| Active | Passive |
|--------|---------|
|  |  |
| **"Interested" Needs features** | **"Unaware" Needs benefits** |

Figure 9.1

But research from the University of Maryland suggests that audiences comprise two types of targets, *active* and *passive* (*Figure 9.1*).

Active audiences are those that seek information about products or services. **For active audiences, stress features**, not benefits in your copy. Why? Because your audiences have already convinced themselves that they need or want what you have to offer. You need only assure them they'll get the right brand, service, warranty, follow-through, etc.

*Example*: A consumer browses the Internet specifically looking for a new refrigerator. This audience knows about refrigerators, probably has done some consumer homework about them, and perhaps even has a specific brand and model in mind. This is an active audience. The shopper needs features copy — product information, warranty, delivery, efficiency, etc.

Passive audiences aren't actively seeking a specific product or service or perhaps even accepting information. They might best be described as "couch potatoes" with respect to a writer's specific purpose.

**For passive audiences, stress benefits**. This group doesn't yet know it needs what you have to offer. They're not "out shopping." By stressing benefits, you'll activate them — convert them to wanting your product or service. Afterward, you can switch to features because then they'll be an active audience.

*Example*:

A consumer, browsing in a shopper's flier, comes across a description of an air mattress. The consumer isn't thinking about air mattresses. The consumer doesn't yet know she needs an air mattress.

This audience needs benefit copy — *an extra bed without the costly expense of mattress and box spring*. Notice how the features of the product are converted to benefits to "activate" this audience.

*Tip*: If you're writing copy to a mixed audience, blended with active and passive types, and you can send only one message piece, such as a marketing brochure or a television commercial, write *benefits first, features second*. Your active audience is seeking information and will wait for the features. But you must capture your passive audience's attention quickly. Early announced benefits will do this. If the passives become actives as they read the copy, they'll eventually get to the features, which they will then be ready for.

*Tip*: Audiences always respond to what's in their best interest. Communicators write far too much copy that focuses on their organizations. Write *to* your audiences, not *about* your organization.

## Use the right "tone"

Tone is a coat of writer attitude paint over the copy. The purpose of imposing tone on copy is to clone the tone in readers' minds.

*Examples*:

*Authoritative tone*: You want to persuade students not to take drugs and you cite evidence that it can cost them their freedom, even their lives.

*Coaxing tone*: You want to persuade employees to give the new share-a-ride program a try before they criticize or condemn it.

*Utilitarian tone*: You want to persuade a public that it will be useful to them to support a particular candidate.

## Use the right "person"

As a writer, you can also control how you want your audience to feel simply by using the right grammatical "person."

*Example*:

• **First person** for authority
  *Take it from me...*

• **Second person** for familiarity
  *You need time for yourself...*

• **Third person** for objectivity
  *Management wants to change the production schedule...*

## Use the right motivators

To pick the right motivator, you simply need to pick the right benefits. Here's how to do it.

You must start by researching your audience. Through research, surveys, demographic studies, national polls, company records, marketing research, VALS study (*see research chapter*) etc., pick the precise motivator that will activate your audience to do what you want. Prove to your audience through *evidence* (experience, cases, etc.) that

they can and will enjoy the benefit (the motivator).

Concentrate on the message. Select the right symbols for the message, offer credible reasons, appeal to emotion, write what you must so your audience gets the right meaning.

*Example*: An organization's policy statement on management's prerogatives concerning employee e-mail :

Your company has a problem with private use of company e-mail services. Your company provides e-mail services to help you do your job. So, you need to keep e-mail channels clear for your customers and stakeholders. You also need the channel to communicate and network with your co-workers about the business of your company.

Unfortunately, many of your co-workers are using e-mail for private purposes. Their behavior causes problems. For example, some workers can't access the e-mail channel to do their jobs. Some employees are unavailable to do their company's business because they're on line conducting personal business. And some employees have used e-mail to criticize the company, its leadership and its employees. That's not only disloyal, it's also dangerous. Outside forces, including competitors and the media, can take advantage of false and unchallenged information to harm our company.

You know from employee publications that employees can't use e-mail for private purposes. You also know that your management has the legal right to monitor all e-mail from company resources. To protect you and your coworkers, the company will exercise its right and monitor all company e-mail.

You can do your part to protect your company and jobs by using e-mail services only for business. Some might say that e-mail for private purposes is a long-standing tradition and is pro-family. Management agrees you occasionally need to communicate with your family and friends while you work.

So, beginning now, the company will relax its rules on using the telephone for personal use, but not e-mail. Please use the privilege judiciously.

**Figure 9.2**

E-mail is the lifeline of the company. It's like your phone at home. You need it free for emergencies, to say hello to someone lonely, to protect your family from an impatient creditor.

Likewise, you need e-mail for your company family here to survive and grow. You're part of that family. So when you observe the e-mail policy you're protecting your company family.

Thank you for respecting e-mail as your contribution to your career with the company. Your respect of this company rule is as important as your work and your word.

Thank you for being the valuable employee you are.

Notice how the memo copy announces the topic, explains proper and improper use of e-mail, explains the law, and outlines the expectations.

The copy overcomes constraints in the audience: loss of traditional right, inability to communicate with family and friends, loss of familiarity on the job.

Emotion plays an influential part through these words: *forces, lonely, self, career, word, hello, protect, family, dangerous, sensitive, respect* and *valuable.*

The symbols are easy to handle: *lifeline, network, creditors, family, out of touch* and *contribution.*

*Tip*: to persuade, tell people what they *want to hear* (using your product, service or idea). Offer sound reasons why they should want to persuade themselves. And always, be credible.

These ideas apply to many types of writing, proposals reports, speeches, resumes, letters and newsletters.

***Persuading is enchanting the willing.***

## Write "audience" copy

Many writers take counsel only with themselves when they write. As a result, their products are "management-minded" writings that appeal only to the writers themselves or offer only management features.

Ask if your copy is *audience-minded* enough. If you *become the audience* when you write — think like them, appreciate what they want, value what they value — then your copy will be on target. A sign of audience-minded writing includes a list of audience benefits rather than management features.

*Example*: A senior residence association flier advertised an upcoming association meeting. On it were listed the topic, date, time, place and the single appeal: "Support Senior Residents." That's a boring appeal. Would seniors leave their homes in the evening to attend a meeting so advertised? In reality, the meeting featured an authority speaking on mental sharpness in older years. It

would have helped had the flier merely mentioned that fact. Still, a speaker and a topic are still only features.

The copywriter should have "become the audience" by researching members of the target audience and asked: "What do I need to do to keep my mind alert in older years?" Answers might involve taking certain vitamins, playing mind exercise games, analyzing and solving local problems, reading and discussing books and poetry, publishing a senior newsletter on health or other interest such as an astronomy or photography, and visiting high school classes for debates and discussions.

If the flier had listed these activities and benefits (from audience research), it would have resonated with senior residents. Add some refreshments and transportation and the place would be packed.

*Tip*: Remember, when you're trying to influence behavior, you might also have to overcome inertia, the final hurdle in persuasion. Some writers use guilt, fear or obligation.

*Example*: *Seniors who associate with other mentally alert seniors tend to stay alert themselves.* (Of course, the meeting helps "associate" them.)

To overcome inertia, you might have to present a family, company, colleague or societal obligation to your readers.

*Example*: *Learn how to stay mentally alert so you can help others.*

Some constrained audiences won't act for themselves, but they will act for others. For example, "life" insurance policies work on the motive of death and obligation to others.

## Persuasive public relations writing products
### *Persuasive letter writing*

In the opening paragraph, recite or recall the precise situation. Don't proceed unless you clearly state you understand the issue.

*Example*: *We're responding to your complaint about our new product.*

or,

*You wrote us about where you can purchase our product in your neighborhood.*

- **Include a "picture" of the benefit**, remedy, result, need satisfied, or other aspects of the topic early in your letter to keep your reader focused.

- **Promise information or action,** but always *satisfaction.* Satisfaction, even the promise of satisfaction, persuades. Include details.

- **Prove that your audience will get what you promise.** Endorsement anecdotes and cases work well. For example, simply saying *"Company policy requires satisfied customers"* won't do. Put yourself, not the company, on the line. Personalize the promise.

- **Ask for action.** Cite specific steps your reader should take to get the satisfaction. Persuasive letters don't rely simply on information transfer. You must instill an attitude that leads to action.

- **Include a P.S.** as often as you can. Research shows the P.S. is the most frequently read part of the letter. But make certain the P.S. contains new information, not previously appearing in the body of the letter.

The law of the persuasive letter is "bonding with your audience."

### Persuasive memo and e-mail writing

Many memos suffer the same failing symptoms—dull, officious and unfocused. Here are some focusing tips:

- Decide why you're writing the memo. Here are four classic memo purposes:

**Announce a position**. Memos efficiently state your position's main points. Include not only your reader's benefit but also your organization's benefit.

**Provide information**. Summarize main points. Use your memo as a "cover" to a longer piece, perhaps a report. Thus, the memo becomes a type of executive summary. Attaching files, paper or electronic (e-mail), fulfills the promise of the information memo.

**Seek action**. Ask for project approvals; seek to get others involved; announce deadlines. Remember, your memo becomes a historical record of activity about your issue. Memos also can become "evidence" at meetings.

**Summarize meetings and agreements**. Memos following a meeting confirm decisions, scheduled actions and assigned responsibilities. Prior to a meeting, memos outline issues and remind people of items they should bring or be prepared to discuss. Used properly, memos can position you as an influential communicator in your organization.

**Use an effective format**. Most memos follow a "logical" pattern — issue/evidence/action. But reversing the order can snap your reader to attention. Try this "reverse logical" format, putting the action first and concluding with your purpose. Here are the three "lines" of an effective memo — the B-E-T formula.

**B** – *Bottom line*. Open with a bottom-line statement. What do you want your audience to know, feel or do? Get to the point. Colleagues appreciate economy of time — theirs.

**E** – *Evidence line*. Offer evidence for your bottom line. Include new research, project history or organizational experience. Name credible people in the organization who support the bottom line. Use logic to connect the bottom line and the anticipated top line.

**T** – *Top line*. The top line goes last. The top line outlines action necessary to implement decisions. If you're writing your memo to a specific person, include specific actions, motivators and appeals for your reader.

*Tip*: Place a deadline at the top of an "action-needed memo." *Example*: "Your advice on this decision will be accepted until 3 p.m. Friday." Prominently display the deadline, perhaps in larger type or different ink color. Requiring deadline action helps your memo rise to the top of your reader's "in" basket.

*Memoranda* means *They must be remembered*. Memos should have such value. And remember that **e-mail is image mail** — yours and your company's.

## Avoid the passive voice

- Generally, the active voice is more persuasive than the passive voice in most copywriting situations. The active voice conforms to the way people actually think, S-V-O, subject-verb-object (*Figure 9.3*).

*Example*: "Employees want a flextime work schedule." Employees (subject), want (verb), schedule (object). People naturally think in this "left-to-right, S-V-O" type logical progression.

Here's the same example written in the passive voice: "A flextime schedule *is desired* by the employees."

This is O-V-S writing (object-verb-subject). Why isn't it persuasive?

Because people don't naturally think in the passive voice. The mind must take the passive syntax, the passive word order, and reorder it from O-V-S to S-V-O. Passive voice is "right-center-left" type thinking. It's unnatural for most people. It takes an extra step. Recall the *Fraction of Selection Formula*. If people have to work too hard to get a

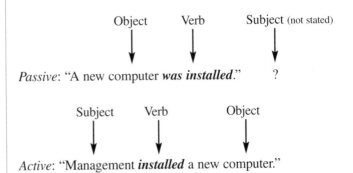

# S - V - O Writing

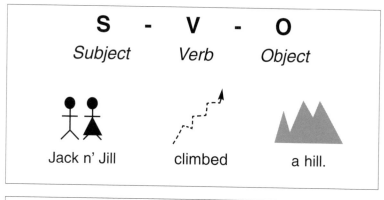

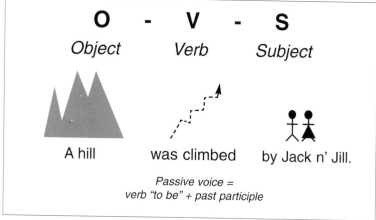

**Figure 9.3**

message, they might not work at all. Mentally reordering syntax could be hard work.

- The passive voice **adds words** to sentences. The passive voice is the verb "to be" plus the past participle of the main verb. That involves two words instead of a single, strong, active verb. Writing in the passive voice unnecessarily increases word count and diminishes reading ease. And that adds impediment effort to the persuasive process.

- The passive voice **avoids responsibility,** and credit. Compare these two examples:

In the passive voice example, no one's responsible for installing the computer. It just "appeared." Unfortunately, the PR copywriter doesn't give credit to management — a key PR task.

*Example*:

An organization copywriter wants to write a persuasive memo to convince employees to get involved in a second annual community relations program — visiting high schools and sharing professional expertise. The tactic is to inspire employees this year by showing how well employees did last year. But if the copywriter writes about what happened last year in the passive voice, it won't connect the company's effort to the benefit the schools enjoyed.

*Poor*: "A lot of children **were helped** last year."

An active voice version would connect the two:

*Better*: "Last year, **your community relations program helped** 500 students learn more about everyday science."

The employee audience connects the program to last year's results and remembers it. The writer will have a better chance to get employees involved in the community relations program this year if they can recall the connection between the company's program and the benefit to the target schools last year.

*Remember*: **If you start a sentence with the object, you must write a passive voice verb.**

*Note*: The passive voice can effectively influence in two special circumstances.

- Use the passive voice when you deliberately want to avoid responsibility.

   *Example*: "A mistake *was made* with your car …"
   Here, the writer deliberately avoids identifying the party responsible for the mistake — the car repair company.

   Managers sometimes ask persuasive copywriters to use the passive voice specifically to avoid responsibility for negative news.

   *Example*:
   "It has **been determined** that e-mail can no longer **be used** for personal reasons. Evidence **was received** by management that the e-mail service **has been abused**."

"it has **been determined** …"  – avoids blaming management

"no longer **be used** …"   – avoids "employee" loss

"evidence **was received** …"  – avoids naming employee informer

"service **has been abused** …" – avoids blaming employees

   Is it persuasive? It could be if the copywriter wants to make certain the audience doesn't connect the bad news to management, innocent employees, an unidentified "snitch" and guilty employees.

   Here, the passive voice guarantees the audience doesn't develop a hostile attitude toward these publics.

- Use the passive voice when the object in your sentence is really more important than the subject and you want to focus your reader's attention on the object.

   *Example*: "The **report** must be improved."

   Here, the copywriter forces the reader to focus on the poor report as the main issue. Who improves it, is secondary. The passive voice can be persuasive in certain responsibility denying contexts.

   In case you forget, "It must **be remembered** that the passive voice should **be avoided**."

## Use picture nouns

   A picture word is worth a thousand nonpicture words. Both types are nouns. Nouns can be friends or foes depending on how you use them (*Figure 9.4*).

   Look at the nouns in your writing. Noun or *nominative* writers generally write weak copy because it lacks punch and zest. It's boring and unconvincing. Verbs do a much better job. But you can make even punchless nouns work for your persuasive efforts.

Take a sample of your writing and put a square around each noun. Then, analyze your nouns. Make certain you write your nouns in the highest possible "degree."

   *Example*: "We sell the finest office **equipment** in the country."

   What do you know about this company's products? Not much. *Equipment* is a low, **third degree word**. This weak writing allows readers to picture anything about *equipment*. As readers, they're out of the writer's control.

   Here's a better version:
   "We sell the finest **technology** in the country."

   Better. Here, the writer does a better job controlling the thinking of readers by offering a **second degree word**, *technology*. As the writer raises the precision level of the noun, readers have less freedom to interpret the words.

   But even at the second degree level, readers can still consider technology to be word processors, calculators, cameras, etc. To further control concepts readers get from the copy, the copywriter raises the noun to the highest level, first degree.

   "We sell the finest **graphic and calculating** computers in the country." Finally, the writer uses **first degree words** (here adjectives and nouns) to *picture* the product. The writer captures the reader who cannot think of anything else except *graphic and calculating computers*. That's controlling, influential copywriting.

   *Remember*: A picture word of a product, service or idea is worth a thousand vague words. Always strive to write "first degree" copy and control the thinking of your audience.

   If you're not controlling thinking, you're not influencing.

## Copywriting strategies

   **Use exit ramps.** When you write promotional copy, keep your paragraphs short. Make certain "white space" (between the graphs) comes early, especially after the first paragraph. Readers can then "exit" or go on to the next paragraph. (Paragraphs shouldn't linger beyond seven lines.)

   "Exit ramps" work because readers make small commitments as they read. They judge the size of the commitment by the size of the paragraphs facing them. Long graphs mean large commitments. If they're unwilling to make the commitment, they "exit."

   *Irony*: Frequent exit ramps actually *keep* people reading because the commitments facing them are small enough that they don't mind making several smaller commitments rather than a single large one.

   **Use the right word.** Using the right word can trigger a desired reaction.

# Picture Words

**Very vague**
*"professional"*

**Getting better**
*"medical personnel"*

**Almost there**
*"doctor"*

**Very picturesque**
*"surgeon"*

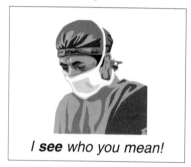

I **see** who you mean!

**Figure 9.4**

*Example*: Harvard psychologist Ellen Langer asked people waiting in line to use a copier: She tested two specifically worded types of requests.

*"May I use the Xerox machine?"* 60 percent agreed.

But when she added "because" to her request, she got higher compliance from those waiting in line. Here are two phrases she tested:

When she asked,

*"May I use the Xerox machine because I'm in a rush?"* 94 percent agreed.

When she asked,

*"May I use the Xerox machine because I need to make copies?"* 93 percent agreed.

Other words and phrases that can inspire agreement are *therefore, consequently, as you can see, it's obvious,* and *so true.*

**Use influential phrases**. Use effective transitions in sales letters: *better still, more important, best of all, how can this benefit you?* and *don't forget.* These transitions control readers' thinking in a subtle way. Readers must think about facts and issues as "better," "more important," etc.

## Special persuasive copywriting circumstances

### *Five-part consumer complaint response strategic writing*

Companies frequently hear from dissatisfied customers and must respond to them. Good companies with excellent public relations vision know how to deal with this situation. Here's a model to help public relations and customer service people handle a difficult situation. You might view these points as five paragraphs or sections of your letter.

### 1. Recite the facts

Repeat the facts of the situation exactly as you learned them. Cite specific correspondence, phone calls, or other contacts between the customer and the organization.

## How Much Do Words Really Matter?

### Doublespeak Defined:
### Cut Through the Bull**** and Get to the Point
*by William Lutz*

William Lutz has fought a long battle to clean up our language by eliminating "doublespeak" words. He says doublespeak is incongruity between what is said or left unsaid, and what really is. It is the incongruity between the word and the referent, between seems and be, between the essential function of language, communication, and what doublespeak does: mislead, distort, deceive, inflate, circumvent, obfuscate.

Lutz says Doublespeak turns lies told by politicians into "strategic misrepresentations," and ordinary sewage sludge into "regulated organic nutrients" that do not stink but "exceed the odor threshold."

Most people know how a switch in adjectives can either irritate or flatter people.

Does someone have a lot of "nerve" or plenty of "courage"?

Some even realize how a change in verbs can alter the meaning of a sentence.

Will you "emphasize" or "hammer away at" their shortcomings?

Do you "gloss over" or "sugar coat" the problem?

When you write, be a wordsmith, not a habitual writer who uses words simply because — well, they were used before.

### 2. Empathize with the consumer

Signal that the customer is right because in the customer's mind, that's the case. Try statements such as:

*How badly you must have felt when you counted on us, but our product (or service) failed you.*

*How upset you must have felt when you arrived and found our store closed five minutes early.*

Don't just sympathize. Empathize. The consumer must know that you both *understand* and *feel* as the consumer does.

### 3. Put the problem at a distance

Position the problem with your organization as an *exception* rather than as the ordinary way you do business. Tell the consumer that the problem is an exception and that your organization stands for better products and services. To support this, cite your record, number of products that haven't failed, and number of satisfied customers. In this section, you want to make the point that your consumer was victimized by an accident, an aberration. Why? Because the consumer can then begin to have confidence that you can solve the problem. Otherwise, the complainer might think the situation is routine and hopeless.

### 4. Cite a specific correcting action

Make the corrective effort specific. Don't promise that a "committee" will look into the problem. Don't write, *"We'll research it and get back to you when we learn something."* Offer a *specific person* who will help or action you'll take to correct the situation. Write, *"I'm asking Ms. Jones to work on this today. Within three days, you'll hear from her. If you want to reach her before then, her number is …"*

### 5. Reinforce empathy, future contact

Repeat your empathic attitude. Leave the name and number of someone the consumer can continue to contact. Cite a date or time you'll get back to the consumer. Send a good will "gift" as a token of regret and your sincerity you're working on the problem.

### *Five-part hostile audience strategic writing*

Every public relations person at one time or another will face a hostile audience, opposition political action group, or harassing editor. Here's a model to help PR counselors deal with these volatile situations.

### 1. Announce your idea and basic evidence

Simply write what you want to happen. Then, list your evidence or arguments to support that point. But don't fully explain your evidence yet. Save your full explanation for a later paragraph. You haven't yet "unfolded the arms" of your hostile audience enough to make them available for your persuasive evidence.

### 2. Recognize your audience's objections

Unless you help your audience become available for persuasion, you'll have a difficult time succeeding. List your audience's main objections to your idea. Use your research. Be honest. Start with the strongest objection. Begin to disarm your audience by recognizing their agenda first before you argue yours. Otherwise, you'll find your audience mentally "in the back of the room" just waiting for you to finish so they can have their say. Because you're writing, your audience might simply trash your copy because they're not a captive audience and don't know when, or if, you'll ever bring up their points.

### 3. Refute each audience objection

One by one, eliminate your audiences' objections by

answering them with your evidence and counter arguments. Be firm. Use rhetorical devices, statistics, winning arguments. This should neutralize hostility and make your audience available for persuasion.

### 4. Argue your position completely

Return to your opening idea statement. Pick up each evidence point and fully expound it. Treat each point as an argument in itself. Use winning arguments, eliminate constraints and stress rewards.

### 5. Conclude with a memorable statement

Repeat your clinching argument and your main appeal — logical, emotional, Maslow's needs, or other persuasion device. Repeat a specific action you want from the audience. Finish with a short memorable phrase that captures your thesis and provides your audience motivation to persuade itself.

### *Winning argument strategy*

The following section will cite an example that uses the "winning argument" formula. Here's what it is.

A winning argument uses a three-part syllogism for effective persuasion.

Part one:   Announce the desired behavior

Part two:   Offer evidence for the desired behavior

Part three: Use a common attitude to bond with the audience.

*Example*:

Part one:   *We need to raise utility rates this year.*

Part two:   *We realized less than 10% profit this past year.*

Part three: *I'm sure you'll agree that unless we realize at least 10% profit, our investors will abandon us and the utility will fail.* (Bonding attitudes are threat of a shut-off and a fair return for investment.)

### *Writing case study – The Employee Health Memo*

Management sent the following memo to company employees to persuade them to get a specific health checkup. We changed only the original organizational information. Look at the original and see if you can make it more persuasive. Afterward, look at the suggested revision and analysis. (*Reprinted with permission of communication briefings.*)

## Employee health memo

### *Weak version*

Free pulmonary screening is offered at Thoracic Community College in conjunction with National Respiratory Week. All employees and their families are invited to visit the campus August 30 and take advantage of this opportunity.

The computerized pulmonary function analyzer will screen for obstructive and restrictive lung diseases. In addition, free blood pressure screening will be offered by college health officials. The screening will be offered both days 10 a.m. until 2 p.m. in the college clinic, located on the first floor of Building "C" on the Bronchial Campus. For further information, call Thoracic nurse, Annie Asthma, at 555-555-5555.

That memo is supposed to get employees to go to a clinic for a health screening. But it probably has little chance to succeed.

The opening paragraph just doesn't make it. The writer assumes that the employees are an active audience and that getting their lungs tested is high on their agenda. The copy focuses on features — the National Respiratory Week, the screening and location. The copy comes across as a cold invitation to a cold audience.

## Guidelines to improve the memo

- The more uninvolved the audience (passive) the more personal the copy should be (stress benefits)

- The more involved the audience (active) the less personal the copy needs to be (stress features).

In the memo, does the writer just *tell* employees that a lung check is good, get them to agree it's good, or get them to *do* it?

The last paragraph shows what the writer wants. The word "information" signals that the writer really only wants to give information. Nothing in the copy says the writer cares whether or not employees get their lungs checked. Had the writer really intended an attitude or behavior change, the copy would have shown that. How?

If the writer had really wanted employees to go for a checkup (behavior), at the very least, the copy would recognize constraints among the employee group and try to remove them. The copy might suggest that the enabling attitude doesn't have to be permanent or difficult to form.

Suppose the writer predicts that employees will think it is too inconvenient to get the test. To overcome that constraint, the writer could remind employees that they "solved a similar *inconvenient* problem" in the past when they donated blood during the annual office blood drive.

The copy could also cite how colleagues overcame a similar constraint to take the test.

The memo never mentions that anyone similar to the target audience had taken or intended to take the test. The writer has placed the full persuasion burden on a management-minded message. Experience shows that such messages don't persuade very well.

Also, the memo doesn't talk to the real audience — all employees with varying reading and comprehension capabilities. A Gunning-Meuller Fog Index analysis shows the copy at a reading level between grades 14 and 15. For example, the copy has 21 words of three syllables. That's difficult copy. It's probably too difficult for the general employee population that reads and comprehends at a lower grade level.

All these factors work against persuasion, if indeed the writer really wanted to persuade.

Here's a more persuasive version of the memo with an analysis of why it might succeed.

### Improved version

#### Breathe Easier About Your Future

*Four employees* who entered the hospital last year with breathing and blood problems have a message for you: Find out before it's *too late*.

We agree. So, we're offering *free* lung and blood pressure tests for you and your family. The *painless tests* take fewer than four minutes. And you can *do it* while you're shopping or returning home.

*Mark* your calendar for Aug. 30-31, during National Respiratory Week.

*Visit* Thoracic Community College, Bronchial Campus, Building C, first floor.

*Stop in* from 10 a.m. to 2 p.m. Questions? *Call* Nurse Annie Asthma at 555-555-5555.

*Your family* deserves a chance to prevent problems that might steal their futures. *Give* them the chance. *Take* them to the free tests — before it's too late.

### Paragraph #1:

The opening graph grabs and holds the audience's attention because the writer judges the employee audience to be **passive about this issue**; hence, the use of a problem and threat. It quickly specifies the purpose of the writing and the bottom line of the sender.

The paragraph also begins the behavior phase of the **winning argument** model. It states the behavior clearly and backs it up with necessary information to stress its importance.

Following researcher Earl Newsome's principle of *familiarity*, the writer uses *trustees* to carry the message to

make it more believable. The message becomes believable because the message sender appears **familiar**. It comes from other similar employees. A cold, organizational, management-minded message won't work as well.

### Paragraph #2:

The writer offers the second part of the winning argument model — the information necessary to appreciate the problem. The writer anticipates employee **objections and constraints** (cost, pain and inconvenience) and diminishes them. Note the strong **identification** with the audience's real concerns.

In addition, the writer **takes credit** (through the active voice) on behalf of the organization, for offering the service. The writing clearly communicates the message points.

### Paragraph #3:

This paragraph specifies the actions necessary to gain the promised rewards. Look at the power verbs that tell the audience exactly what to do. Nothing is left for employees to conclude on their own.

*Find out* about pulmonary disease …   (Information)

*Mark* your calendar for Aug 30 …       (Behavior)

*Give* your family a future with you …  (Attitude)

*Stop in* at the community college …   (Behavior)

The writer *crafted* this persuasive message, not merely wrote it.

### Paragraph #4:

The writer judges that employees might not go to the clinic for their own benefit. (They're an "unavailable" audience. Refer to this idea in Chapter 3.) So the author writes copy to help employees become at least a "disposed" audience by asking them to go for their families' sakes. Hence, the writer introduces the third phase of the winning argument model—the bonding **attitude**.

**The writer** uses a commonly held value, responsibility for family welfare, to bond the audience with the writer and the desired behavior.

Finally, anticipating that personal inertia might still constrain employees, the writer overcomes this *final constraint* by appealing to *family security* as a higher motivator than mere *personal safety*. The writer takes no chances the employee audience might forget the message and leaves them with a memorable statement that summarizes the message points. ■

# Tips

1. The right to tell your side of the story is an exercise of your First Amendment. To write effective copy, first ask yourself, "Why am I writing this product?" The answer to your question is the writing's purpose and you must fulfill it.

2. In any piece of writing, circle all your verbs, put squares around your nouns, and draw triangles around your adjectives and adverbs. Then, you can easily analyze your writing for strong verbs, picturesque nouns, and strong words that don't need many qualifiers.

3. Effective persuaders always write to their audiences, not from their bosses or organizations.

4. The verb "to be" is not a verb — it's an existence word. Its subject does nothing — it just exists. Fewer than five percent of your verbs should be this weak existence word.

5. If you want to write an effective product, such as a memo, you should read memos for 15 minutes before you start writing. Such "genre reading" primes the writing pump and yields more effective memo copy — not just copy.

6. If your copy doesn't seem to "move" along, check transitions between your sentences and paragraphs. Written properly, transitions at the end of writing elements make the reader want to read more. Example: At the end of a paragraph promoting complete consumption of an antibiotic prescription for safety, the reader hears about some patients who became ill by not finishing the prescription as directed. Then the transition enticed the reader to the next paragraph: "And getting ill isn't all that can happen for not finishing your prescription as the horror tale of a forgetful mother shockingly reminds us." The reader must read the next paragraph.

7. If you want to test the effectiveness of your letter or e-mail, ask someone to read it first before you send it. If your reader doesn't understand what you're saying, rewrite it. You can't argue that your reader doesn't "understand." You won't be able to climb into your letter's envelope or through your computer's wiring to help your real reader "understand."

8. If you're writing copy to a mixed audience of active and passive publics, write benefits first and features second. A passive audience must read the benefits quickly or it will stop reading. An active public can wait for the features, while the benefits confirm the active public's decision to be active in the first place.

9. Never argue your points first to a hostile audience. They can't hear you out until you give a hearing to their issues first.

10. Go through your copy and conduct a *that* and *which* clause hunt. Rid your copy of an excessive number of these clauses. But if you must use them, make certain to use a that clause if the material following the word is essential to the word. Use a which clause, set apart by commas, if the material following the word is not essential to the word.

**Questions for classroom discussion**

1. What's the easiest way to reduce the Fog Index from a grade 21 grade level to a grade 9 level?

2. If you're conducting a training session on effective writing for management trainees who will have the responsibility to help others write better, which five key recommendations will you offer?

3. Read a daily newspaper and select three outstanding leads. Why do you think those leads are so good?

4. A pompous manager wrote an article for your company magazine. The problem: It's loaded with jargon and written many levels above the reading level of most employees. How would you address the problem?

5. Rewrite the last sentence to make it more persuasive. Eliminate the passive voice, weak verbs and vague nouns. Change the tone from objective third person to familiar second person. "Employees should be aware that company equipment cannot be used for personal reasons and is against the rules."

**Additional writing assignments**

1. Write a lead announcing your appointment as the first full-time public relations director for a local hospital. You were hired primarily to improve morale through better internal communication and to assist the development director with a $10 million fund raising effort.

2. Write a brief memo (100-words) to all staff members asking for ideas for media coverage.

3. Conduct an Internet search of companies and organizations for examples of news releases. Analyze the leads' news value.

4. Interview a top writer for a public relations firm or organization. Identify the expert's top tips for effective copywriting. Ask about the writer's approach to copy strategy, copy platform and audience focus.

5. Stop by a professional office (doctor's office for example) and pick up a marketing or informational brochure from the literature rack in the waiting room. Analyze the writing for effective principles. If the example is a persuasive piece, look for strong and weak items. Rewrite the piece according to your perception of the target audience and writer's purpose.

**Internet assignment: Online writing tutors**

Log on to one of the online writing tutoring organizations such as Paradigm Online Writing Assistant (**www.powa.org**). Try a sample writing exercise many of them offer. Review three sites and prepare a report for your class comparing the curricula of the three services.

Deliver the report in class, preferably calling up the sites on a "smart classroom" computer and specify the following:

- Ease of using an online writing tutoring service
- Main aspects of the curriculum offered by the three services
- Evaluation of the on-screen copy on the site
- Applicability to public relations practice (look for persuasive copywriting, business writing, and product writing, such as newsletters, brochures, etc.)

Name_____Date_____

## CASE STUDY WRITING ASSIGNMENTS

## Option I

### Case Study: New Public Affairs Manager Faces Tough Assignment

Pick a class partner to complete the following:

Assume you work as the media relations coordinator at DDQ industries. Your new company partner just graduated with honors and landed a new job — also at DDQ.

**The details**: Your partner will begin work next week as the public affairs manager for DDQ Industries, a government contracting firm in Pinetown, N.J.

**The job**: directing community relations, media relations and government relations for the 35-year-old munitions manufacturer. Your partner also will oversee the company's internal and external publications, run the annual meeting, manage a staff of seven and enjoy a large window office.

DDQ has been under fire in Congress, as well as the local and national media, for payoffs to contracting officials. The company hasn't yet been officially charged with anything, but several federal investigations are under way.

The company had sales of $155 million last year, up $13 million from the year before. Sales have nearly doubled over the last five years, despite a massive warehouse explosion killing 18 last year. DDQ employs more than 500 in six manufacturing locations, all located in New Jersey.

**Your task**: Write a news release for your partner's hometown newspaper announcing the appointment. Take the information relevant to the story from this fact sheet. Interview your class partner to gather additional background information and ambitions and include it in your release where appropriate.

**Tip**: Review personnel announcement releases available on many corporate web sites for guidance on style and content. Also, be sure to review personnel announcement stories appearing in newspapers to assess what the media want in these types of stories.

## Option 2

### Case Study: Getting Publicity for a Speech

Find a copy of a speech made by an executive of major company. Good place to look — on company web sites. Look for web site areas managed by the public relations department.

Review the speech and consider how it might be used to generate publicity in local media, either the location of company headquarters or location of the speech.

Next, search media web sites to see if you can find coverage of this speech, or other coverage on the issue the speech covers.

*See other side*

Name_____Date_____

Finally, assume you work as a public relations writer for this company. Prepare a memo to your boss, the company's vice president of public relations, with your recommendations on how to pursue publicity for this speech. Cite specific issues or information in the speech that you believe is newsworthy. Include the lead paragraph of a news release you'd prepare for local newspapers. Also, suggest changes you might make in the speech to enhance its news value.

## Required exercise

## Assignment: Editing for style and usage

Consult a media stylebook, such as the *Associated Press Stylebook and Briefing on Media Law*, to correct style or usage errors in the following statements.

Correct each sentence and list the heading, in the stylebook, under which you found the guidance for your correction.

1.  J.C. Penney, Incorporated announced plans for a new store.

    Heading: _____

2.  We interviewed nineteen applicants.

    Heading: _____

3.  The principal kept his hands-off the matter.

    Heading: _____

4.  The professor is an expert on the middle ages.

    Heading: _____

5.  Deng Xiaopang offered an answer. Xiaopang said little, however.

    Heading: _____

6.  He lives at 7 Morning Cir.

    Heading: _____

7.  The class starts at 10 am Tuesday.

    Heading: _____

Name _____ Date _____

8.  The doctor that went to jail is moving here.

    Heading: _____

9.  Richard Nixon was a republican.

    Heading: _____

10. The robbers convinced him to open the vault.

    Heading: _____

---

**Answers**

1.  J.C. Penney Inc. (incorporated)
2.  19 (numerals)
3.  hands off (hands off/hands-off)
4.  Middle Ages (historical periods)
5.  Deng said little … (Chinese names)
6.  Circle (addresses)
7.  a.m. (a.m., p.m.)
8.  who went (who, whom/essential clauses)
9.  Republican (political party)
10. persuaded (convince, persuade)

---

# Chapter 10

# Communicating in Special Circumstances

## SECTION 1: USING SPECIAL EVENTS IN PUBLIC RELATIONS

**PRaxiom** *Special events can form or change opinion more quickly than any other PR channel.*

### What Section 1 covers

This section will show you the power of special events to convey important messages to your targeted audiences in a dramatic, memorable way. You can use events to gain exposure of important publics to your organization, get publics to try your product or services, or gain media attention for your position on issues.

### Marketing publicity vs. PR publicity

To appreciate the function of special events, it's necessary to understand the difference between marketing publicity and public relations publicity.

Public relations publicity differs from marketing publicity because it offers three special qualities marketing doesn't: objectivity, believability and reach. Applied to special events, the three characteristics work well.

*Objectivity* is achieved because the special event usually involves parties and motives outside the organization such as an organization-sponsored walk-a-thon for cancer.

*Believability* is achieved because the public relations event works to earn, not pay for, publicity attention.

*Reach* is achieved because the special event attracts targets defined by the nature of the event.

*Example*: A fast food restaurant gives free sandwiches to youngsters whose bikes pass local police inspection on restaurant property on Saturday mornings.

Meanwhile, advertising, a part of marketing, also helps promote events.

Special events use face-to-face communication or media channels to build traffic by important publics. They also increase awareness of products, services or organizations. And they induce trial of products and services or participation in an organization's activity.

*Examples*:

**Build traffic**. Special sales such as a giant supermarket "Can-Can" annual January sale attract customers. Canned goods are half price.

**Increase issue awareness**. Free mammogram tests by a local hospital raise awareness of the test's benefit.

**Increase organizational awareness**. To raise its image as a socially responsible company in Chicago, the Sara Lee Baking Company started an adopt-a-school program and selected all-African-American Harper High School. It also picked NFL football player Willie Gault as a spokesperson.

The event raised student achievement with programs like Peer Tutorial Program, Nutrition Bowl, Celebrity Speakeasies with Chicago personalities, and marketing classes using Sara Lee's marketing executives. Result: Sales rose because customers perceived Sara Lee as a socially responsible company.

**Induce trial.** A home show exposes homeowners to a variety of products with live demonstrations, free samples and discounts.

**Induce participation.** Rowan University's PRSSA chapter featured a student setting a *Guinness Book of World Records* for sit-ups in a Levi campus competition

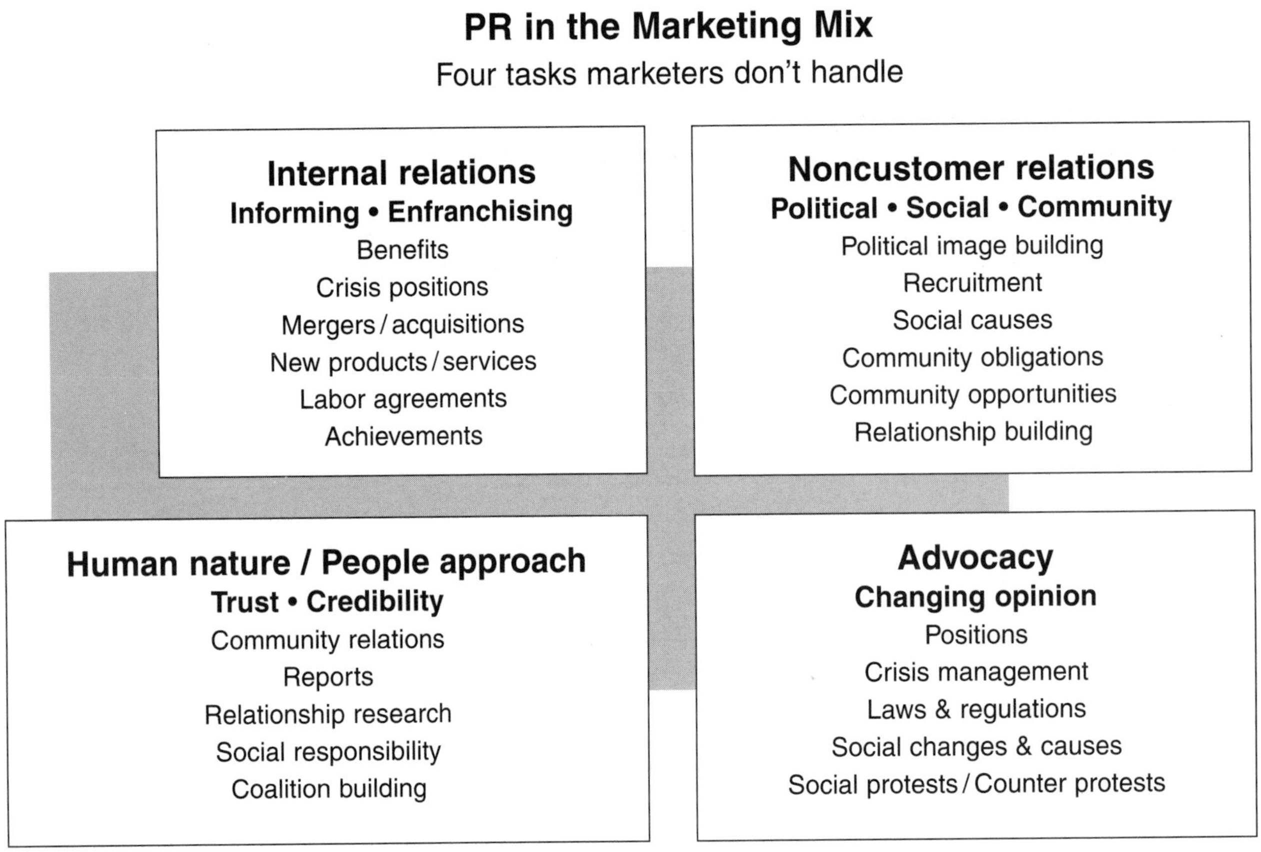

## PR in the Marketing Mix
### Four tasks marketers don't handle

**Internal relations**
**Informing • Enfranchising**
Benefits
Crisis positions
Mergers / acquisitions
New products / services
Labor agreements
Achievements

**Noncustomer relations**
**Political • Social • Community**
Political image building
Recruitment
Social causes
Community obligations
Community opportunities
Relationship building

**Human nature / People approach**
**Trust • Credibility**
Community relations
Reports
Relationship research
Social responsibility
Coalition building

**Advocacy**
**Changing opinion**
Positions
Crisis management
Laws & regulations
Social changes & causes
Social protests / Counter protests

**Figure 10.1**

wearing Levi jeans. The university won first place in the national competition.

## Special event characteristics

Practitioners use special events for a variety of purposes: attract attention, raise funds, build image, satisfy social needs, exercise corporate citizenship, promote employee benefits, publicize products, stage protests, conduct celebrations and anniversaries, enhance important actions, and others.

According to Grunig and Hunt (Managing PR), organizations generally use two types of special events, *functional* and *institutional*.

*Functional events* help organizations achieve their objectives by contributing useful tactics. For example, an organization can donate funds to build a health center in its community and offer free health screenings. One of the organization's objectives is a satisfied, motivated, healthy work force. The organization provides free access to the center for its employees. Therefore, the event is *useful* to the organization because as a tactic, it helps achieve a PR objective.

*Institutional events* build good will for an organization so it can achieve its objectives. They differ from functional

events because they simply build image. For example, an organization can sponsor a parade in a community for an Independence Day celebration. The organization believes that by sponsoring the parade it will gain a positive relationship with its key audiences. Later, when it's needed, the good will produces desired behavior from the audience.

According to the Public Relations Society of America, many special events share some of the following characteristics.

• **Attract media attention**. Media can help send public relations messages to key target publics.

*Example*: A special event, such as a basketball marathon for needy urban families, might entice a television or newspaper story. When the PR motive is publicity or awareness, the PR practitioner will consider the event successful only if the media attend and carry the event's message to important targets.

• **Offer news value**. If the media are gateways to actual target publics, the event must carry news value for the media's viewers and readers. Clever practitioners will pitch their event with a news angle they know the media will seize on.

*Example*: A safety-conscious action group, protesting the use of automobile air bags for children, stages a series of crash demonstrations to draw attention to its point that children are injured more in crashes involving air bags than in crashes without the bags. The media attend the event because of the social news value for their viewers and readers.

• **Attract target publics**. The virtue of special events is their ability to be so many things to so many people and to do it in an entertaining way.

*Example*: The Bicentennial Celebration of the United States encouraged American citizens to celebrate their history. Public relations special events coordinators staged a cross-country wagon train from east to west reenacting the pioneer migration westward and the opening of America. Along the way, the event attracted citizens to celebrate their history by greeting the wagon train and participating in local historical special events.

• **Convey important messages**. Special events uniquely connect messages suitable for key audiences.

*Example*: Many sports teams "adopt" diseases or causes and stage events on their behalf. The Philadelphia Eagles professional football team stages events for the "Eagles Fly for Leukemia."

• **Positively connect the event and organization**. The best events cleverly reflect an organization's mission.

*Example*: A bank celebrates the opening of a new branch by inviting local youngsters to dig for buried coins at the branch's groundbreaking ceremony. The event conjures the image of a bank (coins) rising out of the ground and marries bank, money and groundbreaking in a single event. It also conjures the image of investing money with the bank and enjoying the interest that arises from the investment.

• **Create memorable images**. Events gain attendance or regard, depending on the purpose, when target publics recall the event, the message, or the organization.

*Example*: The Midas Muffler Corporation and the Better Hearing Institution jointly stage a special event to reduce troublesome and unnecessary broken muffler noise in communities.

• **Create a bandwagon effect**. Some events start the ball rolling for others to imitate or start their own.

*Example*: Rowan University PRSSA took its local organ donor special event day and started a national PRSSA competition for the best special events day encouraging organ donor card signatures and conversations with family members about the wish to donate one's organs after death.

Special events coordinators often tie their event to

## Special Event Types

| | |
|---|---|
| Adoption (diseases, schools) | Letter-writing campaign |
| Anniversary | Living history recording |
| Annual meeting | Media tour (junket) |
| Appearance (VIP) | Media party |
| Art contest | Meeting (general) |
| Auction | Naming contest |
| Autograph party | Neighborhood cleanup |
| Award | News conference |
| Bake-off | Open house |
| Barbecue | Pageant |
| Blog | Parade |
| Boycott | Plant tour |
| Car wash | Proclamation |
| Carnival | Product demonstration |
| Celebrity appearance | Protest |
| Charity bazaar | Report presentation |
| Citation | Research presentation |
| Conference | Reunion |
| Contest | Roundtable discussion |
| Convention | Sale |
| Cook-off | Seminar |
| Cornerstone laying | Socratic dialogue |
| Debate | Spaghetti dinner |
| Dedicated Day, Week | Speakers bureau |
| Dedication | Speech |
| Demonstration | Spokesperson tour |
| Dinner | Sporting event |
| Essay contest | Stunt |
| Exhibit | Talk show appearance |
| Fashion show | Tasting |
| Flea market | Thon (Walk-a-thon, Telethon, etc.) |
| Fund raiser | |
| Giveaway | Time capsule interment |
| Grand opening | Time capsule exhumation |
| Ground breaking | Tournament |
| Hospitality event | Tree planting |
| Information booth | World record attempt |
| Internet chat room | |

holidays or other national or local commemorations. They also barter with other organizations in a give-and-take, in which both organizations stage the event for their own purposes.

*Example*: A popular soft drink company promises to provide free beverages to a local youth softball team raising funds through barbecues in exchange for gaining the right be one of the official sponsors of the softball championship tournament.

# How to Plan and Conduct a Special Event

## Special events steps

- **Decide purpose and theme**. Remember to attach a memorable name, slogan, music or other memory "triggers" to the event. Consider advertising hooks.

- **Appoint a coordinator**. The coordinator must handle many details at a time, keep to a schedule, stay calm in a crisis, and love responsibility. The coordinator must also have management's confidence and support.

- **Set date, time, site, speakers**. Coordinating calendars seems like a simple task. But allow nine months advance time to make certain you have no competition for date, time or place.

- **Write a special event plan**. The plan should include tasks, budget and timetable. Share the plan with all employees and others involved in carrying out the plan.

- **Set up and staff committees.** The following committees and their responsibilities represent a reasonable event architecture.

  *Site committee.* Parking, health, security, housekeeping, conference accommodations, audiovisuals, lecterns, microphones, traffic, guides, exhibits, media rooms, signage, telephones, handicapped access, smoking/nonsmoking accommodations, decorations

  *Publicity committee.* Promotion, advertising, public relations, media relations, television, radio, media releases, media kits, photography, videography, Web site, media credentials, internal communication, letters, printing, posters, flyers, brochures, programs, communication center

  *Finance committee.* Budget, housekeeping, insurance, permits, income, expenses, fees

  *Hospitality committee.* Food service, spouse tours and accommodations, VIP arrangements, entertainment, greeting, housing, contests, prizes, promotions, mementos

  *Reservation committee.* Agendas, invitations, program copy, participants' materials, name badges, seating, tours, telephone marketing, message center

  *Speaker/presenter committee.* Biographies, stipends, advance liaison, handout reproduction, transportation, thank-you correspondence

- **Promote the event**. When you invite the media, point out the visual and public interest aspects of the event. Don't neglect the specialized media in your field.

- **Carry out the event**. Ask for progress reports from committees. Allow 6-8 weeks for print materials. Practice each phase of the event, looking for breakdowns.

- **Evaluate your event**. Interview participants, conduct focus groups of key players and targets. Ask for that final "debriefing report" from coordinators. After some time, check again if key messages, attitudes or behaviors were successfully sent, received, formed or performed. Check your accomplishments against your objectives.

---

It's obvious that special events combine imagination with strategic activity to gain an organization's public relations goals

## Planning special events

Kathy Schoch Ziprik, West Virginia building products marketing and public relations consultant, offers practical experience advice for conducting special events.

Students hear the words "special events" and probably decide this unique area of public relations is perfect for them. After all, special events are oftentimes large parties, gala fund raisers or enticing sports events — impressive and interesting incidents associated with celebrations. Who wouldn't want to coordinate an event that sounds like so much fun?

Look deeper at special events and you'll discover intricately designed events that require intense coordination.

Ever hear the old expression, "Don't sweat the details"? Guaranteed, a special events coordinator did not make that expression famous. Public relations people working on special events sweat every detail. The best friend a special events coordinator has is a checklist, closely followed by a detailed timeline leading up to and including the special event itself.

If you are eager to coordinate special events, ask yourself some serious questions. Are you extremely organized? Can you juggle dozens of small details while keeping the "big picture" in mind? Are you good at delegating work to others? Can you really visualize every element of the event beforehand? These are all skills you need to successfully coordinate a special event of any size.

## How special events happen
### First Steps

Most organizations have a good reason to host a special event. Perhaps the event is meant to support other company goals, generate publicity for a new product, or celebrate successful completion of a job. Whatever the reason, PR practitioners first define the event and its contents.

Frequently, brainstorming with others helps develop a creative idea for an event. After defining the parameters of the event, the goals and target audiences come next. Marrying the event with a working budget and general timeline is the final step.

### Moving forward

Once practitioners decide on a special event concept, the coordinator organizes a special event plan. A step-by-step game plan and creation of a detailed timeline are necessary elements of the planning process. Thinking the event through, both forward and backward, helps coordinators detect tiny but important details that could get lost.

Every special event must have contingency plans. Consider what elements could cause your event to fail. Bad weather? Low attendance? A natural disaster that distracts media attention? Prepare for the unexpected for every event and make certain you consider the "doom and gloom" alternatives that could disrupt your event.

### Hosting the event

The best special event coordinators leave nothing to chance. They work out every detail long before the actual event takes place. All preparations, from audio visual equipment to signage to bathroom paper, is carefully checked beforehand.

Communication during a special event assumes several meanings. The coordinator must be in touch with co-workers and team members to assure the event runs smoothly. At the same time, the coordinator must effectively communicate with other audiences such as event participants, media, employees, and the general public. Identify all audiences before the event, assign responsibility to team members for communication roles, and assure that you "cover" all your important audiences.

### The party's not over

Once a special event ends, a seasoned coordinator will tell you that the work is just starting. Make certain to consider postevent debriefing meetings, thank-you notes to participants, summary news releases, and media monitoring for coverage.

The best way to host a special event is to continually refine your coordination talents. This means you should learn something from every element of the special event you just hosted. While the event is fresh in your mind, create a written report for your files. You may think you'll never forget the event, but time will fade your memory. You'll find the detailed reports essential when it comes time to start planning your next special event.

**Figure 10.2. Elephant Brunch**

## Special events case study: Hosting an Elephant Brunch

### First Steps

Special events aren't just magically born, they're created. Some special events gain public attention for a "product" and to influence sales. This was the situation in 1989 with the new Sunday Brunch offered at the Hyatt Regency Atlanta.

Hotel management challenged PR special event coordinators to create a unique event that would generate community awareness of a new Sunday Brunch offered at the hotel. Through research, counselors discovered the yearly arrival of Ringling Brothers and Barnum Bailey Circus coincided with the startup of the new brunch.

Using creative brainstorming, coordinators conceived the idea to bring the elephants to the hotel to "sample" brunch items. Circus management loved the idea because it attracted publicity to the arrival of the circus in town. And it took the circus's publicity plans a step further, incorporating an elephant parade down the major street in the city to the hotel.

### Moving forward

Exacting details for the elephant parade included researching specific foods the elephants could (and could not) eat and coordinating the menu with the chef. Next, coordinators worked with city officials to close the streets to vehicle traffic during the parade. PR people coordinated every detail from "scooping elephant poop," to training tuxedoed waiters, serving the elephants, reviewing insurance and employee policies, and securing appropriate linen for the brunch tables.

Preparing for the unexpected, coordinators selected an alternate time and date in case of rain. Extra hotel and circus staff served as human barricades between elephants and onlookers. Off-duty police and ambulance workers were on hand as a precaution. And, because the elephants were to gather on the circular front drive of the hotel, coordinators created signs to re-direct traffic flow into the hotel. More hotel logo signs were added so television cameras always captured the hotel logo in every shot.

### Hosting the event

Timing and accurate communication were assured during the event by using walkie talkies throughout the route and having employees staged at different areas. Securing an elephant for the hotel's general manager (who also carried a walkie-talkie) to ride allowed coordinators to have minute-by-minute progress reports during the parade.

Gaining media attention for the event was easy, especially when each local television station received its own elephant. Reporters rode elephants bareback to the hotel's driveway where the elephants feasted on tables mounded high with vegetables and fruits. Reporters were treated inside to a sampling of more creative foods, the same menu offered at the new brunch, and a private meeting with the executive chef.

### The party's not over

Once reporters and elephants departed, the work wasn't over. Aside from the obvious mess that 10 elephants leave behind, cleanup was needed inside the hotel as well. And, because the hotel did not wish to appear cavalier about giving food away to animals when so many needy people were hungry in the city, the hotel made a large food delivery the same afternoon to a local homeless shelter.

The short-term results of the unique special event were immediate. The evening brought coverage on all three network affiliates, plus newspaper coverage the following day. Coordinators immediately sent letters and complimentary invitations to the "real" Sunday Brunch for all participants to generate long-term interest in the brunch.

While the hotel did have a few disappointed children each Sunday who expected to see elephants at the brunch, the interest level was high enough to make the weekly brunch a financial success for the hotel. Creativity, a small budget, and an enormous amount of coordination made this special event an overwhelming success for the Hyatt Regency Atlanta.

*Kathy Schoch Ziprik has worked for Six Flags Great Adventure theme park, Hyatt Hotels and Georgia-Pacific Corporation. She was president of PRSSA national in 1980 and 1981.*

## Special Event Case Study "Media Monkey Business"

Hudson, Ohio based PR agency Akhia Public Relations wanted to publicize an alliance between K&M International, a toy manufacturer and Helping Hands, a not-for-profit organization providing capuchin monkeys to severely disabled people who cannot perform everyday tasks such as dressing themselves. The monkeys assist the handicapped persons with daily tasks.

Akhia had created the "Wild Republic" brand for its client K&M to market its stuffed animals. Some proceeds from the line, which comprised 30 different monkeys with Velcro hands and feet, would be donated to Helping Hands.

To gain publicity for the alliance, Akhia arranged pitch visits to the media and brought along Ayla, a 7-year-old, 8-pound, female capuchin monkey to dramatize the line and the alliance.

To avoid charges that the PR firm was merely using Ayla to make profit, Akhia limited the visits. The firm always carefully stated that Ayla's efforts would bring needed funds to Helping Hands for her efforts.

Akhia's efforts resulted in high profile product placements, including "The Drew Carey Show," "ER," "Chicago Hope," and a Sally Field movie.

The goal of the program is to raise enough money to double the number of monkeys Helping Hands can place annually. The cost of breeding, training and placing monkey helpers with a life span of 30 to 40 years is $25,000. The organization provides free lifetime support services for its monkeys.

**Figure 10.3 Monkey Business**

## Tips

1. Always appoint your most logical, creative and organized employee as coordinator of your special events.

2. The most powerful and memorable events are those in which target publics can see a connection between the nature of the event and the organization's objective.

3. Tie some of your special events to local or national celebrations.

4. Don't complete your special event plan without adding a contingency plan for unforeseen hitches.

5. Put yourself in the role of an attendee of your own event. Walk through the process, from receiving publicity and registering to completing an evaluation form. The drill will help you avoid missing important components.

---

**Special events questions**

1. What special asset does special events add to the practitioner's arsenal of communication channels that marketing publicity doesn't?

2. Identify three types of occasions when practitioners could use special events in their campaigns.

3. If you want the media to attend your special event, what must you guarantee they will get from the event?

4. If you had two top people from among five volunteers to help you with an event, which two special event committees would you assign them to? Why?

---

**Internet special events assignment**

Connect with the ISES International Special Events Society Web site, or a similar Web site, and locate a practitioner from its list of members.

Conduct an on-line interview with the practitioner. Identify yourself as a student and ask to conduct a mock search for a special events consultant for your event.

Suggest a type of event from the list on the Web site and ask what the practitioner could do for you and why you should hire the person or firm.

E-mail the results of your search to your professor's, college's or department's Web site.

In class, compare your search and the searches of other students. Then, answer these questions.

- What are the hallmarks of a certified special events planner?

- What virtues of a special events cooordinator did the practitioner stress?

- What questions did the practitioner ask you about your event? Would you hire the coordinator you interviewed? Why?

Name _____ Date _____

## Marketing a Failing Coffee House

To stay in business, a small neighborhood coffee house needs more customers. It needs to fill the house every night, all night.

There's room in the establishment for 60 patrons, six at each of 10 tables. The establishment employs six people. The owner asks you to devise a six-month series of events to increase awareness of the shop and attendance. You may add some specialty items to the present coffee-only menu. The coffee house owner gives you a limited budget of $10,000 for events. Sketch a series of special events to achieve your client's purposes.

1. Design a research plan to discover how to retain **faithful customers** and attract **new customers**.
   (*Tip*: Use the hypothetical research results (*see below*), to decide the type of research that will produce these data. Consider this a "Jeopardy-type" exercise. If the data are the answer, what is the research question? Keep your budget in mind. Research is part of your budget.)

To answer the following questions, use these hypothetical research results.

- Local media have virtually ignored the coffee house.

- The establishment is running about 30 patrons on a weekend night, 20 on a weekday night.

- Patrons like the coffee but complain the establishment has no attractive ambiance.

- The shop offers a couple of magazines and newspapers for casual reading.

- The shop offers plain croissants and scones.

- Smoking is not allowed, But there is a "cigars under the stars" every Wednesday and Friday evening for three outdoor tables.

- Some patrons complain about the cigar smoke as they enter the building. But cigar smokers are among the most regular customers.

- Passersby complain that lack of signage conceals the shop's location from the street.

- Patrons comprise a mix of demographic types — coffee lovers; well educated; conversationalists; arts lovers; music lovers; well read; gourmands; at-home cooks; 21-40 years old; 30% couples, 70% singles; 60% female, 40% male; 90% straight, 10% gay.

- The shop has an underused kitchen.

- Employees are bored with the establishment's sameness. Many feel they can contribute to the shop by doing more than just pouring coffee.

- Ownership that inherited the business lacks growth vision but is willing to experiment.

- A university is located nearby.

Name _____ Date _____

_____

Using these research data, answer these questions.

2. What types of events would attract local media coverage so your audiences receive additional promotion from the media coverage?

_____

_____

_____

_____

_____

_____

3. What types of events would segment your audiences on different evenings?

_____

_____

_____

_____

_____

_____

4. What types of events will attract new customer interest and experimentation?

_____

_____

_____

_____

_____

_____

5. What types of events will capitalize on employee talent and motivation?

_____

_____

_____

_____

*See other side*

Name_____Date _____

6. What types of events will expand kitchen use, menu item and customer identification with the coffee house?

_____

_____

_____

_____

7. What types of events will take advantage of the nearby pool of university students and professors?

_____

_____

_____

_____

8. Create a single event that is not located at the shop, can move about, incorporates visuals, sound, people and coffee shop fare, and positions the shop as a special place for special people.

_____

_____

_____

_____

_____

_____

_____

_____

_____

_____

_____

_____

# SECTION 2: MANAGING CRISES IN PUBLIC RELATIONS

## PRaxiom *PR crises are best handled by being first in informing, second in reacting, and last in speculating.*

## What Section 2 covers

The approaches, suggestions and case solutions in this section will protect you from making crucial errors during a crisis. You'll learn how to put distance between yourself and an offending person or event. You'll also learn how to deflect responsibility when you don't deserve it. And you'll appreciate how the best practitioners distract media and public attention from dwelling on their crises.

This section will also reveal to you the thesis of the crises managers' guidebook — stop the bleeding, manage the crisis, and restore reputation. You'll learn the dirty dozen mistakes poor crises managers make, but also the suitcase of proven techniques to handle internal, external and media relations during a crisis.

## Crisis management

Crisis public relations is crisis management and damage mitigation. Unfortunately, organizations sometimes face difficult challenges such as disasters, emergencies, and catastrophes — events that threaten image, reputation or even the organization's survival.

Public relations practitioners are among the first personnel called in a crisis. During the Exxon Valdez oil spill in Prudhoe Bay, engineers and public relations people were among the first employees Exxon sent to the scene.

## Emergencies, disasters and catastrophes

Every crisis, whether it's an emergency or not, forces an organization to solve the problem and restore reputation or image if it's been lost. In an oil spill catastrophe, for example, a company needs to clean the spill *and* handle media relations, community relations, employee relations, and government relations. While technical managers handle the physical problem, PR counselors handle the reputational problem.

A crisis can have an emergency or chronic nature. The great fire at Six Flags, Great Adventure (NJ) a number of

years ago was a critical emergency. But the tobacco companies have been in a chronic crisis state for years trying to settle potential liability lawsuits with states, the federal government and living and deceased smokers' families. And even the giant Microsoft Company was sued by the government for monopolistic marketing practices.

Disasters and catastrophes present special problems for counselors. Many times, death and injury occur.

The terrorist attack on New York's twin towers on September 11, 2001 caused great loss of life and property. Some companies lost most of their employees. Others lost financial records, employee benefits records, and more. The disaster challenged the crisis management skills of government and private organizations alike. For example, the Social Security Administration did a magnificent job of reassembling staff, restoring records, and helping thousands in need.

And a TWA airline crash off Nova Scotia resulted in 280 deaths amid terrorist conspiracy theories.

In cases like these, PR practitioners must be careful not to speculate about death or injury. That is unprofessional and unfair to families of potential victims waiting for word about their loved ones.

The bombing of the Federal Trade building in Oklahoma City included many deaths and injuries. Government public relations people had to respond to media and family inquiries about the safety of workers and visitors. Likewise, PR people for the 1996 Olympics in Atlanta had to justify security arrangements when a bomb in the People's Park killed two visitors to the games.

Disasters, or potential disasters, could occur naturally or be caused by humans, such as the Three Mile Island near-meltdown of nuclear reactor #2. Natural disasters, such as the devastating Hurricanes Andrew, Charlie, Frances, Ivan and Jeanne (2004) that ravaged Florida and the eastern seaboard, test the professionalism of public relations practitioners of local, state and federal communities. Many times, these disasters raise questions among the public about precautionary actions that could have or should have been taken. The great natural fires in

Yellowstone National Park raised the question of controlled burning. Controlled burning is necessary to eliminate potential kindling for a larger fire. Ironically, public relations people had to explain why the controlled burning, a standard practice, had not taken place. In that case, two public relations philosophies competed for public opinion. One said all controlled burning is bad and forests should be left entirely untouched by humans. The other philosophy said it was precisely the lack of controlled burning of underbrush and dead trees that fed the great fire.

Emergencies, disasters and catastrophes require expert media relations skills by PR professionals. They also demand clear thinking and a compassionate attitude. But compassion, even for victims, is frequently tempered by lawyers who want to limit organizational liability, even if their organizations are at least partly responsible for damage, injury and death. In litigation, lawyers write precise texts for public relations spokespersons. The PR professional is often in the middle of a debate about the best way to handle crisis issues.

## A dirty dozen defects

Many crises display harmful characteristics and challenge PR practitioners to overcome them. Ironically, the wisdom for sound public relations crisis management comes from deterring defects in communication during a crisis. Here are a dirty dozen defects to deter.

**1. Misunderstood**. The organization's position is often misunderstood, or worse, intentionally misinterpreted. When activist groups attack an organization for an action or position they don't agree with, they frequently exaggerate or fabricate issues or facts to make their point. They have learned from a more-than-willing media that dramatic, contentious copy makes good reading and viewing news.

*Example*: Consumer advocate groups challenged the practices of HMOs making medical decisions about paying for medical procedures. The advocates said doctors, not accountants, should make those decisions. The media generally sided with consumers on the issue, making it difficult for PR people to get a hearing for their side of the medical/financial story.

*Example*: The former owners of the Love Canal property were found innocent of deceiving the public about the toxic waste buried beneath the ground on which residents later, against company advice, erected a school.

**2. Mixed messaging**. Too many organizational voices garble messages to the media and other publics. Frequently, public relations people have to deny misinformation or sort the truth from among dozens of statements and rumors.

*Example*: On October 31, 1999, an Egyptian airliner crashed 70 miles off the New England coast on its way from New York to Cairo. All 216 persons on board died. Early voice recorder and data recorder information salvaged from the ocean bottom indicated that back-up co-pilot Gamil al-Battuti intentionally crashed the Boeing jet in a successful suicide. Newsweek reported that Egyptian investigators secretly agreed with U.S. findings. The Egyptian government and family of the co-pilot thought the American government and the American media jumped to the conclusion too quickly.

**3. Speculative statements**. Speculation about facts creates confusing noise in the communication channel.

*Example*: During the administration of President George W. Bush, a senior advisor speculated that "outsourcing" of jobs actually helps grow the economy. Although he was technically correct, political opponents of the president jumped on the statement, charging that the president favored exporting American jobs overseas.

**4. Mismanaged programs**. Many crises don't have a central command controlling information flow.

*Example*: The infamous May 13, 1985 "MOVE" fire in Philadelphia destroyed 61 row houses, and left 250 people homeless. Of the 11 people killed in the fire, five

**MOVE fire
of 1985**

**Figure 10.4**

Philadelphia • May 13, 1985

Eleven people were killed in the fire, including five children.

were children. Police officers arrived at the MOVE home to serve arrest warrants on four MOVE members, and were met with gunfire. Police fired back, touching off a 90-minute gun battle. Later that day, police dropped a bomb on the MOVE row house from a state police helicopter. The bomb missed its target, a fortified bunker on the roof, and started the fire that burned an entire city block (*Figure 10.4*). In that crisis, no central information center was established early enough to control and correct information flow. The city and the police department suffered severe image loss.

**5. Defensive players**. Sometimes managers become defensive about issues and lose the opportunity to calm situations and get their organization's position across.

*Example*: Catholic bishops did not do the right thing when they covered up incidents of sexual abuse by priests, thereby putting the church's reputation above the interests of its parishioners. Ironically, by making decisions that ostensibly put the Church's reputation first, the bishops greatly diminished it.

Cover-ups almost never work. Why? Because today almost anyone can disseminate information quickly and widely on the Internet and in the 24-hour news cycle on cable television where it can be seen by millions. According to Ronald J. Alsop, the Internet is a key source of story ideas for many mainstream news reporters and editors.[1]

**6. Distrusting media**. Media tend to distrust both profit and not-for-profit organizations' motives and actions. This situation calls for experienced counselors who can gain the media's trust and respect to get a decent hearing for the organization's point of view.

*Example*: In 2004, a New Jersey school district wanted to expand its schools through a public referendum. It properly sent literature to its constituents explaining student enrollment growth and the condition of its aging school buildings. But before the media relations plan was executed, a single, embittered long-time resident, who had once been a member of the school board, thought he should have been consulted by the district. He was seeking to relive his past influential role. He hounded the local reporter for days to do a negative story on the project. As media many times do, the reporter (even though young and inexperienced) jumped at the chance to participate in a "newsworthy" contentious issue. His paper published a story below a headline that blared, "***District newsletter upsets residents***" (*Figure 10.5*).

**Figure 10.5**

The article quoted no residents other than the *single disaffected resident*. In fact, the lead paragraph of the story said many residents were "upset" and others were "just up in arms." A meeting with the reporter revealed *he had no sources, other than a couple of phone calls* on which to base the story. After listening to the district's PR people, he apologized for the story and the deceptive headline and promised to "cooperate" with the district to get its point of view across. But serious damage had already been done.

Irresponsible media representatives sometimes simply invent contention to create a story. It most often happens when editor and publisher values conflict with an organization's values as in political, religious, social, governmental and corporate activity. This type of proactive journalism plagues PR practitioners.

**7. Careless communicators**. Preoccupied with demands of the crisis, many PR counselors and managers fail to communicate the organization's position to internal publics and external stakeholders.

*Example*: A large Midwestern casino typifies the way many employees feel about communication in gaming operations. A dealer explained and complained how he felt about management's relationship with employees. He said employees are like mushrooms. They're kept in the dark and occasionally covered with manure. Many other employees complained about not knowing what's going on most of the time, and when they do hear from top management, it tends to be ivory tower pronouncements.

Internal communication in this organization typically consists of a newsletter, an occasional employee meeting, and pounds and pounds of memos with numbing operational

---

1. Alsop, Ronald J. (2004). *The 18 Immutable Laws of Corporate Reputation Creating, Protecting and Repairing Your Most Valuable Asset*, CyberAlert®, Inc.

details that few employees read and fewer still comprehend. One mid-level manager pointed to a pile of papers on his desk and said, "I've got a four-inch stack of memos here, and I still don't know what's going on." The typical company newsletter, according to the majority of employees, is outdated, boring, and self-serving for management. Most employees say they don't read the company newsletter at all and certainly not cover-to-cover. Employees below upper management level almost invariably name "The Grapevine," the informal word-of-mouth communication network present in all large organizations, as their most vital and dependable information source.

**8. Unavailable spokespersons.** In the threatening atmosphere of a crisis, many organizational managers either retreat or are unavailable to the media and other key publics.

*Example*: Gorilla in the grocery store. This example is related by Denise Judlowski, a former University of Iowa student who was interning at a Chicago area grocery chain.

A shopper was about to buy a stuffed toy "talking" gorilla for her son. But she noticed that the gorilla's voice sounded more ethnic than other talking toys made by the same company. The woman took offense to the African-American-sounding gorilla and immediately called the customer relations line.

She spoke with the PR director's secretary, the only other public relations employee within the grocery chain besides the director. The woman stated her case and was immediately cut off. The secretary often received strange phone calls on the customer relations line, and did not think to report this particular incident to her boss.

After her failed call to the customer relations department, the woman took her case to a well-known *Chicago Sun Times* columnist. He printed a story the following day, not only discussing the toy gorilla, but also adding racism by mentioning that another store from the chain had been given a nasty, racist nickname by area residents and customers. The reporter used the grocery store's nickname as his only example, thus creating a reputation problem for the chain.

Many things went wrong during this crisis situation. The person who answered the customer relations line did not know how to negotiate a solution with the customer. She should have shared the situation with her boss. PR customer service people should be available around the clock for "service."

**9. Reactive communicators**. When a crisis hits, many

organizations have no plan to confront it and manage it. They make up the rules as the crisis unfolds. Such reaction leaves employees and spokespersons out on a limb and disconnected from information, positions and responses. It also forces the organization to play defense. Instead of the organization controlling the issues, the issues control and victimize the organization.

> ### When you're forced to react defensively, the issues control you.

*Example*: A few years ago, environmental groups and Green parties worldwide called for a boycott of the ExxonMobil Company for its failure to take responsibility for its role in global warming. The groups wanted ExxonMobil to comply with the Kyoto Protocol that set binding emissions reduction targets. Environmentalists viewed the US company as instrumental in convincing President George W. Bush to abandon the protocol.

ExxonMobil went on the defensive with a spate of editorials defending the company's position on global warming. ExxonMobil acknowledged its concerns about the boycott when it announced its launch of a public relations blitz with advertisements in the *The New York Times*, *The Wall Street Journal*, and *The Washington Post*.

But the anti-Exxon groups didn't give up. They countered by agitating shareholders to pass resolutions to force ExxonMobil to "confess" their complicity in global warming and take a more active role in combating the warming. A leader of anti-Exxon forces gloated about the crisis pressure they brought to bear on ExxonMobil

As attacks and counterattacks continued, ExxonMobil found itself reacting instead of anticipating these issues and mapping a strategic, orderly campaign.

*Note*: A year later, this article appeared: "Greenpeace, which is urging a boycott of ExxonMobil because of its anti-global warming treaty stance, has been sued by the energy giant in France for trademark infringement. That has provided a rich PR opportunity for the media savvy environmental group," O'Dwyer's PR reports. Greenpeace altered the Esso logo by replacing the "ss" with dollar signs. ExxonMobil says that the Greenpeace-altered logo resembles the insignia of the elite Nazi SS army and that it is a "repulsion." According to O'Dwyer's, ExxonMobil fears the E$$O logo "will drive consumers away from its brand." [2]

**10. Spin doctors**. We're all used to politicians

---

2. *O'Dwyer's PR Daily*, June 26, 2002.

spinning events to their advantage. But public relations practitioners take a big hit when their organizations force them to blatantly spin.

*Example*: Canada's Liberal government in British Columbia fired its entire communications division, 300 unionized civil servants, and replaced them with 180 nonunion political appointees to ensure that government information providers are "committed to the goals of the Liberal administration." Union president George Heyman says Premier Gordon Campbell is "using reorganization as an excuse to lay off workers and replace them with political hacks. If the premier wants partisan spin doctors instead of communications professionals, then the Liberal Party of B.C. should foot the bill, not taxpayers." [3]

**11. Panicked practitioners**. Too many practitioners panic in a crisis and abandon the cardinal rule of acquiring research before taking action. Consequently, they become guessers instead of planners, the worst kind of practice for communicators with livelihoods at stake.

*Example*: A CEO is told that his employees are unhappy. Without conducting research, he assumes that more communication will solve the problem. So he starts a newsletter. But they still remain unhappy. Undaunted, he arranges a picnic, complete with a softball game and tee shirts. They like the food, games and gifts and think he's a nice guy, but they're still unhappy. So he asks his PR director (finally) to conduct a survey to find out what's wrong. Results from poorly worded survey questions reveal that employees are unhappy with "relationship with management." Not until the PR director suggests focus group studies does the CEO finally learn that employees don't agree with their health care package. The CEO was trying to communicate his way out of a problem that required instead action and negotiation.

**12. Spun out of control**. Many public relations professionals fail to counter spin false interpretations of issues by adversaries. And some don't bother to develop allies in calmer times that will support the organization in critical times.

*Example*: Let's assume that two major political opponents have settled into patterns of behavior. One politician decides that attacking his opponent and issues works. It allows the attacker to grab headlines and put his opponent on the defensive. Sometimes the attacks don't use facts, just innuendo and suggestion and worse, an attacker stereotypes the behavior of the other politician as, "Well, even if you didn't do it this time, you have done it in the

past or at least that's what you stand for." Now the other politician tries to defend himself every time he's attacked. He tries to be "fair" and accommodating. *Result*: He appears weak. He gives away the high ground to his opponent. The politician has an option. He can counter spin or counter attack. If he can gain the media's attention, he can do the same to his opponent as his opponent is doing to him. Should he exercise the option? Would he seem to be as out of control as his opponent? On the other hand, counter attacking might also result in actually disparaging the attack technique. Perhaps the politician should mimic his opponent, demonstrating to others the cheap nature of his opponent's tactics.

PR minds will differ about the strategic advantage of the politician mimicking an out-of-control opponent or not responding to an attack for fear that it will "keep the controversy alive."

> *Crises give you the chance to reclaim mission, restate positions, and relive achievements.*

When organizations do not see opportunity, even in a crisis, their PR practitioners lose the chance to *reclaim* their organization's mission, *restate* their organization's position, and *relive* the organization's accomplishments.

## Three crisis rules

Frequently, organizations come under attack from adversaries for perceived wrongdoing such as marketing a "dangerous" product. Even when organizations are at least partly responsible for some of the issues adversaries accuse them of, organizations must be very careful to walk on the right sides of the triangular lines of *accepting responsibility*, *disclaiming responsibility*, and *restoring reputation*. Each of these three communication activities plays a major role in crisis management.

Certainly sound public relations philosophy encourages counselors to be truthful about their organization's role in causing some ill effect, even unintentionally. But PR counselors don't have to admit responsibility for things their organizations aren't responsible for. And they're always charged with rehabilitating lost image or reputation.

Here are three principles counselors should follow when they're accused of being responsible for a crisis.

### *Distance*

In any crisis, put distance between your organization and offending parties, issues or policies. State that the offending party, issue or policy is an exception, not the rule of your organization.

*Example*: A college quarterback was accused of

3. Canada.com, June 28, 2002.

"throwing" a football game. In the locker room after the game, he tearfully confessed to the coach. The media overheard the confession and seized the issue to write stories that disparaged the athletic program and "asked" if other student athletes at the college might also be involved.

Assembling the media later, the sports information officer put *distance* between the student and the institution saying the quarterback confessed to activity that did not represent the values of the school. He added that such behavior, if true, was not typical of other athletes at the college. He also advised the media that the quarterback had a right to legal representation — distancing the act even more.

> **Spinners never allow their audiences to breathe logical air.**

## Distraction

Don't let media or adversaries *dwell on your problem issue.* Distract them from doing this by pointing to your successes in other instances. If you don't do this, night after night, talk show after talk show, you'll be asked to explain your organization's role in a negative situation. Key publics, including customers and employees, won't be able to come up for the "air" that would cleanse the situation.

*Example*: When a company recalls a failed product, but has other products on the market, it carefully separates its failed products from its successful products. "We're not just the failed product. We're more than that," said Proctor and Gamble when it recalled its Rely tampon because the super absorbent tampon was targeted as the cause of toxic shock syndrome in women. "We're Ivory Soap, 99 and 44/100ths% pure, and it floats," the company reminded wary customers. The company was **distracting** customers from the negative story.

*Note*: "Spinners" use **distraction** as their key tactic.

• When they're accused of something, they remind us that their adversaries did worse things.

• When they're asked a question they don't want to answer, they reiterate the good things they've done.

• When they're asked for facts to back up their assertions, they claim the facts are well known or the questioner never asks others for facts.

• When they lack support for their opinion, they offer universal acceptance for their point of view: "All Americans feel the same way…."

*They never allow their audiences to breathe logical air.*

## Deflection

Don't let your adversary or investigative media attribute more to your organization than your organization is actually responsible for. Be especially on the lookout for leading media questions that, if answered with a vague nod, will be reported as confirming the point of the question.

*Example*: During the height of the poisoned Tylenol scare, eager reporters shouted to harried PR spokespersons that workers from the plant that produced the tainted pills must have been responsible for the horrible accident. "What else could be the cause?" they shouted. But savvy and cool-headed PR spokespersons said it was too early to blame plant workers. After all, someone could have tampered with the pills after they left the plant, on route to the store, or in the retail store itself prior to purchase.

As it turned out, plant employees were exonerated. The pills had been tampered with on the store shelf, not in the factory. PR spokespersons *deflected* responsibility for something that hadn't been proved, but some irresponsible media representatives wanted to assume.

## Getting ready to make a crisis plan

Every public relations practitioner should remember three principles of crisis management plans. **Write** the plan. **Communicate** it to all employees. **Rehearse** it.

Every organization should have a crisis management plan. No one knows when a disaster will strike, or a catastrophe will befall a company, or a product will fail. Because organizations face so many types of crises, no plan can anticipate all the needs of an organization. But some principles are common to all plans.

## Internal decisions

• **Create lists of important personnel**. Know where decision makers need to be when a crisis strikes. Include the board president, CEO, solicitor, managers and communicators.

• **Centralize information gathering and dissemination**. When an airliner crashed into a San Diego community near a high school, only expert corralling of media representatives prevented misinformation.

• **Keep emergency equipment in a special place**. Try to reserve it for an emergency. *Example*s: battery-operated equipment, fully charged phones, golf cart for transportation. Label the equipment "Emergency use only" so it will be there for the crisis.

• **Appoint a single spokesperson**. Employees and the media must have reliable information from the organization. And the organization wants reliable information going out.

Decide beforehand who will make decisions and who will communicate the decisions to all internal and external publics. Make certain employees know who is in charge of decisions and information.

## Information dissemination

• **Clear and centralize communication channels.** Use the organization's Web site, human "runners," walkie-talkies, internet, pagers, e-mail, and print technology for rapid dissemination of information and directions.

• **Specify employee information channels**. Make certain employees know where they can get the latest information about the crisis. Also provide employees a way to get information, rumors and questions to the central information area.

• **Practice the three D's of crisis communication** — *distance, distraction* and *deflection.*

Don't speculate about death, injuries, damage, or loss of your organization's image without knowledge and approval. Don't "allow" employees to speak freely to the media. Ask their cooperation in controlling information. Role-play crises with them so they know how dangerous it can be to speak without knowledge to the media.

## Media relations

• **Update media lists**. Include both print and electronic media. Make certain to include television personnel. Select certain representatives for a news "pool" who will give information to other media colleagues. Also, be ready for national coverage.

*Example*: A Decatur, Georgia school board expelled six students for two years for fighting. The Rev. Jesse Jackson claimed the expulsion was racially motivated and demonstrated against it on the school's campus. He was arrested during the process. But the national media played it up night after night.

• Prepare crisis media kits containing "evergreen" material such as company and management background information, photos, fact sheets, and explanations of processes.

*Example*: If an unauthorized relative should somehow remove a child from a nursery school, school officials should be prepared to provide the media and authorities copies of the school's policy and procedure process for identifying relatives authorized to pick up children.

## Research in crisis management

The best helper in a crisis is research. It plays an important role identifying causes of problems (as opposed to symptoms), key audiences, appropriate messages, efficient channels, and measurement techniques.

## Credibility in crisis management

John Moscatelli, accredited member of the Public Relations Society of America, is a senior counselor at Anne Klein & Associates, a New Jersey consulting firm. He offers this advice about crisis management to PR counselors.

Credibility determines communication outcome during a crisis. Personal and organizational credibility is essential to a win–win crisis management mentality.

*The news media mediate news they would love to set your agenda for your crisis response. Don t let them.*

Too often, we respond to a crisis from a position of loss, dread or fear of failure. We would be psychologically better off if we anticipated a positive outcome as we approach a crisis.

Once a crisis arrives, you can't do anything to avert it. It could be the crash of an airliner at sea, a leaking oil tanker, or an executive accused of sexual harassment.

You'll succeed at crisis management if you've built a reputation with your stakeholders as an honest and credible practitioner. Credibility builds over time, action by action, statement by statement. Yet you can destroy your credibility instantly with a thoughtless word or a careless act as you respond to a crisis.

You cannot tamper with your personal credibility or your organization's when a crisis hits. Then, you'll need the edge credibility gives you. Credibility is a fragile strength. It can shield you from outrageous claims by critics, detractors and second guessers.

During a crisis, it's unlikely you'll be able to publicly say all you know or think you know about an issue. You might have to protect an investigation. Law or lawyers might prevent you from speaking or counsel you against it to protect your position in court.

Never allow your co-workers — public relations counselors, legal department, human resources or others — to persuade you to shade the truth or lie, even a little. In a crisis, truth is your weapon and credibility is your shield. Surrender truth and you'll lose credibility too.

Never allow the news media to set the agenda for your crisis response activities. In virtually every case, you'll have key stakeholders who need to hear what you have to say as quickly and directly as you can tell them. The news media, by the nature of their business, mediate the news.

Reporters insert themselves between the sources of the news (you) and their audiences (your stakeholders). Most importantly, they interpret for their audiences what the news really is and means. They play an important role in communication during a crisis.

But influential as they are, the news media do not totally control communication. In fact, you do if you exercise control and you're believable. In this age of rapid personal communication, via the Internet, e-mail, teleconferences, and satellite links, you can take your message directly to your key stakeholders.

Your stakeholders might hear other messages from other vested interest groups and from the news media. These messages might vary from what you're saying. They might call into question your interpretation of the facts. This is where your credibility becomes all important.

If the crisis is straightforward and requires only a recitation of the facts, you shouldn't have much problem relaying the information. But if the crisis raises questions, doubts or concerns, as most crises do, you'll need more than just being on the right side of an issue. You'll need credibility.

You must be accessible to the media and stakeholders. You also need to respond quickly, be accurate, and avoid speculation. But without credibility, speed will only hasten detractors' attacks; accuracy will only poison the channels; and all utterances will become speculation.

The best form of crisis management is crisis prevention. Your best preparation is the daily perfecting of your own credibility.

*Author's note about the case study on the opposite page.*
*(Read the case first.)*

**"Storming the Corporate Gates"**

What did "storming the bank's gates" teach PR counselors of like-minded protest groups? Did the eventual action of the bank, refusing involvement in the deal, position the bank as "sensitive" to the demands of the protestors? Or did it teach disaffected groups that you can bring an organization to its knees if you exert enough public pressure using terrorist, invasive methods to exert that pressure?

Sometimes, in their zeal to accommodate groups that disagree with their policies or practices and that have the media's attention, or to appear to be on the politically correct side of issues, organizations capitulate to aggressive protest groups and compromise their policies.

The bank cited "business concerns" for its refusal to finance the deal. Did it unintentionally also add a chapter to the civil disobedience manual of disaffected groups, "How to Provoke a Corporate Crisis and Succeed"? ∎

# Crisis case study: "Storming the corporate gates"

*The scene*: corporate headquarters of a major Philadelphia-based bank. On a quiet midmorning in late summer, and on a day the boss was on vacation, corporate public relations received a call from the chairman's secretary, asking that someone from the department come up to the executive floor right away. She said a "local television crew and a couple of protesters" were outside the chairman's office.

The elevator doors opened and what I thought was going to be a small disturbance turned out to be more than 75 placard-waving highly vocal protesters trying to storm the chairman's office. They were accompanied by four local television crews, local radio and print reporters and "still" news photographers. Corporate security had been called but hadn't arrived yet.

My first thought was, "How did these people get past security?" I decided the answer to that question was an internal problem we could deal with later. I was more concerned with the identity of the protesters, their issues, and what they wanted from us. The chairman let it be known that he wasn't coming out of his office — period. The situation was volatile, highly emotional and threatened to deteriorate quickly.

The first thing to do was to get control of the situation and lower the tension. Ignoring the television crews and lights and microphones in my face, I calmly asked who was in charge. A spokesperson for the protesters said they were employees of a company being sold and whose jobs were going overseas. Having failed to get any satisfaction from old or new owners, they were targeting the bank because one of its subsidiaries had been asked to finance the buyout.

Out of range of the crowd, I immediately got on the phone and contacted the local senior executives who supervised that subsidiary. We asked them to get on the scene as soon as possible. The group arrived a few minutes later and included the bank president and a couple of senior executives who knew the details of the buyout proposal. At that point, the bank hadn't made a decision on the proposal. During the president's briefing, I counseled executives to respond to protesters' concerns with facts as we knew them.

By then, security had arrived. We arranged to move the protesters and the media to a private conference room (and away from the chairman's door). In this way, we were able to control the environment and at the same time, provide a forum for the protesters to air their concerns.

The bank president took the lead as the company's spokesperson. He responded openly, with facts, even though the crowd tried to shout him down on several occasions.

The bank acknowledged that a financing proposal had been made, but our fundamental message was that it was under review and the bank hadn't decided anything about it yet. We repeated the message several times. Although it wasn't what the protesters wanted to hear, it was the truth. Discussions reached a stalemate and the protesters left the building in an orderly way.

Returning to my office (it was late in the afternoon), I immediately wrote a report for the boss. The report recounted in detail everything that had happened from the initial phone call, the steps we took, the concerns and the issues, our communication counsel, and the company's response. We expected an internal review of the incident at the highest level in the corporation.

That evening's local news coverage presented a balanced report of the protest and accurately reported both sides of the issue.

We practiced these crisis principles:

- Stay calm in an emergency
- Gain control of the situation as quickly as possible
- Understand the issues
- Understand the facts of the situation
- Formulate an appropriate response
- Provide a forum for different viewpoints
- Respond with facts.

Later, several reporters complimented us on how we handled the situation.

*Postscript*: Eventually, the bank decided *not* to finance the buyout. The official reason cited was "business concerns." I believe potential damage to our public image and reputation figured in the decision.

*Gregg Feistman is a faculty member at Temple University, Philadelphia, and member of the Philadelphia Chapter of PRSA. He practices in the Delaware Valley.*

# Crisis case study: The great fire at Six Flags

What constitutes the worst type of crisis situation? Loss of life, say many public relations practitioners. Being involved in a crisis where people die can profoundly impact an organization and its employees and target audiences.

Most responsible companies and organizations have strategic crisis plans to guide members of the communication team during a crisis situation. Organizations without a plan are thrown into chaos and lose valuable communication time when a crisis occurs.

At Six Flags Great Adventure in Jackson, New Jersey, we were caught in the midstages of creating our crisis plan when disaster struck. A fire burned down a haunted castle attraction in the park, turning us quickly from an amusement park in a small central New Jersey town to the key focus of national news stories. What brought us there so quickly? Seven teenagers, all on school trips to the popular amusement park, were trapped in the burning structure and died on the night of May 11, 1984.

From a public relations standpoint, many things went wrong. Management at the parent company of the theme park, located in Chicago and removed from the immediacy of the situation, refused to acknowledge the potential negative impact of the disaster at hand.

On-site, the public relations team scrambled to handle hundreds of media calls, the arrival of helicopters carrying television crews, and dozens of media members who camped out for days at the facility.

Where was the road map to guide the team through this crisis? The park didn't have an existing crisis plan. I had written one just weeks earlier and a secretary had typed it, ready to present to the senior public relations manager and marketing director the following week. That left just the secretary and me with knowledge about where to set up the media briefing area, how to staff it, and procedures to handle incoming calls. Other key management members jumped in and tried to help along the way. But without a practiced plan in place, mistakes were made and the park's reputation was severely damaged.

Compounding the park's immediate problem of dealing with the parents of the deceased and grieving employees, was the wish of corporate management that park operations immediately return to normal. The fire occurred around 7 p.m. on a Friday. The park opened for business as usual the next morning. To the world, there was no sign or message of condolence regarding the activities of the previous night. This decision permanently impressed on the media and area residents that the park's management was uncaring and interested only in making money. That single decision negatively impacted attendance at the facility for years to come. Many school districts rescinded plans to send their senior classes to the park for senior trips.

Attendance at the park immediately plummeted after the fire. The long-term public relations strategies required to redeem the park's reputation and rebuild business were detailed and costly.

To restore the park's reputation, PR practitioners included the following objectives in their campaign.
• Certify the park's safety
• Educate the public
• Portray management as responsible and caring

It took years for these steps to rebuild business. Many of the activities could have been eliminated if the parent company or park management had the foresight to have responsible public relations crisis plans in place at the time of the accident.

*This case is crisis public relations experience Kathy Schoch Ziprik encountered while she was PR director at Six Flags, Great Adventure in Jackson, New Jersey. Presently she is a building materials PR consultant working in West Virginia.*

Crisis Management Kit

# Strategic Actions in a Crisis

## Tactics Kit For Crisis Management

**I - E - M**

Internal tactics

External tactics

Media relations tactics

### Internal relations crisis tactics checklist

☐ Decision-making hierarchy

☐ Decision makers' communication plan

☐ Information

☐ Dissemination hierarchy

☐ Information dissemination channels and equipment

☐ Internal plan for each manager and employee

☐ Internal communication channels and items

☐ Print, electronic and face-to-face channels (e-mail, print and electronic billboards, print and electronic newsletters, flyers, briefing areas, fact sheets, position statements, newsletters, Q & A)

### External relations crisis tactics checklist

☐ Position statements for damage and information control

☐ Position statements for reputation management

☐ Letters, letters-to-the-editor, op-eds, advertorials, advertising

☐ Supporting documentation: floor plans, policies, case law, financial performance records, media clips, etc.

☐ Fact sheets, illustrations for interviews, reports and testimony

☐ List of influential radio and television talk shows, speeches to influential Key Communicator groups

☐ Plan to counteract lobbying efforts by hostile groups (demonstrations, political lobbying, grass-roots lobbying)

☐ Rumor defusing mechanism

### Media relations crisis tactics checklist

☐ Common media information area for disseminating information, conferencing, faxing, phoning, printing, copying, e-mailing

☐ Media information kits: video news releases, organizational and personnel backgrounders, audio tapes, videotapes, photography (including digital files), Web sites, brochures, newsletters

☐ Q & A sheets, position papers, fact sheets for news conferences

# Tips

1. Important publics will better appreciate what you try to do in a crisis when they know what you know about the issues and believe you.

2. Persuade management to conduct a full role-play rehearsal of your crisis communication plan.

3. Because so much crisis management activity focuses on outside publics, remember to inform internal publics of your positions and actions.

4. If you have a choice to play offense or defense in a crisis, go on offense; at least you'll have the ball. When you play defense, the other team calls the plays.

5. Phrase all your statements to the media and key publics in positive terms. That will cause you to frame your positions as assets to your organization and to the community. Negative statements in a crisis dwell only on what you're "not" doing, usually bad news for your image.

## Questions for classroom discussion

1. Why is the first priority in a crisis to limit damage?

2. What circumstance would allow you to speculate about important issues in a disaster, such as injuries or deaths?

3. If you're debating which advice to follow in a crisis, your best public relations judgment or your lawyer's admonition, which will you follow? How will you make your decision?

4. What three things should you do with a crisis communication plan?

5. What important role can research play in a crisis?

## Internet assignment

Log on to the Internet site of one of these three public relations sites.

**www.prcentral.com**
> Review the material for the relationship between PR counselors and lawyers when an organization faces a crisis.

**www.amcity.com**
> Review the material for inside tips on handling a crisis.

**www.prsa.org**
> Review an article from *Tactics* on how to assemble a PR crisis team.

*For each of the articles, report your analysis to your class.*

Name _____ Date _____

## Broken glass more irritating than pepper

It's 2 a.m. and you're awakened in New York by a phone call from your Dallas food seasoning operation. Apparently, a shopper returned home after purchasing a bottle of your hot red pepper seeds. After she shook them onto her evening meal and tried to eat, she discovered ground glass in her food. She's as mad as your pepper is hot and she's making a lot of demands, including threatening to hurt your company any way she can.

1. Whom will you contact?

_____

_____

_____

_____

2. What are the first three things you will do?

a. _____

b. _____

c. _____

3. What research should you conduct?

_____

_____

_____

_____

4. Whom will you involve? Tonight? Tomorrow? Later in the week?

Tonight _____

Tomorrow _____

Later _____

*See other side*

Name _____ Date _____

1. Select two items from each of the three major sections of the Tactics Kit for Crisis Management below (two from **internal relations**, two from **external relations**, and two from **media relations**).

2. The items you select should be those you think are most important and immediately needed for this case.

3. After you select the items, write them in the spaces provided and specify the message of the tactics you selected.

*Example*:

✔ Fact sheets for news conference

*Message/content*: History of the pepper product, annual sales, testimonials from satisfied customers, product health safety procedures, plant inspection dates, local health certifications.

## Internal relations

✔ (Kit tactic) _____

Message/content: _____

✔ (Kit tactic) _____

Message/content: _____

## External relations

✔ (Kit tactic) _____

Message/content: _____

✔ (Kit tactic) _____

Message/content: _____

## Media relations

✔ (Kit tactic) _____

Message/content: _____

✔ (Kit tactic) _____

Message/content: _____

Name_____Date_____

# Tactics Kit For Crisis Management

## Internal relations crisis tactics checklist

☐ Decision-making hierarchy

☐ Decision makers' communication plan

☐ Information dissemination hierarchy

☐ Information dissemination channels and equipment

☐ Internal plan for each manager and employee

☐ Internal communication channels and items

☐ Print, electronic and face-to-face channels (e-mail, print and electronic billboards, print and electronic newsletters, fliers, briefing areas, fact sheets, position statements, newsletters, Q & A)

## External relations crisis tactics checklist

☐ Position statements for damage and information control

☐ Position statements for reputation management

☐ Letters, letters-to-the-editor, op-eds, advertorials, advertising

☐ Supporting documentation: floor plans, policies, case law, financial performance records, media clips, etc.

☐ Fact sheets, illustrations for interviews, reports and testimony

☐ List of influential radio and television talk shows, speeches to influential Key Communicator groups

☐ Plan to counteract lobbying efforts by hostile groups (demonstrations, political lobbying, grass roots lobbying)

☐ Rumor defusing mechanism

## Media relations crisis tactics checklist

☐ Common media information area for disseminating information, conferencing, faxing, phoning, printing, copying, e-mailing

☐ Media information kits: video news releases, organizational and personnel backgrounders, audio tapes, videotapes, photography (including digital files), Web sites, brochures, newsletters

☐ Q & A sheets, position papers, fact sheets for news conferences

# Chapter 11

# Communicating in the Networked Age

**PRaxiom** *Your ability to package information so that it informs, persuades, clarifies or teaches is a skill with increasing value.*

## What this chapter covers

This chapter will reintroduce you in a new way to the networked world of digits and quantum communication. It will open to you possibilities of new relationships with audiences — cyber relationships, where audiences never physically meet, yet know what each wants and needs.

For the PR practitioner, making a living in this quantum world will require more than a remote control and cell phone. Every day, masters of the electron devise new databases, new information brokers, and new ways to make us all more public people. If PR practitioners do not enter the new orbit, they risk becoming one of the wide-eyed left behinds at the water cooler, mouthing yet another "gee whiz."

To survive and make a difference in the new age, practitioners will have to come of age in a world where no one grows old.

## New opportunities for PR practitioners in a digital world

Today's digital world offers both challenges and opportunities for PR practitioners. The Internet in particular has blurred the boundaries of a number of disciplines, such as advertising, public relations, publishing and broadcasting, and added an unprecedented level of networked interaction that has redefined our concept of community.

For communicators, the age of mass communication is fading, and a new age of networked communication is taking its place. Having prospered in a world of mass communication, PR practitioners must now reposition themselves for the global network.

The challenge for public relations professionals is to provide credible leadership in the application of the technology, within the context of their positions as a facilitators of public dialog and understanding. As we evolve as an information society, their skill to package information so that it informs, persuades, clarifies or teaches will increase in value. That value is further enhanced, if as Edward Bernays foresaw nearly a century ago, they base their PR practice on solid social science.

Just as Bernays defined PR in the twentieth century as "applied social science," today's masters of networked communication have begun calling their profession "applied social technology." To become effective *social technologists* they need to be well grounded in all three fields: digital technology, the communication arts, and the social sciences.

## Advances in computers and communication technology

The networked world springs from advances in computer and communication technologies. The personal computer lets us do individual work — word processing, desktop publishing, budgeting, illustration, mail list management, and more. Add a network connection, and it becomes a communications device — a pipeline — that lets us send or receive information and make contact with groups or individuals around the world.

Where the PC is a tool that extends or magnifies our individual capabilities, the networked computer enhances both individual and group powers in new and previously unimaginable ways. The ultimate network, the Internet, has taken us down two revolutionary tracks simultaneously—the World Wide Web and e-mail. Each has taken us into its own unique global network, and each has already begun to reshape the world.

## Digital tools for PR practitioners

For PR practitioners, we may look at computer use as a collection of distinct, often related, digital tools. These tools affect the way we practice PR, allowing us to do work faster, better, more accurately, with fewer people, and at less cost. They can also make your life more hectic, and they are certainly contributing to your target audiences feeling overloaded, overstressed and overexposed to communication.

*The World Wide Web is the world s largest and most diverse reference library.*

**1. Communication and network tools**: Thanks to the Internet, the networked computer has emerged as a powerful communication appliance.

- The World Wide Web is the world's largest and most diverse reference library, newspaper, community discussion forum, video conference medium, and more.

- E-mail has largely replaced the fax, the business letter, the typed or printed news release, and the messenger services that hand-delivered news releases to the media.

- While crafting content is an important focus in your use of these Internet tools, you will also need some understanding of the network technology itself. The quality, reliability and especially the security of your connection to the Internet are just as critical as the words and images you put into this communication pipeline.

**2. Productivity tools**: Many of us use computers as individual workstations to help us do our work faster, better, or even permit us to do things that were not possible before. Some PC-based examples:

- *Word processing* replaced typewriters, speeding written communication and greatly reducing the number of typists needed to support an organization.

- *Desktop publishing* replaced typesetters. Together with digital imaging, it has radically reduced the cost and time to go to press. When the output is a PDF document, desktop publishing may even eliminate the printing press.

- *Drawing, graphics and presentation tools* have completely changed the way we design and produce collateral materials and multimedia presentations. Users of computer graphics tools routinely produce digital photos and videos that can blur our very perception of reality.

- *Information managers*, such as desktop databases, contact managers, personal organizers and project managers, help us organize our days and the people with whom we work. Electronic spreadsheets help us manage budgets. Database managers let us target our media lists or e-mail lists and customize letters to targeted publics.

**3. Knowledge base tools**: Computers can overwhelm us with data and information; but they have also provided us the tools to find and share more useful knowledge:

- Data warehouses and data mining tools help us find hidden relationships and capture insights that had been obscured by the flood of digital data.

- Online information services help us engage in more sophisticated research, do it faster and at lower cost.

- Web sites, together with search engines, located on the Internet, Intranets and Extranets give us instant access to global or corporate knowledge. When we publish electronic Web pages, we can share knowledge around the world, or target narrow audiences within a defined network.

*Know the difference between types of Web sites: Internet, Intranet and Extranet.*

We will start with programs for your personal computer (also called the desktop). PCs can run a whole set of productivity applications that have fundamentally altered the way we do our work. In selecting applications, you should give careful thought to how much time you have available to use them. Ask yourself, "Will I use this program daily?" If your answer is, "no," you need to look at the program's complexity. Many of the most enticing and powerful tools are also very complex. An occasional user cannot master them.

**Operating system**: Application software is written to run on top of a specific operating system (OS). The OS is the interface to the higher level language of application programs, turning their instructions into the machine language that your computer understands. All PCs on the market today offer an operating system that supports a Graphical User Interface (GUI), such as the Macintosh OS X and Microsoft's various flavors of Windows. Nearly all important desktop software is being developed for the Windows environment first. Some observers expected that Java's platform independence would make it the operating system of the future, or at least a strong alternative to Windows, but that hasn't happened. Another alternative, Unix, is popular for Web servers (see "Networking" below). Linux, an open-source version of Unix, is emerging as a serious contender in the server market.

On desktop PCs, Linux has a small but avid base among the more technologically adventuresome.

**Word processor**: In the '70s and early '80s, electric typewriters (dominated by the IBM Selectric) ruled every office in America. They are gone today, and so are many of the secretaries who used them. Most of today's PR practitioners type their own news releases, as they compose them, on PC-based word processors. Dedicated word processors by Wang and Xerox had a brief run in many larger organizations but couldn't keep up with the advance of PCs.

Today there are just two major word processing programs: WordPerfect and Microsoft Word. These programs have become so powerful that they now perform may tasks that once required a dedicated page layout program (see Desktop Publishing below). They are also now capable of publishing Web pages in HTML (Hyper Text Markup Language). Thanks to Microsoft Office (a suite of applications including word processor, spreadsheet and data base manager) MS Word dominates the market. If you want a job, you need to know how to use the entire MS Office suite. The Mac and Windows interfaces are sufficiently similar, so that if you know the program on one platform, you can use it on the other without having to relearn basics.

**Electronic Spreadsheet**: Spreadsheets were the first of what the trade press called a *killer app* — an application so powerful it caused people to buy new computers just so they could use the program. Spreadsheets remain an important tool for creating and tracking PR budgets. They also have powerful graphing tools and some database tools that can help in presenting research data, campaign results, or budget comparisons. The two major programs are Excel by Microsoft and Lotus 1-2-3. Microsoft dominates in this category, too.

**Communication hardware and software**: A number of different hardware and software solutions let computers communicate with other computers. Modems, for example, are used to communicate digital information, the language of computers, over analog phone lines. A fax modem also lets you send and receive faxes directly from your computer. Those connecting to a digital network (cable, DSL or a LAN), will need an Ethernet card, also called a network interface card (NIC). Wireless communication (WiFi) is another alternative that is growing in popularity.

Communication between computers remained one of the more difficult applications to master until the Internet offered an easier solution. Today, e-mail, file transfer and

## More on networks and Web sites

You may use, or have a hand in creating, three different types of Web sites: Internet, Extranet or Intranet. All use the same technology but differ in where the Web site is hosted and who has permission to view its pages. To understand these Webs, it is useful to start with the types of networks you can use to access to them:

- **LAN**. A Local Area Network links the computers within a limited area — a room, a floor, a building or a campus. Today, the LAN is most likely connected to the Internet via a broadband connection and provides secure Internet access to all its users through a firewall.

- **WAN**. A Wide Area Network connects computers spread over a large geographic area. It may provide a secure, private network around the globe to those who have been granted access. A WAN may be connected via dedicated phone lines, or it may "tunnel" through the Internet, using an encrypted VPN — Virtual Private Network.

- **Internet**. Public Web sites connected to the Internet are part of the World Wide Web. These sites are open to all, and visitors are anonymous (unless you choose to reveal

your identity, as when you make a purchase on an e-commerce site).

- **Extranet**. An extranet also resides on the Internet, but these Web sites require a user account, and you must log-in and enter a password to gain access. Extranets may have multiple levels of permissions, allowing registered visitors to view only those pages for which they have been granted permission.

- **Intranet**. Intranets reside on a LAN or WAN and are available only to those who are logged into the network. Like the Extranet, Intranets have varying permission levels, so that sensitive financial information, for example, may be limited to those managers who need it.

### Selecting and using digital PR tools

This text lists an overview of the many digital tools you may need in PR. Some of these tools you will use daily. Others you will need only occasionally, and still others you may never use but nevertheless need to understand how others use them.

Web browsing can all be accomplished from a simple interface. Netscape was the first to popularize Web browsing, but Microsoft's Internet Explorer has become the dominant Web browser. AOL (who bought Netscape), Opera and Mozilla Foxfire offer additional alternatives. Microsoft neatly ties together e-mail, group calendars and contact lists with its Outlook program. Eudora also offers a popular e-mail reader with similar capabilities.

**Networking**: Internal networks allow organizations to share printers and files and support local e-mail. Local area networks require a combination of hardware and software. Novel dominated the network software market before Windows NT took the lead. Various flavors of Unix (especially Linux) also have a strong following for network client-server applications and for Web servers. In addition to a network server, computers need a hardware interface to the network. Ethernet is now the preferred method for making that connection between computers and a network.

**Desktop publishing (DTP)**: For those who have an interest in the graphics side of public relations, DTP is an essential tool, or set of tools, to master. For those who think of themselves as essentially writers, the power and the economics of DTP and Web publishing are forcing them to take a hand in the layout and presentation of their words. DTP is one desktop application that Microsoft does not dominate. Adobe's In-Design (formerly PageMaker) and QuarkXpress are the current page layout leaders. Quark has been the preference of ad agencies and graphic designers (who favor Macs), while the Adobe product has tended to lead among corporate users who have standardized on PCs.

**Web publishing**: Web publishing does not have a clear winner as of this writing. The newer word processor, presentation and page layout programs are able to output Web pages, but with mixed results. There are many other programs designed to help you manage links and databases, generate HTML code, or create specialized files or graphics you display on the Web. Among the leaders are Macromedia's HomePage, Dreamweaver and Flash, Adobe's GoLive and Acrobat, and Microsoft FrontPage. More discussion of DTP and Web publishing will follow later in this chapter.

**Presentation software**: Computer-based presentations have replaced the 35mm slide show and the overhead projector. Presentations are now done directly from light, easy-to-carry notebook computers. For one-on-one presentations, the computer's own color screen is adequate.

*Computer-based presentations have replaced the slide show and overhead projector.*

For groups the PC can be attached to a larger external monitor or to an LCD projector. Projectors have also become light and portable. You can scan color photos, or capture images with digital cameras. Using software such as Microsoft PowerPoint, you can integrate graphics, words, sound, animation and video into a presentation. You can also publish presentations to the Web or burn on a CD or DVD.

**Desktop video (DTV)**: This set of computer tools may have as much impact on the public relations profession as desktop publishing. DTV is making video less costly and more accessible to smaller organizations. Even more than desktop publishing, however, DTV involves a steep learning curve and demands creative and technical skills to use it effectively. It is not for the occasional user. Among the DTV tools, animation software offers interesting possibilities for enhancing communication. In addition to the gee-whiz effects that have become too common in commercial and corporate video, animation is a powerful tool for seeing inside a process (or an idea) that cannot be photographed in real life.

**Database applications**: Although databases have been around from the beginning of the computer age, they have not yet been as widely adopted by PC users (including PR professionals) as word processing or electronic spread-sheets. Databases are powerful information tools, but because of their power they can be hard to learn and use. A database program is actually a high-level programming language that requires users to understand the rules and logic of how they work. Of course not all the people putting information in and taking information out of a database need to know how to create the database application; they just need to know enough to use it. Windows and MAC interfaces have made databases friendlier to use, and Web browsers are making databases even more accessible.

Among the Windows database programs, Microsoft's Access (another MS Office suite application) has the lead. If you had to choose one database program to learn today, Access is probably the safest choice. Another application that uses database technology and is getting a lot of use today is the *Personal Information Manager* (PIM). These database tools use electronic versions of familiar paper devices such as personal phone books, appointment calendars and to-do lists. Most are very easy to use, once you have entered all your data. For those who work all day at a computer, PIMs are handier and easier to maintain than their paper counterparts. Electronic pocket organizers, such as the Palm Pilot and Blackberry, also make these programs more portable.

**CD ROM, DVD and interactive multi-media**: The CD ROM quickly became a very inexpensive way to publish large quantities of electronic data. Huge databases, such as the US census, encyclopedias, and other reference works, and software applications are published on CDs. The DVD looks the same but holds even more data on a single disk. CD/DVDs may be interactive. What happens next depends on what the user chooses or how he or she answers a question. It thus holds great potential for training (not to mention interesting PR possibilities). CD/DVDs can display color photos, animation, plus play stereo sound and video clips (entire feature films in the case of DVDs). PR applications include digital media kits with high resolution photos, multimedia news releases and video news releases.

## Why Moore's Law says this chapter is obsolete before you can read it

Understanding today's technology starts with an understanding of the microprocessor, the heart and soul of the digital world. Most of the tools a PR practitioner now uses, from fax to cell phone to pocket organizer or notebook computer, depend on the microprocessor.

The speed of change in the digital world makes preparing a textbook chapter on digital PR tools a challenging task. It is impossible to provide hard rules for selecting or using digital tools when our hardware purchases are obsolete before we get them home, and when software companies can rise, prosper and disappear in less time than you will take to complete a degree.

Intel cofounder Gordon Moore predicted high-tech's breathtaking pace of change in the early 1970s. According to the legend, he was preparing an industry speech. Using logarithmic paper, he plotted the growing number of transistors (indicating performance) integrated into each new generation of Intel microprocessors. The plot was a straight line, showing that transistor count doubles every 18 months (or, inversely, price per transistor is half what it was 18 months before). Moore's Law was born, and it has held true since. *See Figure 11.1.*

## Moore's Law

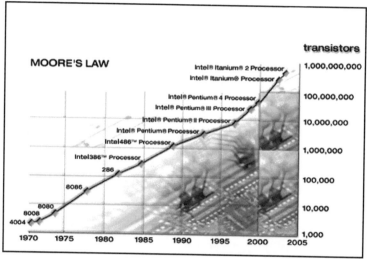

| | Year of Introduction | Transistors |
|---|---|---|
| 4004 | 1971 | 2,250 |
| 8008 | 1972 | 2,500 |
| 8080 | 1974 | 5,000 |
| 8086 | 1978 | 29,000 |
| 286 | 1982 | 120,000 |
| 386™ processor | 1985 | 275,000 |
| 486™ DX processor | 1989 | 1,180,000 |
| Pentium® processor | 1993 | 3,100,000 |
| Pentium II processor | 1997 | 7,500,000 |
| Pentium III processor | 1999 | 24,000,000 |
| Pentium 4 processor | 2000 | 42,000,000 |

Source: http://www.intel.com/research/silicon/mooreslaw.htm

**Figure 11.1**

After more than a quarter-century of this continual doubling, we have reached a point where each increment yields millions of additional transistors. With no end in sight to this rate of increase, computer technology has begun to change the landscape for everyone, in every organization, in every corner of the world.

Microprocessor technology is driving down prices and raising the value of services and products in virtually every sector of the economy. The turmoil of constant change presents a twofold challenge for PR practitioners:

- The technology itself forces you into a constant cycle of upgrading your tools and your skills.
- The effect of technology-driven change on your publics is making the practice of PR more problematic than ever.

## Desktop publishing, Web publishing and PR

Desktop and Web publishing play such large roles in so many PR activities that they demand further discussion in this chapter. DTP provides a set of prepress tools that handle type, page layout, and graphics functions. Some of the most popular graphics tools used for DTP are also the preferred tools for preparing Web graphics.

While DTP put many typesetters out of business, and has made a dent in traditional graphic arts businesses, others have become service bureaus to desktop publishers, producing final film and doing other finishing touches that require more expensive equipment or more skilled operators. DTP has moved from simple publications to high-end film output, color separations, and image enhancement (such as photo retouching and digital airbrushing). Many organizations are now producing professional, camera-ready four-color brochures and advertisements without the assistance of outside designers. With the wide acceptance of the Adobe PDF file, most publishers now accept ads as PDFs in place of film.

## Basic DTP equipment

**The computer**: At the moment Macs are used more by graphics professionals and service bureaus than Windows-based PCs. However, all the major graphics applications are available on both platforms, and PCs tend to cost less. Although service bureaus are largely Mac equipped, most have no trouble accepting Windows files. Mac has for some time been able to read and write to DOS disks, and there are now some good applications available that will let Windows machines read, open or convert Mac files and write to Mac disks. If you plan to produce color

publications, buy lots of RAM. Also buy the fastest, most powerful processor you can afford and lots of disk storage capacity. Large capacity removable media can be useful, such as a Zip disk, for sending large graphic files to a service bureau. However, CDs and DVDs do the same job and hold even more data. A broadband Internet connection is also desirable for quick transfer of large files via FTP (File Transfer Protocol). *Flash drives* the size of a key can store thousands of documents.

**Graphics software**: Adobe Illustrator is probably the most widely used high end drawing program for the Mac platform and has become popular for Windows. Corel Draw is another popular Windows program. Graphics programs are fairly easy to use for simple drawings. The more complex features take time to learn. Illustrations may be vector drawings or bitmaps. Vector drawings are more scalable, make for smaller file size but can be more difficult to print or move from one platform to another (such as from MAC to Windows). Bitmap files must be larger when used for high resolution output, lose quality when scaled up to larger sizes, but are easier to use across different platforms.

*Use databases to track media contacts, employees, customers, association members, alumni and suppliers.*

**Scanners and photo editing software**: Desktop flatbed scanners are now very close in quality to the high-end drum scanners used by printers. They can be used to acquire photo images (even from color slides), drawings, signatures, documents, or anything else you can fit on the glass. With optical character recognition software (OCR) you can scan and edit documents in your word processor or import them into a database. Adobe Photoshop and other programs can alter your scanned image in unlimited ways. This ability to alter photo images has created some serious public relations issues. We can no longer say, "the camera never lies," because the image can be manipulated so easily and so convincingly. Controversies have arisen when magazines published altered pictures that showed people together in situations that did not happen.

**Page layout programs**: The most popular publishing programs are QuarkXPress and Adobe InDesign. Both efficiently handle long documents. Although not easy programs to master, they are essential tools for any public relations professional interested in print communication.

**Printers**: Color printers, both laser and ink jet, are dropping in price and increasing in quality. They can make your communication more effective and faster and may be used for color proofing, short-run color handouts, and many other uses. If you plan to create comprehensive layout presentations, such as magazine spreads or tabloid pages, your printer should be large enough to output an 11-by-17-inch bleed page.

## Using digital information in public relations

Commercial online services and the Internet give you access to vast libraries of information. In addition, organizations use user-developed databases to manage their own data, such as mailing lists, financial data and even customer manuals and support services.

**Database PR**: Personal computers make it easier to create and use databases. They even let you download data from mainframe computers and make more productive use of the information than was possible with the big central machines.

Media contacts, employees, customers, prospects, association members, alumni, and suppliers are some of the publics you can track with databases. The power of the database goes beyond a convenient way to generate mailing lists: you can track the history of your organization's contact with every individual. This powerful idea has emerged as the basis of a whole new marketing paradigm — *database marketing*. A contact management program, a specialized database program, can be used straight out of the box, with no custom programming, to track every contact with an individual or group: every phone call, birthday or anniversary, every service call, for every customer or prospect. This idea is also called *relationship marketing*. We could also call it *personalized public relations*. These tools have helped to shift our thinking from mass communication to personal communication.

**Online information**: Virtually all the commercial online information services may be accessed through the World Wide Web. They may, however, charge a fee for access to all their information — either as an annual subscription or a per-use fee charged to your credit card. Others are supported by online advertising. Some of the better known online information services include Lexis-Nexis (a law database with 100 U.S. newspapers), PR Newswire. U.S. census data, dating back to its beginning in 1890, is also available online (and on CD ROM).

Online information searches on the Internet are aided by search engines and catalogs. The catalogs, like Yahoo, are organized into categories. Web sites and other Internet sources, such as news group archives, are reviewed by editors who make judgments about what to list and how to list it. Also useful are catalogs devoted to a single subject area. A favorite for many journalists is My Virtual Reference Desk (www.refdesk.com), which provides links to virtually every foreign and domestic newspaper with an online

presence, plus dictionaries, encyclopedias, and more.

Search engines, such as Google, use an automated *robot* or *Web crawler* to index virtually every word on the Internet. Search engine software may also be used by some organizations to index their own Intranet. Some search tools will actually index the indexes, making an automated search of as many catalogs and indexes as you choose to include.Mac's Tiger (OS) powerfully indexes every word in your computer.

PR managers can use online information sources to monitor breaking news, spot trends, develop historical perspective on issues, or research competition. Some skill is needed in developing search strategies that will help you wade through the thousands of articles available online. Be sure to read the online help and examples offered by each of the search sites. Every site handles searches differently.

Learn how to minimize time wasted online. One trick used by the more experienced online PR practitioners: Limit your focus to the one best-of-category site for each category you need to follow. Master its capabilities and provide feedback to its developers so they continue to serve your needs.

## Other electronic tools

**Voice mail**: Voice mail is replacing real people who answer phones. When it works, it can make life easier for people who no longer have secretaries to answer for them. Voice mail also makes it more efficient for callers to leave a detailed message. Too often, however, voice mail is poorly implemented and becomes a public relations problem for the organization, alienating its publics.

**Fax machines**: The fax machine has become commonplace in today's offices but may be largely replaced by e-mail and PCs that can send and receive faxes. Faxes have become an indispensable medium for exchanging information between PR offices and the media, from news conference announcements to last-minute fact checking before a story is published. The marriage of fax and PC has brought us fax-back or fax-on-demand, which automates caller requests for any number of information sheets, or fax brochures. This technology has been eclipsed by the World Wide Web and Internet FTP sites that let your publics browse for the information they need and easily print or download any files they find of interest.

**Teleconferencing and video conferencing**: The telephone can be extended beyond the usual one-on-one contact. Special 800 (or 888) numbers and well-trained and equipped call centers can be set up to support PR campaigns, or to handle calls from stockholders or concerned consumers during a crisis. Reporters who can't attend a news confer-

# Effective management of discussion list e-mail

*by Adam Boettiger*

Managing incoming e-mail is a skill that most of us need to master. I get over 150 messages per day and it takes me about 30-45 minutes per day to process my mail. So when people complain about getting 10 messages per day from a discussion list, it makes me wonder whether they are managing their mail. After all, it isn't the discussion list that is causing you problems. It is your inability to effectively manage your own e-mail that is the problem.

A number of skills will help you deal with e-mail more effectively, but I think it's important to first understand why you have joined a discussion list in the first place and how you can get the most out of any discussion list.

Thousands of discussion lists appear on the Internet, on topics ranging from Internet advertising to pet psychology to Uncle Bob's hernia. Anyone with access to e-mail has the capability to start a **discussion list, a collection of blogs.** Your task is to find quality lists that directly relate to your industry or your interests. You do this to:

- Learn from others in the industry as they share their experiences. Learn from the mistakes and advice of others more experienced than you. It will save you time and money.

- Network yourself to others within your industry.

- Establish business relationships that could lead to new business for you or your company.

- Participate in lists that are specific to your industry to establish yourself as an expert or a knowledgeable participant in the eyes of your peers or potential clients.

- Stay current on trends within your industry.

But do you have the time to read a discussion list? If you are serious about your job, and your job has anything to do with online communication, you are doing yourself, your career and your company a serious disservice by not staying current on lists that pertain to your industry.

The more you know about your online job and this industry, the more you'll begin to realize how much you don't know, because this industry changes on a daily basis. Learning is an ongoing process, especially on the Internet. It is very easy to get "information overload" in this industry. I'm online ten hours a day for my job. I get the majority of my industry news via e-mail, but the truth is that I really enjoy the physical act of holding a newspaper in my hands or reading a book after work. It's my escape from the information overload of cyberspace.

## Tips on taking control of your e-mail discussion lists

- Join only *well-filtered discussion lists* and only those that are directly pertinent to your business, industry or personal interests. Many lists on the Net are un-moderated. An unmoderated list means that every single post that members send to the list address is then distributed to list members — even posts that simply say, "Yeah, I agree with what Fred said....Bob." There are many unmoderated lists that are extremely valuable, but I have found that the number of posts distributed on an un-moderated list is much higher per day than a moderated list. Many unmoderated lists reach postings of 60 messages plus per day or more, as members reply and hold their discussion by e-mail. It can be quite overwhelming at times.

By contrast, a moderated list means that posts are submitted to a human being who then selects the best 10-15 per day for passing to the list. Yes, there are drawbacks to this type of arrangement, mainly that not everyone's post is included in the list; but overall, there is a much higher signal-to-noise ratio on moderated lists, and this is generally appreciated by list members.

- **Always subscribe to the individual post version** of a discussion list if it is available and not the digest or compilation version. The only time I would recommend subscribing to a digest version of a list is if you enjoy printing it out and reading it as a paper publication.

Personal preferences are obviously up to you, but for many people, a post-by-post version works best. As posts come in, you're able to see the Subject Header in your e-mail program without even opening the message. You can quickly delete the subjects you have no interest in, open those you do have an interest in, forward a single post to a friend or coworker, or file it for later reference. Try doing this with a large digest. It's also pretty overwhelming when several 30K digests stack up for reading.

- **Use a good e-mail program with filters and mailboxes.** Set up a mailbox for each discussion list or newsletter that you subscribe to. Set a filter for each list that will automatically place posts from that list into the mailbox. Set aside time each day to quickly scan this mailbox and *Subject* lines of the messages. *Filters and mailboxes are a godsend*. Use a good e-mail program and read the manual to take full advantage of these features. They will save you time and help you keep your sanity.

*continued on next page*

• **Learn to scan the *Subject Line* without opening the message.** Scanning is probably the most valuable skill you will learn online, and it will reduce the time you spend on reading your e-mail by at least 30%. Scan the *Subject Headers* of your mail without opening the messages. Open and respond only to those that require immediate response, such as client messages, raises from your boss, etc. You'll find that you can delete many of your incoming messages simply by looking at the *Subject Line* without even opening the message. Anything that you don't have to open up and read saves you time.

Using most e-mail programs, you can even set a filter to look for a specific address or domain in the headers and when a message from that person or client arrives, your program will play a sound and even file the message in a special mailbox or change the priority so you know to read those messages first.

• **If you don't like getting junk e-mail, just delete it and move on.** It takes 0.5 seconds to delete a message and an average of 15 minutes to become involved in an exchange of e-mail with someone who sent you the junk. If you are avidly against spam, then delete the message and just don't ever buy anything from that merchant. If no one bought products that were advertised by spamming, it would not be profitable and would not exist.

If you are trying to save time, learn to use your delete key. It will be your new best friend as you learn to manage your e-mail.

• **Scan the first paragraph.** The art of scanning goes beyond looking at subject headers. Once you've deleted the unopened messages you are not interested in, read only the first paragraph of these messages you are interested in. You can tell from the first paragraph whether it requires your attention. If it doesn't require immediate attention, leave it for when you have time. Prioritize your responses, and only reply to those messages that absolutely require a reply.

• **Don't feel obligated to reply to everyone who writes to you.** It's not scanning your e-mail that takes time; it is replying. Learn to be brief and painfully direct in your responses. Know that the person you are replying to or sending a message to is just as busy. If you sent someone a message, chances are they received it. Don't be insulted if you don't receive a "Thank you" back or a continuation of dialog. They'll read your information and act on it or delete it as they see fit.

If the message needs a reply but you don't have time for a long thought-out message, leave it in your inbox until you can get to it. When you do reply, be brief and state the purpose of your message in the first paragraph. Often it is this first paragraph that will determine whether they will continue reading. Most recipients appreciate brevity.

• **Use the telephone** and include your number in a "signature" at the end of every message you send. E-mail is wonderful, but often you can save a 15-minute message-writing session by making a two-minute call. You can't do this, however, unless the person included a phone number in the message. Most e-mail programs will allow you to attach a standard signature block at the end of every message with your contact information. Use it.

• **Set your e-mail program** so that it will not download messages over 40K in size unless you tell it to.

*Adam Boettiger is founder and moderator of I-Advertising, an Internet advertising discussion list. A free e-mail discussion forum, I-Advertising is received each day by more than 7,000 industry professionals in 90 countries*

---

ence can join in through conference calls. Increasing computer power, improved communication technologies and the Internet have also made live video a viable alternative to bringing a group together in the same room.

## Internet PR

You need to know how to use the Internet in the practice of PR for two reasons. First, you need to be aware of what's being said about your organization on the Internet. You especially need to be prepared with the tools and knowledge to fight the firestorms of controversy that can arise so quickly on the Internet. You also need to be proactive on the Internet (within the limits of net etiquette) to promote your client's or employer's viewpoint.

Second, the Internet provides fast, powerful and surprisingly low cost channels for you to reach the media and your key publics through online announcements and news releases, participation in unmoderated newsgroups (Usenet) or moderated e-mail discussion groups. You can also contribute to (or create your own) e-mail newsletters and glossary, and participate in or host live chat and online discussion.

There are so many Internet channels that your organization might be contributing to, or at least monitoring, that the task can quickly grow beyond the ability of the largest and most dedicated public relations department. One solution is to enlist your network of **key communicators** to help you follow the discussion, news and rumors that

> ## Offer a free e-mail newsletter subscription to develop a lasting relationship with Web visitors.

flow across the Internet. Indeed, the Net provides a whole new set of ways to organize, motivate and stay in contact with your key communicators.

The best place to learn about PR online is to get yourself online. One good starting point is Steve O'Keefe's useful Web site at http://www.patronsaintpr.com. O'Keefe, author of *Publicity on the Internet* (John Wiley & Sons), provides well-organized lists with brief descriptions and direct links to all the Internet resources he spent years discovering. Among the free services is a Web site registration list that helps you register your Web site with the top search engines and directories. Among the PR services are links to lists of media e-mail addresses and "Firefighting Resources" links to sites that help you track what people are posting online about your organization.

O'Keefe urges Internet PR practitioners to have stock materials prepared in advance in a variety of formats (such as text, html, e-mail auto-respond documents, high-resolution graphics, and low-res graphics) so that you can quickly respond to situations and opportunities when they arise. Some electronic materials he suggests you have at hand: product brochures, employee profiles, photos of key staff, several stock signature files, basic company news release, and canned customer service replies.

"If you see your company being attacked," O'Keefe explains, "you can respond quickly. If you find a review of your product, you can offer a JPEG graphic to go with it. If a journalist is looking for someone to interview, you'll have a bio and photo on hand. Advance preparation reduces time-wasting and helps you jump on opportunities at net speed."

## Web site creation and promotion

Many PR professionals produce or collaborate in Web site production. While there are many technical issues involved in Web development that may be beyond the scope of most PR practitioners, your professional skills can play a key role in determining the success of your site.

Both content and presentation play a critical role in attracting new visitors to your Web site, and they are the deciding factors in determining if visitors stay long enough to be persuaded by what you present. Building a good Web site requires orchestrating the varied talents of technical and creative people so that they are focused on delivering an experience that will attract and satisfy your target publics.

## Elements of effective Web communication

The first rule of the Web communication is that *information must be free*. Marketers have long known that "free" is one of those magic words for drawing public attention, and on the Web freely giving information has become the norm. Detailed product information that companies once kept closely guarded is now offered freely on their Web sites.

**Free but worth registering for**: While their information is free, companies — especially business-to-business companies — are learning that visitors will provide their contact information for the privilege of downloading "premium" information. These downloads are usually PDF files of "white papers" (technical articles), catalogs or color brochures. For some companies, Web site registrations have become their single largest source of sales leads, surpassing even paid advertising.

**Other free things you can offer**: Try offering a little software utility that is relevant to your target audience, neat screen saver graphics, or daily cartoons. Offering a free e-mail newsletter subscription is an excellent way to develop a lasting relationship with Web visitors.

> ## Personalize e-mail to editors.

Other content that will draw and keep visitors includes answers to *frequently asked questions (FAQs)*, with a form so that visitors can easily send questions to experts in your organization. Visitors also like to be able to access *databases* for useful information, to look up a local contact, or access support services. Some sites maintain membership areas where only registered users can visit. Every site should have a *newsroom* for the media, where you can post your news releases (others like to read them, too).

Highly targeted free information, however it is packaged, remains the strongest magnet to your Web pages. Add a button that reads: *"e-mail this story to a friend,"* and you can expand your reach beyond those who visit your site.

Sites can also benefit by increasing the visibility of actions they want visitors to take. One Web site increased registration for its e-mail newsletter by a factor of 30 by making a subscription form the first thing a visitor sees when arriving at its home page. Subscribing is not required to gain access to the site, but the form makes it hard to overlook the opportunity. Likewise, if you want people to invite your CEO to speak to their groups, or want them to attend one of your seminars, make the offer highly visible, and make it easy to send a response.

Interestingly, when you offer an *e-mail newsletter*, you

# Target and personalize your e-mail to editors

*By Paul J. Krupin*

1. **Think, think, think** before you write. Ask yourself why you are writing, and what are you trying to accomplish by writing. Put yourself in the position of the person reading your message. You are a busy media professional. What would *you* do upon receiving your message? Publish it or toss it?

2. **Target narrowly and carefully**. Go for quality contacts, not quantity. Don't broadcast a query or news release or announcement to irrelevant media. Pick your target media carefully, based on the industry or readership you are targeting. Study the media you are writing to. Write the way the editors write. Make it easy for them to use your material.

3. **Keep it short.** Trim your e-mail message so it fills one to three screens. Keep it three to four paragraphs, tops. Don't try to sell the media your product. Do try to get their interest so they will make a request for more information.

4. **Keep the subject and content of your message relevant to your target** — it's got to be newsworthy and timely. The subject should intrigue them enough to read your message. Propose problem-solving articles that explain the benefits or techniques associated with a strategy, technique, product or service. This sidebar is an example of a short, useful e-mail that got ink for its author's service.

5. **Use a two-step approach** if you're seeking publicity for a product or service, or want to get reviews for a new book or software — a query with a hook and news angle before transmitting a longer news release or article. Offer to send review copies of products to those who request them. To avoid angry replies and complaints about unsolicited e-mail, some suggest going so far as to send a very brief e-mail requesting permission to send a news release. Others view that as a waste of time. "Don't make them beg," they say. "Just send it, but make sure you make it good."

6. **Tailor the submittal to the media** editorial style or content. Go to a library, read it on-line, or write and ask for a free media kit and a sample copy of the magazine or journal. Study the style and content of the media. Then write the way they like it. Seek to develop a longer term relationship as a regular contributor.

7. **Address each e-mail message separately** to an individual media target. Take your time and personalize each email. Don't ever send to multiple addresses. It's the easiest way to get deleted without being read.

8. **Reread**, reread, and reread and **rewrite**, rewrite, rewrite before you click the send button.

9. **Be brutally honest** with yourself, and with your media contacts. Don't make claims about your product or service you can't prove.

10. **Follow up** in a timely manner, with precision writing and professionalism.

---

Krupin has one final word of advice: While you can and should use e-mail to get news coverage, you shouldn't rely on e-mail alone. When used together with conventional PR (mail, paper, phone and fax), you get the maximum effect. You cultivate relationships with media by becoming known as a valuable contributor. When you give them what their readers want, they give you the publicity.

*US All Media E-mail Directory* (**http://www.owt.com/dircon**) lists more than 10,000 electronic-mail (e-mail) addresses for key editors, columnists, correspondents and executives at magazines, newspapers, radio, TV and news syndicates across the United States and Canada.

*Paul J. Krupin created a widely known media e-mail database called The US All Media E-Mail Directory in 1994. In 1996 he co-created IMEDIAFAX (www.Imediafax.com), an online service that transmits news releases to custom targeted media lists via fax and e-mail. Through IMEDIAFAX Krupin has sent out thousands of news releases a year. These guidelines for using e-mail to get news coverage are based on the "10 Commandments for E-mail PR" posted on his Web site.*

---

are tapping into the power of print media to promote your Web site. When people are able to print out a short, useful newsletter on their own printer, and read your news away from their computer, you have created a medium that gives them the immediacy of electronic age, and the ease, comfort and flexibility-of-use of the print media.

People also value sites that keep them up to date on other sites with a ***links page*** of interesting sites that are relevant to your industry. Also offer ***contests***, stage **Web events**, list the ***trade shows*** you'll be exhibiting at, and offer *seminars* (or be a speaker). Each site needs to develop its Web personality to become a memorable place to visit.

## Web site promotion

When it comes to bringing visitors to their shiny new Home Pages on the World Wide Web, many organizations

## The 5 C's of Web site communication

1. **Content**. Eye candy is fun and may draw attention. But you will leave visitors feeling empty and cheated if you don't provide content that fills their needs for useful information.

2. **Context**. What you offer online must be relevant to your target audience(s). Make sure you are designing and writing with your visitor's perspective and interests in mind. If your Web navigation looks like your company organization chart, you may be talking more to yourself than to your audience.

3. **Continuity**. The tone and character of your online Web content must fit your offline public image.

4. **Community**. Despite the large numbers of people the Web serves, it is not a mass medium. You are addressing one person at a time. You are hosting a Web community of individuals, who expect to develop a relationship with you and to have interactive experiences. When a visitor contacts you by filling out a form on your Web site, you must answer promptly.

5. **Change**. Your Web site has to change often enough to bring back your target audience(s), but remain useful and understandable to new visitors.

seem to be following the "Field of Dreams" movie philosophy: "If you build it, they will come."

But putting up a Web site, without a plan for attracting qualified traffic to your pages, is like a new business expecting customers to call them just because they have installed a telephone. Following are some of the techniques available to bring qualified visitors to your site.

*Search engines*. Search engines or directories can be the central focus for your Web promotion, because this is where Web surfers often turn first when they look for information on a new topic. Danny Sullivan's Search Engine Watch site (http://www.searchenginewatch.com) offers frequently updated information on the main search engines, how they function, how often they are updated, and how to improve your site's visibility on them.

Each search site posts detailed directions for submitting information to it, or requesting a visit to a new site. Those serious about registering need to visit at least the major search sites and read and follow their registration instructions.

Although there are hundreds of search engines, you will find that most referrals come from just a few; so it is a good idea to focus on those that are most often used by your audience.

*Multiple URLs*. An inexpensive and effective way to help people find your Web site is to register multiple URLs, all pointing to the same site. If a company has multiple brand names, each brand could have its own URL. Having multiple doorways leading to your Web site gives you an opportunity for increased exposure in the search engines and increases the number of avenues for people to find your site.

*Links, listings, malls and online "trade shows."* Many Web promoters place their greatest efforts in finding good links, with focused sites that enjoy good traffic. Most sites get more visitors from links than from any other source. Find sites that match your target audience, and link or advertise with them.

Only about 20 percent of the traffic to most sites will come from search engines. Try getting cooperative cross-linking agreements with noncompetitive, similar industry sites. Also look for database listings serving your market, and sites that provide hot lists and Web site reviews.

Many trade magazines and buyers' guides are now offering online directories. These listings may be free, paid, or discounted or free to those who advertise in their print publications. The best online directories include links to the Web sites of the companies they list. Many industry-specific online malls have also been set up with directory listings of suppliers to that industry.

Another venue creating interest on the Web is the *online virtual trade show*. Some are linked to an established show; others are part of an online mall. These virtual shows give organizations an opportunity to show their products or services at a fraction of the cost of exhibiting at a trade show, and the exhibition is open 24 hours a day, seven days a week, for as long as a year.

Today's Web technology offers many ways to create online trade shows. You can offer audio or video clips of key presentations, let visitors download handouts, host live chat or moderated discussions, and create interactive virtual exhibit halls.

### Offline Web promotion

Despite the natural appeal for online promotion to attract online visitors, much of the most productive work will be done offline. Collateral materials such as **business cards, letterhead** and **brochures** all need to include your Web address. Remember, the most important people to attract to your Web site are the people you are now doing business with.

*Ad specialties* are another effective way to promote awareness of your Web site. Web addresses are printed on

T-shirts, clothing, bags, golf balls, and other imaginative or useful give-aways.

## Advertising: print, radio and TV

From a simple *tag line* to overt promotion of your Web site, Web awareness needs to be part of your ongoing advertising program. Analysis of Web site activity has demonstrated that *print advertising* drives traffic to your Web site. In one study, a review of Web logs (file transmission activity) indicated that the number of hits nearly doubled on days when the site was promoted in an advertisement. Even the simple inclusion of the URL address in the tag line increased Web activity by nearly 50 percent. Likewise, *television* advertising has been found effective in promoting Web sites to new visitors, though its cost may prove too high.

## Using public relations to promote your Web site

Just as in your advertising, you should include your Web site address in all news releases, and it should inform news sources that a complete inventory of news releases and backgrounders is available in your *online news room*. Treat your Web site as you'd treat a new product launch. Send out *announcements* of a new site, or new features or enhancements to an existing site. *Stage events*, contests, or tie-ins with radio or TV stations, trade publications or other organizations that will give your Web site exposure to a target audience.

Generate *feature story* placements. Many trade journals, newspaper business pages and newsletters are hungry for Web "how to" stories and success stories. Become a *resource* on Web news. When an event or issue arises that puts the Web in the news, provide your local news or trade press outlets with relevant commentary, insights, or business perspective.

Finally, don't forget *internal communication*. Inform the troops of upcoming Web promotions, so that people responding to an online program will find someone on the other end who knows what the promotion is about.

## Future trends in computer technology

We have reviewed in this chapter some of the powerful computer tools, such as word processing, graphics and data base applications, that have greatly enhanced individual performance. Although the future of technology is impossible to predict with any certainty, following are some near-term trends we will see:

- Shift from PC-centric to Web-centric applications. Technology is moving from the desktop to far more complex applications that seek to enhance group

performance. Expect to see wider adoption of enterprise-wide applications, such as Customer Relationship Management (CRM) and Knowledge Management (KM). Group productivity, information sharing, and collaboration tools are forcing organizations to look more closely at their processes; perhaps even reengineer them. These massive organizational restructurings may have an important PR component in promoting greater user acceptance and compliance to working in different ways.

- Simplicity on the surface, complexity underneath. The effort to simplify the user interface and make it more friendly has added far greater complexity to the underlying code. Operating systems and applications are getting easier to use but harder to troubleshoot when there is a problem. The Internet brought us easier communication and access to information across the globe, but with it came *spam* and complex security issues. The most hopeful sign in user interface design has come from the World Wide Web, which demonstrates that the best interfaces don't require a user manual or training.

- Apple announced it will switch from IBM to Intel chips for its new computer line by 2006.

- New futuristic, portable, hand-held PDAs (Personal Digital Assistants) will do virtually every function — voice activated commands, global positioning, e-mail, phone, voice mail, camera, Internet, MP3 player, and even a keyboard in case you get bored.

- The excitement is gone but the upgrades keep coming. When it comes to computers and software, we seem to be suffering *upgrade exhaustion*. Businesses and consumers have, on occasion, shown some tendency to resist this relentless march of progress. But as long as Moore's Law remains in force, it will be hard to stay off the upgrade merry-go-round for long. ■

# Tips

1. Many PR practitioners call PR in the twentieth century "applied social technology."

2. To be an effective social technologist, you'll need to be well-grounded in three fields: digital technology, the communication arts, and the social sciences.

3. You may create and/or use three different types of Web sites: Internet, Extranet, or Intranet.

4. Presentations are now done directly from light, easy-to-carry notebook computers, replacing slide shows and overhead projectors.

5. Many organizations are now producing high-end films: output, color separations, and image enhancement.

6. Adobe InDesign and QuarkXPress are the most popular publishing programs.

7. Track media contacts, employees, customers, prospects, association members, alumni and suppliers with databases.

8. An excellent source for learning about PR online is Steve O'Keefe's Web site at http://www.patronsaintpr.com.

9. Address each e-mail message to an individual media target. (Personalize each e-mail.) Don't ever send to multiple addresses.

10. Participate in lists that are specific to your industry. This establishes you as an expert in the eyes of peers and potential clients.

Name _____ Date _____

_____

*Answer these questions:*

1. What's the difference between Internet and Intranet?

_____

_____

_____

_____

_____

2. On what does personalized public relations, often called relationship marketing, depend for success?

_____

_____

_____

_____

_____

3. What implications does Moore's Law have for PR practitioners capitalizing on today's technology?

_____

_____

_____

_____

_____

4. Macs are used more by graphics professionals. Why then do many companies buy PCs?

_____

_____

_____

_____

_____

# Chapter 12

# Staying Legal in the Workplace

**PRaxiom** *The practitioner's legal stool rests on three important legs — truth, disclosure and checking.*

## What this chapter covers

Many ideas in this chapter come from writings and speeches by Gerhart L. Klein, Esquire, partner and principal in the New Jersey public relations firm, Anne Klein & Associates. Jerry Klein is a public relations practitioner, lawyer and frequent speaker for the Public Relations Society of America. PRSA offers a PR primer and other resources of Klein's ideas about public relations and the law.

In this chapter, you'll learn how public relations law differs from public relation ethics. You'll learn how counselors can avoid legal communication minefields in areas such as speech, confidentiality, privacy, ownership and contracts. The chapter offers this advice to all communicators: You're responsible for the content of your communication even though you're only a conduit for it.

## Legal involvements for the practitioner

Public relations people live in a litigious society. Publics of all kinds — consumers, employees, vendors, suppliers — all believe that suing organizations for violation of some perceived right can redeem their prestige or reputation, punish the organization, and gain monetary compensation for harm.

Even the government sues organizations.

The government sued the Microsoft Corporation for violation of free trade and an attempt to monopolize use of its software by computer consumers.

Individual states and the federal government sued tobacco companies for compensation for medical treatment of their citizens from illnesses allegedly caused by tobacco products. In 1998, nearly every state joined in a signed settlement by the states' attorneys general amounting to an out-of-court settlement of approximately $74 billion. As part of the settlement, tobacco companies agreed to sponsor programs to prevent young people from beginning a smoking habit.

Numerous government-instigated product recalls cause companies to lose millions of dollars. In some cases, company executives, including public relations practitioners, face civil, even criminal charges. Whether it's the

percentage of real juice in "100% real orange juice" (Tropicana), amount of harm caused by silicon breast implants (Dow/Corning), or the equation between the protection of super absorbent tampons and level of alleged harm by toxic shock syndrome (Proctor & Gamble), companies risk legal problems by merely opening their doors for business each day.

In addition, people sue other people for all sorts of physical, emotional or monetary injuries, both real and imagined. Almost anyone can sue another for anything. And public relations practitioners are not immune from suits that claim they participated in some communication or counseling wrongdoing. Plaintiffs might or might not win. But PR practitioners will have to defend themselves, even if they're innocent. And that could be expensive. *It's important for PR people to have liability insurance*, provided either by their organizations or themselves.

## Law vs. ethics

Practitioners distinguish between legal activity and ethical activity. Law tells PR practitioners what they *must* do. Ethics suggests what PR practitioners *should* do. The chapter on ethical behavior goes into depth about ethical and unethical behavior.

As you read ethical codes, such as PRSA's Member Code of Ethics 2000 (www.PRSA.org), you'll probably conclude that some activities mentioned as examples are both unethical and illegal. For example, the Code prohibits corruption of the channels of integrity of the media or government that

**In doubt? Check with your lawyer. No doubt? Check with your lawyer.**

could be construed as bribery or extortion. The Code also proscribes releasing false or misleading financial information. So do the Securities and Exchange Commission regulations. Conversely, much illegal activity is probably also unethical. But there are exceptions.

For example, a local ordinance might prohibit placing flyers under car windshields in a shopping center. But a well-intentioned communicator wants to draw attention to a special take-back-the-neighborhood rally and the best way to attract attention is through the direct-delivery flyer. The communicator risks running afoul of the law for a higher good and so has no ethical problem with it.

Similarly, civil rights marches and sit-ins witness people breaking laws for higher reasons, according to them. The civil rights marches of the 60s and anti-abortion sit-ins of the '80s and '90s are examples. Modern day "ethical lawbreakers" include Gavin Newsom, mayor of San Francisco. In 2004, he violated California law by issuing licenses to and marrying about 4,000 homosexual couples. In August of that same year, the California Supreme Court voided the same-sex marriages sanctioned in San Francisco and ruled unanimously that the mayor overstepped his authority by issuing licenses to gay and lesbian couples.

But the mayor said he was responding to a higher call he recognized in the U.S. Constitution. The mayor felt justified breaking the law because he saw the law as unethical.

But what should a PR counselor for a city like San Francisco do if the mayor asks the counselor to publicize the issuance of gay and lesbian licenses, take pictures of the weddings, and issue news releases? Later in this chapter, you'll learn that a counselor in this position can't defend his actions by saying he was "told to do it."

PR practitioners who willingly participate in these illegal activities accept the legal risks. But they have no moral compunction about their behavior.

In 1998, Dr. Jack Kevorkian administered lethal drugs to a terminally ill and suffering patient, contrary to Michigan law. He wanted to be arrested and tried so he could make a test case for physician-assisted suicide and demonstrate the need for a euthanasia law. In his mind, his illegal act was ethical.

**But even legal acts can be unethical.** For example, a federal environmental law might allow only a certain amount of toxic chemical to be released into local streams from a manufacturing process. But everyone, including the manufacturer and government officials, knows the law is outdated and the allowable amount should be much less. The manufacturer refuses to voluntarily reduce the amount of toxic chemical and company PR people are involved in making the argument that the company is "doing nothing wrong" [illegal]. Here, the act might be entirely legal, but appear unethical to many, including the community, the government, and possibly the PR people themselves. For a full discussion on how PR practitioners can resolve this and other ethical dilemmas, see the chapter on ethics.

So, when PR people consider certain courses of action, they should consider both the legal and ethical nature of their activity.

## Reduce exposure

PR people must vigilantly reduce their exposure to lawsuits, so that if they are sued, they have a better chance to win. To do that, practitioners should know how the law affects them, whether they work in a PR agency, are in-house employees or sole practitioners. It doesn't matter if PR counselors practice in profit or nonprofit environments. All are subject to the law.

PR and the law is a broad topic because PR law involves not only everyday business law but also an overlay of First Amendment concerns.

To keep current with laws and legal decisions affecting practitioners, students should consult the body of knowledge from PRSA. In addition, many PR agencies and corporations publish pamphlets on various legal topics.

Also, PR periodicals are a good source of information about PR law. PRSA's publications, *The Strategist* and *Tactics,* publish articles about various legal topics.

Jerry Klein offers a word of caution about practicing PR and staying legal. He advises that if practitioners have legal problems, they shouldn't become do-it-yourself lawyers. He suggests practitioners know the general picture from books, pamphlets and articles. These sources can help identify potential legal problems. But once counselors have identified the problem, **they should consult their organization's solicitor or personal lawyer for guidance.**

Every legal problem is unique. Problems might appear to be similar to published cases, but specific circumstances could influence what can or should be done. Talk to a lawyer before acting. Even if your lawyer merely confirms a contemplated action, you'll be on firmer, more comfortable ground.

## First Amendment

The First Amendment to the *United States Constitution* protects most of what PR people can say, even on behalf of commercial clients. It also protects PR counselors' right to access information. The court explicitly upheld that right in the *Virginia Pharmacy* case.

One example of that right in action is the **Freedom of Information Act (FOIA),** which gives practitioners the right to look at material in the federal government's files. The act says any citizen has the right to see any record the government has, unless it's covered by one of several exceptions.

Now, the FOIA does exempt trade secrets and confidential business information the government has collected. But the definition of what constitutes a trade secret or what's really confidential is generally limited.

The implication for PR professionals is that counselors might be able to get a lot of information about competitors from the government. The flip side, of course, is that competitors could do the same. Freedom of Information is a two-edged sword, but in some cases, it may be the ideal research activity.

To learn more about using the Freedom of Information Act, consult a federal government booklet titled, *Citizen's Guide on Using the Freedom of Information Act and Privacy Act of 1974 to Request Government Records: First Report, June 23, 2003*

*(GPO Stock 052-071-01407-1; available from the U.S. Government Printing Office for $7.00 — http://bookstore .gpo.gov).*

## Broadcast law

Another area where both the right to speak and the right to hear are implicated is broadcasting, particularly with the *Fairness Doctrine*, the *Personal Attack Rule*, and the *Equal Time Rule*.

The **Fairness Doctrine** once required broadcast licensees to provide coverage of controversial issues of interest in the community and to provide a reasonable opportunity for the presentation of contrasting views. The doctrine came under attack for a number of years. And in 1987, the Federal Communication Commission (FCC) formally abolished it, calling it an infringement on the First Amendment rights of broadcasters.

That doesn't mean broadcasters don't have to be fair anymore. But it does mean that broadcasters now have a lot more leeway in what they put on and keep off the air without the FCC threatening loss of their licenses.

It also means that the PR practitioners have lost some leverage. Under the old Fairness Doctrine, broadcasters were required to provide balance on controversial issues.

Often that meant an opportunity for a company or client to get some airtime. Now, broadcasters no longer need to make those opportunities available. Although many of them do and will continue to, the Fairness Doctrine no longer requires it.

A corollary of the Fairness Doctrine was the **Personal Attack Rule**. The rule said that when an attack was made over the airways on the honesty, character or integrity of an individual or group during a broadcast about a controversial issue of public importance, the broadcaster had to notify the attacked party and offer a reasonable opportunity to respond.

> *Abolition of the Fairness Doctrine led to the rise of talk radio.*

Originally, the rule applied to any personal attack, but later it was narrowed to attacks that related only to issues of public concern. Over the years, the rule was read more and more narrowly. **Now both the Fairness Doctrine and the Personal Attack rule are gone**. That doesn't mean broadcasters can attack people with impunity. Victims of personal attacks on radio and TV will still have remedy under libel and slander laws.

One rule the FCC did not repeal was the **Equal Time Rule**. The Commission couldn't repeal the rule because it's a section of the U.S. Communication Act — a federal law, not a regulation like the other two — and has been expressly upheld by the Supreme Court. Because the law is an act of Congress, only Congress can control its destiny. The Equal Time Rule says that if a broadcaster allows a political candidate to use the airwaves, it must offer other candidates equal time. Equal time is more like "similar opportunity" rather than a specific number of minutes or time of day. For example, the six o'clock news would have to devote equal time to news coverage of other candidates. Bona fide news and interview shows are exempt from the rule.

**The Equal Time Rule is still alive and well**, and is interpreted quite literally. A 1980s Florida case involved a local TV news anchorman who was running for political office. The court ruled that he was covered by the Equal Time rule even though his newscasts were not political broadcasts. That means the mere act of being on the air, while a candidate, constitutes an unfair advantage over other candidates. He had to decide either to give up his newscasting or to stop campaigning. Similarly when Patrick Buchanan ran for president in 1992, 1996 and 2000, he had to quit hosting the CNN Crossfire Show or his opponents could have complained to CNN that his appearances, without similar access for them, violated the Equal Time Rule. The Equal Time Rule was also the reason viewers didn't see any Ronald Reagan movies on television while he was campaigning for president.

### Fairness Doctrine

Broadcast
FCC rule
Controversial issue
Opportunity for opposing viewpoints
Repealed by FCC in 1987

### Personal Attack Rule

Broadcast
FCC rule
Individual's character or integrity attacked
Could be a controversial issue
Reasonable opportunity to respond
Repealed by FCC

### Equal Time Rule

Broadcast
Communication Act
Equal time for political opponents
Still in effect

## Confidentiality

A Boston advertising agency once pitched for Microsoft business, by claiming it had just hired two people from the ad agency that handled a Microsoft competitor's software. The agency allegedly wanted to use knowledge of its competitor's plans as an advantage to woo Microsoft's business. But business confidentiality agreements required the new agency employees not to offer proprietary information, and the agency hiring them not to seek it. Had the advertising agency actually offered the information to Microsoft, it would have constituted yet a third legal and also unethical violation.

Revealing a client's or employer's confidential information not only violates the PRSA code but it can also subject a practitioner to liability for damages. In most states, it doesn't make any difference whether or not an employee signed a confidentiality agreement. The owner of the information can still have a claim to the privacy of its corporate information.

And it also doesn't matter that the confidential information doesn't rise to the level of a trade secret. But if it does, liability will be even greater.

## Trade secrets

A trade secret is confidential business information, unknown to the rest of the industry, requiring time, effort and money to develop, and giving the person having it a competitive advantage.

PR practitioners often come into contact with trade secrets and other confidential information. They owe companies or clients a duty to safeguard that information, and make certain it doesn't leak to unauthorized people. In fact, some clients ask their PR agencies to sign confidentiality agreements before they'll hire them. Some companies and agencies do the same when they hire individual employees.

You should be careful about what you sign and should not make unrealistic promises. Some companies are overzealous about confidentiality, and will try to get PR people to pledge never to reveal anything they're ever told, whether it's confidential or not.

Jerry Klein believes that position is extreme and suggests that most companies will be satisfied with a simple confidentiality clause like this one:

*"I understand that certain information which you may divulge to me may be confidential or proprietary in nature. I agree not to disclose such information to others, except as may be approved by you for purposes of your communication program."*

Can PR practitioners be required to disclose confidential information in a legal proceeding? Doctors, lawyers and clergy enjoy what's called "privilege." It means they cannot be forced to reveal confidences. **PR people do not have a similar privilege**.

What happens if a PR counselor works for a company that is named in a lawsuit? The counselor can be subpoenaed and forced to disclose anything the company revealed to the counselor. And because the PR counselor lacks legal privilege, there's not much the counselor can do but comply with the legal request.

*Note*: It doesn't matter if the counselor works full-time for the party or is hired as an outside counselor. Neither has legal privilege.

Conversations and correspondence that occurred before litigation started usually can't be protected. Klein suggests a way that counselors can protect themselves, to some degree, after a lawsuit has been filed. Counselors should make certain that the company lawyer is involved in any conversations the PR counselor has with the company about the subject of the litigation. In this way, the conversations are protected by attorney-client privilege. The conversations are considered work product of the legal team.

In the case of outside PR counsel, the company should hire the lawyer and the lawyer should hire the PR counsel as a litigation support consultant. That way, information the outside PR counsel acquires is protected by the lawyer's privilege against disclosing the work product.

## Privacy

The major difference between confidentiality and privacy is that the duty to maintain confidentiality generally arises out of a relationship among people sharing confidential information, such as employer and employee. Invasion of the right of privacy can involve anyone, even people unknown to the parties.

Four major types of invasion of privacy can subject counselors to lawsuits and potential liability.

• The first is ***intrusion into solitude***. That can include things like going into someone's home uninvited, or eavesdropping on a telephone call, or otherwise prying into someone's private affairs.

• The second is ***false light*** and involves portraying someone negatively. A classic example is using a picture of someone to illustrate a story that talks about wrongdoing. Juxtaposing the picture with the story can imply that the person in the picture is one of the wrongdoers. Assuming, of course, that the person is not a wrongdoer, the action would place that person in a false light (negative).

It's also possible to place someone in *positive false light*. For example, if a PR director mistakenly announces to all employees in the company newsletter that a new employee has a college degree and won numerous awards, the employee could suffer serious embarrassment when it's learned the information is incorrect.

• The third is ***public disclosure of private information***, which is self-explanatory.

• Finally, ***appropriation of one's name or likeness*** is the most common, and the one that's most likely to affect PR practitioners. The typical example is using someone's picture without permission. To avoid that problem, always use a **photo consent release** (*Figure 12.1*).

(Sample Photographic Release)

I _____ hereby grant to the AlphaBetaGamma Organization the right to use my photograph and/or visage reproduction in any matter — either for internal communication purposes or external marketing purposes.

Further, I waive all right to any compensation that might be due to me or my heirs that might accrue from use of the photograph or photographs.

I grant this permission in perpetuity.

Name (print)_____

Signature (sign) _____

Date _____

Option: Name and signature of responsible party, guardian, parent or power of attorney.

_____
Name and signature

_____
Address

_____
Contact information (phone/fax/e-mail

_____
Name of organization representation          Date

**Figure 12.1**

For a good discussion of privacy in general look at the September 1987 issue of *PR Journal*.

PR practitioners must consider monitoring electronic communication. Two types are generally troublesome — telephone and e-mail. The simple act of listening in on someone's phone conversation can be an invasion of privacy. It can also be a criminal offense.

Can PR people tape a telephone conversation? Federal law says someone can tape the conversation if one party to the conversation consents. If you're one of the parties to the conversation, you can tape it assuming it's not going to be broadcast. For broadcast, both parties must consent. The FCC requires a beeper on any line that's being recorded. But counselors must check individual state law. If a state says it's illegal, it will supersede a general federal law. Over a dozen states have laws more restrictive than federal law; they require two-party consent.

*Example*: Linda Tripp was indicted by the State of Maryland for recording her phone conversations with Monica Lewinsky, about her relationship with President William Clinton. Maryland requires two-party consent.

Klein suggests that the safest course is to **get the consent of everyone involved** and get that consent on tape.

In their book, *The Law of Public Communication*, authors Kent Middleton and Bill Chamberlain contend that surreptitious recordings may not be an intrusion in business settings, where expectations of privacy are lower, particularly if no deceit is used to gain entry.[1] Often, many organizations will play a recorded message during consumer business calls warning that the conversation could be recorded for quality control.

**E-mail presents a different problem**. It's recognized that employers have the right to monitor all employee e-mail. Management should alert employees to its right. The right comes from the notion that if organizations provide time, location or equipment for employee e-mail communication of company business, then the organization owns the communication. It's also presumed by the company that employees will not use company time, location or equipment for personal use. There's abundant case law defending company rights in this area.

*Note*: In this chapter, we're discussing the legal aspects of e-mail. Employees have sued their companies on the grounds that invading their e-mail amounted to an illegal invasion of their privacy. Employees generally lose

> **Organizations have legal access rights to all employee e-mail.**

these legal challenges. For an ethical discussion of this issue, see the chapter on ethics.

## Financial public relations

To gain a brief overview of many complex laws, practitioners should consider at least three important aspects of financial communications — requirement of *timely disclosure*, *prohibition of insider trading*, and *quiet registration* rules.

## Timely disclosure

Timely disclosure is a general requirement for companies that sell securities. Material information, information that a reasonable investor might consider important in making an investment decision, must be disclosed according to three characteristics. It must be *public*. It must be *timely*. It must be *universal*, i.e., done in a manner that all investors, analysts, and others with an interest **have equal access to the information**.

Timely sometimes means immediate, although not always. In general, the more important the information, the faster it should be disclosed. The Securities and Exchange Commission (SEC) requires quarterly reports of financial information from corporations.

One of the most controversial issues of timely disclosure deals with the disclosure of material information related to merger talks. Many courts have ruled that companies do not have to disclose merger talks until the price and terms are agreed upon. On the other hand, the SEC took the position that some merger talks were material even before agreement was reached.

The Supreme Court decided the issue and agreed with the SEC. Companies must decide on a case-by-case basis whether the existence of the merger talks themselves is material enough to require disclosure even before the parties formally agree.

The court suggested that "no comment" was still a permissible response to questions about merger talks. Klein thinks the decision also suggests there may be times, in particular circumstances, when "no comment" may be misleading, and therefore illegal. He believes that an outright denial that merger talks are going on, when in fact they are, would be false and misleading and violate securities laws.

These areas will be unclear because so much depends upon the particular circumstances involved. But some rules involve specific, routine matters in financial communications that advise about exactly what should be disclosed and when.

1. Middleton, K.R., & Chamberlain, B.F., (1998). *The Law of Public Communication*. White Plains, NY: Longman, Inc., p. 194.

In the *McDonnell Douglass* case, the Tenth Circuit Court ruled that the *business judgment rule* permits a corporation to wait to release information until it is "available and ripe for publication."

In the famous *Texas Gulf Sulphur* case, the appeals court said it was not improper for the company to withhold promising drilling results until it acquired adjacent drilling property.

**Insider Trading**

Figure 12.2

## Insider trading

One of the purposes of the timely disclosure rules is to prevent insider trading. Insider trading occurs when an "insider," someone with access to material information about a company the rest of the investing public doesn't have, uses the information to advantageously trade the stock of the company.

For purposes of those rules, **anyone who comes into contact with insider material, privy information before the information becomes public, is considered an insider**. That includes not only corporate officers, employees, and inside PR people, but also outside consultants, like lawyers, accountants, investment bankers and public relations consultants. If a maintenance worker discovers material information on a scrap of paper in a company wastebasket before the information has been disclosed, the maintenance worker possesses insider information and thus, is an "insider."

To clarify things, the Supreme Court has ruled that an insider is anyone who has privy information that would affect the value of the company's publicly traded stock. In addition, PR counselors are supposed to be prepared to dis-

close on whose behalf they are communicating information.

Can insiders legally pass insider information to outsiders? The case of investment broker Ivan Boesky reveals that an investment firm accounts manager becomes an insider when he passes on insider information to his investment clients.

Insider trading can plague company executives and their outside PR counsel. The most celebrated example involved a national PRSA president. He allegedly placed a buy order for his own client's stock after he learned in private conversations that another company was about to take over his client's company, but before the news became public. He quickly withdrew the buy order after a phone call from a broker alerted his client that its own PR counsel had just placed a significant buy order. Even though he did not actually buy his client's stock, the mere phone call to his broker was enough to force him to resign his PRSA presidency.

Another key requirement is that financial information, when it is released, not be false or misleading. And it has to be sufficiently complete so it doesn't mislead. That imposes on the PR practitioner an obligation to make a reasonable investigation to determine the truth of the information being disseminated.

## Quiet registration period

The quiet registration period is the time after a new securities offering has been filed with the SEC but before the registration becomes effective. During that period, a company can't use any written communication, except a preliminary prospectus, to sell company securities. PR counselors must be careful to avoid generating publicity that would be out of the ordinary routine, or that could bring unusual attention to the company. Something like that could be viewed as part of the selling effort, and would violate the law.

When the search engine Google™ offered its shares publicly for the first time, it had to be careful about generating so much publicity that the government might view the publicity as an effort to boost the value of the stock.

Rules governing financial communications are extremely detailed, even down to the point size of type required for annual financial reporting. Those engaged in financial PR must become familiar with those rules to avoid legal trouble. A useful guide is a government publication titled, *A plain English handbook: How to create clear SEC disclosure documents.*[2]

2. A plain English handbook: How to create clear SEC disclosure documents. (1998). United States. SE 1.36:EN 3. [0904-A]. http://purl.access.gpo.gov/GPO/LPS2340

## Conduit theory

Professional communicators once tried to protect themselves from legal liability through a practice they referred to as the "conduit" excuse. Those communicators, including PR practitioners, asserted that for all communication activities, they are merely communication *conduits* for decisions, messages and activities made by management, above their level. They contend they are not liable or responsible for misinformation or the effects of misinformation they transmit, but do not create. **But courts have found that professional communicators do not enjoy such immunity**. This strategy is akin to the famous Nuremberg defense, in which Hitler's top brass tried to avoid responsibility for war crimes by asserting that they were "just carrying out orders."

Two famous cases in particular clearly specify that organizational communicators do not have immunity from the effects of communication acts in which they participate.

### *Texas Gulf Sulphur v. SEC*

The Securities and Exchange Commission set forth conditions for "insider issues" public relations activity:

- Number and kind of channels PR practitioners use to satisfy the SEC requirement of "full and timely disclosure" of material information
- Truthfulness of the information
- Responsibility and liability of PR counselors for accuracy and truthfulness of information.

In this case, officers of the company were guilty of fraud for misleading the public while insiders bought stock. News releases played down the importance of mineral samples taken at a Canadian mine. After the samples were found, and before the press releases were issued, corporate insiders bought their own stock. The courts found that the communicators who put out the releases were liable for the information and its effects. (See, *The Law of Public Communication, op. cit. page 312 ff for a discussion of this case.*)

### *Pig 'n Whistle v. SEC*

A Chicago-based restaurant, headed by Paul Pickle, was negotiating for the purchase of the Mary Ann Baking Company and the Holiday Lodge near Lake Tahoe. Outside PR consultants, the Financial Relations Board, issued news releases, which the SEC charged contained fraudulent, untrue and misleading information about the stock transactions and registration. The two releases contributed to an increase in the value of the stock. The PR consultants were found not to have immunity, even though, as they contended, they merely communicated information given to them by management.

### Ask before acting

The conduit theory does not hold. *Communicators are liable for information they communicate,* whether or not they know of its truth, falsity or existence. These cases should inspire PR counselors to query their employers about accuracy and truthfulness of information they're expected to communicate. Beyond the SEC, this lack of immunity would have repercussions in other sensitive areas such as invasion of privacy, liable, copyright, etc.

Does this mean counselors have to cross-examine their company or client's management about the information they're given to put out? Probably. Prudent personal protection would involve counselors exercising due diligence, even with their employers, about information they're asked to disseminate. Don't blindly send out anything without investigating its accuracy.

If you have put out information that is no longer true, you could be obliged to correct or update the information. If *someone else* puts out information about your client or company that's not true, you normally have no obligation to correct that information. But if the person who put it out has some special relationship with your company or client, you might need to correct it. And, of course, your correction would have to be complete and accurate.

Professor Scott Cutlip's article in the January 1985 issue of *PR Journal* contains important information about financial communication and a model hold-harmless clause. *Every PR firm or PR counselor should have such a clause in every contract with every client,* whether or not it's related to financial communication. Counselors often must rely on what their clients tell them. A hold-harmless clause will at least offer some legal protection in the event that something a client approved and asked counselors to put out might come back to haunt them.

*Example*: Outside public relations consultants estimate (and include in their bids) printing costs for publications for clients. Should the estimate prove too low because of a change in the economy or cost of raw materials, the counselors are held harmless for the increased costs and are not liable to pay the difference.

## Responsibility for professional conduct

While this chapter deals mainly with PR counselors' liability under the law, the conduit discussion raises the question of responsibility for one's actions. If counselors could be ethically responsible for the effects of their work, they might be legally liable as well. Some arguments in court go to the intention or motive behind the act, as well as to physical participation in it.

David Martinson (*PR Quarterly*, Winter 1994-95) argues that true professionalism requires that PR counselors take responsibility for their actions, even if they're forced to do something they don't entirely agree with.

Martinson argues that there's a difference between formally participating in an action and materially participating in it. Formal participation involves intending the effects of an activity. Material participation involves merely cooperating in the act without intending the effects.

For example, a public relations counselor for a government agency is part of a decision-making team trying to decide on a policy of economic sanctions on another country. Political counselors at the table argue national security issues. Military counselors argue capability. The public relations counselor argues public opinion.

Public opinion issues might involve constituents disagreeing with sanctioning another country, even for national security reasons. They might believe that hardship to innocent citizens does not outweigh the security issue. The public relations counselor would be required to help explain and defend the policy to the media, the public and other nations.

What happens if the public relations counselor doesn't personally agree with the policy? Does the counselor resign, or merely act as a material conduit for the information? Can the counselor participate in the communication without intending all the effects or being responsible for them?

Martinson raises the classic principle of *double effect* to help counselors resolve the ethical dilemma. Counselors may participate in questionable activities without ethically accepting the consequences if they conclude:

- The act is good in itself or is at least indifferent
- The good effect does not directly result from the bad act
- The good effect is as important as the bad effect
- The bad effect is not intended, only allowed

How does the principle of double effect apply to the activity of the PR counselor developing and communicating a government's policy of economic sanctions to another country?

The counselor can argue that the sanctions are not negative acts in themselves. But that might be hard to believe even for the counselor. As long as food, clothing and medicine are allowed through the embargo, the counselor can claim the act is harsh, but not evil.

The good effect of bringing the other country around to behave in a way the international community wants does not come directly from the innocent deaths of citizens. Perhaps. But suppose the other country's leader claims that the deaths were the deciding factor?

The counselor can argue that bringing the country in line with the international community is as important or more important than the lives of the innocents. The rogue country, unless brought into line, could launch lethal weapons causing the deaths of hundreds of thousands of innocent victims.

> *Copyright protects only the expression of ideas, not the ideas themselves.*

The counselor could also legitimately argue that the deaths of innocent citizens aren't intended.

Two counselors might answer these questions differently and come to different conclusions. Are they responsible for the effects of their public relations activity? They probably are, depending on their answers.

Could this thinking be applied to legal cases? Lawyers need to answer this question in the light of allowable defenses in court.

Public relations practitioners must use rational arguments to justify their behavior. They should also use an ethical decision-making model such as the one outlined in the chapter on ethics.

## Copyright

Copyright affects things PR people deal with all the time — writings, pictures, graphics materials and audio-visual works.

The copyright law provides a way to protect works from being used by other people without the author's consent. It also means the PR practitioner can't use other people's work without their consent.

Copyright protects the particular tangible expression of an idea. In other words, it protects the order in which the words are written. Copyright does not protect the ideas those words express. And copyright law says that copyright owners have exclusive right for a limited time to use their works. For works created after January 1, 1978, they are protected for the life of the author plus 70 years.

The Copyright Act states that "anyone who violates any of the exclusive rights of the copyright owner ... is an infringer of the copyright."

For PR people, copyright issues center on two issues — using other people's copyrighted material, and preventing others from using their material.

## Using material of others

With respect to using the works of other people, a lot of unauthorized copying goes on. But the law allows an exception — the *fair use exception*. Section 107 of the Copyright Act outlines the conditions under which copyrighted material can be fairly used by others without violating the law. The "fair use" conditions are four:

- First, the **purpose and the character of the use**, whether for commercial or noncommercial use. Educational uses are favored over commercial uses. Also, a judgment about whether the use adds value to the work affects fair use.

- Second, **nature of the copyrighted work**. Courts have more broadly protected fictional works than factual works.

- Third, how **much of the work** is copied. Obviously, copying a whole document is less protected than copying a page or two.

- Fourth, **effect of the use upon the potential market** for the value of the copyrighted work. If the use decreases the value of the work to the author (e.g., distributing it widely for "free"), it probably isn't fair use.

Nicole B. Casarez, writing in the *Public Relations Quarterly*, (Fall 1997) uses a lawsuit and decision against the Texaco Corporation to exemplify how photocopying copyrighted materials, even for internal research uses, might violate the law.

In that case, some scientific and technical journal publishers filed a class action copyright infringement lawsuit against Texaco. The suit claimed that Texaco employees made unauthorized photocopies of journal articles to use in their research.

Here's the situation: the plaintiffs were members of the Copyright Clearance Center, a center established in 1978 to sell photocopy licenses to businesses, schools, libraries and copy shops.

Texaco agreed that only *one* company researcher would photocopy materials. The researcher made single copies of eight complete articles from eight issues of a particular journal and *placed them in his research files*, making them available to everyone in the company. But the company had purchased only *three* subscriptions to the journal.

The court disagreed with Texaco and said Texaco violated three of the four factors justifying fair use of copyrighted material.

- Factor one: *character of the use*. Texaco violated the law because it intended to use the research to increase its profitability; hence it was a commercial use.

- Factor two: *nature of the work*. Texaco did not violate the law because the work was factual rather than fictional.

- Factor three: *amount copied*. Texaco violated the law because the researcher copied entire articles from each issue.

- Factor four: *effect of the copying*. Texaco violated the law because it deprived the publishers of additional revenue from the additional licenses necessary to copy all the articles, thereby harming their entire licensing system. (The court did not believe, however, that the journal itself lost any significant revenue.)

Rather than appeal the decision to the Supreme Court, Texaco settled out of court, paying a seven-figure settlement and retroactive licensing fee to the Clearance Center.

*Extensively copying of protected materials, even for internal use, could violate copyright law.*

Casarez makes six points PR practitioners should consider:

1. **Observe organizational photocopying practices**. Monitor practices and look out for articles being copied for *everyone* in the company but supported by only *one* subscription.

2. **Work with legal counsel to draft a policy** governing the use of copyrighted material. Make certain the policy contains ongoing advisory practices because the copyright law and the fair use provision are complex.

3. **Never copy newsletters cover-to-cover without permission**. Courts have carved out special protection for small newsletters. It would be better to buy additional subscriptions or an upgraded subscription that permits photocopying.

4. **Purchase additional article reprints or additional subscriptions**. Company research should identify the most popular newsletters and journals being copied.

5. **Obtain permission for copying articles for the company's clipping file**. Publications might give you permission for free or for a modest fee.

6. **Purchase a photocopying license** from the Copyright Clearance Center (CCC) to photocopy copyrighted material registered with the CCC.

The company currently (2005) manages rights relating to over 1.75 million works and represents more than 9,600 publishers and hundreds of thousands of authors and other creators, directly or through their representatives. CCC-licensed customers in the U.S. number over 10,000 corporations and subsidiaries (including 92 of the Fortune

100 companies), as well as thousands of government agencies, law firms, document suppliers, libraries, academic institutions, copy shops and bookstores.[3]

Casarez adds a note about the Texaco ruling. The court made a point that its ruling concerned copies made by a for-profit institution, not by individuals. She wonders if a sole PR practitioner, or a not-for-profit organization, has more leeway with the fair use clause.

PR practitioners should minimize exposure to lawsuits by monitoring their copying practices, purchasing additional subscriptions, and consulting their organizational solicitors about policy and practice.

*Note*: you can copy copyrighted material without permission. But keep in mind that you can be sued, and if you do, you have the burden to establish the fair use defense. You're better off making the extra effort to get permission first.

## Protecting material

The second PR application of copyright law involves proposals, logos, themes, jingles, ads, reports, PR campaign plans, research and other public relations work products.

PR firms (and consultants) are concerned about protecting proposals they write and use to pitch accounts to prospective clients. If a clients doesn't eventually hire a PR firm, the firm doesn't want the lost client to use its ideas independently or give them to another firm.

To solve such a potential problem, put a copyright notice on all your proposals. The copyright notice consists of the letter c inside a circle ©, or the word *copyright*, or the abbreviation *Copr.*, together with the year and the name of the copyright owner.

*Examples*:

- Copyright 2005 by Donald Bagin and Anthony Fulginiti
- © 2005 by Donald Bagin and Anthony Fulginiti
- Copyright © 2005 by Donald Bagin and Anthony Fulginiti

Putting a copyright notice on proposals is a good idea, because it deters some from unauthorized use. *But a copyright protects only the particular expression of ideas, not the underlying ideas themselves.* So even if you copyright your proposal, the copyright probably won't help if a would-be client steals your ideas but not the words you used to express them.

3. The Copyright Clearance Center offers multiple licenses. A company can first copy documents, then seek a license for the material copied. Or the company can pay an up-front annual fee. (For information about photocopy licenses, contact the CCC at 222 Rosewood Drive, Danvers, MA 01923; phone 978-750-8400; fax 978-646-8600; online at http://www.copyright.com)

## Protection Marks

### copyright
Protects works for life of the author plus 70 years
*example:*
© 2005 by Kendall/Hunt

### trademark
Exclusive use of word, name or symbol
*example:*
XEROX™

### registered trademark
Trademark registered with the U.S. Office of Patents and Trademarks
*example:*
iTunes®

### service mark
Protects services rather than products
*example:* **merry** ^SM **maids**

**Figure 12.3**

Counselors do have some protection (*Figure 12.3*). They can sue for misappropriation of intellectual property or ideas. The basis for the suit would be an expressed or implied contract between the parties. The basis could also be the claim that by unjustly appropriating an idea, others have (illegally) enriched themselves.

Counselors should consider putting a notice on their proposals warning against misappropriation.

*Example*:

"The strategic ideas expressed in this proposal are the property of *Public Relations Counselors*. Any independent use of these ideas, apart from a contractual relationship with *Public Relations Counselors*, constitutes a violation of property rights. In that event, *Public Relations Counselors* will be entitled to compensation for any gain, monetary or otherwise, enjoyed by the offending party."

Even that kind of notice presents two drawbacks. First, counselors can't prevent others from using ideas that don't have some degree of novelty and originality. If a proposal suggests that the client should develop a media kit and schedule media tours, counselors can't stop the client from hiring another agency to develop a media kit and begin media tours for them.

The second problem is more a client relations problem than a legal problem. Some prospective clients are turned off by that kind of notice. Counselors will have to decide to accept that risk in return for protection. It may come down to the nature of the relationship with the client (past, present and future) and how much protection counselors really need.

### PR/Legal advice

- Soften a client's negative feeling about your proprietary warning. State that if the client employs you, ideas in the proposal and others you develop under contract with the client become the client's property. Stress that you feel so strongly about intellectual property rights, that you will use those ideas with other clients only with their permission and never with their competitors. Your firm ethic on the issue can work to the advantage of both you and your prospective client.

- It helps if the client understands that by engaging you, the client prevents a competitor from accessing your ideas.

## Ownership

Who owns copyrights? Generally, the creator of the work owns the copyright. But in the case of a so-called "work for hire," the employer owns the copyright. It's clear that if an employee in a traditional work setting creates the work as part of the job, the employer owns the copyright.

One of the most famous cases is the development of the silicon chip. The inventor employee got the idea during lunch one day while at work. Years later, he received a $50,000 reward from the company for his "good idea."

Had he developed the idea on his own, in his garage, and researched it privately, he would have owned rights to the patent.

> **Never put anything you want to protect into public domain without a copyright symbol.**

But what about freelancers? What if a company or an agency hires a freelancer to write something for a client? Who owns the copyright? The copyright statute seems to say that the freelancer owns it, and some courts are deciding that way. Other courts are still following a line of decisions that were decided under the old law, which put a lot of weight on who effectively controlled the work.

To avoid later legal woes, counselors and freelancers should develop specific agreements with clients and companies on who owns copyrights.

Another point about copyrights. If counselors want to sue for copyright infringement, they must have first registered the copyright. Registering is not difficult. It requires filling out a form and sending a nominal fee and some samples of the copyrighted work. You can get forms from the Copyright Office in Washington or online at www.gov.org.

## Trademark

Trademark is a different type of protection for intellectual property. Trademark gives exclusive use of a particular word, name or symbol to identify a company's products. In other words, trademarks are brand names. Kleenex™, Xerox™, Coca-Cola™ and NutraSweet™ are all examples of trademarks.

*Example*: Canon™ developed a radio ad in which a "voice" advised a consumer looking for a good photocopier that Canon copies were just as good as, " … well you know the name." The friendly voice refrained from using the word "Xerox" to mean "copies." When the consumer later used the word Xerox inadvertently, the voice quickly interrupted and said the consumer couldn't do that because "Xerox" is a trade name, and it was illegal to use it without Xerox's permission. It was a clever ad, using a legal principle, to contrast Canon and Xerox technologies and reposition Canon in the mind of the consumer.

In everyday reality, companies that market common products like Kleenex™, Q-Tips™, Band-Aids™ and Xerox™ probably benignly accept consumers bending the law and calling common products by their trademark names.

In discussing companies and their trademarks, this text uses the trademark symbol (™) even though the text is an academic exposition of the concept of trademark. They're protected symbols.

A company that sells services rather than products can have something similar to a trademark — a service mark. *Example*: (ᔆᴹ)

To own a trademark or service mark a company needs only to create it and use it in commerce in a way that indicates it's a trademark. The company could do that by using capital letters or a special typeface or something else to distinguish it from the surrounding text.

*Example*: Merry Maidsᔆᴹ cleaning service.

Counselors should use the trademark symbol, a superscript ™, or the service mark symbol, a superscript ᔆᴹ. If a company registers its trademark with the U.S. Office of Patents and Trademarks, it can use the registration symbol, which is the letter R in a circle, ®, similar to the copyright symbol. *Example*: iTunes® (Apple Corporation).

Trademarks are protected under common law, so counselors don't have to register them. However, registration carries with it a presumption of ownership.

So a registered trademark has a stronger position in the case of a conflict with someone else's unregistered trademark.

PR practitioners must be careful not to infringe on other companies' trademarks in their writings. For example, if a counselor issues a news release about a community event at which refreshments will be served, they don't want to say "Coke will be served," because Coke is a registered trademark of the Coca-Cola™ Company.

They should write instead that "refreshments" will be served, or "cola" will be served. But suppose the special event is a fund raiser in conjunction with the Coca-Cola company. In that case, Coca-Cola will be served and the copy can make a point of saying that. But the copywriter should also use the trademark symbol.

Companies that own popular trademarks, like Coke and Xerox, spend a lot of time and money trying to make sure people don't use their trademarks improperly. Companies can lose their trademarks if they allow them to become *generic terms.*

The best known example is aspirin. Aspirin used to be a trademark. But people started using the word aspirin to describe any brand of acetylsalicylic acid. So eventually, the company lost the trademark, Aspirin.

## Regulation of speech

The *Federal Trade Commission Act* prohibits false or misleading advertising. Most states also have similar laws. In the context of these types of laws, advertising could include what most people would call public relations. Counselors should be careful about the truthfulness of their communication to avoid a suit and a defense based on an exception — that it was an exercise of free speech.

The *Federal Regulation of Lobbying Act* requires anyone representing the interests of others in Washington to register and file income and expense reports. More than half the states have similar laws. By interpretation of the Supreme Court, the federal act generally does not apply unless someone is communicating directly with members of Congress. But if counselors do some work intended to affect the outcome of legislation, they should discuss with their lawyers what they can and cannot do.

The *Federal Foreign Agents Act* says that anyone in the United States who acts as PR counsel for a foreign government, or almost anyone else outside the United States, must register with the attorney general. There's a significant exception. If PR counsel works exclusively on matters involving private, nonpolitical trade or commerce,

> **The essence of libel is the falsity of a statement, not its nastiness.**

registration is not required. But any time counselors work for clients outside the United States, they should carefully review the situation to see if they should register.

Sometimes counselors can't say what they want to say because it might violate another law. An example is antitrust law activity. Certain types of communication are considered anti-competitive, and thus a violation of antitrust laws. In general, counselors should not discuss anything related to price, cost, production, contract bidding, marketing plans, or anything else related to suppliers or customers with anyone who works for a competitor, especially if the counselors work for a large company in a major industry.

Counselors must avoid the appearance they are colluding with competitors to fix market prices or to cooperatively control the flow of goods, information or services.

## Libel and slander

Defamation is "de-faming" another, taking away "fame" or reputation. Two types merit consideration, libel and slander. Historically, libel refers to written defamation, while slander is spoken defamation. Courts have different rules for handling each type. As a practical matter today however, there is little difference. (*See Figure 12.4, Libel Chart, on the next page.*)

In general, defamation is any *untrue* statement that tends to injure another person's reputation. The person injured by the defamation can sue and must **prove** four things:

1. **Statement was false.**

2. **Statement is capable of injuring reputation.**
   In many cases, the complaining party must prove that reputation was **actually** damaged.

3. **Third party heard or read the statement** — published

4. **Statement identifies the injured party,** either directly or by implication. (Defamatory comments about groups more than 100 are probably safe; 100 or fewer need qualify comment; 15 or fewer are probably libelous.)

Someone sued for defaming another can offer a number of defenses. The major defense is that the statement was true or at least substantially true. *Truth is an absolute defense in a libel or slander suit.* That means you can say practically anything about someone, if it's true. The one caution — truth can sometimes invade privacy.

# Is it libel?

| Statement is probably not libelous | CHARACTERISTIC | Statement is probably libelous |
|---|---|---|
| Defendant can prove statement is factually true, or retracts or apologizes | **False** | Defendant cannot prove statement is a true fact |
| Actual harm cannot be proved | **Damaging** | Negatively affects someone's position, property, character, or exposes one to hate, contempt, ridicule or financial loss |
| Person cannot be identified | **Specific** | Names or implies a specific person, not just a member of a group |
| No third party learns of the statement | **Published** | Communicated to a third party by appearing in print or other durable form (film, audio, etc.) — slander if spoken |
| Protected speech — reviews, editorial, cartoon, comedy show, political punditry, journalist reporting news, officially quoted minutes or proceedings | **Privileged** | Comment is not protected by any recognized, legal privileges |
| Comment on facts fairly stated | **Fair comment** | Comment was maliciously made |
| *NY Times v. Sullivan* requires actual malice if the figure is elected official or inserts oneself into a public dispute | **Public figure** | Made with reckless disregard for discovering truth, or knowledge of actual falsity (actual malice) |

**Figure 12.4**

Sued parties can also claim a legally recognized privilege. For example, fair, accurate and opinionated reporting on governmental proceedings is generally privileged, as is some business communication between private parties. Reporters and columnists can say for example, that a particular governmental action is bad for the country and that politicians who legislated it were motivated by greed, politics and selfishness. Or someone can call agents of the government "dumb."

Defendants can claim their statements were expressions of opinion rather than facts. Unfortunately, it's often difficult to predict what the court will consider opinion as opposed to fact.

The First Amendment specially affects defamation actions. In particular, a plaintiff, who is a public official or a so-called public figure, has a heavier burden of proof that defamation took place than does a private individual.

In *New York Times v. Sullivan*,[4] the Supreme Court defined the defense standard for public figures. If the plaintiff is a public figure, the plaintiff must prove that the defendant made the statement **with knowledge of its falsehood or with reckless disregard for truth** (actual malice). That means the statement was made without applying the kind of judgment an ordinary person would apply or was made with actual malice toward the plaintiff.

In some cases, it can make a difference if the topic of discussion is a matter of significant public interest such as public controversy on landfills, abortion or gun control. Public figures are elected officials or others who willingly insert themselves into public controversies on a matter of significant public interest.

4. For an excellent discussion of this case, refer to *The Law of Public Communication*, op cit, pp. 100-108.

For example, if you write a letter to the editor on behalf of your company complaining about something or stating your company's position on an issue, you willingly insert yourself into a public controversy. If someone responds to your letter with another letter-to-the-editor, claiming that you're an idiot, you now have the same heavier burden of proof a public figure has. If you sue, you'll have to prove actual malice. By the way, the other letter writer also becomes a public figure.

## Herbert v. Lando

A significant case decided by the Supreme Court on the question of libel was *Herbert v. Lando*. Colonel Herbert was allegedly involved in a massacre in Vietnam involving noncombatants. Lando was producer of CBS's *60 Minutes*.

During an interview for *60 Minutes*, Herbert told what he thought was his version of the story and believed it would be shown as such. But when the show aired, Herbert was upset because much of what he thought exonerated him was "left on the cutting room floor" by the editor. Herbert sued *60 Minutes* and producer Lando for defamation of character because of the way the story was edited.

The case went to trial. Herbert's lawyers called Mike Wallace and producer Lando of *60 Minutes* to testify. Because Herbert was a public figure, he had to prove negligence or actual malice by Lando, or Wallace, or both. Herbert's lawyers asked Wallace and Lando if they exercised "malice" against Herbert when they edited the tape. Both Wallace and Lando refused to answer the question on the grounds that it violated their freedom of the press privilege. Herbert didn't see it that way. He believed that journalists' rights end where his begin. He appealed to the Supreme Court to compel the witnesses, Lando and Wallace, to answer the questions.

The Supreme Court ruled in *Herbert v. Lando* that Herbert's **right as a plaintiff to prove that he was libeled superseded the journalists' right to free expression**. Lando and Wallace never testified because *60 Minutes* chose to settle the suit with Herbert out of court.

But much to the chagrin of journalists, the ruling laid down an important legal principle. When it comes to a public figure plaintiff's right to force testimony if a defendant is guilty of actual malice, the defendant will lose, **even if the defendant is a journalist**. This case involved a clash of rights. The courts decided that public good is better served when individual rights, rather than free press rights in liable cases, are protected.

Remember also that defamation can ensnare storytellers and rumor mongers. Anyone who repeats a defamatory statement can also be held liable. That means if a PR practitioner's organization libels someone in a news release, issued by the practitioner, the practitioner can be held liable. And so can the newspaper that prints the news release. And logically, so can the person who delivers the paper. But that never happens.

> **Everyone involved in making or disseminating a libelous statement can be sued.**

That's a good enough reason to be careful about what goes into news releases. Recall that the conduit theory does not protect PR people. They are not immune from libel lawsuits even if they "merely communicate" libelous statements.

## Contracts

Like any other business, public relations is a business based on contracts — contracts between agencies and clients, between employers and employees, between purchasers and vendors. Too often, however, PR people rely on oral instead of written contracts. That can get them into a lot of trouble if a dispute arises over who promised to do what, or what the terms and conditions of the agreement were.

As that great legal mind, Casey Stengel, once said, "Verbal contracts aren't worth the paper they're printed on." There are two "Caseyisms" here. Verbal contracts aren't written, they're spoken. And because they're spoken, they're oral, not verbal. Even written contracts are verbal.

That's not to say that oral contracts aren't binding or enforceable — they are. The problem comes in proving the oral agreement. If all the counselor has is a recollection of what was said, versus the recollection of the client, employee or vendor, it's more difficult to resolve disagreements. When the agreement is printed, proving a case is easier and usually avoids disagreements.

## Professional services contracts

### *PR / Legal advice*

When you're drafting a client or agency agreement, be specific about fees and other charges, and terms of payment. Klein recommends that agencies include a paragraph specifying that the client must pay interest if payments are late, and that the client pays interest, costs and attorney fees if the matter goes to court. Clients should not have a problem with that kind of provision, because it takes effect only if they violate their agreement by paying late or not paying at all. That's important, because if a firm does sue, it can't get its attorney's fees reimbursed unless it has that provision in the contract.

## Employee contracts

### PR / Legal advice

Make an employment agreement just as specific as an agency-client agreement. It ought to specify the job, how much it pays, how long it will last, and obligations of respective parties. Also it's important to include a confidentiality clause to bind employees to keep confidential matters confidential.

## Noncompete clauses

### PR / Legal advice

Many employers ask for a noncompete clause (called a *restrictive covenant*), to prevent employees from working for a competitor soon after leaving the company.

These clauses are legal, but they must be reasonable. Companies can't expect PR employees to stop practicing public relations entirely just because they no longer work for the company. Courts won't enforce unreasonable noncompete clauses. Klein suggests that for restrictive covenants to be enforceable, they must be:

- Reasonable in both duration and geographic scope
- Supported by some consideration
- Reasonably necessary to protect the employer's interest
- Able to show irreparable harm if employees violate it

The question of "consideration" is often the sticking point. If the noncompete clause is part of the original employment agreement, it's probably legal. But if the employer comes around after employment begins and gives the employee a noncompete agreement to sign, that, by itself, is generally not enforceable. To be legal, it would need to be accompanied by some sort of return consideration such as promotion or other value the employer gives in return for the promise not to compete.

## Personal references

### PR / Legal advice

What should counselors be concerned about when they're asked for references by employees leaving their employment? *You have no obligation to give references.* In fact, case law from human resources literature reports that some workers sued their former employers claiming that something written or said over the phone by their former employer to a prospective employer caused the employee not to get the job.

If you're going to write or speak a recommendation, make certain it's true and complete enough so it's not misleading. Remember, even true but negative recom-

mendations can form the basis for a lawsuit by casting former employees in *false negative light* and hurting their chances for employment.

## Outsourcing

### PR / Legal advice

Some companies hire part-time or full-time workers called freelancers so employers don't have to calculate and deduct payroll taxes. These workers could be considered legal employees. This arrangement is bad for both employers and employees. It's bad for employers because they could later be liable for the taxes they didn't withhold. It's bad for employees because they're not covered for things like social security, unemployment or disability benefits.

The IRS feuds with companies about classifying certain employees as legally independent contractors (including PR counselors) and thus not full-time employees. The debate focuses on *who controls the time and schedule of the outsourced freelancer*. It also involves the issue of an office — whether the outside consultant is provided an office on site and because of that, comes more closely under the employer's control. Another issue involves the amount of time an outside consultant spends with the same client each week.

Generally, if an independent PR contractor takes orders on when to work, where to work, and how to work, the IRS considers that person an employee. If the individual is simply required to produce an end result, without regard to when, where and how it's done, the PR counselor is more likely to be considered an independent contractor.

Before you make a contract either as an employer or an employee, consult your solicitor for current IRS guidelines on who can be considered a part-time or full-time employee.

## PR counselors and legal counselors

Some would say that, by nature, public relations counselors tend to be open and favor full communication to influence public opinion. They would also say that lawyers, by profession, have a different agenda. They serve their clients' interests by keeping them out of trouble. They tend to be more closed and protective in their approach to communication.

Jeffrey Corbin, writing in *Public Relations Quarterly*, focuses on the problem of how each party plays a role in corporate decision making. Corbin, an attorney and PR counselor, believes there should be a synergistic relationship between the two.

The role of each is to help top management make decisions. Each must give management the best advice based on their areas of concern — legal safety from the legal counselor, positive public opinion from the public relations counselor. Neither party should second guess or cave in to the other. Top management needs both viewpoints.

Consider the similarities and differences between the two practices. Also, consider how public relations counselors can gain respect for their advice and role in the same way lawyers do.

- **Both have roles at the management table**. Or they should. Public relations counselors must demand a place at the decision-making table, not wait until legal counsel has constructed messages solely around legal points, leaving little room for public opinion and image positions.

- **Both use principles**. Lawyers have the body of law to dramatically capture top management's attention because there's a penalty compulsion to pay attention to lawyers. Public relations counselors have their public opinion formation models and persuasion theories. And they also have their ethical principles.

- **Both use cases**. But public relations counselors don't seem to use cases sufficiently enough in their practice. They should practice more like lawyers — cite cases to support their counsel. Top decision makers should respond positively to this tactic because they're used to getting cases and scenarios from their lawyers.

- **Both deal with managing forces inside and outside the organization**. Lawyers and PR counselors alike practice preventive action, damage control and crisis management.

- **Both deal with communication**. Even though lawyers might not consider the communication aspects of their counsel, they need PR people to communicate legal positions both internally and externally, positions that might be hard to understand and accept. PR people are expert at presenting and persuasively explaining difficult positions.

Public relations counselors can serve as bridges between the harsh realities of the law and the opinion of internal and external publics.

## Licensing and accreditation

Today, no license for public relations counselors exists. Neither does it exist for journalists, advertisers or dozens of other job titles, in which communication is the main activity.

Can counselors be licensed to practice public relations? The prevailing feeling among most professionals and societies they belong to is no, they cannot. Here's the reasoning.

To create a "license to communicate" counselors would have to submit to a test or fulfillment of criteria by government, probably state government. Some professionals do submit to government criteria, such as medical doctors, accountants, lawyers, and others.

If public relations practitioners were to submit to government control of their speech rights, they would compromise the free speech guarantee of the First Amendment to the Constitution.

> *Public relations is not an activity in a vacuum or without sponsorship.*

Like journalists, public relations counselors conduct their profession by the free exchange of ideas, in print, in specialized electronic communication such as the Internet and e-mail, on radio and television, and in face-to-face special events. Like journalists, who also cannot be controlled or licensed by the government, **public relations counselors cannot be prohibited or allowed to speak by government fiat or license**.

Like journalists, advertisers, marketers, artists and other "speech and idea" people, public relations counselors must be free in a free society to inform and persuade without government intervention. The right is so strongly protected that these communication professionals can even speak against the government, without restraint.

Why would licensing be important? Without a license to guide it, the public does not know if the communicator it deals with is knowledgeable, experienced, professional, ethical and accountable to an outside authority. **The absence of a license creates uncertainty in the marketplace**. An analogy would be an unlicensed surgeon about to operate, or an unlicensed lawyer advising on the law.

But uncertainty may be the price the public must pay. Without a licensing system to guide it, the public will always wonder if communicators it hires will have the characteristics a license presumes. In the place of certainty about these characteristics, consumers instead get "freely speaking communicators," who are unfettered by government control.

Is there an alternative to licensing that would provide some comfort to the public that communicators have the characteristics licensing would provide? In his last years, Edward Bernays pushed hard for a compromise. He believed that professional societies, such as the Public Relations Society of America, could establish criteria for professional preparation and conduct.

# Profession vs. Professionalism

Distinguish between "profession" and "professionalism." Profession might include the notion of licensing, but professionalism would not.

"Profession" implies scrutiny by peers or the state. Professionalism implies professional behavior only.

The definition of these two words involves criteria lists. Depending upon who structures the criteria lists and how, different answers could emerge.

Is public relations a profession? The answer to the question depends on the definition of a profession. Many authors and thinkers have tackled this issue and tried to define the elements of a profession. Here is a criterion list of most often agreed-to characteristics of a profession:

- **Discrete body of knowledge**
  The body of knowledge must be organized in a way that can be identified and studied as such.

- **Body of knowledge taught in a university**
  Every true profession is recognized as a bona fide college subject or major.

- **Professional association of members**
  Knowledge and skill transfer happens when professionals associate. Professionals working in isolation would not learn and develop as easily. Association also allows for testing and validating of ideas and procedures.

- **Interaction between academics and practitioners of the profession**
  Academics research issues and provide innovation for practitioner use. Practitioners provide current problems and issues for research and skills upgrading. The important part of this association is identification, development and protection of the body of knowledge of the profession.

- **Practices in the public interest or for the public good**
  The practice must be essentially for the well being of clients, e.g., health from medicine, protection from law; safety from electricians, etc.)

- **Independent control of the profession**
  The profession controls its own body of knowledge, professional development of its members, and professional practice. Its own practice causes its own growth. It can introduce new concepts and skills independent of outside influence.

- **Exhibits a code of ethical conduct**
  Without a code of conduct, an important guarantee to consumers would be missing, trust that the PR

practitioner is working in the best interest of the consumer and society.

- **Licensed by the government**
  Licensing does not take away from the profession the ability to define and develop itself. Licensing endorses what the profession first says is necessary about itself. Licensing is an artifact. It has no independent validity apart from its association with a test created in conjunction with the profession and administered by a government entity.

Is public relations a profession? Using the criteria list in this sidebar, public relations can claim:

- Public relations has a *discrete body of knowledge*. Although eclectic, coming from psychology, the social sciences, journalism, graphic arts, research, and others, it has organized itself into an articulated body of knowledge.

- Public relations is *taught in colleges and universities* across the country, both as major courses of study and as single offerings, even in graduate schools. Many textbooks, such as this one, explain its various disciplines and skills.

- Public relations counselors can *associate with colleagues* in local, state, national and even international societies and associations. Small local associations provide important networking and skill building; larger associations and societies provide national accreditation programs, contests, awards and research grant possibilities.

- Public relations *academics and practitioners interact* through the networking services of their associations. The Internet has networked them in more productive ways. PR practitioners can download and use research everyday without other time-consuming research modes. And few personal libraries can compete with the Internet for pure search capability.

- Public relations works for the *public interest* and public good. As a service "profession," PR provides communication to all segments of society to reach their goals through exposition and ideas and persuasive techniques. *Example*: Public relations for an organ donation organization is communication for public good.

- Public relations *controls its own growth* and development as a communication discipline. No outside forces determine what public relations is or does.

*continued on opposite page*

## Profession vs. Professionalism (continued)

- Public relations societies and associations have *ethical codes*. Indeed, codes exist only in those societies. But the codes are specific and cover specific circumstances and conditions. One might argue that practitioners who do not belong to local or national associations would have to demonstrate to clients and bosses that they subscribe to ethical principles similar to those outlined in the codes of national associations.

- Public relations **does not offer licensing** to its members. Although it offers professional accreditation, it does not

have the ability, with government sanctions, to rid itself of charlatans in the profession. For that reason, many think *public relations is not a profession*. But that is not to say that its members do not act professionally.

The same can be said for journalism, advertising, marketing, promotion, publicity, special events, research and other disciplines. They are not professions under the criteria outlined in the sidebar. They cannot control membership in their own practice through licensing without violating the First Amendment.

The state would agree to the criteria. Professional societies would then conduct a "scrutiny," perhaps a test, to willing members. If members passed the scrutiny, they would be awarded a "license" by the government, which would be merely an "endorsement" of the professional society's scrutiny. That has not happened. It might never happen, because the mere act of government having any role in the process troubles many.

It's possible that Bernays's idea can go as far as societies establishing criteria and testing for them, without government intervention. If all communication societies could agree on a common set of criteria, including demonstrated knowledge, practical experience and allegiance to ethical codes, they might be able to supervise the scrutiny themselves and grant "certificates" that would be *surrogates to licensing*.

Many communication societies already conduct professional accreditation programs. The Public Relations Society of America offers the "APR" (Accredited in Public Relations); and for senior members with significant contribution to the professional practice, the additional "Fellow" designation. Other societies with accreditation programs include the International Association of Business Communicators (IABC), the National School Public Relations Association (NSPRA), and others.

These societies offer a variety of ascertainments. They include written tests, in-person interview examinations, portfolios, experience resumes, qualifying years of professional practice and similar evidence activities. The tests usually focus on knowledge of the professional practice, strategic thinking and ethical problem solving. Most of them include the application of knowledge to practical challenges.

Consumers who see accreditation initials after a practitioner's name have some assurance that the

practitioner submitted to the scrutiny of peers and received their endorsement.

## Litigation public relations

Can public relations practitioners become involved in setting forth the best possible case for clients accused of misdeeds by public prosecutors or the media? Does that practice undermine the integrity of the legal process? Do PR advocacy litigants engage in activity that tends to corrupt the channels of integrity of the media or government?

What is *litigation public relations*? Sometimes the media attack organizations as, what James Lukaszewski calls, "the other prosecutors." When the media attack, organizations necessarily defend themselves. This defense can occur any time prior to formal legal action. Among his ten principles of litigation public relations, Dirk Gibson ("Litigation Public Relations: Fundamental Assumptions" *PRQ* Spring 1998) asserts that **litigation public relations is inevitable because the court of public opinion starts long before any trial or other legal activity**.

The media love a public fight, fair or unfair. Adversaries, to a larger extent, and the media, to a lesser extent, will do what they can to give life to a story. Some might even advance rumor and speculation about organizational wrongdoing to prompt a response. If organizations don't respond, they surrender the field to opponents who then control public opinion. And public opinion could guide judicial proceedings, especially selection of potential jurors.

For example, when President William Clinton was charged with perjury and obstruction of justice and suffered two articles of impeachment from the House of Representatives, the major argument made by virtually all his defenders was that the majority of the public didn't want impeachment. His defenders spent less time disputing the facts of the case and more time suggesting that public opinion should determine the outcome of the judicial process. Because of such reliance on public opinion, PR practitioners wonder if they should participate in a public debate on behalf of either side in a legal process to influence public opinion.

The Constitutional question of a conflict between free speech and the right of defendants to a fair trial raises concerns about the propriety of PR activity prior to a trial or other judicial proceeding. But some argue that the conflict should not inhibit the accused from exercising their right to speak in their defense prior to trial. Certainly, pretrial publicity could influence a jury. But such influence might be necessary to counter the effort of an opponent trying to do the same thing. No law prohibits defendants, their legal counsel, or their public relations counsel from speaking publicly on issues prior to trial. In some cases, a judge might "muzzle" everyone involved in a case. But that's a legal, not an ethical issue. And in that case, if the defendant is muzzled, so also by inclusion are legal and PR counsel.

## Plaintiffs and defendants are PR clients

Consider the role of public relations in pretrial publicity in the light of the client/counsel relationship. Public relations practitioners should ethically and legally be able to do what a defendant can do. Public relations is not an activity in a vacuum or without sponsorship. If the accused can speak prior to a trial, so can the accused's public relations counsel. If a jury is prejudiced by the communication activity, then free speech prejudiced it. Some counselors believe that the higher offense would be "chilled speech," especially if the other side is courting public opinion. Fairness and justice would require a like response.

## British rule

Gibson cites the nanny trial of a young British woman accused of responsibility for the death of a child under her care. In that case, the British woman was going on trial in America. The British public was offended over the amount of pretrial publicity. In Britain, news organizations are prohibited from covering cases on trial until a verdict is in. The British focused on the issue — the danger of publicity activity aimed at influencing public opinion prior to a trial. But in America, such activity is allowed.

## Media role in litigation PR

Finally, the media play a major role in litigation public relations. Influence is a circle. Litigants feed their side of the story to the media. The media repeat messages they think are important to the public or they think the public should think important. Their coverage influences the

public (including potential jurors) and litigants. Media coverage spawns more messages from litigants. And a news cycle develops.

Is litigation public relations harmful? It probably depends on which social rule you believe is more important — justice or free speech. And the ethics of each act will follow the decision you make. Like other issues in society, a gain in one area could mean a loss in another ■

# Tips

1. If you intend to use photographs of employees, always have them sign releases giving you permission to use the photographs for either internal publicity or external marketing.

2. Never accept information about a company or its stock from someone inside the company who claims the information isn't known by many people. If you acquire such information, don't use it.

3. As best you can, find out if the information you're being asked to communicate is accurate. Don't accept information on blind faith, not even from your boss.

4. Don't use other people's material, copy, art work, music, strategies or other products without permission.

5. Acquire a multiple copy license from the publisher of an article you like before you photocopy the article for all your employees.

6. If in doubt, remember you have more leeway to copy factual material than fictional material.

7. Don't tape a phone conversation with another without first checking with the laws of the state where the taping will take place. (One- or two-party consent might be necessary)

8. If you need to say something negative about someone, make certain it's the truth.

9. Don't practice public relations as though you have a privilege that can't be penetrated in court. You don't.

10. If you're ever in doubt about the legality of an action, consult your organization's attorney or your personal attorney. Protect yourself by acquiring professional liability insurance.

**Questions for classroom discussion**

1. If a television talk show makes negative comments about a candidate for political office, does the show have to offer equal time to the candidate to rebut the comments? Would it make any difference if the show made no comment, but invited one of the candidate's opponents to be a frequent guest host during the campaign period?

2. If an employee comes up with a good idea on the job and the company makes a lot of money from it, can the employee use the same idea with a second company after leaving the first company? Suppose the employee changed the idea and claimed it was a new idea? What legal issues are involved?

3. In a doctor's office one day, you read an important article on time management. You decide to give it to all 50 of your employees. How much of the article can you copy without infringing on the copyright? Does it make any difference that you do not have a personal or company subscription? What can you do?

4. How "defaming" must a libelous statement be for a plaintiff to win a suit in court? What guidelines did the legal decision, *New York Times v. Sullivan* lay out for defendant public figures to win a libel lawsuit?

5. With respect to stock, company mergers and other financial issues, what constitutes an "insider" according to the Securities and Exchange Commission?

**Internet assignment**

Search the Internet for an example of a company facing a legal challenge. Observe the response of the company. Evaluate it for the force of its legal backdrop. An example would be the Microsoft Corporation challenge to America On Line (AOL) for restricting AOL members from using Netscape for mail and other communication.

*Ask these questions about what you find:*

- Is the challenge legal or ethical?

- Does it seem the organization consulted legal counsel for its response?

- Are any individuals mentioned in the challenge?

- What are the specific legal allegations — privacy, copyright, free trade and contracts?

- Did the company say anything it should not have in its response?

- What would you do differently?

Name_____Date_____

## PR law case: Anatomy or ADnatomy?

You're having lunch with a medical student friend who shows you some original anatomical drawings of human hands and arms. You friend says she's not going to do anything with them. But you're working on the public relations part of a computer company account. You think the drawings would be perfect for ads showing how friendly the company's computers are to the user's body. You use the drawings. Your friend is upset when she sees her work in full-page newspaper ads.

1. Can the student sue you for a portion of the profits your company will make and win in court?

_____

_____

_____

2. What could the student have done to protect her work?

_____

_____

_____

3. What should you have done before using her work?

_____

_____

_____

4. What will you tell your boss?

_____

_____

_____

*See other side*

Name _____ Date _____

Following the appearance of the ads, your former friend speaks negatively about you to anyone who will listen, and even takes out an ad saying her ideas were stolen and calls you a thief. Answer these additional questions:

5. Can you sue her for libel and slander?

_____

_____

_____

6. Will you have the additional burden of a public figure to prosecute a suit against her?

_____

_____

_____

7. What will you have to prove if you file suit?

_____

_____

_____

8. Finally, add to the story additional legal complications you predict could occur in such a scenario.

_____

_____

_____

# Chapter 13

# Staying Ethical in the Workplace

## PRaxiom
*The ought of ethics, not the naught of law, makes us ponder what we have wrought.*

## What this chapter covers

In this chapter, you'll learn how public relations counselors form moral principles and fashion ethical behavior. An easy-to-use model will help you make ethical decisions about problematic issues. You'll also learn why public relations counselors and their organizations clash over ethical differences and how they can resolve their dilemmas.

You'll learn about propaganda, spinning and why some people believe that their organization or cause allows for any behavior, simply because their motives are noble. You'll reason with others about principles, philosophers, values and loyalties and the part they play in everyday decisions about what *ought* to be done.

The ought of ethics, not the naught of law, makes us ponder what we have wrought.

## Ethics on the job

When public relations people go to work, they frequently apply a personal ethical tone to many decisions. For example:

- Can public relations practitioners, on their own and for a "higher purpose," tell the media something about their organizations that their organizations don't want known?

- Can they work for an organization with a different customer philosophy from their own?

- Can they ever lie, even for a good cause?

How can PR people rightly decide? The key to ethical practice lies in what is "right" and "proper." Law deals with what counselors must do in the workplace. Ethics deals with what counselors (and their organizations) ought to do. This chapter is about ethical behavior.

## Morals and ethics

First, distinguish between a *moral* and an *ethic*.

- **A moral is an inward guiding principle residing within the person. It comes from upbringing, religion, education, genetic makeup, life experiences and other influences.**

- **An ethic is an outward behavior resulting from a moral principle.**

For example, the inward moral principle that lying to the media is wrong, prevents PR people from lying to them. Their outward behavior is honesty or truth telling.

But if you believed your company had done something questionable, (according to your moral principle), then you might tell the media about it because you think the public should know (ethical behavior). You might lose your job, but your ethic would correspond to your moral.

But suppose your company management follows a different moral. It doesn't think it did anything questionable. Its moral about the issue differs from yours. Your company might also believe the public doesn't have a right to know everything it does. And, say its executives, the company's experience shows that the media are biased and will distort whatever the company tells them. So, its inward guiding principle (moral) tells the company to shield certain information from the media (ethic). Who's more moral and consequently more ethical, you or your company?

To understand these two important concepts another way, recall the difference between an attitude and a behavior in the chapter on public opinion.

- **An attitude is an inward predisposition to act.**
- **An opinion is the outward expression of that disposition.**

So we can say:

*A moral is to an ethic as an attitude is to an opinion.*

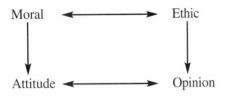

## Workplace ethics

Why is this difference important in the workplace?

Organization specialists distinguish between moral decision making and ethical decision-making. In moral decision making, you establish principles to guide your actions. In ethical decision-making, you apply the principles to specific issues and produce behaviors you can live with.

Because on-the-job ethics depends on moral principles, the workplace debate is about the principles workers and their organizations follow. If the principles conflict, behavior differs, and people become uncomfortable.

So the real debate about differing ethical behavior should focus on moral decision-making. That's the philosophical battleground. That's where managers would disagree.

## Boardwalk boards – environment versus utility

Here's an example. A seaside community doesn't know what to do about an environmental action group's unrest over its decision to harvest hardwood from South American rain forests to redeck its "boardwalk" or promenade

**Poor boardwalk wood**

**Figure 13.1**

(*Figures 13.1 and 13.2*). The seaside community has the **right** to buy and install the wood. There's nothing illegal about it. The wood is the best economical product, lasting 50 years as opposed to more conventional pine lasting about 10 years. The hardwood is more durable, more beautiful, more economical, and easier to walk and ride bikes on.

But the environmental group believes that using "rain forest" wood would deplete the environment of certain species of plants and animals, some providing important drugs for society. They don't believe that durability, beauty or economy outweigh the harmful ecological effects.

The town government doesn't agree with the environmental group about its research on the environment, citing that the wood is replaceable and the "threatened" species suffer no great harm. But this problem isn't going to be fought in the lab. It will be a public opinion street fight.

It's a huge public relations challenge. What's the community to do?

Moral decision making for the community involves a

**New boardwalk hardwood**

**Figure 13.2**

process of deciding the principles or values that will guide its decision. Then it must match its principles against those of the ecology group.

- If they don't align, the community must argue its case in the public relations arena.
- If it succeeds, it can buy the wood without controversy.
- If it fails, it can still buy the wood. But it probably will begin a long public relations battle for what's "right" and "best" for the community and world.
- If community leaders can't gain sufficient access to their publics, it will fail. And if a key channel, the media, side with the environmental group, the community could fail to get its message across.
- If the community doesn't attract important allies to its side, it will fail.
- If the community can't rally public opinion to its side, it will fail.

Sometimes, when organizations want ethical behavior they can live with, they change their morals to fit the situation.

In the case, if the community feels it would lose more in public opinion than it would gain in economic benefit, it might adjust its values. It will raise public image value above economics and aesthetics values and not buy the wood.

The public relations practitioner will counsel management about the feasibility of doing that. But the community won't re-rank its morals until it assesses that its residents are aligned with the ecology group. Why re-rank morals if you don't have to?

Conversely, organizations sometimes stick to their original morals ranking, no matter the cost. Then, the public relations practitioner will communicate the organization's position and try to win the contest for public opinion. *The most challenging public relations activity is getting important publics to adopt your moral stance.*

This example is based on a real case. The community eventually did *not* purchase the hardwood from South America, even though the company it had purchased from in the past replanted the trees. So the community sided with the environmental group, re-ranked its morals and changed its proposed behavior.

**Outcome**: Today, the cheaper, less environmentally sensitive pine wood the community installed is badly deteriorated, buckled and splintered. Conversely, hardwood sections of the boardwalk the community had installed *10 years earlier,* sits side-by-side with the newer deteriorated wood in stark contrast and needing replacement — again.

## Developing workplace morals

To develop a set of morals, ask yourself:

- Do I believe in absolute right and wrong?
- Do I believe in relative rightness and wrongness about things? Do some situations allow me to relax my ideas about what's right and wrong?
- Does my company believe that some things are right no matter the cost? And some things are wrong because of cost?
- Do I believe there is a line I cannot cross, even for my organization?
- Are my internal guiding principles based on things outside me, such as family expectations, church rules, or civil laws? Or are my principles personal conclusions I've reached from inside forces such as religious beliefs, understanding how society works, or political philosophy?
- Do I believe I should never harm anyone? Or is it all right to allow some harm for a greater good?
- If my employer asks me to do something contrary to my internal principles, should I do it because I'm an employee, or should I put my personal principles above the organization's?
- Is my moral attitude ever more important than the company's moral attitude? When?
- Is it ever justifiable to disobey a law for a greater public or company good?
- As an employee, should I be expected to make personal moral accommodations on the job?
- Is there a limit on what my employer can ask me to do?
- Is there a difference between actively deceiving someone and merely doing something that causes others to deceive themselves?
- Is it all right to have a "divided self" on the job, with each "self" comfortably deciding things differently?
- Is it possible to have one set of personal ethics and a different set of business ethics?

## Forming moral principles

Answers to these questions can help you form moral principles to make ethical decisions. On the job, you'll encounter moral principles of co-workers, bosses, customers, suppliers, the media and many others. Then, you'll retain your principles no matter what; or you'll accommodate your principles at the request of others; or you'll abandon your principles and adopt others' principles.

All ethical business decisions have a moral basis. *There's no such thing as a valueless decision.*

## Ethical clashes

The clash of moral principles causes all ethical conflict on the job. A universal set of morals would make all ethical decisions easy. Some academic researchers, such as Professor Dean Kruckberg, advocate a universal ethics code for all public relations practitioners. If it ever exists, it would assume that all practitioners would also adopt the same moral principles behind the code. If practitioners followed the code but didn't internally adopt the principles, they would suffer cognitive dissonance — the clash between their moral principles and the national ethical code they're obliged to follow.

## Ethical codes

The biggest problem with ethical codes is the moral assumptions behind them. For example, why would your morals be better than your boss's? Why would your co-workers' morals be better than yours? Why would your customers' morals be better than everyone else's?

On the job, the "rightness" or "wrongness" of decisions doesn't depend on whether they come from "good" or "bad" morals. Rather, right or wrong decisions depend on whether others see your actions as acceptable or unacceptable. You don't usually have to justify your actions to yourself, only to others.

Notice how ethical debates eventually focus, not on the activity, but on the *inspiring principle.*

In the case about which wood the seaside community should buy, the debate transcends wood buying and centers on dueling responsibilities (values) — to the local community or to the world community. Both values are "good." Ethical decisions emanating from each would also be "good." To buy the wood is "good" (it's based on a community value). Not to buy the wood is also "good" (it's based on a world community value). If you role-played this debate in class, you should hear arguments about values, not actions.

## Making moral decisions

As a public relations practitioner, how would you make moral decisions on the job? Here are some helpful techniques:

- **Check if your morals would do harm**. Ask yourself: Will my morals allow an action that will do more harm to others than good to my organization?

- **Check if you share your morals with others in your organization.** The axiom, "right is right if no one is right and wrong is wrong if everyone is wrong," is absolutist and might even be heroic against opposition. But it can insulate you from others who are more "flexible.".

- **Check if your morals have a universal ring to them.** Honesty, truth telling and justice are generally universally positive values. Stealing, lying and cheating are generally universal negative values.

- **Check if you can comfortably rearrange your morals "ranking."** You might have to accommodate an action you think you should or shouldn't do. Example: You might value honesty. But in advertising a product, you have no responsibility to name every person who used your product but didn't like it. Sometimes, you'll re-rank values because one value will become more important than another.

- **Check if you can justify your morals.** Chris MacDonald, from the Centre for Applied Ethics at the University of British Columbia in Vancouver, says that your morals should have better reasons for them than reasons against them. And others should agree that your reasons are reasonable. This type of justification differs from simply "rationalizing" your moral reasons. It reminds one of the childhood taunt, "I have a right to my opinion." Yes, you do. But do you have any evidence for it?

- **Check that your morals support society's important systems.** Society gets along only because of certain expectations, such as justice, obedience to common laws, civil rights, personal freedom and privacy. You could decide that your morals are more important than one of these values. But you should pick your moral over these values only if a great harm will come if you abandoned your moral.

*Example*: To prevent harassment cases and protect the company from liability, an employer might decide to routinely monitor all e-mail messages. "Personal privacy" drops a rung below "company safety" on the organization's values ladder.

- **Check if your morals maintain loyalty to important relationships.** In public relations, an organization must maintain credibility and reinforce networks among important audiences.

- **Check if your morals come from sound philosophical or theological principles.** For example, Aristotle's principle, "The greatest good for the greatest number," might authorize you to grant a special privilege to one employee but not to another. However, Immanuel Kant's principle, "What's good for one is good for all," might lead you to a different ethical decision. Unions frequently use this Kantian principle and sometimes force companies to use it to indiscriminately protect members' rights.

• **Check if your morals can withstand a "playing out" scenario.** Apply your morals to cases and carry them to logical conclusions to see if you still want to value them as highly.

*Tip*: During a public relations debate, apply your opponent's morals to a real situation. Many times, your opponent's moral will lead to an unacceptable action, forcing your opponent to adjust or abandon the value – in public.

*Example*: If a company is under attack for marketing tobacco products because the products are harmful to health (value), the logical playing out of that value would question why other products that also cause medical harm aren't under attack. Examples: fatty foods, sugar, alcohol, caffeine, processed foods, and others. That could lead to a public admission that indeed, the tobacco industry is being unfairly singled out.

• **Check if your moral principles can withstand scrutiny by challenges and questions from colleagues.** You won't know if your morals are worth keeping until you've shared them with others. As Socrates would have done, discuss your moral positions with others. Recall Socrates's dictum: "The unexamined life isn't worth living."

> *"And if I tell you that it is the greatest good for a human being to have discussions every day about virtue and the other things you hear me talking about, examining myself and others, and that the unexamined life is not livable for a human being, you will be even less persuaded."*

Socrates (469-399 BCE), Greek philosopher. Speech to the court, while on trial on charges of impiety and corruption. Quoted in Plato's *Apology*.

In developing your moral positions, you'll be answering the questions: Who are you? What are you willing to do?

## Applying moral principles on the job

Here are examples of how conflicting moral principles create ethical dilemmas for public relations counselors:

• **Love Canal**. Pesticides poisoned wildlife and industrial waste products and contaminated drinking water. In more severe cases, homeowners evacuated their homes in the Love Canal area, Niagara Falls, New York, in 1978. A community knowingly built homes over the New York toxic waste site. The company was not guilty. It warned the community not to build there. But initially, it took a public relations hit for creating the problem and turning the site over to the community.

Love Canal raised ethical issues about a company's responsibility to be a good corporate community citizen and do no harm to its neighbors' environment. The case demonstrated that even if companies produce harmful materials from production, they can commit to clean the waste and restore the community.

• **Bhopal**. On Dec. 3, 1984, the worst industrial accident in history occurred in Bhopal, India when a toxic gas leak from a Union Carbide insecticide plant killed 4,000 people and seriously injured 30,000 to 40,000. The Indian government sued on behalf of more than 500,000 victims. In 1989, India settled for $470 million in damages and exempted company employees from criminal prosecution. The Indian judiciary rejected that exemption in 1991, and the company's Indian assets were seized (1992) after its officials failed to appear to face charges.

Bhopal forced companies to rethink safety features involved in industrial enterprises. It also alerted company executives that they could be held personally liable for their company's decisions.

• **Exxon Valdez**. Alaska's greatest economic boom occurred after the extensive oil discoveries of 1968. Huge offshore deposits found in 1980 promised future development. But on March 24, 1989, shortly after midnight, an Exxon oil tanker, the Exxon Valdez, bringing oil from Prudhoe Bay, struck Bligh Reef in Prince William Sound and spilled more than 11 million gallons of crude oil causing severe economic and environmental damage.

Public relations practitioners received a field lesson in community and media relations from this ecological catastrophe. The accident demonstrated that a company's responsibility extends to the training and performance of its employees. The expensive cleanup demonstrated how companies should behave when they're responsible for environmental devastation.

### Morals and religion

"Thus while the law permits the Americans to do what they please, religion prevents them from conceiving, and forbids them to commit, what is rash or unjust. But they all agree in respect to the duties which are due from man to man."

*– Alexis de Tocqueville*

Many morals do come from religious codes as de Tocqueville writes. But religion need not be the only infusing motive supporting morals. Notions of right and wrong can derive from the notion of a supreme being, or from the notion of secular fairness among people. While law creates an *order* obligation, morals create a *fairness* obligation. And religion creates a *relationship* obligation among persons, the focus of religious morality.

> *Should employees*
> *be nice to customers*
> *because they deserve courtesy,*
> *or because the company says*
> *the practice will lead*
> *to a better bottom line?*
> *Which motive better ennobles*
> *the company, respects customers,*
> *and motivates employees?*

• **Three Mile Island**. Three Mile Island is the site of a nuclear power plant south of Harrisburg, Pa. On Mar. 28, 1979, the cooling system of the No. 2 nuclear reactor failed. It led to reactor overheating and partial meltdown of its uranium core. The accident produced hydrogen gas and raised fears of an explosion and dispersal of radioactivity. Some radioactive water and gases were released and thousands living near the plant left before the 12-day crisis ended. A federal investigation assigned blame to human, mechanical and design errors. The accident increased public concern over the dangers of nuclear power and slowed construction of other reactors.

This case emphasized that in disasters, ethical behavior means telling the truth to the community and the media. Public relations practitioners and company executives learned hard lessons from accusations that company personnel were not as honest as they should have been about the causes and effects of the disaster.

## Personal ethical dilemmas

Ecological disasters involve serious ethical questions most PR practitioners won't have to face. But they will face other issues that involve them more personally. Here are some examples:

• **Customer service etiquette**. Many companies promote good customer service practices. Do they do it because customers are people who deserve recognition and cultivation? Or do they do it because the service leads to a better bottom line? This ethical question plays out in how front line employees, like retail and customer service associates, deal with customers.

• **Harassment or discrimination: sexual, ethnic or racial.** More than any other behavior, this negative activity comes from deep-seated moral principles. Companies feel obliged to take these cases on because of the moral impressions on important publics.

A recent New Jersey court case found a company guilty of improperly dismissing an employee accused of sexual harassment. The employee won millions of dollars in a settlement. Will the company think twice in the future about dismissing an employee for this cause? PR counselors are drawn into these cases to advise their organizations about ethical behavior and communicate the organization's position.

• **Accepting kickbacks and inducements**. Many companies have written policies about this practice. But an organization's private culture may be the one practiced. If everyone in an industry does it, on both sides, is it ethical? Does society have a right to know about these deals?

• **Blowing the whistle on other employees**. An employee agonizes over telling management something it should know about another employee. The conflict arises between loyalty to a colleague and loyalty to management. The employee solves the loyalty conflict according to the closeness of the relationship, i.e., the "nearer" one is to the object of loyalty (company or employee) the more compelling the reason to be faithful.

• **Taking credit for another's work**. Managers frequently take credit. But it's understood that if the boss looks good, the employee keeps a job. It may be contractually ethical, but humanly unethical.

• **Underevaluating employees**. To dismiss employees or "set employees straight," managers deliberately under-evaluate them. Some managers say the practice is ethically permissible because of "business necessity."

• **Occult compensation**. Some employees secretly compensate themselves. *Examples*: expenses, materials, supplies from work. Some employees make unauthorized telephone calls, use Internet time, take longer lunches and take supplies from the cabinet, etc., because they feel their organizations have not sufficiently rewarded them for their work or their value. Is it occult justice or occult stealing?

## Public disclosure issues

• **Sticking to what's legal**. Legal departments often constrain PR practitioners to communicate "only what the organization is legally doing." If pressed to admit that something might be legal but unethical, they struggle with conflicting responsibilities to their organization and to their constituent publics.

• **Interpreting research data**. Not every research study or research finding need be publicly reported, particularly if the study is private. But is the company obliged to make certain that release of selective information doesn't misrepresent the whole study? Does withholding even private information create a false impression about the company?

## Public interest issues

• **The role of organizations in society.** Society wants businesses and organizations to help solve society's problems. If society perceives that businesses and organizations are acting only for themselves, society loses trust and organizations lose credibility.

Public relations practitioners, who are responsible for organizational credibility, work to make their organization's activities coincide with society's needs. If the activities are "too organizational," do they become unethical? Are organizations unethical if the media say they are?

• **Organizational mission statements and positions.** The beginning of organizational ethical behavior lies in the statements that define the organization. PR practitioners advise about the content of these mission statements, positions and codes of conduct.

It's the job of public relations to remain firm in its belief that organizations work in the public interest and must act socially responsibly when they do.

• **Special interest groups.** The lobbying of special interest groups asks PR people to counsel management to behave in a way acceptable to the group's point of view. Practitioners must help their organizations decide if the groups really represent society's best interest. They must also warn about accommodating the groups just "to get them off the organization's back" or because it's the right thing to do. Accommodating a group, just to relieve public relations pressure, could be unethical because the accommodation bows to the moral principal that public opinion alone is an organization's most valued principle. That impression could conflict with the company's real mission.

## Media relations issues

• **Telling all.** Do the media have the right to know everything a public relations person knows about an organization? PR practitioners balance the rights of their organizations and the rights of the public, with the media asserting they act as advocates for the public.

A PR spokesperson engages in a unique conscience/duty struggle. Only the public relations function in an organization has the responsibility to hold hands with employers and the public simultaneously, with each hand holder demanding complete allegiance.

• **"Spinning" news events.** Public relations practitioners who manage communication for political persons and governmental agencies are frequently asked to "spin" news events and clients' activities to their clients' advantage. If they agree to spin, are PR people compromising any moral principles?

In the national election of 1996, one party resorted to questionable fund raising tactics because "the other side had more money." The side who engaged in the tactics thought it had the "moral right" to raise funds from questionable sources. In fact, "spinners" of the tactics at the time said, "America had to be saved." *(Note: spinning is also done by the media. It's media bias.)*

• **Bartering for favorable coverage.** Whether it's extortion by the media or bribery by the PR practitioner, the practice of bartering advertising or money or privilege for favorable "coverage" by the media is condemned by both media and public relations canons of ethics. A public relations person can't offer advertising, tickets, discounts or amenities for favorable coverage of their organizations. And the media can't ask for them.

It's not the purpose of this book to list all possible circumstances and situations public relations practitioners face. Rather, students should recognize that a well developed moral code, applied to circumstances in a logical, humane way, could answer all questions of ethical behavior, no matter how uncomfortable the answers might be.

## Making ethical decisions

Develop a systematic process to make ethical decisions on the job. To do so, first look at how ethical decision making historically developed. Look also at how the responsibility for applying an ethical tone to decisions is "shared" within an organization.

## Historical development

James Grunig, University of Maryland, traces this development in his book, *Managing Public Relations*.

Prior to the 1940s, public relations communication focused on the language PR practitioners used to describe the issues facing their organizations. It dealt with substance. For example, a company interested in selling cars asked its marketing people to dwell on the car's features, construction and appearance. In that era, what people knew about the product was considered important.

After 1940, public relations practitioners realized that persuasive techniques with car buyers could be as effective as providing information about the cars themselves. The switch to focusing on the audience ushered in the era of persuasive communication or behavioral communication. It also ushered in the possibility of ethical misbehavior by coercing or manipulating people to buy something they really didn't want or didn't need. Nevertheless, the sale was important and the *caveat emptor*, buyer beware, era arrived.

Organizations had a free hand in making the economy grow. Sales, sales promotion, advertising, public relations and other marketing disciplines participated in getting the behavior they wanted by a specific technique — saying what the public needed to hear to get it to behave a certain way.

But since the 1980s, the emphasis in public relations communication shifted to the speaker. Is the speaker reliable? Consumers taught communicators that the way people perceived their organization, its management, its work philosophy, its production techniques, would affect how they felt about the company. So consumer attitudes became important.

Is your information about the car you're selling me truthful? Are you selling me this car because it's the best purchase for me? As you make my car, are you dealing with your employees in a way I approve? These became public relations, not sales questions.

Consider the difference between an organization's former "hard marketing" efforts (knowledge leading to behavior) and its later "soft marketing" efforts (attitudes leading to behavior). Both involve ethics. But how?

## Ethos and pathos (Identity and Image)

Hard marketing persuades audiences by legitimizing the product through advertising, point of purchase displays, demonstrations, product literature, etc. (*Figure 13.3*).

Soft marketing persuades audiences by legitimizing

## Ethos ~ Pathos
### Identity & Image

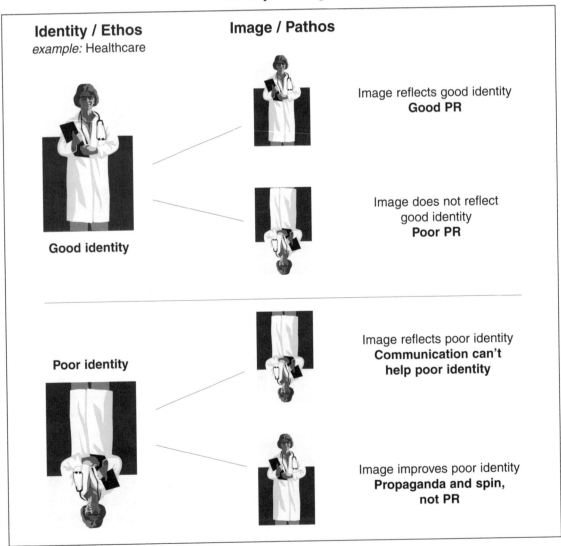

**Identity / Ethos**
*example:* Healthcare

**Good identity**

**Poor identity**

**Image / Pathos**

Image reflects good identity
**Good PR**

Image does not reflect good identity
**Poor PR**

Image reflects poor identity
**Communication can't help poor identity**

Image improves poor identity
**Propaganda and spin, not PR**

**Figure 13.3**

the speaker or seller through public relations.

In terms of ancient and successful Greek rhetoric, total marketing focuses on two consumer issues:

- Ethos: the identity and personality of an organization that eventually gives rise to the image.
- Pathos: the image of an organization in the consumer's mind.

Here's a picture of the selling/buying process:

Ethos (identity) → Pathos (image) → Consumer Decision

Public relations focuses on both the ethos and the pathos.

- First, public relations counsels about what the organization is and does in society (ethos/identity), including the responsiveness of its products and services to society's needs.

- Second, public relations helps communicate the identity to target publics so they're well disposed toward the company and its products and services (pathos/image).

Before the rise of public relations, hard marketing controlled both the identity and the image. But the rise of public relations coincided with organizations learning that consumers wanted more than product information before they would buy a company's products or services. They wanted to know and like the company. They wanted to know the company was on their side. They wanted to know the products and services were made for them.

Hence, public relations counseled management on its identity and position in society and communicated that image to consumers.

Total marketing suddenly involved public relations.

New ethical questions arose. Is the company a good enough company to do business with (socially responsible)? Does it make its products responsibly (employee relations and environmental considerations)? Does the company care about me as a consumer (customer service, product liability)?

*Marketing had acquired a new, necessary partner in public relations to answer the ethical concerns.*

Note that "ethos" and "ethics" come from the same root — what an organization does — its activity in the marketplace, including ethical activity.

In the best public relations world, an organization's ethos (actual identity) earns an audience's pathos (image of the identity). And public relations works to make that happen by counseling organizations to be socially responsible. But it doesn't always succeed. Re-enter ethical concerns.

For example, suppose the car company mistreats its workers or makes its cars from environmentally insensitive

materials. Certainly its ethos/identity isn't very good. But what's marketing to do? It will still advertise and offer discounts and publish literature. Are these communication efforts ethical? Could PR practitioners ethically keep representing the company? What if consumers band together and protest the ethos/identity of the car company? Can hard marketing alone (with advertising) forcibly shape a workable pathos/image in the public and get the company through its emerging crisis without public relations help? Should it try? Should public relations practitioners dare to help the company communicate an image that doesn't resemble its identity? Wouldn't that be unethical?

More and more, public relations is called upon to point the moral barometer needle to "Fair" or "Stormy" for organizational decisions. *Public relations is responsible for what a company is and what it stands for.* And if what it stands for won't work in society, PR is obliged to try to change it.

## Ethical alignment

Businesses and organizations live in complicated historical, social, political and economic conditions. *Alignment* is the process by which businesses and organizations identify with or instigate change in the society in which they operate.

Alignment has been called *applied ethics.* Organizations orient society to themselves or themselves to society. And they depend on public relations to be deeply involved in the process. When public relations is absent from the process (because it hasn't been invited to participate or worse, doesn't exist in an organization) who does the aligning? Who holds the hand of the public? Who advises management about a proper ethos?

Public relations, perhaps alone among an organization's functions, stimulates sound moral identity that leads to sound ethical decisions.

## How PR practitioners make personal ethical decisions

PR practitioners form their own moral decisions by looking within themselves and considering their personal values. They also look at a match between their values and society's to see if their values can withstand the test of different situations, if they harm more than help, and if they're rooted in sound philosophical or theological principles.

Appropriate ethical decisions rest on all these factors, but most importantly, they build upon sound philosophical principles.

Ethics cannot spring from mere whim. Ethical behavior is morally based. It must be based on mores or customs, be repeatable and be reliable. Whim has none of these characteristics. When you're on the job, people should be able to see the principles behind your decisions.

*Example*: A public relations practitioner went to dinner with a colleague from another department within the company. During dinner, the PR person confessed that she felt uncomfortable recently explaining and defending a company position she

> **Political correctness can be morals tyranny.**

didn't personally agree with. Her friend asked her if she would ever do it again.

"It depends on the issue," she explained.

Her friend wanted to know how she could stand by the company in one instance and not in another.

"It's a no-brainer," said the practitioner. "Some issues involve the welfare of a lot more people than just me. When that happens, the welfare of the many wins out. I would not defend the company if the welfare of many customers or the public would be harmed."

Whether she actually knew it or not, the PR professional was following Aristotle's principle of the *greatest good for the greatest number*. The professional knew the principle and was able to defend her decision. But if she had been acting merely on whim, she probably would have answered,

"Oh, I don't know. It depends on which side of the bed I got out of that morning." That kind of ethical decision-making is unreliable, and so is the practitioner.

Now suppose her friend countered with,

"I don't agree with you. I would do anything to make the company look good and keep my job. I don't have any life and death responsibility for customers, employees or anyone else. Whatever works."

The two might have continued dinner and perhaps stayed friends for a long time. But not likely. The colleague bases her ethical decisions on Mill's principle of utility — *whatever is useful is ethical*. No matter what you think of the colleague's ethics, they are rooted in customs, are philosophically based and are repeatable and reliable. She doesn't look out for herself on whim. Her position is very philosophical.

These two friends will behave very differently on the job.

## "Right decisions"

This textbook provides no answers for the "right" ethical decisions. All decisions have several "right" and "correct" aspects to them depending on the motive of the decider. In the example, both friends at dinner thought they would do the "right" thing.

The PR practitioner thought the "right" action involved looking out for the welfare of others. Her friend thought the "right" action was to look out for herself and her family.

Then there's the "right" thing for the boss. Would the boss choose the PR person's ethics over her friend's? What's "right" for the boss and the company? Does the boss want an employee who always looks out for herself? Or does the boss want an employee who looks out for customers or constituents, despite the cost to the boss or the employee?

The second kind of employee would constantly remind the boss of the organization's priorities.

*Another example*: Is it "right" for a corporation to make as much profit as it can after it properly takes care of its employees? Ask shareholders that question and you'll get an affirmative answer. Ask representatives of the company's union and you'll probably get a "let's talk about it" answer. Ask political action groups averse to the corporation's very existence and you'll get a "no way, it's evil" response.

Yet if the union had cause to strike the corporation, you might see the union accuse management of "unethical" business practice. Or, if the union demanded that most of the profit be turned over to the employees, you might see management charge the union with "unethical" practices. And of course, what shareholder's see as a just compensation for their risk, political activists see as greed. Who's "right"?

So, what's "right" is often in the eye of the beholder. And if you apply the "I can sleep at night with my decision" test to most decisions on the job, most people would sleep well, despite the fact that others might be kept awake because of their decision.

## A practical dilemma

Is there any answer to this apparent dilemma that any decision could be considered ethical? Some PR thinkers advocate an international public relations code of ethics. That might allow judgment of ethical decisions by a common norm despite individual rationalizations. But an international ethical code presupposes agreement to an international set of moral principles. Would a canon in such a code calling for truthful dealing with the media apply equally in Cuba as in the United States? The media in a controlled socialist country often are the arm of the government, not independent observers. What obligation would a PR practitioner in such a country have to be truthful to the media?

Later in this chapter, we'll suggest a way to look at ethical decisions by PR practitioners.

## Toward a practical decision-making model

To make an ethical decision, public relations practitioners need a principled systematic process. The process must lead them to conclusions that serve their moral principles. The process must also serve the business and organizational needs of their employers. In addition, it must serve society.

## Teleology

*The end is more important than the means*

Several models can help. Some base ethical decisions on *teleology*. The ethical nature of decisions arises from the *purpose* or *goal* of the person making the decision. It allows the decision maker to justify the means because the end or purpose is noble.

During the 1996 national political elections, the Democratic party confessed to "improper" fund-raising techniques and subsequently returned some large campaign donations. But the fund raisers justified their actions on the basis that the Republican party had more money. To keep pace, the Democrats said they had to raise sufficient funds to match their opponent's kitty. The controversial fund raising spawned senate hearings on the issue. It's interesting to review the public relations efforts by both political camps during the controversy.

## Teleology and spinning

"Spinning" has its roots in teleology. After all, if you've done something you think is noble and good, but some question your actions, you're forced to put the best "spin" on the facts. And usually, the best rationalization for questionable tactics is a "good purpose."

Public relations people are asked to justify an organization's actions on the basis of the organization's overall mission. Professional politicians frequently employ "spinners" to explain their actions. Spinners usually argue:

• *The action is OK because of the "big picture."*
• *The action is OK because my employer means well.*

But teleological spinners have no credibility. They cannot persuade open-minded people that any action by well meaning people or organizations is automatically ethical.

You can challenge teleological decision makers to rethink their goal by challenging the ethics of their tactics.

## Public relations and spinning

If public relations counselors subscribe to the teleological model of ethics, they probably think their spinning is ethical. Conflict arises when the media think that when public relations practitioners spin for their organizations, they're automatically unethical. The conflict happens

because the media have a different purpose in society. They don't represent a person or organization. They don't have to defend decisions or actions. When the media try to hold public relations people to the same standards as theirs, the values difference promotes the perception in their minds of unethical behavior by PR people.

On the other hand, when some media employ questionable tactics "to get the story" (even though this is the highest good for some media representatives) about a business or organization, they're accused by public relations practitioners of employing unethical means.

*Examples:*
• During the Three Mile Island disaster rumors circulated that the media had their ears against doors to private "no media allowed" rooms to overhear what managers and public relations people were planning.
• ABC sent reporters undercover to lie in employment applications to gain access to the Food Lion Corporation. Then they wrote expose´ stories about meat handling. For

> *Teleologists don t let the way get in their way.*

ABC producers, the higher purpose of protecting the public authenticated their ethically questionable news gathering practices.

## Deontology

*The means are as important as the end*

Deontology is a rules-based system that advocates absolutes. Violate the absolutes and you behave unethically. Most codes of professional conduct use the deontological approach because they require adherence to specific canons of conduct.

For example, the Public Relations Society of America tells its members that double dipping is unethical. When practitioners "double dip," they perform the same task for two fees from different clients, without telling the clients. Unless you disclose to both clients what you're doing, you're can't ethically double dip. But disclosure does change the ethical nature of some actions.

Purpose usually doesn't matter as much to deontologists as it does to teleologists. It makes no difference to a deontologist that you stole because you had to pay your rent; or that one of your clients deceived you and deserved a deceit in return. For deontologists, the end does not justify the means. Means are judged in themselves.

By the way, "spinners" are not deontologists — far from it. Deontologists have a "true north" on their moral compass.

# Potter Model
## Path to an Ethical Decision

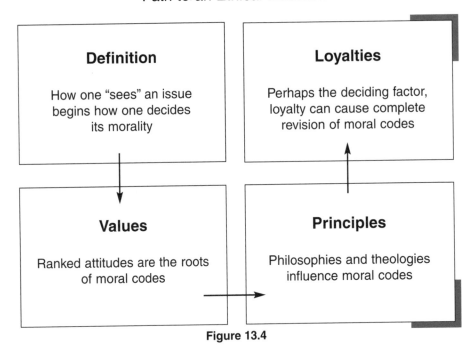

| Definition | Loyalties |
|---|---|
| How one "sees" an issue begins how one decides its morality | Perhaps the deciding factor, loyalty can cause complete revision of moral codes |
| Values | Principles |
| Ranked attitudes are the roots of moral codes | Philosophies and theologies influence moral codes |

**Figure 13.4**

## Situational ethics

The Nineties saw a blossoming, especially in politics and business, of *situational ethics*. This philosophy says that the ethics of behavior is determined by the situation. What may be unethical one day, might be ethical the next. This is the ultimate utilitarian or "useful" philosophy. What is useful is ethical. What is not useful is unethical.

Politicians, business people, public relations practitioners and others who practice situational ethics will appear before cameras and on talk shows and explain, "I did it, but it was right because in this situation …" Situational ethics is a relative of teleology. Morals relate to the moment. The "here and now" shapes ethics.

## The Potter Model

An effective decision-making model is adapted from Dr. Ralph Potter of the Harvard Divinity School. Potter devised a four-stage questioning process for ethical concerns about issues. The four stages are contained in a box of four quadrants — the "Potter Box." By checking in with each quadrant of the box, a decision maker can be comfortable with the result because it came from an orderly process (*Figure 13.4*).

The four quadrants of the Potter Box are:

Definition
Values
Principles
Loyalties

## Definition – "Think" something

The definition of an issue begins its ethical make up. How one "sees" something can pretty much, by itself, determine the ethical outcome. For example, if a PR practitioner defines a media inquiry as an "attack," the practitioner might "justifiably" withhold information from the "enemy."

But if the PR person sees the inquiry as an honest effort by a media representative to get a story, the practitioner might use the question as an opportunity to get the organization's message out.

## Values – "Feel" something

Values are moral attitudes that define a person. They are core beliefs about oneself, society, purpose of organizations, justice, fairness, equality, etc. When applied to specific issues, they bend the decision in the same manner that gravity curves space. The decision maker gravitates in the direction of the value. To go against one's values is to get into serious cognitive dissonance.

## Principles – "Know" something

Principles are philosophies and theologies that guide everyday behavior. PR counselors can use some of the many philosophies available or use their own. This text will offer five for your consideration.

## Loyalties – "Want" something

This is the affective part of decision making. It has little to do with reasoning or analytical application of principles or values to issues. Instead, loyalty asks the decision maker in an ethical quandary to choose a side based on *relationships*. And the reason for choosing may be as uncomplicated as favoring a good boss or a benevolent organization over a competing guiding principle.

Returning to principles in the Potter Box, look to influential philosophies to guide you. Here are five that influence much daily behavior.

## Aristotle's Golden Mean
### *(Aristotle ~ 384-322 BCE)*

*"Greatest good for the greatest number"*

This philosophy stresses moderation. Virtuous living is moderate living, no excesses. It finds the moderate or middle ground between two extremes of excess and deficiency. For Aristotle (*Figure 13.5*), the result of the search for the middle ground was justice, wisdom, courage and temperance. But the middle ground isn't always the midpoint between the two choices. Rather, it's a position in the middle relative to extreme choices.

*Example*:

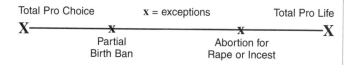

Total Pro Choice     x = exceptions     Total Pro Life

Partial Birth Ban     Abortion for Rape or Incest

In the example, both exceptions are middle ground choices, but not midpoints. From the viewpoint of each extreme camp: a partial birth ban still allows all abortions less radical; abortions for rape and incest still bans all abortions more radical.

Selecting the middle ground also involves picking the right time, serving the greatest number of people, fulfilling the greatest number of purposes, etc.

In employee relations, practitioners seeking consensus from employees might use this philosophy. Practitioners will use it to influence publics to consider the "bigger picture" about an organization instead of focusing on a single failing or indiscretion, such as a product recall.

*Example*: In the 1980s, Proctor and Gamble suffered negative publicity over its super absorbent tampon, *Rely*. Reportedly, some users developed toxic shock syndrome from the tampons. Proctor and Gamble appropriately accepted responsibility but cautioned that the company stood for more than the tampons (the big picture). P&G

## Aristotle

Detail from the fresco *The School of Athens* by Raphael

**Figure 13.5**

also noted that it had only a small portion of the super absorbent tampon market and suggested that other companies should accept some of the responsibility.

## Kant's Categorical Imperative
### *(Immanuel Kant ~ 1724-1804)*

*"What is good for one is good for all."*

This philosophy requires that a decision become "law." It's categorical because it's uncompromising. There are no exceptions. It's imperative because it logically forces decision makers to behave toward everyone as they would behave toward one. Kant would ask, "Do you want your decision applied universally?"

*Examples*:

• Lying would always be wrong, even to save a life. If fetuses were ruled to be persons, abortion would be inappropriate in all cases. If supervisors were to allow one employee to go home early, they must allow everyone to go home early under the same circumstances.

• In public relations practice, this philosophy might guide decisions about employee relations: Every employee has an equal right to information, protection from harassment, opportunity for promotion. It also guides relationships with unions, which traditionally use this philosophy to gain "equal treatment" for its members.

Many educational institutions, for example, have a difficult time instituting merit pay because teachers' unions object to that kind of positive "discrimination" of their members, and instead bargain for an "even playing field" for all.

## Mill's Principle of Utility
### (John Stuart Mill ~ 1806-1873)

*"What is useful is right."*

This philosophy values usefulness. Its utilitarianism measures the right amount of desirable good over avoidable evil. The philosophy authenticates self-pleasure and "meism" — looking out for number one. But it's also applied to decisions about relationships.

Utilitarians seek the best balance of good options over bad ones and spread of this balance widely.

Some utilitarians try to oblige others to their rule of "useful" activity.

*Examples:*
• Watergate perpetrators calculated the consequences of available options and picked the option offering minimal loss. The practical decision became the ethical one.

• When President William Clinton lied about a sexual affair with an intern in the Oval Office, he argued in his apology to the country that the lie was "ethical" because it was practical. It avoided evil (embarrassment to his family and loss of his presidency) and caused good (the lie was designed to keep him in office.)

In public relations, a practitioner might have to explain to the media and the public why a utilitarian boss favored the welfare of shareholders (declaring a larger dividend) over loss to consumers (delivering a product of less quality) in a tough economic decision.

Representing the decisions of others, based on a philosophy they don't agree with, gives PR practitioners their most challenging ethical dilemmas.

## Rawls's Veil of Ignorance
### (John Rawls ~ 1921-2002)

*"Eliminate roles to justly decide."*

This philosophy focuses on the idea that justice emerges when people negotiate without social differentiations. Fairness is paramount.

The veil of ignorance assumes that if negotiating parties step behind a veil and exchange positions or roles (reversing social differentiation), they will negotiate as though they were the other person and emerge with a fair decision for both.

Of course, the issue doesn't always have to be negotiations. It could simply be policy-making, or customer relations.

*Examples:*
• In customer relations, management will ask front line clerks and sales associates to treat all customers as though they were their own family members.

• In media relations it's possible, but much tougher, to ask media representatives to "see" the organization's position in their coverage of a story. Sometimes, a PR practitioner must point out that the angle of a story (or even a headline) might harm an organization more than it benefits society.

• In employee relations, how will management and labor successfully handle employee requests if each side does its decision-making without appreciating the other's position?

The veil is not another name for utility. It's virtuous, fair action, not action that simply benefits the majority.

## Judeo/Christian Principle

*"Treat others as you would be treated yourself"*

A Chinese philosophy asks the same —*"To love all men everywhere alike."*

Love is personal, not legal. It's unlike Kant's categorical imperative. It's more like the biblical notion of "agape," a love feast of unselfish, other-directed love. It's distinct from friendship, charity and benevolence. It's blind to color, age and status. It's akin to Carl Rogers's unconditional positive regard.

*Examples:*
• Obviously this philosophy/theology has great meaning for customer relations. It's hard to imagine an organization deliberately harming the public or society while subscribing to this philosophy. Why? Because the quality of the decision exceeds traditional roles. It's no longer seller/buyer. Now, it's neighbor/neighbor.

• Community relations benefits from this philosophy. It infuses a vision of corporate responsibility for the community in which the corporation does business. A public relations axiom says that effective organizations should demonstrate a civic responsibility to their communities.

• Finally, there's the notion of duty. Duty and right are reciprocal notions. If you have a right to something from me, I have a duty to provide it to you. (*Example*: free speech opportunity.)

Many organizations today publish and display customers', or patients', or employees' Bills of Rights. These "rights" come from a community business philosophy and obligate the organization and its employees to regard those rights. The Bills are an effective way to communicate to everyone in the organization, the moral philosophy guiding the organization's ethical behavior. They also demonstrate that organizations' ethics begin at the top.

# Recall or keep quiet

Here's an example of how an application of the Potter Box results in two different decisions about the same PR issue.

## Issue

A computer company introduced its new computer with a processor designed to provide special timesaving functions. The company receives notice from its subcontracted chip provider that the processor will not do what it's supposed to. But the subcontractor assures the company that consumers won't notice the missing feature. They also say that they will provide a chip that will do the same job "in the near future."

Over 2,000 computers have been sold and another 10,000 are ordered and ready for shipment. Expensive national advertising is already booked, including national television ads. The company is not a giant in the industry. It needs these sales to remain in business.

The CEO calls in the company's PR director and hires an outside PR firm and asks both for advice. Should the company recall the product; announce the problem but do nothing else; take the hit and risk bankruptcy; or say nothing, because no noticeable harm will occur. When the new chip comes in, the company can less expensively replace the defective chip with a free "product upgrade."

Here's how each PR counselor reasoned about the ethical challenge and arrived at different advice to the CEO. Read the boxes in this order:

Definition ⟶ Values ⟶ Principles ⟶ Loyalties

This is the order most people progress in their thinking about ethical decisions. Definition is the instinctive grasp of the problem. Values are the "check with self." Principles are the "check with others." And loyalty is predicting life with self and others after the decision.

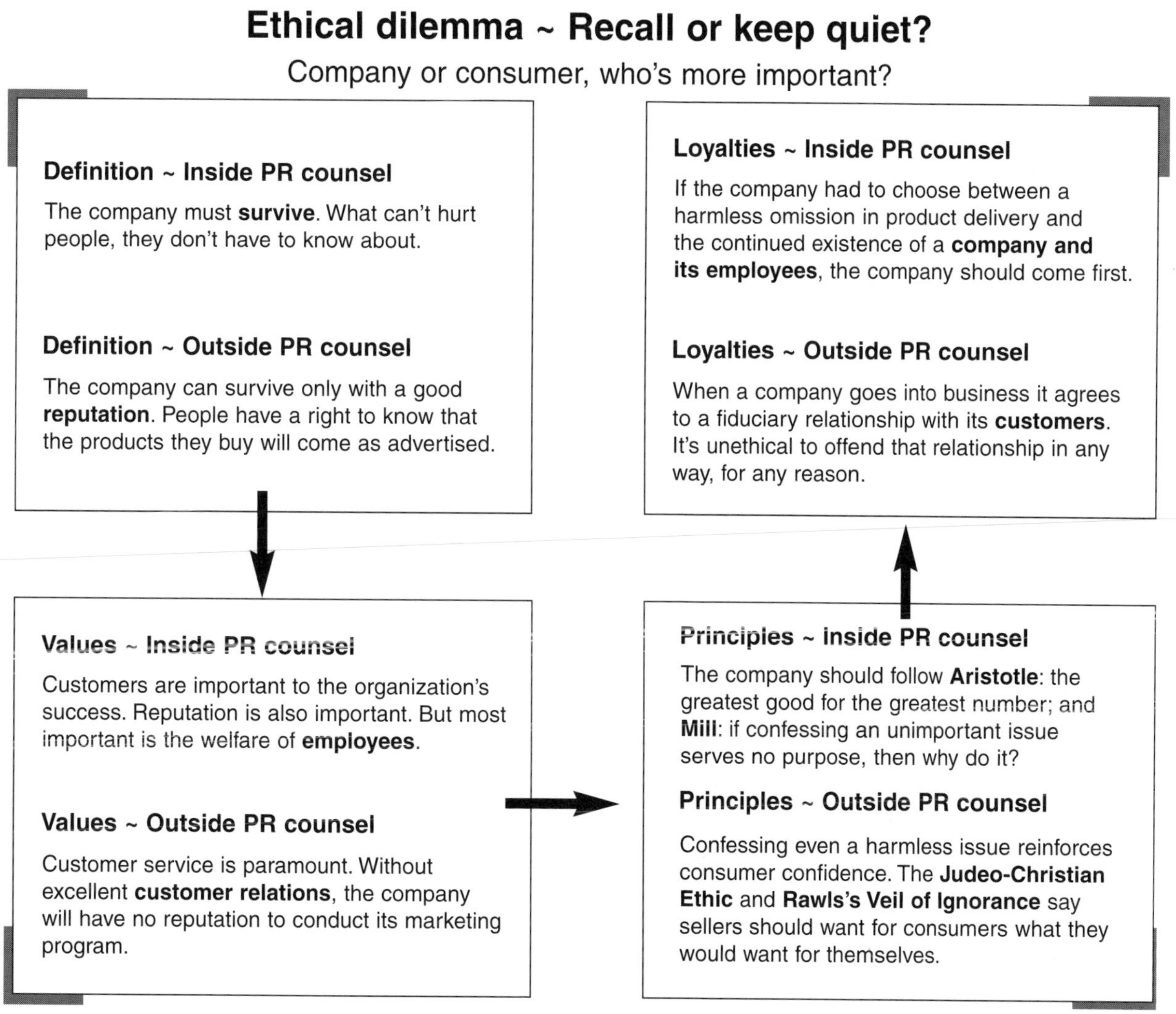

# Ethical dilemma ~ Recall or keep quiet?

## Company or consumer, who's more important?

### Definition ~ Inside PR counsel

The company must **survive**. What can't hurt people, they don't have to know about.

### Definition ~ Outside PR counsel

The company can survive only with a good **reputation**. People have a right to know that the products they buy will come as advertised.

### Values ~ Inside PR counsel

Customers are important to the organization's success. Reputation is also important. But most important is the welfare of **employees**.

### Values ~ Outside PR counsel

Customer service is paramount. Without excellent **customer relations**, the company will have no reputation to conduct its marketing program.

### Principles ~ Inside PR counsel

The company should follow **Aristotle**: the greatest good for the greatest number; and **Mill**: if confessing an unimportant issue serves no purpose, then why do it?

### Principles ~ Outside PR counsel

Confessing even a harmless issue reinforces consumer confidence. The **Judeo-Christian Ethic** and **Rawls's Veil of Ignorance** say sellers should want for consumers what they would want for themselves.

### Loyalties ~ Inside PR counsel

If the company had to choose between a harmless omission in product delivery and the continued existence of a **company and its employees**, the company should come first.

### Loyalties ~ Outside PR counsel

When a company goes into business it agrees to a fiduciary relationship with its **customers**. It's unethical to offend that relationship in any way, for any reason.

**Figure 13.6**

> *Learn as much as you can about the person asking for the behavior and the issues involved. Don t make a premature judgment until you conduct this preliminary analysis.*

## Potter ethical decision-making model

How inside and outside PR counselors could reach different ethical decisions about the same problem and why the company's ethics depends on which moral counsel it follows (*Figure 13.6*).

## Ethical decision ~ Internal PR Counsel

### *Make no announcement.*

Quietly replace the chips at a later time with no cost to the consumer. No harm, no foul. The company avoids the risk of bankruptcy. Employees and shareholders suffer no loss.

## Ethical decision ~ External PR Counsel

### *Announce the error.*

Hold all shipments. Promise publicly (with ads) replacement for the computers shipped. Rely on the goodwill of consumers to appreciate the company's honesty by holding their computers until the new chip is in. Loss in sales now will result in sale's gain later from maintaining reputation.

## What to do?

If you were the CEO, which advice would you follow? Why? How would you evaluate the reasoning of the two decisions? Would you apply any different definition, value, principle or loyalty to the problem? Would you consider responsibility to other computer companies as a factor in your decision, i.e., if you hurt your company, you hurt the whole industry?

If a "whistleblower" from inside your company would later speak to the media about the defective chip shipment, how would you feel then about following internal PR counsel's advice?

Organizations should make an ethical decision in such a way that if they appeared on the 6 p.m. news they would be comfortable with their decision — either way. Carefully look at the boldface copy in each of the four boxes for a consistency clue by each position.

## Ethical decision-making process

### *Steps*

1. **Accept the decision-making challenge with an open mind.** Discover the motive behind the request for the asked-for behavior. Learn as much as you can about the person asking for the behavior and the issues involved. Don't make a premature judgment until you conduct this preliminary analysis.

2. **Analyze the issue.** List the major points. Where is the conflict with accepted norms? See if the actors in the drama have conducted their own ethical analysis. If they have, look at the principles and values they employed. Are they the same as those you would employ?

3. **Check your own preliminary reaction.** Is the asked-for behavior more important than your expected behavior?

Expected behavior ⟷ Asked-for behavior

What do your instincts say you should do? Why? Would you feel uncomfortable with a particular decision? Why?

4. **Go inside yourself and investigate your personal identity and image**. It's important in this activity to check your moral codes – your *actual* moral code and your *perceived* moral code. Revisit the section in this chapter on developing a moral code for your ethical decisions. How will a choice of action satisfy your personal code or be perceived by others?

*Example*: Suppose one choice brings you into conflict with society's moral codes? Are you willing to stand on your own?

5. **Next, check in with your organization**. What is its mission? Does the asked-for behavior fulfill the mission? Which of several options will serve the organization best – both your organization's professed identity and its public image? Look at your organization's five-year plan and its communication objectives. Which behavior will you be able to defend as being most consistent with the organization's plan? How are the values espoused by your organization for its employees and customers fulfilled in the proposed behavior?

6. **Finally, check in with society.** What does society expect from you and your organization? Which of several proposed behaviors will society best agree with? Does the behavior satisfy a valid public interest? Will the proposed behavior gain esteem and reputation for you and your organization? Will you be congratulated for behaving in a socially responsible manner?

7. **Establish your moral position and make your ethical decision**. Then be prepared to explain and defend your position, not from a "gut ethical feeling" but from a reasoned, informed approach **based on moral principles and a dispassionate situation analysis**.

Informed ethical decisions, no matter the consequences, are the most comfortably defensible. Indeed, two public relations practitioners, reasoning to an ethical decision from divergent moral positions, can both sleep at night, knowing their decisions were consciously principled.

*Note*: One of the most important products of ethical decision-making is *morals clarification*. Like the public opinion formation process (see chapter on public opinion) our morals lie dormant or latent until something triggers a need for advice from them. It will happen that you will probably be asked to consider re-ranking your moral code as you calculate the effects of decisions thrust upon you. You will change them or not depending on how "core" your moral code is to you.

## Accountability vs. responsibility

Accountability involves fulfilling expectations such as contracts, promises and mandates. Sometimes, practitioners do things they don't personally agree with but must because they have promised to do them.

The most ethical behavior is to keep your promises, especially public ones. If you don't, your public will see only your broken promise, not the moral code that compelled you to break the promise for a higher personal moral.

**Case example**: *Integrity in politics*

A politician promises not to raise taxes. But after she gets into office, she learns that without more taxes, she won't be able to take care of social issues important to her. In addition, she's under enormous pressure to raise taxes by her opponents who have latched onto the social issues as their own. She doesn't want that to happen. Should her PR counsel advise her to keep her public promise, or follow her social moral code and raise taxes? What principles will guide the PR counselor — personal, political or societal?

*Scenario One*

The counselor tells the politician that he joined her because of his belief in her integrity. She must keep her word. To break it would disillusion not only him, but also others who believed in her. She must put politics second behind personal integrity. Besides, personal integrity is the best politics. He feels so strongly about it that if she ignores his advice, he will leave her, publicly. For him, loyalty will not trump absolute moral codes.

*Scenario Two*

The politician believes she is really a good person. If she raises taxes, she needs to explain why she changed her mind. She'll never fully succeed because her opponents won't let her off the hook. And they'll take the issues she wants for themselves.

She believes Aristotle is right, "the greatest good for the greatest number." She can have her cake and eat it too if she calculates that more people will benefit from the increased taxes than will complain about paying them.

The question is: Will she be able to persuade her constituents, opponents and the media that she is honestly making an Aristotelian decision and not one based on Mills's utilitarianism.

*Decision*

She announces a tax rise, proclaims that her switch in moral stance is really personal and not political (her willingness to take a hit proves that); and her PR counselor resigns.

Responsibility involves fulfilling obligations, whether voluntary or not. Many on-the-job conflicts in public relations involve conflicting responsibilities. Frequently both (or more) responsibilities are valid. When this happens, following one of the four philosophical principles offered in this chapter might help you rank the responsibilities and **clarify your morals**.

**Case example**: *Sexual harassment in the workplace*

A supervisor is supposed to report any sexual harassment circumstance on the job. One day, he sees a picture on the wall of a colleague's private office that has been construed as "mildly offensive" to just one employee who "doesn't want to make a fuss" and doesn't want him to report the employee. He doesn't personally think the material is offensive. Colleagues and other employees he's checked with share his "not offensive" opinion. But his obligation to the organization (he learned in sexual harassment training) is to report any incident, however minor (even one based on just one person's very strict moral code). But he also senses an obligation to his colleague to respect his private tastes and free speech rights. Should he report it or not?

*Scenario One*

The employee reports his colleague, feels good about doing what the company wanted, but feels bad about disloyalty to his colleague and his apparent statement to the rest of the employees: "I value loyalty to the company above all." For him, when he was hired, loyalty to the company became a deep moral code, not just an optional workplace to-do item. He also feels that if he keeps quiet for his friend, he would have to keep quiet for every other

## PR Bronze Anvil

The anvil is a symbol of PRSA's awards for excellent practice.

**Figure 13.7**

case of potential sexual harassment he comes across because he is thoroughly Kantian — "What's good for one is good for all."

*Will he sleep at night?*

### Scenario Two

The employee keeps quiet about what's on his colleague's wall. He feels he's kept a friend, but been disloyal to the company and signaled to other employees that in future company mandates, don't count on him to be a company man.

He's driven by loyalty to real people, not corporate entities. He thinks that he would want the same deal from his colleagues — nondisclosure — if he were found doing something the company didn't sanction, such as using e-mail for personal use. He's a Rawls-behind-the-veil man, and steeped in Judeo-Christian empathy. When the time

comes, he'll want the same dispensation he's now conferring on his friend.

He'll pay a price. In fact, he's asked the next day by his boss, who also saw the offensive material, if he feels he has a career with the company?

*Will he sleep at night?*

## PR's contribution to an ethical climate

The Public Relations Society of America (PRSA) uses the anvil as its symbol of the management contribution of public relations in the workplace (*Figure 13.7*). The anvil is perhaps also the best symbol of ethical contribution. PRSA envisions that decisions in an organization need a sturdy template on which the vagaries of business decisions can acquire form; hence, the anvil.

PRSA sees the anvil as the public relations function in an organization — that all decisions will acquire moral and ethical form by pressing against the PR anvil, which won't yield to inside or outside interests. The anvil will keep its shape because it represents the unchangeable moral code organization's use to fashion ethical decisions. Organizations press their raw facts against the PR anvil and come away with form, ethical form.

PRSA's highest achievement awards are the gold, silver and bronze anvils for contributions to the profession, including ethical character and practice.

Recall the image of public relations people holding their organizations with one hand and society with the other. No other person or function in an organization has this responsibility — to represent an organization's constituents and the organization at the same time. For that reason, public relations is aptly suited to help organizations form their ethical decisions. This is especially true when those decisions relate to external constituents such as customers, clients, the media, governmental agencies, associations and others.

Public relations advocates for an organization's constituents at the decision-making table. Frequently, PR people are the only ones at the table that might object to proposed action on the basis that **moral codes relating to interests both inside outside the organization must guide organizational decisions**.

## Ethics in the information age

The information age, the cyber age, and the communi-cation age present new ethical challenges to practitioners. Ownership of information and information channels also offer new challenges.

• **E-mail**. Who owns the e-mail in an organization? Most human resource literature contends that companies own all e-mail communication in their organizations, even personal communication, and can monitor them at will. Explaining this management right to employees will challenge internal communicators.

• **Internet**. Management can control use of the Internet by employees during work hours. And research by employees during work hours, or with organization equipment, belongs to the organization.

• **Cyber messages**. Messages sent on voice mail or e-mail outside the organization affect the image of the company. All organization employees have an ethical responsibility to send writing, content and graphics that frame the organization in the light it wants to be seen.

• **Free speech**. Office communication through real speech, posters, signs, tee shirts, and other channels can offend or violate others' rights. The content can be about sex, religion, politics, gender, ethnicity or perceived offensive speech and activity. Counseling management about ethical norms and communicating them to employees will challenge communicators.

• **Copyright**. Software, licensed to a single person or a single company, cannot be used by others, even by employees privately, without paying additional rights fees. Sharing such software is illegal and could be unethical.

• **Shareware**. Downloaded shareware from the Internet often carries with it the obligation to send a small fee to the creator. No one will arrest you if you don't send it. But you will know if you don't.

• **Plagiarism**. Acquiring information off the Internet and using it to do business without crediting the source can pose an ethical problem. Information on the Internet is public and free, but also is "owned." Like books in a public bookstore – the information is public and free if you just want to browse, but you can't steal a chapter and use it as your own without attribution. ■

## Tips

1. When you're analyzing ethical behavior always look for the moral behind it. Clashes about ethics are usually clashes about morals.

2. When you identify the moral behind your ethical act, ask around if anyone shares your moral code. Shared morals lead to shared ethical behavior.

3. Before deciding to "blow the whistle" on another employee or on your organization, take time to clarify your morals, then let principles, values and loyalties help you decide.

4. Before putting your name on a product (report, plan, video, ad, etc.) check to see if you're taking more credit than you deserve.

5. Remember, reputation comes more from what an organization or its members do than from what an organization or others say about it.

6. Being honest with the media doesn't mean telling them everything you know about your organization. It means telling them everything your organization allows you to tell them. You might not have a say in this except to advise, conform, or resign.

7. Never barter with the media for favorable coverage. The only favorable ethical coverage is coverage you earn.

8. Before you begin making an ethical decision, know exactly what your final fall back position is — the moral position you cannot surrender.

9. Don't lose a business colleague in a dispute over whose position is "right" on an issue. Rather, clarify the moral behind the position, and agree to disagree if both morals are unchangeable. It's all right if your moral loses, as long as you don't lose your moral. And you don't have to be enthusiastic about a colleague persuading your company to do something you don't believe in. Your public disenchantment keeps the tension between moral choices alive, and that's the healthiest business environment.

10. If you're debating an ethical decision, think of what your decision will look and sound like on the evening news. Go with the image you'll be comfortable with, because it could be a signal from your moral core.

# Public Relations Society of America
# Excerpts from the Member Code of Ethics 2000

(Courtesy of Public Relations Society of America, www.prsa.org)

- Professional Values
- Principles of Conduct
- Commitment and Compliance

This Code applies to PRSA members. The Public Relations Society of America (PRSA) is committed to ethical practices. The level of public trust PRSA members seek, as we serve the public good, means we have taken on a special obligation to operate ethically.

The value of member reputation depends upon the ethical conduct of everyone affiliated with the Public Relations Society of America. Each of us sets an example for each other — as well as other professionals — by our pursuit of excellence with powerful standards of performance, professionalism, and ethical conduct.

This statement presents the core values of PRSA members and, more broadly, of the public relations profession. These values provide the foundation for the Member Code of Ethics and set the industry standard for the professional practice of public relations. These values are the fundamental beliefs that guide our behaviors and decision-making process. We believe our professional values are vital to the integrity of the profession as a whole.

## ADVOCACY

We serve the public interest by acting as responsible advocates for those we represent. We provide a voice in the marketplace of ideas, facts, and viewpoints to aid informed public debate.

## HONESTY

We adhere to the highest standards of accuracy and truth in advancing the interests of those we represent and in communicating with the public.

## EXPERTISE

We acquire and responsibly use specialized knowledge and experience. We advance the profession through continued professional development, research, and education. We build mutual understanding, credibility, and relationships among a wide array of institutions and audiences.

## INDEPENDENCE

We provide objective counsel to those we represent. We are accountable for our actions.

## LOYALTY

We are faithful to those we represent, while honoring our obligation to serve the public interest.

## FAIRNESS

We deal fairly with clients, employers, competitors, peers.

## FREE FLOW OF INFORMATION

*Core Principle*

**Protecting and advancing the free flow of accurate and truthful information is essential to serving the public interest and contributing to informed decision making in a democratic society.**

*Intent*

- To maintain the integrity of relationships with the media, government officials, and the public.
- To aid informed decision-making.

*Guidelines*

*A member shall:*

- Preserve the integrity of the process of communication.
- Be honest and accurate in all communications.
- Act promptly to correct erroneous communications for which the practitioner is responsible.
- Preserve the free flow of unprejudiced information when giving or receiving gifts by ensuring that gifts are nominal, legal, and infrequent.

*Example of Improper Conduct*

- A member representing a ski manufacturer gives a pair of expensive racing skis to a sports magazine columnist, to influence the columnist to write favorable articles about the product.

## COMPETITION

*Core Principle*

**Promoting healthy and fair competition among professionals preserves an ethical climate while fostering a robust business environment.**

*Intent*

- To promote respect and fair competition among public relations professionals.
- To serve the public interest by providing the widest choice of practitioner options.

*Guidelines*

*A member shall:*

- Follow ethical hiring practices designed to respect free and open competition without deliberately undermining a competitor.
- Preserve intellectual property rights in the marketplace.

*Example of Improper Conduct*

- A member employed by a "client organization" shares helpful information with a counseling firm that is competing with others for the organization's business.

## DISCLOSURE OF INFORMATION
### Core Principle
**Open communication fosters informed decision making in a democratic society.**

*Intent*

• To build trust with the public by revealing all information needed for responsible decision making.

*Guidelines*

*A member shall:*

• Be honest and accurate in all communications.
• Act promptly to correct erroneous communications for which the member is responsible.
• Investigate the truthfulness and accuracy of information released on behalf of those represented.
• Reveal the sponsors for causes and interests represented.
• Disclose financial interest (such as stock ownership) in a client's organization.
• Avoid deceptive practices.

*Examples of Improper Conduct*

• Front groups: A member implements "grass roots" campaigns or letter-writing campaigns to legislators on behalf of undisclosed interest groups.
• Lying by omission: A practitioner for a corporation knowingly fails to release financial information, giving a misleading impression of the corporation's performance.

## SAFEGUARDING CONFIDENCES
### Core Principle
**Client trust requires appropriate protection of confidential and private information.**

*Intent*

To protect the privacy rights of clients, organizations, and individuals by safeguarding confidential information.

*Guidelines*

*A member shall:*

• Safeguard the confidences and privacy rights of present, former, and prospective clients and employees.
• Protect privileged, confidential, or insider information gained from a client or organization.
• Immediately advise an appropriate authority if a member discovers that confidential information is being divulged by an employee of a client company or organization.

*Example of Improper Conduct*

• A member changes jobs, takes confidential information, and uses that information in the new position to the detriment of the former employer.

*To view the full PRSA Member Code 2000, log on to: www.prsa.org*

## CONFLICTS OF INTEREST
### Core Principle
**Avoiding real, potential or perceived conflicts of interest builds the trust of clients, employers, and the publics.**

*Intent*

• To earn trust and mutual respect with clients or employers.
• To build trust with the public by avoiding or ending situations that put one's personal or professional interests in conflict with society's interests.

*Guidelines*

*A member shall:*

• Act in the best interests of the client or employer, even subordinating the member's personal interests.
• Avoid actions and circumstances that may appear to compromise good business judgment or create a conflict between personal and professional interests.
• Disclose promptly any existing or potential conflict of interest to affected clients or organizations.
• Encourage clients and customers to determine if a conflict exists after notifying all affected parties.

*Example of Improper Conduct*

• The member fails to disclose that he or she has a strong financial interest in a client's chief competitor.

## ENHANCING THE PROFESSION
### Core Principle
**Public relations professionals work constantly to strengthen the public's trust in the profession.**

*Intent*

• To build respect and credibility with the public for the profession of public relations.
• To improve, adapt and expand professional practices.

*Guidelines*

*A member shall:*

• Acknowledge that there is an obligation to protect and enhance the profession.
• Keep informed and educated about practices in the profession to ensure ethical conduct.
• Actively pursue personal professional development.
• Decline representation of clients or organizations that urge or require actions contrary to this Code.
• Accurately define what public relations activities can accomplish.
• Counsel subordinates in proper ethical decision making.
• Require that subordinates adhere to the ethical requirements of the Code.
• Report ethical violations, whether committed by PRSA members or not, to the appropriate authority.

*Example of Improper Conduct*

• A PRSA member declares publicly that a product the client sells is safe, without disclosing evidence to the contrary.

**Questions for classroom discussion**

1. Why is it important that your moral principles have a "universal ring" to them?

2. It has been said that a universal ethics code can reduce ethical clashes on the job. Do you think a universal workplace ethical code is feasible? If it is, will it practically reduce ethical clashes? Why?

3. Ethical alignment has been called applied ethics. What are the chief considerations about aligning an organization's ethics with society's needs?

4. Which aspect of the Potter Model do you think contributes to most ethical decisions in organizations? Which aspect contributes most to your ethical decisions? After reading this chapter, are you rethinking how you'll make ethical decisions?

5. Of the five philosophers or philosophies outlined in the ethical decision-making process — Aristotle, Kant, Mill, Rawls, and Judeo/Christian ethic — does any fit best with conducting an effective customer relations program? Employee relations program? Media relations program?

**Internet assignment**

The Internet offers Web sites for many newspapers and magazines in the country. Reporters often report what they believe to be unethical practices by businesses and organizations. In writing their stories, they quote "watchdog organizations" that frequently attack the ethics of business and organizations.

Find such an attack on the Internet. Also find the organization's response. Analyze the response according to the organizational ethical principles in this chapter. What do you think of the attack, of the coverage, of the response? Are they all ethical? Why?

Name_____Date_____

## Potter Model Case Study

After reading the following case, assume the parts of both groups trying to make an ethical decision. Then fill in the boxes in the Potter Model for making an ethical decision for each group. By doing this you be able to see both points of view in establishing moral bases for the decision.

Remember, for each group, use words in the DEFINITION BOX that show the starting position of each group – the way they think the decision should ultimately be made.

Name moral principles in the VALUES BOX each group wants to adhere to.

In the PRINCIPLES BOX, cite a philosopher, philosophy, theology or other guiding cultural norm for each group.

Finally, in the LOYALTY BOX, cite what you think each group's ultimate fidelity would be. Remember, it doesn't mean that loyalty alone will determine the final ethical decision, just that it should be part of the process.

Then write the ethical behavior for each group that will logically come from your work. Afterward, select the one you think you agree with and explain why — perhaps using the Potter Model to help you decide.

## Potter Model Case Facts

A Southern California vegetable and fruit growing and packaging company employs some illegal aliens to work the fields and prepare some of the food for shipment overseas. There, foreign workers can, bottle and package the food for sale around the world, including the United States.

The company has come under fire from local unions, the media and even some internal managers for unethically stealing some jobs from American workers by employing some illegal aliens. The company's image is suffering from these different attacks.

The company contends that local unions want to own the company, not just work there. Investors would pull out and the company would fold if it gave in to union demands for full union hiring and high pay scales. It also contends that it needs these workers to stay in business — a business that produces enough food to feed a tenth of the hungry in underdeveloped countries. It agrees with managers that the company and its employees need a better image. So, it calls a community meeting and asks, "Shall we stop hiring some illegal aliens, stop sending some jobs overseas, hire only local union workers and pay union scale? And if we do that, we'll be in business for only one more harvest. Then, we'll have no investors, no taxes to local communities, no employees, and no food production and distribution, because we won't make enough to stay in business.

*See other side*

Name _____ Date _____

**Potter Model Work Sheet**

| Definition ~ Keep company same | Loyalties ~ Keep company same |
|---|---|
| Definition ~ Change company | Loyalties ~ Change company |
| Values ~ Keep company same | Principles ~ Keep company same |
| Values ~ Change company | Principles ~ Change company |

**Figure 13.10**

*Practical Public Relations: Theories and Techniques That Make a Difference*

Name _____ Date _____

_____

Final ethical decision of those who want to keep the company the same

_____

_____

_____

_____

Final ethical decision of those who want to change the company

_____

_____

_____

_____

Your opinion of the best ethical decision of what the company should do.

_____

_____

_____

_____

_____

_____

# Chapter 14

# Planning a PR Program

---

## PRaxiom  *What you conceive, planning can achieve.*

---

### What this chapter covers

In this chapter, you'll learn how to make a simple, workable public relations plan or campaign for any size project, such as introducing a new product or service or changing an organization's image. You'll understand the purpose for each part of the plan and you'll learn how to write logical and creative ideas that work.

The chapter walks you through the planning process in three easy stages — *Learn, Think* and *Plan*.

As you tour the planning process, you'll learn how to convert the basic planning model into a basic public relations plan. Even beginner practitioners can become successful planners using this process. Planning can be fun. It beats guessing — something public relations practitioners cannot afford to do.

### Strategic thinking and planning

Public relations practitioners do an important part of their work when they develop a communication plan and conduct a communication/public relations campaign or program.

The plan is important because it tells everyone in the organization who is involved in the program, exactly what they have to do, when they have to do it, and how to measure the results of their work.

Practitioners plan in many ways. Some veterans believe that nothing is really new in public relations. What worked before can work again. Frequently these practitioners will use old campaign techniques and apply them to new problems.

This dangerous practice assumes that a practitioner will face identical issues and identical audiences with identical needs. Although some situations present similar

challenges, a fund-raising campaign, or a grand opening special event, it's unlikely that every element will be exactly the same.

Other researchers guess about the right thing to do. They say they have an "intuition" for public relations that makes them successful practitioners. They might succeed at times by chance, but their unprofessional technique makes them merely lucky technicians, not professionals.

What makes a professional planner? Public relations planning is a combination of left and right brain activity. The left brain logically analyzes the challenge and available information, and plans a strategic approach to solve the challenge. The right brain contributes creative communication approaches.

Public relations is like medicine and law — there's a science and an art to the practice. Some say public relations is an art applied to a science.

The professional planner engages in strategic thinking, then maps out a strategic plan. The difference between strategic thinking and strategic planning is like the difference between architects' ideas, notes and conversations and their blueprints.

Strategic thinkers first sketch an ambition. They assess the nature of a problem, separate the problem into components, and fashion workable solutions.

Next, strategic planners schedule practical activities to achieve the ambition. They supply blueprints for the thinkers' approaches. It's their responsibility to actually achieve the ambition.

*What you can conceive, planning can achieve.*

### Preparing to make a public relations plan

Here are some things you should do before you develop a public relations plan.

---

## Tips for using resources effectively

- Precisely **define your task** to discover if you can actually reach your goal. But don't avoid important objectives such as persuasion and image change because you think they'll cost too much. Remember, the success of many campaigns depends on what you say, not on how many dollars you spend saying it.

- **Teach others** in your organization to do public relations work. Show employees they are the natural front line for PR efforts. Every willing employee who appreciates and works for the goals of the organization saves you time and money carrying out campaigns.

- If you have limited dollars, **narrow your audience list** to those you can reach several times. Reach a smaller audience a few times rather than a larger audience once.

- If you're persuading, and you must choose among media, **select a face-to-face channel** rather than print or electronic channel.

- To gain maximum mileage from your effort and budget, **try a special event** for your campaign. The event generates publicity and attracts target audiences more efficiently than most other channels.

- **Do your research carefully.** If you have limited funds, be sure to select the right channel to do the job. Shop around for the best price for a graphic designer, electronic presentation expert, annual report artist, printer, etc. Sometimes, you'll do better if you sub-contract a job ("outsourcing") rather than spend hours and days doing it yourself and getting little else done.

- **Cooperate with marketing and human resources.** Make certain you're not duplicating efforts in research, media selection, etc. Also, try cooperating with another organization with a similar ambition. By pooling efforts, you can get a lot more for your dollars.

  *Example*: An insurance company can team with the American Cancer Society to encourage annual health checkups.

- When you're about to write a plan, **look at other successful plans** in your business area. Others may have done a similar project on a "shoestring budget." Why spend to learn things already known?

  *Example*: PRSA offers its competitive Silver Anvil Awards for the best PR plans in the country. Use these ideas and strategies.

- **Use volunteers.** It's surprising how efficiently volunteers can conduct research, take pictures, staff information tables, etc., if you spend a little time training them.

- **Be creative.** Don't routinely do things the "old way." Invent new tactics and channels. Read about the successful work of others in your field.

---

- **Get to know your client or manager and the problem as well as possible**. Do as much research as necessary. Look at documents, talk to people, review history, and conduct studies. The key to successful planning is to bond with your client or boss. Bonding means that you know the problem issues as well as they do.

- **Assemble a team.** Sometimes two or three can do the job. Larger teams can do the job more quickly, with a richer array of ideas. Make certain the team enrolls strategic thinkers and planners. If you're alone, you can make the plan yourself. But check your work with someone else before you actually carry out the plan.

- **Be open**. Shed old ideas. Get your boss or client to allow you to suggest new ways to solve problems.

- **Ask for sufficient resources**. Make certain the organization you're dealing with has sufficient time, personnel and funds to solve the problem. Your responsibility includes counseling your organization if it's trying to climb too high with too small a ladder. It also means you can't over promise results.

- **Ask for commitment.** Public relations campaigns require work. They involve research, which clients and bosses are sometimes unwilling to fund. They also involve creative activities, which can be criticized by Monday morning quarterbacks.

### Key plan elements

Most planning methods have these elements in common.

- Precampaign research
- An analysis of audiences involved, including audience segments
- An ability to make messages that effectively get audiences to support your objectives
- An understanding of how people process and use information (motivation)

# PR Planning Process

 **Learn**

- Record issue history
- Collect issue data
- Describe issue "as is" (*Real State*)

**2 Think**

- Describe issue as it should be (*Ideal State*)
- Identify audiences
- Write messages
- Select channels
- Estimate competition
- Count resources

**3 Plan**

- State goal
- Write objectives
- Design strategies
- Pick tactics
- Evaluate success

**Figure 14.1**

- Credible channels to carry your messages to your audiences such as believable spokespersons and creative presentations
- Practical knowledge of how specific media channels effectively carry certain messages
- Use of behavioral objectives or management by objectives (MBO) including a realistic expectation of what you can accomplish

## How to make a PR plan

Your PR plan will combine three activities: *learn*, *think* and *plan*. Each activity will ask you to perform specific tasks (*Figure 14.1*).

### LEARN

- Record the history of your issue.
- Collect new data about your issue.
- Describe your issue as it now exists — the "**real state**" description.

### THINK

- Describe your issue as it should be — the **ideal state** your client or boss desires. Include how your plan will position the organization in the market-place, in the industry, and among the media.
- Identify your important **audiences** — include audience segments and analyze how each audience has acted in the past and is likely to act in the future.
- Construct appropriate **messages** for each of your audiences.
- Select appropriate **channels** and media to carry those messages.

- Evaluate **competition** for your messages or other **constraints** in your audiences.
- Calculate available and acquirable **resources.**

### PLAN

- State a **goal**
- Fashion **objectives**
- Design **strategies**
- Select **tactics**
- **Evaluate** success

## PR PLAN ELEMENTS

### I. Learn — situation analysis (Part 1)

In this phase, diagnose the situation, key audiences and resources. Some planners call this activity a *situation analysis*. Such an analysis is a methodical checklist to help you understand the situation as well as you can. You cannot write an effective plan unless you bond with clients and managers by understanding the issues, problem or challenge as well as they do, and better.

Access to information inside the organization is crucial for an effective analysis. Remember, quality research makes quality plans.

### 1. Record the history of the issue

- **Interview your client, boss or principals** who know about or are responsible for the outcome of the issue. For some issues, interview employees, customers, vendors, suppliers, experts, government officials, and media.

- **Interview potential target audiences.** This is an

important part of data collection. Save the information for the thinking part of the planning process.

During the interviews, look for your audiences' impressions about the issue, stories or anecdotes about what happened in the past, and their opinions about what went right and what went wrong. Don't prejudge the information. Just collect it. If you delegate others to do this, make certain they have the same pure research attitude. Also, check your client's experiences with the issues, including strategies tried.

• **Search available literature and databases on the topic.** Look for other organizations that dealt with the same issue. Look at public relations magazines and publications such as *Public Relations Quarterly* and the PRSA *Strategist* for case studies about the issue. Make certain to scour the Internet using search engines such as Yahoo™, Google™, and Ask Jeeves™ for relevant web sites.

Don't neglect the literature inside an organization either. Check letters, newsletters, news releases, memos, e-mail and other copy for background on the issue.

Remember, you're looking to do two things in this activity: get up to speed so you know as much as anyone else in the organization about the issues and their history; and gain planning power from information authority and credibility.

## 2. Collect new data about the issue

The difference between research *actions* and research *questions* is the difference between data that you can discover only by probing (*research actions*); and data you merely need to identify and collect (*research questions*).

• **Develop a list** of research questions. Get answers to the questions through interviews and invited opinion.

• **Invite opinion** from audiences key to the issue. Save these data for later use in the thinking stage.

• **Acquire preferred messages** for the PR plan. It's important to start acquiring messages from key audiences you'll later use in the plan. *Remember, audiences themselves will give you messages that will work with them.*

For example, suppose you're conducting a campaign to reduce binge drinking among first year students on a college campus. You'll want to know what positive messages will influence first-year students to avoid binge drinking.

Recent successes in actual college campaigns used positive messages to tell students that the majority of college students do not binge drink. In this phase of learning, discover if such messages will work with your student population.

• **Acquire preferred channels** for the plan. Discover channels that could work to deliver those messages. Using the same binge drinking example, ask students which channels would be effective — face-to-face meetings with student campaign managers, leaders of fraternities and sororities supporting the campaign, or perhaps colorful and attention-catching posters throughout the campus.

## 3. Describe how things are — the "real state" description

• **Picture your key issues** as they exist at the moment. The "now" snapshot includes the history of the issue, the behavior of key players and audiences, tactics tried, messages sent, resources expended, success and failure, and attitudes toward potential messages and channels.

• **Write a statement** that combines what you learned. Call it the "where-we-are" statement. Share the statement with your client, boss or others who commissioned the plan. This crucial "moment" in the planning process bonds you with those responsible for the plan. When you bond with them and the issues, you can authoritatively write the plan. The plan components become believable and acceptable. The *Real State Analysis Statement* will be the most authoritative part of the plan because it is fact-based. Other parts of the plan will be speculative — researched yes, but still speculative, such as what you will try to do and how you'll try to do it.

## II. THINK – situation analysis (Part 2)

### 1. Describe the issue as it should be — the "ideal" state

• **Include "positioning" your issue.** For example, if you want avoidance of binge drinking to be among the top three resolutions first-year college students make, then state it that way. It will help specify the planning process.

The ideal picture represents the large purpose of the campaign — the big picture. Describe the ideal in terms of outcome, what you want to happen. The outcome or purpose generally involves an audience that you hope will act a certain way by the end of the program.

*Example: The majority of first-year college students will avoid binge drinking because of the positive college experiences that follow from avoiding the practice.*

• **Make certain communication and public relations can accomplish the ideal.** Some issues cannot be changed, even with the help of communication, because other variables control the situation.

*Example:* The head of United Way a few years ago was accused of taking too large a salary compared to other executives in not-for-profit organizations. Only the executive's resignation could persuade former contributors to begin making contributions again. Contributors had reduced their contributions because they didn't want their donations going to executives' bloated salaries.

## 2. Identify important audiences related to the issue

• **Divide your major audiences into smaller, manageable segments** before you try to approach them. Consider using this list of types of segmented audiences:

- Direct targets – users of the information
- Indirect targets – gatekeepers who give you access to direct targets
- Influential people or groups who control others' opinions
- Involved people, such as activists, organizers, political action groups
- Role models
- Media

Your list could be longer. It will vary with your plan. Select only audience segments you need for your plan.

*Example*: "All first-year students" is a large audience. If you tried to reach this audience as described, you could fashion messages and select channels only in a general way. That process won't be as effective as fashioning messages and selecting channels for more narrowly defined audiences.

You could segment or divide major audience members according to their status, their association with Greek organizations, their gender, and their commuter/resident status. The larger audience now becomes:

- Matriculated or nonmatriculated
- Fraternity or sorority members and nonmembers
- Males and females
- Residents and commuters

*Examples*:

- *First year students who pledge to fraternities and sororities*
- *First year students who live on campus*
- *First year students who control campus social events*

• **Next, analyze how each segment acts or is likely to act toward the issue.** This is called a *behavioral analysis*. For example: How do students and segments of the student body best receive information? Are their attitudes about excessive drinking so ingrained that they will be difficult to change? Who are their leaders, those they believe and follow? What will be necessary to overcome their desire to "cut loose" because they're away from home? Will they be responsive to messages discovered in the learning phase of planning?

An analysis of how audiences behave is essential to an effective plan. Public relations is not a guessing game. It's a science with an artistic touch. The artistic intuition comes from how much psychology the practitioner knows. Behavior, the bulk of public relations work, comes from the psychology of audiences.

So a model develops (*Figure 14.2*):

Audience identification → audience segmentation → audience behavioral analysis → messages and channels from the analysis → communication to audiences → audience behavior → public relations success.

- Finally, estimate the effort you'll have to expend to reach and inform or persuade your targeted audiences. Ask strategic questions such as:
- Can I reach enough of them to make a difference?
- Do I have to reach all members of the targeted group or just the leaders?
- How available are they to receive my messages?
- What preliminary messages must I send to prepare the way before I send the major messages?
- Do I have access to the channels they use?
- Do I have to increase my credibility with them first before I reach out them?
- How many times will I have to reach them to make a difference?
- Do I have the available talent and resources to do the job?
- Do I have the time?
- Can I reach them in time before they act otherwise?

The most successful practitioners ask themselves such questions.

## 3. Construct the right messages for the right audiences

Here you should review the material in the research chapter for creating effective messages.

Ask yourself if your messages are appropriate.

- Do my messages consider the ambition of the organization promoting the public relations plan?
- Do my messages take care of the information needs of the audience?
- Do my messages help my audience get what it wants as well as what I want?
- Do my messages tell my audience what to do (behavior) as well as what it should know and feel?
- Do my messages conform to the research I discovered in the *learn* phase of my planning process?

## Building Toward Success
### Planning Model

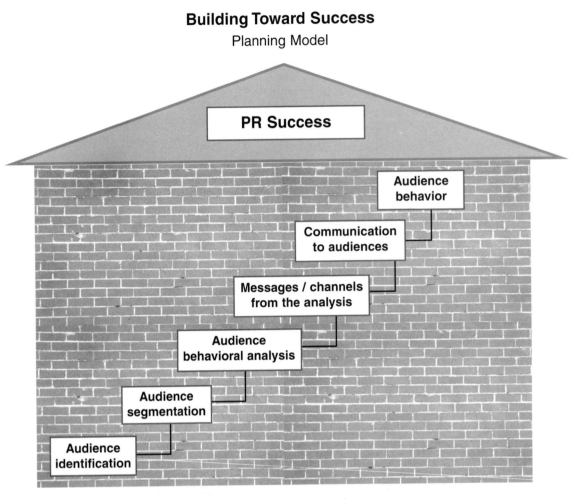

**PR Success**

Audience behavior

Communication to audiences

Messages / channels from the analysis

Audience behavioral analysis

Audience segmentation

Audience identification

**Figure 14.2 Building upward, block by block, toward a plan.**

- Do my messages contain what one researcher calls the (*UPP – Unique Persuasive Proposition*)? Do my messages push my audience's "hot button"?
- Do my messages effectively carry the theme of my campaign?

If a specific audience behavior is supposed to result from your public relations plan, then you must discover factors within your audience that might prevent the desired behavior. The best moments for PR practitioners are the times when they correctly blend research with psychology to understand why audiences behave or don't behave in certain ways. Once you learn about your audiences, you can fashion messages to overcome constraints in your audience and gain the desired behavior.

You can see how important the learning phase of the planning process is from the necessity to fashion appropriate messages.

In the example on binge drinking, messages come from target population research. But they also come from

client ambition — the university. In this example you'll see how a university adopted a national anti-binge drinking campaign. The campaign used positive messages:

- *Students will avoid binge drinking if they see that nonbinge drinkers are among the majority of students on campus.*
- *Nonbinge drinkers do better academically and socially in college than binge drinkers.*

These messages came from national research in the LEARN phase of that campaign.

### 4. Select appropriate channels and media

Messages arrive at target audiences through channels. In this *think* phase of the planning process, you can choose from the whole menu of channels that are varieties of the four major media types — face to face, print, electronic and special events.

In this phase, you must consider three things — the audiences you want to reach; the messages you want to send; and the channels you will use. All three must complement one another or your plan might not work. This is the M-A-C Triad mentioned in the research chapter.

## 5. Evaluate competition

Consider competition in the traditional sense, that an organization's product or service competes with yours for the public's attention or resources. To fashion an effective plan, you need to know what your competition is up to.

In the LEARN phase, look at your competition's PR efforts. You'll be in better position to succeed with your audiences if you know other messages they get each day. You can counter the messages, or perhaps even learn from them. Try to perceive if your competitors' messages come from research. What do they know that you should? If your competitor uses experienced PR practitioners, then you should be able to look backward from the messages and channels to the audience analysis, to the purpose, and then to the research in the *learn* phase.

In addition, by studying the competition your audience faces, even if not from a "competitor," you can overcome resistance to your messages.

*Example*: In the binge drinking program, the competition is not for the time and attention of first-year students. It's from first-year student attitudes of being "free" and "of age" and "being one of the crowd."

You cannot mount an effective program without looking at competition in all its manifestations.

## 6. Calculate available and acquirable resources

Before you finish thinking about your plan design, estimate resources available to deliver your messages to your audiences. Consider the following:

- Will you need expensive mass media such as advertising in the newspapers or on radio, television or the Internet?
- Do you need special talent, such as trained talk show guests, or artists or planners?
- Do you have to train people for special events or fund-raising campaigns?
- Does the organization you're working for have PR talent or volunteers who can help you, or do you have to bring in your own people at extra expense?
- Do you have the right equipment and supplies for the job such as computers, special software, or research tools?
- Do you have access to printers, suppliers, and vendors?
- Does the organization you're working for have effective relationships with the media or will you have to develop them?

- Do you have sufficient time for your tactics to work?

These and many other questions about available and acquirable resources will control what you'll be able to do.

*Caution*: Unless you know how much public relations tools and tactics cost, you could over-plan — schedule more tactics than you have resources to accomplish. Don't underestimate what tactics cost. Costs will vary across the country.

## III. Public relations plan

### PLAN

- State a goal
- Fashion objectives
- Design strategies
- Select tactics
- Evaluate success

When you have completed the thinking phase of the planning process, you should know your ambition, your key audiences (and a lot more about them), your major and minor messages and themes, the best channels for each audience, and resources to get the job done.

In constructing a PR program, practitioners put all the elements together — issues, audiences, messages and channels and blend them into a logical action plan.

The action plan is called a PR program or PR campaign. It takes the basic public relations model, the M-A-C Triad, and makes it a public relations plan.

Note how each element of the model becomes a corresponding element of the plan (*Figure 14.3*).

— Issues become the major goals of the plan.
— Many objectives develop from an audience viewpoint.
— Strategies carry strategic messages.
— And channels are very tactical.

### Conversion Model — Plan

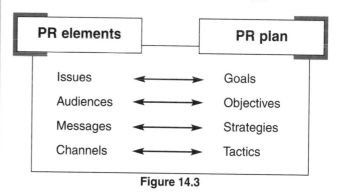

**Figure 14.3**

Before specifying the parts of the plan. let's first see how the transformation from the M-A-C Triad to a full-blown plan takes place. Here's an example of how practitioners decide which channels to select for specific audiences. Consider the following case.

## Mini-Case – Why HMOs aren't paying

A health maintenance organization (HMO) wants to get the word out to both subscribers and critics that it makes medically sound decisions when it pays for or denies health care services. The national company has been under attack in the media for its "unethical practices."

Audience profiling research by the organization reveals that a deep-seated mistrust exists among its subscribers. Personal customer experience and unfavorable media "investigative stories" have fueled the mistrust. Research also shows that the audience is not likely to change its mind unless the company demonstrates a dramatic change in policy. What to do?

First, the company decides to review its policy to see if indeed it's too restrictive. That's the first message. Both subscribers and media want that.

The second message promises a new review procedure for denied requests by an independent ombudsman (a patient advocate within the company) who would have an independent panel of medical and insurance people to help with the review. The company promises to abide by the ombudsman's decision, who can't be fired for reversing "too many" of the denied requests. How to deliver these two new messages?

The company's PR people reason that such a dramatic change in practice deserves some face-to-face techniques and some control techniques for both audiences. Because of the variety of medical cases people face each day, the company's public relations people also want the ability to answer questions and clarify issues.

Here's what the PR practitioners for the HMO decide to do:

**Audience**
*Subscribers*
    **Message 1**
    Policy review
        **Channel 1**
        Letter
            **Rationale**
            *The simplicity of this message demands nothing more than an announcement with some explanation.*
        **Channel 2**
        Hot line

            **Rationale**
            *Feedback from subscribers provides opportunity to clarify issues and gain new information that could help with other tactics.*
    **Message 2**
    Ombudsman appointment
        **Channel 1**
        Special event
            **Rationale**
            *The ombudsman will secure talk show and newsmaker appearances on national radio and television. The PR office will secure these bookings by teasing producers with the topical nature of the subject. Other collateral media efforts will entice the producers to book the ombudsman or other PR spokespersons.*
        **Channel 2**
        Advertising
            **Rationale**
            *The company will use some national newspaper and magazine advertising to guarantee control of the message and its exposure.*
**Audience**
*Media*
    **Messages**
    Policy review
    Ombudsman appointment
        **Channel**
        News conference
            **Rationale**
            *The conference will attract national media attention. Snappy media kits will contain news releases and position statements. And a question-and-answer session will provide sound bites for the electronic media. Finally, electronic media will receive a videotape outlining the company's position, explaining how the new process will work.*

## PR plan components

### Goals — Objectives — Strategies — Tactics

A PR plan comprises four action steps:

**1. State a goal**. A goal is your overarching ambition. It's necessarily ambitious and states what you hope to accomplish. Your plan isn't necessarily unsuccessful if you can't accomplish your entire goal. Consider your goal a target, a picture of the state of affairs that helps your organization achieve its public relations aims.

*Example goal:* Establish a positive reputation for Heal-Me-Now HMO among subscribers and the media.

**2. Fashion objectives**. An objective is a portion of your goal. Consider objectives as "whats" you have to accomplish. You cannot divide the goal into just one objective because then it would be a goal itself. Carefully look at your task and logically divide it into manageable parts. Then write each part in measurable terms. Note the measurable terms in the following examples of objectives:

*Example*:

- **Reverse the negative media coverage** about Heal-Me-Now HMO's decision making on providing health care.

- **Recapture subscribers' confidence** in Heal-Me-Now HMO's ability to provide unbiased health care decision making.

- Rally the HMO industry to **support Heal-Me-Now as a pro-patient insurance company**.

Remember, a valid objective must specify task achievement in a way you can measure when you complete the plan.

**3. Design Strategies**. A strategy is an *approach* to achieve the objective. A strategy is partly "what" you must do and partly "how" you'll do it. Look at strategies as *causes* and objectives as *effects*. Strategies declare what your audience will know, feel or do or what must be in place at the completion of the strategy. Strategies creatively connect audiences and messages. A well-conceived strategy has an undisguised message.

*Example strategies*: Based on the first objective in the example above …

- Influence the media to feel they have **access to counterbalancing information** on the issue.

- Position the HMO as an **organization responsive to customer requests**.

- Respond to specific allegations so the **media's agenda philosophically changes**.

Note that in these strategies a specific verb describes the ambition in terms of management, practitioner or audience behavior. **Strategies merge ambition and action**. But note also, the wording does not mention or describe *how* the ambition/action will be done. Strategies are not techniques. Strategies are *ambition actions*. The *how-to* or *practical action* work is left to tactics.

*Tip*: View your ambition and your message as the same concept.

In the example above: "**Influence** the media to feel they have access to counterbalancing information on the issue." The *ambition* is to get the media to *sense access*. That's also one of the campaign messages. You could

develop as many strategies as there are audiences and messages.

**4. Select tactics**. A tactic is a specific *practical action* that fulfills the ambition of the strategy. Tactics connect your audiences, messages and channels in a specific way.

They're characterized by three specific expenditures — agent, cost and time (memorably A-C-T, for taking **a-c-t**ion, which they do).

An activity is not a tactic unless a specific agent does it, has a specific cost, and occurs in a specific time frame. One way to distinguish a strategy from a tactic is to ask:

| | |
|---|---|
| Who will do it? | **A**gent |
| What will it cost? | **C**ost |
| When and how long will it happen? | **T**ime |

So t**act**ic has the word **act** in it to help you remember that it must have these three elements to be a true tactic.

Here are some examples of tactics for the first strategy in the example above:

*Tactic examples*

- The PR office will conduct a **news conference** corresponding to the launch of talk show appearances and advertising.

- The PR office will disseminate a series of three **news releases** focusing on the need to control medical care costs.

- The PR office will arrange **editorial board visits** with media printing negative news about the organization to positively influence future editorial comment.

All three tactics deal with the first strategy only. As with the objective/strategy connection, so also the strategy/ tactic connection requires at least two tactics for each strategy.

Note that unlike a tactic, you can't assign cost, responsibility or time to a *strategy*.

*Example*:

Strategy: *Influence* the media to feel they have access to counterbalancing information on the issue.

What does "influence" mean?
How much does "influence" cost?
Who will do the "influencing?"
When will the "influencing" take place.

Notice how the three components of a tactic are missing in strategy wording.

# How research helps

The *learn* or research phase of the planning process will help you write objectives, strategies and tactics in the following ways:

- Research helps with analysis or the thinking phase of the process, the cornerstone of the PR plan. **Research pre-thinks analysis.**

- You can't properly fashion objectives unless you properly frame issues. **Research frames issues**.

- To write effective strategies you should consult with experienced and creative practitioners. They can reveal to you ways to divide your objectives. They can also share their successful standards for measuring your strategies. **Research reveals strategic approaches**.

- Research is essential to develop and carry out successful tactics. Media placements, special events costs, speaker availability, etc, all require that you know what's possible before "booking" it. **Research authenticates tactics**.

- And research helps you detect information, attitude or behavior change in your audiences. **Research measures achievement.**

**5. Evaluate success.** To complete the research sandwich (formative and evaluative) evaluate each objective, strategy and tactic to demonstrate the level of your plan's success.

- To evaluate if you achieved your objectives, demonstrate how well you reached the measurable terms of the objective. You can be partially successful, too. In the example above …

*Example objective: Reverse the negative media coverage about Heal-Me-Now HMO's decision making on providing health care.*

… you might reduce the negative media coverage by 75 percent but not entirely eliminate it. Is that success? You might negotiate what's acceptable to client, boss and you. But without measurement, you have no basis for negotiation.

- To evaluate your strategies' successes, demonstrate that you accomplished your strategies' purposes. Remember, strategies aren't like tactics. You can't put your measuring hands around them as well as you can with tactics, which are more specific. To measure if you achieved the strategy's purpose in the above example …

*Influence the media to feel they have access to counterbalancing information on the issue.*

… you need to prove that the media have gained access. You can do this by pointing to disseminated media kits, conversations with media representatives, or better, facts from the media kits showing up in media stories.

- To evaluate the success of your tactics, demonstrate that you delivered them on time, on budget, and that your messages reached your intended targets. You don't have to prove that your messages worked, (that's the job of the strategies), merely that you delivered them. In addition, you can demonstrate that your tactics were the proper ones, that you selected the right channel for the message and the audience. In the above example …

*The PR office will conduct a news conference corresponding to the launch of talk show appearances and advertising.*

… you must demonstrate that the conference took place, was well attended (because the tactics involve tasks such as invitations), and coincided with the launch. Remember, you must demonstrate that the channel (news conference) was appropriate to the audience (media) and message (delivery of counterbalancing information).

When you measure tactics, look at process measurement, "Did I do it right?" and effect measurement, "Did it work?" Avoid declaring the tactic was the wrong choice because the effect didn't happen.

Perhaps you sent a poor invitation or held the news conference when a snowstorm hit town and no one showed up.

*Right tactic + wrong execution = no effect*

Perhaps you sent a brilliantly written news release, but the media wanted to meet your organization's people in person, not through a printed argument.

*Wrong tactic + right execution = no effect*

Perhaps you called the perfect news conference — site, refreshments, media kits — but no one showed up because you called it in the middle of a community crisis.

*Right tactic and execution +poor timing = no effect*

## Model PR plan

Here's a public relations plan adapted from a project by a public relations senior university class. The plan focused on helping students avoid incidents of binge drinking.

### *Goal*

"Within three years, reduce incidence of binge drinking on the college campus by 16% among first-year students through a positive message campaign."

### *Objective 1.0*

**Create a positive culture that encourages students to become part of an on-campus positive movement.**

*Analysis: To encourage students to fully participate in the positive messaging of the campaign, planners decided to promote a positive university-wide culture.*

## Strategy 1.1

**Provide age-specific experiences for students that will encourage them to spend more time with students who do not binge drink.**

*Analysis*: Audience analysis suggests that first-year students, need models to emulate during college years. Research shows that more good things than bad things happen to students who do not binge drink — higher grades, a broader college experience, etc.

## Tactic 1.1.1

**Sponsor a Halloween bash, "Hall-O-Week," in the Student Center ballroom the last week of October.**

*Analysis*: By conducting this event in October, planners want students to get early positive modeling and mentoring.

## Tactic 1.1.2

**Advertise "Hall-O-Week" with two ads in the college newspaper, with 10 public service announcements on the college radio station, through two flyers, three posters, inter- office mail, letters to campus organizations, and a "crier" in the student center. Make certain the event messages gain the sponsorship of the campus-wide task force on binge drinking.**

*Analysis*: Messages came from research in the LEARN portion of the campaign. The invitations do not simply advertise the features of the event. They heavily promote the benefits — "meet the best the university has to offer." Because research showed that the majority of students do not binge drink, the "best of the university" is among the majority of students.

## Strategy 1.2

**Create a "(name) U Spirit" (name of University) on campus that will bond students so when they're tempted to binge drink, students will have access to a like-minded, nonbinge-drinking support group.**

*Analysis*: The planning team considered Spirit an essential attitude to condition the audience to positive messaging. Notice how the strategy reveals the thinking of the planners about the psychology of the audience.

## Tactic 1.2.1

**For one week, student volunteers will distribute "(Name) U Spirit" paraphernalia to students in the student center during lunch hours.**

*Analysis*: Students must see that students like themselves are willing to speak out for moderation in a licentious society and encourage others to be moderate in their drinking habits. When the time comes, the target audience might be encouraged to stand up for themselves and avoid binge drinking.

## Tactic 1.2.2

**Host a live talk show on the college radio station, in the Student Center, to discuss "Drinking in College in America" and provide the tape to the state public television network and C-Span. Audience participation in this public event will stimulate spirit.**

*Analysis*: Spirit comes from prestige and common purpose. The talk show should accomplish both.

## Strategy 1.3

**Using the results of the most recent campus Student Satisfaction Inventory, write and design advertisements and feature articles highlighting positive SSI findings throughout the previous academic year.**

*Analysis*: The Student Satisfaction Inventory contains many references to positive experiences by students. If planners can tie those findings to the statistics that the majority of students do not binge drink, they can imply in their messages to students that they too, can share in such positive experiences.

## Tactic 1.3.1

**Submit two full-page, black and white advertisements to the college newspaper focusing on the researched messages that students who do not binge drink do better in classes and social life than those who do.**

*Analysis*: Notice how the tactic includes the audience, messages and channel.

## Tactic 1.3.2

**Submit two feature articles, one to the university newsletter to students, and the other to the faculty/staff newsletter. The student newsletter article will focus on successful students that have an anti-traditional view about college drinking. The faculty/staff newsletter article will focus on other universities that have successfully conducted an antibinge drinking campaign.**

*Analysis*: The target audience must continue to read and hear about students with nontraditional drinking attitudes. They must sense that "they have company" in this campaign effort. By citing other universities, planners send the subtle message that students can become part of a "movement."

## Objective 2.0

**The campus will unite to send consistent, positive alcohol-related messages prior to orientation.**

*Analysis*: Traditional campus campaigns had focused on negative messaging — "People who drink don't get good scores." For the new campaign to succeed, it must prevent negative and mixed messages from reaching the target. Because other organizations on campus conduct anti-alcohol campaigns of their own, but with negative messaging, planners must get their cooperation to blend the messages, run their campaign at a different time of the year, or end their efforts in favor of the positive message campaign.

### Strategy 2.1

Key Communicators will agree to use only positive alcohol-related messages prior to orientation.

*Analysis*: To succeed, planners must persuade influential administrators and student groups to avoid mixed messages, especially to incoming first-year students.

### Tactic 2.1.1

Prior to orientation, Key Communicators will establish a task force comprising members from each campus organization.

*Analysis*: The strategy should persuade influential leaders from the target organizations to join the campaign effort.

### Tactic 2.1.2

Conduct a workshop to educate task force members how to disseminate positive alcohol-related messages.

*Analysis*: The workshop format provides the opportunity to draw successful managers of similar campaigns to the campus. The infusion of outside talent and experts should influence task force members to coordinate alcohol-related messages.

### Tactic 2.1.3

Create and distribute a pamphlet to task force members explaining how to relay only positive messages regarding alcohol usage.

*Analysis*: Campaigners frequently use print pieces to get "message endurance." If key people missed the workshop, they would have information provided by the campaign sponsors, not merely by workshop attendees.

### Tactic 2.1.4

Faculty will receive a monthly "newsletter/memo" highlighting positive achievements.

*Analysis*: Faculty are a gatekeeper audience in this plan. As influentials, they must have the same information as the planners so they can endorse the project and pass the information on to their students. For example, results of the student attitude survey will inform faculty that less than half the student body binge drinks. Note the use of a newsletter/memo to facilitate quick information intake.

### Strategy 2.2

Evaluate strategy 2.1 for effectiveness in two areas: the use of only positive messages and the dissemination of those messages to target audiences.

*Analysis*: Dissemination of messages alone will not prove that the audience internalized the messages. Never mistake dissemination for total communication.

### Tactic 2.2.1

Conduct four one-hour focus groups at the end of the semester to discover message points students received and remembered about binge drinking.

*Analysis*: Focus groups won't provide scientific data. But they will give planners rich information about reception, internalization, recall and influence of campaign messages. A print survey or intercept interviews might not be able to accomplish what focus groups can.

### Tactic 2.2.2

Conduct a content analysis of messages from campus organizations to determine the effectiveness of the pamphlet and workshop on task force members' behavior regarding positive messaging.

*Analysis*: Planners selected a content analysis as the research method because it can identify all the channels and provide a comprehensive analysis.

### Objective 3.0

Use positive messages to reduce binge drinking on and off the campus, by all students, by three percent in the first year, five percent in the second year, and eight percent in the third year.

*Analysis*: Objectives clearly state the ambition in measurable terms with specific behavior by clearly defined audiences. The amount of behavior change depends on personnel, time and money. By analyzing their resources, planners determined the reasonable percent of change possible.

### Strategy 3.1

Inform students through positive messaging within an extensive media campaign that the majority of university students do not binge drink and encourage them to adopt the attitude that they are not captive to a minority drinking culture.

*Analysis*: Sometimes strategies will only inform audiences or change their attitudes without going after behavior change. It's the cumulative effort of all the strategies that should produce the desired behavior.

Notice how the strategy accomplishes part of the ambition of the objective by going after the real "blocking" attitude — "All college students binge drink and I want to be part of the majority crowd."

### Tactic 3.1.1

Disseminate a "Did you know?" message through announcements on the college radio station and on the local cable access channel, college newspaper advertisements, and in flyers and posters stating that the majority of university students do not binge drink.

*Analysis*: The "Did-you-know?" campaign directly places major messages in play for pickup by the larger target audience. The effort is "pantactical" – a shotgun approach for broad reach.

### Tactic 3.1.2

Randomly ask on-campus students to state the binge-drinking rate on campus. Correct answers earn monetary rewards, such as coupons for the campus bookstore.

*Analysis*: The use of a game approach to disseminate information should do the job with this audience.

### Strategy 3.2

Provide highly publicized alternative activities for students who do not want to binge drink.

*Analysis*: To prove that a counter culture exists, planners must persuade college authorities to provide alternative activities. "Actions speak louder than words."

### Tactic 3.2.1

Sponsor a "Friday Night Coffee Hour" with entertainment participation activities to complement a nondrinking event such as a "Jeopardy-style" contest and demonstration/discussion of student projects.

*Analysis*: To approach segmented audiences, planners narrow channels and messages. Remember that special events in PR campaigns are powerful channels.

### Tactic 3.2.2

Sponsor the "Pajama Jammy Jam," a lock-in event in the student center with movies, dancing and DJ contests, food and other forms of entertainment.

*Analysis*: Lock-in events are becoming popular on college campuses to encourage stay-on-campus movements. Planners must conceive of ways to network the nonbinge drinking and pre-binge drinking audience segments.

### Tactic 3.2.3

Sponsor a pool party in the recreation center.

*Analysis*: Creative planners use the assets of the college community to deliver their messages and network their audiences.

### Strategy 3.3

Evaluate the effectiveness of the media and special events campaign.

*Analysis*: Proper evaluation includes message delivery and retention, attitude change and behavior change.

### Tactic 3.3.1

Conduct intercept studies and focus groups.

*Analysis*: Planners will be certain to include all segments in the studies, especially first-year students. They will also include first-year students that decided to binge drink to discover which portions of the campaign did not work with them.

### Tactic 3.3.2

Conduct a "postmortem" analysis of the campaign design.

*Analysis*: Each aspect of the campaign must be analyzed — objectives, strategies and tactics.

## Final note

Because public relations is an art applied to a science, it's important to know how to evaluate each aspect of the plan. Given the same challenge (goal), two groups of planners should theoretically come up with the same objectives (the science of the profession).

But strategies and tactics are part science and part art. The two groups of planners will almost certainly not come up with the same strategies and tactics.

The art part of the profession depends on the artist. Education, experience, preference for certain media and channels, and depth of psychological knowledge inspire strategies and tactics. When organizations hire PR people, they should look at the "artistic" makeup of the candidate as well as knowledge of the science of the profession.

You should remember three things about the PR mind when you look for a PR job or hire PR people.

- Look at the left brain. Planning is highly logical. Tearing a challenge apart and reassembling it in constituent parts takes methodical thinking. Make certain to include your left brain assets in your resume or pool of candidates.

- Look at the right brain. Planning is highly artistic. Selecting the right tactic to make subtle changes in an audience's attitude, psychological makeup or behavior takes deft skill. Your right brain achievements could get you or other candidates into the final interview.

- Look at the whole brain. The most valuable players on the PR team are those who can see the big picture. They don't fall in love with their own preferences for certain tactics or tools. They know a logical connection from an illogical disconnect, and they appreciate self relations as much as media relations. Present yourself as a whole-brain practitioner or hire one. ■

## Tips

1. Never agree to develop a PR plan without research. You'll only be guessing and you probably won't achieve your objectives.

2. In developing the ideal state analysis, ask your clients to picture how they want things to be.

3. Before you write strategies, list audiences and messages from your research for each objective. Then create a strategy for each pairing.

4. Never start to write a plan until your boss or client has signed off on your situation analysis.

5. The best source for meaningful messages for audiences is from the audiences themselves. Study them. Ask them directly if you can.

6. Hire or appoint planners who know the full array of media and channels available and what each can do to and for an audience. Beware of engaging narrowly focused planners, print-bound, for example.

7. Make certain your planning team comprises both left- and right-brain thinkers.

8. Allow free brainstorming when you're trying to develop tactics. Don't be too quickly judgmental. Because of the creative nature of this part of the process, you can turn off some planners early in the process.

9. Test for the validity of objectives by continually asking: How will this objective get us to the goal?

10. If you don't believe in the planning process, your boss or client won't either.

---

**Questions for classroom discussion**

1. Characterize the activity in each of the planning stages, Learn, Think and Plan, and suggest why they are labeled that way.

2. Why is the Situation Analysis (Part I — Real State Analysis) so important to a consultant? To a counselor? To a planner?

3. In the design pictured, how does each PR element on the left become the corresponding part of a PR plan on the right?

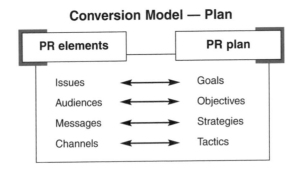

**Conversion Model — Plan**

| PR elements | | PR plan |
|---|---|---|
| Issues | ←→ | Goals |
| Audiences | ←→ | Objectives |
| Messages | ←→ | Strategies |
| Channels | ←→ | Tactics |

4. What three special characteristics of tactics distinguish them from strategies?

5. How would you respond if a client asked you why it's necessary to spend any money on research in making a PR plan?

Name_____Date _____

## PR Planning – M.D. or D.O.? Osteopathy Needs Sympathy

As PR director for a hospital staffed primarily by doctors of osteopathy (D.O. after their names), you continually struggle to prove to your community that your hospital can be trusted as much as a hospital staffed by medical doctors (M.D. after their names). Develop a PR model for the specific issue in the example below, then convert that model to a mini-PR plan (with one objective only). Use the conversion scheme pictured:

### Conversion Model — Plan

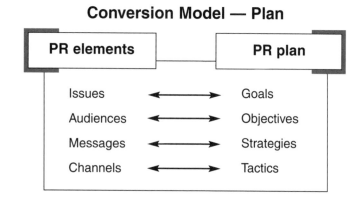

| PR elements | | PR plan |
|---|---|---|
| Issues | ⟷ | Goals |
| Audiences | ⟷ | Objectives |
| Messages | ⟷ | Strategies |
| Channels | ⟷ | Tactics |

**Issue**: Rumors circulate in the community that hospital D.O. radiologists might not see the same important things on X-rays, CAT scans and MRIs as M.D. radiologists might, especially at an M.D. university hospital. The rumors are accompanied by "horror stories" of misread films, misdiagnoses and poor treatment.

Issue /Goal

_____

_____

Audiences /Objective

_____

_____

_____

_____

*See other side*

Name _____ Date _____

**Practical case study**

Messages / Strategies

_____

_____

_____

Channels / Tactics

_____

_____

_____

## Mini PR Plan

Goal _____

Objective 1.0 _____

Strategy 1.1 _____

_____

Tactic 1.1.1 _____

_____

Tactic 1.1.2 _____

_____

Strategy 1.2 _____

_____

Tactic 1.2.1 _____

_____

Tactic 1.2.2 _____

_____

# Chapter 15

# Getting Ahead in Public Relations

**PRaxiom** *Parties who want milk should not seat themselves on a stool in the middle of a field in hope that the cows will back up to them.*

*Elbert Hubbard*

## What this chapter covers

You'll learn how to prepare for a public relations position, how to start your career and how to succeed as you move up the PR ladder. You'll also see which traits bosses respect and how networking can help your future. The chapter also introduces you to careers in college relations, school PR, healthcare PR, political PR, government PR, sports PR and agency PR.

You'll also read about the advantages of joining a professional or preprofessional student public relations group as an important step for anyone who communicates.

## What success in PR looks like

To succeed in public relations, you need many of the following skills and traits:

• **Ability to write**. Frequently, you'll become the final say on word choices such as *affect* or *effect*, and on whether it can be said better in 40 words or seven. Therefore, you should take as many courses as you possibly can in real-world writing. Basic writing at most colleges prepares you to write for teachers of basic writing. When you want to begin a career in public relations, however, you have to demonstrate that you're capable of writing journalistically and in a way that conveys your message to people at many different levels. In addition to taking writing courses, try to serve an internship with an excellent writer who will improve your writing. Most entry level positions will require the ability to write. You'll need:

• **Discipline to determine which of many responsibilities must get done today.** Missing the deadline on something that is ultra-important could cost you your job.

• **Ability to think logically and to plan strategically**. When you're trying to persuade upper-level management

that you should *zig* when they want to *zag*, you've got to be able to present arguments in a logical way and show the implications of possible strategies and decisions.

• **Ability to talk the language of CEOs and vice presidents.** Find out what they're reading and read some of those same publications so you will know the jargon and understand the bottom-line mentality that drives colleagues and bosses. If possible, take one course in basic accounting or at least read a book in accounting so you'll have some feel for the language they're using.

• **Ability to get along with people.** Although almost all who are attracted to public relations say they get along well with people, it's more than just being a nice person. It means going out of your way to work effectively with people who disagree with you. It means being able to argue with someone in a management meeting and then go to lunch with the person and not hold grudges. It means being pleasant to custodians as well as those above you on the corporate ladder. When push comes to shove and it's time to downsize, if all things are equal, bosses much prefer to keep the pleasant people who get along with everyone rather than the malcontents.

• **Ability to take the blame for bosses while they take the credit for many of your accomplishments.** PR beginners who bask in the glory of college newspaper bylines frequently have trouble adapting to a world where they do most of the work behind the scenes but someone else gets the credit. Even worse is the situation where you have recommended strategy A, but the boss picked strategy B and then allowed the rest of the world to think that the PR person was responsible for strategy B that failed.

• **Ability to determine what's working.** In a world that is more and more concerned with bottom-line effectiveness, the public relations professional must be able to show how the public relations program has contributed to the overall success of the organization. This means coming up with ways to measure effectiveness.

• **Ability to establish rapport with secretaries and others** who play a key role in the communication process of an organization. The authors' numerous workshops conducted with thousands of secretaries clearly show that secretaries appreciate being told when they do a good job, what the priorities are and when bosses will be available. They tend to work much harder for bosses who communicate on a regular basis with them and show their gratitude for jobs well done.

*People who smile are perceived to be 10% more intelligent than those who don t.*

• **Ability to suggest ideas and accept rejection of those ideas.** Find out if your boss prefers things on a 3 x 5 card or in her mailbox at lunch, or at a meeting early in the morning before anyone else arrives. Realize that the boss may accept only one of every five ideas submitted. Realize though that at the end of the year, if 10 of your suggestions have been accepted and 40 have been rejected, that the 10 should please your boss. One of the greatest complaints bosses have is that their employees aren't offering new ideas.

• **Walk briskly to communicate that you're serious about your work.** People who walk with an apparent purpose are perceived as having more commitment and purpose in their lives.

• **Smile.** Research indicates that people who smile are perceived to be 10% more intelligent than people who don't.

## Preparing to get your first public relations position

Competition for entry level public relations positions is fierce. To enhance the chance that you'll succeed in your quest for that first job, you should seriously consider the following suggestions:

• **Impress a public relations professor.** Do outstanding work in that professor's class. Ask intelligent questions that show your interest in discussion topics. Demonstrate that you're reading the text and articles about public relations areas that prompt your interest. Then seek that professor's help in finding a solid internship.

• **Land an internship** that enables you to build a portfolio that demonstrates you're capable of accomplishing certain public relations tasks. While serving the internship, build a solid relationship with your supervisor. *Remember*: This person will play a key role in your recommendations. If properly chosen, the internship

supervisor will be blessed with a large number of contacts and will be able to set you up with interview possibilities both in and out of the organization where you were interning.

Be sure the internship opportunity allows you to do serious public relations work. If you realize you're doing secretarial or "gofer" jobs only, talk to your supervisor and your college intern overseer to solve the problem. If you complete the internship without a variety of professional level portfolio fillers, you've wasted your time.

While working at the internship site, strive to be humble while working with all kinds of people — from top bosses to custodians. Future would-be employers will always ask how you got along with people. Be observant. Notice how the people with the kinds of jobs you want dress, how they write memos, how they treat peers and others, and how they always meet deadlines.

• **Volunteer** to take on an occasional volunteer public relations project for a church group, a college fraternity or sorority, or a local nonprofit organization such as The Red Cross, The Cancer Society, etc. Vary the assignments you complete so your portfolio will show some breadth.

• **Select elective courses that will make you more employable.** It's far better to list courses in social psychology and advanced graphics than it is to take courses that end in time for the afternoon soaps. Completing courses that will help you seem more ready to do the jobs needed will be more advantageous than raising your cumulative average by a tenth of a point by enrolling in easy courses.

• **Attend meetings of on-campus groups** that discuss topics and introduce you to speakers who might in some way help you network to identify possible job openings. If a speaker offers information on a topic that turns you on, consider asking a question during or after the session. You might also follow up with a letter that shares an article you read on the topic. This could lead to an invitation to serve an internship. If your campus has a chapter of the Public Relations Student Society of America, you should avail yourself of the opportunity to work on the chapter's newsletter or to serve as an account executive for the student agency.

• As graduation nears, tell as many people as you can that **you're seeking a public relations position**. Don't limit your audience to people who work in public relations positions. You never know who has a cousin who works for someone who just yesterday decided to hire a new public relations person.

• Check with key professors to gain their permission to list them as references. Their support can mean quite a bit with some of the people who might be considering you for a position. If possible, **acquire a written recommendation** you can keep in case the professor is not available over the summer. Don't expect your favorite prof to write the recommendation six hours after requested — especially if it's finals week and grades must be turned in 48 hours from your request.

• When preparing your résumé, **focus on accomplishments and specific skills** you can bring to the job. Many companies use computer scanners to match their needs with what candidates offer. Be sure to communicate as many abilities as you can. Also, use white paper or a very light-colored paper to guarantee that scanners will handle the material well. Here's a tip to separate your résumé from the many others that will arrive at the same time as yours. Offer a closing section headed with "Some Things That Don't Fit in Any of the Above Categories." One graduate wrote: *As a four-year varsity soccer player at State University, I learned the value of teamwork. But I still enjoy going one-on-one with the MAC.* In that brief statement, he communicated that he was a self-starter and a team player — two characteristics every employer cherishes.

• Write a cover letter that immediately communicates that **you are indeed a good writer.** Avoid the first paragraph loaded with the words that your competitors will be using. Example:

*In response to your advertisement in the May 15 Sun Times, I wish to apply for the position of public relations assistant.*

Write something that clearly lets the reader know you can use the language to get attention. Send the cover letter and résumé in a large envelope so you won't have to fold the pages.

• If granted an interview, do your homework. Many job-seekers **botch the interview by failing to prepare questions about the organization.** Chances are good that you know someone who knows someone who works there. Learn about the expected dress, how to find the location and the background of the people you'll be meeting. Send a thank-you note as soon as possible; if possible, include one thought you forgot to offer. If you receive a letter telling you the job went to someone else, show a touch of class by sending another note expressing your continued interest in the company. Surprise research finding: About 10 percent of jobs go to people who had been rejected because the first choice turned down the position.

## Getting ahead in the field of public relations

*Suggestions from Wilma Matthews, ABC, a public relations seminar leader, writer and consultant. She is author of a manual on media relations, published June 1998 by the International Association of Business Communicators, and co-author of* **On Deadline: Managing Media Relations**.

Getting ahead in any field presents challenges. Organizations continue to flatten the management structure so there are fewer places to "get ahead" to. Public relations positions are no longer clearly defined to accommodate just one job skill; instead, they are flexible, pliable positions that call for the mixing of several skills and abilities. Clients and companies continue to stretch the definition of public relations to meet their needs.

> **Problem solving is a key attribute for leadership in public relations.**

Regardless of what happens to management styles, company structures and job descriptions, three common attributes are needed at the leadership levels of public relations: **the attainment of knowledge, the giving away of knowledge, and problem solving**.

Acquiring knowledge is a career-long process. It does not end with formal education and often only begins at that point.

If you set your sights on public relations management and leadership, the scope of knowledge you must acquire is great. You must learn — to some degree — about all the tools and tactics of public relations. You must learn how to develop strategies, set them to plans, implement them correctly and measure them absolutely. You must be familiar with the many types of research necessary to give strength to your public relations programs. You must learn to advise, counsel, negotiate, facilitate and teach.

Learn to serve multiple clients in many industries with varied needs. This also makes it easier for you to learn the business of business, a second — or third — language, and the next communication technology.

As you are learning and acquiring knowledge, you also must be giving it away, every day, to clients, co-workers, managers, executives and others. You give away your knowledge in the work you perform and the success with which you perform it. *With each piece of knowledge you give away, you must learn another piece to replace it.*

Finally, you must be able to solve problems. While this sounds simple, it is often the difference between getting ahead in public relations and simply having a job in public relations. The art and science of public relations is problem solving. This means determining if there is a problem, what the problem is, offering a solution, and implementing the solution — successfully. Problems can range from determining why a media plan didn't work, to anticipating constituents' responses to a megamerger.

These three attributes are crucial to your success, in whatever field you choose.

## Follow-up is important

Remember that the best public relations ideas won't bear the fruits you expect if you don't dot all the I's and cross all the T's. The best plans in the world fall flat if someone doesn't follow up to make sure all the things that need to be taken care of are indeed taken care of.

> **Be sure to dot all the I s and cross all the T s.**

*Example*: An orange grove company developed a strong marketing/public relations program including a well written promotional brochure that enticed people to call. The tone of the material clearly communicated that this was a family-run business that cared about customers. The copy enticed the reader to try the product.

*The problem*: When this writer and a couple of friends called to order, we received, on about 10 different occasions, the phone message that all order takers were busy, but that our order was very important. We waited between five and 10 minutes in each instance and finally gave up. Then this writer called in the evening and was told that the hours were from 9 a.m. to 5 p.m. and that somebody would call me between 9 a.m. and 10 a.m. the following morning. No one ever did.

Let's hope that the public relations/marketing people who developed the excellent brochure were not blamed for a lack of orders. The brochure did its job. But the people responsible for other components didn't.

*Another example*: A casino wanted to attract people who use the simulcast facilities to place bets on horse races around the country. They did a lot of public relations/marketing things well, including a photo ID for members of the Turf Club that they initiated. They went out of their way to make an individual TV available and a functional work area for people who called to reserve a spot. They definitely wanted serious bettors to bet at this casino.

*One problem*: When bettors made reservations to stay overnight, they had to stand in a registration line that was sometimes 90 minutes long. When the simulcast folks were asked to do something to allow bettors to register at the VIP desk, they were told that desk didn't accept poker players and simulcast bettors. Needless to say, the bettors went elsewhere.

There's more to public relations and marketing than just doing those things that get the attention of would-be customers. There must be serious follow-up to make these plans work.

- **Find ways to make your boss look good**. Generate ideas that will propel your boss to a promotion. If your boss is promoted, chances are good that you will too.

- **Carve out a small slice of the public relations pie** and excel in that area. You might become an expert on annual reports or using the Intranet to communicate effectively, or applying survey results to public relations recommendations.

- **Be familiar with all the research on this topic**. Read journal articles and attend seminars that focus on the narrow area that you've identified. Get to know the experts in that particular field and share ideas with them. *Write articles on the topic* and offer to speak to folks to share what you know. This could very well lead to your becoming a recognized expert in the field.

- **Network**. If there is no local chapter of a public relations group in your area, then start your own networking system. You can do this by selecting local members of national associations and getting together with them periodically. You might also try to identify people with similar responsibilities who will be attending regional or national meetings of communication organizations. One public relations executive who moved up the ladder quickly used this approach: He wrote 10 of the top people in the field and said that he would like to have a 90-minute meeting. He asked each person to bring a one-page summary with 11 copies of his or her best idea. Each person then explained the idea in a five-minute presentation. Everyone went away with 10 new ideas and got to know some outstanding practitioners. All the folks then felt comfortable calling on each other with questions and problems.

- **Invest in your professional growth**. Remember all the money that you're spending on your college education; your education shouldn't stop when you get a degree. A true professional will invest his or her money to belong to PR organizations and to purchase publications that will enable professional growth to continue.

- Always remember that **you're not working for someone else** even though someone else may be signing your paycheck. Remember that you're constantly working for **you** and the reputation you're building.

- **Learn to say "no."** If you're recognized as someone who gets the job done, more people are going to ask you to do another job. You constantly have to take a look at your schedule to see what can work. Ask yourself this question: "If I add this to my responsibilities, what can I drop?" Sometimes you have to say "no" to be able to accomplish the other things that you've already committed to get done.

- **Don't bad-mouth anyone**. You never know who is related to whom. There might come a day when your request for expenses for a trip to Hawaii for the company will be turned down by your business manager. You might not realize it, but the person you bad mouthed the business manager to might be his or her paramour.

- **Be a self-starter**. Everybody wants to hire someone who comes up with ideas and starts working on something new when his or her assignments are done.

- **Be a prudent risk-taker**. Only people who are willing to take risks, supported by solid data, will make it to the big time.

- **Be polite**. People in generations that preceded you are still impressed with "please" and "thank you." When asking a secretary to do something, preface it with "please" even though you don't have to.

- **Be a team player**. This is something that more and more employers look for.

---

## Professional associations you should consider

- **Public Relations Society of America**
  33 Irving Place, New York, NY 10003

- **International Assn. of Business Communicators**
  870 Market Street, San Francisco, CA 94102

- **Women in Communications, Inc.**, (open to women and men) 2101 Wilson Blvd., Office 417, Arlington, VA 22201

- **National School Public Relations Association**
  15948 Derwood Road, Rockville, MD 20855

- **National Association of Government Communicators,** 80 South Hurley Street, Alexandria, VA 22304

- **Council for Advancement and Support of Education**, 11 DuPont Circle, Washington, DC 20036 (attracts public relations people working with colleges and universities).

---

Many of these associations conduct seminars and workshops. They also prepare publications and membership lists that could be helpful.

## Positions you might consider

### College and university public relations

If you enjoy being on a college campus, you might consider pursuing a career in college public relations. On most campuses, a variety of opportunities might attract you. Titles that in some way deal with public relations: *college relations director, assistant college relations director, media relations coordinator, internal communication specialist, assistant to the president* (includes speech-writing responsibilities), *sports information officer, alumni affairs director, fund-raising and development director, marketing director*, and others.

*Note*: The combination of marketing and public relations efforts has been discussed elsewhere. Suffice it to say that colleges that would never consider "marketing" 10 years ago have since launched large campaigns to attract students. This means that people from the admissions office work closely with the public relations people and others on campus to build a collection of materials, advertisements and other programs to be sure that enrollment is where the college feels it should be. Without such efforts, competitors tend to attract those students who might have gone to your institution.

When planning a public relations campaign for a college or university, you must work closely with the president, provost and deans to determine the institution's goals. Then, you should develop a public relations plan that helps meet those goals. *Example*: If you want to raise the profile of faculty quality, then you need to come up with efforts that will gain academic exposure for key faculty members. This means working with the heads of departments and establishing rapport with the movers and shakers among the faculty who are speaking, publishing and doing an outstanding job in the classroom. If publishing is important, public relations people might offer seminars or workshops on how to enhance the chance of being published.

The office might also provide a **list of faculty names, areas of expertise and phone numbers** so that your institution will be considered a solid source of knowledgeable professors to address current topics of interest that the media will be covering.

If you think a campus career in public relations might attract you, you're in a good position to prepare for it by taking advantage of the many internships usually available on campuses. Check with your faculty members who teach

---

## Publications you should know about

- *pr reporter*, P.O. Box 600, Exeter, NH 03833

- *PR News*, Phillips Publishing, Inc.
  7811 Montrose Rd., Potomac, MD 20854

- *Public Relations Quarterly*
  P.O. Box 311, Rhinebeck, NY 12571

- *Public Relations Tactics*, Public Relations Society of
  America, 33 Irving Place, New York 10003

- *Public Relations Strategist* (PRSA)
  33 Irving Place, New York, NY 10003

- *Public Relations Review*
  10606 Mantz Road, Silver Springs, MD 20903

- *Communication World*
  870 Market Street, San Francisco, CA 94102

- *O'Dwyer's Newsletter*,
  271 Madison Ave., New York, NY 10016

- *The Journal of School Public Relations*
  4501 Farber Blvd, Suite 200, Lanham, MD 20706

- *Communication Briefings*
  1101 King St., Suite 110, Alexandria, VA 22314

- *The Ragan Report*
  407 S. Dearborne St., Chicago, IL 60605

public relations and also with the public relations people on campus. You might build a variety of experience to add to your portfolio. This kind of experience can make you a serious candidate for positions that arise because people doing the hiring usually prefer to call upon people who know the campus; this allows them to come aboard, not needing a month or two of orientation regarding where to go for what.

## Working for a public relations firm or agency

*Joanie L. Flatt, Joanie L. Flatt & Associates, LTD., is located in Mesa, Arizona.*

If you want to work for my public relations firm, you must bring certain qualities to the job. If you do, I can teach you the rest of what you need to know.

What are the "must haves?"

1. You have to be able to THINK! It means you have to be able to look beyond what you're doing at any given time and **strategically think what impact your actions or activities today will have tomorrow**, the next day, the next week, or the next month. For every action, there will

be reactions and consequences. If you work in our firm, you have to be able to think through several steps ahead before you launch a strategy, implement a tactic or make a recommendation to a client.

2. You have to be able to WRITE and EDIT! I look for writing that is crisp and well organized. **Spelling, punctuation and grammar must be perfect**. Your writing needs to communicate effectively, which means it must be well organized. If you don't grab the reader at the beginning, just as a good lead does, you've failed. And if you burden your writing with superfluous adjectives, adverbs and flowery phrases, it won't cut it in our shop.

3. You have to have a CUSTOMER SERVICE mindset. We're an agency. We have clients, and they are our customers. They also have customers, both internal and external. Your job, as an agency public relations professional, is to understand how to effectively serve our clients and treat them as valued customers. **Your job is also to thoroughly understand our customers' customers**. We don't just crank out news releases, strategic plans and special events. We help our clients communicate and achieve specific goals. And your job, if you're working for an agency like ours, is always to remember that our objectives as a business are: retain our good customers; retire our "bad" customers, which means knowing the difference between good and bad clients; and to grow our firm with a good mix of getting new business through new clients and increasing the work we do for existing clients. When you work for an agency, it's your responsibility to be part of that process.

4. **You must have impeccable ethics and business standards**. As a public relations professional, if you lose your job, chances are you can always get another one. However, if you lose your reputation, you can't easily regain it. The same is true for the agency. Just as an unethical client can reflect negatively on an agency, an unethical employee can be even more lethal. That's why we don't tolerate either.

Think strategically, write and edit well, understand that you're in a customer service business and maintain high ethical standards at all times. These are the keys to a successful career in agency public relations.

## School PR professionals do it all

*Rich Bagin, ASPR, APR, Executive Director*
*National School Public Relations Association*

Let me let you in on a secret that can be one of the best steps you can take for a career in public relations.

If you want to avoid being locked into the early-career repetitive assignments of media calls or writing about everyone else's promotions for a staid corporate newsletter, then a position in school public relations may be just the foundation you need for a career in public relations.

> **School public relations professionals do it all.**

That's because school public relations professionals do it all.

Today more than 2,000 school PR professionals in the United States and Canada are sitting at management tables with their CEOs (superintendents of schools) and other cabinet officials and counseling them on key public issues. They are also hosting local cable TV and radio shows, managing their system's websites, publishing internal and external newsletters, serving as the chief spokesperson for their systems, analyzing their public opinion research, providing public relations training for school leaders, and much more.

Just look at these experiences encountered by members of the National School Public Relations Association:

You are asked to lead a public opinion campaign to pass a bond referendum for four new schools because class size is skyrocketing to nearly 40 students per class in your elementary schools. And, of course, your community is like many others, with nearly 75% of voters not having kids in your schools. You also have a politically active senior citizen contingent that rarely votes for any tax increases.

You are called upon to create a strategy in reputation management because three of your schools were recently cited by the state as being "the worst in the state."

Your boss was pleased with the "op-ed" piece you wrote and placed, but she jumped all over you because "they" used that unflattering picture again. And she didn't like the headline on the op-ed piece.

Principals in your elementary schools say that the new "charter school" is getting all the publicity, and that their schools are just as good or even better than the "charter" school. They want results and help now.

It's the Wednesday before Thanksgiving and just about every elementary school teacher (at least it seems that way) expects you to be there to take a photo for the local paper.

The new brochure you produced for the new central administration building has a major typo in it. A headline says that the new office "enchances" efficiency instead of enhancing it. It's Wednesday and the Open House/Dedication is on Saturday.

These experiences and the myriad of ongoing duties of being the communication professional for multimillion dollar businesses like school districts prove to be a great professional and rewarding experience for those in school

public relations. In the communication industry, there might not be a more noble and redeeming function than to help today's children receive a great education.

## Healthcare public relations – where opportunities abound

*Joyce McFadden is public relations director for Southern County Hospital, Manahawkin, New Jersey.*

Pick up a newspaper or tune in to the evening news and you'll realize that healthcare is a dynamic business. A quick look at some major issues in healthcare — each with major implications for the well-being of every individual in our society — demonstrates the scope and changing nature of the healthcare system. A few topics commanding national attention:

- Extraordinary technological advancements introducing far-reaching ethical questions
- Unprecedented scientific research shedding light on diseases that were once mysteries and cures that were once elusive
- Alternative medicine and the relationship between spirituality and health and healing
- Debate over national health insurance and the future of Medicare
- Cost control initiatives and the controversies surrounding managed care
- Mergers, alliances and government regulations surrounding healthcare delivery

Even Wall Street watches various sectors of the healthcare industry more carefully than ever. And competition is as alive in the nonprofit sectors of healthcare as it is for the profit sector.

And while the scope of the changes in the broader healthcare industry is impressive, so is healthcare on a more focused level, such as in a specific delivery setting. Successful communication for a hospital or other health provider organization requires a strategy of identifying specific audiences and communicating effectively to each. For example, in a hospital setting, *one might first think of patients as the audience.* Their communication needs are unique and often present the challenge of successfully sharing important information despite the barriers of anxiety, physical impairment or discomfort that may be present.

Consider possible communication needs for other groups relative to the same hospital environment but with very different information needs and healthcare backgrounds: physicians and other healthcare professionals, nonclinical support staff, volunteers, patients' families, visitors, other health-related agencies in the community, school personnel, churches and civic groups, community members, emergency squads, insurers, and government agencies.

For public relations professionals, media representatives are always primary audiences for important consideration. Daily, they bring an unending appetite for healthcare news, both negative and positive. Their readers, viewers and listeners have demonstrated a strong desire for all types of healthcare information.

What the healthcare business embodies then is a very complex, rapidly changing collection of information and issues. Audiences for this information and related issues are numerous and varied but they all depend on good information usually provided by the public relations person.

## Ask questions before accepting a job in governmental public relations

*Albert E. Holliday has spent 15 years working in public relations capacities for and with governmental agencies, including a state department of education. He started the* **Journal of Educational Relations** *in 1975 and* **Pennsylvania Magazine** *in 1981, and served as publisher of both. He is based in Camp Hill, Pennsylvania.*

If I were considering another position with a governmental agency, I'd want to ask certain questions before accepting a job as director of its public relations department. These would be:

1. What does the agency head expect of me? Change the agency's image? Start new publications? Build employee morale? Impress members of the state legislature? Are these expectations reasonable?

2. Do I have the background or aptitude to accomplish the assigned tasks?

3. Would I have enough staff funding to operate properly? Would I control a budget?

4. Would I have the right to bring in new staff, possibly to replace existing staff members who do not measure up to my standards? Could I transfer any staff elsewhere, or are they locked in?

5. Where would I, and my office, be on the organization chart? Would I report to the CEO daily or to a third deputy secretary far removed from the power?

6. What do members of the media covering the agency think of the CEO and/or other agency officials? Do they mention agency "problems" that were not brought up in my interviews?

7. How am I going to be evaluated, and by whom?

8. Why did the previous director leave? Can I talk with that person for insights into the agency?

9. Can I support the agency's goals and operations with enthusiasm? (For example, if I am opposed to gambling, I'd have difficulty working for the state lottery commission.)

10. Will I be working as the CEO's PR person or as the PR director for the agency? Does the CEO have political ambitions that can have an impact on my work?

These questions should provide information that will allow you to decide: Is this job for me? Can I handle it? Will it lead to something else in the near or not-too-distant future, depending on my goals?

If you would have to move family/residence to take a new job with a governmental agency, especially in a new career track, you might want to commute for a month or so. That should allow enough time to be sure the job is suited to you and it is safe to establish a new home base. (People who have had successful careers as journalists with commercial media may have difficulty adjusting to the layers of bureaucracy in governmental employment and the amount of time it takes to obtain approvals for action.)

A new college graduate, looking for the first professional job, will probably be offered an assistant's position. In that case, questions 2, 3, 7 and 9 are of most importance. I want to be sure that I would be compatible with my immediate supervisor, and that my perception of the job's scope is in line with that person's perception.

As an assistant director, I'd also want to envision future job growth opportunities that could result from my successful performance of my duties. For example, could I become director in a reasonable length of time, or would I be able to establish a track record in the new job allowing me to gain a more responsible position elsewhere?

While governmental employment is thought to be secure, that is not usually the case for public relations people at the executive level. Many CEOs of governmental agencies serve at the whim of a governor or president, or at the favor of voters, in the case of a mayor, member of Congress, or state legislator. The PR person closest to the CEO often rises or falls as the boss does.

*That means: Don't step on too many toes on your way to the top, and keep your résumé up to date.*

## Political public relations: Helping make a difference in causes you believe in

*David J. Byrd, political consultant; former Associate Commissioner, New Jersey Department of Commerce and Economic Development, served as associate public relations director for the Republican Black Caucus.*

A primary objective of any political group is to control and manage a consensus viewpoint. The fastest way to accomplish that is through the use of effective political public relations. Political public relations communicates the power of ideas and concerns within political organizations (nations, states, counties, cities, school boards, parent-teacher organizations, etc.) in both internal and external affairs.

Communication of your ideas and how those ideas shape political organizations and activities puts you on the cutting edge of using public relations politically. Your consensus is your muscle and a small consensus translates into weak political muscle.

Managing your consensus and remaining under the umbrella of its support are never easy. During colonial times, civic activists published leaflets, delivered blistering critiques from a soapbox, and organized small groups to promote change. Today's technology has given civic activists more tools. The emergence of the Internet and World Wide Web enables anyone, virtually, to reach out and touch anyone through web pages, e-mail and electronic publishing.

However, before one can have a stampede, all the cattle or constituents must agree to go in one direction. Explain your viewpoint, get others to support your ideas, and be sensitive to the needs of those around you. Doing so puts you at the forefront of using public relations politically.

Some political public relations essentials are necessary to manage the communication of your ideas:

*Research.* Do your homework and know both sides of an issue. Be ready to explain why your position is more appealing than that of your opposition. Tell the whole story before you are forced to do so. Your credibility is at stake.

*Be clear.* While serving as Joint Chiefs Chairman during the Persian Gulf War, Gen. Colin Powell said "Our strategy in going after this army is very simple. First we are going to cut it off, then we are going to kill it." No misunderstanding there.

*No jargon, please.* Lawyer-like answers and weasel words are apt to leave your audience confused and unconvinced.

*Repetition.* Some research shows a radio ad has to run at least seven times before a person "hears" it. Something becomes habitual after you do it at least 21 times. Rome wasn't built in one day and it took the Congress 40 years to change political party leadership.

*New isn't necessarily better.* Sophisticated marketing campaigns combined with electronic technology can create some dazzling results. However, a single well written letter to the editor or to an elected representative can still have an impact.

Taking the first step to get involved in political public relations is fairly easy. Just ask friends, relatives and acquaintances if they know a candidate who might appreciate some volunteer public relations help. Do whatever needs to be done while getting to know the public relations professionals behind the scenes. Demonstrate your conscientiousness, be available when needed and recognize the importance of deadlines. Campaigns are relatively short and getting copy in for a brochure a day late could be damaging to the effort and to your reputation. ∎

## Tips

1. Impress one PR professor who can serve as a reference.

2. Do all you can to become an outstanding writer.

3. Be nice to everyone in your organization, not just to the people near and at the top of the organizational chart.

4. To move up professionally, become active in professional organizations such as the Public Relations Society of America.

5. Follow up. Be sure someone is tending to detail.

6. Find ways to make your boss look good.

7. Network with other PR practitioners. This will help you move up in the field.

8. Say "no" when you receive requests that would subtract from time needed for your goals.

9. Smile. Research indicates smilers are perceived to be more intelligent than nonsmilers.

10. Learn to measure PR effectiveness to show the bottom-line contributions of PR.

Name _____ Date _____

1. If you're being interviewed for an entry level public relations position, what are three good questions you might ask to let people know you've done your homework and that you know something about the practice of public relations?

_____

_____

_____

_____

2. A new chief executive officer has been named and she's communicated that she's a no-nonsense person who's concerned about one thing only: the bottom line. You've been asked to meet with her to discuss the role that public relations can play in helping the organization become more profitable. What suggestions would you share with her?

_____

_____

_____

_____

3. To position yourself for your first full-time PR position, name three things you should do.

_____

_____

_____

4. What is the importance of networking in job-seeking? How might you use it?

_____

_____

_____

_____

_____

_____

# Glossary

## A

**accountability** – fulfilling expectations such as contracts, promises and mandates

**Adobe Illustrator**™ – one of the most widely used, high-end drawing programs for the Macintosh platform; also available for Windows

**Adobe InDesign**™ – one of the leading desktop publishing programs in PC and MAC formats

**advertorial** – paid position message placed in an editorial context

**advisory panels** – representatives from a target public appointed to advise an organization about its policies or activities and generally stratified according to certain population characteristics

**advocacy/issue advertising** – indirect portrayal of a company or organization by adoption of a position on a particular issue and used to influence public opinion about an issue or organization

**agate** – 5.5 pt. type; 14 agate lines equals one inch

**A-I-D-A** – discussion process by which audiences adopt concepts, attitudes and behavior — attention, interest, desire and adoption

**alignment** – process by which businesses and organizations identify with or instigate change in the values of the society in which they operate — also called "applied ethics"

**annual report** – management's financial statement to stockholders, security analysts and other publics

**"Alumni"** – industry term referring to retirees who might be tapped for part-time employment or consulting; in touch with an organization to gain information about financial planning and other areas of interest

**anvil** – blacksmith's hardened steel form on which the smith shapes metal — adopted by the Public Relations Society of America as the symbol for PR because public relations is seen as the anvil on which society's institutions and organizations forge their ethical practices; Gold, Silver and Bronze Anvils are annual awards by the Society for excellent practices and products

**APR** – accreditation designation by the Public Relations Society of America for members who demonstrate command of theory and successful practice

**Aristotle's Golden Mean** – philosophical-ethical principle stating: "The greatest good for the greatest number" and stressing moderation and virtuous living or ethical middle ground between extremes of excess and deficiency

**ascender** – part of a lowercase letter that extends above the x-height

**Associated Press (AP)** – news gathering service providing information to print and broadcast media

**attitude** – internal predisposition to act; a mental construct arising from education, background, genes, experience, etc. and causing behavior

**audience-minded** – message constructed more with audience benefits in mind rather than organization product or service features

**audience segmentation** – fracturing an audience into approachable groups according to fixed criteria and based on research

**author alterations** – changes authors make on printers' proofs or galleys

## B

**backgrounder** – in-depth information supporting a story (generally for the media)

**balance** – distribution of visual (or optical) weight throughout a page

**balance, asymmetric** – uneven distribution of visual aid on a page

**balance, symmetric** – even distribution of visual weight of elements on a page

**bartering** – unethical practice of trading advertising, professional advantage, or benefits for favorable media coverage

**baseline** – invisible line on which uppercase letters and bowls of lowercase letters rest

**beat** – reporter's regular area of responsibility, such as "the education beat"

**behavioral analysis** – methodical investigation of motivations and behavior of selected target publics as part of a situation analysis

**belief** – highly ranked attitude that cannot be proved or disproved

**Bhopal** – catastrophic industrial accident in Bhopal, India, in which a toxic gas leak from a Union Carbide insecticide plant killed 4,000 people and seriously injured 30,000 to 40,000 (Indian government settled for $470 million in damages and exempted company employees from criminal liability)

**biased sampling** – prejudiced selection of a sample that denies each member of a universe an equal chance for selection

**billboard** – strategically placed sign on busy highways to reach a captive audience of commuters who drive across the same bridge, or on the same road each day, usually limited to seven words and about eight seconds of attention

**bleeds** – ink printed to the very edge of the page

**blow up** – enlarged visual size of any item

**blue line** – common form of a proof or sample of piece to be printed showing all elements together with all color breaks

**bold type** – blacker, heavier type than surrounding type

**booklet** – usually 24 pages-plus with more structure, photos and illustrations than brochures

**box** – line outline often used to highlight type and surrounding text

**brainstorming** – nonjudgmental idea session to generate information, creative ideas, or solutions to problems

**brand** – symbol or campaign used to identify a product or service and distinguish it from the competition

**brochure** – publication, usually six pages or more, traditionally produced and distributed to a special public for a specific purpose

**business-to-business** – advertising usually appearing in trade journals or the trade press, and featuring messages from one business to another, such as a software company selling its services to accountants, physicians, insurance companies, etc.

**byline** – reporter's name preceding a story

# C

**caption** – editorial material accompanying a photo or illustration without an accompanying story (see *cutline*)

**case study/history** – analysis of a communication program in marketing, public relations or advertising to detect success. or failure

**cause-related marketing** – sponsorship strategy combining marketing and public relations — e.g., American Express donating portion of money charged to its cards to restore the Statue of Liberty

**CD Rom** – disk on which at least 650 megabytes of data can be inexpensively written and/or rewritten and stored for retrieval, e.g., encyclopedias, U.S. Census, and other reference works

**cell** – intersection of two research factors, frequently in research findings such as surveys or content analyses; e.g., number of residents who are parents and middle aged

**center (geometric)** – exact center point on a page

**center (optical)** – a point where the eye naturally falls onto a page, about five units from the bottom of the page and three units from the top

**certainty** – persuasive principle predicting that certain things target publics rely on and value will remain unchanged

**characteristic** – attribute of a population under study

    *demographic* – circumstantial attribute such as geographic location or age

    *psychographic* – personality attribute such as attitude

    *ergraphic* – work or employment attribute

**CIA cards** – cards given to employees to encourage them to give a card to a coworker *caught in the act* of doing something special

**circular** – usually a single-sheet publication of low cost

**clip art** – commercially prepared artwork available in books and via computer to reduce cost of photography and custom artwork, usually without permission

**clippings** – collection of mentions (clips) of a specific organization or topic from a variety of publications, as well as from broadcasts that companies access for a fee

**closed questions** – questions that control or limit audience responses – forced choice responses

**cluster sampling** – sample selection of a geographic community or area from which larger clusters representing the area are selected followed by additional smaller clusters within each large cluster to represent smaller and smaller units comprising the sample

**cognitive dissonance** – Leon Festinger's theory that a mismatch between mind (attitude) and act (behavior) will create an uncomfortable imbalance within a person — most people resolve the imbalance by changing the attitude, the behavior, or both

**commitment** – persuasive principle that relies on the notion that a series of small commitments can more reliably lead to a larger commitment

**communicating** – aspect of public relations practice that tactically conveys an organization's identity to key publics for desired recognition, image and support

**communication** – act of disseminating messages to target audiences to influence audiences' opinions of an organization (the organization's image)

**communication audit** – comprehensive analysis of the efficacy of an organization's methods of communication, or opinion of members of an organization about communication issues

**comprehensive layout (comp)** – drawing or mock-up providing a detailed picture of the final printed piece

**conduit theory** – theory that communicators, including PR practitioners, believe they're merely conduits for management decisions, messages and activities and are not liable for misinformation or the effects of misinformation — found illegal by courts

**condensed type** – narrower type than regular face, allowing more words to fit in a column, but reducing legibility

**confidence level** – reliability that a finding from a probability study will be the same if repeated samples were drawn in the same manner — (for 95% confidence, the same finding will appear 95 times out of 100 if repeated samples were selected 100 times using the same random selection process)

**confidence interval** – confidence that the random sample can be extraploated to a specific percentage of the population, e.g. 95% confidence means that 95% of the population under study falls within the study's error.

**constrained audience** – audience experiencing internal or external pressure to resist providing a desired behavior

**contact list** – persuasive principle that relies on listed target publics

**content analysis** – discovery of information about a series of items through a systematic analysis resulting in factual statements, including frequencies and percentages of each item against selected categories or against the whole

**controlled experiment** – experiment that tests a hypothesis and controls variables

**convincing** – motivating a person to change a deeply held attitude

**cooperative ad** – ad in which manufacturer shares costs with a retailer – also two organizations cooperating with each other

**copy** – text of the message point(s)

**Corel Draw™** – popular graphics program for Windows and Macintosh platforms

**cost per thousand** – cost of exposing a message to each 1,000 members of a target audience

**counseling** –public relations activity of advising an organization about its mission and activity (the organization's identity) to achieve desired image and support from key publics

**cropping** – altering the size or shape of a photo or illustration to fit a desired space or to eliminate unwanted elements

**cross-referenced telephone directory** – telephone directory listing all streets, residences, businesses, etc., with their listed telephone numbers in a community, in street order

**crosstabulations** – analysis of a set of questionnaire responses with another set(s) to make factual findings about either set in relationship to the other

**cut-line** – editorial comment accompanying an illustration that supports a story (see *caption*)

**cyber messages** – messages sent on voice mail or e-mail outside the organization and affecting the image of the organization

**cyber plagiarism** – acquiring information off the Internet and using it to conduct business without crediting the source

# D

**data analysis** - critical examination of information according to a purpose

**dateline** – city location of a release story following a headline or sub-headline

**deadline** – time by which material must be received

**deflection strategy** – crisis PR strategy in which an organization publicly refuses to accept responsibility for crisis aspects for which it is not responsible

**Delphi Study** – research technique to develop a consensus response to a problem or issue using a pyramid approach to increasingly refined responses

**demographic profile** – study of an audience that details identifying characteristics such as geography, age, sex, marital status, and ergraphic (occupational) information

**deontology** – principle advocating absolute moral principles and giving rise to a rules-based ethical system – adherence to specific canons of conduct

**descender** – part of the lowercase letter that extends below the baseline

**diary** – personal record of activities (usually about the use of time or selection of activities) or opinion about campaign items

**dichotomous responses** – two mutually exclusive choices such as agree/disagree, effective/ineffective, present/absent, will vote/won't vote

**diffusion theory** – theory that postulates the manner in which ideas and messages are inserted into society, circulate, and gain acceptance

**direct marketing** – use of many media, creating direct mail and catalogs, and soliciting immediate customer response by mail or telephone

**directory advertising** – yellow pages or yellow book advertising creating widespread awareness or use (nearly all adults refer to these directories during the course of a year)

**discussion list e-mail** – Adam Boettiger's approach to finding quality lists related to an industry or interest

**display type** – type larger than 14 pts., usually for headlines

**distance strategy** – crisis PR strategy in which an organization puts distance between itself and an offending issue, person or event to protect its reputation

**distraction strategy** – crisis PR strategy in which an organization distracts media and other public attention from an incident involving the organization and instead focuses public attention on its successful enterprises to protect its reputation

**document search** – systematic analysis of literature, databases and files on focused issues

**download** – electronic news release directly acquired from an organization's computer into a media representative's computer

**dummy** – mechanical put together, folded or collated exactly resembling the final product

**duotones** –two halftone plates from a one-color illustration and etched to produce a two-tone effect

# E

**"effecktancy"** – technique to generate employee suggestions

**e-mail** – communicating through online messages

**embargo** – use prohibition placed on a news release until time and date specified on the release

**error gap** – gap between the highest and lowest percentage after sampling error has been applied to a finding; e.g. finding of 50% with error of ±5% yields a gap of 45% to 55%

**Equal Time Rule** – federal law requiring broadcast stations to provide equal opportunity for opponents of political candidates for whom the station provided a platform for the candidate's views

**ethic** – outward behavior resulting from an inward moral principle

**ethos** – identity and personality of an organization – what an organization is and does

**exclusive** – story limited to a single representative of the media and not shared with all media

**exit ramp** – space between short paragraphs in copy offering readers the opportunity to exit the copy but actually enticing them to read on because of the minor commitment brief paragraphs elicit (paragraphs shouldn't linger beyond seven lines.)

**external publication** – publication distributed by an organization to customers, community, and other external publics

**extranet** – Internet network requiring user account, log in and password

**extrapolation** – data from a randomly selected sample population scientifically extended to include the larger population (universe)

**Exxon Valdez** – Exxon oil tanker bringing oil from Prudhoe Bay in 1989 that spilled 10 million gallons of oil near the port of Valdez, Alaska, causing severe economic and environmental damage and public relations ethical and crisis challenges

# F

**fact sheet** – statement of facts about an issue or person, generally the basis for a media relations effort

**Fairness Doctrine** – Federal Communication Commission (FCC) broadcast regulation requiring broadcasters to provide balanced coverage, such as opposing points of view, on controversial issues (repealed in 1987)

**familiarity** – one of Earl Newsome's principles of persuasion in which a message sender resembles an important characteristic of the audience, such as age or vested interest

**fax** – short for "facsimile," a reproduction of printed matter sent by telephone connection

**FCC** – Federal Communications Commission – regulates broadcasting

**FDA** – Food and Drug Administration

**feature** – story focusing on human interest

**F-I-C-A** – Earl Newsome's four principles of persuasion — familiarity, identification, clarity and action

**filler** – short informational tidbit used to fill space when laying out a page (not as important as it once was before desktop publishing provided more flexibility)

**flag** – nameplate on a newspaper or newsletter appearing on the front page and occupying about 20 percent of the layout

**flyer** – single-sheet publication, usually used to announce an event or similar idea

**focal point** – main point of visual interest to which the eye is first drawn

**focus group** – nonprobable, controlled questioning of six to eight carefully selected participants from a target audience to discover attitudes and opinion about certain issues (qualitative research)

**Fog Index** – formula used to determine the reading grade level of copy

**folio** – page number

**Food and Drug Administration** – federal agency exercising considerable jurisdictional influence on prescription drug labeling — also regulating tobacco advertising

**formal research** – organized, methodical, scientific research telling researchers what is objectively true about the audience or data under study

**Fraction of Selection Formula** – Wilbur Schramm's formula to make messages more persuasive to constrained audiences by elaborating on the merit of a benefit and diminishing the effort to get the benefit

**free** – especially effective word in direct marketing and ad headlines

**Freedom of Information Act** – federal law guaranteeing the public, including PR practitioners, the right to look at material in the federal government's files

**freelancer** – writer or artist available on a per-story basis or retainer

**frequency** – number of times an item or answer to a question appears in a study, such as a survey

# G

**gatekeeper audience** – intermediary audience capable of allowing access to direct target audiences and influencing them

**glossy** – smooth, shiny photograph

**Golden Mean** – Greek philosopher Pythagoras's formula stating the relationship of the small segment of a line to the larger segment of a line is equal to the ratio of the large segment to the entire line (Not Aristotle's Golden Mean – a philosophical principle)

**ground thirds** – division of a page into thirds and designed as one-third and two-third page units

**Gunning-Meuller Fog Index** – readability measurement technique revealing the grade level of copy and its reading ease score by computing the relationship of average sentence length and number of trisyllabic words in a 100-word sample

**gutter** – space between two pages of a publication

# H

**halftones** – photographs, charcoals or other illustrations that contain graduated tones of black and white, ash or shades of gray (sometimes called mesotints)

**Herbert vs. Lando** – Supreme Court ruling requiring media defendants in public figure libel and slander cases to testify at trial about reckless disregard for truth or actual malice of their statements and actions that prompted the lawsuit

**hold harmless clause** – contract clause offering some legal protection for public relations counselors in the event a client-approved item might legally implicate them

**house ad** – ad prepared by an organization for use in its own publication — e.g., television station promo announcing its own new fall programming

# I

**IABC** – International Association of Business Communicators

**ideal state analysis** – statement of an organization's goals and objectives predicated on the issues in a real state analysis

**identification** – one of Earl Newsome's principles of persuasion in which a sender's message identifies with an audience's ambition

**identity** – what an organization is and does

**"I have an idea" card** – cards distributed to employees to register good ideas and returned to the immediate boss with a copy to person in charge of idea generation for an organization — if boss doesn't respond within a designated period, person charged with idea responsibility brings up the idea

**image** – how important publics perceive what an organization is and does

**InDesign** – popular desktop publishing program by Adobe in both PC and Mac formats

**influence** – factors indirectly or intangibly affecting a person or a course of events

**infomercial** – an information video sponsored by branded products and services

**informal research** – nonscientific method to acquire a nonprobable description of population under study, without extrapolating information from a scientific sample

**insider trading** – using privy or insider information to unfairly trade publicly held stocks by taking advantage of a general public that does not have the information

**institutional advertising** – also called organizational or image advertising

**Internet** – interconnected public web sites, open to all, enabling anonymous visitation — (World Wide Web is part of the Internet)

**integrated marketing communications (IMC)** – attempt to reach organizations' publics by combining public relations, marketing and advertising into an integrated program

**intercept interview** – survey conducted as an interview or questionnaire administered to a target population in motion such as exiting stores (exit studies), on the sidewalk (person-in-the-street studies), in service establishments, such as restaurants (roaming studies), and on transportation vehicles (transit studies)

**internal publication** – publication distributed to employee or membership groups

**interview** – focused conversation with a target audience to discover information level, prevailing attitudes, and/or behavior about certain issues

**Intranet** – in-house electronic network, residing as a LAN or WAN, and available only to those logged onto the network, with requisite permission level

**invitation to cover** – invitation to reporters and editors about upcoming news events to allow media time to plan attendant coverage

# J

**Judeo/Christian Principle** – philosophical-ethical principle stating: "Treat others as you would want to be treated" — love is personal, not legal, and ethical behavior is based on unselfish, other-directed love

**jump** – story continued on another page

**justification** – lines of published copy ending evenly at the same point for a formal look

# K

**Kant's Categorical Imperative** – philosophical-ethical principle stating: "What is good for one is good for all" — categorical because it admits no exceptions; imperative because it requires decision makers to behave toward all as they would behave toward one

**key communicators** – selected and appointed group of influential community members providing an organization with information and opinions about issues, rumors, etc. and accepting information from the organization about key issues for dissemination to the communicator's sphere of influence

**kill** – to discard part or all of a story

**killer app** – strong reason motivating a public to buy and use personal computers and applications for which consumers have an overwhelming need

# L

**LAN** – local area network that links computers within a limited area — room, floor, building or a campus, with or without a router

**laser printer** – printer outputting camera-ready mechanicals, including film

**latent attitude** – unexpressed attitude strong enough to erupt into behavior at the instigation of a triggering incident, event or message

**lead** – pronounced "leed," first sentence or paragraph of a news release, tipping a reporter or editor about a story possibility

**leading** – pronounced "ledding" (line spacing), white space between lines of type

**Likert Scale** – response set that uses five options, generally verbs, responding to statement questions, such as agree/disagree, measuring both quality and strength of responses

**line spacing** – see *leading*

**lobbying** – grass roots efforts mobilizing public relations and other communication tactics to research, analyze and influence regulatory proposals and legislation

**Love Canal** – environmental public relations case in which pesticides poisoned wildlife and industrial waste products contaminated drinking water in land donated to a Niagara Falls, New York community (donor company was exonerated; community was at fault for building homes and school on the site against company warning)

**lower case** – small letters

# M

**M-A-C Triad** – complementary relationship between message, audience and channel necessary for successful public relations communication

**make good** – publishing or broadcasting free, an ad or a commercial that did not run properly because of media error

**management-minded** – messages constructed more with organization's product or service features in mind rather than audience benefits

**margin** – area of white space on edges of pages

**marketing** – process of counting and executing conception, pricing, promotion and distribution of ideas, goods and services to create exchanges to realize individual or organizational objectives

**Maslow's Hierarchy of Needs** – pyramid of human needs, ascending from basic needs to higher personal fulfillment needs; expresses concept that people care for needs at the bottom of the pyramid before caring for needs higher up

**mass sentiment** – latent attitudes within a public toward potential issues

**masthead** – box on the editorial page listing publication's mission and staff involved in preparation and distribution of the publication

**meaning** – mental cognition of a message almost wholly in control of the message's receiver

**mechanical (paste-up)** – camera-ready copy a printer uses to produce a job, often skipped because of modern computer desktop publishing, and instead, directly filmed

**media kit** – package of materials containing information about an organization or an issue

**message** –coded cognition, attitude or volition in a communication transaction

**Mill's Principle of Utility** – philosophical-ethical principle stating: "What is useful is right" — utilitarian practice seeking the best balance of good options over bad ones and spread widely

**modem** – device to communicate digital information, the language of computers, over phone lines

**moral** – inward guiding attitudinal principle from upbringing, religion, education, genetic makeup, life experiences, and other influences

**more** – signification at the bottom of each nonfinal page of a news release

**muckrakers** – term applied by Theodore Roosevelt to turn-of-the-century investigative journalists who attacked New York police, spawning the rise of journalists-become-publicists to defend organizations

# N

**network analysis** – research technique within a communication audit in which all aspects of an employee's communication, incoming and outgoing, content and process, print, electronic, face-to-face, etc., are analyzed for effectiveness

**networking** – sharing printers, files and local e-mail requiring specialized hardware and software — also, identifying and communicating with others in a similar field to assure necessary access

**news and photo memo** – print attachment providing date, time and contact personnel (with phone numbers) to encourage editors and reporters to provide coverage for newsworthy events

**news conference (press conference)** – assembly of media and organization personnel to provide in-depth information about a newsworthy issue and providing media opportunity to question the organization

**Newsome's persuasion principles** – researcher Earl Newsome's theory that all persuasive messages/messengers exhibit four characteristics: familiarity to the audience; identification with audience needs; clear expression of persuader's meaning; and reflection of the persuader's values by calling for imitative action by the audience

**newspaper clips** – collection of appearances of newspaper or other publication articles about an organization; if generated by the public relations function — called "hits"

**New York Times v. Sullivan** – Supreme Court ruling that defined the defense standard for public figures in libel and slander cases — public figure plaintiffs must prove the defendant's statement was made with knowledge of falsity or reckless disregard for the truth (known as NY Times "actual malice")

**nonscientific sample** – representative members selected in nonrandom fashion, usually with deliberate or accidental bias, or by members selecting themselves

**NSPRA** – National School Public Relations Association

# O

**observation** – systematic visual recording of activities to collect data for analysis

**occult compensation** – private and secret compensation by an employee of company material to compensate for perceived inadequate pay or benefits

**off the record** – information to reporters they're not permitted to use

**one-on-one meeting** – meeting between a manager and every relevant reporting employee to develop rapport and generate ideas for more efficient mutual responsibility

**one-three-six** – research technique generating suggestions from employees

**online conferences** – news conference on the web (e-conference)

**op-ed** – short for "opposite editorial," message from and about an organization appearing on the page opposite the editorial page — unpaid if invited by a newspaper or instigated by a PR office; "advertorial" if paid for

**one-way communication** – communication that does not seek or allow for audience feedback

**operating system** – software that controls the application and use of hardware resources such as memory, central processing unit (CPU) time, hard disk space, and peripheral devices (speakers or mouse) — foundation for applications programs such as Microsoft Office, converting application language into language a computer understands

**opinion** – outward expression of an attitude, in any form — purchase, vote, letter, speech; the effect of a temporary or lasting attitude

# P

**pamphlet** – usually an 8½" x 11" sheet folded twice, creating six panels; sometimes a single 8½" x 14" sheet folded twice, creating six panels, or folded three times, creating eight panels (usually smaller than a brochure with fewer photos, illustrations and colors)

**pathos** – image of an organization — what a public believes or perceives an organization is and does

**percentage** – ratio of a set of items compared to the whole set

**Personal Attack Rule** – Federal Communication Commission (FCC) broadcast regulation requiring notification of an attacked person (honesty, character or integrity) about a controversial issue of public importance and offering reasonable opportunity to respond (repealed 1987)

**persuasion** – motivating one to perform a desired behavior even if it apparently goes against a deeply held attitude — the behavior can arise from even a temporary attitude a person adopts for the occasion

**picture word** – word that characterizes issues through the use of a memorable image that is easy to take in, entertains as it informs, and allows audiences to infer personal experiences associated with the image

**Pig 'n' Whistle Case** – conduit theory case in which courts found that public relations communicators for a Chicago-based restaurant were not immune from liability for misinformation contained in fraudulent, untrue and misleading news releases about a company merger

**pitch letter** –one-page or less written appeal that describes a good story and encourages media recipients to cover the story

**point** – printer's standard unit of measure; 72 pts. equal one inch

**position paper** – expression of an organization's position on a specific issue including definition, justification, argument and benefit to both society and the organization from adoption of the organization's position

**position statement** – statement by an organization laying out its position on an important issue, generally for internal and external publics

**Potter Model** – ethical decision-making model from Dr. Ralph Potter of the Harvard Divinity School using a four-stage questioning process for making an ethical decision: definition, values, principles and loyalties

**PowerPoint**™ – computer application that integrates graphics, words, sounds, and animation into a comprehensive visual presentation

**press agentry** – one-way mechanistic communication model, sometimes called the propaganda model, in which an organization draws publicity attention to itself, without audience feedback, and through one-sided messages

**press junket** (press tour) – tour of interested media, sponsored by an organization, to gain attention for a product, service or issue

**principle of double effect** – philosophical notion that someone can ethically engage in an activity with bad consequences if they intend only the good consequences

**probability** – conclusion researchers draw that the information they derive from a scientific sample validly and reliably reflects the larger universe — only random sampling yields probability

**probability survey** – obtaining information from an audience through a questionnaire in writing, over the phone, or in person, in a formal or scientific way

**propaganda** – manipulation technique in which the persuader offers a target public information about only one side of an issue

**proportional sample** – sample that guarantees reflection of certain population characteristics in the same proportion as they exist in the universe population

**protocol** – research regimen for focus group or survey — the number and order of research questions or activities

**PRSA** – Public Relations Society of America

**psychographic profile** – study of an audience listing attitudinal characteristics that detail "who" the audience is — likes or dislikes, preferences, inclinations, leaning on positions

**public affairs** – practice of public relations dealing with government relations

**public figure** – anyone who is actually a public figure by holding or being elected to a public office or who willingly inserts oneself into a public controversy

**public information communication** – one-way mechanistic communication style, often called the publicity model, in which an organization sends messages to important audiences, without audience feedback, to influence image, attitudes and opinion

**public interest** – organizational behavior generally consistent with public and societal needs rather than organizational needs — public interest activity could also be socially responsible

**publicity on the Internet** – source developed by Steve O'Keefe providing well organized lists with brief descriptions and direct links to all the Internet resources he discovered

**public opinion** – accumulation of individual opinion, about an important issue, in public debate, affecting the lives of a public

**public relations** – organized and systematic, two-way communication between an organization (or person) and its publics resulting in relationships that foster understanding and behavioral acceptance by the publics of the organization's (or person's) purposes

**public relations audit** – comprehensive analysis of achievement of an organization's public relations goals (methods to conduct the analysis)

**public relations publicity** –techniques designed to attract the attention of important publics and characterized by objectivity, believability and reach

**Public Relations Society of America** –– largest national professional organization of public relations professionals offering accreditation, library resources, workshops, competitions, honors and awards, industry specific sections, and other professional resources

**Public Relations Student Society of America** – largest national pre-professional student public relations society offering networking, workshops, competitions and other resources

**Public Relations Quarterly** – professional publication containing original and applied research

**public service announcement (PSA)** – usually a minute or shorter, free time provided by the broadcast media for not-for-profit organization's ad — also, occasionally paid for by corporations to support a not-for-profit cause

# Q

**qualitative research** – research method describing a situation, population or database under study such as attitudes and opinions, newspaper clips, etc. without necessarily measuring it

**quality circle** – management/employee meeting to mutually develop quality work goals and standards, assess progress, and solve problems

**quantitative research** – method to measure information about a population or database under study such as attitudes and opinions, newspaper clips, etc. and quantifying it

**QuarkXPress™** – leading desktop publishing program for MAC and PC platforms

**questionnaire** – question and answer instrument used in survey studies

**questions, closed** – questions that control or limit audience responses — forced choice responses

**questions, open** – questions that allow respondents to answer in any manner they wish

**quick-print shop** – shop that handles small runs (one to a few thousand copies)

**quiet registration period** – period after new securities offering has been filed with the SEC and before the registration becomes effective

# R

**random digit dialing** – telephone sampling method in which the sample of random phone numbers is selected from a computer-generated list

**random sampling** – random selection of a sample population from a universe in a way that each member of the universe has an equal chance to be selected

**Rawls's Veil of Ignorance** – philosophical-ethical principle stating: "Elimination of roles frees people to make equitable decisions" — focuses on the idea that justice emerges when people negotiate without social differentiation

**reach** – percentage of unduplicated numbers (of a target public) exposed to a media vehicle at least once during a specific period of time

**readability** – level of reading ease of copy determined by one of several formulas such as the Gunning-Mueller Fog Index

**readability study** – analysis of the readability of copy within an organization's publications or literature

**real state analysis** – statement (situation analysis) of actual issues about an organization prior to developing a PR program

**research protocol** – research instrument such as a questionnaire in a survey, or sequenced research actions in a focus group

**response set** – response pattern in questionnaires designed to acquire information in a form easy to tabulate and analyze

**reverse printing** – text of art in light on a dark background, usually white on black

**rhythm** – the repetition of similar shapes, sizes, textures and like elements in a design

**rightsizing** – euphemistic synonym for downsizing or reducing the number of employees

**rules** – physical lines added to a page to provide visual separation of layout elements

**rumor control center** – source that quickly identifies rumors and provides information to correct facts or perceptions

# S

**sample** – selected portion of a universe

**sampling** – selection technique to identify a target population sample of a larger universe for a research study

**sampling error** – mathematical chance, due to the sample selection process, that the finding of a probability study will differ from the same finding if the whole universe were studied

**sans serif type** – typeface without decorative strokes or "feet"

**scarcity** – persuasive principle that audiences will value what's scarce, will value it more if told reliable information about it is also scarce, or that the persuader alone has the information

**screens** – tints of color used to highlight blocks of text or to cover an entire page to give the illusion of colored paper

**Securities and Exchange Commission** – federal bureau monitoring financial information flow including the corporate quarterly report, and controlling publicly held stock transactions

**self-analysis** – record of participant's role in a communication program and impressions of the efficacy of the program's tactics

**semantic differential** – response set seeking shades of attitude in surveys, using bipolar adjectives such as good/bad, effective/ineffective, informative/uninformative, and modifying them with six adverbs, three on each side of the scale, corresponding to each adjective

**serif type** – typeface distinguished by "feet" or decorative strokes at the ends of letters

**set solid** –type set without proportional space between the horizontal lines

**Shannon-Weaver Communication Model** – model developed by researchers Claude Shannon and Earl Weaver theorizing that human communication comprises mechanistic components analogous to a telephone system — sender, message, channel, noise, receiver and feedback

**shareware** – software programs placed in the public domain with little or no fee to users and focusing on chores such as determining reading ease and correct grammar and syntax of copy

**sheet-fed print shops** – shop for medium-size runs of several hundred to more than 50,000

**Silver Anvil Awards** – PRSA's annual top awards for the best public relations plans among its members

**simple random sampling** – sample selection by drawing representatives in lottery fashion from equally available members of a universe

**situation analysis** – result of methodical investigation into a public relations challenge as a preamble and premise to a public relations plan or campaign (also for advertising)

**situational ethics** – philosophy advocating ethical behavior based on the conditions of the situation a person faces — a utilitarian philosophy authorizing the useful course of action as the ethical course

**slug line** – notation at the upper left of a printed story page identifying the story (reappears on every subsequent page of the story)

**social responsibility** – organizational behavior consistent with the values of relevant publics and societies

**social technologists** —technologist well grounded in digital technology, communication arts, and social sciences

**Socratic Dialogue** – controlled discussion by a facilitator using a case scenario and role-playing professionals to reveal attitudes and opinions about issues

**sole practitioner** – public relations practitioner practicing alone within a one-person PR firm or office

**special event** – public relations technique designed to build traffic by important publics; increase awareness of products, services or organizations; induce trial of products or services; or participate in an organization's activity

**spin doctor** – propagandist who favorably interprets messages and issues to clients' advantage without regard for a balanced analysis

**spinning** – unwavering subjective interpretation of news events or incidents to gain favorable opinion for a person or organization

**spokesperson tour** – personal appearance tour of trained spokespersons to make public speeches, appear on radio and television talks shows, conduct news conferences, and host community forums to gain exposure for an organization's message

**stakeholder** – any member of a public with a vested interest in the success of an organization

**strategic thinking** – process of assessing a public relations issue or challenge, differentiating its components, and fashioning a workable strategic response

**strategic planning** – operationalizing broad public relations strategic approaches by scheduling activities in a protocol

*Strategist* – publication of the Public Relations Society of America containing articles, case studies and original and applied research

**strategy** – general approach to reach an objective; generally conditioning an audience to receive the message contained in the strategy

**stratified sample** – sample which guarantees certain population characteristics so the sample resembles the universe as closely as possible, such as demographic or psychographic characteristics

**stet** —proofreader's instructive word that copy should remain as originally written (from Latin meaning "let it stand.")

**survey** – study of a universe by sampling or census using a questionnaire instrument and administered in person, on the phone, over the internet, by mail, or in publications

**study** – research activity depending on location and availability of target populations

*mall study* – questions shoppers traveling through a mall or entering or exiting stores

*exit study* – questions a population as it leaves a polling place or establishment

*person-in-the-street study* – questions passers-by on the sidewalk

*roaming study* – questions patrons in an establishment, such as diners in a restaurant

*transit study* – questions travelers in transportation vehicles

**stylebook** – writer's guide to correct grammar and usage, such as *The Associated Press Stylebook and Media Briefing on Law*

**subhead** – small heading placed between paragraphs in the body of a news story to break up long copy blocks

**S-W-O-T analysis** – analytical method by which organizations identify important issues categorized under strengths, weaknesses, opportunities and threats

**systematic random sampling** – scientific sample selection using a systemic, repeated internal (every "nth" item) of the collected items in a universe population, such as phone numbers, news clippings, ads, and other data

# T

**tactic** – specific channel technique to deliver a strategic message to a target audience comprising specific agent, cost and time frame

**talent** – people (actors) in audio or visual promotions

**technology assessment** – part of a communication audit — analysis of effectiveness of an organization's entire technology communication component

**teleology** – principle that the ethical nature of decisions arises from the purpose or goal of the decision maker

**testimonial** – endorsement from a satisfied user in an ad or direct marketing promotion

**Texas Gulf Sulphur Case** – conduit case in which courts found that public relations communicators who distribute misleading news releases are liable for the misinformation and its effects

**text blocks** – chunks of information in a visual unit that contains a written message, usually set in columns

**thirty (-30-)** – signal at the end of a news release or a newspaper story to designate the end

**30-3-30** – reader types: 30-second readers scan the copy; three-minute readers read most of the copy quickly; and 30-minute readers read all of the copy

**Three Mile Island** – site of a nuclear power plant and public relations disaster south of Harrisburg, Pennsylvania when the cooling system of the No. 2 nuclear reactor failed and led to reactor overheating and threatened meltdown of the plant's uranium core on March 28, 1979

**thumbnail** – small rough drawing of a page layout

**timely disclosure** – requirement for companies that publicly sell securities to disclose material information (information a reasonable investor considers important in making investments) in a public, timely and universal manner so every interested party has equal access to the information

**transit advertisement** —ads usually appearing (on cards) on cars and buses, and in taxis, trains and subways, and designed to reach a captive traveling public

**Two-Step Flow Theory** – theory that the flow of influence begins with media setting the agenda, influentials picking up ideas and messages from the media, endorsing them, and influencing target publics to know, feel or do something about the agenda

**two-way communication** – dynamic correspondence between an organization and its publics characterized by feedback for either group's benefit

**two-way asymmetric communication** – two-way dynamic, unbalanced communication model, between an organization and its publics, often called the persuasion model, in which an organization researches audiences to learn the best messages to use to persuade them to agree to a proposition the organization has already decided

**two-way symmetric communication** – two-way, dynamic, balanced communication model between an organization and its publics, often called the negotiated consensus model, in which an organization corresponds with its audiences to discover mutually beneficial identities for both the organization and its publics

**typeface** – a specific type design (also *font*)

**type size** – measurement in points from the bottom of the descender to the top of the ascender, or the height of a capital letter

**typo** – typographical error

# U

**uc & lc** – uppercase and lowercase

**uncertainty** – persuasive principle which relies on target publics being empowered to experiment and take a "safe risk" on changing things they value — also used to make publics uncomfortable with consequences if they do not provide a desired behavior, such as effects of failing to buckle seat belts

**unique selling proposition** – characteristic that differentiates a generic product's organization from organizations marketing similar products — e.g., "Double Your Pleasure, Double Your Fun, Doublemint, Doublemint, Doublemint Gum"

**unity** – layout harmony – how well or poorly elements on a page work together

**unique persuasive proposition** – motivating appeal in persuasive public relations practice

**universe** – entire population under study

**UPP** – unique persuasive proposition

**uppercase** – all capital letters

**USP** – unique selling proposition

# V

**VALS** – Values and Lifestyle Study — psychographic study examining values and lifestyle of an audience from SRI International, business researchers and consultants

**variable** – influencing factor in a research study; independent variables intentionally placed by researchers; dependent variables are uncontrolled outcomes; sometimes occurring in a population without researcher control or knowledge, e.g., bias.

**video news release (VNR)** – a 60- to 90-second video tape presenting an organization's message in a news format accessible by television stations

# W

**WAN** – wide area network that connects computers, or two or more LANs, spread over a large geographic area and providing a secure, private network around the globe to those granted access

**web-fed print shop** – shop best serving medium-to-large run jobs from 30,000 to multimillions

**webzine** – magazine approach developed for web use

**whistleblower** – employee or other person who reveals unethical behavior by one of society's institutions or organizations

**whistle blowing** – revelation of ethical misdeeds of a company (to the public) or other employees (to management) by an employee resolving a serious ethical loyalty conflict

**white space** – element of design where nothing is printed, also called design space

**wire service** – electronic switchboard-type news service, collecting and redistributing news from organizations to media designated by a PR practitioner from regional to national., e.g., PR Newswire and Business Wire

# X

**x-height** – the height (or depth) of the bodies of lowercase letters

# Bibliography

## Chapter 1 ~ Public Relations in Society

Aronoff, Craig, & Baskin, Otis W. (1992). *Public relations: Profession and practice* (3rd ed.). Dubuque, IA: Wm. C. Brown.

Cutlip, Scott M. (1994). *The unseen power: A history of public relations.* Hillsdale, NJ: Lawrence Erlbaum.

Fulginiti, Anthony J. et al. (1988). *Power-packed PR: Ideas that work.* Blackwood, NJ: Communication Publication and Resources.

Heath, R. L., & Vasquez, G. (2001). *Handbook of public relations.* Thousand Oaks, CA: Sage.

Lesly, Philip. (1983). *Lesly's public relations handbook* (3rd ed.). Englewood Cliffs, NJ: Prentice Hall.

Seitel, F. P. (2001). *The practice of public relations.* Upper Saddle River, NJ: Prentice Hall.

## Chapter 2 ~ How Public Relations Works

Bourne, James. (2000, December18). The cost of PR. *PR Week*, 20-27.

Cutlip, Scott M., & Center, Allen H., & Broom, Glen M. (1990). *Effective public relations* (8th ed.). Englewood Cliffs, NJ: Prentice Hall.

Dilenschneider, Robert.& Forrestal, Dan (1987). *Public relations handbook (*3rd. ed.*).* Chicago, IL: Dartnell.

Dozier, David M., & Grunig, Larissa A. The organization of the public relations function, in Grunig, James E. (Ed.). *Excellence in public relations and communication management.* (1992) Hillsdale, NJ: Erlbaum. 395-418.

Grunig, James E. (Ed.) (1992). *Excellence in public relations and communication management.* Hillsdale, NJ: Erlbaum.

Heath, Robert L. (1990). Corporate issues management: Theoretical underpinnings and research foundations. *Public Relations Research Annual, 2,* 33.

Hunt, Todd, & Grunig, James E. (1997). *Public relations techniques* (2nd ed.). Fort Worth, TX: Harcourt Brace.

Keichty, Greg, & Springston, Jeff. (Summer 1996). Elaborating on Public Relations Roles. *Journalism and Mass Communication Quarterly*, 467-477.

Wilcox, Dennis L., Ault, Philip H., & Agee, Warren K. (2000). *Public relations: Strategies and tactics* (5th ed.). New York: HarperCollins.

## Chapter 3 ~ Managing Public Opinion

Fulginiti, Anthony J. (1998). *101 ways to influence people on the job.* Alexandria, VA: Briefings Publishing Group.

Glasser, Theodore L., & Salmon, Charles T. (Ed.). (1995) *Public opinion and the communication of consent.* New York: Gillford.

Hallahan, Kirk. (2000). Enhancing motivation, ability, and opportunity to process public relations messages. *Public Relations Review, 26 (4)*, 463-480.

Mewman, Kelli B. (2001, July). The power of emotion. *Public Relations Tactics*, 27.

Pearson, Ron. (1989). Beyond ethical relativism in public relations: Co-orientation, rules, and the idea of communication symmetry. *Public Relations Research Annual*, 1, 67-86.

Ponder, Stephen. (Autumn 1995). Popular propaganda: The food administration in World War 1. *Journalism & Mass Communication Quarterly*, 539-550.

## Chapter 4 ~ Using Research in Public Relations

Alreck, Pamela R., & Settle, Robert B. (1994). *The survey research handbook* (2nd ed.). Burr Ridge, IL: Irwin.

Babbie, E. R., (2001). *The practice of social research* (9th ed.). Belmont, CA: Wadsworth.

Brody, E. W. (ed.). (1991). *New technology and public relations: On to the future.* Sarasota, FL: Institute for Public Relations Research and Education.

Broom, Glen M., & Dozier, David M. (1990). *Using research in public relations: Applications to program management.* Englewood Cliffs, NJ: Prentice-Hall.

Cutlip, Scott M., & Center, Allen H., & Broom, Glen M. (1994). Step four: Evaluating the program, In *Effective Public Relations* (7th ed.). Englewood Cliffs, NJ: Prentice Hall.

Grunig, Larissa A. (1990, Summer). Using focus group research in public relations. *Public Relations Review*, 36-49.

Kerlinger, F. N. (2000). *Foundations of behavioral research* (4th ed.). New York: Holt, Rinehart & Winston.

Keyton, Joann. (2000). *Communication research: Asking questions, finding answers*. Mountain View, CA: Mayfield.

Krueger, R. A., & Casey, M. A. (2000). *Focus groups: A practical guide for applied research* (3rd ed.). Thousand Oaks, CA: Sage.

Lindemann, Walter K. (1993, Spring). An effectiveness yardstick to measure public relations success. *Public Relations Quarterly, 38*, 15.

Ludwig, Barbara. (1997, October). Predicting the future: Have you considered using the delphi methodology? *Journal of Extension, 35* (5).

Osgood, C., Suci, G., & Tannenbaum, P. (1957). *The measurement of meaning*. Urbana: University of Illinois Press.

Rubin, R.B., Rubin, Alan M., & Piele, Linda J. (2000). *Communication research: Strategies and sources* (5th ed.). Belmont CA: Wadsworth.

Simpson,, Andrea L. (1992, Summer). Ten rules of research. *Public Relations Quarterly, 37*, 27.

Stempel, Guido, & Westley, Bruce. (1995). *Research methods in mass communication*. Englewood Cliffs, NJ: Prentice Hall.

Stone, Gerald C. (1996, Winter). Public relations telephone surveys: Avoiding methodological debacles. *Public Relations Review, 2*, 327.

*Using research to plan and evaluate public relations*. Special Issue. (1990, Summer). *Public Relations Review*, 16.

Wimmer, R., & Dominick, J. (2003). *Mass media research* (7th ed.). Belmont, CA: Wadsworth.

## Chapter 5 ~ Managing Relationships with Employees

Best practices in internal communications. (1998, May). *Public Relations Tactics, 5*, 10.

D'Aprix, Roger. (1984). Employee communication. In Kanter, Bill *Experts in action: Inside public relations*. New York: Longman,

Farinelle, Jean L. (March 1992). Motivating your staff. *Public Relations Journal, 48*, 18.

Fulginiti, Anthony J. (1994). *How to deal with people on the job: The best ideas in person-to-person communication*. Blackwood, NJ: Communication Publications and Resources.

Howard, Carole M. (Spring 1996). Face-to-face communications: Payback is worth the effort. *Public Relations Quarterly, 40*, 11.

Kaufman, B.E., & Beaumont, R.A., & Helfgott, R.B. (2003). *Industrial relations to human resources and beyond: The evolving process of employee relations management*. Armonk, NY: Sharpe.

Klubnid, Joan P. (1994). *Rewarding and recognizing employees*. Burr Ridge, IL: Irwin.

O'Connor, James V. (1990, June). Building internal communications. *Public Relations Journal, 46*, 29-33.

Selame, Elinor. (1997, Summer). Public relations' role and responsibility in reflecting changes in companies' culture, structure, products and services. *Public Relations Quarterly, 42*, 12-17.

Suzaki, K. (2002). *Results from the heart: How mini-company management captures everyone's talents and helps them find meaning and purpose at work*. New York: Free Press.

## Chapter 6 ~ Working with the Media

*Bacon's Media Alerts*. Chicago: Bacon's. Published annually with bimonthly updates; publicity opportunities.

*Bacon's Publicity Checker*. Chicago: Bacon's. Published annually with quarterly supplements.

Beckman, Carol. (1996, September). Nine things to remember when talking to a reporter. *Public Relations Tactics, 3*, 13.

*Burrelle's Media Directories*. Livingston, NJ: Burrelle's. Published annually.

Caruthers, Dewey. (1998, October). Media placement: An art that gets no respect. *Public Relations Tactics, 5*, 23.

Collins, David. (1994, Fall). Ten rules of editorial etiquette. *Public Relations Quarterly, 39*, 8.

Dilenschneider, Robert L. (1992, Summer). Use ingenuity in media relations. *Public Relations Quarterly, 37*, 13.

Dilenschneider, Robert L. (1990). *Power and influence*. New York: Prentice Hall

*Gale Directory of Publications*. Detroit: Gale Research. Published annually.

Howard, Carole E., & Mathews, Wilma K. (1998). *On deadline: Managing media relations* (2nd ed.). Prospect Heights, IL: Waveland.

Howard, Carole M. (1996, Summer). 10 media lessons learned the hard way. *Public Relations Strategist, 2*, 45.

Owen, Ann R., & Karrh, James A. (1996, Winter). Video news releases: Effects on viewer recall and attitudes. *Public Relations Review, 22*, 369.

Martin, Dick. (1990). *Executive's guide to handling a press interview*. Babylon, NY: Pilot.

*Public Relations Tactics, 11* (2004, June) 4-31.

Rabin, Phil. (1999, July 26). How to create a top-notch PSA. *PR Week*, 21.

Webster, Natalie. (1990, July). Build confidence with media training. *Public Relations Journal, 46*, 25-26.

Stewart, S. (2003). *Media training 101: A guide to meeting the press*. New York: Wiley.

Wimmer, Roger D., & Dominick, Joseph. (2000). *Mass media research: An introduction*. Belmont, CA: Wadsworth.

Yale, D. R., & Carothers, A. J. (2001). *The publicity handbook: The inside scoop from more than 100 journalists and public relations professionals on how to get great publicity coverage in print, online, and on the air.* Chicago, IL. NTC.

## Chapter 7 ~ Using Advertising, Marketing, and Lobbying in Public Relations

Arens, William F. (2003). *Contemporary advertising* (9th ed.) Chicago: Irwin Professional Publications.

Bagin, Don, & Gallagher, Donald R. (2001). *The school and community relations* (8th ed.). Needham Heights, MA: Pearson.

Bivens, Thomas. (1988). Print advertising. In *Handbook for public relations writing.* Lincolnwood, IL: NTC Business Bks.

Bruno, Alicia. (1995). *A study on the value of preparing public relations students using an integrated marketing curriculum* (Master's thesis, Rowan University, Glassboro NJ).

Bullmore, J. (2003). *Behind the scenes in advertising (Mark III): Brands, business and beyond.* Henley-on-Thames: World Advertising Research Centre.

Caywood, Clarke L. (Ed.). (1997). *The handbook of strategic public relations & integrated communications.* New York: McGraw Hill.

Kitchen, P.J. (2003). *Future of marketing: Critical 21st Century perspectives.* New York: Palgrave Macmillan.

Kotler, Philip, & Andreasen, Alan R. (1987). *Strategic marketing for nonprofit organizations* (3rd ed.). Englewood Cliffs, NJ: Prentice Hall.

Kotler, Philip, & Armstrong, Gary. (1991). *Principles of marketing* (5th ed.). Englewood Cliffs, NJ: Prentice Hall.

Nelson, Roy Paul. (1989). *The design of advertising* (6th ed.). Dubuque, IA: Brown.

Ries, Al, & Trout, Jack. (1986). *Positioning: The battle for your mind.* New York: McGraw-Hill.

Sethi, S. Prakash. (1987). *Handbook of advocacy advertising concepts, strategies and applications.* Cambridge, MA: Ballinger.

Stone, Bob. (1988). *Successful direct marketing methods.* Chicago, IL. NTC .

Zabin, J., & Brebach, G. (2004). *Precision marketing: The new rules for attracting, retaining, and leveraging profitable customers.* Hoboken, NJ: Wiley.

## Chapter 8 ~ Preparing Public Relations Publications

*Publication Manual of the American Psychological Association* (4th ed.) (1996). Washington, DC: American Psychological Association.

Alexander, Michael. (1985, July). Picture-perfect photographs help sell story ideas. *Public Relations Journal.* 5-7

Bivens, Thomas. (1998). Newsletters and house publications. In *Handbook of public relations writing.* Lincolnwood, IL: NTC.

Cuddy, Claudia. (2003). *Communicating with QuarkXPress: Integrating principles of design and techniques of layout.* Dubuque, IA: Kendall/Hunt.

Gordon, Judy A. (1989, November). Desktop publishing: Separating dreams from reality, *Public Relations Journal.* 24-30.

Hudson, Howard. (1988). *Publishing newsletters* (2nd ed.). New York: Scribners.

Miller, Allen, (1988, April) Workshop: How to develop a direct mail piece. *Public Relations Journal.* 31-32.

Nelson, Roy Paul. (1983). *Publication design* (3rd ed.). Dubuque, IA: Brown.

Poor, Suzanne. (1990, May/June). Desktop publishing Report: it's nifty, but is it necessary? *Creative New Jersey,* 8-9.

## Chapter 9 ~ Writing Effective Public Relations Messages

Cialdini, Robert B. (1984) *Influence: The new psychology of modern persuasion.* New York: Quill.

Cross, Mary. (1987). *Persuasive business writing.* New York: American Management Association.

Elsbree, Langdon & Mulderig, Gerald P. *The Heath handbook* (11th ed.). Lexington MA: D.C. Heath.

Fulginiti, Anthony J., & Gillespie, Jack R. (1989). *Power-packed writing that works.* Blackwood, NJ: Communication Publications and Resources.

Funkhouser, Ray G. (1986). *The power of persuasion.* New York: Random House.

*Glossary of Misused Words & Phrases** (1989). Alexandria,VA: Communication Publications and Resources

Goldstein, Norm. (Ed.). (1992). *Associated Press stylebook and briefing on media law.* New York: The Associated Press.

Hacker, Diana. (2000). *Rules for writers* (4th ed.). Boston, MA: Bedford/St. Martin's.

Hayakawa, S. I. (Ed.). (1968). *Use the right word.* Pleasantville, NY: The Readers Digest Association

Lutz, William D. (1999) *Doublespeak defined: Cut through the bull**** and get to the point.* New York: Harper Resource.

Maggio, Rosalie. (1997) *Talking about people: A guide to fair and accurate language.* Phoenix: Oryx .

Newsom, Doug, & Carrell, Bob. (1998). *Public relations writing: Form & style* (5th ed.). Belmont, CA: Wadsworth.

Partridge, Edic. (1983). *A short etymological dictionary of modern English.* New York: Greenwich.

Rice, Scott. (1993). *Right words right place*s. Belmont, CA: Wadsworth.

Treadwell, Donald, & Treadwell, Jill B. (2000) *Public relations writing: Principles in practice.* Boston MA: Allyn and Bacon.

Warriner, John E. (1963). *English grammar and composition, grade 10.* New York: Harcourt, Brace, & World.

## Chapter 10 ~ Communicating in Special Circumstances

Benoit, William L. (1997, Summer). Image repair discourse and crisis communication. *The Public Relations Review, 23,* 177-186.

Bernstein, Alan B. (1990). *The emergency public relations manual* (3rd ed.). Highland Park, NJ: Pase.

Budd, John F. Jr. (1998, Fall). The downside of crisis management. *The Public Relations Strategist, 4,* 36.

Carney, Ann. (1993, August). Prepare for business-related crises. *The Public Relations Journal, 49,* 34.

Coombs, Timothy W. (1996). An analytic framework for crisis situations: Better response from a better understanding of the situation. *Journal of Public Relations Research, 8* (2), 79-106.

Curtis, Carlton L. (1989). Special events: How they're planned and organized, in Cantor, Bill & Burger, Chester (Eds.). *Experts in action: Inside public relations* (2nd ed.). New York: Longman.

DeVito, Joseph A. (1990) *The elements of public speaking* (4th ed.). New York: HarperCollins.

Dilenschneider, Robert L. (1993, Spring). You: Ready for trouble. *The Public Relations Quarterly, 38,* 29.

Green, Peter Sheldon. (1994). *Reputation is everything.* Burr Ridge, IL: Irwin.

Kaufman, Jeffrey B., et al. (1994, July-August) The myth of full disclosure: A look at organizational communication during crises. *Business Horizons, 37,* 29.

Lerbinger, Otto. (1997) *The crisis manager: Facing risk and responsibility.* Mahay, NJ: Lawrence Erlbaum.

Pines, W.L. (1985, Summer). How to handle PR crisis: Five Dos and Don'ts. *Public Relations Quarterly, 16.*

Wiley, Frank W. (1997, July). Anticipation: Key to crisis management. *Communication World,* 34-35.

## Chapter 11 ~ Communicating in the Networked Age

Angell, David, & Heslop, Brent. (1995). *The Internet business companion.* Reading, MA: Addison-Wesley.

Bergman, Robert E., & Moore, Thomas V. (1990). *Managing interactive video/multimedia projects.* Englewood Cliffs, NJ: Educational Technology Publications.

Cameron, Glen T. (1991). The advisory board of the future: expert systems in public relations, in W. Brody (Ed.), *New technology and public relations.* Sarasota FL: Institute for Public Relations Research and Education.

Dessart, George. (1982). *More than you want to know about PSAs: A guide to production and placement of elective public service announcements on radio and television.* National Broadcast Association for Community Affairs.

Haig, M. (2000). *E-PR: The essential guide to using public relations on the Internet.* Dove, NH. Kagan Page.

Holtz, S. (1999). *Public relations on the NET.* New York: AMACOM.

Howard, Carole M. (2000, Spring). Technology and tabloids: How the new media world is changing our jobs. *Public Relations Quarterly,* 8-12.

Hughes, Kevin. (Oct. 1993). *Entering the World-Wide Web: A guide to cyberspace.* Honolulu Community College.

Kent, Michael L. & Taylor, Maureen. (Fall 1998). Building dialogic relationships through the World Wide Web. *Public Relations Review,* 335-350.

Marlow, Eugene. (1996). *Electronic public relations.* Belmont, CA: Wadsworth.

Marlow, Eugene. (1994, August/September). Sophisticated news videos gain wide acceptance. *Public Relations Journal.*

Middleberg, D. (2001). *Winning PR in the wired world.* New York: McGraw-Hill.

O'Keefe, Steve. (2000). *Complete guide to Internet publicity: Creating and launching online campaigns.* New York: Wiley.

Porter, L. V., Shallot L. M., & Cameron, G. T. (2000). New technologies and public relations: Exploring practitioners' use of online resources to earn a seat at the management table. *Journalism and Mass Communication Quarterly, 78*(1), 172-190.

## Chapter 12 ~ Staying Legal in the Workplace

Green, Leanne. (2001, May). Examining electronic press clips and copyrights. *Public Relations Tactics,* 12.

Greenberger, Robert S. (2001, July 3). More courts are granting advertisements First Amendment protection. *Wall Street Journal,* B1.

Haggerty, James. (2001, April 9). Communicating when clients are in court. *PRWeek,* 20.

Lawrence, John & Timberg, Bernard (1989). *Fair use and free inquiry: Copyright law and the new media* (2nd ed.). Norwood, NJ: Ablex.

McGuire, George. (2000, December). Intellectual property issues for PR professionals. *PR Tactics,* 6.

Middleton, Kent R., & Chamberlin, Bill. (1988). *The law of public communication.* White Plains, NY: Longman.

Reber, Bryan H., Cropp, Fritz, & Cameron, Glen T. (2001). Mythic battles: Examining the lawyer-public relations counselor dynamic. *Journal of Public Relations Research. 13*(3), 187-218.

Tripoli, Lori. (2000, August 14). As trials go public, PR seats itself courtside. *PRWeek,* 17.

## Chapter 13 ~ Staying Ethical in the Workplace

Budd, John F. (2000, Fall). The incredible credibility dilemma. *Public Relations Quarterly*, 22-26.

Kemper, Cynthia L. (2001, April/May). Living in spin: Have 21st Century communicators stopped telling the truth? *Communication World*, 6-9.

Martinson, David L. (2000, Fall). Ethical decision making in public relations: What would Aristotle say? *Public Relations Quarterly*, 18-21.

## Chapter 14 ~ Planning a Public Relations Program

Broom, Glen M., & Dozier, David M. (1990). *Writing program goals and objectives in using research in public relations: Applications to program management.* Englewood Cliffs, NJ: Prentice-Hall, 39-44.

Hauss, Deborah. (1993, February). Setting benchmarks leads to effective programs, *Public Relations Journal, 49,* 16ff.

Kendall, Robert. (1996). *Public relations campaign strategies* (2nd ed.). New York: HarperCollins.

Tucker, Kerry, & Broom, (1993, November). Managing issues: A bridge to strategic planning. *Public Relations Journal*, 38-40.

Wilcox, Dennis L., Cameron, Glen T., Ault, Philip H., & Agee, Warren K. (2003). *Public relations: Strategies and tactics* (7th ed.). Boston, MA: Pearson.`

## Chapter 15 ~ Getting Ahead in Public Relations

Burnett, M., (2001). *Dare to succeed: How to survive and thrive in the game of life.* New York: Hyperion Books.

DeRossitt, James. (2003).*The rules of ruthlessness: Getting ahead in business when being good isn't good enough.* Antioch, IL: Center of the Universe.

Gray, John. *How to get what you want at work: A practical guide for improving communication and getting results.* New York: HarperCollins.

Miller, Gordon. (2001). *Getting ahead in today's job market.* New York: Bantam Doubleday Dell Publishing Group.

Tildon, Scott (Ed.) (1986) *Getting ahead.* Blackwood, NJ: Communication Publications and Resources.

Waldroop, J. (2000). *Maximum success: Changing the twelve behavior patterns that keep you from getting ahead.* New York: Currency/Doubleday.

Wellington, Sheila. (2001). *Be your own mentor.* New York: Catalyst, Inc., Random House Inc.

# Index

## A

ability/capability, 23, 24–27
accountability, 347
   responsibility vs., 309–310
accreditation and licensing, 285–287
action, 49, 327
action plan, 41
active audience, 167, 211, 211f
ad components, 142–143
Adams, Samuel, 7
Adobe Illustrator™, 347
Adobe InDesign™, 258, 347
advertising
   business-to-business, 137–138, 348
   direct mail, 145, 157
   directory, 137, 349
   global, 146
   image, 137, 351
   institutional, 139, 139f, 351
   issue, 138, 347
   objective, 140
   outdoor, 145
   political, 137
   PR, 138–140
   PR vs., 135–137
   print, 265
   radio, 119–120, 144, 265
   retail, 137
   special, 145
   "street-furniture," 146
   traditional, 147
   transit, 145, 357
   types of, 137–138
   video game, 147
*Advertising Age,* 149
advertising campaign
   budget for, 148
   creative plan for, 141–143
   evaluation tools for, 147–148
   features/benefits of, 141, 141f
   media plan for, 143–147
   media self-regulation of, 149–150
   questions for, 151–152
   regulation of, 143, 148–149

   situation analysis used in, 140–141, 141f, 321, 356
   tips for, 150
Advertising Council, 140
*Advertising Theory and Practice,* 181
advertorial, 140, 347
advisory panels/committee, 68, 97, 347
advocacy/issue advertising, 138, 347
advocates, 1
*Aeneid* (Virgil), 7
agate, 347
A-I-D-A, 347
Akhia Public Relations, 232
alignment, 301, 347
Alsop, Ronald J., 239
"Alumni," 347
AMA (American Marketing Association), 153
American Advertising Federation, 149
*American Journal of Psychology,* 175
American Management Association, 101
American Marketing Association. *See* AMA
American Red Cross, 140
analysis
   behavioral, 323, 348
   content, 67, 81–82, 82f, 146, 349
   data, 68, 349
   ideal state, 322, 351
   network, 353
   of product, 140–141
   of public opinion, 43–45
   for ranking, 25–27
   real state, 355
   self, 69, 355
   situation, 140–141, 141f, 321, 356
Anne Klein & Associates, 269
annual report, 347
anvil, 310, 310f, 347, 356
AOL, 256
aperture, 143
applied ethics, 301
APR, 347
Arens, 142

Aristotle. *See* Golden Mean (Aristotle)
Arthur W. Page Society, 95
ascender, 347
Ask Jeeves, 322
"Ask Questions Before Accepting a Job in Governmental Public Relations," 342
*The Associated Press Stylebook and Briefing on Media Law,* 206
Association of National Advertisers, 139
asymmetric balance, 172, 347
asymmetric two-way PR models, 3
Atlanta *Braves,* 43
attitude, 220, 347. *See also* Information→Attitudes→Behavior
   changes in, 41
   definition of, 40
   influence on, 41
   latent, 45, 352
   source of, 41
audience(s). *See also* I-S-P-R; MAC Triad
   active, 167, 211, 211f
   constrained, 53f, 53–54, 349
   copy for, 213
   hostile, challenge of, 58
   identification of, 21–22, 220, 321, 323, 324f
   passive, 167, 211f, 211–212
   persuasion relating to, 51–52
   publications relating to, 166
   segmentation of, 22, 143, 347
   writing relating to, 201–202
audience identification wheel, 21f
   external in, 21
   intermediary in, 21
   internal in, 21
   special in, 21
audience, profile of
   demographic, 22–23, 140, 348–354, 349
   psychographic, 22–23, 140, 348, 354
   VALS, 22–23, 140, 212, 357